THE IRISH RACE IN THE PAST AND THE PRESENT

by
Rev. Aug. J. Thebaud, S.J.

First published in 1873

Published by Left of Brain Books

Copyright © 2023 Left of Brain Books

ISBN 978-1-396-32522-9

First Edition

All rights reserved. No part of this publication may be reproduced, distributed, or transmitted in any form or by any means, including photocopying, recording, or other electronic or mechanical methods, without the prior written permission of the publisher, except in the case of brief quotations permitted by copyright law. Left of Brain Books is a division of Left Of Brain Onboarding Pty Ltd.

PUBLISHER'S PREFACE

About the Book

"The Irish people are a Western European ethnic group who originate in Ireland, in north western Europe. People of Irish ethnicity outside of Ireland are common in many western countries, particularly in English-speaking countries. The largest number of people of Irish descent live in the United States -- about ten times more than in Ireland itself."

(Quote from wikipedia.org)

About the Author

Augustus Thebaud (1807 - 1885)

"Jesuit educator and publicist, b. at Nantes, France, 20 Nov., 1807; d. at St. John's College, Fordham, New York, 17 Dec., 1885. Father Thebaud was the son of a worthy but not wealthy merchant who was married to his pious wife in the dark days of the Terror by a loyal priest, a circumstance which eloquently proves their earnest Catholicity. Their children were brought up with great care and given the best religious education which France at that time afforded. Young Thebaud studied at first in the preparatory seminary at Nantes, then entered the grand seminaire and was ordained to the secular priesthood at the usual age. After three years of parochial work in his native city, he entered the Society of Jesus in Italy, on 27 Nov., 1835, whence he returned to France in 1837 to pursue a course of scientific studies at the Sorbonne under Ampere and other distinguished professors. He landed in the United States on 18 Dec., 1838, and was called to the chair of chemistry at St. Mary's College, Kentucky, where he became rector in 1846. Before the end of that year however the Jesuits left Kentucky to take charge of St. John's College, Fordham, New York, which had been transferred to them by Archbishop Hughes. Father Thebaud was the first Jesuit President of St. John's, a position which he held from 1846 to 1851 and again from 1860 to 1863. In the interval he taught the sciences for two years, 1851- 52, under Father Larkin, and the following eight years he spent as the pastor of St. Joseph's Church at Troy. To this charge he returned after his second rectorship at Fordham and filled the position from 1863-69, and again from 1873-74. The intervening years we find him at first in Montreal and then at St. Joseph's Church, Hudson City, New Jersey. After spending another year at Fordham, he was assigned to St. Francis Xavier's parish, New York, where he passed the rest of his days."

(Quote from wikisource.org)

CONTENTS

PUBLISHER'S PREFACE
PREFACE 1
    THE CELTIC RACE 24
    THE WORLD UNDER THE LEAD OF THE EUROPEAN RACES.--MISSION OF THE IRISH RACE IN THE MOVEMENT 67
    THE IRISH BETTER PREPARED TO RECEIVE CHRISTIANITY THAN OTHER NATIONS 91
    HOW THE IRISH RECEIVED CHRISTIANITY 119
    THE CHRISTIAN IRISH AND THE PAGAN DANES 144
    THE IRISH FREE CLANS AND ANGLO-NORMAN FEUDALISM 175
    IRELAND SEPARATED FROM EUROPE.-A TRIPLE EPISODE 206
    THE IRISH AND THE TUDORS--HENRY VIII. 225
    THE IRISH AND THE TUDORS.--ELIZABETH.--THE UNDAUNTED NOBILITY.-- THE SUFFERING CHURCH 257
    ENGLAND PREPARED FOR THE RECEPTION OF PROTESTANTISM--IRELAND NOT 286
    THE IRISH AND THE STUARTS.--LOYALTY AND CONFISCATION 318
    A CENTURY OF GLOOM.--THE PENAL LAWS 349
    RESURRECTION.-DELUSIVE HOPES 389
    RESURRECTION.-EMIGRATION 443
    THE "EXODUS" AND ITS EFFECTS 501
    MORAL FORCE ALL-SUFFICIENT FOR THE RESURRECTION OF IRELAND 551

PREFACE

COUNT JOSEPH DE MAISTRE, in his "Principe Generateur des Constitutions Politiques" (Par. LXI.), says: "All nations manifest a particular and distinctive character, which deserves to be attentively considered."

This thought of the great Catholic writer requires some development.

It is not by a succession of periods of progress and decay only That nations manifest their life and individuality. Taking any one of them at any period of its existence, and comparing it with others, peculiarities immediately show themselves which give it a particular physiognomy whereby it may be at once distinguished from any other; so that, in those agglomerations of men which we call nations or races, we see the variety everywhere observable in Nature, the variety by which God manifests the infinite activity of his creative power.

When we take two extreme types of the human species--the Ashantee of Guinea, for instance, and any individual of one of the great civilized communities of Europe-the phenomenon of which we speak strikes us at once. But it may be remarked also, in comparing nations which have lived for ages in contiguity, and held constant intercourse one with the other from the time they began their national life, whose only boundary-line has been a mountain-chain or the banks of a broad river. They have each striking peculiarities which individualize and stamp them with a character of their own.

How different are the peoples divided by the Rhine or by the Pyrenees! How unlike those which the Straits of Dover run between! And in Asia, what have the conterminous Chinese and Hindoos in common beyond the general characteristics of the human species which belong to all the children of Adam?

But what we must chiefly insist upon in the investigation we are Now undertaking is, that the life of each is manifested by a special physiognomy deeply imprinted in their whole history, which we here call character. What each of them is their history shows; and there is no better means of judging of them than by reviewing the various events which compose their life.

For the various events which go to form what is called the history of a nation are its individual actions, the spontaneous energy of its life; and, as a man shows what he is by his acts, so does a nation or a race by the facts of its history.

When we compare the vast despotisms of Asia, crystallized into forms which have scarcely changed since the first settlement of man in those immense plains, with the active and ever-moving smaller groups of Europeans settled in the west of the Old World since the dispersion of mankind, we see at a glance how the characters of both may be read in their respective annals. And, coming down gradually to less extreme cases, we recognize the same phenomenon manifested even in contiguous tribes, springing long ago, perhaps, from the same stock, but which have been formed into distinct nations by distinct ancestors, although they acknowledge a common origin. The antagonism in their character is immediately brought out by what historians or annalists have to say of them.

Are not the cruelty and rapacity of the old Scandinavian race Still visible in their descendants? And the spirit of organization displayed by them from the beginning in the seizure, survey, and distribution of land--in the building of cities and castles--in the wise speculations of an extensive commerce--may not all these characteristics be read everywhere in the annals of the nations sprung from that original stock, grouped thousands of years ago around the Baltic and the Northern Seas?

How different appear the pastoral and agricultural tribes which have, for the same length of time, inhabited the Swiss valleys and mountains! With a multitude of usages, differing all, more or less, from each other; with, perhaps, a wretched administration of internal affairs; with frequent complaints of individuals, and partial conflicts among the rulers of those small communities--with all these defects, their simple and ever-uniform chronicles reveal to us at once the simplicity and peaceful disposition of their character; and, looking at them through the long ages of an obscure life, we at once recognize the cause of their general happiness in their constant want of ambition.

And if, in the course of centuries, the character of a nation has changed--an event which seldom takes place, and when it does is due always to radical causes--its history will immediately make known to us the cause of the change, and point out unmistakably its origin and source.

Why is it, for instance, that the French nation, after having lived for near a thousand years under a single dynasty, cannot now find a government agreeable to its modern aspirations? It is insufficient to ascribe the fact to the fickleness of the French temper. During ten centuries no European nation has been more uniform and more attached to its government. If to-day the case is altogether reversed, the fact cannot be explained except by a radical change in the character of the nation. Firmly fixed by its own national determination of purpose and by the deep studies of the Middle Ages--nowhere more remarkable than in Paris, which was at that time the centre of the activity of Catholic Europe--the French mind, first thrown by Protestantism into the vortex of controversy, gradually declined to the consideration of mere philosophical utopias, until, rejecting at last its long-received convictions, it abandoned itself to the ever-shifting delusions of opinions and theories, which led finally to skepticism and unbelief in every branch of knowledge, even the most necessary to the happiness of any community of men. Other causes, no doubt, might also be assigned for the remarkable change now under our consideration. The one we have pointed out was the chief.

To the same causes, acting now on a larger scale throughout Europe, we ascribe the same radical changes which we see taking place in the various nations composing it: every thing brought everywhere in question; the mind of all unsettled; a real anarchy of intellect spreading wider and wider even in countries which until now had stood firm against it. Hence constant revolutions unheard of hitherto; nothing stable; and men expecting with awe a more frightful and radical overturning still of every thing that makes life valuable and dear.

Are not these tragic convulsions the black and spotted types wherein we read the altered character of modern nations; are they not the natural expression of their fitful and delirious life?

These considerations, which might be indefinitely prolonged, show the truth of the phrase of Joseph de Maistre that "all nations manifest a particular and distinctive character, which deserves to be attentively considered."

The fact is, in this kind of study is contained the only possible philosophy of history for modern times.

With respect to ages that have passed away, to nations which have run their full course, a nobler study is possible--the more so because inspired writers have traced the way. Thus Bossuet wrote his celebrated "Discours." But he stopped wisely at the coming of our Lord. As to the events anterior to that great epoch, he spoke often like a prophet of ancient times; he seemed at times to be initiated in the designs of God himself. And, in truth, he had them traced by the very Spirit of God; and, lifted by his elevated mind to the level of those sublime thoughts, he had only to touch them with the magic of his style.

But of subsequent times he did not speak, except to rehearse the well-known facts of modern history, whose secret is not yet revealed, because their development is still being worked out, and no conclusion has been reached which might furnish the key to the whole.

There remains, therefore, but one thing to do: to consider each nation apart, and read its character in its history. Should this be done for all, the only practical philosophy of modern history would be written. For then we should have accomplished morally for men what, in the physical order, zoologists accomplish for the immense number of living beings which God has spread over the surface of the earth. They might be classified according to a certain order of the ascending or descending moral scale. We could judge them rightly, conformably with the standard of right or wrong, which is in the absolute possession of the Christian conscience. Brilliant but baneful qualities would no longer impose on the credulity of mankind, and men would not be led astray in their judgments by the rule of expediency or success which generally dictates to historians the estimate they form and inculcate on their readers of the worth of some nations, and the insignificance or even odiousness of others.

In the impossibility under which we labor of penetrating, at the present time, the real designs of Providence with respect to the various races of men, so great an undertaking, embracing the principal, if not all, modern races, would be one of the most useful efforts of human genius for the spread of truth and virtue among men.

Our purport is not of such vast import. We shall take in these pages for the object of our study one of the smallest and, apparently, most insignificant nations of modern Europe--the Irish. For several ages they have lost even what generally constitutes the basis of nationality, self-government; yet they have preserved their individuality as strongly marked as though they were still ruled by the O'Neill dynasty.

And we may here remark that the number of a people and the size of its territory have absolutely no bearing on the estimate which we ought to form of its character. Who would say that the Chinese are the most interesting and commendable nation on the surface of the globe? They are certainly the most ancient and most populous; their code of precise and formal morality is the most exact and clear that philosophers could ever dictate, and succeed in giving as law to a great people. That code has been followed during a long series of ages. Most discoveries of modern European science were known to them long before they were found out among us; agriculture, that first of arts, which most economists consider as the great test whereby to judge of the worth of a nation, is and always has been carried by them to a perfection unknown to us. Yet, the smallest European nationality is, in truth, more interesting and instructive than the vast Celestial Empire can ever be--whose long annals are all compassed within a few hundred pages of a frigid narrative, void of life, and altogether void of soul.

But why do we select, among so many others, the Irish nation, which is so little known, of such little influence, whose history occupies only a few lines in the general annals of the world, and whose very ownership has rested in the hands of foreigners for centuries?

We select it, first, because it is and always has been thoroughly Catholic, from the day when it first embraced Christianity; and this, under the circumstances, we take to be the best proof, not only of supreme good sense, but, moreover, of an elevated, even a sublime character. In their martyrdom of three centuries, the Irish have displayed the greatness of soul of a Polycarp, and the simplicity of an Agnes. And the Catholicity which they have always professed has been, from the beginning, of a thorough and uncompromising character. All modern European nations, it is true, have had their birth in the bosom of the Church. She had nursed them all, educated them all, made them all what they were, when they began to think of emancipating themselves from her; and the Catholic, that is, the Christian religion, in its essence, is supernatural; the creed of the apostles, the sacramental system; the very history of Christianity, transport man directly into a region far beyond the earth.

Wherever the Christian religion has been preached, nations have awakened to this new sense of faith in the supernatural, and it is there they have tasted of that strong food which made and which makes them still so superior to all other races of men. But, as we shall see, in no country has this been the case so thoroughly as in Ireland. Whatever may have been the cause, the Irish were at once, and have ever since continued, thoroughly impregnated with supernatural ideas. For several centuries after St. Patrick the island was "the Isle of Saints," a place midway between heaven and earth, where angels and the saints of heaven came to dwell with mere mortals. The Christian belief was adopted by them to the letter; and, if Christianity is truth, ought it not to be so? Such a nation, then, which received such a thorough Christian education--an education never repudiated one iota during the ages following its reception--deserves a thorough examination at our hands.

We select it, secondly, because the Irish have successfully refused ever since to enter into the various currents of European opinion, although, by position and still more by religion, they formed a part of Europe. They have thus retained a character of their own, unlike that of any other nation. To this day, they stand firm in their admirable stubbornness; and thus, when Europe shall be shaken and tottering, they will still stand firm. In the words of Moore, addressed to his own country:

> "The nations have fallen and thou still art young;
> Thy sun is just rising when others are set;
> And though slavery's cloud o'er thy morning hath hung,
> The full noon of freedom shall beam round thee yet."

That constant refusal of the Irish to fall in with the rapid torrent of European thought and progress, as it is called, is the strangest phenomenon in their history, and gives them at first an outlandish look, which many have not hesitated to call barbarism. We hope thoroughly to vindicate their character from such a foul aspersion, and to show this phenomenon as the secret cause of their final success, which is now all but secured; and this feature alone of their national life adds to their character an interest which we find in no other Christian nation.

We select it, thirdly, because there is no doubt that the Irish is the most ancient nationality of Western Europe; and although, as in the case of the Chinese, the advantage of going up to the very cradle of mankind is not sufficient to impart interest to frigid annals, when that prerogative is united to a vivid life and an exuberant individuality, nothing contributes more to render a nation worthy of study than hoariness of age, and its derivation from a certain and definite primitive stock.

It is true that, in reading the first chapters of all the various histories of Ireland, the foreign reader is struck and almost shocked by the dogmatism of the writers, who invariably, and with a truly Irish assurance, begin with one of the sons of Japhet, and, following the Hebrew or Septuagint chronology, describe without flinching the various colonizations of Erin, not omitting the synchronism of Assyrian, Persian, Greek, and Roman history. A smile is at first the natural consequence of such assertions; and, indeed, there is no obligation whatever to believe that every thing happened exactly as they relate.

But when the large quartos and octavos which are now published from time to time by the students of Irish antiquarian lore are opened, read, and pondered over, at least one consequence is drawn from them which strikes the reader with astonishment. "There can be no doubt," every candid mind says to itself, "that this nation has preceded in time all those which have flourished on the earth, with the exception, perhaps, of the Chinese, and that it remains the same to-day." At least, many years before Christ, a race of men inhabited Ireland exactly identical with its present population (except that it did not enjoy the light of the true religion), yet very superior to it in point of material well-being. Not a race of cannibals, as the credulous Diodorus Siculus, on the strength of some vague tradition, was pleased to delineate; but a people acquainted with the use of the precious metals, with the manufacture of fine tissues, fond of music and of song, enjoying its literature and its books; often disturbed, it is true, by feuds and contentions, but, on the whole, living happily under the patriarchal rule of the clan system.

The ruins which are now explored, the relics of antiquity which are often exhumed, the very implements and utensils preserved by the careful hand of the antiquarian--every thing, so different from the rude flint arrows and barbarous weapons of our North American Indians and of the European savages of the Stone period, denotes a state of civilization, astonishing indeed, when we reflect that real objects of art embellished the dwellings of Irishmen probably before the foundation of Rome, and perhaps when Greece was as yet in a state of heroic barbarism.

And this high antiquity is proved by literature as well as by art. "The ancient Irish," says one of their latest historians, M. Haverty, "attributed the utmost importance to the accuracy of their Historic compositions for social reasons. Their whole system of society--every question as to right of property--turned upon the descent of families and the principle of clanship; so that it cannot be supposed that mere fables would be tolerated instead of facts, where every social claim was to be decided on their authority. A man's name is scarcely mentioned in our annals without the addition of his forefathers for several generations--a thing which rarely occurs in those of other countries.

"Again, when we arrive at the era of Christianity in Ireland, we find that our ancient annals stand the test of verification by science with a success which not only establishes their character for truthfulness at that period, but vindicates the records of preceding dates involved in it."

The most confirmed skeptic cannot refuse to believe that at the introduction of Christianity into Ireland, in 432, the whole island was governed by institutions exactly similar to those of Gaul when Julius Caesar entered it 400 years before; that this state must have existed for a long time anterior to that date; and that the reception of the new religion, with all the circumstances which attended it, introduced the nation at once into a happy and social state, which other European countries, at that time convulsed by barbarian invasions, did not attain till several centuries later.

These various considerations would alone suffice to show the real importance of the study we undertake; but a much more powerful incentive to it exists in the very nature of the annals of the nation itself.

Ireland is a country which, during the last thousand years, has maintained a constant struggle against three powerful enemies, and has finally conquered them all.

The first stage of the conflict was that against the Northmen. It lasted three centuries, and ended in the almost complete disappearance of this foe.

The second act of the great drama occupied a period of four Hundred years, during which all the resources of the Irish clans were arrayed against Anglo-Norman feudalism, which had finally to succumb; so that Erin remained the only spot in Europe where feudal institutions never prevailed.

The last part of this fearful trilogy was a conflict of three centuries with Protestantism; and the final victory is no longer doubtful.

Can any other modern people offer to the meditation, and, we must say, to the admiration of the Christian reader, a more interesting spectacle? The only European nation which can almost compete with the constancy and never-dying energy of Ireland is the Spanish in its struggle of seven centuries with the Moors.

We have thought, therefore, that there might be some real interest and profit to be derived from the study of this eventful national life--an interest and a profit which will appear as we study it more in detail.

It may be said that the threefold conflict which we have outlined might be condensed into the surprising fact that all efforts to drag Ireland into the current of European affairs and influence have invariably failed. This is the key to the understanding of her whole history.

Even originally, when it formed but a small portion of the great Celtic race, here existed in the Irish branch a peculiarity of its own, which stamped it with features easy to be distinguished. The gross idolatry of the Gauls never prevailed among the Irish; the Bardic system was more fully developed among them than among any other Celtic nation. Song, festivity, humor, ruled there much more universally than elsewhere. There were among them more harpers and poets than even genealogists and antiquarians, although the branches of study represented by these last were certainly as well cultivated among them as among the Celts of Gaul, Spain, or Italy.

But it is chiefly after the introduction of Christianity among them, when it appeared finally decreed that they should belong morally and socially to Europe, it is chiefly then that their purpose, however unconscious they may have been of its tendency, seems more defined of opening up for themselves a path of their own. And in this they followed only the promptings of Nature.

The only people in Europe which remained untouched by what is called Roman civilization--never having seen a Roman soldier on their shores; never having been blessed by the construction of Roman baths and amphitheatres; never having listened to the declamations of Roman rhetoricians and sophists, nor received the decrees of Roman praetors, nor been subject to the exactions of the Roman fisc--they never saw among them, in halls and basilicas erected under the direction of Roman architects, Roman judges, governors, proconsuls, enforcing the decrees of the Caesars against the introduction or propagation of the Christian religion. Hence it entered in to them without opposition and bloodshed.

But the new religion, far from depriving them of their characteristics, consecrated and made them lasting. They had their primitive traditions and tastes, their patriarchal government and manners, their ideas of true freedom and honor, reaching back almost to the cradle of mankind. They resolved to hold these against all comers, and they have been faithful to their resolve down to our own times. Fourteen hundred years of history since Patrick preached to them proves it clearly enough.

First, then, although the Germanic tribes of the first invasion, as it is called, did not reach their shore, for the reason that the Germans, as little as the Celts, never possessed a navy--although neither Frank, nor Vandal, nor Hun, renewed among them the horrors witnessed in Gaul, Spain, Italy, and Africa--they could not remain safe from the Scandinavian pirates, whose vessels scoured all the northern seas before they could enter the Mediterranean through the Straits of Gibraltar.

The Northmen, the Danes, came and tried to establish themselves among them and inculcate their northern manners, system, and municipal life. They succeeded in England, Holland, the north of France, and the south of

Italy; in a word, wherever the wind had driven their hide-bound boats. The Irish was the only nation of Western Europe which beat them back, and refused to receive the boon of their higher civilization.

As soon as the glories of the reign of Charlemagne had gone down in a sunset of splendor, the Northmen entered unopposed all the great rivers of France and Spain. They speedily conquered England. On all sides they ravaged the country and destroyed the population, whose only defence consisted in prayers to Heaven, with here and there an heroic bishop or count. In Ireland alone the Danes found to their cost that the Irish spear was thrust with a steady and firm hand; and after two hundred years of struggle not only had they not arrived at the survey and division of the soil, as wherever else they had set foot, but, after Clontarf, the few cities they still occupied were compelled to pay tribute to the Irish Ard-Righ. Hence all attempts to substitute the Scandinavian social system for that of the Irish septs and clans were forever frustrated. City life and maritime enterprises, together with commerce and trade, were as scornfully rejected as the worship of Thor and Odin.

Soon after this first victory of Ireland over Northern Europe, the Anglo-Norman invasion originated a second struggle of longer duration and mightier import. The English Strongbow replaced the Danes with Norman freebooters, who occupied the precise spots which the new owners had reconquered from the Northmen, and never an inch more. Then a great spectacle was offered to the world, which has too much escaped the observation of historians, and to which we intend to draw the attention of our readers.

The primitive, simple, patriarchal system of clanship was Confronted by the stern, young, ferocious feudal system, which was then beginning to prevail all over Europe. The question was, Would Ireland consent to become European as Europe was then organizing herself? The struggle, as we shall see, between the Irish and the English in the twelfth century and later on, was merely a contest between the sept system and feudalism, involving, it is true, the possession of land. And, at the end of a contest lasting four hundred years, feudalism was so thoroughly defeated that the English of the Pale adopted the Irish manners, customs, and even language, and formed only new septs among the old ones.

Hence Ireland escaped all the commotions produced in Europe by the consequences of the feudal system:

I. Serfdom, which was generally substituted for slavery, never existed in Ireland, slavery having disappeared before the entry of the Anglo-Normans.

II. The universal oppression of the lower classes, which caused the simultaneous rising of the communes all over Europe, never having existed in Ireland, we shall not be surprised to find no mention in Irish history of that wide-spread institution of the eleventh and following centuries.

III. An immense advantage which Ireland derived from her isolation, on which she always insisted, was her being altogether freed from the fearful mediaeval heresies which convulsed France particularly for a long period, and which invariably came from the East.

For Erin remained so completely shut off from the rest of Europe, that, in spite of its ardent Catholicism, the Crusades were never preached to its inhabitants; and, if some individual Irishman joined the ranks of the warriors led to Palestine by Richard Coeur de Lion, the nation was in no way affected by the good or bad results which everywhere ensued from the marching of the Christian armies against the Moslem.

The sects which sprang from Manicheism were certainly an evil consequence of the holy wars; and it would be a great error to think that those heresies were short-lived and affected only for a brief space of time the social and moral state of Europe. It may be said that their fearfully disorganizing influence lasts to this day. If modern secret societies do not, in point of fact, derive their existence directly from the Bulgarism and Manicheism of the Middle Ages, there is no doubt that those dark errors, which Imposed on all their adepts a stern secrecy, paved the way for the conspiracies of our times. Hence Ireland, not having felt the effect of the former heresies, is in our days almost free from the universal contagion now decomposing the social fabric on all sides.

But it is chiefly in modern times that the successful resistance offered by Ireland to many wide-spread European evils, and its strong attachment to its old customs, will evoke our wonder.

Clanship reigned still over more than four-fifths of the island when the Portuguese were conquering a great part of India, and the Spaniards making Central and South America a province of their almost universal monarchy.

The poets, harpers, antiquarians, genealogists, and students of Brehon law, still held full sway over almost the whole island, when the revival of pagan learning was, we may say, convulsing Italy, giving a new direction to the ideas of Germany, and penetrating France, Holland, and Switzerland. Happy were the Irish to escape that brilliant but fatal invasion of mythology and Grecian art and literature! Had they not received enough of Greek and Latin lore at the hands of their first apostles and missionaries, and through the instrumentality of the numerous amanuenses and miniaturists in their monasteries and convents? Those holy men had brought them what Christian Rome had purified of the old pagan dross, and sanctified by the new Divine Spirit.

Virgin Ireland having thus remained undefiled, and never having even been agitated by all those earlier causes of succeeding revolutions, Protestantism, the final explosion of them all, could make no impression on her--a fact which remains to this day the brightest proof of her strength and vigor.

But, before speaking of this last conflict, we must meet an objection which will naturally present itself.

To steadily refuse to enter into the current of European thought, and object to submit in any way to its influence, is, pretend many, really to reject the claims of civilization, and persist in refusing to enter upon the path of progress. The North American savage has always been most persistent in this stubborn opposition to civilized life, and no one has as yet considered this a praiseworthy attribute. The more barbarous a tribe, the more firmly it adheres to its traditions, the more pertinaciously it follows the customs of its ancestors. They are immovable, and cannot be brought to adopt usages new to them, even when they see the immense advantages they would reap from their adoption. Hence the greater number of writers, chiefly English, who have treated of Irish affairs, unhesitatingly call them barbarians, precisely on account of their stubbornness in rejecting the advances of the Anglo-Norman invaders. Sir John Davies, the attorney-general of James I., could scarcely write a page on the subject without reverting to this idea.

We answer that the Irish, even before their conversion to Christianity, but chiefly after, were not barbarians; they never opposed true progress; and they became, in fact, in the sixth, seventh, and eighth centuries, the moral and scientific educators of the greater part of Europe. What they refused to adopt they were right in rejecting. But, as there are still many men who, without ever having studied the question, do not hesitate, even in our days, to throw barbarism in their teeth, and attribute to it the pitiable condition which the Irish to-day present to the world, we add a few further considerations on this point.

First, then, we say, barbarians have no history; and the Irish certainly had a history long before St. Patrick converted them. Until lately, it is true, the common opinion of writers on Ireland was adverse to this assertion of ours; but, after the labors of modern antiquarians--of such men as O'Donovan, Todd, E. O'Curry, and others--there can no longer be any doubt on the subject. If Julius Caesar was right in stating that the Druids of Gaul confined themselves to oral teaching--and the statement may very well be questioned, with the light of present information on the subject--it is now proved that the Ollamhs of Erin kept written annals which went back to a very remote age of the world. The numerous histories and chronicles written by monks of the sixth and following centuries, the authenticity of which cannot be denied, evidently presuppose anterior compositions dating much farther back than the introduction of our holy religion into Ireland, which the Christian annalists had in their hands when they wrote their books, sometimes in Latin, sometimes in old Irish, sometimes in a strange medley of both languages. It is now known that St. Patrick brought to Ireland the Roman alphabet only, and that it was thenceforth used not merely for the ritual of the Church, and the dissemination of the Bible and of the works of the Holy Fathers, but likewise for the transcription, in these newly-consecrated symbols of thought, of the old manuscripts of the island; which soon disappeared, in the far greater number of instances at least, owing to the favor in which the Roman characters were held by the people and their instructors the bishops and monks. Let those precious old symbols be called Ogham, or by any other name--there must have been something of the kind.

If any one insists that such was not the case, he must of necessity admit that the oral teaching of the Ollamhs was so perfect and so universally current in the same formulas all over the island, that such oral teaching really took the place of writing; and in this case, also, which is scarcely possible, however, Ireland had an authentic history. This last supposition, certainly, can hardly be credited; and yet, if the first be rejected, it must be admitted, since it cannot be imagined that subsequent Irish historians, numerous as they became in time, could have agreed so well together, and remained so consistent with themselves, and so perfectly accurate in their descriptions of places and things in general, without anterior authentic documents of some kind or other, on which they could rely. Any person who has merely glanced at the astonishing production called the "Annals of the Four Masters," must necessarily be of this opinion.

In no nation in the world are there found so many old histories, annals, chronicles, etc., as among the Irish; and that fact alone suffices to prove that in periods most ancient they were truly a civilized nation, since they attached such importance to the records of events then taking place among them.

But the Irish were, moreover, a branch of the great Celtic race, whose renown for wisdom, science, and valor, was spread through all parts, particularly among the Greeks. The few details we purpose giving on the subject will convince the reader that among the nations of antiquity they held a prominent position; and not only were they possessed of a civilization of their own, not despicable even in the eyes of a Roman--of the great Julius himself--but they were ever most susceptible of every kind of progress, and consequently eager to adopt all the social benefits which their intercourse with Rome brought them. At least, they did so as soon as, acknowledging the superior power of the enemy, they had the good sense to feel that it was all-important to imitate him. Hence sprang that Gallo-Roman civilization which obtained during the first five or six centuries of the Christian era--a civilization which the barbarians of the North endeavored to destroy, but to which they themselves finally yielded, by embracing Christianity, and gradually changing their language and customs.

Everywhere--in Gaul, Italy, Britain, and Ireland--did the Celts manifest that susceptibility to progress which is the invariable mark of a state antagonistic to barbarism. In this they totally differed from the Vandals and Huns, whom it took the Church such a dreary period to conquer, and whom no other power save the religion of Christ could have subdued.

These few words are sufficient for our present purpose. We proceed to show that, in their stubborn opposition to many a current of European opinion, they acted rightly.

They acted rightly, first of all, in excluding from their course of studies at Bangor, Clonfert, Armagh, Clonmacnoise, and other places, the subtleties of Greek philosophy, which occasioned heresies in Europe and Asia during the first ages of the Church, and were the cause of so many social and political convulsions. By adhering strictly---a little too strictly, perhaps--to their traditional method of developing thought, they kept error far from their universities, and presented, in the sixth, seventh, and eighth centuries, the remarkable spectacle in Ireland, France, Germany, Switzerland, and even Northern Italy, of numerous schools wherein no wrangling found a place, and whence never issued a single proposition which Rome found reason to censure. They were at that time the educators of Christian Europe, and not even a breath of suspicion was ever raised against any one of their innumerable teachers. If their mind, in general, did not on that account attain the acuteness of the French, Italians, or Germans, it was at all times safer and more guarded. Even their later hostility to the English Pale, after the eleventh century, was most useful, from its warning against the teachings of prelates sent from the English Universities of Oxford and Cambridge; and Rome seems to have approved of that opposition, by using all her power in appointing to Irish sees, even within the Pale, prelates chosen from the Augustinian, Dominican, Franciscan, and Carmelite orders, in preference to secular ecclesiastics educated in the great seats of English learning.

Thus the Irish, by opening their schools gratuitously to all Europe, but chiefly to Anglo-Saxon England, were not only of immense service to the Church, but showed how fully they appreciated the benefits of true civilization, and how ready they were to extend it by their traditional teaching. Nor did they confine themselves to receiving scholars in their midst: they sent abroad, during those ages, armies of zealous missionaries and learned men to Christianize the heathen, or educate the newly-converted Germanic tribes in Merovingian and Carlovingian Gaul, in Anglo-Saxon and Scandinavian England, in Lombardian Italy, in the very hives of those ferocious tribes which peopled the ever-moving and at that time convulsed Germany.

II. They were right in refusing to submit to the Scandinavian yoke, and accept from those who would impose it their taste for city life, and the spirit of maritime enterprise and extensive commerce. We shall see that this was at the bottom of their two centuries of struggle with the Danes; that they were animated throughout that conflict by their ardent zeal for the Christian religion, which the Northmen came to destroy. There is no need of dwelling on this point, as we are not aware that any one, even their bitterest enemies, has found fault with them here.

III. They were right in opposing feudalism, and steadily refusing to admit it on their soil. Feudal Europe beheld with surprise the inhabitants of a small island on the verge of the Western Continent level to the ground the feudal castles as soon as they were built; reject with scorn the invaders' claim to their soil, after they had signed papers which they could not understand; hold fast to their patriarchal usages in opposition to the new-born European notions of paramount kings, of dukes, earls, counts, and viscounts; fight for four hundred years against what the whole of Europe had everywhere else accepted, and conquer in the end; so that the Irish of to-day can say with just pride, "Our island has never submitted to mediaeval feudalism."

And hence the island has escaped the modern results of the system, which we all witness to-day in the terrible hostility of class arrayed against class, the poor against the rich, the lower orders against the higher. The opposition in Ireland between the oppressed and the oppressor is of a very different character, is we shall see later. But the fact is, that the clan system, with all its striking defects, had at least this immense advantage, that the clansmen did not look upon their chieftains as "lords and masters," but as men of the same blood, true relations, and friends; neither did the heads of the clans look on their men as villeins, serfs, or chattels, but as companions-in-arms, foster-brothers, supporters, and allies. Hence the opposition which exists in our days throughout Europe between class and class, has never existed in Ireland. Let a son of their old chiefs, if one can yet be found, go back to them, even but for a few days, after centuries of estrangement, and they are ready to welcome him yet, as a loyal nation would welcome her long-absent king, as a family would receive a father it esteemed lost. We knowing what manner a son of a French McMahon was lately received among them.

All hostility is reserved for the foreigner, the invader, the oppressor of centuries, because, in the opinion of the natives, these have no real right to dwell on a soil they have impoverished, and which they tried in vain to enslave. This, at least, is their feeling. But the sons of the soil, whether rich or poor, high or low, are all united in a holy brotherhood. This state of things they have preserved by the exclusion of feudalism.

IV. The Irish were right in not accepting from Europe what is known as the "revival of learning;" at least, as carried almost to the excess of modern paganism by its first promoters.

This "revival" did not reach Ireland. Many will, doubtless, attribute this fact to the almost total exclusion then supposed to exist of Ireland from all European intercourse. It would be a great error to imagine such to have been the cause. Indeed, at that very time, Ireland was more in daily contact with Italy, France, and Spain, than had been the case since the eighth century.

If the Irish were right in holding steadfast to the line of their traditional studies, in rejecting the city life and commercial spirit of the Danes, in opposing Anglo-Norman feudalism, and, finally, in not accepting the more than doubtful advantages flowing from the literary revival of the fifteenth century; if, in all this, they did not oppose true progress, but merely wished to advance in the peculiar path opened up to them by the Christianity which they had received more fully, with more earnestness, and with a view to a greater development of the supernatural idea, than any other European nation--then, beyond all other modes, did they display their strength of will and their undying national vitality in their resistance to Protestantism--a resistance which has been called opposition to progress, but the success of which to-day proves beyond question that they were right.

It was, the reader may remark, a resistance to the whole of Northern Europe, wherein their island was included. For, the whole of Northern Europe rebelled against the Church at the beginning of the sixteenth century, to enter upon a new road of progress and civilization, as it has been called, ending finally in the frightful abyss of materialism and atheism which now gapes under the feet of modern nations--an abyss in whose yawning womb nullus ordo, sed sempiternus horror habitat. The end of that progress is now plain enough: political and social convulsions, without any other probable issue than final anarchy, unless nations consent at last to retrace their steps and reorganize Christendom.

But this was not apparent to the eyes of ordinary thinkers in the sixteenth and seventeenth centuries. Only a few great minds saw the logical consequences of the premises laid down by Protestantism, and predicted something of what we now see.

The Irish was the only northern nation which, to a man, opposed the terrible delusion, and, at the cost of all that is dear, waged against it a relentless war.

"To a man;" for, in spite of all the wiles of Henry VIII., who brought every resource of his political talent into play, in order to win over to his side the great chieftains of the nation--in spite of all the efforts of Elizabeth, who either tried to overcome their resistance by her numerous armies, or, by the allurements of her court, strove her best, like her father, to woo to her allegiance the great leaders of the chief clans, particularly O'Neill of Tyrone--at the end of her long reign, after nearly a hundred years of Protestantism, only sixty Irishmen of all classes had received the new religion.

At first, the struggle assumed a character more political than religious, and Queen Elizabeth did her best to give it, apparently, that character. But for her, religion meant politics; and, had the Irish consented to accept the religious changes introduced by her father and herself, there would have been no question of "rebellion," and no army would have been sent to crush it. The Irish chieftains knew this well; hence, whenever the queen came to terms with them, the first article on which they invariably insisted was the freedom of their religion.

But, under the Stuarts, and later on, the mask was entirely thrown aside, and the question between England and Ireland reduced itself, we may say, to one of religion merely. All the political entanglements in which the Irish found themselves involved by their loyalty to the Stuarts and their opposition to the Roundheads, never constituted the chief difficulty of their position. They were "Papists:" this was their great crime in the eyes of their enemies. Cromwell would certainly never have endeavored to exterminate them as he did, had they apostatized and become ranting Puritans. One of our main points in the following pages will be to give prominence to this view of the question. If it had been understood from the first, the army of heroes who died for their God and their country would long ere this have been enrolled in the number of Christian martyrs.

The subsequent policy of England, chiefly after the English Revolution of 1688 and the defeat of James II., clearly shows the soundness of our interpretation of history. The "penal code," under Queen Anne, and later on, at least has the merit of being free from hypocrisy and cant. It is an open religious persecution, as, in fact, it had been from the beginning.

We shall have, therefore, before our eyes the great spectacle of a nation suffering a martyrdom of three centuries. All the persecutions of the Christians under the Roman emperors pale before this long era of penalty and blood. The Irish, by numerous decrees of English kings and parliaments, were deprived of every thing which a man not guilty of crime has a right to enjoy. Land, citizenship, the right of education, of acquiring property, of living on their own soil--every thing was denied them, and death in every form was decreed, in every line of the new Protestant code, to men, women, and even children, whose only crime consisted in remaining faithful to their religion.

But chiefly during the Cromwellian war and the nine years of the Protector's reign were they doomed to absolute, unrelenting destruction. Never has any thing in the whole history of mankind equalled it in horror, unless the devastation of Asia and Eastern Europe under Zengis and Timour.

There is, therefore, at the bottom of the Irish character, hidden under an appearance of light-headedness, mutability of feeling--nay, at times, futility and even childishness--a depth of according to the eternal laws which God gave to mankind. Nothing else is in their mind; they are pursuing no guilty and shadowy Utopia. Who knows, then, whether their small island may not yet become the beacon-light which, guiding other nations, shall at a future day save Europe from the universal shipwreck which threatens her? The providential mission of Ireland is far from being accomplished, and men may yet see that not in vain has she been tried so long in the crucible of affliction.

Another part of the providential plan as affecting her will show itself, and excite our admiration, in the latter portion of the work we undertake.

The Irish are no longer confined to the small island which gave them birth. From the beginning of their great woes, they have known the bitterness of exile. Their nobility were the first to leave in a body a land wherein they could no longer exist; and, during the seventeenth and eighteenth centuries, they made the Irish name illustrious on all the battle-fields of Europe. At the same time, many of their priests and monks, unable longer to labor among their countrymen, spent their lives in the libraries, of Italy, Belgium, and Spain, and gave to the world those immense works so precious now to the antiquarian and historian. Every one knows what Montalembert, in particular, found in them. They may be said to have preserved the annals of their nation from total ruin; and the names of the O'Clearys, of Ward and Wadding, of Colgan and Lynch, are becoming better known and appreciated every day, as their voluminous works are more studied and better understood.

But much more remarkable still is the immense spread of the people itself during the present age, so fruitful in happy results for the Church of Christ and the good of mankind. We may say that the labors of the Irish missionaries during the seventh and eighth centuries are to-day eclipsed by the truly missionary work of a whole nation spread now over North America, the West India Islands, the East Indies, and the wilds of Australia; in a word, wherever the English language is spoken. Whatever may have been the visible causes of that strange "exodus," there is an invisible cause clear enough to any one who meditates on the designs of God over his Church. There is no presumption in attributing to God himself what could only come from Him. The catholicity of the Church was to be spread and preserved through and in all those vast regions colonized now by the adventurous English nation; and no better, no more simple way of effecting this could be conceived than the one whose workings we see in those colonies so distant from the mother-country.

This, for the time being, is the chief providential mission of Ireland, and it is truly a noble one, undertaken and executed in a noble manner by so many thousands, nay millions, of men and women--poor, indeed, in worldly goods when they start on their career, but rich in faith; and it is as true now as it has ever been from the beginning of Christianity, that haec est victoria nostra, fides vestra.

These few words of our Preface would not suffice to prepare the reader for the high importance of this stupendous phenomenon. We We purpose, therefore, devoting our second chapter to the subject, as a preparation for the very interesting details we shall furnish subsequently, as it is proper that, from the very threshold, an idea may be formed of the edifice, and of the entire proportions it is destined to assume.

We have so far sketched, as briefly as possible, what the following pages will develop; and the reader may now begin to understand what we said at starting, that no other nation in Europe offers so interesting an object of study and reflection.

Plato has said that the most meritorious spectacle in the eyes of God was that of "a just man struggling with adversity." What must it be when a whole nation, during nine long ages, offers to Heaven the most sublime virtues in the midst of the extremest trials? Are not the great lessons which such a contest presents worthy of study and admiration?

We purpose studying them, although we cannot pretend to render full justice to such a theme. And, returning for a moment to the considerations with which we started, we can truly say that, in the whole range of modern history, it would be difficult, if not impossible, to find a national life to compare with that of poor, despised Ireland. Neither do we pretend to write the history itself; our object is more humble: we merely pen some considerations suggested naturally by the facts which we suppose to be already known, with the purpose of arriving at a true appreciation of the character of the people. For it is the people itself we study; the reader will meet with comparatively few individual names.

We shall find, moreover, that the nation has never varied. Its history is an unbroken series of the same heroic facts, the same terrible misfortunes. The actors change continually; the outward circumstances at every moment present new aspects, so that the interest never flags; but the spirit of the struggle is ever the same, and the latest descendants of the first O'Neills and O'Donnells burn with the same sacred fire, and are inspired by the same heroic aspirations, as their fathers.

Happily, the gloom is at length lighted up by returning day. The contest has lost its ferocity, and we are no longer surrounded by the deadly shade which obscured the sky a hundred years ago. Then it was hard to believe that the nation could ever rise; her final success seemed almost an impossibility. We now see that those who then despaired sinned against

Providence, which waited for its own time to arrive and vindicate its ways. And it is chiefly on account of the bright hope which begins to dawn that our subject should possess for all a lively interest, and fill the Catholic heart with glowing sympathy and ardent thankfulness to God.

THE CELTIC RACE

NATIONS which preserve, as it were, a perpetual youth, should be studied from their origin. Never having totally changed, some of their present features may be recognized at the very cradle of their existence, and the strangeness of the fact sets out in bolder relief their actual peculiarities. Hence we consider it to our purpose to examine the Celtic race first, as we may know it from ancient records: What it was; what it did; what were its distinctive features; what its manners and chief characteristics. A strong light will thus be thrown even on the Irish of our own days. Our words must necessarily be few on so extensive a subject; but, few as they are, they will not be unimportant in our investigations.

In all the works of God, side by side with the general order resulting from seemingly symmetric laws, an astonishing variety of details everywhere shows itself, producing on the mind of man the idea of infinity, as effectually as the wonderful aspect of a seemingly boundless universe. This variety is visible, first in the heavenly bodies, as they are called; star differing from star, planet from planet; even the most minute asteroids never showing themselves to us two alike, but always offering differences in size, of form, of composition.

This variety is visible to us chiefly on our globe; in the infinite multiplicity of its animal forms, in the wonderful insect tribes, and in the brilliant shells floating in the ocean; visible also in the incredible number of trees, shrubs, herbs, down to the most minute vegetable organisms, spread with such reckless abundance on the surface of our dwelling; visible, finally, in the infinity of different shapes assumed by inorganic matter.

But what is yet more wonderful and seemingly unaccountable is that, taking every species of being in particular, and looking at any two individuals of the same species, we would consider it an astonishing effect of chance, were we to meet with two objects of our study perfectly alike. The mineralogist notices it, if he finds in the same group of crystals two altogether similar; the botanist would express his astonishment if, on comparing two specimens of the same plant, he found no difference between them. The same may be said of birds, of reptiles, of mammalia, of the same kind. A close observer will even easily detect dissimilarities between the double organs of the same person, between the two eyes of his neighbor, the two hands of a friend, the two feet of a stranger whom he meets.

It is therefore but consistent with general analogy that in the moral as well as in the physical faculties of man, the same ever-recurring variety should appear, in the features of the face, in the shape of the limbs, in the moving of the muscles, as well as in the activity of thought, in the mobility of humor, in the combination of passions, propensities, sympathies, and aversions.

But, at the same time, with all these peculiarities perceptible in individuals, men, when studied attentively, show themselves in groups, as it were, distinguished from other groups by peculiarities of their own, which are generally called characteristics of race; and although, according to various systems, these characteristics are made to expand or contract at will, to serve an a priori purpose, and sustain a preconcerted theory, yet there are, with respect to them, startling facts which no one can gainsay, and which are worthy of serious attention.

Two of these facts may be stated in the following propositions:

I. At the cradle of a race or nation there must have been a type imprinted on its progenitor, and passing from him to all his posterity, which distinguishes it from all others.

II. The character of a race once established, cannot be eradicated without an almost total disappearance of the people.

The proofs of these propositions would require long details altogether foreign to our present purpose, as we are not writing on ethnology. We will take them for granted, as otherwise we may say that the whole history of man would be unintelligible. If, however, writers are found who apply to their notion of race all the inflexibility of physical laws, and who represent history as a rigid system of facts chained together by a kind of fatality; if a school has sprung up among historians to do away with the moral responsibility of individuals and of nations, it is scarcely necessary to tell the reader that nothing is so far from our mind as to adopt ideas destructive, in fact, to all morality.

It is our belief that there is no more "necessity" in the leanings of race with respect to nations, than there is in the corrupt instincts of our fallen nature with respect to individuals. The teachings of faith have clearly decided this in the latter case, and the consequence of this authoritative decision carries with it the determination of the former.

According to the doctrine of St. Augustine, nations are rewarded or punished in this world, because there is no future existence for them; but the fact of rewards and punishments awarded them shows that their life is not a series of necessary sequences such as prevail in physics, and that the manifestations or phenomena of history, past, present, or future, cannot resolve themselves into the workings of absolute laws.

Race, in our opinion, is only one of those mysterious forces which play upon the individual from the cradle to the grave, which affect alike all the members of the same family, and give it a peculiarity of its own, without, however, interfering in the least with the moral freedom of the individual; and as in him there is free-will, so also in the family itself to which he belongs may God find cause for approval or disapproval. The heart of a Christian ought to be too full of gratitude and respect for Divine Providence to take any other view of history.

It would be presumptuous on our part to attempt an explanation of the object God proposed to himself in originating such a diversity in human society. We can only say that it appears He did not wish all mankind to be ever subject to the same rule, the same government and institutions. His Church alone was to bear the character of universality. Outside of her, variety was to be the rule in human affairs as in all things else. A universal despotism was never to become possible.

This at once explains why the posterity of Japhet is so different from that of Sem and of Cham.

In each of those great primitive stocks, an all-wise Providence introduced a large number of sub-races, if we may be allowed to call them so, out of which are sprung the various nations whose intermingling forms the web of human history. Our object is to consider only the Celtic branch. For, whatever may be the various theories propounded on the subject of the colonization of Ireland, from whatever part of the globe the primitive inhabitants may be supposed to have come, one thing is certain, to-day the race is yet one, in spite of the foreign blood infused into it by so many men of other stocks. Although the race was at one time on the verge of extinction by Cromwell, it has finally absorbed all the others; it has conquered; and, whoever has to deal with true Irishmen, feels at once that he deals with a primitive people, whose ancestors dwelt on the island thousands of years ago. Some slight differences may be observed in the people of the various provinces of the island; there maybe various dialects in their language, different appearance in their looks, some slight divergence in their disposition or manners; it cannot be other wise, since, as we have seen, no two individuals of the human family can be found perfectly alike. But, in spite of all this, they remain Celts to this day; they belong undoubtedly, to that stock formerly wide-spread throughout Europe, and now almost confined to their island; for the character of the same race in Wales, Scotland, and Brittany, has not been, and could not be, kept so pure as in Erin; so that in our age the inhabitants of those countries have become more and more fused with their British and Gallic neighbors.

We must, therefore, at the beginning of this investigation, state briefly what we know of the Celtic race in ancient times, and examine whether the Irish of to-day do not reproduce its chief characteristics.

We do not propose, however, in the present study, referring to the physical peculiarities of the Celtic tribes; we do not know what those were two or three thousand years ago. We must confine ourselves to moral propensities and to manners, and for this view of the subject we have sufficient materials whereon to draw.

We first remark in this race an immense power of expansion, when not checked by truly insurmountable obstacles; a power of expansion which did not necessitate for its workings an uninhabited and wild territory, but which could show its energy and make its force felt in the midst of already thickly-settled regions, and among adverse and warlike nations.

As far as history can carry us back, the whole of Western Europe, namely, Gaul, a part of Spain, Northern Italy, and what we call to-day the British Isles, are found to be peopled by a race apparently of the same origin, divided into an immense number of small republics; governed patriarchally in the form of clans, called by Julius Caesar, "Civitates." The Greeks called them Celts, "Keltai." They do not appear to have adopted a common name for themselves, as the idea of what we call nationality would never seem to have occurred to them. Yet the name of Gaels in the British Isles, and of Gauls in France and Northern Italy, seems identical. Not only did they fill the large expanse of territory we have mentioned, but they multiplied so fast, that they were compelled to send out armed colonies in every direction, set as they were in the midst of thickly-peopled regions.

We possess few details of their first invasion of Spain; but Roman history has made us all acquainted with their valor. It was in the first days of the Republic that an army of Gauls took possession of Rome, and the names of Manlius and Camillus are no better known in history than that of Brenn, called by Livy, Brennus. His celebrated answer, "Vae victis," will live as long as the world.

Later on, in the second century before Christ, we see another army of Celts starting from Pannonia, on the Danube, where they had previously settled, to invade Greece. Another Brenn is at the head of it. Macedonia and Albania were soon conquered; and, it is said, some of the peculiarities of the race may still be remarked in many Albanians. Thessaly could not resist the impetuosity of the invaders; the Thermopylae were occupied by Gallic battalions, and that celebrated defile, where three hundred Spartans once detained the whole army of Xerxes, could offer no obstacle to Celtic bravery. Hellas, sacred Hellas, came then under the power of the Gauls, and the Temple of Delphi was already in sight of Brenn and his warriors, when, according to Greek historians, a violent earthquake, the work of the offended gods, threw confusion into the Celtic ranks, which were subsequently easily defeated and destroyed by the Greeks.

A branch of this army of the Delphic Brenn had separated from the main body on the frontiers of Thrace, taken possession of Byzantium, the future Constantinople, and, crossing the straits, established itself in the Heart of Asia Minor, and there founded the state of Galatia, or Gallo-Greece, which so long bore their name, and for several centuries influenced the affairs of Asia and of the whole Orient, where they established a social state congenial to their tastes and customs. But the Romans soon after invading Asia Minor, the twelve clannish republics formerly founded were, according to Strabo, first reduced to three, then to two, until finally Julius Caesar made Dejotar king of the whole country.

The Celts could not easily brook such a change of social relations; but, unable to cope against Roman power, they came, as usual, to wrangle among themselves. The majority pronounced for another chieftain, named Bogitar, and succeeded in forming a party in Rome in his favor. Clodius, in an assembly of the Roman people, obtained a decree confirmatory of his authority, and he took possession of Pessinuntum, and of the celebrated Temple of Cybele.

The history of this branch of the Celts, nevertheless, did not close with the evil fortunes of their last king. According to Justinus, they swarmed all over Asia. Having lost their autonomy as a nation, they became, as it were, the Swiss mercenaries of the whole Orient. Egypt, Syria, Pontus, called them to their defence. "Such," says Justinus, "was the terror excited by their name, and the constant success of their undertakings, that no king on his throne thought himself secure, and no fallen prince imagined himself able to recover his power, except with the help of the ever-ready Celts of those countries."

This short sketch suffices to show their power of expansion in ancient times among thickly-settled populations. When we have shown, farther on, how to-day they are spreading all over the world, not looking to wild and desert countries, but to large centres of population in the English colonies, we shall be able to convince ourselves that they still present the same characteristic. If they do not bear arms in their hands, it is owing to altered circumstances; but their actual expansion bears a close resemblance to that of ancient times, and the similarity of effect shows the similarity of character.

We pass now to a new feature in the race, which has not, to our knowledge, been sufficiently dwelt upon. All their migrations in old times were across continents; and if, occasionally, they crossed the Mediterranean Sea, they did so always in foreign vessels.

The Celtic race, as we have seen, occupied the whole of Western Europe. They had, therefore, numerous harbors on the Atlantic, and some excellent ones on the Mediterranean. Many passed the greater portion of their lives on the sea, supporting themselves by fishing; yet they never thought of constructing and arming large fleets; they never fought at sea in vessels of their own, with the single exception of the naval battle between Julius Caesar and the Veneti, off the coast of Armorica, where, in one day, the Roman general destroyed the only maritime armament which the Celts ever possessed.

And even this fact is not an exception to the general rule; for M. de Penhouet, the greatest antiquarian, perhaps, in Celtic lore in Brittany, has proved that the Veneti of Western Gaul were not really Celts, but rather a colony of Carthaginians, the only one probably remaining, in the time of Caesar, of those once numerous foreign colonies of the old enemies of Rome.

Still this strange anomaly, an anomaly which is observable in no other people living on an extensive coast, was not produced by ignorance of the uses and importance of large fleets. From the first they held constant intercourse with the great navigators of antiquity. The Celtic harbors teemed with the craft of hardy seamen, who came from Phoenicia, Carthage, and finally from Rome. Heeren, in his researches on the Phoenicians, proves it for that very early age, and mentions the strange fact that the name of Ireland with them was the "Holy Isle." For several centuries, the Carthaginians, in particular, used the harbors of Spain, of Gaul, even of Erin and Britain, as their own. The Celtic inhabitants of those countries allowed them to settle peaceably among them, to trade with them, to use their cities as emporiums, to call them, in fact, Carthaginian harbors, although that African nation never really colonized the country, does not appear to have made war on the inhabitants in order to occupy it, except in a few instances, when thwarted, probably, in their commercial enterprises; but they always lived on peaceful terms with the aborigines, whom they benefited by their trade, and, doubtless, enlightened by the narrative of their expeditions in distant lands.

Is it not a strikingly strange fact that, under such circumstances, the Celts should never have thought of possessing vessels of their own, if not to push the enterprises of an extensive commerce, for which they never showed the slightest inclination, at least for the purpose of shipping their colonies abroad, and crossing directly to Greece from Celtiberia, for instance, or from their Italian colony of the Veneti, replaced in modern times by maritime Venice? Yet so it was; and the great classic scholar, Heeren, in his learned researches on the Phoenicians and Carthaginians, remarks it with surprise. The chief reason which he assigns for the success of those southern navigators from Carthage in establishing their colonies everywhere, is the fact of no people in Spain, Gaul, or the British Isles, possessing at the time a navy of their own; and, finding it so surprising, he does not attempt to explain it, as indeed it really remains without any possible explanation, save the lack of inclination springing from the natural promptings of the race.

What renders it more surprising still is, that individually they had no aversion to a seafaring life; not only many of them subsisted by fishing, but their curraghs covered the sea all along their extensive coasts. They could pass from island to island in their small craft. Thus the Celts of Erin frequently crossed over to Scotland, to the Hebrides, from rock to rock, and in Christian times they went as far as the Faroe group, even as far as Iceland, which some of them appear to have attempted to colonize long before the Norwegian outlaws went there; and some even say that from Erin came the first Europeans who landed on frozen Greenland years before the Icelandic Northmen planted establishments in that dreary country. The Celts, therefore, and those of Erin chiefly, were a seafaring race.

But to construct a fleet, to provision and arm it, to fill it with the flower of their youth, and send them over the ocean to plunder and slay the inhabitants for the purpose of colonizing the countries they had previously devastated, such was never the character of the Celts. They never engaged extensively in trade, or what is often synonymous, piracy. Before becoming christianized, the Celts of Ireland crossed over the narrow channel which divided them from Britain, and frequently carried home slaves; they also passed occasionally to Armorica, and their annals speak of warlike expeditions to that country; but their efforts at navigation were always on an extremely limited scale, in spite of the many inducements offered by their geographical position. The fact is striking when we compare them in that particular with the Scandinavian free-rovers of the Northern Ocean.

It is, therefore, very remarkable that, whenever they got on board a boat, it was always a single and open vessel. They did so in pagan times, when the largest portion of Western Europe was theirs; they continued to do so after they became Christians. The race has always appeared opposed to the operations of an extensive commerce, and to the spreading of their power by large fleets.

The ancient annals of Ireland speak, indeed, of naval expeditions; but these expeditions were always undertaken by a few persons in one, two, or, at most, three boats, as that of the sons of Ua Corra; and such facts consequently strengthen our view. The only fact which seems contradictory is supposed to have occurred during the Danish wars, when Callaghan, King of Cashel, is said to have been caught in an ambush, and conveyed a captive by the Danes, first to Dublin, then to Armagh, and finally to Dundalk.

The troops of Kennedy, son of Lorcan, are said to have been supported by a fleet of fifty sail, commanded by Falvey Finn, a Kerry chieftain. We need not repeat the story so well known to all readers of Irish history. But this fact is found only in the work of Keating, and the best critics accept it merely as an historical romance, which Keating thought proper to insert in his history. Still, even supposing the truth of the story, all that we may conclude from it is that the seafaring Danes, at the end of their long wars, had taught the Irish to use the sea as a battlefield, to the extent of undertaking a small expedition in order to liberate a beloved chieftain.

It is very remarkable, also, that according to the annals of Ireland, the naval expeditions nearly always bore a religious character, never one of trade or barter, with the exception of the tale of Brescan, who was swallowed up with his fifty curraghs, in which he traded between Ireland and Scotland.

Nearly all the other maritime excursions are voyages undertaken with a Christian or Godlike object. Thus our holy religion was carried over to Scotland and the Hebrides by Columbkill and his brother monks, who evangelized those numerous groups of small islands. Crossing in their skiffs, and planting the cross on some far-seen rock or promontory, they perched their monastic cells on the bold bluffs overlooking the ocean.

No more was the warrior on carnage bent to be seen on the seaboards of Ulster or the western coast of Albania, as Scotland was then called; only unarmed men dressed in humble monastic garb trod those wave-beaten shores. At early morning they left the cove of their convent; they spread their single sail, and plied their well-worn oars, crossing from Colombsay to Iona, or from the harbor of Bangor to the nearest shore of the Isle of Man.

At noon they may have met a brother in the middle of the strait in his shell of a boat, bouncing over the water toward the point they had left. And the holy sign of the cross passed from one monk to the other, and the word of benison was carried through the air, forward and back, and the heaven above was propitious, and the wave below was obedient, while the hearts of the two brothers were softened by holy feelings; and nothing in the air around, on the dimly-visible shores, on the surface of the heaving waves, was seen or heard save what might raise the soul to heaven and the heart to God.

In concluding this portion of our subject, we will merely refer to the fact that neither the Celts of Gaul or Britain, nor those of Ireland, ever opposed an organized fleet to the numerous hostile naval armaments by which their country was invaded. When the Roman fleet, commanded by Caesar, landed in Great Britain, when the innumerable Danish expeditions attacked Ireland, whenever the Anglo-Normans arrived in the island during the four hundred years of the colony of the Pale, we never hear of a Celtic fleet opposed to the invaders. Italian, Spanish, and French fleets came in oftentimes to the help of the Irish; yet never do we read that the island had a single vessel to join the friendly expedition. We may safely conclude, then, that the race has never felt any inclination for sending large expeditions to sea, whether for extensive trading, or for political and warlike purposes. They have always used the vessels of other nations, and it is no surprise, therefore, to find them now crowding English ships in their migrations to colonize other countries. It is one of the propensities of the race.

A third feature of Celtic character and mind now attracts our attention, namely, a peculiar literature, art, music, and poetry, wherein their very soul is portrayed, and which belongs exclusively to them. Some very interesting considerations will naturally flow from this short investigation. It is the study of the constitution of the Celtic mind.

In Celtic countries literature was the perfect expression of the social state of the people. Literature must naturally be so everywhere, but it was most emphatically so among the Celts. With them it became a state institution, totally unknown to other nations. Literature and art sprang naturally from the clan system, and consequently adopted a form not to be found elsewhere. Being, moreover, of an entirely traditional cast, those pursuits imparted to their minds a steady, conservative, traditional spirit, which has resulted in the happiest consequences for the race, preserving it from theoretical vagaries, and holding it aloof, even in our days, from the aberrations which all men now deplore in other European nations, and whose effects we behold in the anarchy of thought. This last consideration adds to this portion of our subject a peculiar and absorbing interest.

The knowledge which Julius Caesar possessed of the Druids and of their literary system was very incomplete; yet he presents to his readers a truly grand spectacle, when he speaks of their numerous schools, frequented by an immense number of the youths of the country, so different from those of Rome, in which his own mind had been trained--"Ad has magnus adolescentium numerus disciplinae causa concurrit:" when he mentions the political and civil subjects submitted to the judgment of literary men-- "de omnibus controversiis publicis privatisque constituunt. ... Si de hereditate, si de finibus controversia est, iidem decernunt:" when he states the length of their studies--"annos nonnulli vicenos in disciplina permanent:" when he finally draws a short sketch of their course of instruction-- "multa de sideribus atque eorum motu, de mundi ac terrarum magnitudine, ... disputant juventutique tradunt."

But, unfortunately, the great author of the "Commentaries" had not sufficiently studied the social state of the Celts in Gaul and Britain; he never mentions the clan institution, even when he speaks of the feuds-- factiones--which invariably split their septs--civitates--into hostile parties. In his eleventh chapter, when describing the contentions which were constantly rife in the cities, villages, even single houses, when remarking the continual shifting of the supreme authority from the Edui to the Sequani, and reciprocally, he seems to be giving in a few phrases the long history of the Irish Celts; yet he does not appear to be aware of the cause of this universal agitation, namely, the clan system, of which he does not say a single world. How could he have perceived the effect of that system on their literature and art?

To understand it at once it suffices to describe in a few words the various branches of studies pursued by their learned men; and, as we are best acquainted with that portion of the subject which concerns Ireland, we will confine ourselves to it. There is no doubt the other agglomerations of Celtic tribes, the Gauls chiefly, enjoyed institutions very similar, if not perfectly alike.

The highest generic name for a learned man or doctor was "ollamh." These ollamhs formed a kind of order in the race, and the privileges bestowed on them were most extensive. "Each one of them was allowed a standing income of twenty-one cows and their grasses," in the chieftain's territory, besides ample refections for himself and his attendants, to the number of twenty-four, including his subordinate tutors, his advanced pupils, and his retinue of servants. He was entitled to have two hounds and six horses, . . . and the privilege of conferring a temporary sanctuary from injury or arrest by carrying his wand, or having it carried around or over the person or place to be protected. His wife also enjoyed certain other valuable privileges.--(Prof. E. Curry, Lecture I.)

But to reach that degree he was to prove for himself, purity of learning, purity of mouth (from satire), purity of hand (from bloodshed), purity of union (in marriage), purity of honesty (from theft), and purity of body (having but one wife).

With the Celts, therefore, learning constituted a kind of priesthood. These were his moral qualifications. His scientific attainments require a little longer consideration, as they form the chief object we have in view.

They may at the outset be stated in a few words. The ollamh was "a man who had arrived at the highest degree of historical learning, and of general literary attainments. He should be an adept in royal synchronisms, should know the boundaries of all the provinces and chieftaincies, and should be able to trace the genealogies of all the tribes of Erin up to the first man.--(Prof. Curry, Lecture X.)

Caesar had already told us of the Druids, "Si de hereditate, si de finibus controversia est iidem decernunt." In this passage he gives us a glimpse of a system which he had not studied sufficiently to embrace in its entirety.

The qualifications of an ollamh which we have just enumerated, that is to say, of the highest doctor in Celtic countries, already prove how their literature grew out of the clan system.

The clan system, of which we shall subsequently speak more at length, rested entirely on history, genealogy, and topography. The authority and rights of the monarch of the whole country, of the so-called kings of the various provinces, of the other chieftains in their several degrees, finally, of all the individuals who composed the nation connected by blood with the chieftains and kings, depended entirely on their various genealogies, out of which grew a complete system of general and personal history. The conflicting rights of the septs demanded also a thorough knowledge of topography for the adjustment of their difficulties. Hence the importance to the whole nation of accuracy in these matters, and of a competent authority to decide on all such questions.

But in Celtic countries, more than in all others, topography was connected with general history, as each river or lake, mountain or hill, tower or hamlet, had received a name from some historical fact recorded in the public annals; so that even now the geographical etymologies frequently throw a sudden and decisive light on disputed points of ancient history. So far, this cannot be called a literature; it might be classed under the name of statistics, or antiquarian lore; and if their history consisted merely of what is contained in the old annals of the race, it would be presumptuous to make a particular alllusion to their literature, and make it one of the chief characteristics of the race. The annals, in fact, were mere chronological and synchronic tables of previous events.

But an immense number of books were written by many of their authors on each particular event interesting to each Celtic tribe: and even now many of those special facts recorded in these books owe their origin to some assertion or hint given in the annals. There is no doubt that long ago their learned men were fully acquainted with all the points of reference which escape the modern antiquarian. History for them, therefore, was very different from what the Greeks and Romans have made it in the models they left us, which we have copied or imitated.

It is only in their detached "historical tales" that they display any skill in description or narration, any remarkable pictures of character, manners, and local traditions; and it seems that in many points they show themselves masters of this beautiful art.

Thus they had stories of battles, of voyages, of invasions, of destructions, of slaughters, of sieges, of tragedies and deaths, of courtships, of military expeditions; and all this strictly historical. For we do not here speak of their "imaginative tales," which give still freer scope to fancy; such as the Fenian and Ossianic poems, which are also founded on facts, but can no more claim the title of history than the novels of Scott or Cooper.

The number of those books was so great that the authentic list of them far surpasses in length what has been preserved of the old Greek and Latin writers. It is true that they have all been saved and transmitted to us by Christian Irishmen of the centuries intervening between the sixth and sixteenth; but it is also perfectly true that whatever was handed down to us by Irish monks and friars came to them from the genuine source, the primitive authors, as our own monks of the West have preserved to us all we know of Greek and Latin authors.

So that the question so long decided in the negative, whether the Irish knew handwriting prior to the Christian era and the coming of St. Patrick, is no longer a question, now that so much is known of their early literature. St. Patrick and his brother monks brought with them the Roman characters and the knowledge of numerous Christian writers who had preceded him; but he could not teach them what had happened in the country before his time, events which form the subject-matter of their annals, historical and imaginative tales and poems. For the Christian authors of Ireland subsequently to transmit those facts to us, they must evidently have copied them from older books, which have since perished.

Prof. E. Curry thinks that the Ogham characters, so often mentioned in the most ancient Irish books, were used in Erin long before the introduction of Christianity there. And he strengthens his opinion by proofs which it is difficult to contradict. Those characters are even now to be seen in some of the oldest books which have been preserved, as well as on many stone monuments, the remote antiquity of which cannot be denied. One well-authenticated fact suffices, however, to set the question at rest: "It is quite certain," says E. Curry, "that the Irish Druids and poets had written books before the coming of St. Patrick in 432; since we find THAT VERY STATEMENT in the ancient Gaelic Tripartite life of the Saint, as well as in the "Annotations of Tirechan" preserved in the Book of Armagh, which were taken by him (Tirechan) from the lips and books of his tutor, St. Mochta, who was the pupil and disciple of St. Patrick himself."

What Caesar, then, states of the Druids, that they committed every thing to memory and used no books, is not strictly true. It must have been true only with regard to their mode of teaching, in that they gave no books to their pupils, but confined themselves to oral instruction.

The order of Ollamh comprised various sub-orders of learned men. And the first of these deserving our attention is the class of "Seanchaidhe," pronounced Shanachy. The ollamh seems to have been the historian of the monarch of the whole country; the shanachy had the care of provincial records. Each chieftain, in fact, down to the humblest, had an officer of this description, who enjoyed privileges inferior only to those of the ollamh, and partook of emoluments graduated according to his usefulness in the state; so that we can already obtain some idea of the honor and respect paid to the national literature and traditions in the person of those who were looked upon in ancient times as their guardians from age to age.

The shanachies were also bound to prove for themselves the moral qualifications of the ollamhs.[1]

A shanachy of any degree, who did not preserve these "purities," lost half his income and dignity, according to law, and was subject to heavy penalties besides.

According to McFirbis, in his book of genealogies, "the historians were so anxious and ardent to preserve the history of Erin, that the description they have left us of the nobleness and dignified manners of the people, should not be wondered at, since they did not refrain from writing even of the undignified artisans, and of the professors of the healing and building arts of ancient times --as shall be shown below, to prove the fidelity of the historians, and the errors of those who make such assertions, as, for instance, that there were no stone buildings in Erin before the coming of the Danes and Anglo-Normans.

"Thus saith an ancient authority: `The first doctor, the first builder, and the first fisherman, that were ever in Erin were--

> Capa, for the healing of the sick,
> In his time was all-powerful;

---

[1] "Purity of hand, bright without wounding,
Purity of mouth, without poisonous satire,
Purity of learning, without reproach,
Purity of husbandship, in marriage."
Many of these details and the following are chiefly derived from
Prof. E. Curry
--(Early Irish Manuscripts.)

> And Luasad, the cunning builder,
> And Laighne, the fisherman.'"

So speaks McFirbis in his quaint and picturesque style.

The literature of the Celts was, therefore, impressed with the character of realistic universality, which has been the great boast of the romantic school. It did not concern itself merely with the great and powerful, but comprised all classes of people, and tried to elevate what is of itself undignified and common in human society. This is no doubt the meaning of the quotation just cited.

Among the Celts, then, each clan had his historian to record the most minute details of every-day history, as well as every fact of importance to the whole clan, and even to the nation at large; and thus we may see how literature with them grew naturally out of their social system. The same may not appear to hold good at first sight with the other classes of literary men; yet it would be easy to discover the link connecting them all, and which was always traditional or matter-of-fact, if we may use that expression.

The next SUB-ORDER was that of File, which is generally translated poet, but its meaning also involves the idea of philosophy or wisdom added to that of poetry.

The File among the Celts was, after all, only an historian writing in verse; for all their poetry resolved itself into annals, "poetic narratives" of great events, or finally "ballads."

It is well known that among all nations poetry has preceded prose; and the first writers that appeared anywhere always wrote in verse. It seems, therefore, that in Celtic tribes the order of File was anterior in point of time to that of Shanachy, and that both must have sprung naturally from the same social system. Hence the monarch of the whole nation had his poets, as also the provincial kings and every minor chieftain.

In course of time their number increased to such an extent in Ireland, that at last they became a nuisance to be abated.

"It is said that in the days of Connor McNassa--several centuries before Christ--there met once 1,200 poets in one company; another time 1,000, and another 700, namely, in the days of Aedh McAinmire and Columcille, in the sixth century after our Saviour. And between these periods Erin always thought that she had more of learned men than she wanted; so that from their numbers and the tax their support imposed upon the public, it was attempted to banish them out of Erin on three different occasions; but they were detained by the Ultonians for hospitality's sake. This is evident from the Amhra Columcille (panegyric of St. Columba). He was the last that kept them in Ireland, and distributed a poet to every territory, and a poet to every king, in order to lighten the burden of the people in general. So that there were people in their following, contemporary with every generation to preserve the history and events of the country at this time. Not these alone, but the kings, and, saints, and churches of Erin preserved their history in like manner."

From this curious passage of McFirbis, it is clear that the Celtic poets proposed to themselves the same object as the historians did; only that they wrote in verse, and no doubt allowed themselves more freedom of fancy, without altering the facts which were to them of paramount importance.

McFirbis, in the previous passage, gives us a succinct account of the action of Columbkill in regard to the poets or bards of his time. But we know many other interesting facts connected with this event, which must be considered as one of the most important in Ireland during the sixth century. The order of poets or bards was a social and political institution, reaching back in point of time to the birth of the nation, enjoying extensive privileges, and without which Celtic life would have been deprived of its warmth and buoyancy. Yet Aed, the monarch of all Ireland, was inclined to abolish the whole order, and banish, or even outlaw, all its members. Being unable to do it of his own authority, he thought of having the measure carried in the assembly of Drumceit, convened for the chief purpose of settling peacefully the relations of Ireland with the Dalriadan colony established in Western Scotland a hundred years before. Columba came from Iona in behalf of Aidan, whom he had crowned a short time previously as King of Albania or Scotland. It seems that the bards or poets were accused of insolence, rapacity, and of selling their services to princes and nobles, instead of calling them to account for their misdeeds.

Columba openly undertook their defence in the general assembly of the nation. Himself a poet, he loved their art, and could not consent to see his native country deprived of it. Such a deprivation in his eyes would almost have seemed a sacrilege.

"He represented," says Montalembert, "that care must be taken not to pull up the good corn with the tares, that the general exile of the poets would be the death of a venerable antiquity, and of that poetry so dear to the country, and so useful to those who knew how to employ it. The king and assembly yielded at length, under condition that the number should be limited, and their profession laid under certain rules."

Dallan Fergall, the chief of the corporation, composed his "Amhra," or Praise of Columbkill, as a mark of gratitude from the whole order. That the works of Celtic poets possessed real literary merit, we have the authority of Spenser for believing. The author of the "Faerie Queene" was not the friend of the Irish, whom he assisted in plundering and destroying under Elizabeth. He could only judge of their books from English translations, not being sufficiently acquainted with the language to understand its niceties. Yet he had to acknowledge that their poems "savoured of sweet wit and good invention, but skilled not of the goodly ornaments of poetry; yet were they sprinkled with some pretty flowers of their natural device, which gave good grace and comeliness to them."

He objected, it is true, to the patriotism of their verse, and pretended that they "seldom choose the doings of good men for the argument of their poems," and became "dangerous and desperate in disobedience and rebellious daring." But this accusation is high praise in our eyes, as showing that the Irish bards of Spenser's time praised and glorified those who proved most courageous in resisting English invasion, and stood firmly on the side of their race against the power of a great queen.

A poet, it seems, required twelve years of study to be master of his art. One-third of that time was devoted to practising the "Teinim Laegha," by which he obtained the power of understanding every thing that it was proper for him to speak of or to say. The next third was employed in learning the "Imas Forosnadh," by which he was enabled to communicate thoroughly his knowledge to other pupils. Finally, the last three years were occupied in "Dichedal," or improvisation, so as to be able to speak in verse on all subjects of his study at a moment's notice.

There were, it appears, seven kinds of verse; and the poet was bound to possess a critical knowledge of them, so as to be a judge of his art, and to pronounce on the compositions submitted to him.

If called upon by any king or chieftain, he was required to relate instantly, seven times fifty stories, namely, five times fifty prime stories, and twice fifty secondary stories.

The prime stories were destructions and preyings, courtships, battles, navigations, tragedies or deaths, expeditions, elopements, and conflagrations.

All those literary compositions were historic tales; and they were not composed for mere amusement, but possessed in the eyes of learned men a real authority in point of fact. If fancy was permitted to adorn them, the facts themselves were to remain unaltered with their chief circumstances. Hence the writers of the various annals of Ireland do not scruple to quote many poems or other tales as authority for the facts of history which they relate.

And such also was heroic poetry among the Greeks. The Hellenic philosophers, historians, and geographers of later times always quoted Homer and Hesiod as authorities for the facts they related in their scientific works. The whole first book of the geography of Strabo, one of the most statistical and positive works of antiquity, has for its object the vindication of the geography of Homer, whom Strabo seems to have considered as a reliable authority on almost every possible subject.

Our limits forbid us to speak more in detail of Celtic historians and poets. We have said enough to show that both had important state duties to perform in the social system of the country, and, while keeping within due bounds, they were esteemed by all as men of great weight and use to the nation. Besides the field of genealogy and history allotted to them to cultivate, their very office tended to promote the love of virtue, and to check immorality and vice. They were careful to watch over the acts and inclinations of their princes and chieftains, seldom failing to brand them with infamy if guilty of crimes, or crown them with honor when they had deserved well of the nation. In ancient Egypt the priests judged the kings after their demise; in Celtic countries they dared to tell them the truth during their lifetime. And this exercised a most salutary effect on the people; for perhaps never in any other country did the admiration for learning, elevation of feeling, and ardent love of justice and right, prevail as in Ireland, at least while enjoying its native institutions and government.

From many of the previous details, the reader will easily see That the literature of the Celts presented features peculiar to Their race, and which supposed a mental constitution seldom found among others. If, in general, the world of letters gives expression In some degree to social wants and habits, among the Celts this expression was complete, and argued a peculiar bent of mind given entirely to traditional lore, and never to philosophical speculations and subtlety. We see in it two elements remarkable for their distinctness. First, an extraordinary fondness for facts and traditions, growing out of the patriarchal origin of society among them; and from this fondness their mind received a particular tendency which was averse to theories and utopias. All things resolved themselves into facts, and they seldom wandered away into the fields of conjectural conclusions. Hence their extraordinary adaptation to the truths of the Christian religion, whose dogmas are all supernatural facts, at once human and divine. Hence have they ever been kept free from that strange mental activity of other European races, which has led them into doubt, unbelief, skepticism, until, in our days, there seem to be no longer any fixed principles as a substratum for religious and social doctrines.

Secondly, we see in the Celtic race a rare and unique outburst of fancy, so well expressed in the "Senchus Mor," their great law compilation, wherein it is related, that when St. Patrick had completed the digest of the laws of the Gael in Ireland, Dubtach, who was a bard as well as a brehon, "put a thread of poetry round it." Poetry everywhere, even in a law-book; poetry inseparable from their thoughts, their speech, their every-day actions; poetry became for them a reality, an indispensable necessity of life. This feature is also certainly characteristic of the Celtic nature.

Hence their literature was inseparable from art; and music and design gushed naturally from the deepest springs of their souls.

Music has always been the handmaid of Poetry; and in our modern languages, even, which are so artificial and removed from primitive enthusiasm and naturalness, no composer of opera would consent to adapt his inspirations to a prose libretto. It was far more so in primitive times; and it maybe said that in those days poetry was never composed unless to be sung or played on instruments. But what has never been seen elsewhere, what Plato dreamed, without ever hoping to see realized, music in Celtic countries became really a state institution, and singers and harpers were necessary officers of princes and kings.

That all Celtic tribes were fond of it and cultivated it thoroughly we have the assertion of all ancient writers who spoke of them. According to Strabo, the Third order of Druids was composed of those whom he calls Umnetai. What were their instruments is not mentioned; and we can now form no opinion of their former musical taste from the rude melodies of the Armoricans, Welsh, and Scotch.

From time immemorial the Irish Celts possessed the harp. Some authors have denied this; and from the fact that the harp was unknown to the Greeks and Romans, and that the Gauls of the time of Julius Caesar do not seem to have been acquainted with it, they conclude that it was not purely native to any of the British islands.

But modern researches have proved that it was certainly used in Erin under the first successors of Ugaine Mor, who was monarch. --Ard-Righ--about the year 633 before Christ, according to the annals of the Four Masters. The story of Labhraid, which seems perfectly authentic, turns altogether on the perfection with which Craftine played on the harp. From that time, at least, the instrument became among the Celts of Ireland a perpetual source of melody.

To judge of their proficiency in its use, it is enough to know to what degree of perfection they had raised it. Mr. Beauford, in his ingenious and learned treatise on the music of Ireland, as cultivated by its bards, creates genuine astonishment by the discoveries into which his researches have led him.

The extraordinary attention which they paid to expression and effect brought about successive improvements in the harp, which at last made it far superior to the Grecian lyre. To make it capable of supporting the human voice in their symphonies, they filled up the intervals of the fifths and thirds in each scale, and increased the number of strings from eighteen to twenty-eight, retaining all the original chromatic tones, but reducing the capacity of the instrument; for, instead of commencing in the lower E in the bass, it commenced in C, a sixth above, and terminated in G in the octave below; and, in consequence, the instrument became much more melodious and capable of accompanying the human voice. Malachi O'Morgair, Archbishop of Armagh, introduced other improvements in it in the twelfth century. Finally, in later times, its capacity was increased from twenty-eight strings to thirty-three, in which state it still remains.

As long as the nation retained its autonomy, the harp was a universal instrument among the inhabitants of Erin. It was found in every house; it was heard wherever you met a few people gathered together. Studied so universally, so completely and perfectly, it gave Irish music in the middle ages a superiority over that of all other nations. It is Cambrensis who remarks that "the attention of these people to musical instruments is worthy of praise, in which their skill is, beyond comparison, superior to any other people; for in these the modulation is not slow and solemn, as in the instruments of Britain, but the sounds are rapid and precipitate, yet sweet and pleasing. It is extraordinary, in such rapidity of the fingers, how the musical proportions are preserved, and the art everywhere inherent among their complicated modulations, and the multitude of intricate notes so sweetly swift, so irregular in their composition, so disorderly in their concords, yet returning to unison and completing the melody."

Giraldus could not express himself better, never before having heard any other music than that of the Anglo-Normans; but it is clear, from the foregoing passage, that Irish art surpassed all his conceptions.

The universality of song among the Irish Celts grew out of their nature, and in time brought out all the refinements of art. Long before Cambrensis's time the whole island resounded with music and mirth, and the king-archbishop, Cormac McCullinan, could not better express his gratitude to his Thomond subjects than by exclaiming--

> "May our truest fidelity ever be given
> To the brave and generous clansmen of Tal;
> And forever royalty rest with their tribe,
> And virtue and valor, and music and song!"

Long before Cormac, we find the same mirthful glee in the Celtic character expressed by a beautiful and well-known passage in the life of St. Bridget: Being yet an unknown girl, she entered, by chance, the dwelling of some provincial king, who was at the time absent, and, getting hold of a harp, her fingers ran over the chords, and her voice rose in song and glee, and the whole family of the royal children, excited by the joyful harmony, surrounded her, immediately grew familiar with her, and treated her as an elder sister whom they might have known all their life; so that the king, coming back, found all his house in an uproar, filled as it was with music and mirth.

Thus the whole island remained during long ages. Never in the whole history of man has the same been the case with any other nation. Plato, no doubt, in his dream of a republic, had something of the kind in his mind, when he wished to constitute harmony as a social and political institution. But he little thought that, when he thus dreamed and wrote, or very shortly after, the very object of his speculation was already, or was soon to be, in actual existence in the most western isle of Europe.

Before Columba's time even the Church had become reconciled to the bards and harpers; and, according to a beautiful legend, Patrick himself had allowed Oisin, or Ossian, and his followers, to sing the praises of ancient heroes. But Columbkill completed the reconciliation of the religious spirit with the bardic influence. Music and poetry were thenceforth identified with ecclesiastical life. Monks and grave bishops played on the harp in the churches, and it is said that this strange spectacle surprised the first Norman invaders of Ireland. To use the words of Montalembert, so well adapted to our subject: "Irish poetry, which was in the days of Patrick and Columba so powerful and so popular, has long undergone, in the country of Ossian, the same fate as the religion of which these great saints were the apostles. Rooted, like it, in the heart of a conquered people, and like it proscribed and persecuted with an unwearying vehemence, it has come ever forth anew from the bloody furrow in which it was supposed to be buried. The bards became the most powerful allies of patriotism, the most dauntless prophets of independence, and also the favorite victims of the cruelty of spoilers and conquerors. They made music and poetry weapons and bulwarks against foreign oppression; and the oppressors used them as they had used the priests and the nobles. A price was set upon their heads. But while the last scions of the royal and noble races, decimated or ruined in Ireland, departed to die out under a foreign sky, amid the miseries of exile, the successor of the bards, the minstrel, whom nothing could tear from his native soil, was pursued, tracked, and taken like a wild beast, or chained and slaughtered like the most dangerous of rebels.

"In the annals of the atrocious legislation, directed by the English against the Irish people, as well before as after the Reformation, special penalties against the minstrels, bards, and rhymers, who sustained the lords and gentlemen, . . . are to be met with at every step.

"Nevertheless, the harp has remained the emblem of Ireland, even in the official arms of the British Empire, and during all last century, the travelling harper, last and pitiful successor of the bards, protected by Columba, was always to be found at the side of the priest, to celebrate the holy mysteries of the proscribed worship. He never ceased to be received with tender respect under the thatched roof of the poor Irish peasant, whom he consoled in his misery and oppression by the plaintive tenderness and solemn sweetness of the music of his fathers."

Could any expression of ours set forth in stronger light the Celtic mind and heart as portrayed in those native elements of music and literature? Could any thing more forcibly depict the real character of the race, materialized, as it were, in its exterior institutions? We were right in saying that among no other race was what is generally a mere adornment to a nation, raised to the dignity of a social and political instrument as it was among the Celts. Hence it was impossible for persecution and oppression to destroy it, and the Celtic nature to-day is still traditional, full of faith, and at the same time poetical and impulsive as when those great features of the race held full sway.

Besides music, several other branches of art, particularly architecture, design, and calligraphy, are worthy our attention, presenting, as they do, features unseen anywhere else; and would enable us still better to understand the character of the Celtic race. But our limits require us to refrain from what might be thought redundant and unnecessary.

We hasten, therefore, to consider another branch of our investigation, one which might be esteemed paramount to all others, and by the consideration of which we might have begun this chapter, only that its importance will be better understood after what has been already said. It is a chief characteristic which grew so perfectly out of the Celtic mind and aptitudes, that long centuries of most adverse circumstances, we may say, a whole host of contrary influences were unable to make the Celts entirely abandon it. We mean the clan system, which, as a system, indeed, has disappeared these three centuries ago, but which may be said to subsist still in the clan spirit, as ardent almost among them as ever.

It is beyond doubt that the patriarchal government was the first established among men. The father ruled the family. As long as he lived he was lawgiver, priest, master; his power was acknowledged as absolute. Hiis children, even after their marriage, remained to a certain extent subject to him. Yet each became in turn the head of a small state, ruled with the primitive simplicity of the first family.

In the East, history shows us that the patriarchal government was succeeded immediately by an extensive and complete despotism. Millions of men soon became the abject slaves of an irresponsible monarch. Assyria, Babylonia, Egypt, appear at once in history as powerful states at the mercy of a despot whose will was law.

But in other more favored lands the family was succeeded by the tribe, a simple development of the former, an agglomeration of men of the same blood, who could all trace their pedigree to the acknowledged head; possessing, consequently, a chief of the same race, either hereditary or elective, according to variable rules always based on tradition. This was the case among the Jews, among the Arabs, with whom the system yet prevails; even it seems primitively in Hindostan, where modern research has brought to light modes of holding property which suppose the same system.

But especially was this the case among the Celts, where the system having subsisted up to recently, it can be better known in all its details. Indeed, their adherence to it, in spite of every obstacle that could oppose it, shows that it was natural to them, congenial to all their inclinations, the only system that could satisfy and make them happy; consequently, a characteristic of the race.

There was a time when the system we speak of ruled many a land, from the Western Irish Sea to the foot of the Caucasus. Everywhere within those limits it presented the same general features; in Ireland alone has it been preserved in all its vigor until the beginning of the seventeenth century, so rooted was it in the Irish blood. Consequently, it can be studied better there. What we say, therefore, will be chiefly derived from the study of

Irish customs, although other Gaelic tribes will also furnish us with data for our observations.

In countries ruled by the clan system, the territory was divided among the clans, each of them occupying a particular district, which was seldom enlarged or diminished. This is seen particularly in Palestine, in ancient Gaul, in the British islands. Hence their hostile encounters had always for object movable plunder of any kind, chiefly cattle; never conquest nor annexation of territory. The word "preying," which is generally used for their expeditions, explains their nature at once. It was only in the event of the extinction of a clan that the topography was altered, and frequently a general repartition of land among neighboring tribes took place.

It is true, when a surplus population compelled them to send abroad swarms of their youth, that the conquest of a foreign country became an absolute necessity. But, on such occasions it was outside of Celtic limits that they spread themselves, taking possession of a territory not their own. They almost invariably respected the land of other clans of the same race, even when most hostile to them; exceptions to this rule are extremely rare. It was thus that they sent large armies of their young men into Northern Italy, along the Danube, into Grecian Albania and Thrace, and finally into the very centre of Asia Minor. The fixing of the geographical position of each tribe was, therefore, a rule among them; and in this they differed from nomadic nations, such as the Tartars in Asia and even the North American Indians, whose hold on the land was too slight to offer any prolonged resistance to invaders. Hence the position of the Gallic civitates was definite, and, so to speak, immovable, as we may see by consulting the maps of ancient Gaul at any time anterior to its thorough conquest by the Romans; not so among the German tribes, whose positions on the maps must differ according to time.

We have already seen that so sacred were the limits of the clan districts, that one of the chief duties of ollamhs and shanachies was to know them and see them preserved.

But if territory was defined in Celtic nations, the right of holding land differed in the case of the chieftain and the clansman. The head of the tribe had a certain well-defined portion assigned to him in virtue of his office, and as long only as he held it; the clansmen held the remainder in common, no particular spot being assigned to any one of them.

As far, therefore, as the holding of land was concerned, there were neither rich nor poor among the Celts; the wealth of the best of them consisted of cattle, house furniture, money, jewelry, and other movable property. In the time of St. Columba, the owner of five cows was thought to be a very poor man, although he could send them to graze on any free land of his tribe. There is no doubt that the almost insurmountable difficulty of the land question at this time originated in the attachment of the people to the old system, which had not yet perished in their affections; and certainly many "agrarian outrages," as they are called, have had their source in the traditions of a people once accustomed to move and act freely in a free territory.

It is needless to call the attention of the reader to another consequence of that state of things, namely, the persistence of territorial possessions. As no individual among them could alienate his portion, no individual or family could absorb the territory to the exclusion of others; no great landed aristocracy consequently could exist, and no part of the land could pass by purchase or in any other way to a different tribe or to an alien race. The force of arms sometimes produced temporary changes, nothing more. It is the same principle which has preserved the small Indian tribes still existing in Canada. Their "reservations," as they are called, having been legalized by the British Government at the time of the conquest from the French, the territory assigned to them would have remained in their occupancy forever in the midst of the ever-shifting possessions of the white race, had not the Ottawa Parliament lately "allowed" those reservations to be divided among the families of the tribes, with power for each to dispose of its portion, a power which will soon banish them from the country of their ancestors.

The preceding observations do not conflict in the least with what is generally said of inheritance by "gavel kind," whereby the property was equally divided among the sons to the exclusion of the daughters; as it is clear that the property to be thus divided was only movable and personal property.

But after the land we must consider the persons under the clan-system. Under this head we shall examine briefly:

I. The political offices, such as the dignities of Ard-Righ or supreme monarch, of the provincial kings, and of the subordinate chieftains.

II. The state of the common people.

III. The bondsmen or slaves.

All literary or civil offices, not political, were hereditary. Hence the professions of ollamh, shanachy, bard, brehon, physician, passed from father to son--a very injudicious arrangement apparently, but it seems nevertheless to have worked well in Ireland. Strange to say, however, these various classes formed no castes as in Egypt or in India, because no one was prevented from embracing those professions, even when not born to them; and, in the end, success in study was the only requisite for reaching the highest round of the literary or professional ladder, as in China.

But a stranger and more dangerous feature of the system was that in political offices the dignities were hereditary as to the family, elective as to the person. Hence the title of Ard-Righ or supreme monarch did not necessarily pass to the eldest son of the former king, but another member of the same family might be elected to the office, and was even designated to it during the lifetime of the actual holder, thus becoming Tanist or heir-apparent. Every one sees at a glance the numberless disadvantages resulting from such an institution, and it must be said that most of the bloody crimes recorded in Irish history sprang from it.

At first sight, the dignity of supreme monarch would almost seem to be a sinecure under the clan system, as the authority attached to it was extremely limited, and is generally compared in its relations to the subordinate kings, as that of metropolitan to suffragan bishops in the Church. Nevertheless, all Celtic nations appear to have attached a great importance to it, and the real misfortunes of Ireland began when contention ran so high for the office that the people were divided in their supreme allegiance, and no Ard-Righ was acknowledged at the same time by all; which happened precisely at the period of the invasion under Strongbow.

Some few facts lately brought to light in the vicissitudes of various branches of the Celtic family show at once how highly all Celts, wherever they might be settled, esteemed the dignity of supreme monarch. It existed, as we have said, in all Celtic countries, and consequently in Gaul; and the passage in the "Commentaries" of Julius Caesar on the subject is too important to be entirely passed over.

After having remarked in the eleventh chapter, "De Bello Gallico," lib. vi., that in Gaul the whole country, each city or clan, and every subdivision of it, even to single houses, presented the strange spectacle of two parties, "factiones," always in presence of and opposed to each other, he says in Chapter XII.: --at the arrival of Caesar in Gaul the Eduans and the Sequanians were contending for the supreme authority--"The latter civitas--clan-- namely, the Sequanians, being inferior in power--because from time immemorial the supreme authority had been vested in the Eduans--had called to its aid the Germans under Ariovist by the inducement of great advantages and promises. After many successful battles, in which the entire nobility of the Eduan clan perished, the Sequanians acquired so much power that they rallied to themselves the greatest number of the allies of their rivals, obliged the Eduans to give as hostages the children of their nobles who had perished, to swear that they would not attempt any thing against their conquerors, and even took possession of a part of their territory, and thus obtained the supreme command of all Gaul."

We see by this passage that there was a supremacy resting in the hands of some one, over the whole nation. The successful tribe had a chief to whom that supremacy belonged. Caesar, it is true, does not speak of a monarch as of a person, but attributes the power to the "civitas," the tribe. It is well known, however, that each tribe had a head, and that in Celtic countries the power was never vested in a body of men, assembly, committee, or board, as we say in modern times, but in the chieftain, whatever may have been his degree.

The author of the "Commentaries" was a Roman in whose eyes the state was every thing, the actual office-holder, dictator, consul, or praetor, a mere instrument for a short time; and he was too apt, like most of his countrymen, to judge of other nations by his own.

We may conclude from the passage quoted that there was a supreme monarch in Gaul as well as in Ireland, and modern historians of Gaul have acknowledged it.

But there is yet a stranger fact, which absolutely cannot be explained, save on the supposition that the Celts everywhere held the supreme dignity of extreme if not absolute importance in their political system.

To give it the preeminence it deserves, we must refer to a subsequent event in the history of the Celts in Britain, since it happened there several centuries after Caesar, and we will quote the words of Augustin Thierry, who relates it:

"After the retreat of the legions, recalled to Italy to protect the centre of the empire and Rome itself against the invasion of the Goths, the Britons ceased to acknowledge the power of the foreign governors set over their provinces and cities. The forms, the offices, the very spirit and language of the Roman administration disappeared; in their place was reconstituted the traditional authority of the clannish chieftains formerly abolished by Roman power. Ancient genealogies carefully preserved by the poets, called in the British language bairdd - bards - helped to discover those who could pretend to the dignity of chieftains of tribes or families, tribe and family being synonymous in their language; and the ties of relationship formed the basis of their social state. Men of the lowest class, among that people, preserved in memory the long line of their ancestry with a care scarcely known to other nations, among the highest lords and princes. All the British Celts, poor or rich, had to establish their genealogy in order fully to enjoy their civil rights and secure their claim of property in the territory of the tribe. The whole belonging to a primitive family, no one could lay any claim to the soil, unless his relationship was well established.

"At the top of this social order, composing a federation of small hereditary sovereignties, the Britons, freed from Roman power, constituted a high national sovereignty; they created a chieftain of chieftains, in their tongue called Penteyrn, that is to say, a king of the whole, in the language of their old annals. And they made him elective.--It was also formerly the custom in Gaul. --The object was to introduce into their system a kind of centralization, which, however, was always loose among Celtic tribes."--(Conquete de l'Angleterre, liv. i.)

It is evident to us that if the Britons constituted a supreme power, when freed from the Roman yoke, it was only because they had possessed it before they became subject to that yoke. It is, therefore, safe to conclude that there was a supreme monarch in Britain and in Gaul as well as in Ireland; and since the Britons, after having lost for several centuries their autonomy of government, thought of reestablishing this supreme authority as soon as they were free to do so, it is clear that they attached a real importance to it, and that it entered as an essential element into the social fabric.

But what in reality was the authority of the Ard-Righ in Ireland, of the Penteyrn in Britain, of the supreme chief in Gaul, whose name, as usual, is not mentioned by Caesar?

First, it is to be remarked that a certain extent of territory was always under his immediate authority. Then, as far as we can gather from history, there was a reciprocity of obligations between the high power and the subordinate kings or chieftains, the former granting subsidies to the latter, who in turn paid tribute to support the munificence or military power of the former.

We know from the Irish annals that the dignity of Ard-Righ was always sustained by alliances with some of the provincial kings, to secure the submission of others, and we have a hint of the same nature in the passage, already quoted, from Caesar, as also taking place in Gaul.

We know also from the "Book of Rights" that the tributes and stipends consisted of bondsmen, silver shields, embroidered cloaks, cattle, weapons, corn, victuals, or any other contribution.

The Ard-Righ, moreover, convened the Feis, or general assembly of the nation, every third year; first at Tara, and after Tara was left to go to ruin in consequence of the curse of St. Ruadhan in the sixth century, wherever the supreme monarch established his residence.

The order of succession to the supreme power was the weakest point of the Irish constitution, and became the cause of by far the greatest portion of the nation's calamities. Theoretically the eldest son--some say the eldest relative--of the monarch succeeded him, when he had no blemish constituting a radical defect: the supreme power, however, alternating in two families. To secure the succession, the heir-apparent was always declared during the life of the supreme king; but this constitutional arrangement caused, perhaps, more crimes and wars than any other social institution among the Celts. The truth is that, after the heir-apparent, sustained by some provincial king, supplanted the reigning monarch, one of the provincial chieftains claimed the crown and succeeded to it by violence.

Yet the general rule that the monarch was to belong to the race of Miledh was adhered to almost without exception. One hundred and eighteen sovereigns, according to the moat accredited annals, governed the whole island from the Milesian conquest to St. Patrick in 432. Of these, sixty were of the family of Heremon, settled in the northern part of the island; twenty-nine of the posterity of Heber, settled in the south; twenty-four of that of Ir; three issued from Lugaid, the son of Ith. All these were of the race of Miledh; one only was a firbolg, or plebeian, and one a woman.

It is certainly very remarkable that for so long a time--nearly two thousand years, according to the best chronologists--Ireland was ruled by princes of the same family. The fact is unparalleled in history, and shows that the people were firmly attached to their constitution, such as it was. It extorted the admiration of Sir John Davies, the attorney-general of James I, and later of Lord Coke.

The functions of the provincial kings of Ulster, Munster, Leinster, and Connaught, were in their several districts the same as those which the Ard-Righ exercised over the whole country. They also had their feuds and alliances with the inferior chieftains, and in peaceful times there was also a reciprocity of obligations between them. Presents were given by the superiors, tributes by the inferiors; deliberations in assembly, mutual agreement for public defence, wars against a common enemy, produced among them traditional rules which were generally followed, or occasional dissensions.

Sometimes a province had two kings, chiefly Munster, which was often divided into north and south. Each king had his heir-apparent, the same as the monarch. Indeed, every hereditary office had, besides its actual holder, its Tanist, with right of succession. Hence causes of division and feuds were needlessly multiplied; yet all the Celtic tribes adhered tenaciously to all those institutions which appeared rooted in their very nature, and which contributed to foster the traditional spirit among them.

For these various offices and their inherent rights were all derived from the universally prevailing family or clannish disposition. Genealogies and traditions ruled the whole, and gave, as we have seen, to their learned men a most important part and function in the social state; and thus what the Greek and Latin authors, Julius Caesar principally, have told us of the Celtic Druids, is literally true of the ollamhs in their various degrees.

But the clannish spirit chiefly showed itself in the authority and rights of every chieftain in his own territory. He was truly the patriarch of all under him, acknowledged as he was to be the head of the family, elected by all to that office at the death of his predecessor, after due consultation with the files and shanachies, to whom were intrusted the guardianship of the laws which governed the clan, and the preservation of the rights of all according to the strict order of their genealogies and the traditional rules to be observed.

The power of the chieftain was immense, although limited on every side by laws and customs. It was based on the deep affection of relationship which is so ardent in the Celtic nature. For all the clansmen were related by blood to the head of the tribe, and each one took a personal pride in the success of his undertakings. No feudal lord could ever expect from his vassals the like self-devotion; for, in feudalism, the sense of honor, in clanship, family affection, was the chief moving power.

In clanship the type was not an army, as in feudalism, but a family. Such a system, doubtless, gave rise to many inconveniences. "The breaking up of all general authority," says the Very Rev. Dean Butler (Introduction to Clyn's "Annals"), "and the multiplication of petty independent principalities, was an abuse incident on feudalism; it was inherent in the very essence of the patriarchal or family system. It began, as feudalism ended, with small independent societies, each with its own separate centre of attraction, each clustering round the lord or the chief, and each rather repelling than attracting all similar societies. Yet it was not without its advantages. If feudalism gave more strength to attack an enemy, clanship secured more happiness at home. The first implied only equality for the few, serfdom or even slavery for the many; the other gave a feeling of equality to all."

It was, no doubt, this feeling of equality, joined to that of relationship, which not only secured more happiness for the Celt, but which so closely bound the nobility of the land to the inferior classes, and gave these latter so ardent an affection for their chieftains. Clanship, therefore, imparted a peculiar character to the whole race, and its effect was so lasting and seemingly ineradicable as to be seen in the nation to-day.

Wherever feudalism previously prevailed, we remark at this time a fearful hatred existing between the two classes of the same nation; and the great majority of modern revolutions had their origin in that terrible antagonism.

The same never existed, and could not exist, in Celtic Countries; and if England, after a conflict of many centuries, had not finally succeeded in destroying or exiling the entire nobility of Ireland, we should, doubtless, see to this very day that tender attachment between high and low, rich and poor, which existed in the island in former ages.

This, therefore, not only imparted a peculiar character to the people, but also gave to each subordinate chieftain an immense power over his clan; and it is doubtful if the whole history of the country can afford a single example of the clansmen refusing obedience to their chief, unless in the case of great criminals placed by their atrocities under the ban of society in former times, and under the ban of the Church, since the establishment of the Christian religion among them.

The previous observations give us an insight into the state of the people in Celtic countries. Since, however, we know that slavery existed among them, we must consider a moment what kind of slavery it was, and how soon it disappeared without passing, as in the rest of Europe, through the ordeal of serfdom.

At the outset, we cannot, as some have done, call slaves the conquered races and poor Milesians, who, according to the ancient annals of Ireland, rose in insurrection and established a king of their own during what is supposed to be the first century of the Christian era. The attacotts, as they were called, were not slaves, but poor agriculturists obliged to pay heavy rents: their very name in the Celtic language means "rent-paying tribes or people." Their oppression never reached the degree of suffering under which the Irish small farmers of our days are groaning. For, according to history, they could in three years prepare from their surplus productions a great feast, to which the monarch and all his chieftains, with their retinue, were invited, to be treacherously assassinated at the end of the banquet. The great plain of Magh Cro, now Moy Cru, near Knockma, in the county of Galway, was required for such a monster feast; profusion of meats, delicacies, and drinks was, of course, a necessity for the entertainment of such a number of high-born and athletic guests, and the feast lasted nine days. Who can suppose that in our times the free cottiers of a whole province in Ireland, after supporting their families and paying their rent, could spare even in three years the money and means requisite to meet the demands of such an occasion? But the simple enunciation of the fact proves at least that the attacotts were no slaves, but at most merely an inferior caste, deprived of many civil rights, and compelled to pay taxes on land, contrary to the universal custom of Celtic countries.

Caesar, it is true, pretends that real slavery existed among the Celts in Gaul. But a close examination of that short passage in his "Commentaries," upon which this opinion is based, will prove to us that the slavery he mentions was a very different thing from that existing among all other nations of antiquity.

"All over Gaul," he says, "there are two classes of men who enjoy all the honors and social standing in the state--the Druids and the knights. The plebeians are looked upon almost as slaves, having no share in public affairs. Many among them, loaded with debt, heavily taxed, or oppressed by the higher class, give themselves in servitude to the nobility, and then, in hos eadem omnia sunt jura quoe dominis in servos, the nobles lord it over them as, with us, masters over their slaves."

It is clear from this very passage that among the Celts no such servile class existed as among the Romans and other nations of antiquity. The plebeians, as Caesar calls them, that is to say, the simple clansmen, held no office in the state, were not summoned to the councils of the nation, and, on that account, were nobodies in the opinion of the writer. But the very name he gives them - plebs - shows that they were no more real slaves than the Roman plebs. They exercised their functions in the state by the elections, and Caesar did not know they could reach public office by application to study, and by being ordained to the rank of file, or shanachy, or brehon, in Ireland, at least: and this gave them a direct share in public affairs.

He adds that debt, taxation, and oppression, obliged a great many to give themselves in servitude, and that then they were among the Celts what slaves were among the Romans.

This assertion of Caesar requires some examination. That there were slaves among the Gaels, and particularly in Ireland, we know from several passages of old writers preserved in the various annals of the country. St. Patrick himself was a slave there in his youth, and we learn from his history and other sources how slaves were generally procured, namely, by piratical expeditions to the coast of Britain or Gaul. The Irish curraghs, in pagan times, started from the eastern or southern shores of the island, and, landing on the continent or on some British isle, they captured women, children, and even men, when the crew of the craft was strong enough to overcome them; the captives were then taken to Ireland and sold there. They lost their rights, were reduced to the state of "chattels," and thus became real slaves. Among the presents made by a superior to an inferior chieftain are mentioned bondsmen and bondsmaids. We cannot be surprised at this, since the same thing took place among the most ancient patriarchal tribes of the East, and the Bible has made us all acquainted with the male and female servants of Abraham, Isaac, and Jacob, who are also called bondsmen and bondswomen. Among the Celts, therefore, slaves were of two kinds: those stolen from foreign tribes, and those who had, as it were, sold themselves, in order to escape a heavier oppression: these latter are the ones mentioned by Caesar.

The number of the first class must always have been very small, at least in Ireland and Britain, since the piratical excursions of the Celtic tribes inhabiting those countries were almost invariably undertaken in curraghs, which could only bring a few of these unfortunate individuals from a foreign country.

As to the other class, whatever Caesar may say of their number in Gaul, making it composed of the greatest part of the plebeians or common clansmen, we have no doubt but that he was mistaken, and that the number of real slaves reduced to that state by their own act must have always been remarkably small.

How could we otherwise account for the numerous armies levied by the Gaulish chieftains against the power of Rome, or by the British and Irish lords in their continual internecine wars? The clansmen engaged in both cases were certainly freemen, fighting with the determination which freedom alone can give, and this consideration of itself suffices to show that the great mass of the Celtic tribes was never reduced to slavery or even to serfdom.

Moreover, the whole drift of the Irish annals goes to prove that slavery never included any perceptible class of the Celtic population; it always remained individual and domestic, never endangering the safety of the state, never tending to insurrection and civil disorder, never requiring the vigilance nor even the care of the masters and lords.

The story of Libran, recorded in the life of St. Columbkill, is so pertinent to our present purpose, and so well adapted to give us a true idea of what voluntary slavery was among the Celtic tribes, that we will give it entire in the words of Montalembert:

"It was one day announced to Columba in Iona that a stranger had just landed from Ireland, and Columba went to meet him in the house reserved for guests, to talk with him in private and question him as to his dwelliing-place, his family, and the cause of his journey. The stranger told him that he had undertaken this painful voyage in order, under the monastic habit and in exile, to expiate his sins. Columba, desirous of trying the reality of his repentance, drew a most repulsive picture of the hardships and difficult obligations of the new life. 'I am ready,' said the stranger, 'to submit to the most cruel and humiliating conditions that thou canst command me.' And, after having made confession, he swore, still upon his knees, to accomplish all the requirements of penitence. 'It is well,' said the abbot: 'now rise from thy knees, seat thyself, and listen. You must first do penance for seven years in the neighboring island of Tirce, after which I will see you again.' 'But,' said the penitent, still agitated by remorse, 'how can I expiate a perjury of which I have not yet spoken? Before I left my country I killed a poor man. I was about to suffer the punishment of death for that crime, and I was already in irons, when one of my relatives, who is very rich, delivered me by paying the composition demanded. I swore that I would serve him all my life; but, after some days of service, I abandoned him, and here I am notwithstanding my oath.' Upon this the saint added that he would only be admitted to the paschal communion after his seven years of penitence.

"When these were completed, Columba, after having given him the communion with his own hand, sent him back to Ireland to his patron, carrying a sword with an ivory handle for his ransom. The patron, however, moved by the entreaties of his wife, gave the penitent his pardon without ransom. 'Why should we accept the price sent us by the holy Columba? We are not worthy of it. The request of such an intercessor should be granted freely. His blessing will do more for us than any ransom.' And immediately he detached the girdle from his waist, which was the ordinary form in Ireland for the manumission of captives or slaves. Columba had, besides, ordered his penitent to remain with his old father and mother until he had rendered to them the last services. This accomplished, his brothers let him go, saying, 'Far be it from us to detain a man who has labored seven years for the salvation of his soul with the holy Columba!' He then returned to Iona, bringing with him the sword which was to have been his ransom. 'Henceforward thou shaft be called Libran, for thou art free and emancipated from all ties,' said Columba; and he immediately admitted him to take the monastic vows."

Servitude, therefore, continued in Ireland after the establishment of Christianity; but how different from the slavery of other European countries, which it took so many ages to destroy, and which had to pass through so many different stages! Although we cannot know precisely when servitude was completely abolished among the Celts, the total silence of the contemporary annals on the subject justifies the belief that the Danes, on their first landing, found no real slaves in the country; and, if the Danes themselves oppressed the people wherever they established their power, they could not make a social institution of slavery. It had never been more than a domestic arrangement; it could not become a state affair, as among the nations of antiquity.

In clannish tribes, therefore, and particularly among the Celts, the personal freedom of the lowest clansman was the rule, deprivation of individual liberty the exception. Hence the manners of the people were altogether free from the abject deportment of slaves and villeins in other nations--a cringing disposition of the lower class toward their superiors, which continues even to this day among the peasantry of Europe, and which patriarchal nations have never known. The Norman invaders of Ireland, in the twelfth century, were struck with the easy freedom of manner and speech of the people, so different from that of the lower orders in feudal countries. They soon even came to like it; and the supercilious followers of Strongbow readily adopted the dress, the habits, the language, and the good-humor of the Celts, in the midst of whom they found themselves settled.

And it is proper here to show what social dispositions and habits were the natural result of the clan system, so as to become characteristic of the race, and to endure forever, as long at least as the race itself. The artless family state of the sept naturally developed a peculiarly social feeling, much less complicated than in nations more artificially constituted, but of a much deeper and more lasting character. In the very nature of the mind of those tribes there must have been a great simplicity of ideas, and on that account an extraordinary tenacity of belief and will. There is no complication and systematic combination of political, moral, and social views, but a few axioms of life adhered to with a most admirable energy; and we therefore find a singleness of purpose, a unity of national and religious feeling, among all the individuals of the tribe.

As nothing is complicated and systematized among them, the political system must be extremely simple, and based entirely on the family. And family ideas being as absolute as they are simple, the political system also becomes absolute and lasting; without improving, it is true, but also without the constant changes which bring misery with revolution to thoughtful, reflective, and systematic nations. What a frightful amount of misfortunes has not logic, as it is called, brought upon the French! It was in the name of logical and metaphysical principles that the fabric of society was destroyed a hundred years ago, to make room for what was then called a more rationally-constituted edifice; but the new building is not yet finished, and God only knows when it will be!

The few axioms lying at the base of the Celtic mind with respect to government are much preferable, because much more conducive to stability, and consequently to peace and order, whatever may have been the local agitation and temporary feuds and divisions. Hence we see the permanence of the supreme authority resting in one family among the Celts through so many ages, in spite of continual wrangling for that supreme power. Hence the permanence of territorial limits in spite of lasting feuds, although territory was not invested in any particular inheriting family, but in a purely moral being called the clan or sept.

As for the moral and social feelings in those tribes, they are not drawn coldly from the mind, and sternly imposed by the external law, in the form of axioms and enactments, as was the case chiefly in Sparta, and as is still the case in the Chinese Empire to-day; but they gush forth impetuously from impulsive and loving hearts, and spread like living waters which no artificially-cut stones can bank and confine, but which must expand freely in the land they fertilize.

Deep affection, then, is with them at the root of all moral and social feelings; and as all those feelings, even the national and patriotic, are merged in real domestic sentiment, a great purity of morals must exist among them, nothing being so conducive thereto as family affections.

Above all, when those purely-natural dispositions are raised to the level of the supernatural ones by a divinely-inspired code, by the sublime elevation of Christian purity, then can there be found nothing on earth more lovely and admirable. Chastity is always attractive to a pure heart; patriarchal guilelessness becomes sacred even to the corrupt, if not altogether hardened, man.

Of course we do not pretend that this happy state of things is without its exceptions; that the light has no shadow, the beauty no occasional blemish. We speak of the generality, or at least of the majority, of cases; for perfection cannot belong to this world.

Yet mysticism is entirely absent from such a moral and religious state, on account, perhaps, of the paucity of ideas by which the heart is ruled, and perhaps also on account of the artless simplicity which characterizes every thing in primitively-constituted nations. And, wonderful to say, without any mysticism there is often among them a perfect holiness of life, adapting itself to all circumstances, climates, and associations. The same heart of a young maiden is capable of embracing a married life or of devoting itself to religious celibacy; and in either case the duties of each are performed with the most perfect simplicity and the highest sanctity. Hence, how often does a trifling circumstance

determine for her her whole subsequent life, and make her either the mother of a family or the devoted spouse of Christ! Yet, the final determination once taken, the whole after-life seems to have been predetermined from infancy as though no other course could have been possible.

There is no doubt that sensual corruption is particularly engendered by an artificial state of society, which necessarily fosters morbidity of imagination and nervous excitability. A primitive and patriarchal life, on the contrary, leads to moderation in all things, and repose of the senses.

Herein is found the explanation of the eagerness with which the Celts everywhere, but particularly in Ireland, as soon as Christianity was preached to them, rushed to a life of perfection and continence. St. Patrick himself expressed his surprise, and showed, by several words in his "Confessio," that he was scarcely prepared for it. "The sons of Irishmen," he says, "and the daughters of their chieftains, want to become monks and virgins of Christ." We know what a multitude of monasteries and nunneries sprang up all over the island in the very days of the first apostle and of his immediate successors. Montalembert remarks that, according to the most reliable and oldest documents, a religious house is scarcely mentioned which contained less than three thousand monks or nuns. It appeared to be a consecrated number; and this took place immediately after the conversion of the island to Christianity, while even still a great number were pagans.

"There was particularly," says St. Patrick, "one blessed Irish girl, gentle born, most beautiful, already of a marriageable age, whom I had baptized. After a few days she came back and told me that a messenger of God had appeared to her, advising her to become a virgin of Christ, and live united to God. Thanks be to the Almighty! Six days after, she obtained, with the greatest joy and avidity, what she wished. The same must be said of all the virgins of God; their parents--those remaining pagans, no doubt--instead of approving of it, persecute them, and load them with obloquy; yet their number increases constantly; and, indeed, of all those that have been thus born to Christ, I cannot give the number, besides those living in holy widowhood, and keeping continency in the midst of the world.

"But those girls chiefly suffer most who are bound to service; they are often subjected to terrors and threats--from pagan masters surely--yet they persevere. The Lord has given his holy grace of purity to those servant-girls; the more they are tempted against chastity, the more able they show themselves to keep it."

Does not this passage, written by St. Patrick, describe precisely what is now of every-day occurrence wherever the Irish emigrate? The Celts, therefore, were evidently at the time of their conversion what they are now; and it has been justly remarked that, of all nations whose records have been kept in the history of the Catholic Church, they have been the only ones whose chieftains, princes, even kings, have shown themselves almost as eager to become, not only Christians, but even monks and priests, as the last of their clansmen and vassals. Every where else the lower orders chiefly have furnished the first followers of Christ, the rich and the great being few at the beginning, and forming only the exception.

The evident consequence of this well-attested fact is that the pagan Celts, even of the highest rank, generally led pure lives, and admired chastity. But there is something more. Morality rests on the sense of duty; the deeper that sense is imprinted in the heart of man, the more man becomes truly moral and holy. It can be almost demonstrated that scarcely any thing gives more solidity to the sense of duty than a simple and patriarchal life. Their views of morals being no more complicated than their views of any thing else; being accustomed to reduce every thing of a spiritual, moral nature to a few feelings and axioms, as it were, but at the same time becoming strongly attached to them on account of the importance which every man naturally bestows on matters of that sort; what among other nations forms a complicated code of morality more or less pure, more or less corrupt, for the nations of which we speak becomes compressed, so to speak, in a nutshell, and, the essence remaining always at the bottom, the idea of duty grows paramount in their minds and hearts, and every thing they do is illumined by that light of the human conscience, which, after all, is for each one of us the voice of God. False issues do not distract their minds, and give a wrong bias to the conscience. Hence Celtic tribes, by their very nature, were strictly conscientious.

So preeminently was this the case with them that spiritual things in their eyes became, as they truly are, real and substantial. Hence their religion was not an exterior thing only. On the contrary, exterior rites were in their eyes only symbolical, and mere emblems of the reality which they covered.

It should, therefore, be no matter of surprise to us to find that for them religion has always been above all things; that they have always sacrificed to it whatever is dear to man on earth. They all seem to feel as instinctively and deeply as the thoroughly cultivated and superior mind of Thomas More did, that eternal things are infinitely superior to whatever is temporal, and that a wise man ought to give up every thing rather than be faithless to his religion.

From the previous remarks, we map conclude, with Mr. Matthew Arnold, who has applied his critical and appreciative mind to the study of the Celtic character, that "the Celtic genius has sentiment as its main basis, with love of beauty, charm, and spirituality for its excellence," but, he adds, "ineffectualness and self-will for its defects." On these last words we may be allowed to make a few concluding observations.

If by "ineffectualness" is understood that, owing to their impulsive nature, the Celts often attempted more than they could accomplish, and thus failed; or that on many occasions of less import they changed their mind, and, after a slight effort, did not persevere in an undertaking just begun, there is no doubt of the truth of the observation. But, if the celebrated writer meant to say that this defect of character always accompanied the Celts in whatever they attempted, and that thus they were constantly foiled and never successful in any thing; or, still worse, that, owing to want of perseverance and of energy, they too soon relaxed in their efforts, and that every enterprise and determination on their part became "ineffectual"--we so far disagree with him that the main object of the following pages will be to contradict these positions, and to show by the history of the race, in Ireland at least, that, owing precisely to their "self-will," they were never ultimately unsuccessful in their aspirations; but that, on the contrary, they have always in the end effected what with their accustomed perseverance and self-will they have at all times stood for. At least this we hope will become evident, whenever they had a great object in view, and with respect to things to which they attached a real and paramount importance.

THE WORLD UNDER THE LEAD OF THE EUROPEAN RACES.--MISSION OF THE IRISH RACE IN THE MOVEMENT

"The old prophecies are being fulfilled; Japhet takes possession of the tents of Sem."--(De Maistre, Lettre au Comte d'Avaray.)

The following considerations will at once demonstrate the importance and reality of the subject which we have undertaken to treat upon:

It was at the second birth of mankind, when the family of Noah, left alone after the flood, was to originate a new state of things, and in its posterity to take possession of all the continents and islands of the globe, that the prophecy alluded to at the head of this chapter was uttered, to be afterward recorded by Moses, and preserved by the Hebrews and the Christians till the end of time.

Never before has it been so near its accomplishment as we see it now; and the great Joseph de Maistre was the first to point this out distinctly. Yet he did not intend to say that it is only in our times that Europe has been placed by Providence at the head of human affairs; he only meant that what the prophet saw and announced six thousand years ago seems now to be on the point of complete realization.

It will be interesting to examine, first, in a general way, how the race of Japhet, to whom Europe was given as a dwelling place, gradually crept more and more into prominence after having at the outset been cast into the shade by the posterity of the two other sons of Noah.

The Asiatic and African races, the posterity of Sem and Cham, appear in our days destitute of all energy, and incapable not only of ruling over foreign races, but even of standing alone and escaping a foreign yoke. It has not been so from the beginning. There was a period of wonderful activity for them. Asia and Africa for many ages were in turn the respective centres of civilization and of human history; and the material relics of their former energy still astonish all European travellers who visit the Pyramids of Egypt, the obelisks and temples of Nubia and Ethiopia, the immense stone structures of Arabia, Petraea and Persia, as well as the stupendous pagodas of Hindostan. How, under a burning sun, men of those now-despised races could raise structures so mighty and so vast in number; how the ancestors of the now-wretched Copt, of the wandering Bedouin, of the effete Persian, of the dreamy Hindoo, could display such mental vigor and such physical endurance as the remains of their architectural skill and even of their literature plainly show, is a mystery which no one has hitherto attempted to solve. Nothing in modern Europe, where such activity now prevails, can compare with what the Eastern and Southern races accomplished thousands of years ago. Ethiopia, now buried in sand and in sleep, was, according to Heeren, the most reliable observer of antiquity in our days, a land of immense commercial enterprise, and wonderful architectural skill and energy. In all probability Egypt received her civilization from this country; and Homer sings of the renowned prosperity of the long-lived and happy Ethiopians. It is useless to repeat here what we have all learned in our youth of Babylon and Nineveh, in Mesopotamia; of Persepolis, in fertile and blooming Iran; of the now ruined mountain-cities of Idumaea and Northern Arabia; of Thebes and Memphis; of Thadmor, in Syria; of Balk and Samarcand, in Central Asia; of the wonderful cities on the banks of the Ganges and in the southern districts of the peninsula of Hindostan.

That the ancestors of the miserable men who continue to exist in all those countries were able to raise fabrics which time seems powerless to destroy, while their descendants can scarcely erect huts for their habitation, which are buried under the sand at the first breath of the storm, is inexplicable, especially when we take into consideration the principles of the modern doctrine of human progress and the indefinite perfectibility of man.

At the time when those Eastern and Southern nations flourished, the sons of Japhet had not yet taken a place in history. Silently and unnoticed they wandered from the cradle of mankind; and, if scripture had not recorded their names, we should be at a loss to-day to reach back to the origin of European nations. Yet were they destined, according to prophecy, to be the future rulers of the world; and their education for that high destiny was a rude and painful one, receiving as they did for their share of the globe its roughest portion: an uninterrupted forest covering all their domain from the central plateau which they had left to the shores of the northern and western ocean, their utmost limit. Many branches of that bold race--audax Japeti genus--fell into a state of barbarism, but a barbarism very different from that of the tribes of Oriental or Southern origin. With them degradation was not final, as it seems to have been with some branches at least of the other stems. They were always reclaimable, always apt to receive education, and, after having existed for centuries in an almost savage state, they were capable of once more attaining the highest civilization. This the Scandinavian and German tribes have satisfactorily demonstrated.

It may even be said that all the branches of the stock of Japhet first fell from their original elevation and passed through real barbarism, to rise again by their own efforts and occupy a prominent position on the stage of history; and this fact has, no doubt, given rise to the fable of the primitive savage state of all men.

That the theory is false is proved at once by the sudden emergence of all Eastern nations into splendor and strength without ever having had barbarous ancestors. But, when they fall, it seems to be forever; and it looks at least problematical whether Western intercourse, and even the intermixture of Western blood, can reinvigorate the apathetic races of Asia. As to their rising of their own accord and assuming once again the lead of the world, no one can for a moment give a second thought to the realization of such a dream.

But how and when did the races of Japhet appear first in history? How and when did the Eastern races begin to fall behind their younger brethren?

A great deal has been written, and with a vast amount of dogmatism, concerning the Pelasgians and their colonizations and conquests on the shore and over the islands of the Mediterranean Sea. But nothing can be proved with certainty in regard to their origin and manners, their rise and fall. In fact, European history begins with that of Greece; and the struggle between Hellas and Persia is at once the brilliant introduction of the sons of Japhet on the stage of the world--the Trojan War being more than half fabulous.

The campaigns of Alexander established the supremacy of the West; and from that epoch the Oriental races begin to fall into that profound slumber wherein they still lie buried, and which the brilliant activity of the Saracens and Moslems broke for a time--now, we must hope, passed away forever.

The downfall of the far Orient was not, however, contemporaneous with the supremacy of Greece over the East. The great peninsula of India was still to show for many ages an astonishing activity under the successive sway of the Hindoos, the Patans, the Moguls, and the Sikhs. China also was to continue for a long time an immense and prosperous empire; but the existence of both these countries was concentrated in themselves, so that the rest of the world felt no result from their internal agitations. Life was gradually ebbing away in the great Mongolian family, and the silent beatings of the pulse that indicated the slow freezing of their blood could neither be heard nor felt beyond their own territorial limits.

Nothing new in literature and the arts is visible among them after the appearance, on their western frontiers, of the sons of Japhet, led by the Macedonian hero. It now seems established that Sanscrit literature, the only, but really surprising proof of intellectual life in Hindostan, is anterior to that epoch.

As to China, the great discoveries which in the hands of the European races have led to such wonderful results, the mariner's compass, the printing-press, gunpowder, paper, bank-notes, remained for the Chinese mere toys or without further improvements after their first discovery. It is not known when those great inventions first appeared among them. They had been in operation for ages before Marco Polo saw them in use, and scarcely understood them himself. Europeans were at that time so little prepared for the reception of those material instruments of civilization, that the publication of his travels only produced incredulity with regard to those mighty engines of good or evil.

But those very proofs of Oriental ingenuity establish the fact of a point of suspension in mental activity among the nations which discovered them. Its exact date is unknown; but every thing tends to prove that it took place long ages ago, and nothing is so well calculated to bring home to our minds the great fact which we are now trying to establish as the simple mention of the two following phenomena in the life of the most remote Eastern nations:

The genius of the East was at one time able to produce literary works of a philosophical and poetical character unsurpassed by those of any other nation. The most learned men of modern times in Europe, when they are in the position to become practically acquainted with them, and peruse them in their original dialects, can scarcely find words to express their astonishment, intimately conversant as they are with the masterpieces of Greece and Rome and of the most polite Christian nations. They find in Sanscrit poems and religious books models of every description; but they chiefly find in them an abundance, a freshness, a mental energy, which fill them with wonder; yet all those high intellectual endowments have disappeared ages ago, no one knows how nor precisely when. It is clear that the nation which produced them has fallen into a kind of unconscious stupor, which has been its mental condition ever since, and which to-day raises puny Europe to the stature of a giant before the fallen colossus.

Again: many ages ago the Mongolian family in China invented many material processes which have been mainly the clause of the rise of Europe in our days. They were really the invention of the Chinese, who neither received them from nor communicated them to any other nation. Ages ago they became known to us accidentally through their instrumentality; but, as we were not at that time prepared for the adoption of such useful discoveries, their mention in a book then read all over Europe excited only ridicule and unbelief. As soon as the Western mind mastered them of itself, they became straightway of immense importance, and gave rise, we may say, to all that we call modern civilization. But in the hands of the Chinese they remained useless and unproductive, as they are to this day, although they may now see what we have done with them. Their mind, therefore, once active enough to invent mighty instruments of material progress, long ago became perfectly incapable of improving on its own invention, so that European vessels convey to their astonished sight what was originally theirs, but so improved and altered as to render the original utterly contemptible and ridiculous. And, what is stranger still, though they can compare their own rude implements with ours, and possess a most acute mind in what is materially useful, they cannot be brought to confess Western superiority. The advantage which they really possessed over us a thousand years ago is still a reality to their blind pride.

But it is time to return to the epoch when the race of Japhet began to put forth its power.

Roman intellectual and physical vigor was the first great force which gave Europe that preeminence she has never since lost; and there was a moment in history when it seemed likely that a nation, or a city rather, was on the point of realizing the prophetic promise made to the sons of Noah.

But an idolatrous nation could not receive that boon; and the Roman sway affected very slightly the African and Asiatic nations, whatever its pretensions may have been.

For, when Rome had subdued what she called Europe, Asia, and Africa -- the whole globe--whenever she found that her empire did not reach the sea, she established there posts of armed men; colonies were sent out and legions distributed along the line; even in some places, as in Britain, walls were constructed, stretching across islands, if not along continents. Whatever country had the happiness of being included between those limits belonged to "the city and the world" -urbi et orbi; beyond was Cimmerian darkness in the North, or burning deserts in the South. Mankind had no right to exist outside of her sway; and, if some roaming barbarians strayed over the inhospitable confines, they could not complain at having their existence swept off from the field of history, so unworthy were they of the name of men. Science itself, the science of those times, had to admit such ideas and dictate them to polished writers. Hence, according to the greatest geographers, mankind could exist neither in tropical nor in arctic regions; and Strabo, dividing the globe into five zones, declared that only two of them were habitable.

We now know how false were those assertions, and indeed how circumscribed was the power of ancient Rome. She pretended to universal as well as to eternal dominion; but she deceived herself in both cases. Under her sway the races of Japhet were not "to dwell in the tents of Sem." She was not worthy of accomplishing the great prophecy which is now under our consideration.

It is, however, undoubtedly due to her that the children of Japhet became the dominant race of the globe, and the Eastern nations, once so active and so powerful, were overshadowed by her glory, and had already fallen into that slumber which seems eternal.

Egypt was reduced so low that a victorious Roman general had only to appear on her borders to insure immediate submission.

Syria and Mesopotamia were fast becoming the frightful deserts they are to-day. Persia dared not move in the awful presence of a few legions scattered along the Tigris; and, if, later on, the Parthian kings made a successful resistance against Rome, it was only owing to the abominable corruption of Roman society at the time; but, in fact, Iran had fallen to rise no more, save spasmodically under Mohammedan rule.

The fact is, that, in the subsequent flood of barbarians which for centuries overwhelmed and destroyed the whole of Europe, we behold, on all sides, streams of Northern European races, members of the same family of Japhet. It was the Goths that ruined Palestine even in the time of St. Jerome. If side by side with Northern nations the Huns appeared, no one knows precisely whence they came. Attila called himself King of the Scythians and the Goths, as well as grandson of Nimrod. He came with his mighty hosts from beyond the Danube; this is all that can be said with certainty of his origin.

The East, therefore, was already dead, and could furnish no powerful foe against that Rome which it detested. It is even in this Oriental supineness that we can find a reason for the duration of the inglorious empire of Constantinople. Rome and the West, though far more vigorous, were overwhelmed by barbarians of the same original stock sent by Providence to "renew its youth like that of the eagle." Constantinople and the East continued for a thousand years longer to drag out their feeble existence, because the far Orient could not send a few of its tribes to touch their walls and cause them to crumble into dust. It is even remarkable that the armies of Mohammed and his successors, in the flush of their new fanaticism, did not dare for a long time to attack the race of Japhet settled on the Bosporus. From their native Arabia they easily overran Egypt and Northern Africa, Syria and Palestine, Mesopotamia and Persia. But Asia Minor and Thrace remained for centuries proof against their fury, and, whenever their fleets appeared in the Bosporus, they were easily defeated by the unworthy successors of Constantine and Theodosius. This fact, which has not been sufficiently noticed, shows conclusively that the energy imparted by Mohammedanism to Oriental nations would have lasted but a short time, and encountered in the West a successful resistance, had not the Turks appeared on the scene, destroyed the Saracen dynasties, and, by infusing the blood of Central Asia into the veins of Eastern and Southern fanatics, prolonged for so many ages the sway of the Crescent over a large portion of the globe.

This was the turning-point in human affairs between the East and the West. We do not write history, and cannot, consequently, enter into details. It is enough to say that a new element, strengthened by a long struggle with

Moslemism, was to give to the West a lasting preponderance which ancient Rome could not possess, and whose developments we see in our days. This new element was the Christian religion, solidly established on the ruins of idolatry and heresy; far more solidly established, consequently, than under the Christian emperors of Rome, while paganism still existed in the capital itself.

The Christian religion, which was to make one society of all the children of Adam; which, at its birth, took the name of universal or catholic (whereas previously all religions had been merely national, and therefore very limited in their effects upon mankind at large); which alone was destined to establish and maintain, through all ages, spite of innumerable obstacles, a real universal sway over all nations and tribes--the Christian religion alone could give one race preponderance over others until all should become, as it were, merged into one.

At first it seemed that Providence destined that high calling for the Semitic branch of the human family. The Hebrew people, trained by God himself, through so many ages, for the highest purposes, finally gave birth to the great Leader who, by redeeming all men, was to gather them all into one family. This Leader, our divine Lord, himself a Hebrew, chose twelve men of the same nation to be the founders of the great edifice. We know how, the divine plan was frustrated by the stubbornness of the Jews, who rejected the corner-stone of the building, to be themselves dashed against its walls and destroyed. The sons of Japhet were substituted for the sons of Sem, Europe for Asia, Rome for Jerusalem; and the real commencement of the lasting preponderance of the West dates from the establishment of the Christian Church in Rome.

See how, from Christianity, the Caucasian race, as we call it, came to be the rulers of the world. A mighty revolution, wherein all the branches of that great race become intermingled and confused, sweeps over the Roman Empire. Every thing seems destroyed by the onset of the barbarians, in order that they, by receiving the only true religion which they found without seeking among those whom they conquered, might become worthy of fulfilling the designs of Providence. All the barriers are overthrown that one institution, called Christendom, may take form and harmony. There are to be no more Romans, nor Gauls, nor Iberians, nor Germans, nor Scandinavians--only Christians. It is a renewed and reinvigorated race of Japhet, imbued with true doctrine, clothed with solid virtues, animated with an overwhelming energy. It is a colossal statue, moulded by popes, chiselled by bishops, set on its feet by Christian emperors and kings, chiefly by Charlemagne, Alfred, Louis IX, and Otho. Is there not perfect unity between those great men divided by such intervals of space and time? Is not their work a universal republic, whose foundations they laid with their own hands?

The rest of the world, still prostrate at the feet of foolish idols, or carried away by human errors and delusions, sinks deeper and deeper into apathy and corruption, while Europe is reserved for mighty purposes in centuries to come. A stream is gathering in the West, which is destined to sweep down and bear away all obstacles, and to cover every continent with its regenerating waters.

That stream is modern European history. It has been recorded in thousands of volumes, many of which, however, are totally unreliable fables of those mighty events. Those only have had the key to its right interpretation who have followed the Christian light given from above, as a star, to guide the wonderful giant in his course. The chief among them were: of old, Augustine, the author of the "City of God;" Orosius, the first to condense the annals of the world into the formula, "divina providentia regitur mundus et homo;" Otho of Freysinguen, in his work "De mutatione rerum;" and the author of "Gesta Dei per Francos;" in modern times, Bossuet and his followers.

The destruction of idolatry was of such vital importance in the regeneration of the world that it sufficed as a dogma to imbue a great branch of the Semitic family with a strong life for several centuries. Moslemism has no other truth to support it than the assertion of God's unity; but, by waging war against the Trinity and, consequently, against the very foundation of Christian belief, it became, for a long time, the greatest obstacle to the dissemination of truth. It prevented the early triumph of the Caucasian race, and galvanized, for a time, the nations of the East and South into a false life.

The ravages of the Tartar hordes under Genghis Khan and his successors were in no sense life, but only a fitful madness.

The European stream was thus impeded in its flood by the new activity of Arabia and Turkomania. It was a struggle in which victory, for a long time, hung in the balance: it required many crusades of the whole of Western Europe; the long heroism of the Spanish and Portuguese nations; the incessant attack and defence of the Templars and the Knights of Malta over the whole surface of the Mediterranean Sea, to secure the preponderance of the West. It was finally decided at Lepanto. Since that great day, Mohammedanism has gradually declined, and there now seems no insurmountable obstacle to the free flowing of the European stream.

This stream, however, is not homogeneous: far from it. Had the Christian element always remained alone in it, or at least supreme, long ere this the victory would have been secure forever, and the Catholic missions alone would have fulfilled the old prophecies and given to the sons of Japhet possession of the tents of Sem--a glorious work so well begun in the East, in India and Japan; in the West, in the whole of America!

But, unfortunately, the policy of the papacy, which was also that of Charlemagne, and of other great Christian sovereigns, was not continued. The Norman feudalism of England and Northern France; the Caesarism of Germany and the Capetian kings; the heresies brought from the East by the Crusaders; the paganism and neo-Platonism of the revival of learning; above all, the fearful upheaval of the whole of Europe by the Protestant schism and heresy, troubled the purity of that great Japhetic stream, and has retarded to our days its momentous and overwhelming impetuosity.

Wonderful, indeed, that in the whole of Europe one small island alone was forever stubbornly opposed to all these aberrations, which has stood her ground firmly, and, we may now say, successfully. The reader already knows that the demonstration of this stupendous fact is the object of the present volume.

Having stood aloof so long from all those wanderings from the right path, she has scarcely appeared in the field of European history save as the victim of Scandinavia and of England. But there is a time in the series of ages for the appearance of all those called by Providence to enact a part. What is a myriad of years for man is not a moment for God; and it would seem that we had reached at last the epoch wherein Ireland is to be rewarded for her steadfastness and fidelity.

The impetus now imparted to European power becomes each day more clearly defined, and, to judge by recent appearances, Irishmen are about to play no inglorious part in it. The power of expansion, so characteristic of them from the beginning, has of late years assumed gigantic proportions. The very hatred of their enemies, the measures adopted by their oppressors to annihilate them, have only served to give them a larger field of operations and a much stronger force. It is not without purpose that God has spread them in such numbers over so many different islands and continents. It is theirs to give to the spread of Japhetism among the sons of Sem its right direction and results. The other races of Western Europe would, had they been left to themselves alone, have converted that great event into a curse for mankind, and perhaps the forerunner of the last calamities; but the Irish, having kept themselves pure, are the true instruments in the hands of God for righting what is wrong and purifying what is corrupt.

Had Europe remained in its entirety as steadfast to the true Christian spirit as the small island which dots the sea on its western border, what an incalculable happiness it would have proved to the whole globe, resting as it does to-day under the lead of the race of Japhet!

But where now are the pure waters which should vivify and fertilize it? Innumerable elements are floating in their midst which can but destroy life and spread barrenness everywhere.

Let us see what Europeans believe; what are the motives which actuate them; what they propose to themselves in disseminating their influence and establishing their dominion; what the real, openly-avowed purposes of the leaders are in the vast scheme which embraces the whole earth; what becomes of foreign races as soon as they come in contact with them.

The bare idea causes the blood of the Christian to curdle in his veins, and he thanks God that his life shall not be prolonged to witness the successful termination of the vast conspiracy against God and humanity.

For, in our days, spite of so many deviations in the course of the great European stream, it is truly a matter of wonder what power it has obtained over the globe in its mastery, its control, its unification. What, then, would have been the result had its course remained constantly under Christian guidance!

It is only a short time since the whole earth has become known to us; and we may say that, for Europe, it has been enough only to know it in order to become at once the mistress of it; such power has the Christian religion given her! The first circumnavigation of the globe under Magellan took place but yesterday, and to-day European ships cover the oceans and seas of the world, bearing in every sail the breath and the spirit of Japhetism. The stubborn ice-fields of the pole can scarcely retard their course, and hardy navigators and adventurous travellers jeopardize their lives in the pursuit of merely theoretical notions, void almost of any practical utility.

The most remote and, up to recently, inaccessible parts of the earth are as open to us, owing to steam, as were the countries bordering on the Mediterranean to the ancients. The Argonautic expedition along the southern coast of the Black Sea was in its day an heroic undertaking. The Phoenician colonies established in Africa and Spain by a race trying for the first time in the history of man to launch their ships on the ocean in order to trade with Northern tribes as far as Ireland and the Baltic, though never losing sight of the coast; the attempts of the Carthaginians to circumnavigate Africa; the three years' voyages of the ships of Solomon in the Red Sea and the Persian Gulf, were one and all far more hazardous undertakings than the long voyages of our steamships across the Indian Ocean to Australia, or around Cape Horn to California and the South Sea Islands, through the Southern and Northern Pacifics.

From all large seaboard cities in any part of the globe, lines of steamers now bear men to every point of the compass, so that the very boards at the entrances of offices, to be found everywhere for the accommodation of travellers, are as indices of works on universal geography.

And the European, still unsatisfied with all he has achieved in speed and comfort, looks to more rapid and easier modes of conveyance. Scientific men have been for many years engaged in experiments by means of which they hope to replace the ocean by the atmosphere as a public highway for nations; and the currents of air rushing in every direction with the velocity of the most rapid winds may yet be used by our children instead of rivers, thenceforth deserted, and of ocean-streams at last left empty and waste as before the voyages of Columbus and De Gama.

All this constitutes a positive and stern fact staring us in the face, and giving to the Caucasian race a power of which our ancestors would never have dreamed. And if all this is to be the only result of man's activity--the attainment of merely worldly purposes--God, whose world this is, may look down on it from heaven as on the work of Titans preparing to attack his rights, and He will know how to turn all these mighty efforts of the sons of Japhet to his own holy designs. He may use a small branch of that great race, preserved purposely from the beginning unsullied by mere thrift, and prepared for his work by long persecution, a consideration which we shall examine later on.

Meanwhile the great mass of the European family is allowed to go on in its wonderful undertaking; and we turn to it yet a short while.

As if to favor still more directly this work of the unification of the globe, Providence has placed at the disposal of the prime movers in the enterprise pecuniary means which no one could have foreseen a few years ago.

In 1846, on a small branch of one of the great rivers of California, a colonist discovers gold carried as dust with the sand, and soon a great part of the country is found to be immensely rich in the precious metal. That first discovery is followed by others equally important, and after a few years gold is found in abundance on both sides of a long range of the Rocky Mountains; again in the north, nearly as high up as the arctic circle. North America, in fact, is found to be a vast gold deposit. Australia soon follows, and that new continent, whose exploration has scarcely begun, is said to be dotted all over by large oases of auriferous rock and gravel. In due time the same news comes from South Africa, where it has been lately reported that diamonds, in addition to gold, enrich the explorer and the workman.

It is needless to speak of mines of silver and mercury after gold and diamonds; but the result is that the European race is straightway provided with an enormous wealth commensurate with the immense commercial and manufacturing enterprises required for the establishment of its supremacy all over the globe.

There is work, therefore, for all the ships afloat; others and larger ones have to be constructed; and modern engineering skill places on the bosom of the deep sea vessels which few, indeed, of the greatest rivers can accommodate in their channels and bays.

All these means of dominion and dissemination once procured, the great work clearly assigned to the race of Japhet may proceed.

Intercourse with the most savage and uncivilized tribes is eagerly cultivated even at the risk of life. New avenues to trade are opened up in places where men, still living in the most primitive state, have few if any wants; and it is considered as part of the keen merchant's skill to fill the minds of these uncouth and unsophisticated barbarians with the desire of every possible luxury. Have we not lately heard that the savages of the Feejee Islands, who were a few years ago cannibals, have now a king seeking the protection of England, if not the annexation of his kingdom to the British empire?

Yes, the material civilization of Europe, the new discoveries of steam and magnetism, the untiring energy of men aiming at universal dominion, give to the Caucasian race such a superiority over the rest of mankind that the time seems to be fast approaching when the manners, the dress, the look even of Europeans, will supersede all other types, and spread everywhere the dead level of our habits.

This fact has already been realized in America, North and South. Geographers may give lengthened descriptions of the original tribes which still possess a shadow of existence; foreign readers may perhaps imagine that the continent is still in the quiet possession of rude and uncivilized races roaming at will over its surface, and allowing some Europeans to occupy certain cities and harbors for the purposes of trade and barter. We know that nothing could be more erroneous. The Europeans are the real possessors, north and south; the Indians are permitted to exist on a few spots contracting year by year into narrower limits. The northern and larger half of the continent is chiefly the dwelling-place of the most active branch of the bold race of Japhet. The first of the iron lines which are to connect its Atlantic and Pacific coasts has recently been laid. Cities spring up all along its track: the harbors of California, Oregon, and Alaska, will soon swarm much more than now with hardy navigators ready to europeanize the various groups of islands scattered over the Pacific. Already in the Sandwich and Tahiti groups the number of Europeans is greatly in excess of that of the natives. Those natives who, in the Philippine Islands, have been preserved by the Catholic Church, will too soon disappear from the surface of the largest ocean of the globe.

Then Eastern Asia will be attacked much more seriously than ever before. Since its discovery, Europeans could only reach it through the long distances which divide Western Europe from China and Japan. But within a short time numerous lines of steamships, starting from San Francisco, Portland, Honolulu, and many other harbors yet nameless, will land travellers in Yokohama, Hakodadi, Yeddo, Shanghai, Canton, and other emporiums of Asia.

Nor will the Americans of the United States be alone in the race. Several governments are preparing to cut a canal through the Isthmus of Panama, or Darien, or Tehuantepec, as has already been done with that of Suez; and soon ships starting from Western Europe will, with the aid of steam, traverse the Atlantic and Pacific Oceans successively as two large lakes to land their passengers and cargoes on the frontiers of China and India.

The Japanese, those Englishmen of the East, are ready to adopt European inventions. They are indeed already expert in many of them, and seem on the alert to conform to European manners. It is said that the nation is divided into two parties on that very question of conformity; before long they will all be of one mind. What an impulse will thus be given to the europeanization of China and Tartary!

In Hindostan, England has fairly begun the work; but the climate of the peninsula offering an obstacle to the introduction of a large number of men of the Caucasian race, it will be more probably from the foot of the Himalaya Mountains that the spread of the race will commence. Already the English and the Russians are concentrating their forces on the Upper Indus. The question merely is, Which nation will be the first to inoculate the dreamy sons of Sem with the spirit and blood of Japhet? It seems that Central Asia will form the rallying-ground for the last efforts of the Titans to unify their power, as it was thence that the power of God first dispersed them.

A glance at the rest of the world as witnessing the same astonishing spectacle, and we pass on. Australia is clearly destined to be entirely European; the number of natives, already insignificant compared to that of the colonists, will soon disappear utterly. Turkey, the Caucasus, Bokhara, are rapidly taking a new shape and adopting Western manners.

The African triangle offers the greatest resistance, owing to its deserts, its terrible climate, and the savage or childish disposition of its inhabitants. Yet the attempt to europeanize it is at this moment in earnest action at its southernmost cape, all along its northern line skirting the Mediterranean, in Egypt chiefly, and also through the Erythrean Gulf in the east; finally, on many points of its western shore, which, strange to say, lags behind, although it formed the first point of discovery by the Portuguese.

To condense all we have just said to a few lines: it looks as though all races of men, except the Caucasian, were undergoing a rapid process of unification or disappearance.

In America certainly the phenomenon is most striking.

In Asia all the native races seem palsied and unable to hold together in the presence of the Russians and the English.

In Africa, Mohammedanism still preserves to the natives a certain activity of life, but even that is fast on the wane.

Finally, in Australia and the Pacific Ocean the disappearance of the natives is still more striking and more sudden in its action than even in America.

This state of things did not exist two hundred years ago; and when the Crusades began the reverse was the case.

We cannot believe that this immense, universal fact is merely an exterior one resulting from new appliances, new comforts, new outward habits; what is called material civilization. We cannot believe that it is merely the dress, houses, culinary regime, the popular customs of those numerous foreign tribes or nations which are undergoing such a wonderful change. This outward phenomenon supposes a substratum, an interior reality of ideas and principles worthy our chief attention as the real cause of all those exterior changes; a cause, nevertheless, which is scarcely thought of in the public estimate of this mighty revolution.

It is the mind of Europe: it is the belief or want of belief, the religious or irreligious views, the grasping ambition, the headlong desire of an impossible or unholy happiness, the reckless sway of unbridled passions, which try to spread themselves among all nations, and bring them all up, or rather down, to the level of intoxicated, tottering, maddened Europe.

If the monstrous scheme succeeds, there will be no more prayer in the villages of the devout Maronites, no more submission to God in the mountains of Armenia, no more simplicity of faith among the shepherds of Chaldea, no more purity of life among the wandering children of Asiatic deserts.

Side by side with truth and virtue many errors and monstrosities will doubtless disappear, but not to be replaced with what is much better.

The muezzin of the mosques will no longer raise his voice from the minarets at noon and nightfall; the simple Lama will no longer believe in the successive incarnations of Buddha; no longer will the superstitious Hindoo cast himself beneath the car of Juggernaut; many another such absurdity and crime will, let us hope, disappear forever. But with what benefit to mankind? After all, is not superstition even better for men than total unbelief? And, when the whole world is reduced to the state of Europe, when what we daily witness there shall be reproduced in all continents and islands, will men really be more virtuous and happy?

We must not think, however, that there is nothing truly good in the stupendous transformation which we have endeavored to sketch. If it really be the accomplishment of the great prophecy mentioned by us at the beginning of this chapter, it is a noble and a glorious event. God will know how to turn it to good account, and it is for us to hail its coming with thankfulness.

There is no doubt that the actual superiority of the race of Japhet, by force of which this wonderful revolution is being accomplished, is the result of Christianity, that is, of Catholicity. It is because Europe, or the agglomeration of the various branches of the race of Japhet, was for fifteen hundred years overshadowed by the true temple of God, his glorious and infallible Church; it is because the education of Europeans is mainly due to the true messengers of God, the Popes and the bishops; it is because the mind of Europe was really formed by the great Catholic thinkers, nurtured in the monasteries and convents of the Church; it is, finally, because Europeans are truly the sons of martyrs and crusaders, that on them devolves the great mission of regenerating and blending into one the whole world.

But, unfortunately, the work is spoiled by adjuncts in the movement which have grown up in the centuries preceding us. In fact, the whole European movement has been thrown on a wrong track, which we have already pointed out as mere material civilization.

Still, in spite of all the dross, there is a great deal of pure metal in the Japhetic movement. Underlying it all runs the doctrine that all men are sprung from the same father, and that all have had the same Redeemer; that, consequently, all are brethren, and that there should be no place among them for castes and classes, as of superior and inferior beings; that the God the Christians adore is alone omnipotent; that idolatry of all kinds ought to disappear, and that ultimately there should be but one flock and one shepherd.

These are saving truths, still held to in the main by the race of Japhet, in spite of some harsh and opposing false assertions, truths which the Catholic Church alone teaches in their purity, and which are yet destined, we hope, to make one of all mankind.

But her claims are yet far from being acknowledged by the leaders in the movement. And who are those leaders? A question all-important.

England is certainly the first and foremost. Endowed with all the characteristics of the Scandinavian race, which we shall touch upon after, deeply infused with the blood of the Danes and Northmen, she has all the indomitable energy, all the systematic grasp of mind and sternness of purpose joined to the wise spirit of compromise and conservatism of the men of the far North; she, of all nations, has inherited their great power of expansion at sea, possessing all the roving propensities of the old Vikings, and the spirit of trade, enterprise, and colonization, of those old Phoenicians of the arctic circle.

The Catholic south of Europe, Spain and Portugal, having, through causes which it is not the place to investigate here, lost their power on the ocean; the temporary maritime supremacy of Holland having passed away, because the people of that flat country were too close and narrow-minded to grasp the world for any length of time; France, the only modern rival of England as a naval power, having been compelled, owing to the revolutions of the last and the present centuries, to concentrate her whole strength on the Continent of Europe; the young giant of the West, America, being yet unable to grasp at once a vast continent and universal sway over the pathways of the ocean, England had free scope for her maritime enterprises, and she threw herself headlong into this career. Out of Europe she is incontestably the first power of the whole world. To give a better idea of the extent of her dominion, we subjoin an abridged sketch from the "History of a Hundred Years," by Cesare Cantu:

"In Europe she has colonies at Heligoland, Gibraltar, Malta, and the Ionian Isles.

"In Africa, Bathurst, Sierra Leone, many establishments on the coast of Guinea, the islands of Mauritius, Rodrigo, Sechelles, Socotora, Ascension, St. Helena, and, most important of all, the Cape Colony.

"In Asia, where she replaced the French and Dutch, she has, besides Ceylon, an empire of 150,000,000 of people in India, the islands of Singapore and Sumatra, part of Malacca, and many establishments in China.

"In America, she is mistress of Canada, New Brunswick, and other eastern provinces; the Lucayes, Bermudas, most of the Antilles, part of Guiana, and the Falkland Isles.

"In the Southern Ocean, the greater part of Australia, Tasmania, Norfolk, Van Diemen's Land, New Zealand, and many other groups of Oceanica are hers.

"What other state can compete with her in the management of colonies, and in the selection of situations from which she could command the sea? Jersey and Guernsey are her keys of the Straits of Dover; from Heligoland she can open or shut the mouths of the Elbe and Weser; from Gibraltar she keeps her eye on Spain and the States of Barbary, and holds the gates of the Mediterranean. With Malta and Corfu she has a like advantage over the Levant. Socotora is for her the key of the Red Sea, whence she commands Eastern Africa and Abyssinia. Ormuz, Chesmi, and Buschir, give her the mastery over the Persian Gulf, and the large rivers which flow into it. Aden secures the communication of Bombay with Suez. Pulo Pinang makes her mistress of the Straits of Malacca, and Singapore, of the passage between China and India. At the Cape of Good Hope her troops form an advanced guard over the Indian Ocean; and from Jamaica she rules the Antilles and trades securely with the rest of Central and South America.

"Englishmen have made a careful survey of the whole of the Mediterranean Sea, of the course of the Indus, the Ganges, the Bramaputra, the Godavery, and other rivers of India; of the whole littoral between Cape Colony and China; England has steamships on the Amazon and Niger, and her vessels are found everywhere on the coast of Chili and Peru."

Other European families try to follow in her footsteps; at their head the United States now stand. Primitively an offshoot of the English stock, the blood of all other Japhetic races has given the latter country an activity and boldness which will render it in time superior in those respects to the mother-country herself.

Yet at this time, even in the presence of the United States, in the presence of all other maritime powers, England stands at the head of the Japhetic movement.

Unfortunately, her first aim, after acquiring wealth and securing her power, is, to exclude the Roman Catholic Church as far as is practicable from the benefit of the system, to oppose her whenever she would follow in the wake of her progress, and either to allow paganism or Mohammedanism to continue in quiet possession wherever they exist, or to substitute for them as far as possible her Protestantism. At all events, the Catholicity of the Church is to be crushed, or at least thwarted, to make room for the catholicity of the English nation.

And it looks as though such, in truth, would have been the result, had not the stubbornness of the Irish character stood in the way; if the Celt of Erin, after centuries of oppression and opposition to the false wanderings of the European stream, had not insisted on following the English lord in his travels, dogging his steps everywhere, entering his ships welcome or unwelcome, rushing on shore with him wherever he thought fit to land, and there planted his shanty and his frame church in the very sight of stately palaces lately erected, and gorgeous temples with storied windows and softly-carpeted floors.

And after a few years the Irish Celt would show himself as active and industrious in his new country as oppression had made him indolent and careless on his own soil; the shanty would be replaced by a house worthy of a man; above all, the humble dwelling which he first raised to his God would disappear to make room for an edifice not altogether unworthy of divine majesty; at least, far above the pretentious structures of the oppressors of his religion. The eyes of men would be again turned to "the city built upon a mountain;" and the character of universality, instead of being wrested from the true Church, would become more resplendent than ever through the steadfast Irish Celt.

Thus the spreading of the Gospel in distant regions would be accomplished without a navy of their own. As their ancestors did in pagan times, they would use the vessels of nations born for thrift and trade; the stately ships of the "Egyptians" would be used by the true "people of God."

For them hath Stephenson perfected the steam-engine, so as to enable vessels to undertake long voyages at sea without the necessary help of sails; for them Brunel and others had spent long years in planning and constructing novel Noah's arks capable of containing all clean and unclean animals; for them the Barings and other wealthy capitalists had embraced the five continents and the isles of the ocean in their financial schemes; the Jews of England, Germany, and France, the Rothschilds and Mendelssohns, had accumulated large amounts of money to lend to ship-building companies; for them, in fine, the long-hidden gold deposits of California, Australia, and many other places, had been discovered at the proper time to replenish the coffers of the godless, that they might undertake to furnish the means of transportation and settlement for the missionaries of God!

And, to prove that this is no exaggeration, it is enough to look at the number of emigrants that were to be carried to foreign parts, and that actually left England for her various colonies or for the United States. For several years one thousand Irish people sailed daily from the ports of Great Britain; and for a great number of years 200,000 at least did so every twelve months. When we come, to contrast the Irish at home with the Irish abroad, we shall give fuller details than are possible here. These few words suffice to show the immense number of vessels and the vast sums that were required for such an extraordinary operation.

This phenomenon is surely curious enough, universal enough, and sufficiently portentous in its consequences, to deserve a thorough inquiry into its causes and the way in which it was brought about.

It will be seen that it all came from the Irish having kept themselves aloof from the other branches of the great Japhetic race in order to join in the general movement at the right time and in their own way, constantly opposed to all the evil that is in it, but using it in the way Providence intended.

The chapters which follow will be devoted to the development of this general idea; the few remarks with which we close the present may tend to set the conclusion which we draw more distinctly before our minds.

There is no doubt that, taking the Irish nation as a whole, we find in it features which are visible in no other European nation; and that, taking Europe as a whole, in all its complexity of habits, manners, tendencies, and ways of life, we have a picture wholly distinct from that of the Irish people. England has striven during the last eight hundred years to shape it and make it the creature of her thought, and England has utterly failed.

The same race of men and women inhabit the isle of Erin to-day as that which held it a thousand years ago, with the distinction that it is now far more wretched and deserving of pity than it was then. The people possess the same primitive habits, simple thoughts, ardent impulsiveness, stubborn spirit, and buoyant disposition, in spite of ages of oppression. In the course of centuries they have not furnished a single man to that army of rash minds which have carried the rest of Europe headlong through lofty, perhaps, but at bottom empty and idle theories, to the brink of that bottomless abyss into which no one can peer without a shudder.

No heresiarch has found place among them; no fanciful philosopher, no holder of fitful and lurid light to deceive nations and lead them astray, no propounder of social theories opposed to those of the Gospel, no inventor of new theogonies and cosmologies--new in name, old in fact-- rediscovered by modern students in the Kings of China, the Vedas of Hindostan, the Zends of Persia, or Eddas of the North; no ardent explorer of Nature, seeking in the bowels of the earth, or on the summits of mountains, or in the depths of the ocean, or the motions of the stars, proofs that God does not exist, or that matter has always existed, that man has made himself, developing his own consciousness out of the instinct of the brute, or even out of the material motions of the zoophyte.

We would beg the reader to bear in mind those insane theories so prevalent to-day, out of which society can hope for nothing but convulsions and calamities, to see how all the nations of Europe have contributed to the baneful result except the Irish; that they alone have furnished no false leader in those wanderings from the right path; that their community has been opposed all through to the adoption of the theories which led to them, have spurned them with contempt, and even refused to inquire into them: with these thoughts and recollections in his mind, he may understand what we mean when we assert that the Irish have stubbornly refused to enter upon the European movement. Although, by the reception of Christianity, they were admitted into the European family, the Christianity which they received was so thoroughly imbibed and so completely carried out that any thing in the least opposed to it was sternly rejected by the whole nation. Hence they became a people of peculiar habits. Rejecting the harsh features of feudalism, not caring for the refinement of the so-called revival of learning, sternly opposed at all times to Protestantism, they would have naught to do with what was rejected or even suspected by the Church, until in our days they offer to the eyes of the world the spectacle we have sketched. Thus have they, not the least by reason of their long martyrdom, become fit instruments for the great work Providence asks of them to-day.

England, the great leader in the material part of the social movement which has been the subject of this chapter, for a long time hesitated to adopt principles altogether subversive to society. In her worldly good sense she endeavored to follow what she imagined a via media in her wisdom, to avoid what seemed to her extremes, but what is in reality the eternal antagonism of truth and falsehood, of order and chaos. Twenty years back there was a unanimity among English writers to speak the language of moderation and good sense whenever a rash author of foreign nations hazarded some dangerous novelties; and in their reviews they immediately pointed out the poison which lay concealed under the covering of science or imagination, and the peril of these ever-increasing new discoveries. If any Englishman sanctioned those theories, he could not form a school among his countrymen, and remained almost alone of his party.

But at last England has given way to the universal spread of temptation, and to-day she runs the race of disorganization as ardent as any, striving to be a leader among other leaders to ruin. Every one is astounded at the sudden and remarkable change. It is truly inexplicable, save by the fearful axiom, Quos Deus vult perdere, dementat. Hence not a few expect soon to see storms sweep over the devoted island of Great Britain, which no longer forms an exception to the universality of the evil we have indicated.

Which, then, is the one safe spot in Europe, whither the tide of folly, or madness rather, has not yet come?

Ireland alone is the answer.

THE IRISH BETTER PREPARED TO RECEIVE CHRISTIANITY THAN OTHER NATIONS

THE introduction of Christianity gave Europe a power over the world which pagan Rome could not possess. All the branches of the Japhetic family combined to form what was with justice and propriety called Christendom. Ireland, by receiving the Gospel, was really making her first entry into the European family; but there were certain peculiarities in her performance of this great act which gave her national life, already deviating from that of other European nations, a unique impulse. The first of those peculiarities consisted in her preparation for the great reception of the faith, and the few obstacles she encountered in her adoption of it, compared with those of the rest of the world.

Providence wisely decreed that redemption should be delayed until a large portion of mankind had attained to the highest civilization. It was not in a time of ignorance and barbarism that the Saviour was born. The Augustan is, undoubtedly, the most intellectual and refined age, in point of literary and artistic taste, that the world has ever seen. A few centuries before, Greece had reached the summit of science and art. No country, in ancient or modern times, has surpassed the acumen of her philosophical writers and the aesthetic perfection of her poets and artists. Rome made use of her to embellish her cities, and inherited her taste for science and literature.

But art and literature embody ideas only; and, as Ozanam says so well: "Beneath the current of ideas which dispute the empire of the world, lies that world itself such as labor has made it, with that treasure of wealth and visible adornment which render it worthy of being the transient sojourn-place of immortal souls. Beneath the true, the good, and the beautiful, lies the useful, which is brightened by their reflection. No people has more keenly appreciated the idea of utility than that of Rome; none has ever laid upon the earth a hand more full of power, or more capable of transforming it; nor more profusely flung the treasures of earth at the feet of humanity . . . .

"At the close of the second century . . the rhetorician Aristides celebrated in the following terms the greatness of the Roman Empire: 'Romans, the whole world beneath your dominion seems to keep a day of festival. From time to time a sound of battle comes to you from the ends of the earth, where you are repelling the Goth, the Moor, or the Arab. But soon that sound is dispersed like a dream. Other are the rivalries and different the conflicts which you excite through the universe. They are combats of glory, rivalries in magnificence between provinces and cities. Through you, gymnasia, aqueducts, porticoes, temples, and schools, are multiplied; the very soil revives, and the earth is but one vast garden!'

"Similar, also, was the language of the stern Tertullian: 'In truth, the world becomes day after day richer and better cultivated; even the islands are no longer solitudes; the rocks have no more terrors for the navigator; everywhere there are habitations, population, law, and life.'

"The legions of Rome had constructed the roads which furrowed mountains, leaped over marshes, and crossed so many different provinces with a like solidity, regularity, and uniformity; and the various races of men were lost in admiration at the sight of the mighty works which were attributed in after-times to Caesar, to Brunehaud, to Abelard!"

It was in the midst of those worldly glories that Christ was born, that he preached, and suffered, that his religion was established and propagated. It found proselytes at once among the most polished and the most learned of men, as well as among slaves and artisans; and thus was it proved that Christianity could satisfy the loftiest aspirations of the most civilized as well as insure the happiness of the most numerous and miserable classes.

But we must reflect that the advanced civilization of Greece and Rome was in fact an immense obstacle to the propagation of truth, and, what is more to be regretted, often gave an unnatural aspect to the Christianity of the first ages in the Roman world-- a half-pagan look--so that the barbarian invasion was almost necessary to destroy every thing of the natural order; that the Church alone remaining face to face with those uncouth children of the North, might begin her mission anew and mould them all into the family called "Christendom." "Christianity," to quote Ozanam again, "shrank from condemning a veneration of the beautiful, although idolatry was contained in it; and as it honored the human mind and the arts it produced, so the persecution of the apostate Julian, in which the study of the classics had been forbidden to the faithful, was the severest of its trials. Literary history possesses no moment of greater interest than that which saw the school with its profane --that is to say pagan--traditions and texts received into the Church. The Fathers, whose christian austerity is our wonder, were passionate in their love of antiquity, which they covered, as it were, with their sacred vestments. . . . By their favor, Virgil traversed the ages of iron without losing a page, and, by right of his Fourth Eclogue, took rank among the prophets and the sibyls. St. Augustine would have blamed paganism less, if, in place of a temple to Cybele, it had raised a shrine to Plato, in which his works might have been publicly read. St. Jerome's dream is well known, and the scourging inflicted upon him by angels for having loved Cicero too well; yet his repentance was but short-lived, since he caused the monks of the Mount of Olives to pass their nights in copying the Ciceronian dialogues, and did not shrink himself from expounding the comic and lyric poets to the children of Bethlehem."

We know already that nothing of the kind existed in Ireland when the Gospel reached her, and that there the new religion assumed a peculiar aspect, which has never varied, and which made her at once and forever a preeminently Christian nation.

Among the Greeks and Romans, literature and art, although accepted by the Church, were nevertheless deeply impregnated with paganism. All their chief acts of social life required a profession of idolatry; even amusements, dramatic representations, and simple games, were religious and consequently pagan exhibitions.

We do not here speak of the attractions of an atheistic and materialist philosophy, of a voluptuous, often, and demoralizing literature and poetry, of an unimaginable prostitution of art to the vilest passions, which the relics of Pompeii too abundantly indicate.

But apart from those excesses of corruption and unbelief, which, no doubt, virtuous pagans themselves abhorred, the approved, correct, and so-called pure life of the best men of pagan Rome necessitated the contamination of idolatrous worship. Apart from the thousand duties, festivals, and the like, decreed or sanctioned by the state, the most ordinary acts of life, the enlisting of the soldier, the starting on a military expedition, the assumption of any civil office or magistracy, the civil oaths in the courts of law, the public bath, the public walk almost, the current terms in conversation, the private reading of the best books, the mere glancing at a multitude of exterior objects, constituted almost as many professions of a false and pagan worship.

How could any one become a Christian and at the same time remain a Greek or a Roman? The gloomy views of the Montanist Tertullian were, to many, frightful truths requiring constant care and self-examen. For the Christian there were two courses open--both excesses, yet either almost unavoidable: on the one side, a terrible rigorism, making life unsupportable, next to impossible; on the other, a laxity of thought and action leading to lukewarmness and sometimes apostasy.

Bearing in mind what was written on the subject in the first three ages of Christianity, not only by Tertullian, but by most orthodox writers, St. Cyprian, Lactantius, Arnobius, and the authors of many Acts of martyrs, we may easily understand how the doctrines of Christianity stood in danger of never taking deep root in the hearts of men surrounded by such temptations, themselves born in paganism, and remaining, after their conversion, exposed to seductions of such an alluring character.

Therefore this same "high civilization," as it is called, in the midst of which Christianity was preached, was a real danger to the inward life of the new disciple of Christ.

How could it be otherwise, when it is a fact now known to all, that, even at the beginning of the fifth century, Rome was almost entirely pagan, at least outwardly, and among her highest classes; so that the poet Claudian, in addressing Honorius at the beginning of his sixth consulship, pointed out to him the site of the capitol still crowned with the Temple of Jove, surrounded by numerous pagan edifices, supporting in air an army of gods; and all around temples, chapels, statues, without number--in fact, the whole Roman and Greek mythology, standing in the City of the Catacombs and of the Popes!

The public calendars, preserved to this day, continued to note the pagan festivals side by side with the feasts of the Saviour and his apostles. Within the city and beyond, throughout Italy and the most remote provinces, idols and their altars were still surrounded by the thronging populace, prostrate at their feet.

If in the cities the new religion already dared display something of its inherent splendor, the whole rural population was still pagan, singing the praises of Ceres and of Bacchus, trembling at Fauns and Satyrs and the numerous divinities of the groves and fountains. Christianity then held the same standing in Italy that in the United States Catholicity holds to-day in the midst of innumerable religious sects.

This is not the place to show how far the paganism of Greece and Rome had corrupted society, and how complete was its rottenness at the time. It has been already shown by several great writers of this century. Enough for our purpose to remark that even some Christian writers, of the age immediately succeeding that of the early martyrs, showed themselves more than half pagans in their tastes and productions. Ausonius in the West, the preceptor of St. Paulinus, is so obscene in some of his poems, so thoroughly pagan in others, that critics have for a long time hesitated to pronounce him a Christian. How many of his contemporaries hovered like him on the confines of Christianity and paganism! When Julian the apostate restored idolatry, many, who had only disgraced the name of Christian, openly returned to the worship of Jupiter and Venus, and their apostasy could scarcely be cause for regret to sincere disciples of our Lord.

In the East the phenomenon is less striking. Strange to say, idolatry did not remain so firmly rooted in the country, where it first took such an alluring shape; and Constantinople was in every sense of the word a Christian city when Rome, in her senate, fought with such persistent tenacity for her altars of Victory, her vestals, and her ancient worship.

Yet there, also, Christian writers were too apt to interfuse the old ideas with the new, and to adopt doctrines placed, as it were, midway between those of Plato and St. Paul. There were bishops even who were a scandal to the Church and yet remained in it. Synesius is the most striking example; whose doctrine was certainly more philosophical than Christian, and whose life, though decorous, was altogether worldly. The history of Arianism shows that others besides Synesius were far removed from the ideal of Christian bishops so worthily represented at the time by many great doctors and holy pontiffs.

Such, in the East as well as in the West, were the perils besetting the true Christian spirit at the very cradle of our holy religion.

Nor was the danger confined to the mythology of paganism, its literature and poetry. Philosophy itself became a real stumbling- block to many, who would fain appear disciples of faith, when they gave themselves up to the most unrestrained wanderings of human reason.

The truth is, that Greek philosophy, divided into so many schools in order to please all tastes, had become a wide-spread institution throughout the Roman world. The mind of the East was best adapted to it, and those who taught it were, consequently, nearly all Greeks. Cicero had made it fashionable among many of his countrymen; and although the Latin mind, always practical to the verge of utilitarianism, was not congenial to utopian speculations, still, as it was the fashion, all intellectual men felt the need of becoming sufficiently acquainted with it to be able to speak of it and even to embrace some particular school. Those patricians, who remained attached to the stern principles of the old republic, became Stoics; while the men of the corrupt aristocracy called themselves, with Horace, members of the "Epicurean herd." Hence the necessity for all to train their minds to scientific speculation, converted the Western world into a hotbed of wild and dangerous doctrines.

In the opinion of some Eastern Fathers of the Church, Greek philosophy had been a preparation for the Gospel, and could be made subservient to the conversion of many. Thus we find St. Justin, the martyr, all his life long glorying in the name of philosopher, and continuing to wear, even after his conversion, the philosopher's cloak so much derided by the scoffer, Lucian.

Still, despite this very respectable opinion, we can entertain no doubt, in view of what happened at the time and of subsequent events, that philosophy grew to be a stumbling-block in the path of Christianity, and originated the worst and most dangerous forms of heresy; that it sowed the seed, in the European mind, of all errors, by creating that speculative tendency of character so peculiar to most branches of the Japhetic race.

Persian Dualism, and, as many think, Pantheistic Buddhism, which were then flourishing in Central and Eastern Asia, infected the Alexandrian schools, and impressed philosophy with a new and dreamy character, which became the source of subsequent and frightful errors. The Neo-Platonism of Porphyry and Plotinus was intended, in the minds of its originators, to lay a scientific basis for polytheism; and, in Jamblichus finally, became an open justification of the most absurd fables of mythology.

But, though this might satisfy Julian and those who followed him in his apostasy, it could not come to be an inner danger to the Church. With many, however, it assumed a form which at once engendered the worst errors of Gnosticism; and Gnosticism was, at first, considered a Christian heresy; so that a man might be a pantheist, of the worst kind, and still call himself Christian. St. John had foreseen the danger from the beginning, and it is said that he wrote his gospel against it because the doctrine openly denied the divinity of Christ. But the sect became much more powerful after his death, and allured many Christians who were disposed, from a misinterpretation of some texts of St. Paul on the struggle between the flesh and the spirit, to embrace a system which professed to explain the origin of that struggle.

The Alexandrian Gnosticism failed to excite in the minds of the holy monks of the East that aversion which we now feel for its tenets, inasmuch as it did not openly anathematize the Scriptures of the Old Law, nay, even preserved a certain outward respect for them, on account of the multitude of Jews living in Alexandria, and particularly because the open system of Dualism, which afterward came from Syria and in the hands of Manes established the existence of two equal and eternal principles of good and evil, found no place in the teachings of Valentinus and his school.c

But even this frightful Syrian Gnosticism, which gave to the principle of evil an origin as ancient and sacred as that of God himself--Manicheism barefaced and radically immoral--so repugnant to our feelings, so monstrous to our more correct ideas, bore a semblance of truth for many minds, at that time inclined toward every thing which came from the East. We know what a firm hold those doctrines took on the great soul of Augustine, who for a long time professed and cherished them. Rome, under the pagan emperors, had received with open arms the Oriental gods and the philosophy which endeavored to explain their mythology; and many gifted minds of the third and fourth centuries lost themselves in the contemplation of those mysteries which from out Central Asia spread a lurid glare over the Western world.

This first danger, however, was warded off by the writings of St. Ignatius of Antioch, St. Irenaeus of Lyons, Clement of Alexandria, Tertullian, Origen,

St. Epiphanius, Theodoret, and others, long before the time of St. Augustine, the last of them. Gnosticism was prevented from any longer imparting a wrong tendency to Christian doctrines, and it died out, until restored during the Crusades to revive in the middle ages in its most malignant form.

But at the very moment of its decline, philosophy entered the Church; almost to wreck her by inspiring Arius and Pelagius. The teachings of the first were clearly Neo-Platonic; of the second, Stoic: and all the errors prevalent in the Church from the third to the sixth century originated in Arianism and Pelagianism.

In Plato, as read in Alexandria, Arius found all the material for his doctrine, which spread like wild-fire over the whole Church. Many things conspired to swell the number of his adherents: the ardent love for philosophy so inherent in the Eastern Church, to the extent of many believing that Plato was almost a Christian, and his doctrines therefore endowed with real authority; the natural disposition of men to adopt the new and a seeming rational explanation of unfathomable mysteries; the apparent agreement of his doctrine with certain passages of Scripture, where the Son is said to be inferior to the Father; but chiefly the satisfaction it afforded to a number of new Christians who had embraced the faith at the conversion of Constantine on political rather than conscientious grounds, and who were at once relieved of the supernatural burden of believing in a God-man, born of a woman, and dying on a cross. Faith reduced to an opinion; religion become a philosophy; a mere man, let his endowments be what they might, recognized as our guide, and not overwhelming us with the dread weight of a divine nature; all this explains the historic phrase of St. Jerome after the Council of Rimini, "The world groaned and wondered to find itself Arian."

Any person acquainted with ecclesiastical history knows how the Church of Christ would have surely become converted into a mere rational school, under the pressure of these doctrines, were it not for the promises of perpetuity which she had received.

We know also what a time it took to establish truth: how many councils had to meet, how many books had to be written, the efforts required from the rulers of the Church, chiefly from the Roman pontiffs, to calm so many storms, to explain so many difficult points of doctrine, to secure the final victory.

And, after all had been accomplished, there still remained the root of the evil engrafted in what we call the philosophical turn of mind of the Western nations--that is to say, in the disposition to call every thing in question, to seek out strange and novel difficulties, to start war-provoking theories in the midst of peace, to aim at founding a new school, or at least to stand forth as the brilliant and startling expounder of old doctrines in a new form, in fine to add a last name to the list, already over-long, of those who have disturbed the world by their skill in dialectics and sophism.

Pelagius followed Arius, and his errors had the same object in view in the long-run, to strip our holy religion of all that is spiritual and divine.

In the time of St. Augustine and St. Jerome, there existed among Christians an extraordinary tendency to embrace all possible philosophical doctrines, even when directly opposed to the first principles of revealed religion; and, within the Church, the danger of subtilizing on every question connected with well- known dogmas was much greater than many imagine.

From the previous reflections we may learn how difficult it was to establish, in pagan Europe, a thoroughly Christian life and doctrine; and that, after society had come to be apparently imbued with the new spirit, it was still too easy to disturb the flowing stream of the heavenly graces of the Gospel. This resulted, we repeat, from causes anterior to Christianity, from sources of evil which the divine religion had to overcome, and which too often impeded its supernatural action. In fact, the ecclesiastical history of those ages is comprised mainly in depicting the almost continual deviations from the straight line of pure doctrine and morality, and the strenuous efforts assiduously made by the rulers of the Church against a never- ceasing falling away.

Having taken this glance at the early workings of Christianity through the rest of the world, we may now turn fairly to the immediate subject we have in hand, and trace its course in Ireland. From the very beginning we are struck by the peculiarities--blessed, indeed--which show themselves, as in all other matters, in its reception of the truth. The island, compared with Europe, is small, it is true; but the heroism displayed by its inhabitants during so many ages, in support of the religion which they received so freely, so generously, and at once, in mind as well as heart, marks it out as worthy of a special account; and, from its unique reception and adherence to the faith, as worthy of, if possible, a natural explanation of such action beyond the promptings of Divine grace, since its astonishing perseverance, its unswerving faith, form to-day as great a characteristic of the nation as they did on the day of its entry into the Christian Church.

We proceed to examine, then, the kind of idolatry which its first apostle encountered on landing in the island, and the ease with which it was destroyed, so as to leave behind no poisonous shoots of the deadly root of evil.

In order to understand the religious system of Ireland previous to the preaching of the Gospel, we must first take a general survey of polytheism, if it can be so called, in all Celtic countries, and of the peculiar character which it bore in Ireland itself.

Of old, throughout all countries, religion possessed certain things in common, which belonged to the rites and creeds of all nations, and were evidently derived from the primitive traditions of mankind, and, consequently, from a true and Divine revelation. Such were the belief in a golden age, in the fall from a happy beginning, in the penalty imposed on sin, which gave a reason for great mundane calamities--the Deluge chiefly--the memory of which lived in the traditions of almost every nation; in the necessity of prayer and expiatory sacrifice; in the transmission of guilt from father to son, expressed in all primitive legislations, and to this day preserved in the Chinese laws and customs; in the existence of good and bad spirits, whence, most probably, arose polytheism; in the hope of the future regeneration of man, represented in Greece by the beautiful myth of Pandora's box; and, finally, in the doctrine of eternal rewards and punishments.

Each one of these strictly true dogmas underwent more or less of alteration in its passage through the various nations of antiquity, but was, nevertheless, everywhere preserved in some shape or form.

At what precise epoch did mankind begin wrongfully to interpret these primitive traditions? When did the worship of idols arise and become universal? No one can tell precisely. All we know for certain is, that a thousand years before Christ idolatry prevailed everywhere, and that even the Jewish people often fell into this sin, and were only brought back by means of punishment to the worship of the true God.

But if error tainted the whole system of worship among nations, it differed in the various races of men according to the variety of their character. Ferocity or mildness of manners, acuteness or obtuseness of understanding, activity or indolence of disposition, a burning, a cold, or a temperate climate, a smiling or dreary country, but chiefly the thousand differences of temper which are as marked among mankind as the almost infinite variety of forms visible in creation, gave to each individual religion its proper and characteristic types, which in after-times, when truth was brought down from heaven for all, imparted to the universal Christian spirit a peculiar outward form in each people, an interior adaptation to its peculiar dispositions, destined in the Divine plan to introduce into the future Catholic Church the beautiful variety requisite to make its very universality possible among mankind.

To enter into details on the Celtic religion would carry us beyond due limits. The question as to whether the ancient Celts were idolaters or not still remains undecided, though in France alone more than six hundred volumes have been written on the subject. Julius Caesar believed that they were worshippers of idols in the same sense as his own countrymen; but he probably stood alone in his opinion. Aristotle, Pythagoras, Polyhistor, Ammianus Marcellinus, considered the Druids as monotheist philosophers. Most of the Greek writers agreed with them, as did all the Alexandrian Fathers of the Church in the third and fourth centuries.

Among the moderns the majority leans to a contrary opinion; nevertheless, many authors of weight, distinguishing the public worship of the common people from the doctrine of the Druids, assert the monotheism of this sacerdotal caste. Samuel F. N. Morus particularly, who, with J. A. Ernesti, was esteemed the master of antiquarian scholarship in Europe during the last century, maintains, in his edition of the "Commentaries" of Caesar, that "human beings, as well as human affairs, fortunes, travels, and wars, were thought by the Celts to be governed and ruled by one supreme God, and that the system of apotheosis, common to nearly all ancient nations, was totally unknown in ancient Gaul, Britain, and the adjacent islands."

The ancient authorities concurring with these conclusions are so numerous and clear spoken that the great historian of Gaul, Amedee Thierry, thinks that such a pure and mystic religion, joined to such a sublime philosophy, could not have been the product of the soil. In his endeavor to investigate its origin, he supposes that it was brought to the west of Europe by the Eastern Cymris of the first invasion; that it was adopted by the higher classes of society, and that the old idolatrous worship remained in force among the lower orders.

The unity and omnipotence of the Godhead, metempsychosis, or the doctrine and the transmigration of soul--not into the bodies of animals, as it obtained and still obtains in the East, but into those of other human beings--the eternal duration of existing substances, material and spiritual, consequently the immortality of the human soul, were the chief dogmas of the Druids, according to the majority of antiquarians.

If this be true, then it can be said boldly that, with the exception of revealed religion in Judea, which was always far more explicit and pure, no system can be found in ancient times superior to that of the Druids, more especially if we add that, in addition to religious teaching, a whole system of physics was also developed in their large academies. "They dispute," says Caesar, "on the stars and their motions, on the size of the universe and of this earth, on the nature of physical things, as well as on the strength and power of the eternal God."

To bring our question home, what were the religious belief and worship of the Irish Celts while still pagans? Very few positive facts are known on the subject; but we have data enough to show what they were not; and in such cases negative proofs are amply sufficient.

It was for a long time the fashion with Irish historians to attribute to their ancestors the wildest forms of ancient idolatry. They appeared to consider it a point of national honor to make the worship of Erin an exact reflex of Eastern, Grecian, or Roman polytheism. They erected on the slightest foundations grand structures of superstitious and abominable rites. Fire-worship, Phoenician or African horrors, the rankest idol-worship, even human sacrifices of the most revolting nature, were, according to them, of almost daily occurrence in Ireland. But, with the advancement of antiquarian knowledge, all those phantoms have successively disappeared; and, the more the ancient customs, literature, and history of the island are studied, the more it becomes clear that the pretended proofs adduced in support of those vagaries are really without foundation.

In the first place, there is not the slightest reason to believe that the human sacrifices customary in Gaul were ever practised in Ireland. No really ancient book makes any mention of them. They were certainly not in vogue at the time of St. Patrick, as he could not have failed to give expression to his horror at them in some shape or form, which expression would have been recorded in one, at least, of the many lives of the saint, written shortly after his death, and abounding in details of every kind. If not, then, during his long apostleship, we may safely conclude that they never took place before, as there was no reason for their discontinuance prior to the propagation of Christianity.

There was a time when all the large cromlechs which abound in the island were believed to be sacrificial stones; and it is highly probable that the opinion so prevalent during the last century with respect to the reality of those cruel rites had its origin in the existence of those rude monuments. After many investigations and excavations around and under cromlechs of all sizes, it is now admitted by all well-informed antiquarians that they had no connection with sacrifices of any kind. They were merely monuments raised over the buried bodies of chieftains or heroes. Many sepulchres of that description have been opened, either under cromlechs or under large mounds; great quantities of ornaments of gold, silver, or precious stones, utensils of various materials, beautiful works of great artistic merit, have been discovered there, and now go to fill the museums of the nation or private cabinets. Nothing connected with religious rites of any description has met the eyes of the learned seekers after truth. Thus it has been ascertained that the old race had reached a high degree of material civilization; but no clew to its religion has been furnished.

As to fire-worship, which not long ago was admitted by all as certainly forming a part of the Celtic religion in Ireland, so little of that opinion remains to-day that it is scarcely deserving of mention. There now remains no doubt that the round towers, formerly so numerous in Ireland, had nothing whatever to do with fire-worship. For a long time they were believed to have been constructed for no other object, and consequently long prior to the coming of St. Patrick. But Dr. Petrie and other antiquarians have all but demonstrated that the round towers never had any connection with superstition or idolatry at all; that they were of Christian origin, always built near some Christian church, and of the same materials, and had for their object to call the faithful to prayer, like the campanile of Italy, to be a place of refuge for the clergy in time of war, and to give to distant villages intimation of any hostile invasion.

The fact in the life of St. Patrick, when he appeared before the court of King Laeghaire, upon which so much reliance is placed as a proof of the existence of fire-worship, is now of proportionate weakness. It seems, to judge by the most reliable and ancient manuscripts, that, after all, the kindling of the king's fire was scarcely a religious act.

McGeoghegan, whose history is compiled, from the best-authenticated documents, says: "When the monarch convened an assembly, or held a festival at Tara, it was customary to make a bonfire on the preceding day, and it was forbidden to light another fire in any other place at the same time, in the territory of Breagh."

This is all; and the probable cause of the prohibition was to do honor to the king. Had it been an act of worship, Patrick, in lighting his own paschal-fire, would not only have shown disrespect to the monarch, but in the eyes of the people committed a sacrilege, which could scarcely have missed mention by the careful historians of the time.

But the proof that we are right in our interpretation of the ceremony is clear, from the following passage, taken from the work of Prof. Curry on "Early Irish Manuscripts:" "We see, by the book of military expeditions, that, when King Dathi-- the immediate predecessor of Laeghaire on the throne of Ire-land-- thought of conquering Britain and Gaul, he invited the states of the nation to meet him at Tara, at the approaching feast of Baltaine (one of the great pagan festivals of ancient Erin) on May-day.

"The feast of Tara this year was solemnized on a scale of splendor never before equalled. The fires of Lailten (now called Lelltown in the north of Ireland) were lighted, and the sports, games, and ceremonies, were conducted with unusual magnificence and solemnity.

"These games and solemnities are said to have been instituted more than a thousand years previously by Lug, in honor of Lailte, the daughter of the King of Spain, and wife of MacEire, the last king of the Firbolg colony. It was at her court that Lug had been fostered, and at her death he had her buried at this place, where he raised an immense mound over her grave, and instituted those annual games in her honor.

"These games were solemnized about the first day of August, and they continued to be observed down to the ninth century"- therefore, in Christian times-and consequently the lighting of the fires had as little connection with fire-worship as the games with pagan rites.

A more serious difficulty meets us in the destruction of Crom Cruagh by St. Patrick, and it is important to consider how far Crom Cruagh could really be called an idol.

With regard to the statues of Celtic gods, all the researches and excavations which the most painstaking of antiquarians have undertaken, especially of late years, have never resulted in the discovery, not of the statue of a god, but of any pagan sign whatever in Ireland. It is clear, from the numerous details of the life of St. Patrick, that he never encountered either temples or the statues of gods in any place, although occasional mention is made of idols. The only fact which startles the reader is the holy zeal which moved him to strike with his "baculus Jesu" the monstrous Crom Cruagh, with its twelve "sub-gods."

In all his travels through Ireland-and there is scarcely a spot which he did not visit and evangelize-St. Patrick meets with only one idol, or rather group of idols, situated in the County Cavan, which was an object of veneration to the people. Nowhere else are idols to be found, or the saint would have thought it his duty to destroy them also. This first fact certainly places the Irish in a position, with regard to idolatry, far different from that of all other polytheist nations. In all other countries it is characteristic of polytheism to multiply the statues of the gods, to expose them in all public places, in their houses, but chiefly within or at the door of edifices erected for the purpose. Yet in Ireland we find nothing of the kind, with the exception of Crom Cruagh. The holy apostle of the nation goes on preaching, baptizing, converting people, without finding any worship of gods of stone or metal; he only hears that there is something of the kind in a particular spot, and he has to travel a great distance in order to see it, and show the people their folly in venerating it.

But what was that idol? According to the majority of expounders of Irish history, it was a golden sphere or ball representing the sun, with twelve cones or pillars of brass, around it, typifying, probably, astronomical signs. St. Patrick, in his "Confessio," seems to allude to Crom Cruagh when he says: "That sun which we behold by the favor of God rises for us every day; but its splendor will not shine forever; nay, even all those who adore it shall be miserably punished."

The Bollandists, in a note on this passage of the "Confessio," think that it might refer to Crom Cruagh, which possibly represented the sun, surrounded by the signs of the twelve months, through which it describes its orbit during the year.

We know that the Druids were, perhaps, better versed in the science of astronomy than the scholars of any other nation at the time. It was not in Gaul and Britain only that they pursued their course of studies for a score of years; the same fact is attested for Ireland by authorities whose testimony is beyond question. May we not suppose that a representation of mere heavenly phenomena, set in a conspicuous position, had in course of time become the object of the superstitious veneration of the people, and that St. Patrick thought it his duty to destroy it? And the attitude of the people at the time of its destruction shows that it could not have borne for them the same sacred character as the statue of Minerva in the Parthenon did for the Greeks or that of Capitoline Jove for the Romans. Can we suppose that St. Paul or St. Peter would have dared to break either of these? And let us remark that the event we discuss occurred at the very beginning of St. Patrick's ministry, and before he had yet acquired that great authority over the minds of all which afterward enabled him fearlessly to accomplish whatever his zeal prompted him to do.

Whatever explanation of the whole occurrence may be given, we doubt if we shall find a better than that we advance, and the considerations arising from it justify the opinion that the Irish Celts were not idolaters like all other peoples of antiquity. They possessed no mythology beyond harmless fairy-tales, no poetical histories of gods and goddesses to please the imagination and the senses, and invest paganism with such an attractive garb as to cause it to become a real obstacle to the spread of Christianity.

Moreover, what we have said concerning the belief in the omnipotence of one supreme God, whatever might be his nature, as the first dogma of Druidism, would seem to have lain deep in the minds of the Irish Celts, and caused their immediate comprehension and reception of monotheism, as preached by St. Patrick, and the facility with which they accepted it. They were certainly, even when pagans, a very religious people; otherwise how could they have embraced the doctrines of Christianity with that ardent eagerness which shall come under our consideration in the next chapter? A nation utterly devoid of faith of any kind is not apt to be moved, as were the Irish, perhaps beyond all other nations, at the first sight of supernatural truths, such as those of Christianity. And so little were they attached to paganism, so visibly imbued with reverence for the supreme God of the universe, that, as soon as announced, they accepted the dogma.

The simple and touching story of the conversion of the two daughters of King Laeghaire will give point and life to this very important consideration. It is taken from the "Book of Armagh," which Prof. O'Curry, who is certainly a competent authority, believes older than the year 727, when the popular Irish traditions regarding St. Patrick must have still been almost as vivid as immediately after his death.

St. Patrick and his attendants being assembled at sunrise at the fountain of Clebach, near Cruachan in Connaught, Ethne and Felimia, daughters of King Laeghaire, came to bathe, and found at the well the holy men.

"And they knew not whence they were, or in what form, or from what people, or from what country; but they supposed them to be fairies--duine sidhe--that is to say, gods of the earth, or a phantasm.

"And the virgins said unto them: 'Who are ye, and whence are ye?'

"And Patrick said unto them: 'It were better for you to confess to our true God, than to inquire concerning our race.'

"The first virgin said: 'Who is God?

"'And where is God?

"'And where is his dwelling-place?

"'Has God sons and daughters, gold and silver?

"'Is he living?

"'Is he beautiful?

"'Did many foster his son?

"'Are his daughters dear and beauteous to men of this world?

"'Is he in heaven or on earth?

"'In the sea?--In rivers?--In mountainous places?--In valleys?

"'Declare unto us the knowledge of him?

"'How shall he be seen?-How shall he be loved?-How is he to be found?

"'Is it in youth?-Is it in old age that he is to be found?'

"But St. Patrick, full of the Holy Ghost, answered and said:

"'Our God is the God of all men-the God of heaven and earth-of the sea and rivers. The God of the sun, and the moon, and all stars. The God of the high mountains, and of the lowly valleys. The God who is above heaven, and in heaven, and under heaven.

"'He has a habitation in the heavens, and the earth, and the sea, and all that are thereon.

"'He inspireth all things. He quickeneth all things. He is over all things.

"'He hath a Son coeternal and coequal with himself. The Son is not younger than the Father, nor the Father older than the Son. And the Holy Ghost breatheth in them. The Father, and the Son, and the Holy Ghost, are not divided.

"'But I desire to unite you to a heavenly King inasmuch as you are daughters of an earthly king. Do you believe?'

"And the virgins said, as of one mouth and one heart: Teach us most diligently how we may believe in the heavenly King. Show us how we may see him face to face, and whatsoever you shall say unto us we will do.'

"And Patrick said: 'Believe ye that by baptism you put off the sin of your father and your mother?'

"They answered him, 'We believe.'

"'Believe ye in repentance after sin? 'We believe . . .' etc.

"And they were baptized, and a white garment was put upon their heads. And they asked to see the face of Christ. And the saint said unto them: 'Ye cannot see the face of Christ except ye taste of death, and except ye receive the sacrifice.'

"And they answered: 'Give us the sacrifice that we may behold the Son our spouse.'

"And they received the eucharist of God, and they slept in death.

"And they were laid out on one bed-covered with garments -and their friends made great lamentations and weeping for them."

This beautiful legend expresses to the letter the way in which the Irish received the faith. Nor was it simple virgins only who understood and believed so suddenly at the preaching of the apostle. The great men of the nation were as eager almost as the common people to receive baptism: the conversion of Dubtach is enough to show this.

He was a Druid, being the chief poet of King Laeghaire--all poets belonging to the order. After the wife, the brothers, and the two daughters of the monarch, he was the most illustrious convert gained by Patrick at the beginning of his apostleship. He became a Christian at the first appearance of the saint at Tara, and immediately began to sing in verse his new belief, as he had formerly sung the heroes of his nation. To the end he remained firm in his faith, and a dear friend to the holy man who had converted him. How could he, and all the chief converts of Patrick, have believed so suddenly and so constantly in the God of the Christians, if their former life had not prepared them for the adoption of the new doctrine, and if the doctrine of monotheism had offered a real difficulty to their understanding? There was, probably, nothing clear and definite in their belief in an omnipotent God, which is said to have been the leading dogma of Druidism; but their simple minds had evidently a leaning toward the doctrine, which induced them to approve of it, as soon as it was presented to them with a solemn affirmation.

In order to elucidate this point, we add a short description of the labors and success of this apostle.

In the year 432, Patrick lands on the island. By that time, some few of the inhabitants may possibly have heard of the Christian religion from the neighboring Britain or Gaul. Palladius had preached the year before in the district known as the present counties of Wexford and Wicklow, erected three churches, and made some converts; but it may be said that Ireland continued in the same state it had preserved for thousands of years: the Druids in possession of religious and scientific supremacy; the chieftains in contention, as in the time of Fingal and Ossian; the people, though in the midst of constant strife, happy enough on their rich soil, cheered by their bards and poets; very few, or no slaves in the country; an abundance of food everywhere; gold, silver, precious stones adorning profusely the persons of their chiefs, their wives, their warriors; rich stuffs, dyed with many colors, to distinguish the various orders of society; a deep religious feeling in their hearts, preparing them for the faith, by inspiring them with lively emotions at the sight of divine power displayed in their mountains, their valleys, their lakes and rivers, and on the swelling bosom of the all-encircling ocean; superstitions of various kinds, indeed, but none of a demoralizing character, none involving marks of cruelty or lust; no revolting statues of Priapus, of Bacchus, of Cybele; no obscene emblems of religion, as in all other lands, to confront Christianity; but over all the island, song, festivity, deep affection for kindred; and, as though blood-relationship could not satisfy their heart, fosterage covering the land with other brothers and sisters; all permeated with a strong attachment to their clan-system and social customs. Such is an exact picture of the Erin of the time, which the study of antiquity brings clearer and clearer before the eyes of the modern student.

Patrick appears among them, leaning on his staff, and bringing them from Rome and Gaul new songs in a new language set to a new melody. He comes to unveil for them what lies hidden, unknown to themselves, in the depths of their hearts. He explains, by the power of one Supreme God, why it is that their mountains are so high, their valley so smiling, their rivers and lakes teeming with life, their fountains so fresh and cool, and that sun of theirs so temperate in its warmth, and the moon and stars, lighted with a soft radiance, shimmering over the deep obscurity of their groves.

He directs them to look into their own consciences, to admit themselves to be sinners in need of redemption, and points out to them in what manner that Supreme God, whom they half knew already, condescended to save man.

Straightway, from all parts of the island, converts flock to him; they come in crowds to be baptized, to embrace the new law by which they may read their own hearts; they are ready to do whatever he wishes; many, not content with the strict commandments enjoined on all, wish to enter on the path of perfection: the men become monks, the women and young girls nuns, that is to say, spouses of Christ. In Munster alone "it would be difficult," says a modern writer, Father Brenan, "to form an estimate of the number of converts he made, and even of the churches and religious establishments he founded."

And so with all the other provinces of the island. The proof's still stand before our eyes. For, as Prof. Curry justly remarks: "No one, who examines for himself, can doubt that at the first preaching in Erin of the glad tidings of salvation, by Saints Palladius and Patrick, those countless Christian churches were built, whose sites and ruins mark so thickly the surface of our country even to this day, still bearing through all the vicissitudes of time and conquest the unchanged names of their original founders."

According to the commonly-received opinion, St. Patrick's apostleship lasted thirty-three years; but, whatever may have been its real duration, certain it is that his feet traversed the whole island several times, and, at his passing, churches and monasteries sprang up in great numbers, and remained to tell the true story of his labors when their founder had passed away.

Nor was it with Ireland as with Rome, Carthage, Antioch, and other great cities of Europe, Africa, and Asia. Not the slaves and artisans alone filled these newly-erected Christian edifices. Some of the first men of the nation received baptism. We have already spoken of the family of Laeghaire. In Connaught, at the first appearance of the man of God, all the inhabitants of that portion of the province now represented by the County Mayo became Christians; and the seven sons of the king of the province were baptized, together with twelve thousand of their clansmen. In Leinster, the Princes Illand and Alind were baptized in a fountain near Naas. In Munster, Aengus, the King of Cashel, with all the nobility of his clan, embraced the faith. A number of chieftains in Thomond are also mentioned; and the whole of the Dalcassian tribe, so celebrated before and after in the annals of Ireland, received, with the waters of baptism, that ardent faith which nothing has been able to tear from them to this day.

Many Druids even, by renouncing their superstitions, abdicated their power over the people. We have mentioned Dubtach; his example was followed by many others, among whom was Fingar, the son of King Clito, who is said to have suffered martyrdom in Brittany; Fiech, pupil of Dubtach, himself a poet, and belonging to the noble house of Hy-Baircha in Leinster, was raised by St. Patrick to the episcopacy, and was the first occupant of the See of Sletty.

Fiech was a regular member of the bardic order of Druids, a poet by profession, esteemed as a learned man even before he embraced Christianity; and during his lifetime he was, as a Christian bishop, consulted by numbers and regarded as an oracle of truth and heavenly wisdom.

Nevertheless, Patrick encountered opposition. Some chieftains declared themselves against him, without daring openly to attack him. Many Druids, called in the old Irish annals magi, tried their utmost to estrange the Irish people from him. But he stood in danger of his life only once. It was, in fact, a war of argument. Long discussions took place, with varied success, ending generally, however, in a victory for truth.

The final result was that, in the second generation after St. Patrick, there existed not a single pagan in the whole of Ireland; the very remembrance of paganism even seemed to have passed away from their minds ever after; hence arises the difficulty of deciding now on the character of that paganism.

After its abolition, nothing remained in the literature of the country, which was at that time much more copious than at present--nothing was left in its monuments or in the inclinations of the people--to imperil the existence of the newly-established Christianity, or of a nature calculated to give a wrong bias to the religious worship of the people, such as we have seen was the case in the rest of Europe.

May we not conclude, then, that Ireland was much better prepared for the new religion than any other country; that, when she was thus admitted by baptism into the European family, she made her entry in a way peculiar to herself, and which secured to her, once for all, her firm and undeviating attachment to truth?

She had nothing to change in her manners after having renounced the few disconnected superstitions to which she had been addicted. Her songs, her bards, her festivities, her patriarchal government, her fosterage, were left to her, Christianized and consecrated by her great apostle; clanship even penetrated into the monasteries, and gave rise later on to some abuses. But, perhaps, the saint thought it better to allow the existence of things which might lead to abuse than violently and at once to subvert customs, rooted by age in the very nature of the people, some of which it cost England, later on, centuries of inconceivable barbarities to eradicate.

As to what exact form, if any, the paganism of the Irish Celts assumed, we have so few data to build upon that it is now next to impossible to shape a system out of them. From the passage of the "Confessio" already quoted, we might infer that they adored the sun; and this passage is very remarkable as the only mention anywhere made by St. Patrick of idolatry among the people. If it was only the emblem of the Supreme Being, then would there have been nothing idolatrous in its worship; and the strong terms in which the saint condemns it perhaps need only express his fear lest the superstition of the ignorant people might convert veneration into positive idolatry. At all events, there was not a statue, or a temple, or a theological system, erected to or connected with it in any shape.

The solemn forms of oaths taken and administered by the Irish kings would also lead us to infer that they paid a superstitious respect to the winds and the other elements. But why should this feeling pass beyond that which even the Christian experiences when confronted by mysteries in the natural as well as the supernatural order? The awe-struck pagan saw the lightning leap, the tempest gather and break over him in majestic fury; heard the great voice of the mighty ocean which laved or lashed his shores: he witnessed these wonderful effects; he knew not whence the tempests or the lightnings came, or the voice of the ocean; he trembled at the unseen power which moved them --at his God.

So his imagination peopled his groves and hill-sides, his rivers and lakes, with harmless fairies; but fairy land has never become among any nation a pandemonium of cruel divinities; and we doubt much if such innocuous superstition can be rightly called even sinful error.

In fact, the only thing which could render paganism truly a danger in Ireland, as opposed to the preaching of Christianity, was the body of men intrusted with the care of religion--the Druids, the magi of the chronicles. But, as we find no traces of bloody sacrifices in Ireland, the Druids there probably never bore the character which they did in Gaul; they cannot be said to have been sacrificing priests; their office consisted merely in pretended divinations, or the workings of incantations or spells. They also introduced superstition into the practice of medicine, and taught the people to venerate the elements or mysterious forces of this world.

Without mentioning any of the many instances which are found in the histories of the workings of these Druidical incantations and spells, the consulting of the clouds, and the ceremonies with which they surrounded their healing art, we go straight to our main point: the ease and suddenness with which all these delusions vanished at the first preaching of the Gospel --a fact very telling on the force which they exercised over the mind of the nation. All natural customs, games, festivities, social relationships, as we have seen, are preserved, many to this day; what is esteemed as their religion, and its ceremonies and superstitions, is dropped at once. The entire Irish mind expanded freely and generously at the simple announcement of a God, present everywhere in the universe, and accepted it. The dogma of the Holy Spirit, not only filling all--complens omnia-- but dwelling in their very souls by grace, and filling them with love and fear, must have appeared natural to them. Their very superstitions must have prepared the way for the truth, a change --or may we not say a more direct and tangible object taking the place of and filling their undefined yearnings--was alone requisite. Otherwise it is a hard fact to explain how, within a few years, all Druidism and magic, incantations, spells, and divinations, were replaced by pure religion, by the doctrine of celestial favors obtained through prayer, by the intercession of a host of saints in heaven, and the belief in Christian miracles and prophecies; whereas, scarcely any thing of Roman or Grecian mythology could be replaced by corresponding Christian practices, although popes did all they could in that regard. Nearly all the errors of the Irish Celts had their corresponding truths and holy practices in Christianity, which could be readily substituted for them, and envelop them immediately with distrust or just oblivion. Hence we do not see, in the subsequent ecclesiastical history of Ireland, any thing to resemble the short sketch we have given of the many dangers arising within the young Christian Church, which had their origin in the former religion of other European nations.

In regarding philosophy and its perils in Ireland, our task will be an easy one, yet not unimportant in its bearings on subsequent considerations. The minds of nations differ as greatly as their physical characteristics; and to study the Irish mind we have only to take into consideration the institutions which swayed it from time immemorial. They were of such a nature that they could but belong to a traditional people. All patriarchal tribes partake of that general character; none, perhaps, so strikingly as the Celts.

People thus disposed have nothing rationalistic in their nature; they accept old facts; and, if they reason upon them, it is to find proofs to support, not motives to doubt them. They never refine their discussions to hair-splitting, synonymous almost with rejection, as seems to be the delight of what we call rationalistic races. It was among these that philosophy was born, and among them it flourishes. They may, by their acute reasoning, enlarge the human mind, open up new horizons, and, if confined within just limits, actually enrich the understanding of man. We are far from pretending that philosophy has only been productive of harm, and that it were a blessed thing had the human intellect always remained, as it were, in a dormant state, without ever striving to grasp at philosophic truth and raise itself above the common level; we hold the great names of Augustine, Anselm, Thomas Aquinas, and so many others, in too great respect to entertain such an opinion.

Yet it cannot be denied that the excessive study of philosophy has produced many evils among men, has often been subservient to error, has, at best, been for many minds the source of a cold and desponding skepticism.

No race of men, perhaps, has been less inclined to follow those intellectual aberrations than the Celtic, owing chiefly to its eminently traditional dispositions.

Before Christianity reached them, the intellectual labors of the Celts were chiefly confined to history and genealogy, medicine and botany, law, song, music, and artistic workings in metals and gems. This was the usual curriculum of Druidic studies. Astronomy and the physical sciences, as well as the knowledge of "the nature of the eternal God," were, according to Caesar, extensively studied in the Gallic schools. Some elements of those intellectual pursuits may also have occupied the attention of the Irish student during the twelve, fifteen, or twenty years of his preparation for being ordained to the highest degree of ollamh. But the oldest and most reliable documents which have been examined so far do not allow us to state positively that such was the case to any great extent.

In Christian times, however, it seems certain that astronomy was better studied in Ireland than anywhere else, as is proved by the extraordinary impulse given to that science by Virgil of Salzburg, who was undoubtedly an Irishman, and educated in his native country.

It is from the Church alone, therefore, that they received their highest intellectual training in the philosophy and theology of the Scriptures and of the Fathers. It is known that, by the introduction of the Latin and Greek tongues into their schools in addition to the vernacular, the Bible in Latin and Greek, and the writings of many Fathers in both languages, as also the most celebrated works of Roman and Greek classical writers, became most interesting subjects of study. They reproduced those works for their own use in the scriptoria of their numerous monasteries. We still possess some of those manuscripts of the sixth and following centuries, and none more beautiful or correct can be found among those left by the English, French, or Italian monastic institutions of the periods mentioned.

During the seventh, eighth, and ninth centuries, the Irish schools became celebrated all over Europe. Young Anglo-Saxons of the best families were sent to receive their education in Innisfail, as the island was then often called; and, from their celebrated institutions of learning, numerous teachers and missionaries went forth to England, Germany (along the Rhine, chiefly), France, and even Switzerland and Italy.

Yet, in the history of all those intellectual labors, we never read of startling theories in philosophy or theology advanced by any of them, unless we except the eccentric John Scotus Erigena, whom Charles the Bald, at whose court he resided, protected even against the just severity of the Church. Without ever having studied theology, he undertook to dogmatize, and would perhaps have originated some heresy, had he found a following in Germany or France.

But he is the only Irishman who ever threatened the peace of the Church, and, through her, of the world. Duns Scotus, if he were Irish, never taught any error, and remained always an accepted leader in Catholic schools. To the honor of Erin be it said, her children have ever been afraid to deviate in the least from the path of faith. And it would be wrong to imagine that the preservation from heresy so peculiar to them, and by which they are broadly distinguished from all other European nations, comes from dulness of intellect and inability to follow out an intricate argumentation. They show the acuteness of their understanding in a thousand ways; in poetry, in romantic tales, in narrative compositions, in legal acumen and extempore arguments, in the study of medicine, chiefly in that masterly eloquence by which so many of them are distinguished. Who shall say that they might not also have reached a high degree of eminence in philosophical discussions and ontological theories? They have always abstained from such studies by reason of a natural disinclination, which does them honor, and which has saved them in modern times, as we shall see in a subsequent chapter, from the innumerable evils which afflict society everywhere else, and by which it is even threatened with destruction.

Thus, among the numerous and versatile progeny of Japhet one small branch has kept itself aloof from the universal movement of the whole family; and, in the very act of accepting Christianity and taking a place in the commonwealth of Western nations, it has known how to do so in its own manner, and has thus secured a firm hold of the saving doctrines imparted to the whole race for a great purpose--the purpose, unfortunately often defeated--of reducing to practice and reality the sublime ideal of the Christian religion.

The details given in this chapter on the various circumstances connected with the introduction of our holy faith into Ireland were necessarily very limited, as our chief object was to speak of the nation's preparation for it.

In the following we treat directly of what could only be touched upon in the latter part of this.

HOW THE IRISH RECEIVED CHRISTIANITY

FOR the conversion of pagans to Christianity, many exterior proofs of revelation were vouchsafed by God to man in addition to the interior impulse of his grace. Those exterior proofs are generally termed "the evidences of religion." They produce their chief effect on inquiring minds which are familiar with the reasoning processes of philosophy, and attach great importance to truth acquired by logical deduction. To this, many pagans of Greece and Rome owed their conversion; by this, in our days, many strangers are brought, on reflection, to the faith of Christ, always presupposing the paramount influence of divine grace on their minds and hearts.

But it is easy to remark that, except in rare cases, those who are gained over to truth by such a process are with some difficulty brought under the influence of the supernatural, which forms the essential groundwork of Christianity. This influence, it is true, is only the effect of the operation of the Holy Ghost on the soul of the convert; but the Holy Ghost acts in conformity with the disposition of the soul; and we know, by what has been said on the character of religion among the Romans and the Greeks in the earlier days of the Church, that it took long ages, the infusion of Northern blood, and the simplicity of new races uncontaminated by heathen mythology, to inspire men with that deep supernatural feeling which in course of time became the distinguishing character of the ages of faith. Ireland imbibed this feeling at once, and thus she received Christianity more thoroughly, at the very beginning, than did any other Western nation.

The fact is--whatever may be thought or said--the Christian religion, with all the loveliness it imparts to this world when rightly understood, though never destroying Nature, but always keeping it in mind, and consecrating it to God, truly endowed, consequently, with the promises of earth as well as those of heaven--the Christian religion is nevertheless fundamentally supernatural, full of awe and mystery, heavenly and incomprehensible, before being earthly and the grateful object of sense.

Without examining the various formularies which heresy compelled an infallible Church to proclaim and impose upon her children from time to time, the Apostles' Creed alone transfers man at once into regions supernatural, into heaven itself. The Trinity, the Incarnation, the Redemption, the mission of the Hold Ghost on earth, the communion of saints, the forgiveness of sins, and the resurrection of the dead, are all mysteries necessitating a revelation on the part of God himself to make them known to and believed by man. Do they not place man, even while on earth, in direct communication with heaven?

The firm believer in those mysteries is already a celestial citizen by faith and hope. He has acquired a new life, new senses, as it were, new faculties of mind and will--all things, evidently, above Nature.

And it is clear, from many passages of the New Testament, that our Lord wished the lives of his disciples to be wholly penetrated with that supernatural essence. They were not to be men of the earth, earthly, but citizens of another country which is heavenly and eternal. Hence the holiness and perfection required of them--a holiness, according to Christ, like that of the celestial Father himself; hence contempt for the things of this world, so strongly recommended by our Lord; hence the assurance that men are called to be sons of God, the eternal Son having become incarnate to acquire for us this glorious privilege; hence, finally, that frequent recommendation in the Gospel to rely on God for the things of this life, and to look above all for spiritual blessings.

That reliance is set forth in such terms, in the Sermon on the Mount, that, taken literally, man should neglect entirely his temporal advantages, forget entirely Nature, and think only of grace, or rather, expect that the things of Nature would be given us by our heavenly Father "who knows that we need them."

Nature, consequently, assumes a new aspect in this system. It is no longer a complexity of temporal goods within reach of the efforts of man, and which it rests with man alone to procure for himself. It is, indeed, a worldly treasure, belonging to God, as all else, and which the hand of God scatters profusely among his creatures. God will not fail to grant to every one what he needs, if he have faith. Thus God is always visible in Nature; and redeemed man, raised far above the beasts of the field, has other eyes than those of the body, when he looks around him on this world.

Had Christianity been literally understood by those who first received it, it would have completely changed the moral, social, and even natural aspect of the universe. The change produced throughout by the new religion was indeed remarkable, but not what it would have been, if the supernatural had taken complete possession of human society. This it did in Ireland, and, it may be said, in Ireland alone.

To begin with the preaching of St. Patrick, we note his care to impart to his converts a sufficient knowledge of the Christian mysteries, but, above all, to make those mysteries influence their lives by acting more powerfully on the new Christian heart than even on the mind.

Thus, in the beautiful legend of Ethne and Felimia, the saint, not content with instructing them on the attributes of God, the Trinity, and other supernatural truths, goes further still; he requires a change in their whole being--that it be spiritualized: by deeply exciting their feelings, by speaking of Christ as their spouse, by making them wish to receive him in the holy Eucharist, even at the expense of their temporal life, he so raises them above Nature that they actually asked to die. "And they received the Eucharist of God, and they slept in death."

Again, in the hymn of Tara, the heavenly spirit, which consists in an intimate union with God and Christ, is so admirably expressed, that we cannot refrain from presenting an extract from it, remarking that this beautiful hymn has been the great prayer of all Irishmen through all ages down even to our own times, though, unfortunately, it is not now so generally known and used by them as formerly:

"At Tara, to-day, may the strength of God pilot me, may the power of God preserve me, may the wisdom of God instruct me, may the eye of God view me, may the ear of God hear me, may the word of God render me eloquent, may the hand of God protect me, may the way of God direct me, may the shield of God defend me, etc.

"Christ be with me, Christ before me, Christ after me, Christ in me, Christ under me, Christ over me, Christ at my right, Christ at my left; . . . Christ be in the heart of each person whom I speak to, Christ in the mouth of each person who speaks to me, Christ in each eye which sees me, Christ in each ear which hears me!"

Could any thing tend more powerfully to make of those whom he converted, true supernatural Christians--forgetful of this world, thinking only of another and a brighter one?

The island, at his coming, was a prey to preternatural superstitions. The Druids possessed, in the opinion of the people, a power beyond that of man; and history shows the same phenomenon in all pagan countries, not excepting those of our time. A real supernatural power was required to overcome that of the magi.

Hence, according to Probus, the magicians to whom the arrival of Patrick had been foretold, prepared themselves for the contest, and several chieftains supported them. Prestiges were, therefore, tried in antagonism to miracles; but, as Moses prevailed over the power of the Egyptian priests, so did Patrick over the Celtic magicians. It is even said that five Druids perished in one of the contests.

The princes were sometimes also punished with death. Recraid, head of a clan, came with his Druids and with words of incantation written under his white garments; he fell dead. Laeghaire himself, the Ard-Righ of all Ireland, whose family became Christian, but who refused to abandon his superstitions, perished with his numerous attendants.

But a more singular phenomenon was, that death, which was often the punishment of unbelief, became as often a boon to be desired by the new Christian converts, so completely were they under the influence of the supernatural. Thus Ruis found it hard to believe. To strengthen his faith, Patrick restored to him his youth, and then gave him the choice between this sweet blessing of life and the happiness of heaven; Ruis preferred to die, like Ethne and Felimia.

Sechnall, the bard, told St. Patrick, one day, that he wished to sing the praises of a saint whom the earth still possessed. "Hasten, then," said Patrick, "for thou art at the gates of death." Sechnall, not only undisturbed, but full of joy, sang a glorious hymn in honor of Patrick, and immediately after died.

Kynrecha came to the convent-door of St. Senan. "What have women in common with monks?" said the holy abbot. "We will not receive thee."

"Before I leave this place," responded Kynrecha, "I offer this prayer to God, that my soul may leave the body." And she sank down and expired.

The various lives of the apostle of Ireland and his successors are full of facts of this nature. Supposing that a high coloring was given to some of these by the writers, one thing is certain: the people who lived during that apostleship believed in them firmly, and handed down their belief to their children. Moreover, nothing was better calculated to give to a primitive people, like the Irish, a strong supernatural spirit and character, than to make them despise the joys of this earth and yearn for a better country.

There are, indeed, too many facts of a similar kind related in the lives of St. Patrick and his fellow-workers, to bear the imputation, not of imposition, but even of delusion. The desire of dying, to be united with Christ; the indifference, at least, as to the prolongation of existence; the readiness, if not the joy, with which the announcement of death was received, are of such frequent mention in those old legends, as matters of ordinary occurrence, surprising no one, that they must be conceded as facts often taking place in those early ages.

And, more striking still, this feeling of accepting death, either as a boon or as a matter of course, and with perfect resignation to the will of God, seems to have been throughout, since the introduction of Christianity, a characteristic of the Irish people. It is often witnessed in our own days, and manifested, equally by the young, the middle-aged, or the old. The young, closing their eyes to that bright life whose sweetness they have as yet scarcely tasted, never murmur at being deprived of it, though hope is to them so alluring; the middle-aged, called away in the midst of projects yet unaccomplished, see the sudden end of all that before interested them, with no other concern than for the children they leave behind them; the old, among other races generally so tenacious of life, are, as a rule, glad that their last hour has come, and speak only of their joy that at last they "go home" to that country whither so many of their friends and kindred have gone before them.

This in itself would stamp the Celtic character with an indelible mark, distinguishing it from all other, even most Christian, peoples.

The second sign we find of the firm hold the supernatural had taken of the Irish from the very beginning is their strong belief in the power of the priesthood. This is so striking among them that they have been called by their enemies and those of the Church "a priest-ridden people." Let us consider if this is a reproach.

If Christianity be true, what is the priesthood? Even among the Greeks, from whom so many heresies formerly sprang before they were smitten into insignificance by schism and its punishment--Turkish slavery--when the great doctors sent them by Providence spoke on the subject, what were their words, and what impression did they make on their supercilious hearers? St. John Chrysostom will answer. His long treatise, written to his friend Basil, is but a glowing description of the great privileges given to the Christian priest by the High-Priest himself--Christ our Lord.

When the great preacher of Antioch, though not yet a priest, describes the awful moment of sacrifice, the altar surrounded by angels descended from heaven, the man consecrated to an office higher than any on earth, and as high as that of the incarnate Son of God--God himself coming down from above and bringing down heaven with him--who can believe in Christianity and fail to be struck with awe?

Who can read the words of Christ, declaring that any one invested with that dignity is sent by him as he was himself sent by his Father, and not feel the innate respect due to such divine honors? Who can read the details of those privileges with respect to the remission of sin, the conferring of grace by the sacraments, the infallible teaching of truth, the power even granted to them sometimes over Nature and disease, without feeling himself transported into a world far above this, and without placing his confidence in what God himself has declared so powerful and preeminent in the regions beyond?

Such, in a few words, is the Christian priesthood, if Christianity possesses any reality and is not an imposture. Among all nations, therefore, where sound faith exists, the greatest respect is shown to the ministers of God; but the Irish have at all times been most persistent in their veneration and trust. And if we would ascertain the cause of their standing in this regard, we shall find that other nations, while firmly believing the words of Christ, keep their eyes open to human frailty, and look more keenly and with more suspicion on the conduct of men invested with so high a dignity, but subject at the same time to earthly passions and sins; while the Irish, on the contrary, abandon themselves with all the impulsiveness of their nature to the feeling uppermost in their hearts, which is ever one of trust and ready reliance.

But this statement, whatever may be its intrinsic value, itself needs a further explanation, which is only to be found in the greater attraction the supernatural always possessed for the Irish nature, when developed by grace. They accept fully and unsuspiciously what is heavenly, because they, more than others, feel that they are made for heaven, and the earth, consequently, has for them fewer attractions. They cling to a world far above this, and whatever belongs to it is dear to them.

Hence, from the first preaching of Christianity among them, all earthly dignities have paled before the heavenly honors of the priesthood. They have been taught by St. Patrick that even the supreme duties of a real Christian king fall far below those of a Christian bishop.

The king, according to the apostle of Ireland - and his words have become a canon of the Irish Church - "has to judge no man unjustly; to be the protector of the stranger, of the widow, and the orphan; to repress theft, punish adultery, not to keep buffoons or unchaste persons; not to exalt iniquity, but to sweep away the impious from the land, exterminate parricides and perjurers; to defend the poor, to appoint just men over the affairs of the kingdom, to consult wise and temperate elders, to defend his native land against its enemies rightfully and stoutly; in all things to put his trust in God."

All this evidently refers only to the exterior polity and administration. But "the bishop must be the hand which supports, the pilot who directs, the anchor that stays, the hammer that strikes, the sun that enlightens, the dew which moistens, the tablet to be written on, the book to be read, the mirror to be seen in, the terror that terrifies, the image of all that is good; and let him be all for all."

Under this metaphorical style we here discern all the interior qualities of a spiritual Christian guide, teaching no less by authority than example.

And, in the opinion of the converts of Patrick, were not the bishops, abbots, and priests, supported by an invisible power, stronger than all visible armies and guards of kings and princes?

"When the King of Cashel dared to contend against the holy abbot Mochoemoc, the first night after the dispute an old man took the king by the hand and led him to the northern city-walls; there he opened the king's eyes, and he beheld all the Irish saints of his own sex in white garments, with Patrick at their head; they were there to protect Mochoemoc, and they filled the plain of Femyn.

"The second night the old man came again and took the king to the southern wall, and there he saw the white-robed glorious army of Ireland's virgins, led by Bridget: they too had come to defend Mochoemoc, and they filled the plain of Monael." [1]

In the annals of no other Christian nation do we see so many examples of the power of the ministers of God to punish the wicked and help and succor the good, as we do in the hagiography of Ireland. Bad kings and chieftains reproved, cursed, punished; the poor assisted, the oppressed delivered from their enemies, the sick restored to health, the dead even raised to life, are occurrences which the reader meets in almost every page of the lives of Irish saints. The Bollandists, accustomed as they were to meet with miracles of that kind, in the lives they published, found in Irish hagiography such a superabundance of them, that they refused to admit into their admirable compilation a great number already published or in manuscript. Nevertheless, the critics of our days, finding nothing impossible to or unworthy of God in the large collection of Colgan and other Irish antiquarians, express their surprise at their exclusion from that of Bollandus.

No one at least will refuse to concede that, true or not, the facts related in those lives are always provocative of piety and redolent of faith. They certainly prove that at all periods of their existence the Irish have manifested a holy avidity for every thing supernatural and miraculous. Do they not know that our Lord has promised gifts of this description to his apostles and their successors? And what the acts of the Apostles and many acts of martyrs positively state as having happened at the very beginning of the Church, is not a whit less extraordinary or physically impossible than any thing related in the Irish legends.

---

[1] Many quotations in this chapter are from the "Legend. Hist." by J. G. Shea.

Every Christian soul naturally abhors the unbelief of a Strauss or of a Renan as to the former; is it not unnatural, then, for the same Christian soul to reject the latter because they fall under the easy sneer of "an Irish legend," and are not contained in Holy Writ?

At all events, the faith of the Irish has never wavered in such matters, and to-day they hold the same confidence in the priests' power that meets us everywhere in the pages of Colgan and Ward. The reason is, that they admit Christianity without reserve; and in its entirety it is supernatural. The criticisms of human reason on holy things hold in their eyes something of the sacrilegious and blasphemous; such criticisms are for them open disrespect for divine things; and, inasmuch as divine things are, in fact, more real than any phenomena under natural laws can be, skepticism in the former case is always more unreasonable than in the latter, supposing always that the narrative of the Divine favors reposes on sufficient authority.

It is clear, therefore, that since the preaching of Christianity in Ireland, the world showed itself to the inhabitants of that country in a different light to that in which other men beheld it. For them, Nature is never separated from its Maker; the hand of God is ever visible in all mundane affairs, and the frightful parting between the spiritual and material worlds, first originated by the Baconian philosophy, which culminates in our days in the almost open negation of the spiritual, and thus materializes all things, is with justice viewed by the children of St. Patrick with a holy horror as leading to atheism, if it be not atheism itself.

Without going to such extremes as the avowed infidels of modern times, all other Christian nations have seemed afraid to draw the logical conclusions whose premises were laid down by revelation. They have tried to follow a via media between truth and error; they have admitted to a certain extent the separation of God and Nature, supposing the act of creation to have passed long ages ago, and not continuing through all time; and thus they are bound by their system to hold that miracles are very extraordinary things, not to be believed prima facie, requiring infinite precautions before admitting the supposition of their having taken place; all which indicates a real repugnance to their admission, and an innate fear of supposing God all-powerful, just, and good. It is the first step to Manicheism and the kindred errors; and most Christian nations having, unfortunately, imbibed the principles of those errors in the philosophy of modern times, have almost lost all faith in the supernatural, and reduced revelation to a meagre and cold system, unrealized and not to be realized in human life.

Not so the Irish Religion has entered deep into their life. It is a thing of every moment and of every place. Nature, God's handiwork, instead of repelling them from God himself, draws them gently but forcibly toward Him, so that they feel themselves to be truly recipients of the blessings of God by being sharers in the blessings of Nature.

And must God's ministers, who have received such extraordinary powers over the supernatural world, be entirely deprived of power over the inferior part of creation? Who can say so, and have true faith in the words of our Lord? Who can say so, and truly call himself the follower and companion of the saints who have all believed so firmly in the constant action of God in this, the lesser part of his creation?

And this faith of the Irish in the power of the priesthood is not a thing of yesterday. It dates from their adoption of Christianity, to continue, we hope, forever. It ought, therefore, to be carefully distinguished from that love for every priest of God which beats so ardently in the hearts of them all, and which was so strengthened by a long community of persecution and suffering.

In Ireland, as in every other Christian country, the priesthood has always sided with the people against their oppressors. During the early ages of Christianity in the island, the bishops, priests, and monks, were often called upon to exercise their authority and power against princes and chiefs of clans, accustomed to plunder, destroy, and kill, on the slightest pretext, and unused to control their fierce passions, inflamed by the rancor of feuds and the pride of strength and bravery. Some of those chieftains even opposed the progress of religion; and it is said that Eochad, King of Ulster, cast his two daughters, whom Patrick had baptized and consecrated to God, into the sea.

For several centuries the heads of clans were generally so unruly and so hard to bring under the yoke of Christ, that the saints, in taking the side of the poor, had to stand as a wall of brass to stem the fury of the great and powerful.

Bridget even, the modest and tender virgin, often spoke harshly of princes and rulers. "While she dwelt in the land of Bregia, King Connal's daughter-in-law came to ask her prayers, for she was barren. Bridget refused to go to receive her; but, leaving her without, she sent one of her maidens. When the nun returned: 'Mother,' she asked, 'why would you not go and see the queen? you pray for the wives of peasants.' 'Because,' said the servant of God, 'the poor and the peasants are almost all good and pious, while the sons of kings are serpents, children of blood and fornication, except a small number of elect. But, after all, as she had recourse to us, go back and tell her that she shall have a son; he will be wicked, and his race shall be accursed, yet he shall reign many years.'"

We might multiply examples such as this, wherein the saints and the ministers of God always side with the poor and the helpless; and their great number in the lives of the old saints at once gives a reason for the deep love which the lower class of the Irish people felt for the holy men who were at once the servants of God and their helpers in every distress.

The same thing is to be found in the whole subsequent history of the island, chiefly in the latter ages of persecution. But, as we said before, this affection and love must be distinguished from the feeling of reverence and awe resulting from the supernatural character of their office. The first feeling is merely a natural one, produced by deeds of benevolence and holy charity fondly remembered by the individuals benefited. The second was the effect of religious faith in the sacredness of the priestly character, and remained in full force even when the poor themselves fell under reproof or threat in consequence of some misdeed or vicious habit.

Hence the universal respect which the whole race entertains for their spiritual rulers, and their unutterable confidence in their high prerogatives. In prosperity as in adversity, in freedom or in subjection, they always preserve an instinctive faith in the unseen power which Christ conferred on those whom He chose to be his ministers. This feeling, which is undoubtedly found among good Christians in all places, is as certainly only found among particular individuals; but among the Irish Celts it is the rule rather than the exception.

Well have they merited, then, in this sense, from the days of St. Patrick down, the title of a "priest-ridden" people, which has been fixed on them as a term of reproach by those for whom all belief in the supernatural is belief in imposture.

Another and a stronger fact still, exemplifying the extent to which the Irish have at all times carried their devotion to the supernatural character of the Christian religion, is the extraordinary ardor with which, from the very beginning, they rushed into the high path of perfection, called the way of "evangelical counsels." Nowhere else were such scenes ever witnessed in Christian history.

For the great mass of people the common way of life is the practice of the commandments of God; it is only the few who feel themselves called on to enter upon another path, and who experience interiorly the need of being "perfect."

In Ireland the case was altogether different from the outset. St. Patrick, notwithstanding his intimate knowledge of the leanings of the race, expresses in his "Confessio" the wonder and delight he experienced when he saw in what manner and in what numbers they begged to be consecrated to God the very first day after their baptism. Yet were they conscious that this very eagerness would excite the greater opposition on the part of their pagan relatives and friends. Thus we read of the fate of Eochad's daughters, and the story of Ethne and Felimia.

The whole nation, in fact, appeared suddenly transported with a holy impetuosity, and lifted at once to the height of Christian life. Monasteries and nunneries could not be constructed fast enough, although they contented themselves with the lightest fabrics--wattles being the ordinary materials for walls, and slender laths for roofs.

Nor was this an ephemeral ardor, like a fire of stubble or straw, flashing into a momentary blaze, to relapse into deeper gloom. It lasted for several centuries; it was still in full flame at the time of Columba, more than two hundred years after Patrick; it grew into a vast conflagration in the seventh and eighth centuries, when multitudes rushed forth from that burning island of the blest to spread the sacred fire through Europe.

How the nation continued to multiply, when so many devoted themselves to a holy celibacy, is only to be explained by the large number of children with which God blessed those who pursued an ordinary life, and who, from what is related in the chronicles of the time, must have been in a minority.

Of the first monasteries and convents erected not a single vestige now remains, because of the perishable materials of which they were constructed; yet each of them contained hundreds, nay thousands, of monks or nuns.

But, even in our days, we are furnished with an ocular demonstration of what men could scarcely bring themselves to believe, or at least would term an exaggeration, did not standing proof remain. God inspired his children with the thought of erecting more substantial structures, of building walls of stone and roofing them in with tiles and metal; and the island was literally covered, not with Gothic castles or luxurious palaces and sumptuous edifices, but with large and commodious buildings and churches, wherein the religious life of the inmates might be carried on with greater comfort and seclusion from the world.

At the time of the Reformation all those asylums of perfection and asceticism were of course profaned, converted to vile or slavish uses, many altogether destroyed to the very foundations; a greater number were allowed to decay gradually and become heaps of ruins.

And what happened when the English Government, unable any longer to resist public opinion, was compelled to consent that a survey be made of the poor and comparatively few remains still in existence, in order to manifest a show of interest for the past history of the island; when commissioners were appointed to publish lists and diagrams of the former dwellings of the "saints," which the "zeal" of the "reformers" had battered down without mercy? To the astonishment of all, it was proved by the ruins still in existence that the greater portion of the island had been once occupied by monasteries and convents of every description. And Prof. O'Curry has stated his conviction, based on local traditions and geographical and topographical names, that a great number of these can be traced back to Patrick and his first companions.

It is clear enough, then, that, from the beginning, the Irish were not only "priest-ridden," but also very attached to "monkish superstitions."

Yet we could not form a complete idea of that attachment were we to limit ourselves to an enumeration of the buildings actually erected, supposing such an enumeration possible at this time. For we know, by many facts related in Irish hagiology, that a great number of those who devoted themselves to a life of penance and austerity, did not dwell even in the humble structures of the first monks, but, deeming themselves unworthy of the society of their brethren, or condemned by a severe but just "friend of their soul," as the confessor was then called, hid themselves in mountain-caves, in the recesses of woods or forests, or banished themselves to crags ever beaten by the waves of the sea.

Yes, there was a time when those dreadful solitudes of the Hebrides, which frighten the modern tourist in his summer explorations, teemed with Christian life, and every rock, cave, and sand-bar had its inhabitant, and that inhabitant an Irish monk.

They sometimes spent seven years on a desert islet doing penance for a single sin. They often passed a lifetime on a rock in the midst of the ocean, alone with God, and enjoying no communion but that of their conscience.

Who knows how many thousands of men have led such a life, shocking, indeed, to the feelings of worldlings, but in reality devoted to the contemplation of what is above Nature--a life, consequently, exalted and holy?

Passing from the solitudes to the numerous hives where the bees of primitive Christianity in Ireland were busy at work constructing their combs and secreting their honey, what do we see? People generally imagine that all monastic establishments have been alike; that those of mediaeval times were simply the reproduction of earlier ones. An abbot, the three vows, austerity, psalmody, study--such are the general features common to all; but those of Ireland had peculiarities which are worthy of examination. We shall find in them a stronger expression of the supernatural, perhaps; certainly a more heavenly cast, a greater forgetfulness of the world, its manners and habits, its passions and aims.

Patrick had learned all he knew of this holy life in the establishment of Lerins, wherein the West reflected more truly than it ever did subsequently the Oriental light of the great founders of monasticism in Palestine and Egypt.

The first thing to be remarked is the want, to a great extent, of a strict system. The Danes, when Christianized, and the Anglo-Normans, introduced this afterwards; but the genius of the Irish race is altogether opposed to it, and the Scandinavian races in following ages could hardly ever bring them under the cold uniformity of an iron rule.

Did St. Patrick establish a rule in the monasteries which he founded? Did St. Columba two centuries later? Did any of the great masters of spiritual life who are known to have exercised an influence on the world of Irish convents? Not only has nothing of the kind been transmitted to us, but no mention of it is made in the lives of holy abbots which we possess.[1] St. Columbanus's rule is the only one which has come down to us; but the monasteries founded by him were all situated in Burgundy, Switzerland, Germany, and Italy--that is to say, out of Ireland, out of the island of saints. He was compelled to furnish his monasteries with a written rule, because they were surrounded by barbarous peoples, some of whom his establishments often received as monks, and to whom the holiness of Ireland was unfamiliar or utterly unknown. But why should the people of God, living in his devoted island, redeemed as soon as born by the waters of baptism, be shackled by enactments which might serve as an obstacle to the action of the Holy Ghost on their free souls?

According to the common opinion, each founder of a monastery had his own rule, which he himself was the first to follow in all its rigor; if disciples came, they were to observe it, or go elsewhere; if, after having embraced it, they found themselves unable to keep it to the letter, the abbot was indulgent, and did not impose on them a burden which they could no longer bear, after having first proved their willingness to practise it.

Thus, it is reported that St. Mochta was the only one who practised his own rule exactly, his monks imitating him as well as they could. St. Fintan, who was inclined to be severe, received this warning in a vision: "Fight unto the end thyself; but beware of being a cause of scandal to others, by requiring all to fight as thou doest, for one clay is weaker than another."

Thus, every founder, every abbot even, left to the guidance of the Holy Spirit, practised austerities which in our days of self-indulgence seem

---

[1] The "Irish Penitentials," quoted at length in Rev. Dr. Moran's "Early Irish Church," are not monastic rules, although many canons have reference to monks.

absolutely incredible, and showed themselves severe to those under their authority. But this severity was tempered by such zeal for the good of souls, and consequently by such an unmistakable charity, that the penitent monk carried his burden not only with resignation, but with joy. This, in after-ages, became a characteristic feature of Irish monasticism.

The life of Columba is full of examples of this holy severity. In St. Patrick's life we read that Colman died of thirst rather than quench it before the time appointed by his master.

How many facts of a similar nature might be mentioned! Enough to say that, after so many ages, in which, thanks to barbarous persecutions, all ecclesiastical and monastic traditions were lost to Ireland, through the sheer impossibility of following them up, the Irish still show a marked predilection for the holy austerity of penance, though the rest of the Christian world seems to have almost totally forgotten it.

But if the Irish convents lacked system, there was at the same time in them an exuberance of feeling, an enthusiastic impulse, which is to be found nowhere else to the same extent, and which we call their second peculiar feature after they received Christianity. This is beautifully expressed in a hymn of the office of St. Finian: "Behold the day of gladness; the clerks applaud and are in joy; the sun of justice, which had been hidden in the clouds, shines forth again."

As soon as this primitive enthusiasm seemed to slacken in the least, reformers appeared to enkindle it again. Such was Bridget, such was Gildas, such were the disciples of St. David of Menevia in Wales, such was any one whom the Spirit of God inspired with love for Ireland. Thus the scenes enacted in the time of Patrick were again and again repeated.

And when a monastery was built, it was not properly a monastery, but a city rather; for the whole country round joined in the goodly work. As some one has said, "it looked as if Ireland was going to cease to be a nation, and become a church."

With regard to the question of ground and the appropriation of landed property, what matters it who is the owner? If it be clan territory, there is the clan with nothing but welcome, applause, and assistance. If it be private, the owner is not consulted even; how could he think of opposing the work of God? Thus, we never read in Irish history - in the earlier stages at least - of those long charters granted in other lands by kings, dukes, and counts, and preserved with such care in the archives of the monastery. It seems that the Danes, after they became Christians, were the first to introduce the custom; after them, the Anglo-Normans, in the true spirit of their race, made a flourishing business of it. The Irish themselves never thought of such at first. There was no fear of any one ever claiming the ground on which God's house stood. The buildings were there: the ground needed to support them: what Irishman could think of driving away the holy inmates and pulling the walls about their ears?

The whole surrounding population is busy erecting them. Long rows of wattles and tessel-work are set in right order; over them a rough roof of boards; within small cells begin to appear, as the slight partitions are erected between them. Symmetry or no symmetery, the position of the ground decides the question; for there is no need of the skill of a surveyor to establish the grade. Does not the rain run its own way, once it begins?

How far and how wide will those long rows reach? They seem the streets of a city; and in truth they are. The place is to receive two, three thousand monks, over and above the students committed to their care. And, in addition to the cells to dwell in, there are the halls wherein to teach; the museums and repositories of manuscripts, of sacred objects; the rooms to write in, translate, compose; the sheds to hold provisions, to prepare and cook them, ready for the meal.

For the most important edifice--the temple of God--alone stones are cut, shaped, and fitted each to each with care and precision. A holy simplicity surrounds the art; yet are there not wanting carven crosses and other divine emblems sculptured out. Within, the heavenly mysteries of religion will be performed. Should you ask, "Why so small?" the answer is ready. That large space empty around holds room enough for the worshippers, whose numbers could be accommodated in no edifice. The minds of Irish architects had not yet expanded to the conception of a St. Peter's. Inside is room enough for the ministers of religion; without, at the tinkling of the bell, in the round tower adjoining, the faithful will join in the services.

Nor was it only in the erection of those edifices that a cheerful impulse, which overlooked or overcame all difficulties, was displayed. The monastic life was not all the time a life of penance and gloomy austerity, but of active work also and overflowing feeling, of true poetry and enthusiastic exultation. We read in the fragments we still possess how, on the arid rock of Iona, Columba remembered his former residence at Derry, with its woods of oaks and the pure waters of its loughs. In all the lives of Irish saints we read of the deep attachment they always preserved for their country, relatives, and friends; what they did and were ready to do for them. And though all this was at bottom but a natural feeling, the extent to which it was carried will make us better acquainted with the Irish character, and explain more clearly that extraordinary expansion of soul which, in the domains of the supernatural, surpassed every thing witnessed elsewhere.

"In a monastery two brothers had lived from childhood. The elder died, and while he was dying the other was laboring in the forest. When he came back, he saw the brethren opening a grave in the cemetery, and thus he learned that his brother was dead. He hastened to the spot where the Abbot Fintan, with some of his monks, were chanting psalms around the corpse, and asked him the favor of dying with his brother, and entering with him into the heavenly kingdom. 'Thy brother is already in heaven,' replied Fintan, 'and you cannot enter together unless he rise again.' Then he knelt in prayer, the angels who had received the holy soul restored it, and the dead man, rising in his bier, called his brother: 'Come,' said he, 'but come quickly; the angels await us.' At the same time he made room beside him, and both, lying down, slept together in death, and ascended together to the kingdom of God."

This anecdote may tend better than any thing else to show us how Nature and grace were united in the Irish soul, to warm it, purify it, exalt it above ordinary feelings and earthly passions, and keep it constantly in a state of energy and vitality unknown to other peoples. For, in what page of the ecclesiastical history of other nations do we read of things such as these?

With regard to their country, also, grace came to the aid of Nature; the supernatural was, therefore, seldom absent from the natural in their minds, and something of this double union has, remained in them in every sense, and has, no doubt, contributed to render their nationality imperishable in spite of persecution. How ardent and pure in the heart of Columba was the love of Ireland, from which he was a voluntary exile! Patrick, also, though not native born, yielded to none in that sacred feeling; one of the three things he sought of God on dying was, that Erin should not "remain forever under a foreign yoke:" Kieran offered the same prayer, and their reason for thus praying was that she was the "island of saints," destined to help out the salvation of many.

Religion has been invariably connected with that acute sentiment ever present in the minds of Irishmen for their country; and it is, doubtless, that holy and supernatural feeling which has preserved a country which enemies strove so strenuously to wrest from them.

But it was not love of country alone, of relatives and friends, which enkindled in their hearts a spirit of enthusiasm; their whole monastic life was one of high-spirited devotedness, and energy, and action, more than human.

We see them laboring in and around their monastic hive. How they pray and chant the divine office; how they study and expound the holy doctrine to their pupils; how they are ever travelling, walking in procession by hundreds and by thousands through the island, the interior spirit not allowing them to stand still. There are so many pilgrimages to perform, so many shrines to venerate, so many works of brotherly love to undertake. Other monks in other countries, indeed, did the same, but seldom with such universal ardor. The whole island, as we said, is one church. On all sides you may meet bishops, and priests, and monks, bearing revered relics, or proceeding to found a new convent, plant another sacred edifice, or establish a house for the needy. The people on the way fall in and follow their footsteps, sharers of the burning enthusiasm. Many-how many!-were thus attracted to this mode of life, wherein there was scarce aught earthly, but all breathing holiness and heavenly grace!

Thus the island was from the beginning a holy island. But zeal for God in their own country alone not being enough for their ardor, those men of God were early moved by the impulse of going abroad to spread the faith. Volumes might be written of their apostleship among barbarous tribes; we have room only for a few words.

They first went to the islands north of them, to the Hebrides, the Faroe Isles, and even Iceland, which they colonized before the Norwegian pirates landed there. Then they evangelized Scotland and the north of England; and, starting from Lindisfarne, they completed the work of the conversion of the Anglo-Saxons, which was begun by St. Augustin and his monks in the south.

Finally, the whole continent of Western Europe offered itself to their zeal, and at once they were ready to enter fully and unreservedly into the current of new ideas and energies which at that time began to renew the face of that portion of the world overspread by barbarians from Germany. Under the Merovingian kings in France, and later on, under the Carlovingian dynasty, they became celebrated in the east of France, on the banks of the Rhine, even in the north through Germany, in the heart of Switzerland, and the north of Italy. This is not the place to attempt even a sketch of their missionary labors, now known to all the students of the history of those times. But we may here mention that at that time the Irish monarchs and rulers became acquainted with continental dynasties and affairs through the necessary intercourse held by the Irish bishops and monks with Rome, the centre of Catholicity. Thus we see that Malachi II corresponded with Charles the Bald, with a view of making a pilgrimage to Rome.

We learn from the yellow-book of Lecain that Conall, son of Coelmuine, brought from Rome the law of Sunday, such as was afterward practised in Ireland.

Over and above the Irish missionaries who kept up a constant correspondence from the Continent of Europe with their native land, it is known that many in those early ages went on pilgrimages to Rome; among others, St. Degan, St. Kilian, the apostle of Franconia; St. Sedulius the younger, who assisted at a Roman council in 721, and was sent by the Pope on a mission to Spain; St. Donatus, afterward Bishop of Fiesole, and his disciple, Andrew. St. Cathald went from Rome to Jerusalem, and on his return was made Bishop of Tarento. Donough, son of Brian Boru, went to Rome in 1063, carrying, it is said, the crown of his father, and there died.

It has been calculated that the ancient Irish monks held from the sixth to the ninth century thirteen monasteries in Scotland, seven in France, twelve in Armoric Gaul, seven in Lotharingia, eleven in Burgundy, nine in Belgium, ten in Alsatia, sixteen in Bavaria, fifteen in Rhaetia, Helvetia, and Suevia, besides several in Thuringia and on the left bank of the Rhine. Ireland was then not only included in, but at the head of, the European movement;

and yet that forms a period in her annals which as yet has scarcely been studied.

The religious zeal which was then so manifest in the island itself burned likewise among many Continental nations, and lasted from the introduction of Christianity to the Danish invasion. What contributed chiefly to make that ardor lasting was, that every thing connected with religion made a part even of their exterior life. Grace had taken entire possession of the national soul. This world was looked upon as a shadow, beautiful only in reflecting something of the beauty of heaven.

Hence were the Irish "the saints." So were they titled by all, and they accepted the title with a genuine and holy simplicity which betokened a truer modesty than the pretended denegation which we might expect. Thus they seemed above temptation. The virgins consecrated to God were as numerous at least as the monks. These had also their processions and pilgrimages; they went forth from houses over-full to found others, not knowing or calculating beforehand the spot where they might rest and "expect resurrection." Such was their language. Sometimes they applied at the doors of monasteries, and if there was no spot in the neighborhood suitable for the sisters, the monks abandoned to them their abode, their buildings and cultivated fields where the crops were growing, taking with them naught save the sacred vessels and the books they might need in the new establishment they went forth to found elsewhere.

Who could imagine, then, that even a thought could enter their minds beyond those of charity and kindness? Were they not dead utterly to worldly passions, and living only to God? It would have been a sacrilege to have profaned the holy island, not only with an unlawful act but even with a worldly imagination. Had not many holy men and women seen angels constantly coming down from heaven, and the souls of the just at their departure going straight from Ireland to heaven? Both in perpetual communication! Had the eyes of all been as pure as those of the best among them, the truth would have been unveiled to all alike, and the "isle of saints" would have shown itself to them as what it really was-a bright country where redemption was a great fact; where the souls of the great majority were truly and actually redeemed in the full sense of the word; where people might enjoy a foretaste of heaven-the very space above their heads being to them at all times a road connecting the heavenly mansions with this sublunary world.

True is it that there were ever in the island a number of great sinners who desecrated the holy spot they dwelt on by their deeds of blood. The Saviour predicted that there should be "tares among the wheat" everywhere until the day of judgment.

It was among the chieftains principally, almost entirely, that sin prevailed. The clan-system, unfortunately, favored deadly feuds, which often drenched all parts of the island in blood. Family quarrels, being in themselves unnatural, led to the most atrocious crimes. The old Greek drama furnishes frightful examples of it, and similar passions sometimes filled the breasts of those leaders of Irish clans. Few of them died in their beds. When carried away by passion, they respected nothing which men generally respect.

It would, however, be an exaggeration to suppose on this account a distinct and complete antagonism to have existed between the clan and the Church, and to class all the princes on the side of evil as opposed to the "saints," whom we have contemplated leading a celestial life. We know from St. Aengus that one of the glories of Ireland is that many of her saints were of princely families, whereas among other nations generally the Gospel was first accepted by the poor and lowly, and found its enemies among the higher and educated classes. But in Ireland the great, side by side with the least of their clansmen, bowed to the yoke of Christ, and the bards and learned men became monks and bishops from the very first preaching of the Word.

The fact is, a great number of kings and chieftains made their station doubly renowned by their virtues, and find place in the chronicle of Irish saints. Who can read, for instance, the story of King Guaire without admiring his faith and true Christian spirit?

It is reported that as St. Caimine and St. Cumain Fota were one day conversing on spiritual things with that holy king of Connaught, Caimine said to Guaire, "O king, could this church be filled on a sudden with whatever thou shouldst wish, what would thy desire be?" "I should wish," replied the king, "to have all the treasures that the church could hold, to devote them to the salvation of souls, the erection of churches, and the wants of Christ's poor." "And what wouldst thou ask?" said the king to Fota. "I would," he replied, "have as many holy books as the church could contain, to give all who seek divine wisdom, to spread among the people the saving doctrine of Christ, and rescue souls from the bondage of Satan." Both then turned to Caimine. "For my part," said he, "were this church filled with men afflicted with every form of suffering and disease, I should ask of God to vouchsafe to assemble in my wretched body all their evils, all their pains, and give me strength to support them patiently, for the love of the Saviour of the world."[1]

Thus the most sublime and supernatural spirit of Christianity became natural to the Irish mind in the great as well as in the lowly, in the rich as well as in the poor. Women rivalled men in that respect.

"Daria was blind from birth. Once, whilst conversing with Bridget, she said: 'Bless my eyes that I may see the world, and gratify my longing.' The night was dark; it grew light for her, and the world appeared to her gaze. But when she had beheld it, she turned again to Bridget. 'Now close my eyes,' said she, 'for the more one is absent from the world, the more present he is before God.'"

Even though one may express doubt as to the reality of this miracle, one thing, at least, is beyond doubt: that the spirit of the words of Daria was congenial to the Irish mind at the time, and that none but one who had first reached the highest point of supernatural life could conceive or give utterance to such a sentiment.

That more than human life and spirit elevated, ennobled, and, as it were, divinized, even the ordinary human and natural feelings, which not only ceased to become dangerous, but became, doubtless, highly pleasing to God and meritorious in his sight. An example may better explain our meaning:

"Ninnid was a young scholar, not over-reverent, whom the influence of Bridget one day suddenly overcame, so that he afterward appeared quite a different being. Bridget announced to him that from his hand she should, for the last time, receive the body and blood of our Lord. Ninnid resolved that his hand should remain pure for so high and holy an office. He enclosed it in an iron case, and wishing at the same time to postpone, as far as lay in his power, the moment that was to take Bridget from the

---

[1] This passage is given in Latin by Colgan (Acts SS.). In the original Irish, translated and published by Dr. Todd--Liber Hymn--there are more details.

world, he set out for Brittany, throwing the key of the box into the sea. But the designs of God are immutable. When Bridget's hour had come, Ninnid was driven by a storm on the Irish coast, and the key was miraculously given up by the deep."

Where, except in Ireland, could such friendship continue for long years, without giving cause not only for the least scandal, but even for the remotest danger? In that island the natural feelings of the human heart were wholly absorbed by heavenly emotions, in which nothing earthly could be found? Hence the celebrated division of the "three orders of the Irish saints," the first being so far above temptation that no regulation was imposed on the Cenobites with respect to their intercourse with women.

"Women were welcome and cared for; they were admitted, so to speak, to the sanctuary; it was shared with them, occupied in common. Double, or even mixed monasteries, so near to each other as to form but one, brought the two sexes together for mutual edification; men became instructors of women; women of men."

Nothing of the kind was ever witnessed elsewhere; nothing of the kind was to be seen ever after. Robert of Arbrissel established something similar in the order, of Fontevrault in France; but there it was a strange and very uncommon exception; in Ireland for two centuries it was the rule. This alone would show how completely the Christian spirit had taken possession of the whole race from the first.

It is this which gives to Irish hagiology a peculiar character, making it appear strange even to the best men of other nations. The elevation of human feeling to such a height of perfection is so unusual that men cannot fail to be surprised wherever they may meet it.

Yet far from appearing strange, almost inexplicable, it would have been recognized as the natural result of the working of the Christian religion, if the spirit brought on earth by our Lord had been more thoroughly diffused among men, if all had been penetrated by it to the same degree, if all had equally understood the meaning of the Gospel preached to them.

But, unfortunately, so many and so great were the obstacles opposed everywhere to the working of the Spirit of God in the souls of men, that comparatively few were capable of being altogether transformed into beings of another nature.

The great mass lagged far behind in the race of perfection. They were admitted to the fold of Christ, and lived generally at least in the practice of the commandments; but the object proposed to himself by the Saviour of mankind was imperfectly carried out on earth. The life of the world was far from being impregnated by the spirit which he brought from heaven.

In the "island of saints" we certainly see a great number open out at once to the fulness of that divine influence. Herein we have the explanation of the deep faith which has ever since been the characteristic of the people. "Centuries have perpetuated the alliance of Catholicity and Ireland. Revolutions have failed to shake it; persecution has not broken it; it has gained strength in blood and tears, and we may believe, after thirteen centuries of trial, that the Roman faith will disappear from Ireland only with the name of Patrick and the last Irishman."

NOTE.-It is known that F. Colgan, a Franciscan, undertook to publish the "Acta Sanctorum Hiberniae." He edited only two volumes: the first under the title of "Trias thaumaturga" containing the various lives of St. Patrick, St. Columba, and St. Bridget:-the second under the general title of "Acta SS."- Barnwall, an Irishman born and educated in France, published the "Histoire Legendaire d'Irlande," in which he collected, without much order, a number of passages of Colgan's "Acta," and Mr. J. G. Shea translated and published it. We have taken from this translation several facts contained in this chapter, the work of the Franciscan being not accessible to us.

Dr. Todd, from Irish MSS., has given a few pages showing the accuracy of Colgan, although the good father did not scruple occasionally to condense and abridge, unless the MSS. he used differed from those of Dr. Todd. The whole is a rich mine of interesting anecdotes, and Montalembert has shown what a skilful writer can find in those pages forgotten since the sixteenth century. Mr. Froude himself has acknowledged that the eighth was the golden age of Ireland.

THE CHRISTIAN IRISH AND THE PAGAN DANES

FOR several centuries the Irish continued in the happy state described in the last chapter. While the whole European Continent was convulsed by the irruptions of the Germanic tribes, and of the Huns, more savage still, the island was at peace, opened her schools to the youth of all countries-- to Anglo-Saxons chiefly--and spread her name abroad as the happy and holy isle, the dwelling of the saints, the land of prodigies, the most blessed spot on the earth. No invading host troubled her; the various Teutonic nations knew less of the sea than the Celts themselves, and no vessel neared the Irish coast save the peaceful curraghs which carried her monks and missionaries abroad, or her own sons in quest of food and adventure.

Providence would seem to have imposed upon the nation the lofty mission of healing the wounds of other nations as they lay helpless in the throes of death, of keeping the doctrines of the Gospel alive in Europe, after those terrible invasions, and of leading into the fold of Christ many a shepherd-less flock. The peaceful messengers who went forth from Ireland became as celebrated as her home schools and monasteries; and well had it been for the Irish could such a national life as this have continued.

But God, who wished to prepare them for still greater things in future ages, who proves by suffering all whom he wishes to use as his best instruments, allowed the fury of the storm to burst suddenly upon them. It was but the beginning of their woes, the first step in that long road to Calvary, where they were to be crucified with him, to be crucified wellnigh to the death before their final and almost miraculous resurrection. The Danes were to be the first torturers of that happy and holy people; the hardy rovers of the northern seas were coming to inaugurate a long era of woe.

The Scandinavian irruption which desolated Europe just as she was beginning to recover from the effects of the first great Germanic wave, may be said to have lasted from the eighth to the twelfth century. Down from the North Sea came the shock; Ireland was consequently one of the first to feel it, and we shall see how she alone withstood and finally overcame it.

The better to understand the fierceness of the attack, let us first consider its origin:

The Baltic Sea and the various gulfs connected with it penetrate deeply the northern portion of the Continent of Europe. Its indentations form two peninsulas: a large one, known under the name of Norway and Sweden, and a lesser one on the southwest, now called Denmark. The first was known to the Romans as Scania; the second was called by them the Cimbric Chersonesus. From Scania is derived the name Scandinavians, afterward given to the inhabitants of the whole country. Besides these two peninsulas, there are several islands scattered through the surrounding sea.

The frozen and barren land which this people inhabited obliged them from time immemorial to depend on the ocean for their sustenance: first, by fishing; later on, by piracy. They soon became expert navigators, though their ships were merely small boats made of a few pieces of timber joined together, and covered with the hide of the walrus and the seal.

It seems, from the Irish annals, that they belonged to two distinct races of men: the Norwegians, fair-haired and of large stature; the Danes dark, and of smaller size. Hence the Irish distinguished the first, whom they called Finn Galls, from the second, whom they named Dubh Galls. By no other European nation was this distinction drawn, the Irish being more exact in observing their foes.

It is the general opinion of modern writers that they belonged to the Teutonic family. The Goths, a Teutonic tribe, dwelt for a long period on the larger peninsula. But whether the Goths were of the same race as the Norwegians or Danes is a question. Certain it is that the various German nations which first overwhelmed the Roman Empire bore many characteristics different from those of the Danes and Norwegians, though the language of all indicated, to a certain extent, a common origin.

The Swedes, the inhabitants of the eastern coast of Scania, do not appear to have taken an important part in the Scandinavian invasions; nor, indeed, have they ever been so fond of maritime enterprises as the two other nations. Moreover, they were at that time in bloody conflict with the Goths, and too busy at home to think of foreign conquest.

For a long time the Scandinavian pirates seem to have confined themselves to scouring their own seas, and plundering the coasts as far as the gulfs of Finland and Bothnia. At length, emboldened by success, they ventured out into the ocean, attacked the nations of Western and Southern Europe, and in the west colonized the frozen shores of the Shetland and Faroe Islands, and soon after Iceland and Greenland.

For several centuries the harbors of Denmark and Norway became the storehouses of all the riches of Europe, and a large trade was carried on between those northern peninsulas and the various islands of the Northern and Arctic Seas, even with the coast of America, of which Greenland seems to form a part.

Those stern and mountainous countries and the restless ocean which divides them were for the Scandinavian pirates what the Mediterranean and the coasts of Spain and Africa had long before been for the Phoenicians and Carthaginians. These peoples were clearly destined to introduce among modern nations the spirit of commerce and enterprise.

But here it is well to consider their religious and social state from which nations chiefly derive their noble or ignoble qualities. We shall find both made up of the rankest idolatry, of cruel manners and revolting customs.

Their system of worship, with its creed and rites, is much more precise in character and better known to us than that of the Celts. If we open the books which were written in Europe at the time of the irruption of these Northmen, and the poems of those savage tribes preserved to our own days, and comprised under the name of Edda, besides the numerous sagas, or songs and ballads, which we still possess, we find mention of three superior gods and a number of inferior deities, which gave a peculiar character to this Northern worship.

They were Thor, the god of the elements, of thunder chiefly; Wodan or Odin, the god of war; and Frigga, the goddess of lust; the long list of others it is unnecessary to give. Their religion, therefore, consisted mainly: 1. In battling with the elements, particularly on the sea, under the protection of Thor; 2. In slaying their enemies, or being themselves slain, as Odin willed

--the giving or receiving death being apparently the great object of existence; 3. In abandoning themselves at the time of victory to all the propensities of corrupt nature, which they took to be the express will of Frigga manifested in their unbridled passions.

Such was Scandinavian mythology in its reality.

Modern investigators, principally in Germany and France, find in the Edda a complete system of cosmogony and of a religion almost inspired, so beautiful do they make it. At least they have made it appear as profound a philosophy as that of old Hindostan and far-off Thibet. By grouping around those three great divinities, which are supposed to be emblematical of the superior natural forces, their numerous progeny, that of Odin especially, together with an incredible number of malicious giants and good-natured ases--a kind of fairy--any skilful theorist, gifted with the requisite imagination, may extract from the whole an almost perfect system of cosmogony and ethics. Then the disgusting legends of the Edda and the sagas are straightway transformed into interesting myths, offsprings of poetry and imagination, and conveying to the mind a philosophy only less than sublime, derived, as they say, from the religion of Zoroaster.

It is, as we said, in Germany and France chiefly that these discoveries have been made. The English, a more sober people, although of Scandinavian blood, do not set so high a value on what is, in the literal sense, so low.

Pity that such pleasing speculations should be mere theoretical bubbles, unable to retain their lightness and their vivid colors in the rude atmosphere of the arctic regions, bursting at the first breath of the north wind! How could sensible men, under such a complicated system of religion and physics, account for the uncouth pirates of the Baltic?

As useless is it to say that they brought it from the place of their origin--Persia, as these theorists affirm. To a man uninfluenced by a preconceived or pet system, it is evident at first sight that no mythology of the East or of the South has ever given rise to that of Scandinavia. There is not the slightest resemblance between it and any other. It must have originated with the Scandinavians themselves; and their long religious tales were only the bloody dreams of their fancy, when, during their dreary winter evenings, they had nothing to do but relate to each other what came uppermost in their gross minds.

Saxo Grammaticus, certainly a competent authority, and Snorry Sturleson, the first to translate the Edda into Latin, who is still considered one of the greatest antiquarians of the nation--both of whom lived in the times we speak of, when this religious system still flourished or was fresh in the minds of all--solved the question ages ago, and demonstrated beforehand the falsehood of those future theories by stating with old-time simplicity that the abominable stories of the Edda and the sagas were founded on real facts in the previous history of those nations, and were consequently never intended by the writers as imaginative myths, representing, under a figurative and repulsive exterior, some semblance of a spiritual and refined doctrine.

We must look to our own more enlightened times to find ingenious interpreters of rude old songs first flung to the breeze nine hundred years ago in the polar seas, and bellowed forth in boisterous and drunken chorus during the ninth and tenth centuries by ferocious, but to modern eyes romantic, pirates reeking with the gore of their enemies.

Because it has pleased some modern pantheist to concoct systems of religion in his cabinet, does it become at once clear that the mythic explanation of those songs is the only one to be admitted, and that the odious facts which those legends express ought to be discarded altogether? At least we hope that, when philosophers come to be the real rulers of the world, they will not give to their subtle and abstract ideas of religion the same pleasant turn and the same concrete expression in every-day life that the worshippers of Odin, Thor, and Frigga, found it agreeable to give when they were masters of the continent and rulers of the seas.

No! The only true meaning of this Northern worship is conveyed in the simple words of Adam of Bremen, when relating what still existed in his own time. (Descript. insularum Aquil., lib. iv.) He describes the solemn sacrifices of Upsala in Sweden thus: "This is their sacrifice; of each and all animals they offer nine heads of the male gender, by whose blood it is their custom to appease the gods. The dead bodies of the victims are suspended in a grove which surrounds the temple. The place is in their eyes invested with such a sacred character that the trees are believed to be divine on account of the blood and gore with which they are besmeared. With the animals, dogs, horses, etc., they suspend likewise men; and a Christian of that country told me that he had himself seen them with his own eyes mixed up together in the grove. But the senseless rites which accompany the sacrifice and the sprinkling of blood are so many, and of so gross and immoral nature, that it is better not to speak of them."

We have here the naked truth, and no meaning whatever could be attached to such ceremonies other than that of the rankest idolatry. To complete the picture, it is proper to state that Thor, Odin, and Frigga, were frightful idols, as represented in the Upsala temple, and the small statues carried by the Scandinavian sailors on their expeditions and set in the place of honor on board their ships, were but diminutive copies of the hideous originals. It is known, moreover, that Odin had existed as a leader of some of their migrations, so that their idolatry resolved itself into hero-worship.

Having spoken of their gods, we have only a word to add on their belief in a future state, for every one is acquainted with their brutal and shocking Walhalla. Yet, such as it was, admittance to its halls could only be aspired to by the warriors and heroes, the great among them; the common herd was not deemed worthy of immortality. Thus aristocratic pride showed itself at the very bottom of their religion.

Of their social state, their government, we know little. They lived under a kind of rude monarchy, subject often to election, when they chose the most savage and the bravest for their ruler. But blood-relationship had little or nothing to do with their system, so different from that of the Celts. The sons of a chieftain could never form a sept, but at his death the eldest replaced him; the younger brothers, deprived of their titles and goods, were forced to separate and acquire a title to rank and honor by piracy; and that right of primogeniture, which was the primary cause of their sea invasions, stamped the feudal system with one of its chief characteristics, a system which probably originated with them. Some, however, entertain a contrary opinion, and suppose that at the death of the father his children shared his inheritance equally.

Of their moral habits we may best judge by their religion. All we know of their history seems to prove that with them might was right, and outlawry the only penalty of their laws.

A man guilty of murder was compelled to quit the country, unless his superior daring and the number of his friends and followers enabled him, by more atrocious and wholesale murders, still to become a great chieftain and even aspire to supreme power. Iceland was colonized by outlaws from Norway; and the frequent changes of dynasty in pagan times prove that among them, as among barbarous tribes generally, brute force was the chief source of law and authority.

That outlawry was not esteemed a stain on the character is sufficiently demonstrated by the fact that the mere accident of birth made outlaws of all the children of chieftains with the exception of the eldest born; the necessity for the younger sons abandoning their home and native country, and roaming the ocean in search of plunder, being exactly equivalent, according to their opinion and customs, to criminal outlawry of whatever character. This, at least, many authors assert without hesitation.

Their domestic habits were fit consequences of such a state of society. There could exist no real tie of kindred, no filial or brotherly affection among men living under such a social system. The gratification of brutal passions and the most utter selfishness constituted the rule for all; and even the fear of an inexorable judge after death could not restrain them during life, as might have been the case among other pagan nations, since the hope of reaching their Walhalla depended for its fulfilment on murder or suicide.

With their system of warfare we are better acquainted than with any thing else belonging to them, as the main burden of their songs was the recital of their barbarous expeditions. It is, indeed, difficult for a modern reader to wade through the whole of their Edda poems, or even their long sagas, so full is their literature of unimaginable cruelties. Yet a general view of it is necessary in order to understand the horror spread throughout Europe by their inhuman warfare.

As soon as the warm breeze of an early spring thaws the ice on his rivers and lakes, the Scandinavian Viking unfurls his sail, fills his rude boat with provisions, and trusts himself to the mercy of the waves. Should he be alone, and not powerful enough to have a fleet at his command, he looks out for a single boat of his own nation--there being no other in those seas. Urged by a mutual impulse, the two crews attack each other at sight; the sea reddens with blood; the savage bravery is equal on both sides; accident alone can decide the contest. One of the crews conquers by the death of all its opponents; the plunder is transferred to the victorious boat; the cup of strong drink passes round, and victory is crowned by drunkenness.

But if the two chieftains have contended from morning till night with equal valor and success, then, filled with admiration for each other, they become friends, unite their forces, and, falling on the first spot where they can land, they pillage, slay, outrage women, and give full sway to their unbridled passions. The more ferocious they are the braver they esteem themselves. It is a positive fact, as we may gather from all their poems and songs, that the Scandinavians alone, probably, of all pagan nations, have had no measure of bravery and military glory beyond the infliction of the most exquisite torture and the most horrible of deaths.

Plunder, which was apparently the motive power of all their expeditions, was to them less attractive than blood; blood, therefore, is the chief burden of their poetry, if poetry it can be called. It would seem as though they were destined by Nature to shed human blood in torrents--the noblest occupation, according to their ideas, in which a brave man could be engaged.

The figures of their rude literature consist for the most part of monstrous warriors and gods, each possessed of many arms to kill a greater number of enemies, or of giant stature to overcome all obstacles, or of enchanted swords which shore steel as easily as linen, and clave the body of an adversary as it would the air.

Then, heated with blood, the Northman is also influenced with lust, for he worships Frigga as well as Odin. But this is not the place to give even an idea of manners too revolting to be presented to the imagination of the reader.

Cantu's Universal History will furnish all the authorities from which the details we have given and many others of the same kind are derived.

We do not propose describing here the horrors of the devastations committed by the Anglo-Saxons and Danes in England, by the Normans in France, Spain, and Italy. All these nations, even the first, were Scandinavians, and naturally fall under our review. The story is already known to those who are acquainted with the history of mediaeval Europe. The only thing which we do not wish to omit is the invariable system of warfare adopted by this people when acting on a large scale.

Arrived on the coast they had determined to ravage, they soon found that in stormy weather they were in a more dangerous position than at sea. Hence they looked for a deep bay, or, better still, the mouth of a large river, and once on its placid bosom they felt themselves masters of the whole country. The terror of the people, the lack of organization for defence, so characteristic of Celtic or purely Germano-Franco society, the savage bravery and reckless impetuosity of the invaders themselves, increased their rashness, and urged them to enter fearlessly into the very heart of a country which lay prostrate with fear before them. All the cities on the river-banks were plundered as they passed, people of whatever age, sex, or condition, were murdered; the churches especially were despoiled of their riches, and the numerous and wealthy monasteries then existing were given to the flames, after the monks and all the inmates even to the schoolchildren, had been promiscuously slaughtered, if they had not escaped by flight.

But, although all were slaughtered promiscuously, a special ferocity was always displayed by the barbarous conqueror toward the unarmed and defenceless ministers of religion. They took a particular delight in their case in adding insult to cruelty; and not without reason did the Church at that time consider as martyrs the priests and monks who were slain by the pagan Scandinavians. Their sanguinary and hideous idolatry showed its hatred of truth and holiness in always manifesting a peculiar atrocity when coming in contact with the Church of Christ and her ministers. And, our chief object in speaking of the stand made by the Irish against the pagan Danes is, to show how the clan-system became in truth the avenger of God's altars and the preserver of the sacred edifices and numerous temples with which, as we have seen, the Island of Saints was so profusely studded, from total annihilation.

Knowing that, when their march of destruction had taken them a great distance from the mouth of the river, the inhabitants might rise in sheer despair and cut them off on their return, the Scandinavian pirates, to guard against such a contingency, looked for some island or projecting rock, difficult of access, which they fortified, and, placing there the plunder which loaded their boats, they left a portion of their forces to guard it, while the remainder continued their route of depredation. In Ireland they found spots admirably adapted for their purpose in the numerous loughs into which many of the rivers run.

This was their invariable system of warfare in the rivers of England; in Germany along system Rhine; along the Seine, the Loire, and the Garonne, in France, as well as on the Tagus and Guadalquivir in Spain, where two at least of their large expeditions penetrated. This continued for several centuries, until at last they thought of occupying the country which they had devastated and depopulated, and they began to form permanent settlements in England, Flanders, France, and even Sicily and Naples.

When that time had arrived, they showed that, hidden under their ferocious exterior, lay a deep and systematic mind, capable of great thoughts and profound designs. Already in their own rude country they had organized commerce on an extensive scale, and their harbors teemed with richly-laden ships, coming from far distances or preparing to start on long voyages. They had become a great colonizing race, and, after establishing their sway in the Hebrides, the Orkneys, the Faroe Islands, Iceland, and Greenland, they made England their own, first by the Jute and Anglo-Saxon tribes, then by the arms of Denmark, which was at that time so powerful that England actually became a colony of Copenhagen; and finally they thought of extending their conquests farther south to the Mediterranean Sea, where their ships rode at anchor in the harbors of fair Sicily.

We know, from many chronicles written at the time, with what care they surveyed all the countries they occupied, confiscating the land after having destroyed or reduced its inhabitants to slavery; dividing it among themselves and establishing their barbarous laws and feudal customs wherever they went. Dudo of St. Quentin, among other writers, describes at length in his rude poem the army of surveyors intrusted by Rollo, the first Duke of Normandy, with the care of drawing up a map of their conquests in France, for the purpose of dividing the whole among his rough followers and vassals.

Of this spirit of organization we intend to speak in the next chapter, when we come to consider the Anglo-Norman invasion of Ireland; but we are not to conclude that the Northmen became straightway civilized, and that the spirit of refinement at once shed its mild manners and gentle habits over their newly-constructed towns and castles. For a long time they remained as barbarous as ever, with only a system more perfect and a method more scientific--if we may apply such expressions to the case--in their plunderings and murderous expeditions.

Of Hastings, their last pagan sea-kong, Dudo, the great admirer of Northmen and the sycophant of the first Norman dukes in France, has left the following terrible character, on reading which in full we scarcely know whether the poem was written in reproach or praise. We translate from the Latin

According to Dudo, he was--

> "A wretch accursed and fierce of heart,
> Unmatched in dark iniquities;
> A scowling pest of deadly hate,
> He throve on savage cruelties.
>
> Blood-thirsty, stained with every crime,
> An artful, cunning, deadly foe,
> Lawless, vaunting, rash, inconstant,
> True well-spring of unending woe!"

Hastings never yielded to the new religion, which he always hated and persecuted. But, even after their conversion to Christianity, his countrymen for a long time retained their inborn love of bloodshed and tyranny; they were in this respect, as in many others, the very reverse of the Irish.

Of Rollo, the first Christian Duke of Normandy, Adhemar, a contemporary writer, says:

"On becoming Christian, he caused many captives to be beheaded in his presence, in honor of the gods whom he had worshipped. And he also distributed a vast amount of money to the Christian churches in honor of the true God in whose name he had received baptism;" which would seem to imply that this transaction occurred on the very day of his baptism.

We may now compare the success which attended the arms of these terrible invaders throughout the rest of Europe with their complete failure in Ireland. It will be seen that the deep attachment of the Irish Celts for their religion, its altars, shrines, and monuments, was the real cause of their final victory. We shall behold a truly Christian people battling against paganism in its most revolting and audacious form.

But, first, how stood the case in England?

"It is not a little extraordinary," says a sagacious writer in the Dublin Review (vol. xxxii., p. 203), "that the three successive conquests of England by the Anglo-Saxons, Danes, and Normans, were in fact conquests made by the same people, and, in the last two instances, over those who were not only descended from the same stock, but who had immigrated from the very same localities. The Jutes, Angles, and Saxons, were for the most part Danes or of Danish origin. Their invasion of England commenced by plunder and ended by conquest. These were overthrown by the Danes and Norwegians in precisely the same manner.

"In the year 875, Roll or Rollo, having been expelled from Norway by Harold Harfager, adopted the profession of a sea-kong, and in the short space of sixteen years became Duke of Normandy and son-in-law of the French king, after having previously repudiated his wife. The sixth duke in succession from Rollo was William, illegitimate son of Robert le Diable and Herleva, a concubine. By the battle of Hastings, which William gained in 1066, over King Harold, who was slain in it, the former became sovereign of England, and instead of the appellation of 'the Bastard,' by which he had been hitherto known, he now obtained the surname of 'the Conqueror.'

"Thus both the Saxon and Danish invaders were subdued by their Norman brethren."

All the Scandinavian invasions of England were, therefore, successful, each in turn giving way before a new one; and it is not a little remarkable that the very year in which Brian Boru dealt a death-blow to the Danes at Clontarf witnessed the complete subjection of England by Canute.

The success of the Northmen in France is still more worthy of attention. Their invasions began soon after the death of Charlemagne. It is said that, before his demise, hearing of the appearance of one of their fleets not far from the mouth of the Rhine, he shed tears, and foretold the innumerable evils it portended. He saw, no doubt, that the long and oft-repeated efforts of his life to subdue and convert the northern Saxons would fail to obtain for his successors the peace he had hoped to win by his sword, and, knowing from the Saxons themselves the relentless ferocity, audacity, and frightful cruelty, inoculated in their Scandinavian blood, he could not but expect for his empire the fierce attacks which were preparing in the arctic seas. All his life had he been a conqueror, and under his sway the Franks, whom he had ever led to victory, acquired a name through Europe for military glory which, he dreaded, would no longer remain untarnished. His forebodings, however, could not be shared by any of those who surrounded him in his old age; his eagle eye alone discerned the coming misfortunes.

Seven times had the great emperor subdued the Saxons. He had crushed them effectually, since he could not otherwise prevent them from disturbing his empire. The Franks, who formed his army, were therefore the real conquerors of Western Europe. Starting from the banks of the Rhine, they subjugated the north as far as the Baltic Sea; they conquered Italy as far south as Beneventum, by their victories over the Lombards; by the subjugation of Aquitaine, they took possession of the whole of France; the only check they had ever received was in the valley of Roncevaux, whence a part of one of their armies was compelled to retreat, without, however, losing Catalonia, which they had won.

Nevertheless, we see them a few years after powerless and stricken with terror at the very name of the Northmen, as soon as Hastings and Rollo appeared. Those sea-rovers established themselves straightway in the very centre of the Frankish dominion; for it was at the mouth of the Rhine, in the island of Walcheren, that they formed their first camp. From Walcheren they swept both banks of the Rhine, and, after enriching themselves with the spoils of monasteries, cathedrals, and palaces, they thought of other countries. Then began the long series of spoliations which desolated the whole of France along the Seine, the Loire, and the Garonne.

Opposition they scarcely encountered. Paris alone, of all the great cities of France, sustained a long siege, and finally bought them off by tribute. The military power of the nation was annihilated all at once, and of all French history this period is undoubtedly the most humiliating to a native of the soil.

And now let us see how the Irish met the same piratical invasions.

We are already acquainted with the chief defect of their political system, namely, its want of centralization. The Ard-Righ was in fact but a nominal ruler, except in the small province which acknowledged his chieftainship only. Throughout the rest of Ireland the provincial kings were independent save in name. Not only were they often reluctant to obey the Ard-Righ, but they were not seldom at open war with him. Nor are we to suppose that, at least in the case of a serious attack from without, their patriotism overcame their private differences, and made them combine together to show a common front against a common foe. In a patriarchal state of government there is scarcely any other form of patriotism than that of the particular sept to which each individual belongs. All the ideas, customs, prejudices, are opposed to united action.

Yet an invasion so formidable as that of the Scandinavian tribes showed itself everywhere to be, would have required all the energies and resources of the whole country united under one powerful chief, particularly when it did not consist of one single fearful irruption.

During two centuries large fleets of dingy, hide-bound barks discharge on the shores of Erin their successive cargoes of human fiends, bent on rapine and carnage, and altogether proof against fear of even the most horrible death, since such death was to them the entry to the eternal realms of their Walhalla.

But, at the period of which we speak, the terrible evil of a want of centralization was greatly aggravated by a change occurring in the line which held the supreme power in the island.

The vigorous rule of a long succession of princes belonging to the northern Hy-Niall line gave way to the ascendency of the southern branch of this great family; and the much more limited patrimony and alliances of this new quasi-dynasty rendered its personal power very inferior to that of the northern branch, and consequently lessened the influence possessed by the ruling family in past times. In Ireland the connections, more or less numerous, by blood relationship with the great families, always exercised a powerful influence over the body of the nation in rendering it docile and amenable to the will of the Ard-Righ.

Mullingar, in West Meath, was the abode of the southern Hy-Nialls, and Malachy of the Shannon, the first Ard-Righ of this line, succeeded King

Niall of Callan in 843. The Danes were already in the country and had committed depredations. Their first descent is mentioned by the Four Masters as taking place at Rathlin on the coast of Antrim in the year 790.

But the country was soon aroused; and religious feelings, always uppermost in the Irish heart, supplied the deficiencies of the constitution of the state and the particularly unfavorable circumstances of the period. The Danes, as usual, first attacked the monasteries and churches, and this alone was enough to kindle in the breasts of the people the spirit of resistance and retaliation. Iona was laid waste in 797, and again in 801 and 805. "To save from the rapacity of the Danes," says Montalembert in his Monks of the West, "a treasure which no pious liberality could replace, the body of S. Columba was carried to Ireland. And it is the unvarying tradition of Irish annals, that it was deposited finally at Down, in an episcopal monastery, not far from the eastern shore of the island, between the great monastery of Bangor in the North, and Dublin the future capital of Ireland, in the South."

Ireland was first assailed by the Danes on the north immediately after they had gained possession of the Hebrides; but the coasts of Germany, Belgium, and France had witnessed their attacks long before. Religion was the first to suffer; and as the Island of Saints was at the time of their descent covered with churches and monasteries, the Scandinavian barbarians found in these a rich harvest which induced them to return again and again. The first expedition consisted of only a few boats and a small body of men. Nevertheless, as their irruptions were unexpected, and the people were unprepared for resistance, many holy edifices suffered from these attacks, and a great number of priests and monks were murdered.

We read that Armagh with its cathedral and monasteries was plundered four times in one month, and in Bangor nine hundred monks were slaughtered in a single day. The majority of the inmates of those houses fled with their books and the relics of their saints at the approach of the invaders, but, returning to their desecrated homes after the departure of the pirates, gave cause for those successive plunderings.

But the Irish did not always fly in dismay, as was the case in England and France. A force was generally mustered in the neighborhood to meet and repel the attack, and in numerous instances the marauders were driven back with slaughter to their ships.

For the clans rallied to the defence of the Church. Though the chieftains and their clansmen might seem to have failed fully to imbibe the spirit of religion, though in their insane feuds they often turned a deaf ear to the remonstrances and reproaches of the bishops and monks, nevertheless Christianity reigned supreme in their inmost hearts. And when they beheld pagans landed on their shores, to insult their faith and destroy the monuments of their religion, to shed the blood of holy men, of consecrated virgins, and of innocent children, they turned that bravery which they had so often used against themselves and for the satisfaction of worthless contentions into a new and a more fitting channel--the defence of their altars and the punishment of sacrilegious outrage.

The clan system was the very best adapted for this kind of warfare, so long as no large fleets came, and the pirates were too few in number and too sagacious in mind to think of venturing far inland. When but a small number of boats arrived, the invaders found in the neighborhood a clan ready to receive them. The clansmen speedily assembled, and, falling on the plundering crews, showed them how different were the free men of a Celtic coast, who were inspired by a genuine love for their faith, from the degenerate sons of the Gallo-Romans.

So the annals of the country tell us that the "foreigners" were destroyed in 812 by the men of Umhall in Mayo; by Corrach, lord of Killarney, in the same year; by the men of Ulidia and by Carbry with the men of Hy-Kinsella in 827; by the clansmen of Hy-Figeinte, near Limerick, in 834, and many more.

But the hydra had a thousand heads, and new expeditions were continually arriving. In the words of Mr. Worsaae, a Danish writer of this century:

"From time immemorial Ireland was celebrated in the Scandinavian north, for its charming situation, its mild climate, and its fertility and beauty. The Kongspell--mirror of Kings--which was compiled in Norway about the year 1200, says that Ireland is almost the best of the lands we are acquainted with although no vines grow there. The Scandinavian Vikings and emigrants, who often contented themselves with such poor countries as Greenland and the islands in the north Atlantic, must, therefore, have especially turned their attention to the 'Emerald Isle,' particularly as it bordered closely upon their colonies in England and Scotland. But to make conquests in Ireland, and to acquire by the sword alone permanent settlements there, was no easy task.... When we consider that neither the Romans nor the Anglo-Saxons ever obtained a footing in that country, although they had conquered England, the adjacent isle, and when we further reflect upon the immense power exerted by the English in later times in order to subdue the Celtic population of the island, we cannot help being surprised at the very considerable Scandinavian settlements which, as early as the ninth century, were formed in that country."

These are the words of a Dane. We shall see what the "very considerable Scandinavian settlements" amounted to; the quotation is worthy of note, as presenting in a few words the motives of those who at any time invaded Ireland, and the stubborn resistance which they met.

The Irish were not dismayed by the constant arrivals of those northern hordes. They met them one after another without considering their complexity and connection. They only saw a troop of fierce barbarians landed on their shores, chiefly intent upon plundering and burning the churches and holy houses which they had erected; they saw their island, hitherto protected by the ocean from foreign attack, and resting in the enjoyment of a constant round of Christian festivals and joyful feasts, now desecrated by the presence and the fury of ferocious pagans; they armed for the defence of all that is dear to man; and though, perhaps, at first beaten and driven back, they mustered in force at a distance to fall on the victors with a swoop of noble birds who fly to the defence of their young.

This kind of contest continued for two hundred years, with the exception of the periods of larger invasions, when a single clan no longer sufficed to avenge the cause of God and humanity, and the Ard-Righ was compelled to throw himself on the scene at the head of the whole collective force of the nation in order to oppose the vast fleets and large armies of the Danes.

The country suffered undoubtedly; the cattle were slain; the fields devastated; the churches and houses burned; the poets silenced or woke their song only to notes of woe; the harpers taught the national instrument the music of sadness; the numerous schools were scattered, though never destroyed; as centuries later, under the Saxon, the people took their books or writing materials to their miserable cottages or hid them in the mountain fastnesses, and thus, for the first time in their history, the hedge school succeeded those of the large monasteries. So the nation continued to live on, the energetic fire which burned in the hearts of the people could not be quenched. They rose and rose again, and often took a noble revenge, never disheartened by the most utter disaster.

On three different occasions this bloody strife assumed a yet more serious and dangerous aspect. It was not a few boats only which came to the shores of the devoted island; but the main power of Scandinavia seemed to combine in order to crush all opposition at a single blow.

When the knowledge of the richness, fertility, and beauty of the island had fully spread throughout Denmark and Norway, a large fleet gathered in the harbors of the Baltic and put to sea. The famous Turgesius or Turgeis--Thorgyl in the Norse--was the leader. The Edda and Sagas of Norway and Denmark have been examined with a view to elucidate this passage in Irish history, but thus far fruitlessly. It is known, however, that many Sagas have been lost which might have contained an account of it. The Irish annals are too unanimous on the subject to leave any possibility of doubt with regard to it; and, whatever may be the opinion of learned men on the early events in the history of Erin, the story of the eighth, ninth, and tenth centuries rests entirely on historical ground, as surely as if the facts had happened a few hundred years ago.

Turgesius landed with his fleet on the northeast coast of the island, and straightway the scattered bands of Scandinavians already in the country acknowledged his leadership and flocked to his standard. McGeoghegan says that "he assumed in his own hands the sovereignty of all the foreigners that were then in Ireland."

From the north he marched southward; and, passing Armagh on his route, attacked and took it, and plundered its shrines, monasteries, and schools. There were then within its walls seven thousand students, according to an ancient roll which Keating says has been discovered at Oxford. These were slaughtered or dispersed, and the same fate attended the nine hundred monks residing in its monasteries.

Foraanan, the primate, fled; and the pagan sea-kong, entering the cathedral, seated himself on the primatial throne, and had himself proclaimed archbishop.--(O'Curry.) He had shortly before devastated

Clonmacnoise and made his wife supreme head of that great ecclesiastical centre, celebrated for its many convents of holy women. The tendency to add insult to outrage, when the object of the outrage is the religion of Christ, is old in the blood of the northern barbarians; and Turgesius was merely setting the example, in his own rude and honest fashion, to the more polished but no less ridiculous assumption of ecclesiastical authority, which was to be witnessed in England, on the part of Henry VIII. and Elizabeth.

The power of the invader was so superior to whatever forces the neighboring Irish clans could muster, that no opposition was even attempted at first by the indignant witnesses of those sacrileges. It is even said that at the very time when the Northmen were pillaging and burning in the northeast of the island, the men of Munster were similarly employed in Bregia; and Conor, the reigning monarch of Ireland, instead of defending the invaded territories, was himself hard at work plundering Leinster to the banks of the river Liffey--(Haverty.) But, doubtless, none of those deluded Irish princes had yet heard of the pagan devastations and insults to their religion, and thus it was easy for the great sea-kong to strengthen and extend his power. For the attainment of his object he employed two powerful agents which would have effectually crushed Ireland forever, if the springs of vitality in the nation had not been more than usually expansive and strong.

The political ability of the Danes began to show itself in Ireland, as it did about the same period (830) in England, and later on in France. Turgesius saw that, in order to subdue the nation, it was necessary to establish military stations in the interior and fortify cities on the coast, where he could receive reinforcements from Scandinavia. These plans he was prompt to put into practice.

His military stations would have been too easily destroyed by the bravery of the Irish, strengthened by the elasticity of their clan-system, if they were, planted on land. He, therefore, set them in the interior lakes which are so numerous in the island, where his navy could repel all the attacks of the natives, unused as they were to naval conflicts. He stationed a part of his fleet on Lough Lee in the upper Shannon, another in Lough Neagh, south of Antrim, a third in Lough Lughmagh or Dundalk bay. These various military positions were strongholds which secured the supremacy of the Scandinavians in the north of the island for a long time. In the south,

Turgesius relied on the various cities which his troops were successively to build or enlarge, namely, Dublin, Limerick, Galway, Cork, Waterford, and Wexford. This first Scandinavian ruler could begin that policy only by establishing his countrymen in Dublin, which they seized in 836.

Up to that time the Irish had scarcely any city worthy of the name. A patriarchal people, they followed the mode of life of the old Eastern patriarchs, who abhorred dwelling in large towns. Until the invasion of the Danes, the island was covered with farm-houses placed at some distance from each other. Here and there large duns or raths, as they were called, formed the dwellings of their chieftains, and became places of refuge for the clansmen in time of danger. Churches and monasteries arose in great numbers from the time of St. Patrick, which were first built in the woods, but soon grew into centres of population, corresponding in many respects to the idea of towns as generally understood.

The Northmen brought with them into Ireland the ideas of cities, commerce, and municipal life, hitherto unknown. The introduction of these supposed a total change necessary in the customs of the natives, and stringent regulations to which the people could not but be radically opposed. And strange was their manner of introduction by these northern hordes. Keating tells us how Turgesius understood them. They were far worse than the imaginary laws of the Athenians as recorded in the "Birds" of Aristophanes. No more stringent rules could be devised, whether for municipal, rural, or social regulations; and, as the Northmen are known to have been of a systematic mind, no stronger proof of this fact could be given.

Keating deplores in the following terms the fierce tyranny of the Danish sea-kong:

"The result of the heavy oppression of this thraldom of the Gaels under the foreigner was, that great weariness thereof came upon the men of Ireland, and the few of the clergy that survived had fled for safety to the forests and wildernesses, where they lived in misery, but passed their time piously and devoutly, and now the same clergy prayed fervently to God to deliver them from that tyranny of Turgesius, and, moreover, they fasted against that tyrant, and they commanded every layman among the faithful, that still remained obedient to their voice, to fast against him likewise. And God then heard their supplications in as far as the delivering of Turgesius into the hands of the Gaels."

Thus in the ninth century the subsequent events of the sixteenth and seventeenth were foreshadowed. The judicious editor of Keating, however, justly remarks, that this description, taken mainly from Cambrensis, is not supported in its entirety by the contemporaneous annals of the island; that the power of the Danes never was as universal and oppressive as is here supposed; and that though each of the facts mentioned may have actually taken place in some part of the country, at some period of the Danish invasion, yet the whole, as representing the actual state of the entire island at the time, is exaggerated and of too sweeping a nature.

It is clear, nevertheless, that the domination of the Northmen could not have been completely established in Ireland, together with their notions of superiority of race, trade on a large scale, and a consequent agglomeration of men in large cities, without the total destruction of the existing social state of the Irish, and consequently something of the frightful tyranny just described.

But the people were too brave, too buoyant, and too ardent in their nature, to bear so readily a yoke so heavy. They were too much attached to their religion, not to sacrifice their lives, if necessary, in order to put an end to the sacrilegious usurpations of a pagan king, profaning, by his audacious assumptions, the noblest, highest, purest, and most sacred dignities of holy Church. A man, stained with the blood of so many prelates and priests, seated on the primatial throne of the country in sheer derision of their most profound feelings; his pagan wife ruling over the city which the virgins of Bridget, the spouses of Christ, had honored and sanctified so long; their religion insulted by those who tried to destroy it--how could such a state of things be endured by the whole race, not yet reduced to the condition to which so many centuries of oppression subsequently brought it down!

Hence Keating could write directly after the passage just quoted: "When the nobles of Ireland saw that Turgesius had brought confusion upon their country, and that he was assuming supreme authority over themselves, and reducing them to thraldom and vassalage, they became inspired with a fortitude of mind, and a loftiness of spirit, and a hardihood and firmness of purpose, that urged them to work in right earnest, and to toil zealously in battle against him and his murdering hordes."

And hereupon the faithful historian gives a long list of engagements in which the Irish were successful, ending with the victory of Malachi at Glas Linni, where we know from the Four Masters that Turgesius himself was taken prisoner and afterward drowned in Lough Uair or Owell in West Meath, by order of the Irish king.

This prince, then monarch of the whole island, atoned for the apathy and the want of patriotism of his predecessors, Conor and the Nialls. He was in truth a saviour of his country, and the death of the oppressor was the signal for a general onslaught upon the "foreigners" in every part of the island.

"The people rose simultaneously, and either massacred them in their towns, or defeated them in the fields, so that, with the exception of a few strongholds, like Dublin, the whole of Ireland was free from the Northmen. Wherever they could escape, they took refuge in their ships, but only to return in more numerous swarms than before." - (M. Haverty.)

It is evident that their deep sense of religion was the chief source of the energy which the Irish then displayed. They had not yet been driven into a fierce resistance by being forcibly deprived of their lands; although the Danes, when they carried their vexatious tyranny into all the details of private life - not allowing lords and ladies of the Irish race to wear rich dresses and appear in a manner befitting their rank - when they went so far as to refuse a bowl of milk to an infant, that a rude soldier might quench his thirst with it - could have scarcely permitted the apparently conquered people to enjoy all the advantages accruing to the owner from the possession of land. Yet in none of the chronicles of the time which we have seen is any mention made of open confiscation, and of the survey and division of the territory among the greedy followers of the sea-kong. We do not yet witness what happened shortly after in Normandy under Rollo, and what was to happen four hundred years later in Ireland. The Scandinavians had not yet attained that degree of civilization which makes men attach a paramount importance to the possession of a fixed part of any territory, and call in surveys, title-deeds, charters, and all the written documents necessitated by a captious and over-scrupulous legislation. The Irish, consequently, did not perceive that their broad acres were passing into the control of a foreign race, and were being taken piecemeal from them, thus bringing them gradually down to the condition of mere serfs and dependants.

What they did see, beyond the possibility of mistake or deception, was their religion outraged, their spiritual rulers, not merely no longer at liberty to practise the duties of their sacred ministry, but hunted down and slaughtered or driven to the mountains and the woods. They saw that pagans were actually ruling their holy isle, and changing a paradise of sanctity into a pandemonium of brutal passion, presided over by a superstitious and cruel idolatry. For surely, although the Irish chronicles fail to speak of it, the minstrels and historians being too full of their own misery to think of looking at the pagan rites of their enemies - those enemies worshipped Thor and Odin and Frigga, and as surely did they detest the Church which they were on a fair way to destroy utterly. This it was which gave the Irish the courage of despair. For this cause chiefly did the whole island fly to arms, fall on their foes and bring down on their heads a fearful retribution. This it was, doubtless, which breathed into the new monarch the energy which he displayed on the field of Glas Linni; and when he ordered the barbarian, now a prisoner in his hands, to be drowned, it was principally as a sign that he detested in him the blasphemer and the persecutor of God's church.

Thus did the first national misfortunes of this Celtic people become the means of enkindling in their hearts a greater love for their religion, and a greater zeal for its preservation in their midst.

Ireland was again free; and, although we have no details concerning the short period of prosperity which followed the overthrow of the tyranny we have touched upon, we have small doubt that the first object of the care of those who, under God, had worked their own deliverance, was to repair the ruins of the desecrated sanctuaries and restore to religion the honor of which it had been stripped.

The Danes themselves came to see that they had acted rashly in striving to deprive the Irish of a religion which was so dear to their hearts; they resolved on a change of policy, as they were still bent on taking possession of the island, which Mr. Worsaae has told us they considered the best country in existence.

They resolved, therefore, to act with more prudence, and to make use of trade and the material blessings which it confers, in order to entice the Irish to their destruction, by allowing the Northmen to carry on business transactions with them and so gradually to dwell among them again. Father Keating tells the story in his quaint and graphic style:

"The plan adopted by them on this occasion was to equip three captains, sprung from the noblest blood of Norway, and to send them with a fleet to Ireland, for the object of obtaining some station for purpose of trade. And with them they accordingly embarked many tempting wares, and many valuable jewels -- with the design of presenting them to the men of Ireland, in the hope of thus securing their friendship; for they believed that they might thus succeed in surreptitiously fixing a grasp upon the Irish soil, and might be enabled to oppress the Irish people again . . . . The three captains, therefore, coming from the ports of Norway, landed in Ireland with their followers, as if for the purpose of demanding peace, and under the pretext of establishing a trade; and there, with the consent of the Irish, who were given to peace, they took possession of some sea-board places, and built three cities thereon, to wit: Waterford, Dublin, and Limerick."

We see, then, the Scandinavians abandoning their first project of conquering the North to fall on the South and confining themselves to a small number of fortified sea-ports.

The first result of this policy was a firmer hold than ever on Dublin, once already occupied by them in 836. "Amlaf, or Olaf, or Olaus, came from Norway to Ireland in 851, so that all the foreign tribes in the island submitted to him, and they extracted rent from the Gaels." - (Four Masters.)

From that time to the twelfth century Dublin became the chief stronghold of the Scandinavians, and no fewer than thirty-five Ostmen, or Danish kings, governed it. They made it an important emporium, and such it continued even after the Scandinavian invasion had ceased. McFirbis says that in his time - 1650 - most of the merchants of Dublin were the descendants of the Norwegian Irish king, Olaf Kwaran; and, to give a stronger impulse to commerce, they were the first to coin money in the country.

The new Scandinavian policy carried out by Amlaf, who tried to establish in Dublin the seat of a kingdom which was to extend over the whole island, resulted therefore only in the establishment of five or six petty principalities, wherein the Northmen, for some time masters, were gradually reduced to a secondary position, and finally confined themselves to the operations of commerce.

Since the attempt of Turgesius to subvert the religion of the country, they never showed the slightest inclination to repeat it; hence they were left in quiet possession of the places which they occupied on the sea-board, and gradually came to embrace Christianity themselves.

Little is known of the circumstances which attended this change of religion on their part; and it is certain that it did not take place till late in the tenth century. Some pretend that Christianity was brought to them from their own country, where it had already been planted by several missionaries and bishops. But it is known that St. Ancharius, the first apostle of Denmark, could not establish himself permanently in that country, and had to direct a few missionaries from Hamburgh, where he fixed his see. It is known, moreover, that Denmark was only truly converted by Canute in the eleventh century, after his conquest of England. As to Norway, the first attempt at its conversion by King Haquin, who had become a Christian at the court of Athelstan in England, was a failure; and although his successor, Harold, appeared to succeed better for a time, paganism was again reestablished, and flourished as late as 995. It was, in fact, Olaf the Holy who, coming from England, in 1017, with the priests Sigefried, Budolf, and Bernard, succeeded in introducing Christianity permanently into Norway, and he made more use of the sword than of the word in his mission.

With regard to the conversion of the Danes in Ireland, it seems that, after all, it was the ever-present spectacle of the workings of Christianity among the Irish which gradually opened their eyes and ears. They came to love the country and the people when they knew them thoroughly; they respected them for their bravery, which they had proved a thousand times; they felt attracted toward them on account of their geniality of temperament and their warm social feelings; even their defects of character and their impulsive nature were pleasing to them. They soon sought their company and relationship; they began to intermarry with them; and from this there was but a step to embracing their religion.

The Danes of Waterford, Cork, and Limerick were, however, the last to abandon paganism, and they seem not to have done so until after Clontarf.

It is very remarkable that, during all those conflicts of the Irish with the Danes, when the Northmen strewed the island with dead and ruins; when they seemed to be planting their domination in the Orkneys, the Hebrides, and even the Isle of Man, on a firm footing; when the seas around England and Ireland swarmed with pirates, and new expeditions started almost every spring from the numerous harbors of the Baltic--the Irish colony of Dal Riada in Scotland, which was literally surrounded by the invaders, succeeded in wresting North Britain from the Picts, drove them into the Lowlands, and so completely rooted them out, that history never more speaks of them, so that to this day the historical problem stands unsolved--What became of the Picts?--various as are the explanations given of their disappearance. And, what is more remarkable still, is, that the Dal Riada colony received constant help from their brothers in Erin, and the first of the dynasty of Scottish kings, in the person of Kenneth McAlpine, was actually set on the throne of Scotland by the arms of the Irish warriors, who, not satisfied apparently with their constant conflicts with the Danes on their own soil, passed over the Eastern Sea to the neighboring coast of Great Britain.

During the last forty years of the tenth century the Danes lived in Ireland as though they belonged to the soil. If they waged war against some provincial king, they became the allies of others. When clan fought clan, Danes were often found on both sides, or if on one only, they soon joined the other. They had been brought to embrace the manners of the natives, and to adopt many of their customs and habits. Yet there always remained a lurking distrust, more or less marked, between the two races; and it was clear that Ireland could never be said to have escaped the danger of subjugation until the Scandinavian element should be rendered powerless.

This antipathy on both sides existed very early even in Church affairs, the Christian natives being looked upon with a jealous eye by the Christian Danes; so that, toward the middle of the tenth century, the Danes of Dublin having succeeded in obtaining a bishop of their own nation, they sent him to England to be consecrated by Lanfranc, the Archbishop of Canterbury, and for a long time the see of Dublin was placed under the jurisdiction of Lanfranc's successors.

This grew into a serious difficulty for Ireland, as the capital of Leinster began to be looked upon as depending, at least spiritually, on England; and later on, at the time of the invasion under Strongbow, the establishment of the English Pale was considerably facilitated by such an arrangement, to which Rome had consented only for the spiritual advantage of her Scandinavian children in Ireland.

And the Irish were right in distrusting every thing foreign on the soil, for, even after becoming Christians, the Danes could not resist the temptation of making a last effort for the subjugation of the country.

Hence arose their last general effort, which resulted in their final overthrow at Clontarf. It does not enter into our purpose to give the story of that great event, known in all its details to the student of Irish history. It is not for us to trace the various steps by which Brian Boru mounted to supreme power, and superseded Malachi, to relate the many partial victories he had already gained over the Northmen, nor to allude to his splendid administration of the government, and the happiness of the Irish under his sway.

But it is our duty to point out the persevering attempts of the Scandinavian race, not only to keep its footing on Irish soil, but to try anew to conquer what it had so often failed to conquer. For, in describing their preparations for this last attempt on a great scale, we but add another proof of that Irish steadfastness which we have already had so many occasions to admire.

In the chronicle of Adhemar, quoted by Lanigan from Labbe (Nova Bibl., MSS., Tom. 2, p.177), it is said that "the Northmen came at that time to Ireland, with an immense fleet, conveying even their wives and children, with a view of extirpating the Irish and occupying in their stead that very wealthy country in which there were twelve cities, with extensive bishoprics and a king."

Labbe thinks the Chronicle was written before the year 1031, so that in his opinion the writer was a contemporary of the facts he relates.

The Irish Annals state, on their side, that "the foreigners were gathered from all the west of Europe, envoys having been despatched into Norway, the Orkneys, the Baltic islands, so that a great number of Vikings came from all parts of Scandinavia, with their families, for the purpose of a permanent settlement."

Similar efforts were made about the same time by the Danes for the lasting conquest of England, which succeeded, Sweyn having been proclaimed king in 1013, and Canute the Great becoming its undisputed ruler in 1017.

It is well known how the attempt failed in Erin, an army of twenty-one thousand freebooters being completely defeated near Dublin by Brian and his sons.

From that time the existence of the Scandinavian race on the Irish soil was a precarious one; they were merely permitted to occupy the sea-ports for the purpose of trade, and soon Irish chieftains replaced their kings in Dublin, Limerick, Waterford, and Cork.

The reader may be curious to learn, in conclusion, what signs the Danes left of their long sojourn on the island. If we listen to mere popular rumor, the country is still full of the ruins of buildings occupied by them. The common people, in pointing out to strangers the remains of edifices, fortifications, raths, duns, even round-towers and churches, either more ancient or more recent than the period of the Norse invasion, ascribe them to the Danes. It is clear that two hundred years of devastations, burnings, and horrors, have left a deep impression on the mind of the Irish; and, as they cannot suppose that such powerful enemies could have remained so long in their midst without leaving wonderful traces of their passage, they often attribute to them the construction of the very edifices which they destroyed. The general accuracy of their traditions seems here at fault. For there is no nation on earth so exact as the Irish in keeping the true remembrance of facts of their past history. Not long ago all Irish peasants were perfectly acquainted with the whole history of their neighborhood; they could tell what clans had succeeded each other, the exact spots where such a party had been overthrown and such another victorious; every village had its sure traditions printed on the minds of its inhabitants, and, by consulting the annals of the nation, the coincidence was often remarkable. How is it, therefore, that they were so universally at fault with respect to the Danes?

A partial explanation has been given which is in itself a proof of the tenacity of Irish memory. It is known that the Tuatha de Danaan were not only skilful in medicine, in the working of metals and in magic, but many buildings are generally attributed to them by the best antiquarians; among others, the great mound of New Grange, on the banks of the Boyne, which is still in perfect preservation, although opened and pillaged by the Danes-- a work reminding the beholder of some Egyptian monument. The coincidence of the name of the Tuatha de Danaan with that of the Danes may have induced many of the illiterate Irish to adopt the universal error into which they fell long ago, of attributing most of the ancient monuments of their country to the Danes.

The fact is, that the ruins of a few unimportant castles and churches are all the landmarks that remain of the Danish domination in Ireland; and even these must have been the product of the latter part of it.

But a more curious proof of the extirpation of every thing Danish in the island is afforded by Mr. Worsaae, whose object in writing his account of the Danes and Norwegians in England, Scotland, and Ireland, was to glorify his own country, Denmark.

He made a special study of the names of places and things, which can be traced to the Scandinavians respectively in the three great divisions of the British Isles; and certainly the language of a conquering people always shows itself in many words of the conquered country, where the subjugation has been of sufficient duration.

In England, chiefly in the northern half of the kingdom, a very great number of Danish names appear and are still preserved in the geography of the country. In Mr. Worsaae's book there is a tabular view of 1,373 Danish and Norwegian names of places in England, and also a list of 100 Danish words, selected from the vulgar tongue, still in use among the people who dwell north of Watling Street.

In Scotland, likewise--in the Highlands and even in the Lowlands--a considerable number of names, or at least of terminations, are still to be met in the geography of the country.

Three or four names of places around Dublin, and the terminations of the names of the cities of Waterford, Wexford, Longford, and a few others, are all that Mr. Worsaae could find in Ireland. So that the language of the Irish, not to speak of their government and laws, remained proof against the long and persevering efforts made by a great and warlike Northern race to invade the country, and substitute its social life for that of the natives.

As a whole, the Scandinavian irruptions were a complete failure. They did not succeed in impressing their own nationality or individuality on any thing in the island, as they did in England, Holland, and the north of France. The few drops of blood which they left in the country have been long ago absorbed in the healthful current of the pure Celtic stream; even the language of the people was not affected by them.

As for the social character of the nation, it was not touched by this fearful aggression. The customs of Scandinavia with respect to government, society, domestic affairs, could not influence the Irish; they refused to admit the systematic thraldom which the sternness of the Northmen would engraft upon their character, and preserved their free manners in spite of all adverse attempts. In this country, Turgesius, Amlaf, Sitrick, and their compeers, failed as signally as other Scandinavian chieftains succeeded in Britain and Normandy.

The municipal system, which has won so much praise, was scornfully abandoned by the Irish to the Danes of the sea port towns, and they continued the agricultural life adapted to their tastes. Towns and cities were not built in the interior till much later by the English.

The clan territories continued to be governed as before. The "Book of Rights" extended its enactments even to the Danish Pale; and the Danes tried to convert it to their own advantage by introducing into it false chapters. How the poem of the Gaels of Ath Cliath first found a place in the "Book of Rights" is still unknown to the best Irish antiquarians. John O'Donovan concludes from a verse in it that it was composed in the tenth century, after the conversion of the Danes of Dublin to Christianity. It proves certainly that the Scandinavians in Ireland, like the English of the Pale later on, had become attached to Erin and Erin's customs--had, in fact, become. Irishmen, to all intents and purposes. Not succeeding in making Northmen of the Irish, they succumbed to the gentle influence of Irish manners and religion.

As for the commercial spirit, the Irish could not be caught by it, even when confronted by the spectacle of the wealth it conferred on the "foreigners." It is stated openly in the annals of the race that their greatest kings, both Malachi and Brian Boru, did not utterly expel the Danes from the country, in order that they might profit by the Scandinavian traders, and receive through them the wines, silks, and other commodities, which the latter imported from the continent of Europe.

The same is true of the sea-faring life. The Irish could never be induced to adopt it as a profession, whatever may have been their fondness for short voyages in their curraghs.

The only baneful effects which the Norse invasion exercised on the Irish were: 1. The interruption of studies on the large, even universal, scale on which, they had previously been conducted; 2. The breaking up of the former constitution of the monarchy, by compelling the several clans which were attacked by the "foreigners" to act independently of the Ard-Righ, so that from that time irresponsible power was divided among a much greater number of chieftains.

But these unfortunate effects of the Norse irruptions affected in no wise the Irish character, language, or institutions, which, in fact, finally triumphed over the character, language, and institutions of the pirates established among them for upward of two centuries.

THE IRISH FREE CLANS AND ANGLO-NORMAN FEUDALISM

THE Danes were subdued, and the Irish at liberty to go on weaving the threads of their history--though, in consequence of the local wars, they had lost the concentrating power of the Ard-Righ--when treachery in their own ranks opened up the way for a far more serious attack from another branch of the great Scandinavian family--the Anglo-Norman.

The manners of the people had been left unchanged; the clan system had not been altered in the least; it had stood the test of previous revolutions; now it was to be confronted by a new system which had just conquered Europe, and spread itself round about the apparently doomed island. Of all places it had taken deep root in England, where it was destined to survive its destruction elsewhere in the convulsions of our modern history. That system, then in full vigor, was feudalism.

In order rightly to understand and form a correct judgment on the question, and its mighty issues, we must state briefly what the chief characteristics of feudalism were in those countries where it flourished.

The feudal system proceeded on the principle that landed property was all derived from the king, as the captain of a conquering army; that it had been distributed by him among his followers on certain conditions, and that it was liable to be forfeited if those conditions were not fulfilled.

The feudal system, moreover, politically considered, supposed the principle that all civil and political rights were derived from the possession of land; that those who possessed no land could possess neither civil nor political rights--were, in fact, not men, but villeins.

Consequently, it reduced nations to a small number of landowners, enjoying all the privileges of citizenship; the masses, deprived of all rights, having no share in the government, no opportunity of rising in the social scale, were forever condemned to villeinage or serfdom.

Feudalism, in our opinion, came first from Scandinavia. The majority of writers derive it from Germany. The question of its origin is too extensive to be included within our present limits, and indeed is unnecessary, as we deal principally with the fact and not with its history.

When the sea-rover had conquered the boat of an enemy, or destroyed a village, he distributed the spoils among his crew. Every thing was handed over to his followers in the form of a gift, and in return these latter were bound to serve him with the greatest ardor and devotedness. In course of time the idea of settling down on some territory which they had devastated and depopulated, presented itself to the minds of the rovers. The sea-kong did by the land what he had been accustomed to do by the plunder: he parcelled it out among his faithful followers-- fideles--giving to each his share of the territory. This was called feoh by the Anglo-Saxons, who were the first to carry out the system on British soil, as Dr. Lingard shows. Thus the word fief was coined, which in due time took its place in all the languages of Europe.

The giver was considered the absolute owner of whatever he gave, as is the commander of a vessel at sea. It was a beneficium conferred by him, to which certain indispensable conditions were attached. Military duty was the first, but not the only one of these. Writers on feudalism mention a great number, the nonfulfilment of which incurred what was called forfeiture.

In countries where the pirates succeeded in establishing themselves, all the native population was either destroyed by them, as Dudo tells us was the case in Normandy, or, as more frequently happened, the sword being unable to carry destruction so far, the inhabitants who survived were reduced to serfdom, and compelled to till the soil for the conquerors; they were thenceforth called villeins or ascripti glebae. It is clear that such only as possessed land could claim civil and political rights in the new states thus called into existence. Hence the owning of land under feudal tenure was the great and only essential characteristic of mediaeval feudalism.

This system, which was first introduced into Britain by the Anglo-Saxons, was brought to a fixed and permanent state by the Normans--followers of William the Conqueror; and, when the time came for treachery to summon the Norman knights to Irish soil, the devoted island found herself face to face with an iron system which at that period crushed and weighed down all Europe.

The Normans had now been settled in England for a hundred years; all the castles in the country were occupied by Norman lords; all bishoprics filled by Norman bishops; all monasteries ruled by Norman abbots. At the head of the state stood the king, at that time Henry II. Here, more than in any other country in Europe, was the king the key-stone to the feudal masonry. Not an inch of ground in England was owned save under his authority, as enjoying the supremum dominium. All the land had been granted by his predecessors as fiefs, with the right of reversion to the crown by forfeiture in case of the violation of feudal obligations. Here was no allodial property, no censitive hereditary domain, as in the rest of, otherwise, feudal Europe. All English lawyers were unanimous in the doctrine that the king alone was the true master of the territory; that tenure under him carried with it all the conditions of feudal tenure, and that any deed or grant proceeding from his authority ought to be so understood.

The south-western portion of Wales was occupied by Norman lords, Flemings for the most part. Two of these, Robert Fitzstephens and Maurice Fitzgerald, sailed to the aid of the Irish King of Leinster. They were the first to land, arriving a full year before Strongbow.

Strongbow came at last. The conditions agreed on beforehand between himself and the Leinster king were fulfilled. He was married to the daughter of Dermod McMurrough, chief of Leinster, acknowledged Righ Dahma, that is, successor to the crown, while the Irish, accustomed for ages to admire valor and bow submissively to the law of conquest, admitted the claim. The English adventurer they looked upon as one of themselves by marriage. Election in such a case was unnecessary, or rather, understood, and Strongbow took the place which was his in their eyes by right of his wife, of head under McMurrough of all the clans of Leinster.

When, a little later, came Henry II. to be acknowledged by Strongbow as his suzerain, and to receive the homage of the presumptive heir of Leinster, submission to him was, in the eyes of the Irish, merely a consequence of their own clan system. They understood the homage rendered to him in a very different sense from that attached to it by feudal nations; and had they had an inkling of the real intentions of the new comers, not one of them would have consented to live under and bow the neck to such a yoke.

In fact, on the small territory where those great events were enacted, two worlds, utterly different from each other, stood face to face. Cambrensis tells us that the English were struck with wonder at what they saw. The imperialism of Rome had never touched Ireland. The Danes, opposed so strenuously from the outset, and finally overcome, had never been able to introduce there their restrictive measures of oppression. The English found the natives in exactly the same state as that in which Julius Caesar found the Gauls twelve hundred years before, except as to religion--the race governed patriarchally by chieftains allied to their subordinates by blood relationship; no unity in the government, no common flag, no private and hereditary property, nothing to bind the tribes together except religion. It was not a nation properly, but rather an agglomeration of small nations often at war each with each, yet all strongly attached to Erin--a mere name, including, nevertherless, the dear idea of country--the chieftains elective, bold, enterprising; the subordinates free, attached to the chief as to a common father, throwing themselves with ardor into all his quarrels, ready to die for him at any moment. Around chief and clansmen circled a large number of brehons, shanachies, poets, bards, and harpers--poetry, music, and war strangely blended together. The religion of Christ spread over all a halo of purity and holiness; large monasteries filled with pious monks, and convents of devout and pure virgins abounded; bishops and priests in the churches chanting psalms, each accompanying himself with a many-stringed harp, gave forth sweet harmony, unheard at the time in any other part of the world.

A most important feature to be considered is their understanding of property. Hereditary right of land with respect to individuals, and the transmission of property of any kind by right of primogeniture, were unknown among them. If a specified amount of territory was assigned to the chieftain, a smaller portion to the bishop, the shanachy, head poet, and other civil officers each in his degree, such property was attached to the office and not to the man who filled it, but passed to his elected successor and not to his own children; while the great bulk of the territory belonged to the clan in common. No one possessed the right to alienate a single rood of it, and, if at times a portion was granted to exiles, to strangers, to a contiguous clan, the whole tribe was consulted on the subject. Over the common land large herds of cattle roamed--the property of individuals who could own nothing, except of a movable nature, beyond their small wooden houses.

This state of things had existed, according to their annals, for several thousand years. Their ancestors had lived happily under such social conditions, which they wished to abide in and hand down to their posterity.

Foreign trade was distasteful to them; in fact, they had no inclination for commerce. Lucre they despised, scarcely knowing the use of money, which had been lately introduced among them. Yet, being refined in their tastes, fond of ornament, of wine at their feasts, loving to adorn the persons of their wives and daughters with silk and gems, they had allowed the Danes to dwell in their seaports, to trade in those commodities, and to import for their use what the land did not produce.

Those seaport towns had been fortified by the Northmen on their first victories when they took possession of them. Throughout the rest of the island, a fortress or a large town was not to be seen. The people, being all agriculturists or graziers, loved to dwell in the country; their houses were built of wattle and clay, yet comfortable and orderly.

The mansions of the chieftains were neither large architectural piles, nor frowning fortresses. They bore the name of raths when used for dwellings; of duns when constructed with a view to resisting an attack. In both cases, they were, in part under ground, in part above; the whole circular in form, built sometimes of large stones, oftener of walls of sodded clay.

Instead of covering their limbs with coats of mail, like the warriors of mediaeval Europe, they wore woollen garments even in war, and for ornaments chains or plates of precious metal. The Norman invaders, clad in heavy mail, were surprised, therefore, to find themselves face to face with men in their estimation unprotected and naked. More astonished were they still at the natural boldness and readiness of the Irish in speaking before their chieftains and princes, not understanding that all were of the same blood and cognizant of the fact.

Still less could they understand the freedom and familiarity existing between the Irish nobility and the poorest of their kinsmen, so different from the haughty bearing of an aristocracy of foreign extraction to the serfs and villeins of a people they had conquered.

The two nations now confronting each other had, therefore, nothing in common, unless, perhaps, an excessive pertinacity of purpose. The new comers belonged to a stern, unyielding, systematic stock, which was destined to give to Europe that great character so superior in our times to that of southern or eastern nations. The natives possessed that strong attachment to their time-honored customs, so peculiar to patriarchal tribes, in whose nature traditions and social habits are so strongly intermingled, that they are ineradicable save by the utter extirpation of the people.

And now the characteristics of both races were to be brought out in strong contrast by the great question of property in the soil, which was at the bottom of the struggle between clanship and feudalism. The Irish, as we have seen, knew nothing of individual property in land, nor of tenure, nor of rent, much less of forfeiture. They were often called upon by their chieftains to contribute to their support in ways not seldom oppressive enough, but the contributions were always in kind.

A new and very different system was to be attempted, to which the Irish at first appeared to consent, because they did not understand it, attaching, as they did, their own ideas to words, which, in the mouths of the invaders, had a very different meaning.

With the Irish "to do homage" meant to acknowledge the superiority of another, either on account of his lawful authority or his success in war; and the consequences of this act were, either the fulfilment of the enactments contained in the "Book of Rights," or submission to temporary conditions guaranteed by hostages. But that the person doing homage became by that act the liegeman of the suzerain for life and hereditarily in his posterity, subject to be deprived of all privileges of citizenship, as well as to the possibility of seeing all his lands forfeited, besides many minor penalties enjoined by the feudal code which often resolved itself into mere might--such a meaning of the word homage could by no possibility enter the mind of an Irishman at that period.

Hence, when, after the atrocities committed by the first invaders, who respected neither treaties nor the dictates of humanity, not even the sanctuary and the sacredness of religious houses, Henry II. came with an army, large and powerful for that time, the Irish people and their chieftains, hoping that he would put an end to the crying tyranny of the Fitzstephens, Fitzgeralds, De Lacys, and others, went to meet him and acknowledge his authority as head chieftain of Leinster through Strongbow, and, perhaps, as the monarch who should restore peace and happiness to the whole island. McCarthy, king of Desmond, was the first Irish prince to pay homage to Henry.

While the king was spending the Christmas festivities in Dublin, many other chieftains arrived; among them O'Carrol of Oriel and O'Rourke of Breffny. Roderic O'Connor of Connaught, till then acknowledged by many as monarch of Ireland, thought at first of fighting, but, as was his custom, he ended by a treaty, wherein, it is said, he acknowledged Henry as his suzerain, and thus placed Ireland at his feet. Ulster alone had not seen the invaders; but, as its inhabitants did not protest with arms in their hands, the Normans pretended that from that moment they were the rightful owners of the island.

Without a moment's delay they began to feudalize the country by dividing the land and building castles. These two operations, which we now turn to, opened the eyes of the Irish to the deception which had been practised upon them, and were the real origin of the momentous struggle which is still being waged today.

Sir John Davies, the English attorney-general of James I., has stated the whole case in a sentence: "All Ireland was by Henry II. cantonized among ten of the English nation; and, though they had not gained possession of one-third of the kingdom, yet in title they were owners and lords of all, so as nothing was left to be granted to the natives."

McCarthy, king of Desmond, had been the first to acknowledge the authority of Henry II., yet McCarthy's lands were among the first, if not the first, bestowed by Henry on his minions. The grant may be seen in Ware, and it is worthy of perusal as a sample of the many grants which followed it, whereby Henry attempted a total revolution in the tenure of land. The charter giving Meath to De Lacy was the only one which by a clause seemed to preserve the old customs of the country as to territory; and yet it was in Meath that the greatest atrocities were committed.

Yet one difficulty presented itself to the invaders: their rights were only on paper, whereas the Irish were still in possession of the greatest part of the island, and once the real purpose of the Normans showed itself, they were no longer disposed to submit to Henry or to any of his appointed lords. The territory had to be wrested from them by force of arms.

The English claimed the whole island as their own. They were, in fact, masters only of the portion occupied by their troops; the remainder was, therefore, to be conquered. And if in Desmond, where the whole strength of the English first fell, they possessed only a little more than one-fourth of the soil, what was the case in the rest of the island, the most of which had not yet seen them?

Long years of war would evidently be required to subdue it, and the systematic mind of the conquerors immediately set about devising the best means for the attainment of their purpose. The lessons gathered from their continental experience suggested these means immediately; they saw that by covering the country with feudal castles they could in the end conquer the most stubborn nation. A thorough revolution was intended. The two systems were so entirely antagonistic to each other that the success of the Norman project involved a change of land tenure, laws, customs, dress--every thing. Even the music of the bards was to be silenced, the poetry of the files to be abolished, the pedigrees of families to be discontinued, the very games of the people to be interrupted and forbidden. A vast number of castles was necessary. The project was a fearful one, cruel, barbarous, worthy of pagan antiquity. It was undertaken with a kind of ferocious alacrity, and in a short time it appeared near realization. But in the long run it failed, and four hundred years later, under the eighth Henry, it was as far from completion as the day on which the second Henry left the island in 1171.

To show the importance which the invaders attached to their system, and the ardor with which they set about putting it in practice, we have only to extract a few passages from the old annals of the islands; they are wonderfully expressive in their simplicity:

"A.D. 1176. The English were driven from Limerick by Donnall O'Brian. An English castle was in process of erection at Kells."--(Four Masters.)

"A.D. 1178. The English built and fortified a castle at Kenlis, the key of those parts of Meath, against the incursions of the Ulster men."--(Ware's Antiquities.)

"A.D. 1180. Hugh De Lacy planted several colonies in Meath, and fortified the country with many castles, for the defence and security of the English."--(Ibid.)

Such enumerations might be prolonged indefinitely; we conclude with the following entry taken from the Four Masters:

"A.D. 1186. Hugh De Lacy, the profaner and destroyer of many churches, Lord of the English of Meath (the Irish cannot call him their lord), Breffni, and Oirghialla, he who had conquered the greater part of Ireland for the English, and of whose English castles all Meath, from the Shannon to the sea, was full, after having finished the castle of Der Magh, set out accompanied by three Englishmen to visit it . . . . One of the men of Tebtha, a youth named O'Miadhaigh, approached him, and with an axe severed his head from his body."

So wide-reaching and comprehensive was the plan of the invaders from the beginning that they felt confident of holding possession of Ireland forever; and to effect this they must certainly have intended to destroy or drive out the native race, or at best to make slaves of as many of them as they chose to keep. Thus they had prophecies manufactured for the purpose, and Cambrensis, in his second book, chapter xxxiii., says confidently: "Prophecies promise a full victory to the English people. . . . and that the island of Hibernia shall be subjected and fortified with castles--literally incastellated, incastellatam--throughout from sea to sea."

Meanwhile, together with the building of castles, the partition of the territory was being carried out. The ten great lords, among whom, according to Sir John Davies, Henry II. had cantonized Ireland, saw the necessity of giving a part of their large estates to their followers that so they might occupy the whole. McGeohegan compiles from Ware the best view of this very interesting and comparatively unexplored subject. Curious details are found there, showing that, with the exception of Ulster, not only the geography, but even the most minute topography of the country, had been well studied by those feudal chieftains. Their characteristic love for system runs all through these transactions.

But the Irish had now seen enough. The whole country was in a blaze. That kind of guerilla war peculiar to the Celtic clans began. The newly built castles were attacked and often captured and destroyed. Strongbow was shut up and besieged in Water-ford, which fell into the hands of the Danes. The latter sided everywhere with the Irish. Limerick changed hands several times, until Donnall O'Brian, who was left in possession, set fire to it rather than see it fall again into the hands of the invaders.

In Meath, where the numerous castles of De Lacy were situated, a war to the knife was being waged. O'Melachlin first tried persuasion, but in conference with De Lacy he dared inveigh loudly against the King of England, and, as his words must have expressed the feelings of the great majority of the people, we give them:

"Notwithstanding his promise of supporting me in the possession of my wealth and dignities, he has sent robbers to invade my patrimony. Avaricious and sparing of his own possessions, he is lavish of those of others, and thus enriches libertines and profligates who have consumed the patrimony of their fathers in debauchery."

This manly protest was answered by the stroke of a dagger from the hand of Raymond Legros, and, after being beheaded, O'Melachlin was buried feet upward as a rebel.

The monarch himself, Roderic O'Connor, finally appeared on the scene, beat the English at Thurles, and, marching into Meath, laid the country waste.

Henry at last saw the necessity of adopting a milder policy, and O'Connor dispatching to England Catholicus O'Duffy, Archbishop of Tuam, Lawrence O'Toole, of Dublin, and Concors, Abbot of St. Brendan, the Treaty of Windsor was concluded, which was really a compromise, and yet remained the true law of the land for four hundred years. It may be seen in Rymer's "Foedera."

Sir John Davies justly remarks that by the treaty "the Irish lords only promised to become tributaries to King Henry II.; and such as pay only tribute, though they are placed by Bodin in the first degree of subjection, yet are not properly subjects, but sovereigns; for though they be less and inferior to the princes to whom they pay tribute, yet they hold all other points of sovereignty.

"And, therefore, though King Henry had the title of Sovereign Lord over the Irish, yet did he not put those things in execution, which are the true marks of sovereignty.

"For to give laws unto a people, to institute magistrates and officers over them, to punish or pardon malefactors, to have the sole authority of making war or peace, are the true marks of sovereignty, which King Henry II. had not in Ireland, but the Irish lords did still retain all those prerogatives to themselves. For they governed their people by the Brehon law; they appointed their own magistrates and officers; . . . . they made war and peace one with another, without control; and this they did not only during the reign of Henry II., but afterward in all times, even until the reign of Queen Elizabeth."

By an article of the treaty the Irish were allowed to live in the Pale if they chose; and even there they could enjoy their customs in peace, as far as the letter of the law went. Many acts of Irish parliaments, it is true, were passed for the purpose of depriving them of that right, but without success.

Edmund Spenser, himself living in the Pale in the reign of Elizabeth, speaks as an eye-witness of "having seen their meeton their ancient accustomed hills, where they debated and settled matters according to the Brehon laws, between family and family, township and township, assembling in large numbers, and going, according to their custom, all armed."

Stanihurst also, a contemporary of Spenser, had witnessed the breaking up of those meetings, and seen "the crowds in long lines, coming down the hills in the wake of each chieftain, he the proudest that could bring the largest company home to his evening supper."

Here would be the proper place to speak of the Brehon law, which remained thus in antagonism to feudal customs for several centuries. Up to recently, however, only vague notions could be given of that code. But at this moment antiquarians are revising and studying it preparatory to publishing the "Senchus Mor" in which the Irish law is contained. It is known that it existed previous to the conversion of Ireland to Christianity, and that the laws of tanistry and of gavelkind, the customs of gossipred and of fostering, were of pagan origin. Patrick revised the code and corrected what could not coincide with the Christian religion. He also introduced into the island many principles of the Roman civil and canon law, which, without destroying the peculiarities natural to the Irish character, invested their code with a more modern and Christian aspect.

Edmund Campian, who afterward died a martyr under Elizabeth, says, in his "Account of Ireland," written in May, 1571: "They (the Irish) speak Latin like a vulgar language, learned in their common schools of leechcraft and law, whereat they begin children, and hold on sixteen or twenty years, conning by rote the aphorisms of Hippocrates, and the Civil Institutes, and a few other parings of these two faculties. I have seen them where they kept school, ten in some one chamber, grovelling upon couches of straw, their books at their noses, themselves lying prostrate, and so to chant out their lessons by piecemeal, being the most part lusty fellows of twenty-five years and upward."

It was then after studies of from sixteen to twenty years that the Brehon judge--the great one of a whole sept, or the inferior one of a single noble family--sat at certain appointed times, in the open air, on a hill generally, having for his seat clods of earth, to decide on the various subjects of difference among neighbors.

Sir James Ware remarks that they were not acquainted with the laws of England. He might have better said, they preferred their own, as not coming from cold and pagan Scandinavia, but from the warm south, the greatest of human law-givers, the jurisconsults of Old Rome, and the holy expounders of the laws of Christian Rome.

What were those laws of England of which Ware speaks? There is no question here of the common law which came into use in times posterior to Henry II., and which the English derived chiefly from the Christian civil and canon law; but of those feudal enactments, which the Anglo-Normans endeavored to introduce into Ireland, for the purpose of supplanting the old law and customs of the natives.

There was, first, the law of territory, if we may so call it, by which the supreme ruler became really owner of the integral soil, which he distributed among his great vassals, to be redistributed by them among inferior vassals.

There was the law of primogeniture, which even to this day obtains in England, and has brought about in that country since the days of William the Conqueror, and in Ireland since the English "plantations" of the sixteenth and seventeenth centuries, the state of things now so well known to Europe.

There was also the long list of feudal conditions to be observed, by the fulfilment of which the great barons and their followers held their lands. For their tenure was liable to homage and fealty, as understood in the feudal sense, to wardships and impediments to marriage, to fines for alienations, to what English legists call primer seizins, rents, reliefs, escheats, and, finally, forfeitures; this last was at all times more strictly observed in England than in any other feudal country, and by its enactments so many noble families have, in the course of ages, been reduced to beggary, and their chiefs often brought to the block. English history is filled with such cases.

The law of wardship, by which no minor, heir, or heiress could have other guardian than the suzerain, and could not marry without his consent, was at all times a great source of wealth to the royal exchequer, and a correspondingly heavy tribute laid on the vassal. So profitable did the English kings find this law, that they speedily introduced it into Church affairs, every bishop's see or monastery being considered, at the death of the incumbent, as a minor, a ward, to be taken care of by the sovereign, who enjoyed the revenues without bothering himself particularly with the charges.

There were, finally, the hunting laws, which forbade any man to hunt or hawk even on his own estate.

Such were the laws of England, which Sir James Ware complains the Irish did not know.

In signing the treaty of Windsor, the English king had apparently recognized in the person of Roderic O'Connor, and in the Irish through him, the chief rights of sovereignty over the whole island, except Leinster and, perhaps, Meath. But, at the same time, a passage or two in the treaty concealed a meaning certainly unperceived by the Irish, but fraught with mischief and misfortune to their country.

First, Roderic O'Connor acknowledged himself and his successors as liegemen of the kings of England; in a second place, the privileges conceded to the Irish were to continue only so long as they remained faithful to their oath of allegiance. We see here the same confusion of ideas, which we remarked on the meaning given to the word homage by either party. The natives of the island understood to be liegemen and under oath in a sense conformable to their usual ideas of subordination; the English invested those words with the feudal meaning.

All the calamities of the four following centuries, and, consequently, all the horrors of the times subsequent to the Protestant Reformation, were to be the penalty of that misunderstanding.

Let us picture to ourselves two races of men so different as the Milesian Celts on the one side, and the Scandinavian Norman French on the other, having concluded such a treaty as that of Windsor, each side resolved to push its own interpretation to the bitter end.

The English are in possession of a territory clearly enough defined, but they are ever on the alert to seize any opportunity of a real or pretended violation of it, in order to extend their limits and subjugate the whole island. Yet they are bound to allow the Brehon Irish to live in their midst, governed by their own customs and laws. Moreover, they acknowledge that the former great Irish lords of the very country which they occupy are not mere Irish, but of noble blood; for, from the beginning, the English recognized five families of the country, known as the "five bloods," as pure and noble, in theory at least.

The Irish without the Pale are acknowledged as perfectly independent, completely beyond English control, with their own magistrates and laws, even that of war; subject only to tribute. But, at the same time, this independence is rendered absolutely insecure by the imposition of conditions, whose meaning is well known and perfectly understood in all the countries conquered by the Scandinavians, but utterly beyond the comprehension of the Irish.

The consequence is clear: war began with the conclusion of the treaty--a war which raged for four centuries, until a new and more powerful incentive to slaughter and desolation showed itself in the Reformation, ushered in by Henry VIII.

First came a general rebellion. This is the word used by Ware, when John, a boy of twelve years of age, was dispatched by his father Henry, with the title of Lord of Ireland, to receive the submission of various Irish lords at Waterford, where he landed. "The young English gentlemen," says Cambrensis, who was a witness of the scene, "used the Irish chieftains with scorn, because," as he says, "their demeanor was rude and barbarous." The Irish naturally resented this treatment from a lad, as they would have resented it from his father; and they retired in wrath to take up arms and raise the whole land to "rebellion."

This solemn protest was not without effect in Europe. At the beginning of the reign of Richard I., Clement III., on appointing, by the king's request, William de Longchamps, Bishop of Ely, as his legate in England, Wales, and Ireland, took good care to limit the authority of this prelate to those parts of Ireland which lay under the jurisdiction of the Earl of Moreton-- that is, of John, brother to Richard. He had power to exercise his jurisdiction "in Anglia,, Wallia, et illis Hiberniae partibus in quibus Joannes Moretonii Comes potestatem habet et dominium."--(Matth. Paris.) It would seem, then, that Clement III. knew nothing of the bull of Adrian IV.

The war, as we said, was incessant. England finally so despaired of conquering the country, that some lords of the court of Henry VI. caused him to write letters to some of his "Irish enemies," urging the latter to effect the conquest of the island in the king's name. This was assuredly a last resource, which history has never recorded of any other nation warring on a rival. But even in this England failed. Those lords--the "Irish enemies" of King Henry VI.--sent his letters to the Duke of York, then Lord-Lieutenant, "and published to the world the shame of England."-- (Sir John Davies.)

The result was that, at the end of the reign of Henry VI., the Irish, in the words of the same author, "became victorious over all, without blood or sweat; only that little canton of land, called the English Pale, containing four small shires; maintained yet a bordering war with the Irish, and retained the form of English government."

Feudalism was thus reduced in Ireland to the small territory lying between the Boyne and the Liffey, subject to the constant annoyance of the O'Moores, O'Byrnes, and O'Cavanaghs. And this state of affairs continued until the period of the so-called Reformation in England.

Ireland proved itself then the only spot in Western Europe where feudal laws and feudal customs could take no root. Through all other nations of the Continent those laws spread by degrees, from the countries invaded by the Northmen, into the most distant parts, modified and mitigated in some instances by the innate power of resistance left by former institutions. In this small island alone, where clanship still held its own, feudalism proved a complete failure. We merely record a fact, suggestive, indeed, of thought, which proves, if no more, at least that the Celtic nature is far more persevering and steady of purpose than is generally supposed.

But a more interesting spectacle still awaits us--that of the English themselves morally overcome and won over by the example of their antagonists, renouncing their feudal usages, and adopting manners which they had at first deemed rude and barbarous.

The treaty of Windsor, which was subsequently confirmed by many diplomatic enactments, obliged King Henry III. of England to address O'Brien of Thomond in the following words: "Rex regi Thomond salutem." The same English monarch was compelled to give O'Neill of Ulster the title of Rex, after having used, inadvertently perhaps, that of Regulus.--(Sir John Davies.) Both O'Brien and O'Neill lived in the midst of a thickly populated Irish district, with a few great English lords shut up in their castles on the borders of the respective territory of the clans.

The Norman lords in many parts of the country lived right in the midst of an Irish population, with its Brehon judges, shanachies, harpers, and other officers, attached to their customs of gossipred, fostering, tanistry, gavelkind, and other usages, which the parliaments of Drogheda, Kilkenny, Dublin, Trim, and other places, were soon to declare lewd and barbarous. The question of the moment was: Which of the two systems, clanship or feudalism, brought thus into close contact and antagonism, was to prevail?

Ere long it began to appear that the aversion first felt by the English lords at such strange customs was not entirely invincible, and many of them even went so far as to choose wives from among the native families. In fact, there lay a great example before their eyes from the outset, in the marriage of Strongbow with Eva, the daughter of McMurrough. Intermarriage soon became the prevailing custom; so that the posterity of the first invaders was, after all, to have Celtic blood in its veins.

Hence, a distinction arose between the English by blood and the English by birth. The first had, indeed, an English name; but they were born in the island, and soon came to be known as degenerate English.--That degeneracy was merely the moral effect of constant intercourse with the natives of their neighborhood. --The others were continually shifting, being always composed of the latest new-comers from England.

It is something well worthy of remark that a residence of a short duration sufficed to blend in unison two natures so opposed as the Irish and the English. The latter, not content with wedding Irish wives, sent their own children to be fostered by their Irish friends; and the children naturally came from the nursery more Irish than their fathers. They objected no longer to becoming gossips for each other at christenings, to adopt the dress of their foster-parents, whose language was in many cases the only one which they brought from their foster-home.

Thus Ireland, even in districts which had been thoroughly devastated by the first invaders, became the old Ireland again; and the song of the bard and the melody of the harper were heard in the English castle as well as in the Irish rath.[1]

The nationalization of their kin, which received a powerful impetus from the fact that the English who lived without the Pale escaped feudal exactions and penalties from the impossibility of enforcing the feudal laws on Irish territory, alarmed the Anglo-Normans by birth, in whose hand rested the engine of the government; and, looking around for a remedy, they could discover nothing better than acts of Parliament.

---

[1] The process of gaining over an Englishman to Irish manners is admirably described in the "Moderate Cavalier," under Cromwell, quoted by Mr. J. P. Prendergast in his second edition of the "Cromwellian Settlement," p. 263. If this process were common with the Protestant officers of Cromwell, how much more so with Catholic Anglo-Normans!

We have not been able to ascertain the precise epoch in which the first Irish Parliament was convened; indeed, to this day, it seems a debated question. The general belief, however, ascribes it to King John. The first mention of it by Ware is under the year 1333, as late as Edward III., more than one hundred and fifty years after the Conquest. But the need of stringent rules to keep the Irish at bay, and prevent the English from "degenerating," became so urgent that, in 1367, the famous Parliament met at Kilkenny, and enacted the bill known as the "Statutes of Kilkenny," in which the matter was fully elaborated, and a new order of things set on foot in Ireland.

The Irish could recognize no other Parliament than their ancient Feis; and, these having been discontinued for several centuries, they showed their appreciation of the new English institution in the manner described by Ware under the year 1413: "On the 11th of the calends of February, the morrow after St. Matthias day, a Parliament began at Dublin, and continued for the space of fifteen days; in which time the Irish burned all that stood in their way, as their usual custom was in times of other Parliaments."

The reader who is acquainted with the enactments which go by the name of the "Statutes of Kilkenny" will scarcely wonder at this mode of proceeding.

Neither at that period, nor later on save once under Henry VIII., was the Irish race represented in those assemblies. In the reign of Edward III. no Irish native nor old English resident assisted at the Parliament of Kilkenny, but only Englishmen newly arrived; for all its acts were directed against the Irish and the degenerate English--against the latter particularly. How the members composing these Parliaments were elected at that time we do not know; but they were not summoned from more than twelve counties, which number, first established by King John, gradually dwindled, until, in the reign of Henry VII., it was reduced to four, so that the Irish Parliament came to be composed of a few men, and those few representatives of purely English interests.

A true history of the times would demand an examination of the various enactments made by these so-called Irish Parliaments, as setting forth more distinctly than any thing else could do the points at variance between the two nations. Our space, however, and indeed our purpose, forbids this. In order to put the reader in possession of at least an idea of the difficulties on either side, we add a few extracts from the very famous "Statutes of Kilkenny."

The preamble sets forth "that already the English in Ireland were mere Irish in their language, names, apparel, and their manner of living, and had rejected the English laws and submitted to the Irish, with whom they had many marriages and alliances, which tended to the utter ruin and destruction of the commonwealth." And then the Statutes go on to enact --we cull from various chapters: "The English cannot any more make peace or war with the Irish without special warrant; it is made penal to the English to permit the Irish to send their cattle to graze upon their land; the Irish could not be presented by the English to any ecclesiastical benefice; they--the Irish--could not be received into any monasteries or religious houses; the English could not entertain any of their bards, or poets, or shanachies, " etc.

This extraordinary legislation proves beyond any amount of facts to what degree the posterity of the first Norman invaders of Ireland had adopted Irish customs, and made themselves one with the natives.

The Irish, therefore, had, in this instance, morally conquered their enemies, and feudalism was defeated. Another example was given of the invariable invasions of the island. The enemy, however successful at the beginning, was compelled finally to give way to the force of resistance in this people; and the time-honored customs of an ancient race survived all attempts at iolent foreign innovations. The posterity of those proud nobles, who, with Giraldus Cambrensis, had found nothing but what was contemptible in this nation, so strange to their eyes, who looked upon them as an easy victim to be despoiled of their land, and that land to be occupied by them, that posterity adopted, within, comparatively speaking, a few years, the life and manners of the mere Irish in their entirety. Feudalism they renounced for the clan. Each of the great English families that first landed in the island had formed a new sept, and the clans of the Geraldines, De Courcys, and others, were admitted into full copartnership with the old Milesian septs. This the two great families of the Burkes in Connaught called their chiefs McWilllams Either and McWilliams Oughter. The Berminghams bad become McYoris; the Dixons, McJordans; the Mangles, McCostellos. Other old English families were called McHubbard,

McDavid, etc.; one of the Geraldine septs was known as McMorice, another as McGibbon; the chief of Dunboyne's house became McPheris.

Meanwhile, "it was manifest," says Sir John Davies, "that those who had the government of Ireland under the crown of England intended to make a perpetual separation and enmity between the English settled in Ireland and the Irish, in the expectation that the English should in the end root out the Irish."

There is no doubt that, if these laws of Kilkenny could have been enforced and carried out, as they were meant to be, the effect hoped for by these legislators might have been the natural result. Yet even much later on, at a period, too, when the English power was considerably increased, under Henry VIII., a very curious discussion of this possibility, which took place at the time, did not by any means promise an easy realization. The following passage of the "State Papers," under the great Tudor, contains a rather sensible view of the subject, and is not so sanguine of the success of the hopes cherished by the attorney-general of James I.:

"The lande is very large--by estimation as large as Englande--so that, to enhabit the whole with new inhabiters, the number would be so great that there is no prince christened that commodiously might spare so many subjects to depart out of his regions. . . . But to enterprise the whole extirpation and totall destruction of all the Irishmen of the lande, it would be a marvellous and sumptuous charge and great difficulty, considering both the lack of enhabitors, and the great hardness and misery these Irishmen can endure, both of hunger, colde, and thirst, and evill lodging, more than the inhabitants of any other lande."

There were, therefore, evidently difficulties in the way; yet it is certain that the question of the total extirpation of the Irish has been entertained for centuries by a class of English statesmen, and confidently looked for by the English nation. Sir John Davies, as we see, attributes no other object to the Statutes of Kilkenny.

But could those statutes be enforced? were they ever enforced? The same writer pretends that they were for "several years;" but the sequel proves that they were not. The reason which he assigns for their execution--that for a certain time after that Parliament there was peace in the island-- leads us to believe the contrary; for if, as he himself justly remarks before, the intention of the legislators was to create a perpetual separation and enmity between the two races, the promulgation and strict execution of those statutes would have immediately enkindled a war which could have ended only with the total extirpation of one race or the other.

And the further fact that it was thought necessary to reenact those odious laws frequently in subsequent Irish Parliaments proves that they were not carried into execution, since new legislation on the subject was demanded.

It is true that events, transmitted to us either through the Irish annals or the English chronicles, show that several attempts were made to enforce those acts of Kilkenny, chiefly against the Fitz-Thomases or Geraldines of Desmond, who pretended, even after their enactment, to be as independent of them as before, and refused to attend the Parliament when convoked, claiming the strange privilege "that the Earls of Desmond should never come to any Parliament or Grand Council, or within any walled town, but at their will or pleasure." And the Desmonds continued in their persistent opposition to the English laws until the reign of Elizabeth.

But it was against Churchmen chiefly that they were carried out in full; for we occasionally meet in the annals of the country with instances where some English prelate in Ireland had been prosecuted for having conferred orders on mere Irishmen, and that some Norman abbots had been deposed for having received mere Irishmen as monks into their monasteries.

With the exception of a few cases of this kind, no proof can be furnished that any material change was brought about in the relations of the old English settlers with their Irish neighbors. In fact, matters progressed so favorably in this friendly direction, that at length the descendants of Strongbow and his followers became, as is well known, "Hibernis Hiberniores," and the judges sent from England could hold their circuit only in the four counties between the Liffey and the Boyne; and the name given to the majority of the old English families was "English rebels," while the natives were called "Irish enemies."

Sir John Davies himself is forced to admit it: "When the civil government grew so weak and so loose that the English lords would not suffer the English laws to be executed within their territories and seigniories, but in place thereof both they and their people embraced the Irish customs, then the state of things, like a game at Irish, was so turned about, that the English, who hoped to make a perfect conquest of the Irish, were by them perfectly and absolutely conquered, because Victi victoribus leges dedere."

The truth could not be expressed in more explicit terms. Yet all has not been said. The same persevering character, making headway against apparently insurmountable obstacles, shows itself conspicuously in the Irish, in the preservation of their land, which, after all, was the great object of contention between the two races.

The first Anglo-Norman invaders, including Henry II himself, had no other object in view than gradually to occupy the whole territory, subject it to the feudal laws, give to Englishmen the position of feudal lords, and reduce the Irish to that of villeins, if they could not succeed in rooting them out.

A few years later, by the Treaty of Windsor, the king seemed to confine his pretensions to Leinster, and perhaps Meath, and expressly allowed the natives to keep their lands in the other districts of the island. Yet none of his former grants, by which "he had cantonned the whole island between ten Englishmen," were recalled; the continued as part of and means to shape the policy of the invaders, and subsequent Parliaments always supposed the validity of those former grants made to Strongbow and his followers.

It is true that those posterior Acts of Parliament did not merely rely for their strength on the first documents, but on the pretence that the Irish chieftains and people outside of Leinster and Meath had justly forfeited their estates by not fulfilling the conditions virtually contained in the Windsor Treaty, in which they had professed homage and submission to the English king. It is clear that, lawfully or unlawfully, the Anglo-Normans were determined to gain possession, sooner or later, of the whole island.

To secure their end, they declared that the natives would not be subject to the English laws, but retain their Brehon laws, which in their eyes were no laws at all, and which the Parliament of Kilkenny had declared to be "lewd customs." Henceforth, then, the natives were out of the pale of the law, could not claim its protection, but became subject to the crown of England, without political, civil, or even human rights.

They were soon, by reason of the constant border wars all around the Pale, declared "alien and enemies." And these expressions became, in the eyes of the English lawyers, identical with the Irish race and the Irish nature; so that at all times, peace or war, even when the Irish fought in the English ranks, aiding the Plantagenets in their furious contests with the Scotch or the French, they were still "Irish enemies;" "aliens" unworthy human rights, villeins in whose veins no noble blood could flow, with the exception of five families.

All the rest were not only ignoble, but not even men; nothing but mere Irish, whom any one might kill, even though serving under the English crown, at a risk of being fined five marks, to be paid to the treasury of the King of England, for having deprived his majesty of a serviceable tool.

This (to modern eyes) astounding social state demands a closer examination in order to see if, at least, it had the merit of finally procuring for the English the possession of the land they coveted.

We find first that Henry II., John, and Henry III., would seem on several occasions to have extended the laws of England all over the island. But all English legists will tell us that those laws were only for the inhabitants of English blood. The mere Irish were always reputed aliens, or, rather, enemies to the crown, so that it was, "by actual fact, often adjudged no felony to kill a mere Irish in time of peace," as Sir John Davies expressly points out.

Five families alone were excepted from the general category and acknowledged to be of noble blood--the O'Neills of Ulster, the O'Melachlins of Meath, the O'Connors of Connaught, the O'Briens of Munster, and the McMurroughs of Leinster.

Those five families, numerous certainly, but forming only as many septs, were, or appeared to be, acknowledged as having a right to their lands, and as able to bring or defend actions at law. We say, appeared to be, because they found themselves on so many occasions ranked as mere Irish, that individuals of those septs, induced by sheer necessity, were often driven, in spite of an almost invincible repugnance, to apply for and accept special charters of naturalization from the English kings. Thus in the reign of Edward IV., O'Neill, on the occasion of his marriage with a daughter of the house of Kildare, was made an English citizen by special act of Parliament.

In reality then, even the most illustrious members of the "five bloods" were scarcely considered as enjoying the full rights of the lowest English vassals, although their ancestors had been acknowledged kings by former Anglo-Norman monarchs in public documents: "Rex Henricus regi O'Neill," etc.

But if there was some shadow of doubt with regard to the political and social rights of those great families, such doubt did not exist for the remainder of the Irish race. They were absolutely without rights. Depriving them of their lands, pillaging their houses, devastating their farms, outraging their wives and daughters, killing them, could not subject the guilty to any civil or criminal action at law. In fact, as we have shown, such acts were in accordance with the spirit, even with the letter of the law, so that the criminal, as we should consider him, had but to plead that the man whom he had robbed or killed was a mere Irishman, and the proceedings were immediately stopped, if this all-important fact were proved; and in case of homicide the murderer escaped by the payment of the fine of five marks to the treasury.

To modern, even to English ears, all this may sound incredible. Many striking examples of the truth of it might be produced. They are to be found in all works which treat of the subject. Sir John Davies, that great Irish hater, evidently takes a genuine delight in depicting several such instances with all their aggravating details, scarcely expecting that every word he wrote would serve to brand forever with shame Anglo-Norman England.

Under such legislation it was clear that life on the borders of the Pale was not only insecure, but that the soil would remain in the grasp of the strongest. Any Anglo-Norman only required the power in order to take possession of the land of his neighbor.

But it is not in man's nature to submit to such galling thraldom as this, without at least an attempt at retaliation. Least of all was it the nature of such a people to submit to such measures--a nation, the most ancient in Europe, dating their ownership of the soil as far back as man's memory could go, civilized before Scandinavia became a nest of pirates, Christianized from the fifth century, and the spreader of literature, civilization, and the holy faith of Christ through England, Scotland, Germany, France, and Northern Italy.

If we have dwelt a little, and only a little, upon the intensity of the contest waged for four hundred years previous to the added atrocities introduced by the Reformation, we have done so advisedly, since it has become a fashion of late to throw a gloss over the past, to ignore it, to let the dead bury their dead--all which would be very well, could it be done, and could writers forget to stamp the Irish as unsociable, barbarous, and bloodthirsty, because with arms in their hands, and a fire ardent and sacred in their souls, they strove again and again to reconquer the territory which had been won from them by fraud, and because they thought it fair to kill in open fight the men who avowed that they could kill them even in peace at a penalty of five marks.

The contest, therefore, never ceased; how could it? But, in that endless conflict between the two races, the loss of territory leaned rather to the English side. If, with the help of their castles, better discipline, and arms, the English at first gained on the natives and extended their possessions beyond the Pale, a reaction soon set in--the Irish had their day of revenge, and entered again into possession of the land of which they had been robbed. In order to repair their losses, the Anglo-Normans had recourse to acts of Parliament, which could bind not only the English of the Pale, but also those of other districts, who, enjoying the privileges of English law, were likewise bound by its provisions.

In order rightly to understand the need and purposes of those enactments, we must return a moment to the days of the conquest.

The case of Strongbow will illustrate many others. He married Eva, the daughter of McMurrough, and thus allied himself to the best families of Leinster. On the death of his father-in-law, he received the whole kingdom as his inheritance. The greater part of his dominions, which he either would not or could not govern himself, he was compelled to distribute, in the usual style, among his followers. He distributed large estates as fiefs among those who had followed his fortunes, but he could not forget his Irish relatives, to whom he had become strongly attached. He secured, therefore, to many Irish families the territory which was formerly theirs, and many of his English adherents, who, like himself, had married daughters of the soil, did the same in their more limited territories. This explains fully why Irish families remained in Leinster after the settlement of the Anglo-Normans there, who established their Pale in it, as also why they continued to possess their lands in the midst of the English as they had formerly done in the midst of the Danes.

The same thing took place in the kingdom of Cork, on the borders of Connaught, and around the seaports of Ulster, wherever the English had established themselves and erected castles and fortifications.

But, over and above the Irish families, which, by their alliance by marriage and fosterage with the English, retained their lands and gradually increased them, many others, natives of the soil, reentered into possession of their former territory by the withdrawal of the Anglo-Norman holders of fiefs. Constant border wars, the necessary consequence of the English policy, could not but discourage in course of time many Englishmen, who, owning large possessions also in England and Wales, preferred to return to their own country rather than remain with their wives and children in a constant state of alarm, compelled to reside within their castles, in dread of an attack at any moment from their Irish neighbors.

Moreover, the vast majority of the Irish, who did not enjoy the benefit of these special privileges, who, deprived of their lands at the first invasion, had remained really outlaws, and never entered into matrimonial or social alliance with their enemies, these men could not consent to starve and perish on their own soil, in the island which they loved and from which they could not--had they so chosen--escape by emigration. One resource remained to them, and they grasped at it. They had their own mountain fastnesses and bogs to fly to, and from those recesses they could harass the invader, and inch by inch win back their lawful inheritance.

They were often even encouraged in their attacks and depredations by the English of the Pale and out of it, who, unwilling longer to submit to the grinding feudal laws and exactions, could prevent the English judges, sheriffs, escheators, and other king's officers from executing the law against them, and thus they held out in their mountains, bogs, and rocky crags, in the midst of the invaders of their soil.

A necessity arose then, on the part of the English rulers, of adopting measures calculated to prevent a further acquisition of territory by the

Irish, if not to extend the English settlements. They saw no other remedy than acts of Parliament, which they thought would at least prevent the subjects of English blood from assisting the Irish to reenter into possession, as was then being done on so extensive a scale.

To effect this they revived the former statutes by which the Irish were placed without the protection of the law, were declared aliens and enemies, and were consequently denied the right of bringing actions in any of the English courts for trespasses on their lands, or for violence done to their persons.

They soon advanced a step beyond this. The Irish were forbidden to purchase land, though the English were at liberty to occupy by force the landed property of the Irish, whenever they were strong enough to do so. An Irishman could acquire neither by gift nor purchase a rood of land which was the property of an Englishman. Thus, in every charter afterward granted to the few Irishmen who applied for them, it was expressly stated that they could purchase land for themselves and their heirs, which, without this special provision, they could not do; while for an Englishman to dispose of his landed property by will, gift, or sale to an Irishman, was equivalent to forfeiting his estate to the crown. The officers of the exchequer were directed by those acts of Parliament to hold inquisitions for the purpose of obtaining returns of such deeds of conveyance, in order to enrich the king's treasury by confiscations and forfeitures; and the statute-rolls, preserved to this day in Dublin and London, show that such prosecutions often took place, with the invariable result of forfeiture.

The decision of the courts was always in favor of the crown, even in cases where the deed of conveyance or will was of no benefit to the person in whose favor it was drawn, but simply a trust for a third person of English race. And the great number of cases in which the inquisitions were set aside, as appears from the Parliament-rolls, for the finding having been malicious and untrue--the parties complained of not being Irish but English--prove what we allege, namely, that an Irishman could not take land by conveyance from an Englishman.

Yet, as Mr. Prendergast justly says: "Notwithstanding these prohibitions and laws of the Irish Parliament, the Irish grew and increased upon the English, and the Celtic customs overspread the feudal, until at length the administration of the feudal law was confined to little more than the few counties lying within the line of the Liffey and the Boyne."

Let us now glance, in conclusion, at the result of more than four centuries of feudal oppression.

Ireland rejected feudalism from the beginning, and this at a time when Europe had been compelled to adopt it, more or less, throughout.

The distinction between lords and villeins, so marked in all other countries, remained at the end as it was at the beginning of the contest, a thing unknown in the island. Even in the Pale, the presence of the O'Moores, O'Byrnes, O'Kavanaghs, and other septs, protested against and openly denied, from moor and glen and mountain fastness, that outrage on humanity, which bestows on the few every thing meant for all. The Brehon law was in full force all over the island, and if the Irish allowed the English judges to ride on their circuits within the four counties, it was on the full understanding that they would administer their justice only to English subjects, and levy their feudal dues, and pronounce their forfeitures and confiscations on such only as acknowledged the king's right on the premises. The laws enacted in the pretended Irish Parliament were only for such as called themselves English by birth; for even the English by blood, whose ancestors had long resided on the island, frequently refused to submit to the laws of Parliament, where they would not sit themselves, although possessing the right to do so.

In vain was the threat of compulsion held up again and again before the eyes of the great lords of Desmond, Thomond, and Connaught. If they chose, they went; if they chose not, they remained at home; and obeyed or disobeyed at will the laws themselves, according as they were able or unable to set them at defiance.

The castles which had been built all over the country by the first invaders, as a means of awing into subjection the surrounding districts, were at the beginning of the fifteenth century no longer feudal castles. They had either been destroyed and levelled to the ground by the Irish, or they were occupied by Irish chieftains; or, stranger still, if their holders were English lords, they were of those who had been won over to Irish manners. In their halls all the old customs of Erin were preserved. One saw therein groups of shanachies, and harpers, and Brehon lawyers, all conversing with their chieftain in the primitive language of the country. Hence were they called degenerate by the "foreigners" living in Dublin Castle. The mansions of the Desmonds, of the Burgos, of the Ormonds, were the headquarters of their respective clans, not the inaccessible fortresses of steel-clad warriors, who alone were possessed of social and civil rights. If the master of the household held sometimes the title of earl, or count, or baron, he was careful never to use it before his retainers, whom he called his clansmen. When he went to Dublin or to London, he donned it with the dress of a knight or a great feudal lord; on his return home he threw it aside, resumed the cloak of the country, and was Irish again.

The subject of feudal titles in Ireland has not been sufficiently studied and elucidated. A clearer light thrown on this question would, we have no doubt, show more conclusively than long discussions with what stubbornness the Irish refused to submit to the reality of feudalism, even when consenting to admit its presence and phraseology. It is a fact not sufficiently dwelt upon, that the few Irishmen, who subsequently consented to receive English titles from the king, were regarded by their countrymen with greater abhorrence than the English themselves, though in most cases the titles were empty ones, which affected nothing in their mode of life. Yet were they looked upon as apostates to their nation, and after the Reformation such a step was often the first to apostasy of religion, the deepest stain on an Irish name.

Feudalism had also its mode of taxation which failed with the rest in Ireland.

In feudal countries the lord imposed no tax on his villeins; these were mere chattels, ascripti gleboe, who tilled the land for their masters, and, as good serfs, could own nothing but the few utensils of their miserable hovels. They were just allowed what sufficed to support their own life and that of their families, and consequently they could bear no additional tax. But, in the complicated state of society brought about by feudalism, the inferior lord was taxed by his superior, a system that ran down the whole feudal scale, and it would take a lawyer to explain aids, talliages, wardships, fines for alienation, seizins, rents, escheats, and finally forfeiture, the heaviest and most common of all in England.

The Irish fought valiantly against the imposition of those burdens, and aided the English settled among them to repudiate them all in course of time.

It must be said, however, that they did not succeed in preventing their own taxes, according to the Book of Rights, from becoming heavier under the ingenuity of the English who were established among them and admitted to all the rights of clanship. We see by documents which have been better studied of late, that the great Anglo-Irish lords had succeeded in increasing the burdens in the shape of exactions, which were never complained of by the Irish.

On this subject Dr. O'Donovan, in the preface to his edition of the "Book of Rights," is worthy of perusal.

But it is chiefly in the very essence of feudalism that the failure of the Anglo-Normans was most signal. Feudalism really consisted in the status given to the land, the possession of which determined and gave all rights, so that, according to it, man was made for the land rather than the land for man. He was placed on the land with the beasts of the field as far as tillage and production went, until the system should round to perfection and finally bring to the surface the new principles of social economy, according to which the greater the number of cattle and the fewer the number of men, the more prosperous and happy might the country be said to be.

The Irish staked their existence against those principles, and won. So complete was their victory that the feudal barons who first came among them finally yielded to clanship, became the chiefs of new clans, and opened their territories to all who chose to send their horses and kine to graze in the chief's domains. In vain did Irish Parliaments issue writs of forfeiture against the English lords who acted thus, for between the law and its execution the clans intervened, and no sheriff or judge could step beyond the bounds of the four counties of the Pale to enforce those acts.

It is told of one of the Irish chieftains that on receiving intimation from a high English official of a sheriff's visit on the next breach of some new law or ordinance, for the safety of which sheriff he would be held responsible, he replied: "You will do well to let me know at the same time what will be the amount of his eric, in case of his murder, that I may beforehand assess it on the clan."

This story may tend better than any thing else to give a clear reason for the failure of feudalism in Ireland.

IRELAND SEPARATED FROM EUROPE.-A TRIPLE EPISODE

WHILE the struggle described in the last chapter was raging, Ireland could have little or no intercourse with the rest of Europe. Heaven alone was witness of the heroism displayed by the free clans wrestling with feudal England. It was only during the internecine wars of the Roses that Erin enjoyed a respite, and then we read that Margaret of Offaly summoned to peaceful contest the bards of the island, while the shrines of Rome and Compostella were thronged with pilgrims, chiefs, and princes, "paying their vows of faith from the Western Isle."

In the mean time Christendom had been witness of mighty events in which Ireland could take no part. The enthusiastic impulse which gave birth to the Crusades, the uprising of the communes against feudal thraldom, the mental activity of numerous universities, starting each day into life, form, among other things, the three great progressive waves in the moving ocean of the time:

I. When Europe in phalanx of steel hurled itself upon Asia and saved Christendom from the yoke of Islam, when the Japhetic race by a mighty effort asserted its right not merely to existence, but to a preponderance in the affairs of the world, Ireland, the nation Christian of Christians, had not a name among men. It was supposed to be a dependency of England, and the envoys sent abroad to all parts by the Holy See to preach the Crusades, never touched her shores to deliver the cross to her warriors. The most chivalrous nation of Christendom was altogether forgotten, and in its ecclesiastical annals no mention is made of the Crusades even by name.

The holy wars, moreover, were set on foot and carried on by the feudal chivalry of Europe, and in fact, wherever the Europeans established their power in the East, that power took the shape of feudalism. But Ireland had rejected this system, and consequently her sons could find no place in the ranks of the knights of Flaners, Normandy, Aquitaine, and England. Their chivalry was of another stamp, and was employed at the time in wresting their social state and territory from the grasp of ruthless invaders.

Hence, not even St. Bernard, the ardent friend of St. Malachi, remembered them, when journeying through Europe to distribute the Cross to whole armies of warriors. Not only did he fail to cross the Channel for the purpose of rousing the Christian enthusiasm of a people ever ready to hearken to a call to arms when a noble cause was at stake; he did not think even of writing a single letter to any bishop or abbot in Ireland, asking them to preach the holy war in his name.

Thus Ireland failed to participate in any of the benefits which accrued to the European nations from the Crusades, as she failed likewise to participate in results less beneficial which also accrued from that powerful agitation.

Among such results is one which has not met with all the attention it deserves. Historians speak at length of the many and wide-spread heresies which infected Europe during the middle ages; but their Eastern origin has not been thoroughly investigated, and we have no doubt that, if it had been, many of them would be found to have come with a returning wave of the Crusades.

All these errors bear at the outset a very Oriental appearance. Paulicians, Petrobrusians, Albigensians, and kindred sects, all started from the principle of dualism, and even at the time were openly accused of Manicheistic ideas. They all involved more or less immoral principles, and rejected, or at least strove to weaken, the commonly-received ideas upon which society, civil and religious, is founded. Had they succeeded in spreading their errors through Europe, it is possible that the invasion would have been more fatal in its consequences than that of Islamism itself. And, even in their failure, they left among European societies the germ of secret associations which have existed from that time down, and which in our days have burst forth undisguised to terrify nations, and cause them to dread the coming of the last days.

To an attentive observer it is clear that the heresies of the twelfth, thirteenth, and fourteenth centuries resemble more the errors of our days than the Protestantism which intervened. Luther's first principles, if carried to their legitimate conclusion, would have inaugurated the socialism and communism of modern times; but he shrank from the consequences of his own doctrines, and the necessity of his standing well with the German princes caused him, during the War of the Peasants, almost to retract his first utterances and take his stand midway between Catholic principles and the thorough nihilism of later times. It is known that in the after-part of his life he endeavored to repair the ruins of every dogma, social and religious, which he at first had tried to subvert and destroy.

The Manicheism of the middle ages was certainly not of so scientific and elaborate a nature as modern socialism; but it would have been productive of like evil results to society had it not been crushed down by the united power of the Church and the state. If it had been successful, it is impossible to imagine what would have become of Europe.

Of its Eastern origin historians say little. We know, however, that, after a residence in the East, the most pious Christians grew lukewarm and less firm in their opposition to the dangerous errors then prevalent in Asia. Tournefort remarked this in his own time, during the reign of Louis XIV.

It is known also that the posterity of the first crusaders in Palestine formed a hybrid race, which, weakened by the influence of the luxurious habits of Eastern countries, became corrupt, and under the name of Pulani practised a feeble Christianity, unfit to cope with the vigorous fanaticism of the Mussulman. Many Europeans came back from those wars wavering in faith, and no one knows how many with faith entirely lost.

It is not, therefore, too much to suppose that the Oriental errors which suddenly burst forth at this time in Western Europe followed in the wake of the returning pilgrims, and it is highly probable, if not absolutely certain, that, had there been no Crusades, Manicheism and the secret societies born of it would never have been known in Italy and France. Hence, one of the first and greatest champions of the Church in controversy with the Albigenses - Peter the Venerable, Abbot of Cluny - at the very beginning of the heresy, found no better means of opposing the new errors than attacking every thing coming from the East. Thus, he wrote his long treatises against the Talmud and the Koran, so much had the Crusades already contributed to introducing into Western Europe the seeds of Asiatic errors. All historians agree in giving an Eastern origin to the Paulicians, Bulgarians, Albigenses, and others of those times.

Manicheism indeed had infested Europe long before. Some Roman emperors had published severe edicts against it. In the fifth century, the heresy still flourished in Italy and Africa, St. Augustine himself being an adept for several years, and by his writings he has made us acquainted with its strongest supporters in his day. He was followed, in his attacks on it, by a great number of Fathers, both Greek and Latin.

But after the barbarian invasions we hear no more of the Manichees for upward of five hundred years. The West had entirely forgotten them. Arianism and Manicheism had apparently perished together. The tenth century is called a period of darkness and ignorance; it at least possessed the advantage of being free from heresy; the dogmas of the Church were unhesitatingly and universally accepted. Western Europe, though cut up by the new-born feudalism into a thousand fragments, was at least one in faith, until that great and powerful union having, in an outburst of enthusiasm, produced the Crusades, we suddenly find Eastern theories and immoralities invading the countries most faithful to the Church.

Raymond VI., Count of Toulouse, the great champion of the Albigenses, was the near descendant of that great Raymond, one of the chiefs of the first Crusade, who might have aspired to the throne of Jerusalem, had not Godfrey de Bouillon won the suffrages of the soldiers of the Cross by his ardent and pure piety. Raymond VI. dwelt in Languedoc, in all the luxurious splendor of an Eastern emir; and he doubtless found the doctrines of dualistic Manicheism more congenial to his taste for pleasure than the stern tenets of the Christian religion. Ambition, it is true, was one of the chief motives which prompted him to place himself at the head of the heretics; he hoped to enrich himself through them by the spoils of the Church; and thus the same power which later on moved the German princes to embrace Lutheranism was already acting on the aspiring Count of Toulouse at the beginning of the thirteenth century. Thus we find him at the head of his troops, plundering churches, ravaging monasteries, outraging and profaning holy things, for the purpose of filling his coffers.

Yet it is also certain that he, the chief of the sectarians, and a great number of the nobility of Southern France, were led to embrace the Albigensian error by the degrading habits which they had previously contracted.

We do not purpose entering into a lengthened discussion on the subject; we merely wish to contrast, with the wide spread of heresy in Western Europe, the great fact of a total absence of it in Ireland; or rather, we should say, and by so saying we confirm our reflection, that errors of a similar nature did invade the Pale in Erin at this time, without touching in any wise the children of the soil.

For, it is a remarkable fact that, at the beginning of the fourteenth century, the name of heresy is mentioned for the first and last time in Catholic Ireland; the new doctrines bearing a close resemblance to some of the errors of the Albigenses, and their chief propagators being all lords of the Pale.

In November of 1235, Pope Benedict XII. wrote a letter on this subject to Edward III. of England, which may be read in F. Brenan's Ecclesiastical History.

It is clear from many things related by Ware in his "Antiquities" that the Vicar of Christ, unable to follow freely his inclinations with respect to the filling of the sees of Erin, and obliged to appoint to bishoprics, at least in many parts of the island, only men of English birth, selected for that purpose members of the various religious orders then existing. Instead of granting episcopal jurisdiction to the feudal nominees of the court, when unworthy, Rome appointed a Franciscan, or a Dominican, a member of some religious community, who was born in England, but at least more independent of the court, of greater sympathy with the people, less swayed by worldly and selfish motives, and consequently readier to obey the mandates of Rome, which were always on the side of justice and morality. Thus we find that in the whole history of Ireland, as a general rule, the bishops chosen from religious orders were acceptable to the people, and true to their duty.

Such a man certainly was Richard Ledred, a Minorite, born in London, whom the Pope made Bishop of Ossory. But on that very account he incurred the hatred of many English officials, and even of worldly prelates, among whom Alexander Bicknor, Archbishop of Dublin, was the most conspicuous. Bieknor was not only archbishop, but had been appointed Lord Justice of Ireland by the king, and later on Lord Deputy; later still he was dispatched by the English Parliament as ambassador to France.

"It had been well," says F. Brenan, "for the archbishop himself, and for those immediately under his jurisdiction, had he abstained from mixing himself up with the state affairs of those times. Ambition formed no inferior trait in the character of Alexander, even long before he had been exalted to a high dignity in the Church. He advanced rapidly into power, stepping from one office into another, until at length he found himself in the midst of the labyrinth, without being able to make his way, unless by means of guides as inexperienced as they were treacherous. It was by causes such as these that he brought himself into serious difficulties, not only with the Archbishop of Armagh, on account of the primacy, but also with his own suffragans, and particularly with the Bishop of Ossory."

Under these circumstances it was that the prelate last mentioned, on visiting his diocese, found unmistakable signs of the spread of heresy among his flock. His diocese at that time formed a part of the English Pale, and Kilkenny, where he had his cathedral, was often the seat of Parliament.

Among those most active for the propagation of the new doctrines were found, the Seneschal of Kilkenny, the Treasurer of Ireland, and the Chief-Justice of the Common Pleas--all English of the Pale. The zealous bishop, fearless of the consequences, openly denounced them, and publicly excommunicated the Treasurer. At once a terrible storm was raised among their English abettors, and, in order to screen the guilty parties, they recriminated against the prelate, and accused him of being a sharer in the crime of Thomas Fitzgilbert, who had burned the castle of Moy Cahir, and killed its owner, Hugh Le Poer. The temporalities of Ledred having been already sequestrated for his boldness in denouncing heretics, he was compelled finally to leave his diocese and fly to Avignon, where he remained in exile for nine years.

The Archbishop of Dublin had been one of his bitterest enemies, and, although not actually accused of heresy himself, he was certainly the abettor of heretics, and had done all in his power to have Ledred arrested for his supposed crimes.

Ware, in his lives of Bicknor and Ledred, is evidently a partisan of the first and an enemy of the second. He pretends that Ledred tacitly acknowledged his guilt in the affair of Le Poer, since he sued for pardon to the king, as though readers of English history did not constantly meet with instances of innocent men compelled to sue for pardon of crimes which they had never committed.

We have fortunately better judges of the characters of both prelates in the two popes, Benedict XII. and Clement VI.: the first believing in the existence of the heresy denounced by Ledred; the second exempting the Bishop of Ossory from the superior jurisdiction of Bicknor, on account of the unjust animosity displayed toward him by this worldly prelate.

The absence of all historical documents in reference to the case leaves us at a loss to know the effect produced on Edward III. by the letter of the Pontiff. It is highly probable that the king preferred to believe Bicknor rather than the Pope, and disregarded the advice of the latter.

In such an event, how was the heresy put down? Simply by the good sense and spirit of faith of the people, or rather by the deep Christian feeling of the native Irish, who were always opposed to innovation, and who remained firm in the traditional belief inherent in the nation by the grace of God. Schism and heresy seem impossible among the children of Erin. If at any time certain novelties have appeared among them, they have speedily vanished like empty vapor. They heard that, in other parts of the Church, in the East chiefly, heresiarchs had arisen and led away into error large numbers of people forming sometimes formidable sects, which threatened the very existence of the religion of Christ; but the face of a heretic they had never beheld. Soon, indeed, they were to be at the mercy of a whole swarm of them, to see a pretended church leagued with the state to bring about their perversion; but as yet they had had no experience of the kind.

Only a few heretics were pointed out to them by the finger of one of their bishops, and his denunciations were confirmed by the judgment of the Holy See. Hence, according to F. Brenan, "the sensation which pervaded all classes became vehement and frightful. The bishop and his clergy came forward, and by solid argument, by the strength and power of truth, opposed and discomfited the enemies of religion."

The feeling here expressed is a natural one for a true Christian at the very mention of heresy. Yet how few nations have experienced a sensation "vehement and frightful" at the appearance of positive error among them!

But, at all periods of their history, such has been the feeling of the Irish people.

Fortunately for them, the number of sectarians was so small as to become insignificant; the English of the Pale were always few in comparison with the natives, and heresy had been, adopted by only a small body.

Error, therefore, could not cause in the island the social and political convulsions which it had produced in France about the same time. There was no need of a second Albigensian war to put it down. There was no need even of the Inquisition, as an ecclesiastical tribunal. The sentence of the bishop, the decree of excommunication pronounced from the foot of the altar, was all that was required.

When we compare this single fact of Irish ecclesiastical history with what was then transpiring in Europe--the most insidious errors spreading throughout; the faith of many becoming unsettled, a general preparation for the social deluge which was impending and so soon to fall--we cannot but conclude that Ireland, in the midst of her misfortunes, was happy in being separated from the rest of the world. The breath of novelty could breathe no contagion on her shores. Happy even was she in not seeing her sons enlist in the army of the Cross, if the result of their victories was, to bring back from the Holy Land the Eastern corruption and the many heresies nestling there and settled, even around the sepulchre of our Lord, during so many ages of separation from the West and open communication with all the wild vagaries of Arabian, Persian, and Indian philosophies.

Even in the midst of such a trial we believe that Ireland would have held steadfast to her faith, as she did later on when heresy came to her with compulsion or death; and this firmness of purpose, which the Irish have always manifested when the question was a change of religion, is worthy our consideration. For the facility with which some nations have, in the course of ages, yielded to the spirit of novelty, and the sturdy resistance opposed to it by others, is a subject that would repay investigation, but which we can only slightly touch upon.

In ancient times the Greek mind, accustomed from the beginning to subtlety of argument, and easily carried away by a rationalism which was innate, offers a striking contrast to the steady traditional spirit of the Latin races in general. Except Pelagiaism and its cognate errors, all the great heresies which afflicted the Church during the first ten centuries, originated in the East; and the various sects catalogued by several of the Greek Fathers, as early as the second and third centuries, astonish the modern reader by the slender web on which their often ridiculous systems are spun, of texture strong enough, however, at the time to form the groundwork for making a disastrous impression on a large number of adherents. The infinity almost of philosophical systems in pagan Greece had prepared the way for the subsequent vagaries of heresy, and we must look to our own times, so prolific of absurd theories, in order to find a parallel to the incredible variety of dogmatic assertions among the Greek heresiarchs of early times.

But, at the outbreak of Protestantism, in the sixteenth century, the world witnessed a still more striking example of diversity in the various branches of the Japhetic family - the nations belonging to the Teutonic and Scandinavian stocks chiefly embracing the error at once with a wonderful spontaneity. The various remnants of the Celtic race and the totality of the Latin nations remained, on the whole, obedient to the guiding voice of the Church of Christ. It is customary with modern writers, when imbued with what are called liberal ideas, to ascribe this difference to the steady, systematic mind of northern nations, and to their innate love of liberty, which could not brook the yoke of spiritual despotism imposed by the Church of Rome. But all this is mere supposition, inadequate to accounting for the fact. The Teutonic and Scandinavian mind is certainly more systematic and apparently more steady than the Celtic; but it is far less so than the Latin. No nation in the whole history of mankind has ever displayed more steadiness and system than the Romans, and the Latin family has inherited those characteristics from Rome. The Spanish race has no equal in steadiness (in the sense here intended of steadfastness), and the French certainly none in system, which it often carried to the verge of absurdity.

As for love of liberty, as distinct from love of license, it had absolutely nothing to do with the great revolution which has been called the Reformation. No nation can relish despotism, and the whole history of Ireland is a living example that her sons are steadily opposed to it to the death. And it is now too late to pretend that the cause of true liberty has been served by the spread of Protestantism over a large portion of Europe. Balmez and others have proved the falsehood of such pretensions. If any modern writers, such as Mr. Bancroft, for instance, men otherwise of sound mind and great ability, continue to assert this, the assertion must proceed from prejudice deeply ingrained, which reflection has not yet succeeded in eradicating, and their opinions on the subject are necessarily confined to bold assertions, of a character which in others they themselves would stigmatize as empty and unfounded.

The reason of the difference lies deeper in the constitution of the human mind, in the Celtic and Latin races on the one side, in the Teutonic and Scandinavian families on the other. Any one who has studied the Irish character in our days--a character which was the same in former ages--will easily see something of that great and happy cause.

The difference lies first in the good sense which enables them to perceive instinctively that the eternal should be preferred to the temporal. If all men kept that distinct perception ever present to their minds, they would not only accept at all times the truths of faith, since faith, according to St. Paul, is "the substance of the things hoped for," but they would remain ever faithful to the moral code given us by God. The Celt indeed will at times lose sight of the eternal in the presence of a temporal temptation; but he is never blind to the knowledge that faith is the groundwork of salvation, and that hope remains as long as that is not surrendered. Therefore he will never surrender it. The need of reviving his faith is rarely called for, when, after a life of sin, the shadow of death reminds him of the duty he owes his own soul. The great truth that, after all, the ETERNAL is every thing, remains always deeply impressed on his mind; and half his labor is spared to the minister of God, when bringing such a man back to a life of virtue. There is scarcely any need of asking an Irishman, "Do you believe?" For, every word that passes his lips, every look and gesture, every expression of feeling, is in fact an act of faith. How easy after this is the work of regeneration!

O happy race, to whom this life is in truth a shadow that passeth away! to whom the unseen is ever present, or comes back so vividly and so readily!

This supposes, as we have said, a sound, good sense, which is characteristic of the race. We may say that this nation possesses the wisdom of Sir Thomas More, who esteemed it folly to lose eternity for a life of twenty years of ease and honors. Is not this, at bottom, the thought which has sustained the nation in that dread martyrdom of three centuries, whose terrible story we have still to tell? Have they not, as a nation, one after another, generation upon generation, lived and passed their lives in contempt, in want, in frightful misery, to die in torments or hidden sufferings, without a gleam of hope from this world for their race, their families, their children, their very name, because they would not surrender their religion, that is to say, truth, which alone could secure the eternal welfare of their souls?

Speak to us, after this, of a steady and systematic mind! Prate to us of the love of liberty, of self-dignity! Where are such things to be found in their reality, on their trial, if not in the scenes and the nation we have just pictured?

A second reason, no less effective, perhaps, than the first, and certainly as remarkable, is the very composition of the Celtic mind, which naturally tends to firm belief, because it is given exclusively to traditions, past events, narratives of poets, historians, and genealogists. Had the Irish at any time turned themselves to criticise, to doubt, to argue, their very existence, as a people, would have ceased. They must go on believing, or all reality vanishes from their minds, accustomed for so many ages to take in that solid knowledge founded, it is true, on hearsay; but how else can truth reach us save by hearsay? Hence, their simple and artless acquiescence in any thing they hear from trustworthy lips - acquiescence ever refused to a known enemy, never to a well-tried friend, even when the facts ascertained are strange, mysterious, unaccounted for, and incredible to minds differently constituted.

Thus, when we read their "Acta Sanctorum," we at once find ourselves in a world so different from our every-day world - a region of wonders, mysteries, of heavenly and supernatural deeds, unequalled in any story of marvellous travel or fable of imaginative romance. Yet, who will say that the writers doubted a single phrase of what they wrote? Is it not clear, from the very words they use, that they would have held it sacrilege to utter a falsehood, when speaking of the blessed saints? And, can the lives of the saints be like those of common mortals? What is there strange in considering that the earth was mysterious and heavenly, when heavenly beings walked upon it? Read the Litany and Festology of Aengus, and doubt if the holy man did not believe all therein contained. Say, if it can be possible, that it is not all true, though apparently incredible. Who can doubt what is asserted with such vehemence of belief? How can that fail to be true which holy men and women have themselves believed, and given to the world to be believed?

This thoroughly explains the simplicity of faith which still distinguishes the Irish people. It explains why no heretic could be found among them, and their intense horror of heresy as soon as known. Nor is it their mind alone which bears the impress of faith: their very exterior is a witness to it. Go into any large city where dwell a number of Irish inhabitants; walk through the public streets, where they walk among the children of other races, and you will easily distinguish them, not only by the modesty of their women and the simple bearing of their men, but by the look of confidence and contentedness stamped on their features. Whoever has a settled faith, is no longer an inquirer, no longer troubled with the anxiety and restlessness of a man plunged in doubt and uncertainty; all the lineaments of the face, all the gestures and attitudes of the body, speak of quietude and repose.

We might render this discussion more effective by the study of the contrary phenomena, by showing how easily races, differently gifted, endowed with the spirit of criticism and argument, sever from the faith and follow the lead of deceptive teachers. Our object here was to describe the Irish, and not to enter into a study of the physiology of other minds; but a word on Germanic and Scandinavian tribes and peoples may not be amiss.

There is no doubt that these races place their "good sense" in a very different line from the Irish; that they are, also, much more given to criticism, what they call "grumbling," and absence of repose.

With regard to the first point - their "good sense" - it is easy to remark their tendency to prefer the temporal to the eternal. For their "good sense" consists in enjoying the things of this life without troubling themselves over-much about another. And, in this observation, there is nothing which can possibly offend them, for such is their open profession and estimate of true wisdom. Hence result their love of comfort, their thrift, their shrewdness in all material and worldly affairs; hence, their constant boasting about their civilization, understanding, thereby, what is pleasing to the senses; hence, also, their success in a life wherein they set their whole happiness. How could they be expected to remain steadfast to a faith which declares war to pleasure, and speaks only of contempt for this world? It is not matter of surprise, then, that their great argument, to prove that theirs is the better and the right religion, is to compare their physical well-being with the inferiority in that regard of Catholic nations.

With regard to the spirit of criticism and argumentation, nothing is so opposed to the spirit of faith; and it is as clear as day that the northern races possess this in an eminent degree. What question, religious or philosophical, can rest intact when brought under the microscopic vision of a German philosopher or an English rationalist? A few years more of criticism, as now understood and practised by them, would leave absolutely nothing which the mind of man could respect and believe.

An attentive observer will surely conclude, after a serious examination of the subject, that it is from petty causes of this character that these races have so easily surrendered their faith, rather than from their systematic minds and love of liberty.

II. The rising of the communes, one of the greatest features of mediaeval Europe, did not extend to Ireland, separated as it then was from the Continent. But, by reason of this very separation, the island remained forever free from the future political commotions of what is known as "the third estate." A few remarks on this subject are requisite, because of the objection brought against the Irish, that they have never known municipal government, and also on account of the false assertions of some philosophical historians, who allege that the Danes and Anglo-Normans, in turn, wrought a great good to Ireland by bringing with them the boon of citizen rights.

What were the causes of the rising of the communes in the eleventh and following centuries? The universality of the fact argues identity of motives, since, without common understanding among various nations, the risings showed themselves at about the same time in Italy, France, Germany, Spain, and England.

In ancient cities, which existed prior to the Germanic invasions, the population, after the scourge had passed, was composed principally of three elements: 1. Free men of the conquering races, who were poor, and had embraced some mechanical pursuit; 2. The remnants of the Roman population, who followed some trade; 3. Freedmen from the rural districts, who, unable to gain a livelihood in the country, had come to reside in the cities, where they could more easily subsist.

Thus, besides the feudal lords and the class of villeins, there was formed everywhere a third class, that of arts and trades.

The juridical power being restricted to the lords, whose rights extended only to the land and the men attached to it, the class of artisans found themselves destitute of legal rights, without a recognition or place even in the jurisprudence, as then existing, consequently in a practically anarchical state. Hence, they formed among themselves their own associations, elected their own magistrates, enacted their own by-laws.

In the cities we have mentioned, the bishop alone held social relations with the lords, whether the feudal chieftain of the vicinity, or the Count of the city. Thus, the bishop often acted as the mediator between the citizens and the privileged class which surrounded them. The great object of the citizens was to obtain a charter of rights from the suzerain, who alone could act with justice and impartiality toward those disfranchised burghers. To this was owed the immense number of charters granted at that time, many of which, lately published, tend better than any thing else to give us an insight into the origin of municipal life in mediaeval Europe.

New cities, either founded by the invaders or springing up of themselves around feudal castles and monasteries, soon experienced the necessity of similar favors, which, as soon as obtained, invested them with a social status unenjoyed before.

The number of freemen, reduced to poverty, or of recent freedmen - freed by the emancipation everywhere set on foot and encouraged by the Church - extended the spread of communes even to the rural districts. Thus, many villages or small towns grew into corporations, and a social state arose, hitherto totally unknown in Europe.

The question has been much discussed, whether those new municipal corporations owed their origin to the municipal system of the Romans, or were altogether disconnected with it. The opinion commonly now accepted is, that the two systems were utterly distinct. In some few instances, a particular Roman municipal city may have passed into a mediaeval corporate town under a new charter and with extended rights; but this was certainly the exception. In the great majority of cases, the newly-chartered cities had never before enjoyed municipal rights.

These few words suffice to show that the communes, wherever they arose, presupposed the existence of feudalism, and the slavery once so widely extended, passing gradually into serfdom.

But neither feudalism nor slavery, in the old pagan sense of the word, nor even serfdom, properly so called, as the doom of the ascripti glebae, ever existed in Ireland. There was, therefore, no need among the Irish for the rising of communes.

Nevertheless, we do find communes existing in Ireland and charters granted to Irish cities by English kings. But they were merely English institutions for the special benefit of the English of the Pale, which were always refused to "the Irish enemy," and which the "Irish enemy," with the exception of a few individual cases, never demanded. Consequently the fact stands almost universally true that the rising of the communes never extended to Ireland, and that, if the Irish never enjoyed the benefit of them, as little did they share in the evil consequences resulting from them.

All those evil consequences had their root in a feeling of bitter hostility between the higher or noble classes, and not only the villeins, whom they ground between them, but also the middle classes, who were dwelling in the cities, emancipating themselves by slow degrees, and forming in course of time the "third estate."

The workings of that hostility form a great part of the history of Europe from the twelfth century down to the present day, and many social convulsions, recorded in the annals of the six ages preceding our own, may be traced to it. The frightful French Revolution was certainly a result of it, although it must be granted that several secondary causes contributed to render the catastrophe more destructive, the chief among which was the spread of infidel doctrines among the higher and middle classes.

But our days witness a still more awful spectacle, the persistent array of the poor against the rich in all countries once Christian, and this may be traced directly to their mediaeval origin now under our consideration; and, the evils preparing for mankind therefrom, future history alone will be able to tell.

In Ireland, this has never been the danger. In the earlier constitution of the nation, there could be no rivalry, no hostility of class with class, as there never existed any social distinction between them; and if, in our days, the poor there as elsewhere seem arrayed against the rich, it is not as class against class, but as the spoiled against the spoiler, the victim against the robber, against the holders of the soil by right of confiscation--a soil upon which the old owners still live, with all the traditions of their history, which have never been completely effaced, and which in our days are springing into new life under the studies of patriotic antiquarians. This fact cannot be denied.

The case of Ireland is so different in this respect from that of other nations, that in no other country have the people been reduced to such a degrading state of pauperism, yet in no other country is the same submission to the existing order of society found among the lower classes. No communism, no socialism has ever been preached there, and, were it preached, it would only be to deaf ears. Until the last two or three centuries, no seed of animosity between high and low, rich and poor, had been sowed in Ireland. The reason of this we have seen in a previous chapter. And if, since the wholesale confiscations of the seventeenth century, the country has been divided into two hostile camps, the fault has never laid with the poor, the despoiled; they have always been the victims, and never uttered open threats of destruction against their oppressors. If in the future men look to great calamities, Ireland is the only quarter from which nothing of the kind is to be feared, and the impending revolution by which she may profit will look to her for no assistance in the subversion of society.

We now leave the reader to appreciate to its full extent the real value of the opinion of modern writers who would justify the successive invasions of the Danes and Anglo-Normans, and also, we suppose, of the Puritans, as praiseworthy attempts to introduce into Ireland the municipal system, so productive of good elsewhere throughout Europe.

There is no doubt that municipal rights have been of immense advantage to European society, as constituted at the time of their introduction. They formed the germ of a new class, destined to be the ruling class of the world, by whom human rights were first to be understood and proclaimed, and the necessary amount of freedom granted to all and secured by just laws justly administered. Christianity is the true source of all those rights, as Christian morality ought to be their standard.

But what an amount of human misery was first required, in order that such blessed results might follow, merely because religion, which was and ever had been steadily working to the same end, was altogether set aside, and its assistance even despised in the mighty change! And after all--we might say in consequence--how limited has the boon practically become! How few are the nations, even in our days, which understand impartiality, moderation, justice! How soon will mankind become sufficiently enlightened to settle down peacefully in the enjoyment of those blessings of civil liberty proclaimed and trumpeted to the four winds of heaven, yet in no place rightly understood and equitably shared?

Ireland never knew those municipal rights from which have flowed so many evils, side by side with so few blessings, because their essential elements were never found there. What the future may develop, no man can say. It is time, however, for all to see that the nation is equal to any rights to which men are said to be entitled.

III. The great intellectual movement set on foot in Europe during the middle ages, by the numerous universities which sprang up everywhere, under the fostering care of Popes or Christian monarchs, failed to reach the island, in consequence of its exclusion from the European family; yet even this was not for her an unmitigated evil, though certainly the greatest loss she sustained. While Europe, during the eighth and ninth centuries, was in total darkness, Ireland alone basked in the light of science, whose lustre, shining in her numerous schools, attracted thither by its brightness the youth of all nations, whom she received with a generosity unbounded. Not content with this, she sent forth her learned and holy men to spread the light abroad and dispel the thick darkness, to establish seats of learning as focuses whence should radiate the light of truth on a world buried in barbarism.

And when the warm sunshine, created or kept alive by her, sheds its rays on Italy, on France, on Germany, and England itself, all her own schools are closed, her once great universities destroyed. Clonard, Clonfert, Armagh, Bangor, Clonmacnoise, are desolate, and the wealthy Anglo-Norman prelates find their purses empty when the question arises of restoring or forming a single centre of intellectual development. The natural consequences should have been darkness, barbarism, gross ignorance. Ireland never fell to that depth of spiritual desolation. Her sons, though deprived of all exterior help, would still feed for centuries on their own literary treasures. All the way down to the Stuart dynasty, the nation preserved, not only her clans, her princes, and her brehon laws, but also her shanachies, her books, her ancient literature and traditions. These the feudal barons could not rob her of; and if they would not repay her, in some measure, for what they took away, by flooding her with the new methods of thought, of knowledge, of scientific investigation, at least they could not destroy her old manuscripts, wipe out from her memory the old songs, snatch the immortal harp from the hands of her bards, nor silence the lips of her priests from giving vent to those bursts of impassioned eloquence which are natural to them and must out. Hence there was no tenth century of darkness for her--let us bear this in mind--light never deserted her, but continued to shine on her from within, despite the refusal of her masters to unlock for her the floodgates of knowledge.

For this reason was it not to her an unmitigated loss; but there is another and, perhaps, a stronger still.

We should be careful not to attribute to what is good the abuse made of it by men; yet the good is sometimes the occasion of evil; and so it was with those great, admirable, and much-to-be-regretted universities.

They imparted to the mind of man an impulse which the pride and ambition of man turned to his intellectual ruin. What was intended for the spread of true knowledge and faith became in the end the source of spiritual pride, the natural fosterer of doubt and negation. Modern science, so called, that incarnation of vanity, sophistry, error, and delusion, comes indirectly from those universities of the middle ages; and it was chiefly at the time of what is called the revival of learning, that the great revolution in science came about, which changed the intellectual gold into dross, the once divine ambrosia of knowledge, served to happy mortals in mediaeval times, into poison.

That pretended "revival of learning" can never be mentioned in connection with Ireland; and the "idolatry of art," and corruption of morals, never crossed the channel which God set between Great Britain and the Island of Saints.

Another revival, though of a very different character, was, however, actually taking place in Erin at that very period, when the Wars of the

Roses gave her breathing-time, which we relate in the words of a modern Irish writer, as a conclusion to the reflections we have indulged in:

"Within this period lived Margaret of Offaly, the beautiful and accomplished queen of O'Carrol, King of Ely. She and her husband were munificent patrons of literature, art, and, science. On Queen Margaret's special invitation, the literati of Ireland and Scotland, to the number of nearly three thousand, held a "session" for the furtherance of literary and scientific interests at her palace near Killeagh, in Offaly, the entire assemblage being the guests of the king and queen during their stay.

"The nave of the great church of Da Sinchell was converted for the occasion into a banqueting-hall, where Margaret herself inaugurated the proceedings by placing two massive chalices of gold, as offerings, on the high altar, and committing two orphan children to the custody of nurses to be fostered at her charge. Robed in cloth of gold, this illustrious lady, who was as distinguished for her beauty as for her generosity, sat in queenly state m one of the galleries of the church, surrounded by the clergy, the brehons, and her private friends, shedding a lustre on the scene which was passing below, while her husband, who had often encountered England's greatest generals in battle, remained mounted on a charger outside the church, to bid the guests welcome and see that order was preserved. The invitations were issued, and the guests arranged according to a list prepared by O'Carrol's chief brehon; and the second entertainment, which took place at Rathangan, was a supplemental one, to embrace such men of learning as had not been brought together at the former feast."--(A.M. O'Sullivan.)

Such was the true "revival of learning" in Ireland--a return to her old traditional teaching. If this peaceful time had been of longer duration, there is no doubt that her old schools would have flourished anew, and men in subsequent ages might have compared the results of the two systems: the one producing with true enlightenment, peace, concord, faith, and piety, though confined to the insignificant compass of one small island; the other resulting in the mental anarchy so rife to-day, and spreading all over the rest of Europe.

THE IRISH AND THE TUDORS--HENRY VIII.

BY losing the only bond of unity--the power vested in the Ard-Righ--which held the various parts of the island together, Ireland lost all power of exercising any combined action. The nations were as numerous as the clans, and the interests as diverse as the families. They possessed, it is true, the same religion, and in the observance of its precepts and practices they often found a remedy for their social evils; but religion, not encountering any opposition from any quarter, with the exception of the minor differences existing between the native clergy and the English dignitaries, was generally considered as out of the question in their wranglings and contentions. We shall see how the blows struck at it by the English monarchs welded into one that people, were the cause of that union now so remarkable among them, and really constituted the only bond that ever linked them together.

Before dwelling on these considerations, let us glance a moment at the state of the country prior to the attempt of introducing Protestantism there.

The English Pale was reduced at this period to one half of five counties in Leinster and Meath; and even within those boundaries the O'Kavanaghs, O'Byrnes, O'Moores and others, retained their customs, their brehon laws, their language and traditions, often making raids into the very neighborhood of the capital, and parading their gallowglasses and kerns within twenty miles of Dublin.

The nobility and the people were in precisely the same state which they had known for centuries. The few Englishmen who had long ago settled in the country had become identified with the natives, had adopted their manners, language, and laws, so offensive at first to the supercilious Anglo-Normans.

But a revolution was impending, owing chiefly to the change lately introduced into the religion of England, by Henry Tudor. It is important to study the first attempt of the kind in Ireland; not only because it became the occasion of establishing for a lengthy period a real unanimity among the people--giving birth to the nation as it were--but also for the right understanding of the word "rebellion," which had been so freely used before toward the natives, and which was now about to receive a new interpretation.

The English had once deceived the Irish, exacting their submission in the twelfth century by foisting upon them the word homage: they would deceive Europe by a constant use, or rather misuse, of the words "rebel" and "rebellion." By the enactment of new laws they pronounce the simple attachment to the old religion of the country a denial of sovereign right, and consequently an act of overt treason; and the Irish shall be butchered mercilessly for the sake of the religion of Christ without winning the name, though they do the crown, of martyrdom; for Europe is to be so effectually deceived, that even the Church will hesitate to proclaim those religious heroes, saints of God.

But the great fact of the birth of a nation, in the midst of those throes of anguish, will lessen their atrocity in the mind of the reader, and explain to some extent the wonderful designs of Providence.

From an English state paper, published by M. Haverty, we learn that, in 1515, a few years before the revolt of Luther, the island was divided into more than sixty separate states, or "regions," "some as big as a shire, some more, some less."

Had it not been for this division and the constant feuds it engendered, in the north between the O'Neills and O'Donnells, in the south between the Geraldines (Desmonds and Kildares) and the Butlers (Ormonds), the authority of the English king would have been easily shaken off. The policy so constantly adopted by England in after-times--a policy well expressed by the Latin adage, Divide et impera--preserved the English power in Ireland, and finally brought the island into outward subjection at least, to Great Britain--a subjection which the Irish conscience and the Irish voice and Irish arms yet did not cease to protest against and deny. But the nation was divided, and it required some great and general calamity to unite them together and make of them one people.

That, even spite of those divisions, they were at the time on the point of driving the English out of the island, we need no better proofs than the words of the English themselves. The Archbishop of Dublin, John Allen, the creature of Wolsey, who was employed by the crafty cardinal to begin the work of the spoliation of convents in the island, and oppose the great Earl of Kildare, dispatched his relative, the secretary of the Dublin Council, to England, to report that "the English laws, manners, and language in Ireland were confined within the narrow compass of twenty miles;" and that, unless the laws were duly enforced, "the little place," as the Pale was called, "would be reduced to the same condition as the remainder of the kingdom;" that is to say, the Pale itself, which had been brought to such insignificant limits, would belong exclusively to the Irish.

It was while affairs were at this pass that the revolt of "silken Thomas" excited the wrath of Henry VIII., and brought about the destruction of almost the whole Kildare family.

It was about this time, also, that Wolsey fell, and Cromwell, having replaced him as Chancellor of England, with Cranmer as Archbishop of Canterbury, the Reformation began in England with the divorce of the king, who shortly after assumed supremacy in spirituals as a prerogative of the crown, and made Parliament -- in those days himself--supreme lawgiver in Church and state.

Cromwell, known in history as the creature and friend of Cranmer, like his protector a secret pervert to the Protestant doctrines of Germany, and the first arch-plotter for the destruction of Catholicity in the British Isles, undertook to save the English power in Ireland by forcing on that country the supremacy of the king in religious matters, knowing well that such a step would drive the Irish into resistance, but believing that he could easily subdue them and make the island English.

Having been appointed, not only Chancellor of England, but also king's vicar-general in temporals and spirituals, Cromwell inquired of his English agents in Ireland the best means of attaining his object--the subjection of the country. Their report is preserved among the state papers, and some of their suggestions deserve our attentive consideration. If Henry VIII. had consented to follow their advice, he would have himself inaugurated the bloody policy so well carried out long after by another Cromwell, the celebrated "Protector."

The report sets forth that the most efficient mode of proceeding was to exterminate the people; but Henry thought it sufficient to gain the nobility over--the people being beneath his notice.

The agents of the vicar-general were right in their atrocious proposal. They knew the Irish nation well, and that the only way to separate Ireland from the See of Peter was to make the country a desert.

Their means of bringing about the destruction of the people was starvation. The corn was to be destroyed systematically, and the cattle killed or driven away. Their operations, it is true, were limited to the borders of the Pale. The gentle Spenser, at a later period, proposed to extend them to all Munster, and it was a special glory reserved for the "Protector" to carry out this policy through almost the whole of the island.

"The very living of the Irishry," says the report, "doth clearly consist in two things: take away the same from them, and they are passed for ever to recover, or yet to annoy any subject Ireland. Take first from them their corn, and as much as cannot be husbanded, and had into the hands of such as shall dwell and inhabit in their lands, to burn and destroy the same, so as the Irishry shall not live thereupon; and then to have their cattle and beasts, which shall be most hardest to come by, and yet, with guides and policy, they may be oft had and taken."

The report goes on to point out, most elaborately and ingeniously, every artifice and plan for carrying this policy into effect. But here we have, condensed, as it were, in a nutshell, and coolly and carefully set forth, the system which was adopted later on, and almost crowned with a fiendish success. But the moment for the execution of this barbarous scheme had not yet come, and we find no positive results following immediately.

This project, complete as it was, was far from being the only one proposed at that time for "rooting out the Irish" from Ireland. Mr. Prendergast, in his "Introduction to the Cromwellian Settlement," says:

"The Irish were never deceived as to the purport of the English, and, though the Pale had not been extended for two hundred and forty years, their firm persuasion in the reign of Henry VIII. was, that the original design was not abandoned. 'Irishmen are of opinion among themselves,' said Justice Cusack to the king, 'that Englishmen will one day banish them from their lands forever.'"

In fact, project after project was then proposed for clearing Ireland of Irish to the Shannon. Some went so far as already to contemplate their utter extirpation; but "there was no precedent for it found in the chronicles of the conquest. Add to this the difficulty of finding people to reinhabit it if suddenly unpeopled.

"The chiefs and gentlemen of the Irish only were to be driven from their properties," according to some of those projects, "and they only were to be driven into exile, while their lands should be given to Englishmen."

"The king, however, seems to have been satisfied with confiscating the estates of the Earl of Kildare and of his family. Fierce and bloody though he was, there was something lion-like in his nature; notwithstanding all those promptings, he left to the Irish and old English their possessions, and seemed even anxious to secure them, but failed to do so for want of time."

We think Mr. Prendergast's judgment of Henry VIII. too favorable. Generosity did not prompt him to spare the people and the nobles, with the exception of the Kildares. We believe that he never contemplated the extirpation of the people, because such a political element could not enter into his mind. As for the nobles, he wished to gain them over, because of the long wars he foresaw necessary to bring about their utter extinction or exile.

He adopted, accordingly, a plan of his own, holding firm to his design of having his new title of "Head of the Church" acknowledged in Ireland as well as in England.

Cromwell commenced his work by two measures which had met with perfect success in the latter country, but which were destined to fire the sister isle from end to end, and make "the people," in course of time, really one. These measures were acts of Parliament: 1. Establishing 'the king's spiritual supremacy; 2. Suppressing, at once, all the monasteries existing in the country, and giving their property to the nobles who were willing to apostatize.

The necessity of convening Parliament resulted from the failure of the first attempt, already made, to establish the king's supremacy. Browne, the successor of Allen in the See of Dublin, a rank Lutheran at heart, had been commissioned by the king and by Cranmer, his consecrator, to establish the new doctrine at once. His want of success, is thoroughly explained in a letter to Cromwell, which is still preserved, and which remains one of the proudest monuments of the steadfastness of the Irish in their religion.

He complains that not only the clergy, but the "common people," were "more zealous in their blindness than the saints and martyrs in truth, in the beginning of the Gospel," and "such was their hostility against him that his life was in danger."

And all this in Dublin, in the heart of the Pale, where the chief antagonist of the new doctrine, "the leader of the people" against this first attempt at schism, was Cromer, the Archbishop of Armagh, an Englishman himself! So that those prelates of England, who, with the exception of the noble Fisher, had all yielded without a murmur of opposition to the will of Henry, could find no followers, not even of their own nation, in Ireland, so much had their faith been strengthened by contact with that of "the common people."

A Parliament was needed, therefore, and that one which was to be the instrument of introducing the great English measure, met for the first time in Dublin, on the 1st of May, 1536; but, being prorogued, it met again in 1537, and did not complete its work until once more summoned in 1541, when the old Irish element was for the first and last time introduced at its sitting, in order, if possible, to consecrate the new doctrine by having it solemnly accepted by the old race.

This Parliament, which was first convened in Dublin, McGeoghegan says, "adjourned to Kilkenny, thence to Cashel, after ward to Limerick, and lastly to Dublin again." The chief cause of these interruptions was the difficulty of bringing an Irish Parliament, even when composed of Englishmen, as was the case up to 1541, to pass the decrees of supremacy, denial of Roman authority, etc., which had been so readily accepted in England.

The Irish Parliaments, as far back as we can see, were composed not only of lords, spiritual and temporal, and of deputies of the Commons, but each diocese possessed also the right to send there three ecclesiastical proctors, who, by reason of their office, owned neither benefice nor fief, and were therefore at liberty to vote, fearless of attainder and confiscation, in accordance with their conscience and their sense of right.

This feature of the Irish assemblies, even when no representative of the native race sat in them, was a fatal obstacle to the success of the scheme devised by Browne and executed by Cromwell. Accordingly, we are not astonished to find that, by an act of despotism not uncommon during the reign of Henry VIII., the proctors were excluded from Parliament, which thus became an obedient tool in the hands of the government.

Not only, therefore, were several state measures carried in accordance with the wish of the king, but the great object proposed by the meeting of this assembly was finally obtained; and, lowing the lead of the English Parliament, Henry VIII. and his successors were confirmed in the title of "Supreme Head of the Church in Ireland," with power of reforming and correcting errors in religion. All appeals to Rome were prohibited, and the Pope's authority declared a usurpation.

Henry, however, foreseeing that all these favorite measures of his policy, being carried by English votes in a purely English assembly, though on Irish soil, would meet with universal opposition from all the native lords, conceived the idea of summoning the great Irish chieftains to a new meeting of Parliament, from which he expected that a moral revolution would be effected in the island. Sir Anthony St. Leger, created deputy in August, 1540, was thought a likely man to be intrusted with so delicate a mission. He conducted it with political prudence, that is to say, with a judicious mixture of kindness and fraud, which succeeded beyond all expectations.

In order to prepare the way for hoodwinking the Irish chieftains, favors of every kind were showered upon them, to wit, titles and estates, chiefly those of suppressed monasteries; and St. Leger, by an alternate use of force and diplomacy, at length effected that the Irish should consent to accept titles. Con O'Neill, the head of the house of Tyrone, went to England, accompanied by O'Kervellan, Bishop of Ologher, and was admitted to an audience by the king. Henry adopted toward those proud Irishmen a policy utterly different from that he had used with the English lords. These latter were merely threatened with his displeasure, and with the feudal penalties he knew so well how to inflict; the others were received at court as favorites and dear friends; a royal courtesy, kind expressions, a smiling face--such were the arms he employed against the "barbarous Irish."

Tyrone, O'Donnell, and others, were not proof against his cunning. The first renounced his title of prince and the glorious name of O'Neill, to receive in return that of Earl of Tyrone. Manus O'Donnell was made Earl of Tyrconnel. Both received back the lands which they had offered to the king, and their example was followed by a great number of inferior lords. Among them, two Magenisses were dubbed knights; Murrough O'Brien, of North Munster, was made Earl of Thomond and Baron of Inchiquin; De Burgo, or McWilliams, was created Earl of Clanricard, and a host of others submitted in like manner, and received the new titles which henceforth became conspicuous in Irish history.

This was the beginning of the gradual suppression of the clans. Many of these nobles, unfortunately, not content with receiving back, at the hands of the king, the lands which had come into their possession from a long line of ancestors, and which really belonged not to them personally, but to the clans whose heads they were, greedily snatched at the estates of religious orders, whose suppression was the first consequence of the schism in Ireland, which will soon occupy our attention.

The Irish chieftains had already seen Wolsey, a cardinal in full communion with Rome, suppress forty monasteries in the island. They might therefore imagine that the confiscation of a still greater number on the part of the king was a thing not altogether incompatible with the religion of the monarch, and that the fact of their sharing in the plunder was not entirely opposed to their titles of Catholics and subjects of Rome. Such is human conscience when blinded by self-interest.

The king thought that he had gained over the nobility,--which was all he wished--and the last session of the previous Parliament of 1536 and the following years might now be held in order to consecrate the unholy work.

"On the 12th of June, 1541," says Mr. Haverty, "a Parliament was held in Dublin, at which the novel sight was witnessed of Irish chieftains sitting for the first time with English lords. O'Brien appeared there by his procurators and attorneys, and Kavanagh, O'More, O'Reilly, McWilliams, and others, took their seats in person, the addresses of the Speaker and of the Lord-

Chancellor being interpreted to them in Irish by the Earl of Ormond. An act was unanimously passed, conferring on Henry VIII. and his successors the title of King of Ireland, instead of that of Lord of Ireland, which the English kings, since the days of John, had hitherto borne. This act was hailed with great rejoicings in Dublin, and on the following Sunday, the lords and gentlemen of Parliament went in procession to St. Patrick's Cathedral, where solemn high mass was sung by Archbishop Browne, after which the law was proclaimed and a Te Deum chanted."

It is worthy of remark that in the session of 1541, at which alone the Irish chieftains appeared, not a word was said of the supremacy of the king in spirituals. Sir James Ware, who gives the various decrees with more detail than usual, makes no mention of this pet measure of the king and of the Lutheran Archbishop Browne, but it was only part and parcel of the Parliament of 1536, prorogued successively to Kilkenny, Cashel, Limerick, and finally again to Dublin. At its first sitting the law of supremacy was passed and proclaimed as law of Ireland. Nothing was said of it in the various sessions that followed, including that of 1541; and yet the Irish chieftains were supposed to have sanctioned it, inasmach as it was a measure previously passed in the same Parliament: and the suppression of various abbeys and monasteries having been openly decreed in the final session, as a result of the king's supremacy--Rome not having been consulted, of course--all the signers of the last decree were supposed to have thereby sanctioned and adopted the previous ones. Thus O'Neill, O'Reilly, O'More, and the rest, without being aware of the fact, became schismatics, though many of them, perhaps all, did not see the connection between the various sessions of that long Parliament. Certainly, if, on leaving the Dublin Cathedral, where they had heard the archbishop's mass and assisted at that solemn Te Deum, they had been told that that act was intended to consecrate the surrender of the religion of their ancestors, and the commencement of a frightful revolution, which would end in the destruction of their national existence, almost of their very race, they would have incredulously laughed to scorn the unwelcome prophet.

But even if, as we may well believe, those Irish lords had really been the victims of deception, and had not, as a body, been corrupted by the sacrilegious gift of suppressed monasteries, the people, their clansmen, prompted by the vivid impressions and unerring instincts of religious faith and patriotic nationality, which were ever living in their breasts, resented the weakness of their chieftains as a national defection and a real apostasy, and took immediate steps to bring the lords to their senses, and to prevent the spread of English corruption.

All who had received titles from Henry, and surrendered to him the deeds of their lands, as if those lands belonged to them personally, and not to the clans collectively, all those, particularly, who had enriched themselves by the plunder of religious houses, and who had taken any part in the destruction of the religious orders so dear to the Irish heart, were soon made to feel the indignation which those events had excited among the native clansmen, north and south. And those of the chieftains who had really been deceived, and had preserved in their hearts all through a strong love for their religion and country, were recalled to a sense of their error, and brought back to a sense of their duty by the unmistakable voice of the "people."

While the nobles were still in England, feted by Henry in his royal palace of Greenwich, renouncing their Irish names to become English earls and barons, the Ulster chief, protesting that he would never again take the name of O'Neill, but content himself with the title of Earl of Tyrone; while O'Brien was being created Earl of Thomond; McWilliams, Earl of Clanricard; O'Donnell, Earl of Tyrconnell; Kavanagh, Baron of Ballyann; and Fitzpatrick, Baron of Ossory; the clans at home, hearing in due time of those real treasons, were concerting plans for making their lords repent of their weakness or treachery, and for administering to them due punishment on their return.

O'Neill, "the first of his race who had accepted an English title," on landing in Ireland, learned that, his people had deposed him, and elected in his stead his son John the Proud, better known as Shane O'Neill; O'Donnell, on his arrival, met most, of his clan, headed by his son, up in arms against him; the new Earl of Clanricard had already been deposed by his people and another McWilliams, with a Gaelic name, elected in his place; and so with the rest.

But, unfortunately, the Government of England was strong enough to support its favorite chieftains, and it found some Irish tools ready at hand to form the nucleus of an Irish party in their favor. Thus, unanimity no longer marked the decisions of the clans; two parties were formed in each of them, the one national, comprising the great bulk of the people, the real, true people; the other English, composed of a few apostate Irishmen, backed by the power of England. Thus, henceforth we hear of the O'Reilly, and the king's O'Reilly, etc.

Henry VIII. seemed, therefore, with the help of his minister, St. Leger, to have succeeded in breaking up the clans, after the Irish national government had been broken up long before. Confusion of titles, property, and traditions became worse confounded. How could the shanachies, bards, and brehons, any longer agree in their pedigrees, songs, and legal decisions? England had thus early adopted in Ireland the stern and coldhearted policy which, centuries later, she used to destroy the native and Mohammedan dynasties in Hindostan. It was not yet divide et impera on a large scale, but the division was pushed as far as lay in the power England, to the very last elements of the social system.

From this time forward, then, we must not be surprised to find England welcoming to her bosom unworthy sons of Ireland, whom she wished to make her tools. There was always, either in Dublin or London, a sufficient supply of materials out of which crown's chiefs might be manufactured; the government made it part of its policy to hold in its hands and train to its purposes certain members of each of the ruling families--of the O'Neills, O'Reillys, O'Donnells, O'Connors, and others.

It was no longer, therefore, the rooting out and exterminating policy which prevailed, but one as fatal in its results, which would have utterly destroyed Irish national feeling, to set up in its place, not only English manners, language, and customs, but also English schism, heresy, philosophical speculations--as the Four Masters have it--finally, materialism and nihilism.

But, in real sober fact, the scheme proved almost an utter failure, owing to the far-seeing good sense of the people. The national spirit revived among the upper classes, both native and of English descent--owing to the decided stand taken by the inferior clansmen.

The Desmonds and Kildares, in the south, the O'Donnells, Maguires, and others, in the north, soon showed themselves animated by a new spirit of ardent Catholicism; created, in fact, a new nation, quite apart from, or rather embracing, clanship, well-nigh destroyed the English power, kept Elizabeth, during the whole of her reign, in constant agitation and fear, and would have succeeded in recovering their independence, and securing freedom of worship, had not their good-nature been imposed upon by the hypocrisy and faithlessness of the Stuarts, to whom they always looked for freedom in the practice of their religion, without ever obtaining it.

Thus did the people, the Irish race, thwart the policy of Henry, who sought to gain over the nobility. Their stubborn resistance to the vastly-increased and constantly-increasing English power, grew at last to such proportions, and became so discouraging to their oppressors, that the old policy of utter extermination was resumed by Cromwell and the Orange party of the following age.

The refusal of the people, that is to say, of the bulk of the nation, to submit to the policy of their chieftains, and the determination to repudiate that policy by deposing its supporters and choosing others in their stead, was most happy in its effect on their whole future history.

The leaders, by accepting the new titles bestowed on them by the English kings, by taking their seats in Parliament, and concurring in the various measures there passed, subjected themselves to a foreign rule, surrendered to this rule the tribe-lands, which it was not in their power to surrender of themselves, gave up, in fact, their nationality, and became English subjects. The action of the clansmen reversed all the fatal consequences resulting from those acts. They remained a nation distinct from the English, whose laws they had never either admitted or accepted. And, as the clan spirit declined, under the policy of England, it only made way for a new and a greater spirit--religious feeling, the bond of a common religion assaulted--which, henceforth, lay at the bottom of the whole struggle--which, for the first time in their history, blended into one whole the broken clans, gave them a unity and a consistency never known till then, and thus the real nation was born.

They might boast, therefore, not only of not having lost their autonomy, but of being more firmly than ever knit together; they could conclude treaties of alliance with foreign powers, without committing treason, and they soon began to use that power; they could even declare war against England, and it was not rebellion. The successors of Henry VIII. acted constantly as though the Irish nation had really subjected itself to English kings and English rule, as though the acceptance of a few titles by a few chieftains (who were deposed by their people as soon as the fact was known) signified an acknowledgment on the part of the Irish people of their absorption by the English feudal system; they appeared "horrified" when they saw the successors of those chieftains reject those titles and resume their own names; and they called the Irish "rebels" and "traitors" for going to war with England--a country they had never acknowledged as their ruler--and introducing into their country Spanish, Italian, and French troops as allies.

The explanation of the whole mystery consisted in the simple fact that the people, the nation, had steadily refused to sanction the act of their leaders; and all the pretensions of English kings, statesmen, and lawyers, were valueless. Those Irishmen who subsequently entered into the various Geraldine and Ulster confederacies, and summoned foreign armies to their aid, were neither rebels nor traitors, but citizens of an independent state, possessing their international rights as citizens of any independent country. This we have seen in a previous chapter, and Sir John Davies has been obliged to confess its truth, admitting the difference between a tributary and a subject nation.

A glance shows us the importance of the almost unanimous outcry of the clansmen of Tyrone, Tyrconnell, and of other parts of Ireland. Owing to the patriotic feeling of these, nothing remained for the English but to punish the Irish people for their resolve of holding to their religion, and to declare a religious war against them, though they called them all the time rebels and traitors. This is the view an impartial historian should take of those mighty events.

But, it is well to look more closely at this new element, which then showed itself for the first time in Irish national life, the people, irrespective of clanship; the people, as influencing the leaders, and thus becoming a living--nay, a ruling power in the state. And, lest any of our readers should not be convinced that such really was the case, we mention here a fact, which will come more prominently before us in the next chapter, that, at the end of Elizabeth's reign, the efforts of all her large armies and her tortuous policy for changing the religion of the country, resulted in the grand total of sixty converts to Protestantism from the noble class, not one of the clansmen turning apostate!

Bridget of Kildare would not have been surprised at this, to judge by what we have previously heard from her.

In order to find the explanation of this wonderful fact, we must compare the Irish people with other nationalities, and we may then easily distinguish its peculiar features, so persistent, so enduring, we may say, indestructible. We shall find that what this people was three hundred years ago, it is to this day, with a greater unity of feeling, devotedness to principle, and higher aims than any people of modern times.

In antiquity, the people, in the Christian sense of the word, never appeared in the field of history. In the despotic countries of Asia and Africa, there was and could be no question of such a thing; it was an inert mass used at will by the despot. The Phoenician states, and Carthage in particular, were mere oligarchies, with commerce for their chief object, and slaves for mercantile or warlike purposes. In the republics of Greece and Italy, the aristocracy ruled, and when, after centuries of bloody struggles and revolutions, the subjects of Rome were finally granted the rights of citizenship, the despotism of the empire suddenly appeared, crushing both plebs and patricians.

Whenever in those ancient governments we find the lower classes unable longer to bear the heavy yoke imposed upon them, revolting against a despotism which had grown insupportable, and claiming their natural rights, it was merely a surging of waves raised to mountain-height by the fury of a sudden storm, but soon allayed and subdued beneath the inflexible will of stern rulers. The people was a mere mob, whose violence, when successful, fatally carried destruction with it; and, though it is seemingly full of a terrible power which nothing can resist, its power lasts but for a very short time. Could it only outlast the destruction of all superior rulers, it would end by destroying itself.

If we would meet with the people, such as we conceive it to be in accordance with our Christian ideas, we must come down to that period of time which followed close upon the organization of Christendom, namely, to the much-abused middle ages. Feudalism, it is true, withstood its expansion for a long time, kept alive the remnants of slavery which it had found in Europe at its birth, or at best invented serfdom as a somewhat milder substitute for the former degradation of man. But feudalism itself was not strong enough to prevent the natural consequences of the vigorous Christianity which at that time prevailed; and kings, dukes, and feudal bishops, were compelled to grant charters which insured the freedom of the subject. Then the people appeared, in the cities first, afterward in the country, where, however, the peasants had still to drag on for a weary time the chains of secular serfdom.

Thus the people lived in Spain, where they fought valiantly under their lords for centuries against the Crescent, so that in some provinces all classes were ennobled, and not a single plebeian was to be found, which simply means that the whole mass of the citizens formed the people. Thus the people had an early existence in Italy, where every city almost became a centre of freedom and activity, notwithstanding strife and continual feuds. Thus the people had its life in France, where the learned men of Catholic universities determined with precision the limits of kingly power, and where the outburst of the Crusades brought all classes together to fight for Christ, forming but one body engaged alike throughout in a holy cause. Thus, finally, the people had its life even in Germany and England, where real liberty, though of later birth, afterward remained more deeply rooted in social life.

In all those countries, it was called populus Christianus; it had its associations, its guilds, its Christian customs, its privileges, its rights. Its existence was acknowledged by law, and it possessed everywhere either Christian codes, or at least local customs for its safeguards. It gradually grew into a great power, and took the name of the "Third Estate," ranking directly after the clergy, and nobility. Its members knew and respected the gradations of the social hierarchy as then existing. The monarchs in most countries, in France chiefly, sided with it whenever the nobles sought to oppress it, and its deputies were heard in the Parliaments of the various nations of Christendom.

How many millions of human beings lived happily during several centuries under these great institutions of mediaeval times! And if the members of the people at that time could seldom rise above their order, except through the Church, this unfortunate inability often prevented dangerous and subversive ambitions, and was thus really the source and cause of, happiness to all. Governments at that period lasted for thousands of years; men could rely on the stability of things, and great enterprises could be undertaken and carried to a successful termination.

But throughout all Europe, with the single exception of Ireland, the people had to contend against the feudal power; and it was only very gradually, and step by step, that it could creep up to its rights. In Ireland, as we have seen, feudalism had failed to strike root; so that the clansmen who represented there what the people did elsewhere, never having been subject to slavery or serfdom, possessed all the liberties which the ordinary class of men can claim. They had always borne their share in the affairs of their own territory, at least by the willing help they afforded to their leaders, during the Danish wars chiefly, and afterward throughout the four hundred years of struggle with the Anglo-Normans. The people were the real conquerors under the lead of their chieftains, and the perpetual enjoyment of their beloved customs was the privilege of the least among them as much as of the proudest of their nobles. They themselves were well aware of this, and to their own efforts no less than to the heads of the clans they attributed the advantages which they had gained.

Thus, when the conduct of their chieftain was not in accordance with what the clansmen considered the right, they were ready to express their disapproval of his actions by deposing him, and placing their allegiance at the service of the man of their choice.

But though this course of action is true of the whole period of their history, more especially from the date of their becoming Christian up to the time when the blows of religious persecution welded them into one people, yet they were divided and often at war among themselves. But no sooner did the work of perversion make itself felt among them, than we behold the clansmen exhibiting a unity of feeling on many points which never marked them before. So that thenceforth the separated clans gradually began to merge into Irishmen.

This unity of feeling showed itself, above all, in the deep love for their religion, which at once became universal and all-pervading. This love had undoubtedly existed before, as it could scarcely have originated and swollen to such proportions all at once; but as the stroke of the hammer reveals the spark, so the force of opposition enkindled the flame and caused it to burst forth into view. At the first blow it showed itself throughout the island, and thus the people became once and forever united.

This unity of feeling was displayed likewise in an ardent love for their country in contradistinction to the special locality of the tribe. Thus arose a true fraternal union with all their countrymen of whatever county or city.

The old antagonism between family and family only appeared at fitful and unguarded intervals; but in general each one grasped the hand of another only as a Catholic and an Irishman.

This is clearly attributable to their religion. Catholicity knows no place; its very name is opposed to restrictions of this character. Could it carry out its purpose, which is that of its Divine founder, it would make one of all nations; and, to a certain extent, it has achieved this task. Differences of character, which are deeply impressed in the nature of various branches of the human family, are indeed never totally obliterated by it; but such differences disappear when kneeling at the same altar and receiving the same sacraments. The Catholic religion is the only one which is, has ever been, and must ever claim to be, universal; the religions of antiquity were purely local.

Since the coming of our Lord, no heresy, no schism has ever pretended to the reality of a catholic existence, and, if the word is self-applied by certain sects, the world laughs at it as a meaningless thing. The Catholic Church alone has truly claimed and possessed such a character.

But if of all men it makes one family with respect to spiritual matters, what unanimity of feeling must it not create in a single nation truly imbued with its spirit, which is attacked for its sake? Until the reign of Henry VIII., the Irish, in their struggle with England, could summon no religious thought to their aid, since England was Catholic also, and the Norman nobles established among them followed the same calendar, possessed the same churches, the same creed, the same sacraments. But as soon as the English power was stamped with heresy, the opposition to that power assumed a religious aspect, and no longer restricted itself to the clans immediately attacked, but spread throughout the whole nation.

To bring the case down to some particular point, in order to render our meaning more clear, a priest or monk, who was hunted down, was no longer sure of refuge in his own district, and among men of his own sept merely, but he was equally welcomed in the castle of the chieftain or the hut of the peasant through the length and breadth of the land. Any Irishman, subject to fine, imprisonment, or torture, for the sake of his religion, did not find sympathy restricted to his own circle of friends or acquaintances, but, even if tried and prosecuted in a corner of the island, far away from his own home, he could count upon the sympathy of as many friends as there were Irish Catholics to witness his sufferings. This state of things was certainly unknown before.

Religion, when deep, is the strongest feeling of the human heart, and endows the nation steeped in it with an unconquerable strength. To judge of the intensity of religious feeling in the Irish, it should be remembered that it was the only legacy left them after every thing else had been taken away, and, though it was the special object of attack, they were to be stripped one by one of their old customs, their own chieftains, their houses of study and of prayer, their religious and secular teachers, nay, of the chance even of educating their children, of the right to possess not merely their own soil, but even to cultivate a few acres of it, nay, of their very language itself, in a word, of all that makes a country dear to man. For ages were they destined to remain outcasts and strangers on the soil which was their own; abject and ignorant paupers, without the faintest possibility of rising in the social scale.

One thing only did they keep in their hearts, their faith, though stripped of all the exterior circumstances which adorn it, and reduced to its simplest elements. But at least it was their religion, to deprive them of which, all the wealth, resources, armies, laws of a powerful nation, were to be strained to the utmost during long ages. How, then, could they fail to love and cherish it, to cling fast to it, as to an inestimable treasure, the only real one indeed they could possess on earth, where all else passes away?

Here, then, always presupposing the paramount influence of the grace of God, lay the secret of that indestructible strength and unwearied energy manifested by Irishmen, from the middle of the sixteenth century down, and we are enabled thus to appreciate the value of that unity which persecution alone fastened upon them.

To the love of religion, which was the origin of that unity, love of country was soon added, and by love of country we here understand the love of the whole island, not merely of the particular sept to which the individual belonged, or of the particular spot in which he happened to be born. Such had been the divisions among the people and the chieftains hitherto, that England could attack one sept without fearing the revolt of the others, nay, was often assisted by an adverse clan. And so thoroughly had the Anglo-Normans adopted the native manners, that the Kildares were frequently at war with the Desmonds, though both belonged to the same

Geraldine family; and the Ormonds kept up a constant feud with both the Geraldine branches. When Henry VIII. almost destroyed the Kildares, we do not find that the Desmonds felt their loss at first; perhaps they even rejoiced at it.

It was the same with the natives, particularly with the O'Neills and the O'Donnells, in the north. The whole island and its general interests seemed the concern of no one, so taken up were they by the affairs of their own particular locality. And this state of feeling had existed from the beginning, even among holy men. The songs of Columba, of Cormac McCullinan, even of the Fenian heroes of old, all celebrated the victories of one sept over another, or the beauties of some one spot in the island, in preference to all others.

Nay, so prevalent was this clannish spirit, even at the beginning of the religious troubles, that Henry VIII., and Elizabeth after him, gained their successes by directing their attacks against particular places, so certain were they that the other districts would not come to the rescue.

The feeling of nationality, of what we call patriotism, wrestled along time in the throes of birth, before coming forth, and it was only during the latter half of Elizabeth's reign that those confederacies were formed, which included the whole country and called in even foreign aid.

But this feeling began to appear as soon as religion was attacked; and therefore do we call this epoch the true birth of a people.

And as it is with the people chiefly that we are concerned, it is to our purpose to remark here that they gradually lost sight of their petty quarrels and local prejudices in losing their chieftains; they began to look for leaders among themselves, and, understanding at last that the whole island was threatened by the invading policy of England, they were to fight for the whole, and not for any special district.

Then, for the first time, did Ireland become a reality to them, an existing personality, a desolate queen weeping over the fate of her children, calling, with the voice of a stricken mother, those who survived to her aid, and worthy, by her beauty and misfortunes, of their most heroic and disinterested efforts.

Religious feeling, then, first made the Irish a nation, and gave them that unity of thought which they now exhibit everywhere, even in the remotest quarters of the globe, wherever they may choose their place of exile. And if there still exists among them something of that former predilection for the place where they first saw the light, the other parts of Erin are at least included in their deep love, and they would shed their blood for their country, irrespective of prejudice of place.

Thus have they come at last to love each other as men of no other nation ever did. In order to understand this thoroughly, we must remember that for ages they, as a people, have been oppressed and held in bondage by a stern and powerful nation. They had to defend themselves in turn against the most open and the most insidious attacks. Bereft in many cases of all the means of defence, they had nothing left them, save their religion, and the support they could afford each other.

If, by any stretch of imagination, we could place ourselves in their position, understand their language when they met each other in their huts, in their morasses and bogs, in their mountain fastnesses and desolate moors, could we only enter into their feelings and see the working of their minds, we might catch a faint conception of the affection which they must have felt for brothers waging the deadly fight against the same enemies, and contending in a seemingly endless and hopeless struggle against the same terrible odds. Union, affection, devotedness, are words too weak to serve here.

For this reason, also, do we find the Irish people stamped with peculiarities which we find in no others. In antiquity, as we have said, the people could never rise to any thing greater than a mob; in modern times such has also often been the case. With the Irish it is not, and could not be so. Their aim has always been too lofty, their struggle of too long duration, their morality too genuine and too pure. For their aim has constantly been to rescue their country; their struggle has lasted nearly three hundred years; their morality has ever been directed by the sweetest religion. Extreme cases of oppression such as theirs may have occasionally given rise to violent outbreaks inevitable in human despair; but, on the whole, it may to their honor be fearlessly said, that they have preserved, almost throughout, a due regard for social hierarchy and all kinds of rights. Many of them have died of hunger, rather than touch the property of a rich and hostile neighbor. Where else can we find such an example?

This union of the people, which was thus brought about by religious persecution, included not only the natives of the old race, but the Anglo-Irish themselves, who were brought by degrees to a unanimity of feeling which they had never known before, although they had previously adopted Irish manners - a unanimity which the Lutheran Archbishop Browne had foreseen and openly denounced beforehand. This was the man who had unwittingly borne testimony to the Irish that "the common people of this isle are more zealous in their blindness than the saints and martyrs were in the truth at the beginning of the Gospel;" the same George Browne, of Dublin, had also been the first to perceive that the religious question was beginning, even under Henry VIII., to unite the native Irish and the descendants of Strongbow's followers, until that time bitterly opposed to each other.

In a letter, dated "Dublin, May, 1538," to the Lord Privy Seal, he said: "It is observed that, ever since his Highness's ancestors had this nation in possession, the old natives have been craving foreign powers to assist and raise them; and now both English race and Irish begin to oppose your lordship's orders" (about supremacy), "and do lay aside their national old quarrels, which, I fear, if any thing will cause a foreigner to invade this nation, that will."

This man, who was altogether worldly and without faith, displayed in this a keen political foresight far above that of the ordinary counsellors of England's king. He openly announced what actually came to pass only toward the middle of Elizabeth's reign, and what the horrors of the Cromwellian wars were to complete - the thorough fusion of Irish and Anglo-Norman Catholics, both transplanted to Connaught, perishing under the sword of the soldier, the rope of the hangman, or dying of starvation in the recesses of their mountains - united forever in the bonds of martyrdom.

The "birth of the Irish people" was to be insured by another measure of the English Government - the suppression of religious houses. We must, in conclusion, turn to this.

In the annals of the Four Masters, under the year 1537, we read: "A heresy and a new error broke out in England, the effect of pride, vainglory, avarice, sensual desire, and the prevalence of a variety of scientific and philosophical speculations, so that the people of England went into opposition to the Pope and to Rome.

"At the same time, they followed a variety of opinions; and, adopting the old law of Moses, after the manner of the Jewish people, they gave the title of Head of the Church of God, during his reign, to the king. They ruined the orders who were permitted to hold worldly possessions, namely, monks, canons regular, nuns, and Brethren of the Cross, etc . . . . They broke into the monasteries, they sold their roofs and bells; so that there was not a monastery from Arran of the Saints to the Iccian Sea that was not broken and scattered, except only a few in Ireland."

And, under 1540, they say: "The English, in every place throughout Ireland, where they established their power, persecuted and banished the nine religious orders, and particularly they destroyed the monastery of Monaghan, and beheaded the guardian and a number of friars."

We may add that, at the restoration of the old faith under Queen Mary, nothing had to be restored in Ireland save the monasteries. These establishments had, almost without exception, been ruthlessly destroyed.

In our previous considerations, we have spoken of no other religious houses in Ireland, save those of the old Columbian order of monks, as it was called, which was a growth of the country, and bore so many marks of Irish peculiarities. This continued until, communications with Rome becoming more frequent, the various orders established in the West were successively introduced into Ireland. Our purpose is not to write a history of monasticism, and therefore we do not intend entering into details on this point, interesting though they are. But we may add that, gradually, the old monasteries - from the Norman invasion chiefly - as well as the new ones which were established, were placed under the rule of the various congregations, acknowledged by the Holy See. It seems that the monasteries founded by St. Columba himself afterward submitted to the rule of St. Benedict, the others, for the most part, embracing that of the canons regular of St. Augustine; but the precise epoch of these changes is not known. It is certain, however, that the Benedictines, Cistercians, and Bernardines, were introduced into the country at a very early date, together with the four mendicant orders of Franciscans, Dominicans, Carmelites, and Augustinians.

The pretext for their destruction was, of course, the same in England as in all the other countries of Europe - their need of reformation; but it does not appear that even this pretence was put forward in the case of the Irish monasteries. The fact was, the breath of suspicion could not rest upon those stainless establishments in the Isle of Saints. In the idea of the natives, their very names had ever been synonymous with holiness and all Christian virtues, and so they continued to enjoy the most unbounded popularity. The fact of the English Government selecting them as a special point of attack is in itself sufficient to vindicate their character from any aspersion. Two measures were deemed necessary and sufficient for the purpose of detaching Ireland from its allegiance to the Holy See, and of introducing schism, if not heresy, into the country. One, and certainly the most efficacious of these, was thought to be the destruction of convents for both sexes. This, we affirm, is ample apology for their inmates.

But this general reflection is not enough for our purpose, which is, to delineate and bring out the true character of the nation. It is, therefore, fitting to give an idea of the extent to which the monastic influence prevailed, and of the nature of the people who cherished, loved, and accepted it at all times.

It may be said that the Christian Church, as established in the island by St. Patrick, rested mainly for its support on the religious orders. In many cases the abbots of monasteries were superior to bishops, and, as a general rule, the hierarchy of the Church was, as it were, subordinate to monastic establishments.[1] At the time we speak of, indeed, such was no longer the case; but the previously-existing state of reciprocal subordination between abbots and bishops during several centuries, in Ireland,, had left deep traces in the nature of the institutions and of the people itself. It may be said that in the mind of an Irishman the existence of Christianity almost presupposed a numerous array of convents and religious houses. And this idea of theirs can scarcely be called a wrong one, nor did they exaggerate the value of religious orders, since their estimate of them was no higher than that of Christ himself and his Church.

If with justice it was said that the French monarchy was established by bishops, with equal justice may it be said that the Irish people had been educated, nay, created by monks. The monks had taken the place left

---

[1] Vide Montalembert's "Monks of the West: Bollandists, Oct.," tome xii., p. 888.

vacant by the Druids, and thus they became for the Christian what the others had been for the pagan Irish. For a long period the Irish monks formed a very considerable portion of the population. In their body were concentrated the gifts of science, art, holiness, even miracles without number, unless we are to suppose that the hagiography of the island was intrusted to the care of idiots incapable of ascertaining current facts. The vast literature of the island, greater indeed than that of any other Christian country at the time, was either the product of monastic intellect and learning, or at least had been translated and preserved by monks. The gifted Eugene O'Curry could fill numbers of the pages of his great work with the bare titles of the books which are known to have issued from the Irish monasteries, of which but a few fragments remain; and no sensible man who has read his book can affect to despise establishments which could produce so many proofs of fancy, intellect, and erudition. The scattered fragments of that rich literature, which had escaped the fury of the Scandinavian, the ignorance and rapacity of the early Anglo-Norman, the blind fanaticism of the Puritan, could still in the seventeenth century furnish materials enough for the immense compilations of the Four Masters, Ward, Wadding, Lynch, and Colgan.

What we have here stated is the simple, unvarnished truth; yet it is but yesterday that the subject has really begun to be studied.

But what is chiefly worthy our attention is, that the monasteries were not only the seats of learning and literature in Ireland, but they constituted and comprised in themselves every thing of value which the nation possessed. As they were found everywhere, there was not room for much else in the department they filled in the island. Take them away, and the country is a blank. So well were the crafty counsellors of Henry VIII. and Elizabeth satisfied of this, that they insisted on the destruction of the monasteries, and turned all their efforts to carry their purpose into effect.

Feudalism had failed in its endeavor to cover the country with castles; the native royalty and inferior chieftainship being engaged in constant bickerings with each other and with the common foe, had been unable to enrich the country with monuments of art and wealthy palaces; the Church alone had accomplished whatever had been effected in this way, and in the Church the monks rather than the bishops had for a long time exercised the preponderating influence. Hence, it may be truly said that

Ireland was essentially a monastic country, more so than any other nation of Christendom.

This fact explains how it happened that the monastic institutions could not be destroyed. The convent-walls might be battered down, the more valuable edifices might be converted into dwellings for the new Protestant aristocracy, their property might go to enrich upstarts, and feed the rapacity of greedy conquerors, but the institution itself could not perish.

It is true that in all Catholic countries this seems also to be the case; but wide is the difference with regard to Ireland. In all places religious establishments have frequently been the object of anti-Christian fury and rage. They have often been destroyed, and seem to have utterly disappeared, when the world has been surprised by their speedy resurrection. The fact is, the Church needs them, and the practice of evangelical counsels must forever be in a state of active operation upon earth, since the grace of God always inspires with it a number of select souls. God is the source; consequently the stream must flow, since the life-spring is eternal and ever-running.

But in other countries besides the one under our consideration religious houses and institutions have sometimes been effectually rooted out, at least for a time. When the French Constituent Assembly, by one of its destructive decrees, closed those establishments all over France, such of them as by their laxity deserved to die, ceased at once to exist, and poured forth their inmates to swell the ranks of a corrupt society, and add religious degradation to the immoral filth of the world. Those religious houses, within whose walls the spirit of God had not ceased to dwell, were indeed closed and emptied; but their inmates endeavored to live their lives of religion in some unknown and obscure spot, until the madness of the Convention, and the Reign of Terror which soon followed, rendered the continuation of the holy exercises of any community absolutely impossible. But mark this well: the holy aims of the monks and nuns found no response in the nation, and, finding themselves almost entirely rejected by a faithless people, with no resting-place in the whole extent of the country, a sudden and total interruption of religious ascetic life in the once most Catholic nation of Europe was the result.

The same may soon come to pass in our days in Italy and Spain, until better times return to those now distracted countries, and the extremities of evil bring them back to something of their primitive faith.

Not so in Ireland: the communities could continue to exist even when turned out-of-doors, because the nation wanted them, and could afford them asylum and peace in the worst periods of persecution. And this great fact of the mutual love between monks, priests, and people, contributed also in no small degree to that union among all, which henceforth became the characteristic feature of a people hitherto split up into hostile clans. Nothing probably tended so much toward effecting the birth of the nation as the deep attachment existing between the Irish and their religious orders. The latter had always preached peace and often reconciled enemies, and brought furious men to the practice of Christian charity and forbearance.

We have seen instances of this when the clans were all powerful and the chieftains thought of nothing but of "preyings," as they called them, compelling their enemies to give "hostages" and devastating the territories of hostile clans. Then the voice of the monk came to be heard in the midst of contending passions, and real miracles were often performed by them in changing into lambs men who resembled roaring lions or devouring wolves; but their action became much more efficacious when nothing was left to the people save their religion and the "friars." These, it is true, could no longer reside within the walls of their convents, but on that very account their life became more truly one with that of the people.

Sometimes they found refuge in the large, hospitable dwellings of the native nobility, where, during the latter part of the reign of Henry VIII. and the whole of that of Elizabeth, the almost independent power of the chieftains could still afford them succor. Sometimes also the humbler dwelling of the farmer or the peasant offered them a sure asylum, wherein they could practise their ministry in almost perfect freedom, owing to the sure and inviolable secrecy of the inmates and neighbors. For a great distance around, the Catholics knew of their abode, were often visited by them, even without mach danger of the fact becoming known to spies and informers. And this brings naturally before us a new feature of the Irish character.

Their nature, which was so expansive and passionate on all other subjects, so that to keep a secret was an impossible feat to them, wore another character when danger to their religion or its ministers required of them to set a seal on their lips. For years frequently, large numbers of priests and religious could not only exist, but move and work among them, without their place of abode becoming known to the swarms of enemies who surrounded them. The nation was trained to prudence and discretion by centuries of oppression and tyranny. Many facts of this nature are known and recorded in the dark annals of those times; but how many more will be known never!

Thus, in the year 1588, during the worst part of Elizabeth's reign, "John O'Malloy, Cornelius Dogherty, and Walfried Ferral, of the order of St. Francis, fell finally victims to the malice of the heretics. They had spent eight years in administering the consolations of religion throughout the mountainous districts of Leinster. Many families of Carlow, Wicklow, and Wexford, had been compelled to take a refuge in the mountains from the fury of the English troops. The good Franciscans shared in all their perils, travelling about from place to place, by night; they visited the sick, consoled the dying, and offered up the sacred mysteries for all. Oftentimes the hard rock was their only bed; but they willingly embraced nakedness, and hunger, and cold, to console their afflicted brethren." - (Moran's Archbishops of Dublin.)

In these few words, we have a picture of the mountain monastery. During those eight years, how many Irish were consoled and comforted by those few laborers, who, driven from their holy home, had chosen to live in the wilderness, and practise their rule among the wandering people of three large counties, receiving in return the substance, the love, and loving secrecy of their flock! We have only to figure to ourselves this scene, or similar, repeated in every corner of the land, and we may then easily understand how the Irish people were brought to the unanimous resolve of standing by each other, and how, from the state of complete division which formerly prevailed, the elements of a compact, solid, and indestructible body, began to form.

We attribute this "birth of a nation" to Henry VIII., because the change which he tried to introduce into the religion of the island constituted the occasion and origin of it; and, although his reign never witnessed that perfect union of the people which came later on, nevertheless, it is true that then it surely began, and its origin was the attempt to establish his spiritual supremacy in Ireland.

This feeling of union and strength in love went on growing, and showed itself more and more, wring the two centuries which followed, when so many scenes similar to the one described were enacted in the remotest parts of the island. God, in his mercy, provided it with many high mountains, difficult of access, whose paths were known only to the natives. In these fastnesses, the holy men, who had been driven from their dwellings and their churches, could rest in peace and attend to the duties of their office. They could even recruit their shattered forces, admit novices, and train them up; and thus their rule continued to be observed, and their existence as a body protracted, long after their enemies imagined that they had perished utterly. As soon as quiet was restored, when persecution abated, and breathing-time was given them, so that they could show themselves, with some safety, more openly, they visited their old abodes, often found some portions of the ruins which admitted of repair, and dwelt again in security where their predecessors had dwelt for centuries.

The peasant's hut would also often afford them shelter; some solitary farm-house on the borders of a lake, or near a deep morass, took the name of their monastery; some cranogue in the lake, or dry spot in the thick of the morass, which they could reach by paths known to themselves only, was their asylum in times of extraordinary danger. In ordinary times, the farm-house, to which they had given the name of their lost monastery, was their convent. It was thus the brothers O'Cleary, and their companions, lived for years, editing the work of the "Four Masters," until, at length, they succeeded in publishing their extraordinary "Annals." The manuscripts which, in spite of the raging persecution, and the "penal laws," they traversed the whole island to collect, were preserved, with a reverend care, in a poor Irish hut. Literary treasures which have since unfortunately perished, but which they saved for a time from the reach of the enemy, and which they perpetuated by having them printed, filled the poor presses and the old furniture of their asylum, and, owing purely to the friendly help of those who had given them shelter, they were enabled to enrich the world with their marvellous compilation.

From the mountain and the hut, on the river-side, the monks were sometimes allowed to move to their former dwellings, at the risk, nevertheless, of their liberty and lives. What their ancestors had done during the

Scandinavian invasions, when the monasteries were so often destroyed and rebuilt, that did the monks of the sixteenth and seventeenth centuries likewise in many parts of the island.

Thus, Father Mooney, a Franciscan, relates that his monastery - that of Multifarnham - having been totally destroyed by Sir Francis Shean, and many monks having been killed, he, with a few others, after long and extraordinary adventures, came back to the spot, then abandoned by the enemy, and "before the feast of the Nativity of our Lord, we built up a little house on the site of the monastery, and there we dwelt who were left after the flight . . . . . Afterward, Father Nehemias Gregan, the father guardian, began to build a church, and to repair the monastery, and for this purpose caused much wood to be cut in the territory of Deabhna McLochlain; and when they had roofed a chapel and some other buildings, there came the soldiers of another Sir Francis Ringtia, and they burned down the monastery again, and carried off some of the brethren captive to Dublin."

This convent of Multifarnham was raised a third time; and, in fact, remained in possession of the Franciscans throughout the persecution, so that to this day the old church has been restored by them, and the modern house, which now forms their convent, is built on the site of the old monastery.

Such for a long time was the case with many other religious establishments; for the same Father Mooney, writing as late as 1624, says: "When Queen Elizabeth strove to make all Ireland fall away from the Catholic faith, and a law was passed proscribing all the members of the religious orders, and giving their monasteries and possessions to the treasury, while all the others took to flight, or at least quitted their houses, and, for safety's sake, lived privately and singly among their friends, and receiving no novices, the order of St. Francis alone ever remained, as it were, unshaken. For, though they were violently driven out of some convents to the great towns, and the convents were profanely turned into dwellings for seculars, and some of the fathers suffered violence, and even death; yet, in the country and other remote places, they ever remained in the convents, celebrating the divine office according to the custom of religious, their preachers preaching to the people and performing their other functions, training up novices and preserving the conventual buildings, holding it sinful to lay aside, or even hide, their religious habit, though for an hour, through any human fear. And, every three years, they held their regular provincial chapters in the woods of the neighborhood, and observed the rule as it is kept in provinces that are in peace."

Thus, when the Cromwellian persecution began, the religious orders were again flourishing in Ireland. They had obtained from the Stuarts some relaxation in the execution of the laws, and, as all at the time were fighting for Charles I. against the Parliamentarians, it was only natural that the authorities did not carry out the barbarous laws to their full extent in the island.

It is no matter of great surprise, therefore, that, in 1641, more than one hundred years after the decree of Henry VIII., the Franciscan order still possessed sixty-two flourishing houses in Ireland, each with a numerous community, besides ten convents of nuns of the order of St. Clare. The acts of the General Chapter of the Dominicans, held in Rome in 1656, referring to the same persecution of Cromwell, state that, when it began, there were forty-three convents of the order, containing about six hundred inmates, of whom only one-fourth survived the calamity. The Jesuits were eighty in number, in 1641, of whom only seventeen remained when the storm had passed away. From a petition presented to the Sacred Congregation, in 1654, we learn that all the Capuchins had been banished, except a few who remained on the island, where they lived as "shepherds," "herdsmen," or "tillers of the soil."

All the decrees of the Parliaments of Henry VIII. and Elizabeth had not succeeded, in the space of a century, in destroying monasticism; the Cromwellian war alone seemed to have done so, as it left the entire nation almost at the last gasp, on the verge of annihilation. Nevertheless, a few years saw the orders again revive and prepare to start their holy work anew. Henry VIII. then, and his vicar, Cromwell, deceived themselves in thinking that they had put an end to monasticism in the land which had been the cradle of so many families of religious. They succeeded only in intensifying the determination of Irishmen not to allow their nationality to be absorbed in that of England. If any thing was calculated to nourish and keep alive that sentiment in their hearts, it was their daily communing with the holy men who shared their distress, their mountain-retreats, their poverty in the bogs, their wretchedness in the woods and glens. If monasticism had created and nurtured the nation on its first becoming Christian, it gave to the people a second birth holier than the first, because consecrated by martyrdom. Henceforth, divided clans and antagonistic septs were to be unknown among them: only Catholic Irishmen were to remain ranked around the successors of "the saints" of old, all determined to be what they were, or die. But as laws, edicts, and measures of fanatic frenzy cannot destroy a nation, the new people was destined to survive for better and brighter days.

We have anticipated the course of events somewhat, in order to pass in review the chief facts connected with the designs of the English Government upon the religious orders. These few words will suffice to give the reader an idea of the new character which such events impressed upon the Irish nation. Every day saw it more compact; every day the resolve to fight to the death for God's cause, grew stronger; the old occasions of division grew less and less, and that unanimity, which suffering for a noble cause naturally gives rise to in the human heart, showed itself more and more. A nation, in truth, was being born in the throes of a wide-spread and long-continued calamity; but long ages were in store in times to come to reward it for the misfortunes of the past.

It is a remarkable thing that, when England, through fear of civil war, was compelled to grant Catholic emancipation in 1829, when Irish agitators succeeded in wrenching it from the enemy, and obtaining it, not only for themselves, but likewise for their English Catholic brethren, the British statesmen, who finally consented to such a tardy measure of justice, steadily refused, nevertheless, to extend the boon to the religious orders. These remained under the ban, and so they remain still. The "penal laws" were never repealed for them, and, even to this day, they are, according to law, strictly prohibited from "receiving novices" under all the barbarous penalties formerly enacted and never abrogated.

But the nation has constantly considered this exception as not to be taken into account. The religious orders now existing are under the protection of the people, and England has never dared to use even a threat against the open violation of these "laws." Dr. Madden, in his interesting work on "Penal Laws," gives prominence to this fact by warmly taking up the old theme of thorough-going Irish Catholicity, by asserting, with force, that "religious orders are necessary to the Church," and that to deny their right to exist, even though it be only on paper in the statute-book, is none the less an outrage against so thoroughly Catholic a nation as the Irish.

The only fact which appears to clash with our reflections is the one well ascertained and mentioned by us, that some native Irish lords occupied certain monasteries and took their share in the sacrilegious plunder. But a few chieftains cannot be said to constitute the nation, and doubtless many of those who yielded to the temptation, listened later to the reproving voice of their conscience, as in the following case, given by Miles O'Reilly, in his "Irish Martyrs:"

"Gelasius O'Cullenan, born of a noble family in Connaught . . . joined the Cistercian order. Having competed his studies in Paris, the monastery of Boyle was destined as the field of his labors. On his arrival in Ireland, he found that the monastery, with its property, had been seized on by one of the neighboring gentry, who was sheltered in his usurpation by the edict of Elizabeth. The abbot . . . went boldly to the usurping nobleman, admonishing him of the guilt he had incurred; and the malediction of Heaven, which he would assuredly draw down upon his family. Moved by his exhortations, the nobleman restored to him the full possession of the monastery and lands; and, some time after, contemplating the holy life of its inmates, . . . he, too, renounced the world and joined the religious institute."

THE IRISH AND THE TUDORS.--ELIZABETH.--THE UNDAUNTED NOBILITY.-- THE SUFFERING CHURCH

ON January 12, 1559, in the second year of the reign of Elizabeth, a Parliament was convened in Dublin to pass the Act of Supremacy; that is to say, to establish Lutheranism in Ireland, as had already been done in England, under the garb of Episcopalianism.

But the attempt was fated to encounter a more determined opposition in Dublin than it had in London.

Sir James Ware says, in reference to it: "At the very beginning of this Parliament, her Majestie's well-wishers found that most of the nobility and Commons--they were all English by blood or birth--were divided in opinion about the ecclesiastical government, which caused the Earl of Sussex (Lord Deputy) to dissolve them, and to go over to England to confer with her Majesty about the affairs of this kingdom.

"These differences were occasioned by the several alterations which had happened in ecclesiastical matters within the compass of twelve years.

"1. King Henry VIII. held the ecclesiastical supremacy with the first-fruits and tenths, maintaining the seven sacraments, with obits and mass for the living and the dead.

"2. King Edward abolished the mass, authorizing the book of common prayers, and the consecration of the bread and wine in the English tongue, and establishing only two sacraments.

"3. Queen Mary, after King Edward's decease, brought all back again to the Church of Rome, and the papal obedience.

"4. Queen Elizabeth, on her first Parliament in England, took away the Pope's supremacy, reserving the tenths and first-fruits to her heirs and successors. She put down the mass, and, for a general uniformity of worship in her dominions, as well in England as in Ireland, she established the book of common prayers, and forbade the use of popish ceremonies."

Such is the very lucid sketch furnished by Ware of the changes which had taken place in religion in England within the brief space of twelve years.

The members of the Irish Parliament, although of English descent, could not so easily reconcile themselves to these rapid changes as their fellows in England had done; in fact, they laid claim to a conscience--a thing seemingly unknown to the English members, or, if known at all, of an exceedingly elastic and slippery nature. Here lay the difficulty: how was it to be overcome? The conversation between Elizabeth and Sussex must have been of a very interesting character.

Returning with private instructions from the queen, the Earl of Sussex again convened the Parliament, which only consisted of the so called representatives of ten counties--Dublin, Meath, West Meath, Louth, Kildare, Carlow, Kilkenny, Waterford, Tipperary, and Wexford. We see that the almost total extinction of the Kildare branch of the Geraldines had extended the English Pale. The other deputies were citizens and burgesses of those towns in which the royal authority predominated. "With such an assembly," says Leland, "it is little wonder that, in despite of clamor and opposition, in a session of a few weeks, the whole ecclesiastical system of Queen Mary was entirely reversed." It is needless to remark that the people had nothing whatever to do with this reversal; it merely looked on, or was already organizing for resistance.

Nevertheless, even in that assembly the queen's agents were obliged to have recourse to fraud and deception, in order to carry her measures, and it cannot be said that they obtained a majority.

"The proceedings," according to Mr. Haverty, "are involved in mystery, and the principal measures are believed to have been carried by means fraudulent and clandestine." And, in a note, he adds: "It is said that the Earl of Sussex, to calm the protests which were made in Parliament, when it was found that the law had been passed by a few members assembled privately, pledged himself solemnly that this statute would not be enforced generally on laymen during the reign of Elizabeth."[1]

Whatever the means adopted to introduce and carry out the new policy, it was certainly enacted that "the queen was the head of the Church of Ireland, the reformed worship was reestablished as under Edward VI., and the book of common prayers, with further alterations, was reintroduced. A fine of twelve pence was imposed on every person who should not attend the new service, for each offence; bishops were to be appointed only by the queen, and consecrated at her bidding. All officers and ministers, ecclesiastical or lay, were bound to take the oath of supremacy, under pain of forfeiture or incapacity; and any one who maintained the spiritual supremacy of the Pope was to forfeit, for his first offence, all his estates, real and personal, or be imprisoned for one year, if not worth twenty pounds; for the second offence, to be liable to praemunire; and for the third, to be guilty of high-treason."

It was understood that those laws would be strictly enforced against all priests and friars, though left generally inoperative for lay people; and, with certain exceptions, mentioned by Dr. Curry, such was the rule observed. Thus, the reign of Elizabeth, which was such a cruel one for ecclesiastics, produced few martyrs among the laity in Ireland. And, for this reason, Sir James Ware is able to boast that, in all the "rebellions" of the Irish against Elizabeth; they falsely complained that their freedom of worship was curtailed, as though they could worship without either priests or churches.

But the law was passed which made it "high-treason" to assert, three times in succession, the spiritual supremacy of the Pope; and, henceforth, whoever should suffer in defence of that Catholic dogma, was to be a traitor and not a martyr.

The woman, seated on the English throne, speedily discovered that it was not so easy a matter to change the religion of the Irish as it had been to subvert completely that of her own people.

---

[1] Dr. Curry, in his "Civil Wars," has collected some curious facts in illustration of this point.

Deprived of religious houses and means of instruction, deprived of priests and churches, no communication with Rome save by stealth, the Irish still showed their oppressors that their consciences were free, and that no acts of Parliament or sentences of iniquitous tribunals could prevent their remaining Catholics.

By promising to deal as lightly with the laity as severely with the clergy, Elizabeth felt confident that the Catholic religion would soon perish in Ireland, and that, with the disappearance of the priests, the churches, sacraments, instruction, and open communion with Rome, would also disappear. To all seeming, her surmises were correct; but the people were silently gathering and uniting together as they had never done before.

The whole of Elizabeth's Irish policy may be comprised under two headings: 1. Her policy toward the nobles, apparently one of compromise and toleration, but really one of destruction, and so rightly did they understand it that they rose and called in foreign aid to their assistance; 2. Her church policy, one of blood and total overthrow, which priests and people, now united forever in the same great cause, resisted from the outset, and finally defeated; and the decrees of high-treason, which were carried out with frightful barbarity, only served to confirm the Irish people in that unanimity which the wily dealings of Henry VIII. had originated.

I. With the nobility Elizabeth hoped to succeed by flattery, cunning, deceit, finally by treachery, and sowing dissension among them; but all her efforts only served to knit them more firmly one to another, and to revive among them the true spirit of nationality and patriotism.

She did not state to them that her great object was to destroy the Catholic Church; nevertheless they should have felt and resented it from the beginning; above all, ought they to have given expression to the contempt they entertained for the bait held out to them that the "laws" would not be executed against them, but against Churchmen only. Had they been truly animated by the feelings which already possessed the hearts of the people, they would have scornfuly rejected the compromise proposed.

But she appeared to allow them perfect freedom in religious matters; she subjected them to no oath, as in England; the new laws were a dead letter as far as regarded the native lords, who lived under other laws and remained silent, as with the lords of the Pale. Yet nothing was of such importance in her eyes as the enforcement of those decrees; consequently, she could only accomplish her designs by deceit. George Browne, the first Protestant Archbishop of Dublin, had predicted that the old Irish race and the Anglo-Irish chieftains would unite and combine with Continental powers in order to establish their independence. The whole policy of Elizabeth's reign would give us reason to believe that she rightly understood the deep remark of the worldly heretic. Hence, although (or, rather, because) the north, Ulster, was at that time the stronghold of Catholic feeling, and the O'Neills and O'Donnells its leaders, she flatters them, has them brought to her court, pardons several "rebellions" of Shane the Proud, and afterward loads with her favors the young Hugh of Tyrone, whom she kept at her own court. She would dazzle them by the splendor of that court, by the royal presents she so royally lavishes upon them, and by the prospect of greater favors still to come. Meanwhile on the south she turns a stern eye, and makes up her mind to destroy what is left of the Geraldine family. This was to be the beginning of the war of extermination, and the nobility which at the time was disunited became firmly consolidated shortly after.

It is needless to go into the glorious and romantic history of the Geraldine family. Elizabeth chose them for the first object of her attack, because they, as Anglo-Irish Catholics, were more odious in her eye than the pure Irish.

She knew that the then Earl of Desmond had escaped almost by miracle from the island with his younger brother John, when the rest of the noble stock had been butchered at Tyburn. She knew that Gerald, after many wanderings, had finally reached Rome, been educated under the care of his kinsman, Cardinal Pole, cherished as a dear son by the reigning Pontiff, had subsequently appeared at the Tuscan court of Cosmo de Medici; that consequently, since his return to Ireland, he might be considered the chief of the Catholic party there, although, to save himself from attainder and hold possession of his immense wealth in Munster, he displayed the greatest reserve in all his actions, appeared to respect the orders of the queen in all things, even in her external policy against the Church; so that if priests were entertained in his castles, it was always by stealth, and they were compelled to lead a life of total retirement.

But, despite all this outward show, Elizabeth knew that Gerald was really a sincere Catholic, that he considered himself a sovereign prince, and would consequently have small scruple about entering into a league against her, not only with the northern Irish chieftains, but even with the Catholic princes of the Continent. She resolved, therefore, to destroy him.

Sidney was sent to Ireland as lord-lieutenant. He travelled first through all Munster, and complained bitterly that the Irish chieftains were destroying the country by their divisions, though perfectly conscious that those divisions were secretly encouraged by England. He appeared to listen to the people, when they complained of their lords, and yet at the holding of assizes he hanged this same people on the flimsiest pretexts, and had them executed wholesale. In one of his dispatches to the home government, he makes complacent allusion to the countless executions which accompanied his triumphant progress through Munster: "I wrote not," he says, "the name of each particular varlet that has died since I arrived, as well by the ordinary course of the law, and the martial law, as flat fighting with them, when they would take food without the good-will of the giver; for I think it is no stuff worthy the loading of my letters with; but I do assure you, the number of them is great, and some of the best, and the rest tremble. For the most part they fight for their dinner, and many of them lose their heads before they are served with supper. Down they go in every corner, and down they shall go, God willing."--(Sidney's Dispatches, Br. M.)

This was the man who announced himself as the avenger of the people on their rulers. He complained chiefly of Gerald of Desmond, and, without any pretext, summoned him with his brother John, carried them prisoners to Dublin, and afterward sent them to the Tower of London. The shanachy of the family relates that then, and then only, Gerald sent a private message to his kinsmen and retainers, appointing his cousin James, son of Maurice, known as James Fitzmaurice, the head and leader in his family during his own absence.

"For James," says the shanachy, "was well known for his attachment to the ancient faith, no less than for his valor and chivalry, and gladly did the people of old Desmond receive these commands, and inviolable was their attachment to him who was now their appointed chieftain."

James began directly to organize the memorable "Geraldine League," upon the fortunes of which, for years, the attention of Christendom was fixed.

This, the first open treaty of Irish lords with the Pope, as a sovereign prince, and with the King of Spain, calls for a few remarks on the right of the Irish to declare open war with England, and choose their own friends and allies, without being rebels.

The English were at this very time so conscious of the weakness of their title to the sovereignty of Ireland, that they were continually striving to prop up their claims by the most absurd pretensions.

In the posthumous act of attainder against Shane O'Neill in the Irish Parliament of 1569, Elizabeth's ministers affected to trace her title to the realm of Ireland back to a period anterior to the Milesian race of kings. They invented a ridiculous story of a "King Gurmondus," son to the noble King Belan of Great Britain, who was lord of Bayon in Spain--they probably meant Bayonne in France--as were many of his successors down to the time of Henry II., who possessed the island after the "comeing of Irishmen into the same lande."--(Haverty, Irish Statutes, 2 Eliz., sess. 3, cap. i.)

These learned men who flourished in the golden reign of Elizabeth must have thought the Irish very easily imposed upon if they imagined they could give ear to such a fabrication, at a time when each great family had its own chronicler to trace its pedigree back to the very source of the race of Miledh.

The title of conquest, at that time a valid one in all countries, had no value with the Irish who never had been and never admitted themselves to have been conquered. Had they not preserved their own laws, customs, language, local governments? Had the English ever even attempted to subject them to their laws? They had openly refused to grant their pretended benefits to those few "degenerate Irishmen" who in sheer despair had applied for them. This policy of separation was adopted by England with the view of "rooting out" the Irish. The English Government could therefore only accept the natural consequence of such a system-- that the Irish race should be left to itself, in the full enjoyment of its own laws and local governments.

The very policy of Henry VIII. and Elizabeth, as displayed in their attempt to break down the clans by favoring "well-disposed Irishmen" and setting them up, by fraudulent elections, as chiefs of the various septs, proves that the English themselves admitted the clans to be real nation--nationes-

-as they were called at the time by Irish chroniclers and by English writers even. It was an acknowledgment of the plain fact that the natives possessed and exercised their own laws of succession and election, their own government and autonomy.

The disappearance of the Ard-Righ, who had held the titular power over the whole country, is no proof that the Irish possessed no government: for they themselves had refused for several centuries to acknowledge his power. The island was split up into several small independent states, each with the right of levying war, and making peace and alliance. Gillapatrick, of Ossory, dispatched his ambassador to Henry VIII. to announce that if he, the English king, did not prevent his deputy, Rufus Pierce, of Dublin, from annoying the clans of Ossory, Gillapatrick would, in self-defence, declare war against the King of England. And the imperious Henry Tudor, instead of laughing at the threat of the chieftain; was shrewd enough to recognize its significance, and prevented it being carried into execution by admitting the cause as valid, and submitting the conduct of his deputy to an investigation.

Moreover, the principles by which Christendom had been ruled for centuries, were just then being broken up by the advent of Protestantism; and novel theories were being introduced for the government of modern nations. What were the old principles, and what the new; and how stood Ireland with respect to each?

In the old organization of Christendom, the key-stone of the whole political edifice was the papacy. Up to the sixteenth century, the Sovereign Pontiff had been acknowledged by all Christian nations as supreme arbiter in international questions, and if England did possess any shadow of authority over Ireland, it was owing to former decisions of popes, who, being misinformed, had allowed the Anglo-Norman kings to establish their power in the island. Whatever may be thought of the bull of Adrian IV., this much is certain: we do not pretend to solve that vexed historical problem.

But, by rebelling against Rome, by rejecting the title of the Pope, England threw away even that claim, and by the bull of excommunication, issued against Elizabeth, the Irish were released from their allegiance to her, supposing that such allegiance had existed, solely built upon this claim.

So well was this understood at the time, that the Roman Pontiffs, as rulers of the Papal States, the Emperors of Germany, as heads of the German Empire, and the Kings of Spain and France, always covertly and sometimes openly received the envoys of O'Neill, Desmond, and O'Donnell, and openly dispatched troops and fleets to assist the Irish in their struggle for their de facto independence.

All this was in perfect accordance, not merely with the authority which Catholic powers still recognized in the Sovereign Pontiff, but even with the new order of things which Protestantism had introduced into Western Europe, and which England, as henceforth a leading Protestant power, had accepted and eagerly embraced. By the rejection of the supreme arbitration of the Popes, on the part of the new heretics, Europe lost its unity as Christendom, and naturally formed itself into two leagues, the Catholic and the Protestant. An oppressed Catholic nationality, above all a weak and powerless one, had therefore the right of appeal to the great Catholic powers for help against oppression. And the pretension of England to the possession of Ireland was the very essence of oppression and tyranny in itself, doubly aggravated by the fact of an apostate and vicious king or queen making it treason for a people, utterly separate and distinct from theirs, to hold fast to its ancient and revered religion.

Who can say, then, that Gregory XIII. was guilty of injustice and of abetting rebellion when, in 1578, he furnished James Fitzmaurice, the great Geraldine, with a fleet and army to fight against Elizabeth? The authority greatest in Catholic eyes, and most worthy of respect in the eyes of all impartial men--the Pope--thus endorsed the patent fact that Ireland was an independent nation, and could wage war against her oppressors. Here we have a stand-point from which to argue the question for future times.

The rash or, perhaps, treacherous share taken by a few Irish chieftains, in the schismatical and heretical as well as unpatriotic decrees of the Parliament of 1541, and in the subsequent ones of 1549, could compromise the Irish nation in nowise, inasmuch as the people, being still even in legal enjoyment of their own government, their chieftains possessed no authority to decide on such questions without the full concurrence of their clans, and these had already pronounced, clearly enough and unmistakably, on the return of their lords from their title-hunting expedition in England.

All the chroniclers of the time agree that "the people" was invariably sound in faith, siding with the chieftains wherever they rose in opposition to oppressive decrees, abandoning them when they showed signs of wavering, even; but, above all, when they ranged themselves with the oppressors of the Church. The English Protestant writers of the period confirm this honorable testimony of the Irish bards, by constantly accusing the natives of a "rebellious" spirit.

The history of the Geraldine struggle is known to all readers of Irish history, and does not enter into the scope of these pages. We have, however, to consider the foreign aid which the chieftains received, from Spain chiefly, and the causes of these failures, which at first would seem to argue a lack of firmness on the part of the Irish themselves. During the Geraldine wars, and later on in what is called the rebellion of Hugh O'Neill and Hugh O'Donnell, the King of Spain sent vessels and troops to the assistance of the Irish. All these expeditions failed, and the destruction of the natives was far greater than it might otherwise have been, in consequence of the greater number of English troops sent to Ireland to face the expected Spanish invasion.

The same ill success attended the French fleet and army dispatched to Limerick by Louis XIV. to assist James II., and, later still, the large fleet and well-appointed troops sent by the French Convention to the aid of the "United Irishmen," in 1798.

In like manner, the Vendeans, on the other side, those French "rebels" against the Convention itself, received their death-blow in consequence of the English who were sent to their succor at Quiberon.

It seems, indeed, a universal historic law that, when a nation or a party in a nation struggles against another, the almost invariable consequence of foreign aid is failure; but no conclusion can be deduced from that fact of lack of bravery, steadfastness, even ultimate success, on the part of those who rise in arms against oppression. Of the many causes which may be assigned to that apparently strange law of history, the chief are:

1. The difficulty of effecting a joint and simultaneous effort between the insurgent forces and the distant friendly power. Help comes either too soon or too late, or lands on a point of the coast where aid is worse than useless, and where it only throws confusion into the ranks of the struggling

native forces, whose plans are thus all disarranged, disconcerted, and thrown into confusion. Add to this the dangers of the sea, the possibly insufficient knowledge of the soundings and of the nature of the coast, the differences of spirit, customs, and language, of the two coalescing forces, and it may be easily concluded that the chances of success, as opposed to those of failure, are but scanty.

2. The forces against which the coalition is made are always immeasurably increased for the very purpose of meeting it, its purport being always known beforehand. In the case under consideration, it were easy to show that Elizabeth was prompted by the fear of Spain to be speedy in crushing the attempted "rebellions" in the south and north. Historians have made a computation of the troops dispatched from England by the queen, and of the treasure spent in these expeditions during her reign, and the result is astonishing for the times. In fact, the whole strength of England was brought into requisition for the purpose of overpowering Ireland.

In our own days, the successful insurrection of Greece against Turkey seems at variance with these considerations. But the independence of the Greeks was brought about rather by the unanimous voice of Europe coercing Turkey than by the few troops sent from France, or by the few English or Poles who volunteered their aid to the insurgents.

The remarks we have made may be further corroborated by the reflection that the successful risings of oppressed nationalities, recorded in modern history, were wholly effected by the unaided forces of the insurgents. Thus, the seven cantons of Switzerland succeeded against Austria, the Venetian Republic against the barbarians of the North, the Portuguese in the Braganza revolution against Spain, and the United Provinces of the Low Countries against Spain and Germany.

The only historical instance which may contravene this general rule is found in the Revolution of the United States of America, where the French cooperation was timely and of real use, chiefly because the foreign aid was placed entirely under the control and at the command of the supreme head of the colonists, General Washington.

These few words suffice for our purpose.

The policy of Elizabeth toward the Irish nobility is well known to our readers. The fate of the house of Desmond was, in her mind, sealed from the beginning. It is now an ascertained fact that she drove the great earl into rebellion, who, for a long time, refused openly to avow his approbation of the confederates' schemes, and even seemed at first to cooperate with the queen's forces, in opposition to them. It was only after his cousin Fitzmaurice and his brother John had been almost ruined that, convinced of the determination of the English Government to seize and occupy Munster with his five or six millions of acres, he boldly stood up for his faith and his country, and perished in the attempt.

It was then that "Protestant plantations" began in Ireland. The confiscated estates of Desmond--which, in reality, did not belong to him but to his tribe--were handed over to companies of "planters out of Devonshire, Dorsetshire, and Somersetshire, out of Lancashire and Cheshire, organized for defence and to be supported by standing forces."--(Prendergast.)

Then the work set on foot by Henry II. in favor of Strongbow, De Lacy, De Courcy, and others, was resumed, after an interval of four hundred years, to be carried through to the end; that is to say, to the complete pauperizing of the native race.

Among the "undertakers" and "planters" introduced into Munster by Elizabeth, a word may not be out of place on Edmund Spenser and Walter Raleigh, the first a great poet, the second a great warrior and courtier. They both united in advocating the extermination of the native race, a policy which Henry VIII. was too high-minded to accept, and Elizabeth too great a despiser of "the people" to notice. To Henry and Elizabeth Tudor the people was nothing; the nobility every thing. Spenser, Raleigh, and other Englishmen of note, who came into daily contact with the nation, saw very well that account should be taken of it, and thought, as Sir John Davies had thought before them, that it ought to be "rooted out." That great question of the Irish people was assuming vaster proportions every day; the people was soon to show itself in all its strength and reality, to be crushed out apparently by Cromwell, but really to be preserved by Providence for a future age, now at hand to-day.

Spenser and Raleigh, being gifted with keener foresight than most of their countrymen, were for the entire destruction of the people, thinking, as did many French revolutionists of our own days, that "only the dead never come back."

The author of the "Faerie Queene," who had taken an active part in the horrible butcheries of the Geraldine war, when all the Irish of Munster were indiscriminately slaughtered, insisted that a similar policy should be adopted for the whole island. In his work "On the State of Ireland," he asks for "large masses of troops to tread down all that standeth before them on foot, and lay on the ground all the stiff-necked people of that land." He urges that the war be carried on not only in the summer but in the winter; "for then, the trees are bare and naked, which use both to hold and house the kerne; the ground is cold and wet, which useth to be his bedding; the air is sharp and bitter, to blow through his naked sides and legs; the kine are barren and without milk, which useth to be his food, besides being all with calf (for the most part), they will through much chasing and driving cast all their calf, and lose all their milk, which should relieve him in the next summer."

Spenser here employs his splendid imagination to present gloatingly such details as the most effective means for the destruction of the hated race. All he demands is, that "the end should be very short," and he gives us an example of the effectiveness and beauty of his system "in the late wars in Munster." For, "notwithstanding that the same" (Munster) "was a most rich and plentiful country, full of corne and cattle, . . . yet ere one yeare and a half they" (the Irish) "were brought to such wretchednesse as that any stony heart would have rued the same. Out of every corner of woods and glynnes, they came creeping forthe upon their hands, for their legges could not beare them; they looked like anatomies of death; they spoke like ghosts crying out of their graves . . . . that in short space there were none almost left, and a most populous and plentiful country suddenly left void of man and beast."

Such is a picture, horribly graphic, of the state to which Munster had been reduced by the policy of England as carried out by a Gilbert, a Peter Carew, and a Cosby; and to this pass the "gentle" Spenser would have wished to see the whole country come.

Even Mr. Froude is compelled to denounce in scathing terms the monsters employed by the queen, and his facts are all derived, he tells us, from existing "state papers."

Writing of the end of the Geraldine war, he says: "The English nation was at that time shuddering over the atrocities of the Duke of Alva. The children in the nurseries were being inflamed to patriotic rage and madness by the tales of Spanish tyranny. Yet, Alva's bloody sword never touched the young, defenceless, or those whose sex even dogs can recognize and respect.

"Sir Peter Carew has been seen murdering women and children, and babies that had scarcely left the breast; but Sir Peter Carew was not called on to answer for his conduct, and remained in favor with the deputy. Gilbert, who was left in command at Kilnallock, was illustrating yet more signally the same tendency. "Nor" was Gilbert a bad man. As time went on, he passed for a brave and chivalrous gentleman, not the least distinguished in that high band of adventurers who carried the English flag into the western hemisphere . . . . above all, a man of 'special piety.' He regarded himself as dealing rather with savage beasts than with human beings (in Ireland), and, when he tracked them to their dens, he strangled the cubs, and rooted out the entire brood.

"The Gilbert method of treatment has this disadvantage, that it must be carried out to the last extremity, or it ought not to be tried at all. The dead do not come back; and if the mothers and babies are slaughtered with the men, the race gives no further trouble; but the work must be done thoroughly; partial and fitful cruelty lays up only a long debt of deserved and ever-deepening hate.

"In justice to the English soldiers, however, it must be said that it was no fault of theirs if any Irish child of that generation was allowed to live to manhood."--(Hist. of Engl., vol. x., p. 507.)

These Munster horrors occurred directly after the defeat of the Irish at Kinsale. Cromwell, therefore, in the atrocities which will come under our notice, only followed out the policy of the "Virgin Queen." And it is but too evident that the English of 1598 were the fathers or grandfathers of those of 1650. Both were inaugurating a system of warfare which had never been adopted before, even among pagans, unless by the Tartar troops under Genghis Khan; a system which in future ages should shape the policy, which was followed, for a short time, by the French Convention in la Vendee.

Raleigh, as well as Spenser, seems to have been a vigorous advocate of this system. It is true that his sole appearance on the scene was on the occasion of the surrender of Smerwick by the Spanish garrison; but the Saxon spirit of the man was displayed in his execution of Lord Grey's orders, who, after, according to all the Irish accounts, promising their lives to the Spaniards, had them executed; and Raleigh appears to have directed that execution, whereby eight hundred prisoners of war were cruelly butchered and flung over the rocks in the sea. From that time out the phrase "Grey's faith" (Graia fides) became a proverb with the Irish.

After having succeeded in crushing Desmond and "planting" Munster, the attention of Elizabeth was directed to the O'Neills and O'Donnells of Ulster. That thrilling history is well known. It is enough to say that O'Donnell from his youth was designedly exasperated by ill-treatment and imprisonment; and that as soon as O'Neill, who had been treated with the greatest apparent kindness by the queen, that he might become a queen's man, showed that he was still an Irishman and a lover of his country, he was marked out as a victim, and all the troops and treasures of England were poured out lavishly to crush him and destroy the royal races of the north.

In that gigantic struggle one feature is remarkable--that, whenever the English Government felt obliged to come to terms with the last asserters of Irish independence, the first condition invariably laid down by O'Neill and O'Donnell was the free exercise of the Catholic religion. For we must not lose sight of the well-ascertained fact that the English queen, who at the very commencement of her reign had had her spiritual supremacy acknowledged by the Irish Parliament under pain of forfeiture, praemunire, and high-treason, insisted all along on the binding obligation of this title; and though at first she had secretly promised that this law should not be enforced against the laity, she showed by all her measures that its observance was of paramount importance in her eyes.

Had the Irish followed the English as a nation, and accepted Protestantism, Elizabeth would scarcely have made war upon them, nor introduced her "plantations." All along the Irish were "traitors" and "rebels" simply because they chose to remain Catholics, and McGeoghegan has well remarked that, "not-withstanding the severe laws enacted by Henry VIII., Edward VI., and Elizabeth, down to James I., it is a well-established truth that, during that period, the number of Irishmen who embraced the 'reformed religion' did not amount to sixty in a country which at the time contained two millions of souls." And McGeoghegan might have added that, of these sixty, not one belonged to the people; they were all native chieftains who sold their religion in order to hold their estates or receive favors from the queen.

Sir James Ware is bold enough to say that, in all her dealings with the Irish nobility, Elizabeth never mentioned religion, and their right of practising it as they wished never came into the question. She certainly never subjected them to any oath, as was the case in England. Technically speaking, this statement seems correct. Yet it is undeniable that Elizabeth allowed no Catholic bishops or priests to remain in the island; permitted the Irish to have none but Protestant school-teachers for their children; bestowed all their churches on heretical ministers; closed, one by one, all the buildings which Catholics used for their worship, as soon as their existence became known to the police; in fact obliged them to practise Protestantism or no religion at all.

In the eyes of Elizabeth a Catholic was a "rebel." Whoever was executed for religion during her reign was executed for "rebellion." The Roman emperors who persecuted the Church during the first three centuries, might have advanced the same pretences And indeed the early Christians were said to be tortured and executed for their "violation of the laws of the empire."

This point will come more clearly before us in considering the second phase of the policy of Elizabeth, her direct interference with the Church.

II. If the policy of England's queen had been one of treachery and deceit toward the nobility, toward the Church it was avowedly one of blood and destruction.

Well-intentioned and otherwise well-informed writers, among them Mr. Prendergast, seem to consider that the main object of the atrocious proceedings we now proceed to glance at was "greed," and that the English Government merely connived at the covetous desires of adventurers and undertakers, who wished to destroy the Irish and occupy their lands; for, as Spenser says "Sure it was a most beautiful and sweete country as any under heaven, being stored throughout with many goodly rivers, replenished with all sorts of fish most abundantly; sprinkled with many very sweete islands, and goodly lakes like little inland seas; adorned with goodly woods; also full of very good ports and havens opening upon England as inviting us to come into them."

Such, according to those writers, was the policy of England from the first landing of Strongbow on the shores of Erin, and even during the preceding four centuries, when both races were Catholic, and the conversion of the natives to Protestantism could not enter the thoughts of the invaders.

This, to a certain extent, is true. Still, it seems very doubtful to us that Elizabeth should have undertaken so many wars in Ireland, which lasted through her whole reign, and on which she employed all the strength and resources of England, merely to please a certain number of nobles who wished to find foreign estates whereon to settle their numerous offspring.

The chief importance, in her eyes, of the conquest was clearly to establish her spiritual superiority in that part of her dominions. She would have left the native nobles at peace, and even conferred on them her choicest favors, had they only consented, as English subjects, to break with Rome. Rome had excommunicated her; Pius V. had released her subjects from their allegiance because of her heresy, and Ireland did not reject the bull of the Pope. This in her eyes constituted the great and unpardonable offence of the Irish. And that, for her, the whole question bore a religious character, will appear more clearly from her conduct toward the Catholic Church throughout her reign. Into this part of our subject the examination of the step taken by Pius V. naturally enters, and, in examining it, we shall see whether, and how far, the Irish can be called rebels and "traitors."

In his history of the Reformation, Dr. Heylin says of Elizae's supremacy could not stand together, and she could not possibly maintain the one without discarding the other." This is perfectly true, and furnishes us with the key to all her church measures.

She pretended to be a Catholic during Mary's reign; but it was merely pretence. To persevere in Catholicity required of her the sacrifice of her political aspirations; for the Church could not admit of her legitimacy, and consequently her title to the crown of England. Hence, upon the death of Mary Tudor, the Queen of Scots immediately assumed the title of Queen of England; and although the Pope, then Pius IV., did not immediately declare himself in favor of Mary Stuart, but reserved his decision for a future period, nevertheless, the view of the case adopted by the Pontiff could not be mistaken. Elizabeth's legitimacy, or, as Heylin has it, "legitimation and the Pope's supremacy could not stand together." No course was left open to her, then, than to reject the pontifical authority, and establish her own in her dominions, as she did not possess faith enough to set her soul above a crown; and the success of her father, Henry VIII., and of her half-brother, Edward VI., encouraged her in this step. This fully explains her policy. It became a principle with her that, to accept the Pope's supremacy in spirituals, was to deny her legitimacy, and consequently to be guilty of treason against her. This made the position of Catholics in England and Ireland a most trying one. But their moral duty was clear enough, and every other obligation had to give way before that. In the persecution which followed they were certainly martyrs to their duty and their religion.

That the question of the succession in England was an open one, must be admitted by every candid man. Who was the legitimate Queen of England at the death of Mary Tudor? The Queen of Scots assumed the title, and, as the legitimate offspring of the sister of Henry VIII., she had the right to it as the nearest direct descendant in the event of Elizabeth's pretensions not being admitted by the nation. The nation at the time was in fact, though not in right, the nobles, who enriched themselves at the expense of the Church, and were therefore deeply interested in the exclusion of Catholic principles. A Parliament composed of the nobles had already acknowledged Elizabeth to the exclusion of the Queen of Scots, and the former decision was reaffirmed as against a "female pretender" supported by a foreign power, namely, France.

England, that is to say, the corrupt nobility of the kingdom, by taking upon itself that decision, refused to submit the question to the arbitration of the Pope; and thus, for the first time, the principles which had guided Christendom for eight hundred years, were discarded. Yet, under Mary, the Catholic Church had been declared the Church of the state; at her death, no change took place; the mass of the people was still Catholic. It took Elizabeth her whole reign to make the English a thoroughly Protestant people. The great mass of the nation came consequently then, even legally, under the law of mediaeval times, which surrendered the decision of such cases into the hands of the Roman Pontiff.

Again, when we reflect that our preset object is the consideration of who was the legitimate Queen of Ireland, the question becomes clearer and simpler still. The supremacy of Henry VIII. had never been acknowledged in the island, even by those who had subscribed to the decrees of the Parliament of 1541 and 1569. The Irish chieftains had not only never assented, but had always preserved their independence in all, save the suzerainty of the English monarchs, and they were at the time, without exception, Catholics. For them, therefore, the Pope was the expounder of the law of succession to the throne, as, up to that time, he had been generally recognized in Europe. Elizabeth, consequently, as an acknowledged illegitimate child, could not become a legitimate queen without a positive declaration and election by the true representatives of the people, approved by the Pope. Her assumption, then, of the supreme government was a mere usurpation. The theory of governments de facto being obeyed as quasi-legitimate had not yet been mooted among lawyers and theologians. With respect to the whole question, there can be no doubt as to the conclusion at which any able constitutional jurist of our days would arrive.

Could usurped rights such as these invest Elizabeth with authority to declare herself paramount not only in political but also in religious matters? And, because she was called queen, can it be considered treason for an Irishman to believe in the spiritual supremacy of the Pope? Yet, unless we look upon as martyrs those who died on the rack and the gibbet in Ireland during her reign, because they refused to admit in a woman the title of Vicar of Christ, to such decision must we come.

The policy of the English queen toward Catholic bishops, priests, and monks, presents the question in a still stronger light. Its chief feature will now come before us, and will show how all of these suffered for Christ. We say all, because not only those are included in the category who held aloof from politics and confined themselves to the exercise of their spiritual functions, but those also who, at the bidding of the Pope, or following the natural promptings of their own inclinations, favored the so-called rebellion of the Geraldine and of the Ulster chieftains. The lives and death of both are now well known, and to both we award the title of heroes and Christian martyrs.

As it would be too long to present here a complete picture of those events, and trace the biography of many of those who suffered persecution at that time, we content ourselves with two faithful representatives of the classes above mentioned--Richard Creagh, Archbishop of Armagh, and Dr. Hurley, Archbishop of Cashel. The case of the great Oliver Plunkett, who suffered under Charles II., and who was the victim of the entire English nation, is beyond our present discussion.

The biography of the first of these has been written by several authors, who, agreeing as to the main facts of his history, differ only in their chronology. Dr. Roothe's account is the longest of all and is intricate, and subject to some confusion with regard to dates; but a sketch of that life, which appeared in the Rambler of April, 1853, is the most consistent and easily reconciled with the well-known facts of the general history of the period, and therefore we follow it:

Richard Creagh, proposed for the See of Armagh by the nuncio, David Wolfe, arrived at Limerick in the August of 1560, at the very beginning of the reign of Elizabeth. Pius IV., who was then Pontiff, had not come to any conclusion respecting the sovereignty of England, and did not openly declare himself in favor of the right of Mary Stuart to the crown. The Pope, not having given any positive injunctions to Archbishop Creagh, with regard to his political conduct, the latter was left free to follow the dictates of his conscience. He came only with a letter, to Shane O'Neill, who, at the time, was almost independent in Ulster.

Not only did the archbishop not take any part in the political measures of the Ulster chieftain, who was often at war with Elizabeth, but he soon came to a disagreement with him on purely conscientious grounds, and finally excommunicated him. In the midst of the many difficulties which surrounded him, he resolved to inculcate peace and loyalty to Elizabeth throughout Ulster, asking of Shane only one favor, that of founding colleges and schools, and thinking that, by remaining loyal to the queen, he might obtain her assistance in founding a university. The good prelate little knew the character of the woman with whom he had to deal, imagining probably that the decree of her spiritual supremacy would remain a dead letter for the priesthood, as had been falsely promised to the laity.

But he was not left long to indulge in these delusions; for, in the act of celebrating mass in a monastery of his diocese, he was betrayed by some informer, and was arrested by a troop of soldiers, who conducted him before the government authorities, by whom he was sent to London and confined in the Tower on January 18,1565. He was there several times interrogated by Cecil and the Recorder of London, who could easily ascertain that the prelate was altogether guiltless of political intrigue.

He escaped miraculously, passed through Louvain, went to Spain, at the time at peace with England, and, wishing to return to Ireland, wrote, through the Spanish ambassador, to Leicester, then all-powerful with the queen, to protest beforehand that, if the Pope should order him to return to his diocese, he intended only to render to Caesar what is Caesar's and to God what is God's. Even then, after his prison experience of several months, he thought that, if he could persuade Elizabeth that he was truly loyal to her, she would forgive him his Catholicity.

Receiving no answer, he set sail for his country, where he landed in August, 1566, and shortly after wrote to Sir Henry Sidney, then lord-deputy, in the very terms he had used with Leicester, and proposing in addition to use his efforts in inducing Shane O'Neill to conclude peace.

What Sidney and his masters in London, Cecil and Leicester, must have thought of the simplicity of this good man, it is impossible to say. They condescended to return no answer to his more than straightforward communication, save the short verbal reply concerning O'Neill: "We have given forth speach of his extermination by war."

The good prelate, after having so clearly defined his position, thought he might safely follow the dictates of his conscience, and govern his flock in peace; but he was soon taken prisoner, in April, 1567, by O'Shaughnessy, who received a special letter of thanks from Elizabeth for his services on this occasion.

By order of the queen, he was tried in Dublin; but, so clear was the case before them, that even a Protestant jury could not convict him. The honest Dublin jurors were therefore cast into prison and heavily fined, while the prelate was once again transferred to London, whence he a second time escaped by the connivance of his jailor.

Retaken in 1567, he was handed over to the queen's officers, under a pledge that his life would be spared. And, in consequence of this pledge alone, was he never brought to trial, but kept a close prisoner in the Tower for eighteen years, until in 1585 he was, according to all reliable accounts, deliberately poisoned.

This simple narrative certainly proves that in Elizabeth's eyes, the mere sustaining the Pope's spiritual supremacy was treason, and every Catholic consequently, because Catholic, a traitor deserving death. True, the Irish prelates, monks, and people, might have imitated the majority of the English nobles and people in accepting the new dogma. In that case, they would have become truly loyal and dutiful subjects, and been admitted to all the rights of citizenship; the nobles would have retained possession of their estates, the gentry obtained seats in the Irish Parliament; while the common people, renouncing clanship, absurd old traditions, the memory of their ancestors, together with their obedience to the See of Rome, would not have been excluded from the benefits of education; would have been allowed to engage in trades and manufactures; would have been permitted to keep their land, or hold it by long leases; would have enjoyed the privilege of dwelling in walled towns and cities, if they felt no inclination for agriculture. They would have become no doubt "a highly-prosperous" nation, as the English and Scotch of our days have become, partakers of all the advantages of the glorious British Constitution, cultivating the fields of their ancestors, and converting their beautiful island into a paradise more enchanting than the rich meadows and wheat-fields of England itself.

On the other hand, they would have obtained all those temporal advantages at the expense of their faith, which no one had a right to take from them; in their opinion, and in that of millions of their fellow-Catholics, they would have forfeited their right to heaven, and the Irish have always been unreasonable enough to prefer heaven to earth. They have preferred, as the holy men of old of whom St. Paul speaks, "to be stoned, cut asunder, tempted, put to death by the sword, to wander about in sheep-skins, in oat-skins; being in want, distressed, afflicted, of whom the word was not worthy; wandering in deserts, in mountains, in dens, and in the caves of the earth, being approved by the testimony of faith:" that is to say, having the testimony of their conscience and the approval of God, and consider-ing this better than worldly prosperity and earthly happiness.

Turning now to those prelates, monks, and priests, who during Elizabeth's reign took part in Irish politics against the queen, can we on that account deny them the title of martyrs to their faith?

Dr. Hurley, Archbishop of Cashel, whose memoirs were published by Miles O'Reilly, may be taken as a type of this class. Suppose, as well grounded, although never proved, the suspicion of the English Government with regard to his political mission. Prelates and priests, generally speaking, were put to death under Elizabeth, or confined to dungeons on mere suspicion, and, as we have seen in the case of the Archbishop of Armagh, even clear proofs of their innocence would not save them.

On his father's side, Dr. Hurley was naturally in the interest of James Geraldine, Earl of Desmond; and, on his mother's, he belonged to the royal family of O' Briens of Munster. Consecrated Archbishop of Cashel at Rome in 1550, under Gregory XIII., during the Geraldine rebellion, he was compelled to use the utmost precaution in entering Ireland. The police of Elizabeth was particularly active at that time in hunting up priests and monks throughout the whole island, but particularly in the south.

The archbishop escaped all these dangers, and he avoided the certain denunciation of Walter Baal, the Mayor of Dublin probably, who was then actually persecuting his mother, Dame Eleanor Birmingham; he fled to the castle of Thomas Fleming, who concealed him in a secret chamber in his house and treated him as a friend. But when everybody thought the danger past, and that it was no longer imprudent for him to mix in the society of the castle, he was suspected by an Anglo-Irishman of the name of Dillon, denounced by him, and finally surrendered by Thomas Fleming, and conveyed to Dublin, where proceedings were set on foot against him by the Irish Council and the queen's ministers in England.

His imprisonment was coincident with the suppression of the rising in Munster, and the Earl of Desmond was beginning that frightful outlaw-life which only ended with his miserable death.

The object of the archbishop's accusers was to connect him with the designs of Rome and the Munster insurrection; and the state papers preserved in London have disclosed to us the correspondence between Adam Loftus, the Protestant Archbishop of Dublin, on the one side, and Walsingham and Cecil on the other.

The only proofs of the Archbishop's having joined the southern confederacy were: 1. Suspicions, as he was consecrated in Rome about the time of the sailing of the expedition under James Fitzmaurice; 2. The information of a certain Christopher Barnwell, then in jail, who was promised his life if he could furnish proofs enough to convict the prelate. The value of the testimony of an "informer" under such circumstances is proverbial; yet all Barnwell could allege was, that "he was present at a conversation in Rome between Dr. Hurley and Cardinal Comensis, the Pope's secretary, and, the result of the whole conversation was, "that the doctor did not know nor believe that the Earl of Kildare had joined the rebellion of Fitzmaurice and Desmond, and he was rebuked by the cardinal for not believing it."

This was considered overwhelming proof against him, in spite of his positive denial. Torture was applied, but the most awful sufferings could not wring from him the acknowledgment of having taken part in the conspiracy. Yet Loftus and Wallop were of opinion that he was a "rebel" and ought to be put to death. The only difficulty which presented itself to the "Lords Justices" of Ireland was, that there was no statute in Ireland against "traitors" who had plotted beyond the seas, and they asked that the archbishop should either be sent to be tried in England, or tried in Ireland by martial law, which would screen them from responsibility.

This last favor was granted them; and the holy archbishop was taken from prison at early dawn, on a Friday, either in May or June, 1584. He was barbarously hanged in a withey (withe) calling on God, and forgiving his torturers with all his heart.

Our purpose is not to inveigh against this judicial murder, and, by further details, increase the horror which every honest man must feel at the narrative of such atrocious proceedings. We will suppose, on the contrary, that the cooperation of the Archbishop of Cashel with Fitzmaurice and Desmond, and even with the Pope and King of Spain, had been clearly proved--as it is certain that, if not in this case, at least in some others, during the reign of Elizabeth, the bishops or priests accused had really taken part in the attempt of the Irish to free themselves from such tyranny--and insist that, even then, the murdered Catholic ecclesiastics really died for their religion, and could be called "rebels" in no sense whatever.

First, the question might arise as to how far the Irish were subject to the English crown. We have seen how, a few years before, Gillapatrick, of Ossory, asserted his right of making war on England, when he felt sufficient provocation. Under Elizabeth the case was still clearer, at least for Catholics, after the excommunication of the queen by Pius V. As we have seen, the chief title of England to Ireland rested on two pretended papal bulls: another Pope could and did recall the grant, which had been founded on misrepresentation. Up to that time, there had been no real subjection by conquest, outside of the Pale, which formed but an insignificant part of the island.

Under such circumstances, it must at least be admitted that a radically and clearly unjust law, imposed by a foreign though perhaps suzerain power, could be justly resisted by force of arms. And such was the case in Ireland. The Queen of England--the Irish Parliament of 1539 had no other authority than that of the queen, and represented no part of the people--had made it rebellion for the Irish to remain faithful to their religion. What could prevent the Irish from resisting such pretension, even at the cost of effusion of blood? The early Christians, under the Roman Empire, it is true, never rose in arms against the bloody edicts of the Caesars or the Antonines; but the cases are not parallel.

Suppose that Greece or Asia Minor had never succumbed to the Roman power, and had become entirely Christian: no one would refuse to admit their right to offer armed resistance to the extension of the edicts of persecution into their territory. On the contrary, it would have been their duty to do so: and every one of their inhabitants, who was taken and executed as a rebel, would have been crowned with the martyr's crown.

At this point, indeed, comes in the consideration of the special motive which animated each belligerent, even when fighting on the right side. We are far from saying that all the Irishmen, particularly the leaders and chieftains who at that time ranged themselves under the banners of the Desmonds or the O'Neills, fought purely for Christ and religion. Many of them, no doubt, engaged in the contest from mere worldly motives, perhaps even for purposes unworthy of Christians; and in this case, those who fell in the struggle were in no sense soldiers of Christ.

But how many such are to be found among the bishops, priests, or monks, who perished under Elizabeth? May it not be said of them that, to a man, they fell for the sake of religion? We may even be bold enough to say that the majority of the common Irish people who lost their lives in those wars may be placed in the same category as their spiritual rulers, being in reality the upholders of right and the champions of Catholicity.

Let it be remembered that, at the period of which we speak, the only real question involved in the contest was gradually assuming more and more a religious character. Henry VIII. and his deputy, St. Leger, had struck a fatal blow at clanship and Irish institutions in general, by bestowing on and compelling the chieftains to accept English titles, and by investing them with new deeds of their lands under feudal tenure. By Elizabeth, the same policy was steadily and successfully pursued, her court being always graced by the presence of young Irish lords, educated under her own eyes, and loaded with all her royal favors. All she asked of them in return was that they should become Queen's men. The repugnance once felt by Irishmen for that gilded slavery was each day becoming less marked. But, while every thing was seemingly working so well for the attainment of Elizabeth's object at the commencement of her reign, a new feature suddenly shows itself, and grows rapidly into prominence--the attachment of the Irish to their religion, and the violent opposition to the change always kept foremost in view by the queen, namely the substitution of her spiritual supremacy for that of the Pope.

Thus we find the Irish leaders, when proclaiming their grievances, either on the eve of war, or the signing of a treaty of peace, always giving their religious convictions the first place on the list. The religious question, then, was becoming more and more the question, and, notwithstanding all her fine assurances that she would not infringe upon the religious predilections of the laity, Elizabeth's great purpose, in Ireland and in England, was to destroy Catholicity, by destroying the priesthood, root and-branch.

The nobles showed how fully convinced they were of this, when they carne to adopt a system of concealment, even of duplicity, to which Irishmen ought never to have been weak enough to submit. Not only were the practices of their religion confined to places where no Englishman or Protestant could penetrate, but gradually they allowed their houses--those sanctuaries of freedom--to be invaded by the pursuivants of the queen, searching for priests or monks "lately arrived from Rome."

Secret apartments were constructed by skilful architects in noblemen's manors; recesses were artfully contrived under the roofs, in roomy staircases, or even in basements and cellars. There the unfortunate minister of religion was confined for weeks and months, creeping forth only at night, to breathe the fresh air at the top of the house or in the thick shrubbery of the adjoining park. All the means of evading the law used by the Christians of the first centuries were reproduced and resorted to in Catholic Ireland by chieftains who possessed the "secret promise" of the queen that their religion should not be interfered with, and that her supremacy should not be enforced against them.

Not thus did the people act: their keen sense of injustice took in at once all the circumstances of the case. It was a religious persecution, nothing else; and this the nobles also felt in their inmost souls. The people saw the ministers of religion hunted down, seized, dragged to prison, tried, convicted, barbarously executed; they recognized it in its reality as a sheer attempt to destroy Catholicity, and as such they opposed it by every means in their power. They beheld the monks and friars treated as though they had been wild beasts; the soldiers falling on them wherever they met them, and putting them to death with every circumstance of cruelty and insult, without trial, without even the identification required for outlaws. Mr. Miles O'Reilly's book, "Irish Martyrs," is full of cases of this kind. Hence the people frequently offered open resistance to the execution of the law; the soldiers had to disperse the mob; but the real mob was the very troop commanded by English officers.

When at length the Irish lords no longer dared offer asylum to the outlawed priesthood in their manors and castles, the hut of the peasant lay open to them still. The greater the quantity of blood poured out by the executors of the barbarous laws, the greater the determination of the people to protect the oppressed and save the Lord's anointed.

Then opened a scene which had never been witnessed, even under the most cruel persecutions of the tyrants of old Rome. The whole strength of the English kingdom had been called into play to crush the Irish nobility during the wars of Ulster and Munster; the whole police of the same kingdom was now put in requisition for the apprehension and destruction of church-men. Nay, from this very occupation, the great police system which since that time has flourished in most European states, arose, being invented or at least perfected for the purpose.

Then, for the first time in modern history, numbers of "spies" and "informers" were paid for the service of English ministers of state. Not only did the cities of England and Ireland, harbor cities chiefly, swarm with them, but they covered the whole country; they were to be found everywhere: around the humble dwelling of the peasant and the artisan, in the streets and on the highways, inspecting every stranger who might be a friar or monk in disguise. They spread through the whole European Continent--along the coast and in the interior of France and Belgium, Italy and Spain, in the churches, convents, and colleges, even in the courts of princes, and, as we have seen in the case of Dr. Hurley, in the very halls of the Vatican. The English state papers have disclosed their secret, and the whole history is now before us.

To support this army of spies and informers, the soldiers of that other army of England, who were employed either in keeping England under the yoke or in crushing freedom and religion out of Ireland, did not disdain to execute the orders which converted them into policemen and sbirri. And it may be said, to their credit, that they executed those orders with a ferocious alacrity unequalled in the annals of military life in other countries. If, during the most fearful commotions in France, the army has been employed for a similar purpose, it must be acknowledged that, as far as the troops were concerned, they performed their unwelcome task with reluctance, and softened down, at least, their execution, by considerate manners and respectful demeanor. But these soldiers of Elizabeth showed themselves, from first to last, full of ferocity. They generally went far beyond the letter of their orders; they took an inhuman delight in adding insult to injury, uniting in their persons the double character of preservers of public order and ruffianly executioners of innocent victims. Many and many a record of their barbarity is kept to this day. We add a few, only to justify our necessarily severe language:

"The Rev. Thaddeus Donald and John Hanly received their martyr's crown on the 10th of August, 1580. They had long labored among the suffering faithful along the southwestern coast of Ireland. When the convent of Bantry was seized by the English troops, these holy men received their wished-for crown of martyrdom. Being conducted to a high rock impending over the sea, they were tied back to back, and precipitated into the waves beneath."

"In the convent of Enniscorthy, Thaddeus O'Meran, father-guardian of the convent, Felix O'Hara, and Henry Layhode, under the government of Henry Wallop, Viceroy of Ireland, were taken prisoners by the soldiers, for five days tortured in various ways, and then slain."

"Rev. Donatus O'Riedy, of Connaught, and parish priest of Coolrah, when the soldiers of Elizabeth rushed into the village, sought refuge in the church; but in vain, for he was there hanged near the high altar, and afterward pierced with swords, 12th of June, 1582."

"While Drury was lord-deputy, about 1577, Fergal Ward, a Franciscan, . . . fell into the hands of the soldiery, and, being scourged with great barbarity, was hanged from the branches of a tree with the cincture of his own religious habit."

In order to find a parallel to atrocities such as these, we must go back to the record of some of the sufferings of the early martyrs--St. Ignatius of Antioch, for instance, who wrote of the guards appointed to conduct him to Italy: "From Syria as far as Rome, I had to fight with wild beasts, on sea and on land, tied night and day to a pack of ten leopards, that is to say, ten soldiers who kept me, and were the more ferocious the more I tried to be kind to them."

Instances of such extreme cruelty are rare, even in the Acts of the early martyrs, but they meet us every moment in the memoirs of the days of Elizabeth. Both the police-spies and the soldier-police were animated with the rage and fury which must have possessed the soul of the queen herself; for, after all, the cruelty practised in her reign, and mostly under her orders, was not necessary in order to secure her throne to her, during life; and, as she could hope for no posterity of her own, it was not the desire of retaining the crown to her children which could excuse so much bloodshed and suffering. She evidently followed the promptings of a cruel heart in those atrocious measures which constitute the feature of the home policy of her reign. The persecution which raged incessantly throughout her long career, in Ireland and England, is surely one of the most bloody in the annals of the Catholic Church.

ENGLAND PREPARED FOR THE RECEPTION OF PROTESTANTISM--IRELAND NOT

IT cost Elizabeth the greater part of her reign in time, and all the growing resources of a united England in material, to establish her spiritual supremacy in Ireland; and yet, when, at her death, Mountjoy received orders to conclude peace on honorable terms with the Ulster chieftains, her darling policy was abandoned; and failure, in fact, confessed.

On the 30th of March, 1603, Hugh O'Neill and Mountjoy met by appointment at Mellifont Abbey, where the terms of peace were exchanged. O'Neill, having declared his submission, was granted amnesty for the past, restored to his rank, notwithstanding his attainder and outlawry, and reinstated in his dignity of Earl of Tyrone. Himself and his people were to enjoy the "full and free exercise of their religion;" new letters-patent were issued restoring to him and other northern chieftains almost the whole of the lands occupied by their respective clans.

O'Neill, on his part, was to renounce forever his title of "O'Neill," and allow English law to prevail in his territory.

How this last condition could agree with the full and free exercise of the Catholic religion, the treaty did not explain; but it is evident that the new acts of Parliament respecting religion were not to be included in the English law admitted by the Ulster chiefs.

Meanwhile, the descendants of Strongbow's companions had been completely subdued in the south, Munster having been devastated, and the Geraldines utterly destroyed. Yet, even there, Protestantism was not acknowledged by such of the inhabitants as were left.

It may be well to compare here the different results which attended the declaration of the queen's supremacy in England and Ireland:

At the commencement of Elizabeth's reign, England was still, outwardly at least, as Catholic as Ireland. Henry VIII. had only aimed at starting a schism; the Protestantism established under Edward had been completely swept away during Mary's short reign. Could Elizabeth only have hoped to be acknowledged queen by the Pope, there can be little doubt that, even for political motives, she would have refrained from disturbing the peace of the country for the sake of introducing heresy. Religion was nothing to her--the crown every thing.

It was not so easy a matter for her to establish heresy as for Henry to introduce schism. All the bishops of Henry's reign, with the exception of Fisher, had renounced their allegiance to Rome, in order to please the sovereign; all the bishops of Mary's nomination remained faithful to Rome; and so difficult was it to find somebody who should consecrate the new prelates created by Elizabeth, that Catholic writers have, we believe, shown beyond question that no one of the intruding prelates was really consecrated.

Nevertheless, at the end of Elizabeth's reign, there is no doubt that the English people, with a few individual exceptions, were Protestant; and Protestants they have ever since remained.

In Dr. Madden's "History of the Penal Laws," we read "Father Campian was betrayed by one of Walsingham's spies, George Eliot, and found secreted in the house of Mr. Yates, of Lyford, in Berkshire, along with two other priests, Messrs. Ford and Collington. Eliot and his officers made a show of their prisoners to the multitude, and the sight of the priests in the hands of the constables was a matter of mockery to the unwise multitude. This was a frequent occurrence in conveying captured priests from one jail to another, or from London to Oxford, or vice versa, and it would seem, instead of finding sympathy from the populace, they met with contumely, insult, and sometimes even brutal violence. This is singular, and not easily accounted for; of the fact, there can be no doubt."

Dr. Madden probably considered that, within a few years after the change of religion, the English people ought to have shown themselves as firm Catholics as did the Irish. But the explanation of the contumely and violence is easy: it was an English and not an Irish populace. The first had altogether forgotten the faith of their childhood, the second could not be brought to forsake it. The difficulty, in accounting for the difference between them, is in getting at its true cause; and to us it seems that one of the chief causes was the difference of race.

The English upper classes, as a whole, were utterly indifferent to religion; the one thing which affected them, soul and body, was their temporal interests, and, to judge by their ready acquiescence in all the changes set forth at the commencement of the last chapter, they would as soon have turned Mussulmen as Calvinists. The lower classes, at first merely passive, became afterward possessed by a genuine fanaticism for the new creed established by the Thirty-nine Articles; so that, from that period until quite recently--and the spirit still lives--an English mob was always ready to demolish Catholic chapels, and establishments of any kind, wherever the piety of a few had succeeded in erecting such, however quietly.

It is evident from the facts mentioned that, prior even to that extraordinary religious revolution called the Reformation, the Catholic faith did not possess a firm hold upon the English mind and heart, whatever may have been the case in previous ages. It is clear that even "the people" in England were not ready to submit to any sacrifice for the sake of their religion.

There is small doubt that Elizabeth foresaw this, and expected but little opposition on the part of the English nobility and people to the changes she purposed effecting. Had she imagined that the nation would have been ready to submit to any sacrifice rather than surrender their religion, she would at least have been more cautious in the promulgation of her measures, even though she had determined to sever her kingdom from Rome. She might have rested content with the schism introduced by her father, and this indeed would have sufficed for the carrying out of her political schemes.

But she knew her countrymen too well to accredit them with a religious devotion which, if they ever possessed, had long ago died out. She saw that England was ripe for heresy, and the result confirmed her worldly sagacity. How came it, then, that the change which was absolutely impossible in Ireland, was so easily effected in the other country? Or, to generalize the question: How is it that, to speak generally, the nations of Northern Europe embraced Protestantism so readily, while those of Southern Europe refused to receive it, or were only slightly affected by it? Ranke has remarked that, when, after the first outbreak in the North, the movement had reached a certain point in time and space, it stopped, and, instead of advancing further, appeared to recede, or at least stood still.

Many Protestant writers have attempted a weak and flippant solution of the question, and we are continually told of the superior enlightenment of the northern races, of their attachment to liberty, of their higher civilization, and other very fine and very easily-quoted things of the same kind, which, at the present moment, are admitted as truths by many, and esteemed as unanswerable explanations of the phenomenon. According to this opinion, therefore, the southern races were more ignorant, less civilized, more readily duped by priestcraft and kingcraft; above all, readier to bow to despotism, and indifferent to freedom.

Catholic writers, Balmez principally, have often given a satisfactory answer to the question; yet, the replies which they have made to the various sophisms touched upon, have seemingly produced no effect on the modern masses, who continue steadfast in their belief of what has been so often refuted. It would be presumptuous and probably quite useless, on our part, to enter into a lengthened discussion of the question. But, when confined to England, it is a kind of test to be applied to all those subjects of civilization and liberty, and is so clear and true that it cannot leave the least room for doubt or hesitation: moreover, as it necessarily enters into the inquiry which forms the heading of this chapter, it cannot be entirely laid aside.

All that we purpose doing is, discovering why the northern nations fell a prey more readily to the disorganizing doctrines of Protestantism than the southern. The general fickleness of the human mind, which is so well brought out by the great Spanish writer, does not strike us as a sufficient cause; for the mind of southern peoples is certainly not less fickle, on many points at least, than that of other races.

In our comparison between the North and the South, we class the Irish with the latter, although, geographically, they belong to the former, and, indeed, constitute the only northern nation which remained faithful to the Church.

First, let us state the broad facts for which we wish to assign some satisfactory reasons.

After the social convulsions which attended the change of religion had subsided somewhat, it was found that Protestantism had invaded the three Scandinavian kingdoms, to the almost total exclusion of Catholicism, to such an extent, indeed, that, until quite recently, it was death or transportation for any person therein to return to the bosom of the mother Church.

The same statement is true, to almost the same extent, of Northern Germany, where open persecution, or rather war, raged until the establishment of "religious peace" toward 1608. Saxony, whence the heresy sprang, was its centre and stronghold in Germany; and the Saxons were Scandinavians, having crossed over from the southern-borders of the Baltic, where, for a long time, they dwelt in constant intercourse with the Danes, Norwegians, and Swedes.

Saxon and Norman England was found to be, at the end of the sixteenth century, almost entirely Protestant, and the persecution of the comparatively few Catholics who survived flourished therein full vigor.

A singular phenomenon presented itself in the Low Countries. That portion of them subsequently known as Holland, which was first invaded and peopled by the Northmen of Walcheren, became almost entirely Protestant, while Belgium, which was originally Celtic, remained Catholic.

Bavaria, Austria, and Switzerland, were divided between Protestantism and Catholicity, and the division exists to this day.

In France a section only of the nobility, which was originally Norman as well as Frank, and under feudalism had become thoroughly permeated by the northern spirit, was found to have embraced the new doctrines, which were repudiated by the people of Celtic origin. It is true that, later on, the Cevennes mountaineers received Protestantism from the old Waldenses; but we are presenting a broad sketch, and do not deny that several minor lineaments may not fall in with the general picture.

In Italy only literary men, in Spain a few rigorist prelates and monks, showed any inclination toward the "reform" party.

On the whole, then, it is safe to conclude that the Scandinavian mind was congenial to Protestantism.

We say the Scandinavian mind, because the Scandinavian race extended, not only through Scandinavia proper, but also through Northern Germany, along the Baltic Sea and German Ocean; through Holland by Walcheren; through a portion of Central and Southern Germany, as far down as Switzerland, which was invaded by Saxons at the time of Charlemagne, and after him, until Otto the Great gave them their final check, and subdued them more thoroughly than the great Charles had succeeded in doing.

Common opinion traces the Scandinavians and Germans back to the same race. In the generic sense, this is true; and all the Indo-Germanic nations may have originally belonged to the same parent stock; but, specifically, differences of so striking a nature present themselves in that immense branch of the human family, that the existence of sub-races of a definite character, presupposing different and sometimes opposite tendencies, must be admitted.

Who can imagine that the Germans proper are identical with the Hindoos, although by language they, in common with the greater part of European nations, may belong to the same parent stock? In like manner, the Germanic tribes, although possessing many things in common with the Scandinavian race, differ from it in various respects.

The best ethnographic writers admit that the Scandinavian race, which they, in our opinion improperly, name Gothic, differed greatly in its language from the Teutonic. The language of the first, retained in its purity in Iceland to this day, soon became mixed up with German proper in Denmark, Sweden, and even in Norway to a great extent. The languages differed therefore originally, as did, consequently, the races. Even at this very moment an effort is being made by Scandinavians to establish the difference between themselves and the Teutons with respect to language and nationality.

How far the religion of both was identical is a difficult question. We believe it very probable that the worship of Thor, Odin, and Frigga, was purely Scandinavian, and penetrated Germany, as far as Switzerland, with the Saxons. Hertha, according to Tacitus, was the supreme goddess of the Germans. She had no place in Scandinavian mythology. Ipsambul, so renowned among the Teutons, was quite unknown in Scandinavia. The Germans, in common with the Celts, considered the building of temples unworthy the Deity; whereas, the Scandinavian temples, chiefly the monstrous one of Upsala, are well known. Many other such facts might be brought out to show the difference of their religions.

The Germans showed themselves from the beginning attached to a country life; and we know how the Frankish Merovingian kings loved to dwell in the country. The Scandinavians only cared for the sea, and manifested by their skill in navigation how they differed from the Germans, who were less inclined even than the Celts for large naval expeditions.

All this is merely given as strong conjecture, not as proof positive amounting to demonstration, of the real difference between the two races--the Germanic and Scandinavian.

But how was Protestantism congenial to the Scandinavian mind? This second question is of still greater importance than the first.

In the earlier portion of the book, we passed in review the character of the tribes, once clustered around the Baltic, with the exception of the Finns, who dwelt along the eastern coast; and, grounding our opinion on unquestionable authorities, we found that character to consist mainly of cruelty, boldness, rapacity, system, and a spirit of enterprise in trade and navigation.

When they embraced Christianity, it undoubtedly modified their character to a great extent, and many holy people lived among them, some of whom the Church has numbered among the saints. But the conquest of these ferocious pirates was undoubtedly the greatest triumph ever achieved by the holy Spouse of Christ.

Yet, even after becoming Christian, they preserved for a long time--we speak not now of the present day--deep features of their former character, among others the old spirit of rapacity, and that systematic boldness which, when occasion demands, is ever ready to intrench upon the rights of others. They soon displayed, also, a general tendency to subject spiritual matters to individual reason, and the great among them to interfere and meddle with religious affairs. The Dukes of Normandy, the Kings of England, and the Saxon Emperors of Germany, seldom ceased disputing the rights of spiritual authority; and the learned among them were forward to question the supremacy of Rome in many things, and to argue against what other people, more religiously inclined, would have admitted without controversy. That spirit of speculation, to which the Irish Four Masters partly ascribed the introduction of Protestantism into England, was rampant in the schools of these northern nations, when a superior civilization gave rise to the erection of universities and colleges in their midst.

But over and above that systematic philosophical spirit, their character was deeply imbued with a material rapacity which, after all, has always constituted the great vice of those northern tribes. It is unnecessary to remind the reader that, in England chiefly, Protestantism was particularly grateful to the avaricious longings of the courtiers of Henry VIII. and Elizabeth. The confiscation of ecclesiastical property and its distribution among the great of the nation was the chief incentive which moved them to adopt the convenient doctrines of the new order, and subvert the old religion of the country. This rapacious spirit showed itself also in Germany, though not so conspicuously as in England; and certainly, in both countries, the universal confiscation of the estates of religious houses, and the robbery of the plate and jewels of the churches, are prominent features in the history of the great Reformation.

William Cobbett has written eloquently on this subject, and marshalled an immense array of facts so difficult of denial that the defenders of Protestantism were compelled to resort to the petty subterfuge of retorting that the great English radical was a mere partisan, who never spoke sincerely, but always supported the theory he happened to take up by exaggerated and distorted facts, which no one was bound to admit on his responsibility. Such was their reply; but the awkward facts remained and remain still unchallenged.

But, since Cobbett, men who could not be accused of partisanship and exaggeration have published authentic accounts of the unbounded rapacity of the Reformers of the sixteenth century, in England particularly, which all impartial men are bound to respect, and not attribute to any unworthy motive, since they are supported even by Protestant authorities. We quote a few, taken from the "History of the Penal Laws" by Dr. R. R. Madden:

"The Earl of Warwick, afterward Duke of Northumberland, was the first of the aristocracy in England who inveighed publicly against the superfluity of episcopal habits, the expense of vestments and surplices, and ended in denouncing altars and the 'mummery' of crucifixes, pictures and images in churches.

"The earl had an eye to the Church plate, and the precious jewels that ornamented the tabernacles and ciboriums. Many courtiers soon were moved by a similar zeal for religion--a lust for the gold, silver, and jewels of the churches. In a short time, not only the property of churches, but the possession of rich bishoprics and sees, were shared among the favorites of Cranmer and the protector (Somerset): as were those of the See of Lincoln, 'with all its manors, save one;' the Bishoprie of Durham, which was allotted to Dudley, Duke of Northumberland; of Bath and Wells, eighteen or twenty of whose manors in Somerset, were made a present of to the protector, with a view of protecting the remainder."

A number of similar details are to be found in the pages of the same author.

Dr. Heylin, a Protestant, says: "That the consideration of profit did advance this work--of the Reformation--as much as any other, if perchance not more, may be collected from an inquiry made two years after, in which (inquiry) it was to be interrogated: `What jewels of gold, or silver crosses, candlesticks, censers, chalices, copes, and other vestments, were then remaining in any of the cathedral or parochial churches, or, otherwise, had been embezzled or taken away?'. . . The leaving," adds Dr. Heylin, "of one chalice to every church, with a cloth or covering for the communion-table, being thought sufficient. The taking down of altars by command, was followed by the substitution of a board, called the Lord's Board, and subsequently of a table, by the determination of Bishop Ridley.

"Many private persons' parlors were hung with altar-cloths, their tables and beds covered with copes, instead of carpets and coverlets, and many made carousing cups of the sacred chalices, as once Belshazzar celebrated his drunken feasts in the sanctified vessels of the Temple. It was a sorry house, not worth the naming, which had not something of this furniture in it, though it were only a fair large cushion made of a cope or altar-cloth, to adorn their windows, and to make their chairs appear to have somewhat in them of a chair of state."

Could such scenes as these have been surpassed by what took place during the ninth, tenth, and eleventh centuries, in the rude towns of Norway and Denmark, at the return of a powerful seakong, with his large fleet, from a piratical excursion into Southern Europe, when the spoils of many a Christian church and wealthy house went to adorn the savage dwellings or those barbarians? Adam of Bremen relates how he saw, with his own eyes, the rich products of European art and industry accumulated in the palace of the King of Denmark, and in the loathsome dwellings of the nobility, or exposed for sale in the public markets of the city.

But rapacity formed only one characteristic of the Scandinavians; the mind of the people, moreover, showed itself, notwithstanding the intricate and monstrous mythology which it had created when pagan, of a rationalistic and anti-supernatural tendency. Their mind was naturally systematic and reasoning; it discussed spiritual matters in all their material aspects, and thus gave rise to those speculations which soon became the source of heresy. Hence, in England and the north of Germany, the power of Rome was always called in question; and as the English mind was altogether Scandinavian, while that of the Germans was mixed with more of a southern disposition, the chief trouble in Germany, between the empire and the Roman Church, lay in the question of investitures, which combined a material and spiritual aspect, whereas, in England, the quarrel was almost invariably of a pecuniary nature, as, for instance, Peter's pence.

Even in the most Catholic times, the English made a bitter grievance of the levying of Peter's pence among them, and of the giving of English benefices to prelates of other nations, which also resolved itself into a question of revenue or money. And so characteristic was the grievance of the whole nation that it was restricted to no class, churchmen and monks being as loud in their denunciations of Rome as the king and the nobles; and thus the theological questions of the papal supremacy and of ecclesiastical authority generally took with them quite a material form. The diatribes of the Benedictine monk Matthew Paris are well known, and their worldly spirit can only excite in us pity that they should have been the chief cause of the destruction of his own order in England and Ireland, and of the total spoliation of the religious houses in whose behalf he imagined that he wrote.

If the harms done by those contemptible wranglings about Peter's pence and benefices had been confined to depriving the pontifical exchequer of a revenue which was cheerfully granted by other nations to aid the Father of the Faithful, the result was to be regretted; but, after all, Christendom would not have suffered in a much more sensible quarter. But in England the question passed immediately to the election of bishops and abbots, and thus the opposition to Rome gradually assumed much vaster proportions.

The nation, also, in the main, sided with the kings against the popes. Every burgher of London, York, or Canterbury, got it into his head that Rome had formed deep designs of spoliation against his private property, and purposed diving deep into his private purse. In such a state of public opinion, respect for spiritual authority could not fail to diminish and finally die out altogether; and, when the voice of the Pontiff was heard on important subjects in which the best interests of the nation were involved, even the clearest proof that Rome was right, and desired only the good of the people, could not entirely dispel the suspicious fears and distrusts which must ever lurk in the mind of the miser against those he imagines wish to rob him.

It is not possible to enter here into further details, but, if the reader wish for stronger proofs of the "questioning spirit," "reasoning mistrust," and "systematic doggedness," natural to the Scandinavian mind, he has only to reflect on what took place in England at the time of the Reformation. Every question respecting the soul, every supernatural aspiration of the Christian, every emotion of a living conscience, appears to be altogether absent from all those English nobles, prelates, theologians, learned university men, even simple priests and monks often, save a very few who, with the noble Thomas More, thought that "twenty years of an easy life could not without folly be compared with an eternity of bliss." The reasoning faculty of the mind, nourished on "speculations," had replaced faith, and, every thing of the supernatural order being obliterated, nothing was left but worldly wisdom and material aspirations for temporal well-being.

By reviewing other characteristics of the Scandinavian race, we might arrive at the same conclusion; but our space forbids us to go into them. After what has been said, however, it is easy to see how well prepared was the English nation for accepting the change of religion almost without a murmur.

There was, indeed, some expression of indignation on the part of the people at the beginning of the reign of Edward VI., when the desecration of the churches began. "Various commotions," says Dr. Madden, "took place in consequence of the reviling of the sacrament, the casting it out of the churches in some places, the tearing down of altars and images; in one of which tumults, one of the authorities was stabbed, in the act of demolishing some objects of veneration in a church.

"The whole kingdom, in short, was in commotion, but particularly Devonshire and Norfolk. In the former county, the insurgents besieged Devon; a noble lord was sent against them, and, being, reenforced by the Walloons--a set of German mercenaries brought over to enable the government to carry out their plans--his lordship defeated these insurgents, and many were executed by martial law."

But this remnant of affection for the religion of their fathers seems to have soon died out, since at the death of Edward the people appeared to have become thoroughly converted to the new doctrines. At the very coronation of Mary, a Catholic clergyman having prayed for the dead and denounced the persecutions of the previous reign, a tumult took place; the preacher was insulted, and compelled to leave the pulpit. What wonder, then, that, at the death of Elizabeth, England was thoroughly Protestant?

We are very far from ignoring the noble examples of attachment to their religion displayed by Christian heroes of every class in England during those disastrous days. The touching biographies of the English martyrs, told in the simple pages of Bishop Challoner, cannot be read without admiration. The feeling produced on the Catholic reader is precisely that arising from a perusal of the Acts of the Christian martyrs under the Roman emperors, which have so often strengthened our faith and drawn tears of sorrow from our eyes. At this moment, particularly when so many details, hitherto hidden, of the lives of Catholics, religious, secular priests, laymen, women, during those times, are coming to light in manuscripts religiously preserved by private families, and at last being published for the edification of all, the story is moving as well as inspiring of the heroism displayed by them, not only on the public scaffold, but in obscure and loathsome jails, in retreats and painful seclusion, continuing during long years of an obscure life, and ending only in a more obscure death, when the victim of persecution was fortunate enough to escape capture. There is no doubt that, when the whole story of the hunted Catholics in England shall be known, as moving a narrative of their virtues will be written as can be furnished by the ecclesiastical annals of any people.

Nevertheless, what has been said of the nation, as a nation, remains a sad fact which cannot be doubted. Those noble exceptions only prove that the promptings of race are not supreme, and that God's grace can exalt human nature from whatever level.

How different were the nations of the Latin and Celtic stock! With them the attachment to the religion of their fathers was not the exception, but the rule, and it is only necessary to bear in mind what the Abbe McGeoghegan has said--that, at the death of Elizabeth, scarcely sixty Irishmen, take them all in all, had professed the new doctrines--in order at once to comprehend the steady tendency toward the path of duty imparted by true nobility of blood. Nor did the Irish stand alone in this steadfastness; it is needless to call to mind how the people generally throughout France, and particularly in Paris, acted at the time when the Huguenot noblemen would have rooted in the soil the errors planted there before, and already bearing fruit in Germany, Switzerland, and England.

It looks as though we had lost sight of the interesting question proposed at the outset, and of which so far not a word has been said--whether Protestantism spread so readily in the North, because it found that region peopled with races better disposed for civilization, if not taking the lead already in that respect, and men ardent for freedom and impatient of servitude of any kind. We stated that the solution of this question, particularly in the case of England, is clear, and consequently not to be discarded on account of previous solutions of the same question, which have scarcely met with any attention from the adverse side.

One thing certainly undeniable is, that neither in its origin, nor even in its consequences, can Protestantism be esteemed as in any sense the promoter of freedom and civilization in the British islands.

It has always struck us as strange that sensible men, acquainted with history, could maintain that an aspiration after freedom and a higher civilization gave to Germany and England a leaning toward Protestantism. We can understand how the state of Europe in the eighteenth and nineteenth centuries may give a coloring to the statement of a partisan writer, desirous of explaining in these modern times the greater amount of freedom really enjoyed in England, and the advanced material prosperity visible generally among Protestant Northern nations. So much we can understand. But, to make Protestantism the origin of freedom and civilization, and ascribe to it what happened subsequent to its spread indeed, but what really resulted from very different causes, passes our comprehension.

As far as freedom goes, the most superficial reader must know that there was not a particle of it left in England when Protestantism commenced; and it were easy to show that there was less of it in Germany than in Italy, Spain, and even France.

Who can mention English freedom in the same breath with Henry and Elizabeth Tudor? How could the actions of those two members of the family advance it in the least degree, and was it not precisely the slavish disposition of the English people at the time which prepared them so admirably for the reception of German heresy? The people were treated like a set of slaves, and stood for nothing in the designs of those great political rulers. In the very highest of the aristocracy, there lingered not a spark of the old brave spirit which wrung Magna Charta from the heart of a weak sovereign. The king or queen could fearlessly trample on every privilege of the nobility, send the proudest lords of the nation to the block, almost without trial, and confiscate to the swelling of the royal purse the immense estates of the first English families. There is no need of proofs for this. The proofs are the records, the headings, as it were, of the history of the times which one may read as he runs; it constitutes the very essence of their history; and events of the sixteenth century in England scarcely present us with any thing else. This state of things was the natural result of the general anarchy which prevailed during the "Wars of the Roses."

A more interesting and intricate question still might be raised here: how to explain the appearance of such a phenomenon in so proud a nation? Had the Catholic religion, which, up to that time, had been the only religion of the country, anything to do with the matter? These questions might furnish material for a very animated discussion. But, with regard to the fact itself-- the slavish disposition of Englishmen at that time under kingly and queenly rule--no doubt can possibly exist.

To show that Catholicity had nothing to do with the introduction of such a despotism, would give rise to a dissertation too long for us to enter upon.

We merely offer a few suggestions, which, we think, will prove sufficient and satisfactory for our purpose to every candid reader:

I. Catholic theology had certainly never brought about such a state of affairs. In all Catholic schools of the day, in England as on the Continent, St. Thomas was the great authority, and his work, "De Regimine Principum," was in the hands of all Catholic students. Luther was the first to reject St. Thomas.

In this book, all were taught that, if, among the various kinds of government, "that of a king is best," in the opinion of the author, "that of a tyrant is the worst." And a tyrant he defines as "any ruler who despises the common good, and seeks his private advantage."

In that book of the great doctor, all may read: "The farther the government recedes from the common weal, the more unjust is it. It recedes farther from the common weal in an oligarchy, in which the welfare of a few is sought, than in a democracy, whose object is the good of the many. . . . But farther still does it recede from the common weal in a tyrannous government, by which the good of one alone is sought."

The general consequence which St. Thomas draws from this doctrine is, that, "if a ruler governs a multitude of freemen for the common good of the multitude, the government will be good and just as becomes freemen."

Such was the political doctrine taught in the Catholic universities of Europe until the sixteenth century; but, in all probability, this golden work, "De Regimine Principum," was no longer the text-book in the English schools of the time of Henry Tudor.

But, when, entering into details, the holy and learned author goes on to contrast the contrary effects produced by freedom and despotism on a nation, how could Henry willingly permit the circulation of such words as the following?

"It is natural that men brought under terror" (a tyrannical government) "should degenerate into beings of a slavish disposition, and become timid and incapable of any manly and daring enterprise--an assertion which is proved by the conduct of countries which have been long subjected to a despotic government. Solomon says: 'When the imperious are in power, men hide away' in order to escape the cruelty of tyrants, nor is it astonishing; for a man governing without law, and according to his own caprice, differs in nothing from a beast of prey. Hence, Solomon designates an impious ruler as a roaring lion and a ravenous bear.'

"Because, therefore, the government of one is to be preferred -- which is the best--and because this government is liable to degenerate into tyranny--which has been proved to be the worst -- hence, the most diligent care is to be taken so to regulate the establishment of a king over the people, that he may not fall into tyranny."

Finally, St. Thomas epitomizes the doctrines of this whole book in his "Summa," as follows: "A tyrannical government is unjust, being administered, not for the common good, but for the private good of the ruler; therefore, its overthrow is not sedition, unless when the subversion of tyranny is so inordinately pursued that the multitude suffers more from its overthrow than from the existence of the government."

The subject might be illustrated by any quantity of extracts from the writings of other great theologians of the middle ages; but what we have said is enough for our purpose. It is manifest that Catholic doctrine cannot have brought about the state of England under the Tudors.

II. Another, and a very important suggestion, is the following: it certainly was not the Catholic hierarchy, least of all the pontifical power, which produced it.

Whatever may have been written derogatory to the institutions existing in Europe during the mediaeval period, several great facts, most favorable to the Catholic religion, have been commonly admitted by Protestant writers, from which we select two. The first of these was originally stated by M. Guizot, in his "Civilization in Europe," namely, that the kingdom of France was created by Christian bishops. Since that first admission, other non-Catholic writers have gone further, and have felt compelled to admit that, as a general rule, the modern European nations have all been created, nurtured, fostered, by Catholic bishops, and that the first free Parliaments of those nations were, in fact, "councils of the Church," either of a purely clerical character and altogether free from the intermixture of lay elements, such as the Councils of Toledo, in Spain, or acting in concert with the representatives of the various classes in the nations.

The clergy, as all readers know, the clerks, were the first to take the lead in civil affairs, being more enlightened than the other classes, and holding in their body all the education of the earlier times. It is unnecessary to add to this fact that, among really Christian people, the voice of religion is listened to before all others. And is it not to-day a well-ascertained fact that, in the main, the influence exerted by the clergy on the formation of modern European kingdoms was in favor of a well-regulated freedom based on the first law--the law of God--that primal source of true liberty and civilization? To the clergy, certainly, and to the monks, is chiefly due the abolition of slavery; and the bishops took a very active and prominent part in the movements of the communes, to which the Third Estate owes its birth.

A malignant ingenuity has been displayed by many writers, in ransacking the pages of history, in order to fasten on certain prelates of the Church charges of despotism and oppression. But, apart from the fact that the narratives so carefully compiled have, in many cases, turned out to be perversions of the truth, and granting even that all these allegations are impartial and true, the general tenor and tendency of the history of those times is now admitted to be ample refutation of such accusations, and impartial writers confess that the ecclesiastical influence, during those ages, was clearly set against the oppression of the people, and finally resulted in the formation of those representative and moderate governments which are the boast of the present age; and that the principles enunciated by the great schoolmen, led by Thomas Aquinas, founded the order of society on justice, religion, and right. The more history is studied honestly, investigated closely, and viewed impartially, the more plainly does the great fact shine forth that the Catholic hierarchy, in the various European nations, constituted the vanguard of true freedom and order.

With regard to the papal power, it is a curious instance of the reversal of human judgment, and a very significant fact, that those very Popes who, a hundred years ago, were looked upon, even by Catholic writers, as the embodiment of supercilious arrogance and sacrilegious presumption, namely, Gregory VII., Innocent III., and Boniface VIII., are now acknowledged to have been the greatest benefactors to Europe in their time, and true models of supreme Christian bishops.

But, if these two facts be admitted, the question recurs, How is it that the governments of several kingdoms, and that of England in particular, had, during the fifteenth and sixteenth centuries, merged into complete and unalloyed despotism? As our present interest in the question is restricted to England, we confine ourselves to that country, and proceed to treat of it in a few words.

Under the Tudors, the government grew to be altogether irresponsible, personal, and despotic, chiefly because under previous reigns, and constantly since the establishment of the Norman line of kings, the authority of Rome, which formed the only great counterpoise to kingly power at the time, had been gradually undermined, while the bishops, being deprived of the aid of the supreme Pontiff, had become mere tools in the hands of the monarchs.

The particular shape which the opposition to Rome took in England, compared with a similar opposition in Germany, has been already touched upon; it was found to be involved chiefly in the question of tribute-money and benefices, the latter being also reduced to a money difficulty. It was seen that the monks and the people sided generally with the kings, and gradually took a dislike and mistrust to every thing coming from Rome; the authority of the monarch, though not precisely strengthened thereby, was left without the control of a superior tribunal to direct him, and consequently the kings, if they chose, were left to follow the impulse of their own caprice, which, according to St. Thomas, forms the characteristic of tyranny.

Other causes, doubtless, contributed to pave the way for and consolidate the despotism of the Kings of England. Among such causes may be mentioned the extraordinary successes which attended the English arms, led by their warrior kings in France, and the frightful convulsions subsequently arising from the Wars of the Roses; but we doubt not the one mentioned above was the chief, and, of itself, would in the long-run have brought about the same result.

Protestantism, therefore, was neither the growth of freedom in England, nor did it plant freedom there at its introduction, inasmuch as the royal power became more absolute than ever by its predominance, and by the first principle which it laid down, that the king was supreme in Church as well as in state. Can its origin in England, then, be accounted for by the existence of a higher civilization, anterior to it in point of time, out of which it grew, or, at least, by a true aspiration toward such.

This question is as easy of solution as the first: There can be no doubt that the nations which remained either entirely or in the main faithful to the Church, in point of learning and civilization, ranked far beyond the Northern nations, where heresy so early found a permanent footing, and that in the South also the tendencies toward a higher civilization were at that time of a most marked and extraordinary character, so much so that the reign of Leo X. has become a household phrase to express the perfection of culture.

England, as a nation, was at that period only just beginning to emerge from barbarism, and in fact was the last of the European nations to adopt civilized customs and manners in the political, civil, and social relations of life.

In politics she was, until that epoch, plunged in frightful dynastic revolutions, and as yet had not learned the first principles of good government. In civil affairs, her code was the most barbarous, her feudal customs the most revolting, her whole history the most appalling of all Christendom. In social habits, she had scarcely been able to retain a few precious fragments of good old Catholic times; and the fearful scenes through which the nation had passed, which, according to J. J. Rousseau, for once expressing the truth, render the reading of that period of her history almost impossible to a humane man, had sunk her almost completely in degradation. The reader will understand that the England here spoken of is the England of three centuries ago, and not of to-day.

If by civilization is understood learning and the fine arts, what, in general phrase, is expressed by culture and refinement, how could England compare at the time with Italy, Flanders, Spain, France, all Latin or Celtic nations? How can it be pretended that she was better fitted for the reception of a more spiritual and elevating religion than any of the countries mentioned?

Two great names may be brought forward as proving that the expressions used are harsh and ill-founded--Shakespeare and Milton; a third, Bacon, we omit for reasons which our space forbids us to give.

Shakespeare, whose name may rank with those of Homer and Dante, was not a product of those times. He was a gift of Heaven. At any other epoch he would have been as great, perhaps greater. What he received from his surroundings and from the "civilization" with which he was blessed, he has handed down to us in the uncouth form, the intricacy of plot and adventures, which would have rendered barbarous a poet less naturally gifted. And, although the question has never been definitely settled, it is probable that he was born and lived a Catholic; and it is strange how Elizabeth, who, tradition tells us, was present at some of his plays, could endure his faithful portrayal of friars and nuns, while she was persecuting their originals so barbarously at the time; strangest of all, how she could bear to look upon the true and noble image of Katherine of Aragon, whom Henry in his good moment pronounces "the queen of earthly queens," contrasted with her own mother, to whom the shrewd old court lady tells the story:

"There was a lady once ('tis an old story), That would not be a queen, that would she not, For all the mud in Egypt:--Have you heard it?"

Thus did Shakespeare contrast Elizabeth's wanton mother with the noble woman whom Henry discarded for a toy. And some critics can only find a reason for the composition of the "Merry Wives of Windsor" and the "Sonnets" as an offering to the lewd queen. Nothing more did he owe to his time.

And Milton, who, though his father was a Catholic, was himself a rank Puritan, something of what we have said of Shakespeare may be said of him. At all events, all his cultivation and taste came from Italy. The poets of that really civilized country had polished his uncouth nature, as it were in spite of itself, and added to the depth of his wonderful genius the beauty and soft harmony of verse that ever flowed freely, and the strength of a nervous and sonorous prose.

Now comes the question: If the origin of Protestantism in England cannot be attributed to freedom and civilization, may it not, at least, be maintained that the natural result of Protestantism was the acquisition of true freedom and of a higher civilization? Is it not true that to-day Protestant nations are in advance of others in both these respects? And to what other cause can such advancement be ascribed than to the "reformed religion?" Is it not the freedom which has come to the human mind, after the rejection of the yoke of spiritual authority, and the proclamation of the rights of individual reason, that has brought about the present advanced state of affairs

We know all these fine-sounding phrases which are so continuously dinned into our ears, and republished day after day in a thousand forms. The question, we admit, is not so easy of solution as the first, and might, indeed, without suspicion of evasion, be discarded as not coming under the head of this chapter, which spoke of origin and not of consequences. Nevertheless, a few words may be devoted to the subject, to prove that the answer must still be in the negative.

The first result of Protestantism was undoubtedly to extinguish as completely as possible the remaining sparks of truly liberal thought promulgated in Europe by the Catholic doctors of the middle ages. Wherever the new doctrines spread, secular rulers were not only freed from pontifical control, but were themselves invested with supreme ecclesiastical power. The effective check which the paternal and bold voice issuing from the Vatican had exercised on kings and princes was in a moment taken away. In Germany, England, and Scandinavia, the kings and petty princes, and dukes even, became each so many popes in their own dominions. And this took place with the consent and frequently at the earnest request of the Reformers.

Even the European states which did not fall away from the old faith of Christendom took advantage, it might almost be said, of the difficult position in which the Holy Father found himself, to countenance new doctrines with respect to the limits of the authority of the Supreme Pontiff; and the new errors which so suddenly appeared in France and elsewhere, during the prevalence and at the extinction of the great schism, limiting the power of the Popes in many matters where it had been considered binding, broke out again, in France principally, under the lead of Protestant or Erastian parliamentarians and legists, under the name of Gallican liberties--pretended liberties, which would really make the Church a subordinate adjunct of the State, instead of what it is, a spiritual living body ruled exclusively by a spiritual head.

How could the cause of true liberty in Europe be promoted by such altered circumstances as these?--to say nothing of the disastrous imprudence with which those blind rulers and so-called theologians took away the key-stone of the European social edifice, which grew weaker from that day forth, until now we see it tottering to its fall.

The introduction of Protestantism, then, was one of the chief causes of the change by which a much greater personal power was transferred to the hands of the sovereign than he had ever before held, and it is no surprise to see the absolutism of emperors and kings, in Christian Europe, date from its coming.

As time passed on, the cause acting on a larger scale, embracing a wider circumference, and drawing within its circle vaster territories, the world saw absolute rule established in England, France, Spain, and Germany. Previous to the sixteenth century, the word 'absolutism' was unknown in Christendom, as was the doctrine of the "divine right of kings" understood and preached as it has since been in England.

But, to furnish details which should render these reflections more striking, would require an unravelling of the whole tangled skein of history during those times.

Nevertheless, we must come to consider the last refuge of Protestant liberalism. Did not the Reformation really emancipate modern nations, and gradually bring about the whole system of representative governments, which, starting from England, have now, in fact, become, more or less, general throughout Europe?

Our answer is, Yes and No. It may be granted that Protestantism did give rise to a certain kind of liberalism very prevalent in our days; but such liberalism is very far from bestowing on nations true liberty and stability; hence their constant agitation, and the perils of society which threaten all, even the specially favored Protestant nations themselves as much as any.

It was indeed the new doctrines which brought about the "Commonwealth" in England, and the subsequent Revolution of 1688; between which two events, however, great differences exist.

The destruction of monarchy under and in the person of Charles I. was the just retribution dealt by Providence to the English kings, who had been the first openly to shake off from a great nation the wise and beneficent yoke of Rome. At all events, one thing is certain, that under the "Protector," the child of the Revolution, as little as under the Protestant Tudors, could the English scarcely be regarded as freemen.

Cromwell banished from their hall the representatives of the people. He could scarcely find epithets opprobrious enough for Magna Charta, which the people considered, and rightly, as the palladium of English liberty. In his scornful order to "take away that bawble," though the "bawble" immediately referred to was the Speaker's mace, the word meant the freedom of the nation. He was as absolute a monarch as ever ruled England. The liberty enjoyed under his regime was as meaningless for every class as for the Catholics, whom he more immediately oppressed, and was ill compensated for by the material prosperity which his genius knew so well how to secure.

It was his despotic rule, in fact, and the fear of anarchy which affrighted the minds of the people at his death--the dread of a government of rival soldiers--which rendered so easy the triumphant restoration of the worthless Stuarts, in the person of the most worthless of them all, Charles II.

The true constitutional liberty of which England may fairly boast was the work of a long series of years subsequent to the Revolution of 1688. It was the work of the whole eighteenth century, in fact, and was grounded on the fragments of old Catholic doctrines and customs. In no sense can it be called the result of Protestantism, save as coming after it in point of time.

Whoever is acquainted with the state of religion and society in England, during the latter part of the seventeenth and the whole of the eighteenth century, needs not to be told that, among the ruling classes, faith in a revealed religion had ceased to exist. The yoke of Rome once shaken off, the human mind was quick to draw all the consequences of the principle of entire independence in religious matters. Tindal, Collins, Hobbes, Shaftesbury, and other philosophers, had openly denounced revelation, and that portion of the nation which esteemed itself enlightened embraced their new doctrines. It would be false to imagine that, in 1700 and afterward, the English were as firm believers in the Church of England's Thirty-nine Articles as they seemed to be at the beginning of this century. The whole of the last century was for all Europe, with the exception of the two peninsulas of Italy and Spain, a period of avowed disbelief.

Even Presbyterian Scotland did not escape the contagion, and some theologians and preachers of the Kirk at that time are now praised for their liberal views of religion, that is, for their want of real faith. The influence of Wesley and his fellow-workers on the English mind, and the dread of the spread of French infidelity and jacobinism, were more extensive and effectual than people are apt to imagine; and there is no doubt that, seventy years ago England was far more of a believing country than she had been for a hundred years before.

But, if even Scotch Presbyterian ministers and Church of England men, such as Laurence Sterne, were unworthy of the name of Christian, what are we to think of those who had to profess no outward faith in Christianity, because of ministerial offices? There is no doubt that, in the mass, they were almost completely void of any faith in revealed religion.

To such men as these is England indebted for the development of her constitution. If Protestantism had any share in it at all, it did not go beyond preparing the way for the destruction of Christianity in the mind and heart of the people; or, rather, constitutional liberty in England has no connection whatever with religion. The English, left to their own ingenuity and skill, displayed a vast amount of statesmanlike qualities in devising for themselves a system of check and counter-check, which protected the subject and defined the rights of the ruler; and this gave the nation an undoubted superiority over their neighbors on the Continent. But it cannot be attributed, except in a very remote manner, to the Protestant doctrine of the independence of the human mind.

Were we to examine the effect which the example of England produced on other nations, we should find that, instead of spreading liberty, it was the cause of the diffusion of an unbridled license under the name of liberalism.

In England itself; the lower orders of society having been kept in ignorance, and consequently in subjection to the ruling classes, and the latter finding it to their interest to preserve order and stability in the state, no frightful commotions could ensue to threaten the destruction of society.

In Continental countries, the middle and even the lowest classes were more readily caught by doctrines which, when kept within due bounds, may be promotive of exterior prosperity, but which, pushed to their extremes and logical consequences, may embroil the whole nation in revolution and calamities.

Such has been the case in our own days, and in days immediately preceding our own; and England is now experiencing the recoil of those convulsions, and seems on the eve of being convulsed herself more terribly, perhaps, than any other nation has yet been.

These few reflections must suffice, as to extend them would go beyond our present scope. But now comes the question, Why was Ireland unprepared for the reception of Protestantism? Why did she reject it absolutely and permanently?

According to the theorists who attribute the success of Protestantism in the North of Europe to a higher civilization and a more ardent love of freedom, the contrary characteristics should distinguish those nations which remained faithful to the Church, and particularly the Irish. Was the lack of a higher civilization and more ardent love for freedom really the cause, then, for Ireland's undergoing so many fearful sacrifices merely for the sake of her religion?

We should not dread entering upon a comparison of the Scandinavian and Celtic races in these two articular points, as they existed at the time of the Tudors. We are confident that a detailed survey of both would result in a glorious vindication of the Irish character, although, owing to six hundred years of cruel wars with Dane and Anglo-Norman, the actual prosperity of the country was far inferior to that of England. But the outline of so vast a subject must content us here.

In judging of the elevation of a nation's sentiments, the first thing that strikes us is the motive assigned by the Irish representatives for refusing to pass the bill of supremacy. "Five or six changes of religion in twelve years were too much for conscientious people." Such was the answer sent back to Elizabeth, and spoken as though easy of comprehension. Had they deemed that their language could have been misunderstood, they would undoubtedly have expressed themselves in stronger terms.

Strange that such an obvious and common-sense remark had never occurred to the intelligent and highly-civilized members of the English Parliament--those ardent lovers of freedom--when applied to by a new

English monarch to acknowledge and confirm, as law, the religious system he had determined to establish!

Apparently, then, at this time, Ireland possessed a conscience which England either laid no claim on, or made no pretensions to; and it might not be too much to lay this down as the first reason why Ireland remained faithful to her religion. In fact, the whole history of the period bears out this general observation. The subserviency of the proud English aristocracy, of those pretended statesmen and legislators, in matters so intimately connected with the soul, its convictions and its morality, shows conclusively that the word "conscience" had no meaning for them, or that, if they were aware of the existence of such a thing, they made so little account of it that they were ready at all times to barter it for position, what they considered honor, and wealth.

On the other hand, the constant, unshaken, and emphatic refusal of the Irish to renounce their religion for the novel "speculations" of pretended theologians--in reality, heretical teachers--at the beck of king or queen; their willingness to submit to all the rigor of extreme penal laws rather than disobey their sense of right, proves too well that they possessed a conscience, knew what it meant, and resolved to follow it. There is not a single fact of their, history, general or particular, taking them collectively as a nation, when, by their actions, they spoke as one people or individually, when priest and friar, great man or mean man, chose to lose position, property, name--life itself--rather than be false to their religion and God--which does not prove that they owned a conscience and obeyed its voice.

Can a nation, deprived of this, be esteemed really free and truly civilized? and can a nation which possesses it be considered barbarous? The answer cannot be doubtful, and is of itself a sufficient solution of the question under examination.

But, to come to more special details. The Irish idea of civilization was certainly of a very different character from that of the English; but was it the less true? From the landing of the first invasion, the Norman nobles and prelates looked down on the invaded people as barbarous and uncouth, as they previously looked down upon the Anglo-Saxons. Later on, they spoke of the Irish customs as "lewd;" and, later still, the majority of them adopted those "lewd customs."

If the question be merely one of refinement of outward manners, and aquaintance with the artificial code established by a society with which the Irish, up to that time, had never come in contact, the Normans may be granted whatever benefit may accrue to them from such, though, even here, the Irish chieftains might later on compare favorably with their foes. For instance, if is doubtful whether Hugh O'Donnell and O'Sullivan Beare, one of whom went to Spain, and the other to Portugal--and the second, Philip II. commanded to be treated as a Spanish grandee--were not as courteous and dignified as Cecil or Walsingham, or Essex or Raleigh, at the court of Elizabeth. And, if we take the case of the descendants of Strongbow's warriors, who became "more Irish than the Irish," there is no reason why we should not prefer the manners and bearing of young Gerald Desmond, when, after leaving Rome, he appeared at the court of Tuscany, to those of the young lords who danced at Windsor, under the eyes of Henry, with Anne Boleyn. But, treating the subject seriously, and examining it more closely, we may find a necessity for reversing the opinion which is too commonly entertained.

Civilization does not consist only, or chiefly, in refinement of manners, but in all things which exalt a nation; and, after the "conscience" of which we have spoken, nothing is so important in making a nation civilized as the institutions under which it lives.

The laws are the great index of a people's civilization, chiefly as regards their execution. Nothing can be more indicative of it than the criminal code of a people.

The law of England at that time compares poorly with the Irish compilation known as the "Senchus Mor," which scholars have only recently been able to study, and which is being printed as we write, and to be illustrated with learned notes. From all accounts given by competent reviewers, it is clear that wisdom, sound judgment, equity, and Christian feeling, constitute the essence of those laws which Edmund Campian found the young Irishmen of his day studying under such strange circumstances and with such ardor and application as to spend sixteen or eighteen years at it.

And in what manner were those very Christian enactments which lay at the foundation of the English legislation executed at the same period? What, for instance, were the features of its criminal code? It is unnecessary to depict what all the world knows.

In extenuation of the barbarous blood-thirstiness which characterized it, it may be said that torture, cruel punishments, and fearful chastisement for slight offences, formed the general features of the criminal code of most Christian nations. They had been handed down by barbarous ancestors, the relics of Scandinavian cruelty for the most part, added to the Roman slave penalties, which were the remnants of pagan inhumanity. This answer would be insufficient when comparing the English with the Brehon law, but it does not hold good even with reference to other Continental nations. In no country at that time was punishment so pitiless as in England. The details, now well known, can only be published for exceptional readers; to find a comparison for them Dr. Madden says:

"We must come down to the reign of terror in France, to the massacres of September, to the wholesale executions of conventional times; to find the mob insulting the victims, and the executioner himself adding personal affront to the disgusting fulfilment of his horrible office."

Passing from the laws to the usages of warfare, and chiefy to domestic strife, here the most vulnerable point in the Irish character shows itself. The constant feuds resulting from the clan system furnish a never-failing theme to those who accuse the Irish of barbarism. Yet is there no parallel to them in the horrors of those dynastic revolutions which preceded the Tudors in England, and which the Tudors only put an end to by the completest despotism, and by shedding the best blood of the country in torrents? The Irish feuds never depopulated the country. It is even admitted by most reliable historians that, while those dissensions were rifest, the land was really teeming with a happy people, and rich in every thing which an agricultural country can enjoy. The great battles of the various clans resulted often in the killing of a few dozen warriors. Such, in fact, was the manner in which chroniclers estimated the gains or losses of each of those victories or defeats.

But, in the Wars of the Roses, England lost a great part of her adult population; so much so, that she was altogether incapacitated from waging war with any external nation. She could not even afford to send any reenforcements to the English Pale in Ireland--not even a few hundred which at times would have proved so serviceable. It was in fact high time and almost a happy thing for England that the crushing despotism of the Tudors came in to save the nation from total ruin.

Finally, can it be said that the Irish were inferior in civilization to the English by reason of their social habits, when Danes, Anglo-Saxons and Normans, in turn, invariably adopted Irish manners in preference to their own, after living a sufficient time in the country to be able to appreciate the difference between the one and the other?

The writers of whom we speak ascribe the spread of Protestantism not only to a higher civilization, or at least a special aptness and fitness for it, but also say that it was due to the greater love for freedom which possessed those who accepted it; whereas the Irish, as they allege, have been forever priest-ridden and cowered under the lash.

The connection between English Protestantism and freedom has been sufficiently touched upon. But in Ireland the whole resistance of the Irish people to the change of religion is the most conspicuous proof which could be advanced of their inherent love for freedom.

What is the meaning of this word "priest-ridden?" If, as attached to the Irish, it means that they have remained faithfully devoted to their spiritual guides, and protected them at cost of life and limb against the execution of barbarous laws, this epithet which is flung at them as a reproach is a glory to them, and a true one.

Are they to be accused of cowardice because they were never bold enough to demolish a single Catholic chapel--a favorite amusement of the English mobs from Elizabeth's reign to Victoria's--or because they could not find the courage in their hearts to mock a martyr at the stake, or imbrue their hands in his blood, as did the nation of a higher civilization and a more ardent love for freedom?

The Irish cower under the lash! It could never be applied, until calculating treachery had first rendered them naked and defenceless, and removed from their reach every weapon of defence. And the man who in such a case receives the lash is a coward, while he who safely applies it is a hero!

Our observations so far have cleared the ground for the right solution and understanding of the present question. It may now be said that the Irish were not prepared for the reception of Protestantism, and remained firm in their faith because--

1. They possessed a conscience.

2. There had existed no religious abuses, worthy of the name, in their country which called for reform. Such abuses had in England and Germany furnished the pretext for a change of religion. It was a mere pretext, for the alleged abuses might all be remedied without intrenching on the domain of faith, and unsettling the religious convictions of the whole nation. There is no greater crime possible than to introduce among people enjoying all the benefits resulting from a firm belief in holy truth a simple doubt, a simple hesitating surmise, calculated to make them waver in the least in what had previously been a solid and well-grounded faith. But to consider that crime carried to the extent of so sapping the foundation of Christian belief as to bring about the inevitable consequence of opening under nations the fearful abyss of atheism and despair--there is no word sufficiently strong to express the indignation which such a course of action must naturally excite. And that the ultimate result of the new heresy was to carry men to the very brink of the abyss is plain enough to-day, and was foreseen by Luther himself. In all probability he had a clear perception of it, since the latter half of his life was devoted to propping up the crumbling walls of his hastily-erected edifice by whatever supports he could steal from the old faith, and fighting hard against all those who had already drawn the ultimate conclusions of his own principles.

For those, then, who in the sixteenth century set in motion the chaos which threatens to overwhelm us to-day, the religious abuses existing at the time can offer no excuse for their destruction of Religion, because stains happened to sully the purity of her outward garment.

But in Ireland no such abuses existed; and consequently there was there not even a pretext for the introduction of Protestantism, and by the very reason of their sense of good and right the Irish were unprepared for heresy.

3. Even had it entered into their minds to wish for a reformation of some kind, they were certainly unprepared for the one offered them. The first reform of the new order was to close the religious houses which the people loved, which were the seats of learning, holiness, and education. Their Catholic ancestors had founded those religious houses; they themselves enjoyed the spiritual and even temporal advantages attached to them, for they constituted in fact the only important and useful establishments which

their country possessed; they had been consecrated by the lives and deaths of a thousand saints within their walls; and they suddenly beheld pretended ministers of a new religion of which they knew nothing, backed by ferocious Walloon or English troopers, turn out or slay their inmates, close them, set them on fire, pillage them, or convert them into private dwellings for the convenience of an imported aristocracy. This was the first act of the "introduction" of the "Reformation" into Ireland. The people were enabled to judge of the sanctity of the new creed at its first appearance among them. And this alone, apart from their firm adherence to the faith of their fathers, was quite enough to justify them in their resistance to such a substitute.

But, above all, when they beheld how the inmates of those holy-houses were treated, when they saw them cast out into the world, penniless, reduced to penury and want, persecuted, declared outcasts, hunted down, insulted by the soldiery, arrested, cruelly beaten, bound hand and foot, and hung up either before the door of their burning monastery, or even in the church itself before the altar--what wonder that they were unprepared to receive the new religion?

The barbarity displayed throughout England and Ireland toward Catholicism was specially fiendish when directed against religious of both sexes; and, as in Ireland no class of persons was more justly and dearly loved, what wonder that the Irish literally hated the religion that came to them from beyond the sea?

Without going over the other aspects of the religious question of the time, and comparing article with article of the new and old beliefs, this single feature of the case alone is sufficient. The process might be carried out with advantage, but is not necessary.

4. The new order of things, in one word, resolved itself into rapacity and wanton bloodshed. And, despite whatever may be said of Irish outrages by those who are never tired of alluding to them, Irish nature is opposed to such excesses. If they are ever guilty of such, it is only when they have previously been outraged themselves, and in such cases they are the first to repent of their action in their cooler moments. On the other hand, the men who first set all these outrages going never find reason to accuse themselves of any thing, are even perfectly satisfied with and convinced of their own perfection; and, as from the first they acted coolly and systemat-

ically, their self-equanimity is never disturbed, they continue unshaken in the calm conviction that they have always been in the right, whatever may have been the consequences of the initiative movement and its steady continuance.

But we repeat advisedly--the Irish nature is opposed to rapacity and wanton shedding of blood, and this formed another strong reason for their opposition to the religious revolution which immersed them in so bloody a baptism.

5. Yet perhaps the most radical and real cause of their persistent refusal to embrace Protestantism lies in their traditional spirit, of which we have previously spoken. There is no rationalistic tendency in their character.

And all the points well considered, which, after all, is the better, the simply traditional or strictly rationalistic nature? What has been the result of those philosophical speculations from which Protestantism sprang? Whither are men tending to-day in consequence of it? Would it not have been better for mankind to have stood by the time-honored traditions of former ages, independently of the strong and convincing claims which Catholicity offers to all? This is said without in the least attributing the fault to sound philosophy, without casting the slightest slur on those truly great and illustrious men who have widened the limits of the human intellect, and deserved well of mankind by the solid truths they have opened up in their works for the benefit and instruction of minds less gifted than their own.

THE IRISH AND THE STUARTS.--LOYALTY AND CONFISCATION

UPON the death of Elizabeth, in 1603, the son of the unfortunate Mary Stuart was called to the throne of England, and for the first time in their history the Irish people accepted English rule, gave their willing submission to an English dynasty, and afterward displayed as great devotedness in supporting the falling cause of their new monarchs, as in defending their religion and nationality.

This feeling of allegiance, born so suddenly and strangely in the Irish breast, cherished so ardently and at the price of so many sacrifices, finally raising the nation to the highest pitch of heroism, is worth studying and investigating its true cause.

What ought to have been the natural effect produced on the Irish people by the arrival of the news that James of Scotland had succeeded to Elizabeth? The first feeling must have been one of deep relief that the hateful tyranny of the Tudors had passed away, to be supplanted by the rule of their kinsmen the Stuarts--kinsmen, because the Scottish line of kings was directly descended from that Dal Riada colony which Ireland had sent so long ago to the shores of Albania, to a branch of which Columbkill belonged.

For those who were not sufficiently versed in antiquarian genealogy to trace his descent so far back, the thought that James was the son of Mary Stuart was sufficient. If any people could sympathize with the ill-starred Queen of Scots, that people was the Irish. It could not enter into their ideas that the son of the murdered Catholic queen, should have feelings uncongenial to their own. It is easy, then, to understand how, when the news of Elizabeth's death and of the accession of James arrived, the sanguine Irish heart leaped with a new hope and joyful expectation.

As for the real disposition of that strangest of monarchs, James I,, writers are at variance. Matthew O'Connor, the elder, who had in his hands the books and manuscripts of Charles O'Connor of Bellingary, is very positive in his assertions on his side of the question:

"James was a determined and implacable enemy to the Catholic religion; he alienated his professors from all attachment to his government by the virulence of his antipathy. One of his first gracious proclamations imported a general jail-delivery, except for 'murderers and papists.' By another proclamation he pledged himself 'never to grant any toleration to the Catholics,' and entailed a curse on his posterity if they granted any."

Turning now to Dr. Madden's "History of the Penal Laws," we shall feel disposed to modify so positive an opinion. There we read:

"It is very evident that his zeal for the Protestant Church had more to do with a hatred of the Puritans than of popery, and that he had a hankering, after all, for the old religion which his mother belonged to, and for which she had been persecuted by the fanatics of Scotland."

Hume seems to support this judgment of Dr. Madden when he says that "the principles of James would have led him to earnestly desire a unity of faith of the Churches which had been separated."

Both opinions, however, agree in the long-run, since Dr. Madden is obliged to confess that "new measures of severity, as the bigotry of the times became urgent, were wrung from the timid king. He had neither moral nor political courage."

Still, on the day of his coronation, the Irish could little imagine what was in store for them at the hands of the son of Mary Stuart; hence their great rejoicing, till the first stroke of bitter disappointment came to open their eyes, and awaken them to the hard reality. This was the flight of Tyrone and Tyrconnell, which had been brought about by treachery and low cunning. These chieftains were, as they deserved to be, the idols of the nation. They were compelled to fly because, as Dr. Anderson, a Protestant minister, says, "artful Cecil had employed one St. Lawrence to entrap the Earls of Tyrone and Tyrconnell, the Lord of Devlin, and other Irish chiefs, into a sham plot which had no evidence but his."

The real cause of their flight was that adventurers and "undertakers" desired to "plant" Ulster, though the final treaty with Mountjoy had left both earls in possession of their lands. That treaty yielded not an acre of plunder, and was consequently in English eyes a failure. The long, bloody, and promising wars of Elizabeth's reign had ended, after all, in forcing coronets on the brows of O'Neill and O'Donnell, with a royal deed added, securing to them their lands, and freedom of worship to all the north.

James was met by the importunate demand for land. O'Neill, O'Donnell, and several other Irish chieftains, were sacrificed to meet this demand; they were compelled to fly; and they had scarcely gone when millions of acres in Ulster were declared to be forfeited to the crown, and thrown open for "planting."

And here a new feature in confiscation presents itself, which was introduced by the first of the Stuart dynasty, and proved far more galling to Irishmen than any thing they had yet encountered in this shape.

In the invasion led by Strongbow, in the absorption of the Kildare estates by Henry VIII., in the annexation of King's and Queen's Counties under Philip and Mary, even in the last "plantation" of Munster by Elizabeth's myrmidons at the end of the Desmond war, the land had been immediately distributed among the chief officers of the victorious armies. The conquered knew that such would be the law of war; the great generals and courtiers who came into possession scarcely disturbed the tenants. A few of the great native and Anglo-Irish families suffered sorely from the spoliation; the people at large scarcely felt it, except by the destruction of clanship and the introduction of feudal grievances. Moreover, the new proprietors were interested in making their tenants happy, and not unfrequently identified themselves with the people--becoming in course of time true Irishmen.

But, with the accession of the first of the Stuarts to the English throne, a great alteration took place in the disposal of the land throughout Ireland.

The Tyrone war had ended five years before, and those who had taken part in the conflict had already received their portion; the vanquished, of misfortune--the conquerors, of gain. James brought in with him from Scotland a host of greedy followers; and all, from first to last, expected to rise with their king into wealth and honor. England was not wide enough to hold them, nor rich enough to satiate their appetites. The puzzled but crafty king saw a way out of his difficulties in Ireland. He no longer limited the distribution of land in that country to soldiers and officers of rank chiefly. He gave it to Scotch adventurers, to London trades companies. He settled it on Protestant colonies whose first use of their power was to evict the former tenants or clansmen, and thus effect a complete change in the social aspect of the north.

Well did they accomplish the task assigned them. Ulster became a Protestant colony, and the soil of that province has ever since remained in the hands of a people alien to the country.

Yet the Ulstermen had been led to believe that James purposed securing them in their possessions; for, according to Mr. Prendergast, in his Introduction to the "Cromwellian settlement:"

"On the 17th of July, 1607, Sir Arthur Chichester, Lord Deputy, accompanied by Sir John Davies and other commissioners, proceeded to Ulster, with powers to inquire what land each man held. There appeared before them, in each county they visited, the chief lords and Irish gentlemen, the heads of creaghts, and the common people, the Brehons and Shanachies, who knew all the septs and families, and took upon themselves to tell what quantity of land every man ought to have. They thus ascertained and booked their several lands, and the Lord-Deputy promised them estates in them. 'He thus,' says Sir John Davies, 'made it a year of jubilee to the poor inhabitants, because every man was to return to his own house, and be restored to his ancient possessions, and they all went home rejoicing.'

"Notwithstanding these promises, the king, in the following year, issued his scheme for the plantation of Ulster, urged to it, it would seem, by Sir Arthur Chichester, who so largely profited by it. . . . It could not be said that the flight of the earls gave occasion for this change, inasmuch as the king, immediately after, issued a proclamation--which he renewed on taking possession of both earls' territories--assuring the inhabitants that they should be protected and preserved in their estates."

It looks, indeed, as though the whole transaction, including the promises and the call for ascertaining the quantity of land occupied by each inhabitant, as also the sham plot into which the earls were inveigled, was but a cunning device to bring about the plantation, in which manors of one thousand, fifteen hundred, and three thousand acres, were offered to such English and Scotch as should undertake to plant their lots with British

Protestants, and engage that no Irish should dwell upon them. Meanwhile, all who had been in arms during Tyrone's war were to be transplanted with their families, cattle, and followers, to waste places in Munster and Connaught, and there set down at a distance from one another.

Over and above this, the Irish were indebted to James for a new project--a most ingenious invention for successful plunder. He was the real author of the celebrated "Commission for the investigation of defective titles."

It would seem that the province of Ulster was too small for the rapacity of those who were constantly urging upon the king a greater thoroughness in his plans. It was clear, moreover, that the English occupation of the other three provinces had hitherto proved a failure. The island had failed to become Anglicised, and it was necessary to begin the work anew.

The new commission was presented to the Irish people in a most alluring guise. That political hypocrisy, which to-day stands for statesmanship, is not a growth of our own times. The intention of James confined itself to putting an end to all uncertainty on the subject of titles, and bestowing on each land-owner one which, for the future, should be unimpeachable. But the result went beyond his intention. This measure became, in fact, an engine of universal spoliation. It failed to secure even those who succeeded in retaining a portion of their former estates in possession, as Strafford made manifest, who, despite all the unimpeachable titles conferred by James, managed to confiscate to his own profit the greater part of the province of Connaught.

It is fitting to give a few details of this new measure of James, in order to show the gratitude which the Irish owed the Stuarts, if on that account only. In "Ireland under English Rule," the Rev. A. Perraud justly remarks: "Most Irish families held possession of their lands but by tradition, and their rights could not be proved by regular title-deeds. By royal command, a general inquiry was instituted, and whoever could not prove his right to the seat of his ancestors, by authentic documents, was mercilessly but juridically despoiled of it; the pen of the lawyer thus making as many conquests as the blade of the mercenary."

The advisers of James--those who aided him in this scheme--were fully alive to its efficiency in serving their ends. A few years previously, Arthur Chichester and Sir John Davies had only to consult the Brehon lawyers and the chroniclers of the tribes, whose duty it was to become thoroughly acquainted with the limits of the various territories, and keep the records in their memory, in order to procure from the Ulster men the proofs of their rights to property. Up to that time the word of those who were authorized, by custom, to pronounce on such subjects, was law to every Irishman. And, indeed, the verdict of these was all-sufficient, inasmuch as the task was not overtaxing to the memory of even an ordinary man, since it consisted in remembering, not the landed property of each individual, but the limits of the territory of each clan.

The clan territories were as precisely marked off as in any European state to-day; and, if any change in frontier occurred, it was the result of war between the neighboring clans, and therefore known to all. To suppose, then, under such a state of land tenure, that the territory of the Maguire clan, for instance, belonged exclusively to Maguire, and that he could prove his title to the property by legal documents, was erroneous--in fact, such a thing was impossible. Yet, such was the ground on which the king based his establishment of the odious commission.

The measure meant nothing less than the simple spoliation of all those who came under its provisions at the time. Matthew O'Connor has furnished some instances of its workings, which may bring into stronger light the enormity of such an attempt.

"The immense possessions of Bryan na Murtha O'Rourke had been granted to his son Teige, by patent; in the first year of the king's reign, and to the heirs male of his body. Teige died, leaving several sons; their titles were clear; no plots or conspiracies could be urged to invalidate them. By the medium of those inquisitions, they were found, one and all, to be bastards. The eldest son, Bryan O'Rourke, vas put off with a miserable pension, and detained in England lest he should claim his inheritance. Yet, in this case, the title was actually in existence.

"In the county of Longford, three-fourths of nine hundred and ninety-nine cartrons, the property of the O'Farrells, were granted to adventurers, to the undoing and beggary of that princely family. Twenty-five of the septs were dispossessed of their all, and to the other septs were assigned mountainous and barren tracts about one-fourth of their former possessions.

"The O'Byrnes, of Wicklow, were robbed of their property by a conspiracy unparalleled even in the annals of those times; fabricated charges of treason, perjury, and even legal murder, were employed; and, though the innocence of those victims of rapacious oppression was established, yet they were never restored."

With regard to the Anglo-Irish, and even such of the natives as had consented to accept titles from the English kings, those titles, some of which went back as far as Strongbow's invasion, were brought under the "inquiry" of the new commission--with what result may be imagined. An astute legist can discover flaws in the best-drawn legal papers. In the eye of the law, the neglect of recording is fatal; and it was proved that many proprietors, whose titles had been bestowed by Henry VIII. and Elizabeth, were not recorded, simply by bribing the clerks who were charged with the office of recording them.

This portion of our subject must present strange features to readers acquainted with the laws concerning property which obtain among civilized nations. In making the necessary studies for this most imperfect sketch, the writer has been surprised at finding that not one of the authors whom he has consulted has spoken of any thing beyond the cruelty of compelling Irish landowners to exhibit title-deeds, which it was known they did not and could not possess. Not a single one has ever said a word of "prescription;" yet, this alone was enough to arrest the proceedings of any English court, if it followed the rules of law which govern civilized communities.

Most of the estates, then declared to be escheated to the king, had been in possession of the families to which the holders belonged, for centuries; we may go so far, in the case of some Irish families and tribes, as to say for thousands of years. But, to disturb property which has been held for even less than a century, would convulse any nation subjected to such a revolutionary process. No country in the world could stand such a test; it would loosen in a day all the bonds that hold society together.

If the commission set on foot by James did not go to the extreme lengths to which it was carried by those who came after him, he it was who established what bore the semblance of a legal precedent for the excesses of Strafford, under Charles I., which reached their utmost limits in the hands of Cromwell's parliamentary commissioners. James set the engine of destruction in action: they worked it to its end. The Irish might justly lay at his door all the woes which ensued to them from the principles emanating from him. Even during his reign they saw, with instinctive horror, the abyss which he had opened up to swallow all their inheritance. The first commission of James commenced its operations by reporting three hundred and eighty-five thousand acres in Leinster alone as "discovered," inasmuch as the titles "were not such as ought" (in their judgment) "to stand in the way of his-Majesty's designs."

Hence, long before the death of James, all the hopes which his accession had raised in the minds of the Irish had vanished; yet, strange to say, they were not cured of their love for the Stuart dynasty. They hailed the coming of Charles, the husband of a Catholic princess, with joy. His marriage took place a year previous to the death of his father; and, to know that Henrietta of France was to be their queen, was enough to assure the Irish that, henceforth, they would enjoy the freedom of their religion. The same motive always awakes in them hope and joy. Men may smile at such an idea, but it is with a profound respect for the Irish character that such a sentence is written. Hope of religious freedom is the noblest sentiment which can move the breast of man; and if there be reason for admiration in the motive which urges men to fight and die for their firesides and families, how much more so in that which causes them to set above all their altars and their God!

This time their hope seemed well-founded; for the treaty concluded between England and France conferred the right on the Catholic princess of educating her children by this marriage till the age of thirteen. And, in addition, conditions favorable to the English Catholics were inserted in the same treaty.

But people were not then aware of the reason for the insertion of those conditions. Hume, later on, being better acquainted with what at the time was a secret, states in his history that "the court of England always pretended, even in the memorials to the French court, that all the conditions favorable to the English Catholics were inserted in the marriage treaty merely to please the Pope, and that their strict execution was, by an agreement with France, secretly dispensed with."

The Irish rejoiced, however; and Charles and his ministers encouraged their expectations. Lord Falkland, in the name of the king, promised that, if the Catholic lords should present Charles, who needed money, with a voluntary tribute, he would in return grant them certain immunities and protections, which acquired later on a great celebrity under the name of "graces."

The chief of these were--to allow "recusants" to practise in the courts of law, and to sue out the livery of their land, merely on taking an act of civil allegiance instead of the oath of supremacy; that the claims of the crown should be limited to the last sixty years--a period long enough in all conscience; and that the inhabitants of Connaught should be allowed to make a new enrolment of their estates, to be accepted by the king. A Parliament was promised to sit in a short time, in order to confirm all these "graces."

The subsidy promised by the Irish lords amounted to the then enormous sum of forty thousand pounds sterling, to be paid annually for three years. Two-thirds of it was paid, according to Matthew O'Connor, but no one of the "graces" was forthcoming, the king finding he had promised more than he could perform.

Instead of enabling the land-owners of Connaught to obtain a new title by a new enrolment, Strafford, with the connivance of Charles, devised a project which would have enabled the king to dispose of the whole province to the enriching of his exchequer. This project consisted in throwing open the whole territory to the court of "defective titles." To legalize this spoliation, the parchment grant, five hundred years old, given to Roderic O'Connor and Richard de Burgo, by Henry II., was set up as rendering invalid the claims of immemorial possession by the Irish, although confirmed by recent compositions.

In the counties of Roscommon, Mayo, and Sligo, juries were found for the crown. The honesty and courageous resistance of a Galway jury prevented the carrying out of the measure in that county. Strafford resented this rebuff deeply; and the brave Galway jurors were punished without mercy for their "contumacy," for they had been told openly to find for the king. Compelled to appear in the Castle chamber, they were each fined four thousand pounds, their estates seized, and themselves imprisoned until their fines should be paid; while the sheriff, who was also fined to the same amount, not being able to pay, died in prison. Such were a few of the "graces" granted the Irish on the accession of Charles I.

Meanwhile, the king's difficulties with his English subjects drove him to turn for hope to the Scotch, upon whom he had attempted to force Episcopalianism. The resistance of the Scotch, and the celebrated Covenant by which they bound themselves, are well known. Charles, finally, granted the Covenanters not only liberty of conscience, but even the religious supremacy of Presbyterianism, paying their army, moreover, for a portion of the time it passed under service in the rebellion against himself.

The example of the Scotch was certainly calculated to inflame the Irish with ardor, and drive them likewise into rebellion. What was the oppression of Scotland compared to that under which Ireland had so long groaned? Surely the final attempt of the chief minister of Charles to rob them of the one province which had hitherto escaped, was enough to open their eyes, and convert their faith in the Stuart dynasty into hatred and determined opposition. Yet were they on the eve of carrying their devotion to this faithless and worthless line to the height of heroism. The generosity of the nature which is in them could find an excuse for Charles. "He would have done us right," they thought, "had he been left free." From the rebellion of his subjects, in England and Scotland, they could only draw one conclusion--that he was the victim of Puritanism, for which they could entertain no feeling but one of horror; and it is a telling fact that their attachment to their religion kept them faithful to the sovereign to whom they had sworn their allegiance, however unworthy he might be.

Thus in the famous rising of 1641, when in one night Ireland, with the exception of a few cities, freed herself from the oppressor (the failure of the plan in Dublin being the only thing which prevented a complete success; the English of the Pale still refusing to combine with the Irish), the native Irish alone, left to their own resources, proclaimed emphatically in explicit terms their loyalty to the king, whom they credited with a just and tolerant disposition, if freed from the restraints imposed upon him by the Puritanical faction. A further fact stranger still, and still more calculated to shake their confidence in the monarch, occurred shortly after, which indeed raises the loyalty of the nation to a height inconceivable and impossible to any people, unless one whose conscience is swayed by the sense of stern duty.

When the Scottish Covenanters, whose rebellion had secured them in possession of all they demanded, heard of the Irish movement, they were at once seized with a fanatical zeal urging them to stamp out the Irish

"Popish rebellion." King Charles, who was then in Edinburgh, expressed his gratification at their proposal, and no time was lost in shipping a force of two thousand Scots across the Channel. They landed at Antrim, when they began those frightful massacres which opened by driving into the sea three thousand Irish inhabitants of the island Magee.

When, according to M. O'Connor's "Irish Catholics," "letters conveying the news of the intended invasion of the Scots were intercepted; when the speeches of leading members in the English Commons, the declaration of the Irish Lord-Justices, and of the principal members of the Dublin Council, countenanced those rumors; when Mr. Pym gave out that he would not leave a Papist in Ireland; when Sir Parsons declared that within a twelve-month not a Catholic should be seen in the whole country; when Sir John Clotworthy affirmed that the conversion of the Papists was to be effected with the Bible in one hand and the sword in the other," and the King all the while seemed to allow and consent to it, the Irish were not in the least dismayed by those rumors, but set about establishing in the convulsed island a sort of order in the name of God and the king!

Then for the first time did native and Anglo-Irish Catholics take common side in a common cause. This was the union which Archbishop Browne had foreseen, which had shown itself in symptoms from time to time, but which had oftener been broken by the old animosity. But, at last, convinced that the only party on which they could rely, and the party which truly supported the reigning dynasty, was that of the Ulster chiefs, the Catholic lords of the Pale threw themselves heart and soul into it, and, under the guidance of the Catholic bishops who then came forward, together they formed the celebrated "Confederation of Kilkenny" in 1642.

Had Charles even then possessed the courage, honesty, or wisdom to recognize and acknowledge his true friends, he might have been spared the fate which overtook him; but all he did was almost to break up the only coalition which stood up boldly in his favor.

A circumstance not yet touched upon meets us here. Protestantism was at this time effecting a complete change in the rules of judgment and conduct which men had hitherto followed. In place of the old principles of political morality which up to this period had regulated the actions of Christians, notions of independence, of subversion of existing governments, of revolutions in Church and state, were for the first time in

Christian history scattered broadcast through the world, and beginning that series of catastrophes which has made European history since, and which is far from being exhausted yet. The Irish stood firm by the old principles, and, though they became victims to their fidelity, they never shrank from the consequences of what they knew to be their duty, and to those principles they remain faithful to-day.

To return from this short digression: The Irish hierarchy, the native Irish and the Anglo-Irish lords of the Pale, had combined together to form the "Confederation of Kilkenny," in which confederation lay the germ of a truly great nation. Early in the struggle the Catholic hierarchy saw that it was for them to take the initiative in the movement, and they took it in right earnest. They could not be impassive spectators when the question at issue was the defence of the Catholic religion, joined this time with the rights of their monarch. They met in provincial synod at Kells, where, after mature deliberation, the cause of the confederates, "God and the king," freedom of worship and loyalty to the legitimate sovereign, was declared just and holy, and, after lifting a warning voice against the barbarities which had commenced on both sides, and ordaining the abolition and oblivion of all distinctions between native Irish and old English, they took measures for convoking a national synod at Kilkenny.

It met on the 10th of May, 1643. An oath of association bound all Catholics throughout the land. It was ordained that a general assembly comprising all the lords spiritual and temporal and the gentry should be held; that the assembly should select members from its body to represent the different provinces and principal cities, to be called the Supreme Council, which should sit from day to day, dispense justice, appoint to offices, and carry on the executive government of the country.

Meanwhile the Irish abroad, the exiles, had heard of the movement, and several prominent chieftains came back to take part in the struggle; while those who remained away helped the cause by gaining the aid of the Catholic sovereigns, and sending home all the funds and munitions of war they could procure. Among these, one of the most conspicuous was the learned Luke Wadding, then at Rome engaged in writing his celebrated works, who dispatched money and arms contributed by the Holy Father. John B. Rinuccini, Archbishop of Fermo, sent by the Pope as Nuncio, sailed in the same ship which conveyed those contributions to Ireland.

The Catholic prelates thus originated a free government with nothing revolutionary in its character, but combining some of the forms of the old Irish Feis with the chief features of modern Parliamentary governments. Matthew O'Connor makes the following just observations on this subject in his "Irish Catholics:"

"The duty of obedience to civil government was so deeply impressed on the Catholic mind, at this period, in Ireland, that it degenerated into passive submission. These impressions originated in religious zeal, and were fostered by persecution. The spiritual authority of the clergy was found requisite to soften those notions, and temper them with ideas of the constitutional, social, and Christian right of resistance in self-defence. The nobility and gentry fully concurred in those proceedings of the clergy, and the nation afterward ratified them in a general convention held at Kilkenny, in the subsequent month of October. The national union seemed to be at last cemented by the wishes of all orders, and the interests of all parties."

The fact is, the nation had been brought to life, and took its stand on a new footing. When the general assembly met, in October, eleven bishops and fourteen lay lords formed what may be called the Irish peerage; two hundred and twenty-six commoners represented the large majority of the Irish constituencies; a great lawyer of the day, Patrick Darcy, was elected chancellor; and a Supreme Council of six members from each province constituted what may be called the Executive.

This government, which really ruled Ireland without any interference until Ormond succeeded in breaking it up, was obeyed and acknowledged throughout the land. It undertook and carried out all the functions of its high office, such as the coining of money, appointing circuit-judges, sending ambassadors abroad, and commissioning officers to direct the operations of the national army. Among these latter, one name is sufficient to vouch for their efficiency: that of Owen Roe O'Neill, who had returned, with many others, from the Continent, in the July of that year, and formally, assumed the command of the army of Ulster.

Owen Roe O'Neill was grand-nephew to Hugh of Tyrone. Unknown, even now, to Europe, his name still lives in the memory of his countrymen. "The head of the Hy-Niall race, the descendant of a hundred kings, the inheritor of their virtues, without a taint of their vices, he would have deserved a crown, and, on a larger theatre, would have acquired the title of a hero."--(M. O'Connor.)

Had Charles recognized this government, which proclaimed him king, discharged from office the traitors, Borlase and Parsons, who plotted against him, and not surrendered his authority to Ormond, Ireland would probably have been saved from the horrors impending, and Charles himself from the scaffold. Whatever the issue might have been, the fact remains that the Irish then proved they could establish a solid government of their own, and that it is an altogether erroneous idea to imagine them incapable of governing themselves.

It is impossible to enter here upon the details of the intricate complications which ensued--complications which were chiefly owing to the plots of Ormond; but, it may be stated fearlessly that, the more the history of those times is studied, the more certainly is the "national" party, with the Nuncio Rinuccini for head and director, recognized as the one which, better than any other, could have saved Ireland. At least, no true Irishman will now pretend that the "peace party," headed by Ormond, which was pitted against the "Nuncionists," could bring good to the country; on the contrary, its subsequent misfortunes are to be ascribed directly to it.

To stigmatize it as it deserves, needs no more than to say that among its chief leaders were Ormond, its head and projector, and Murrough O'Brien, of Inchiquin, to this day justly known as Murrough of the burnings. These two men were the product of the "refined policy" of England to kill Catholicism in the higher classes by the operation of one of the laws that governed the oppressed nation--wardship.

Both Inchiquin and Ormond were born of Catholic fathers, and all their relations, during their lives, remained Catholics. But, their fathers dying during the minority of both, the law took their education out of the hands of the nearest kin, to give it to English Protestant wardens, in the name of the king, who was supposed by the law to be their legitimate guardian. This was one of the fruits of feudalism. They were duly brought up by these wardens in the Protestant religion, and received a Protestant education. They grew up, fully impressed with the idea that the country which gave them birth was a barbarous country; the parents to whom they owed their lives were idolaters; and their fellow-countrymen a set of villains, only fitted to become, and forever remain, paupers and slaves.

There is no exaggeration in these expressions, as anybody must concede who has studied the opinions and prejudices entertained by the English with regard to the Irish, from that period down almost to our own days. At any rate, to one acquainted with the workings of the "Court of Wards," there is nothing surprising in the fact that Ormond, the descendant of so many illustrious men of the great Butler family--a family at all times so attached to the Catholic faith, and which afterward furnished so many victims to the transplantation schemes of Cromwell--should himself become an inveterate enemy to the religion of his own parents, and to those who professed it; and that he should employ the great gifts which God had granted him, solely to scheme against this religion, and prevent his native countrymen from receiving even the scanty advantages which Charles at one time was willing to concede to them, through Lord Glanmorgan.

It was Ormond who prevented the execution of the treaty between that lord and the confederates, the provisions of which were--

1. The Catholics of Ireland were to enjoy the free and public exercise of their religion.

2. They were to hold, and have secure for their use, all the Catholic churches not then in actual possession of Protestants.

3. They were to be exempt from the jurisdiction of the Protestant clergy.

But, thanks to his education, such provisions were too much for Ormond, the son of a Catholic father, and whose mother, at the very time living a pious and excellent life, would have rejoiced to see those advantages secured to her Church and herself, in common with the rest of her countrymen and women.

In like manner, Murrough O'Brien, the Baron of Inchiquin, the descendant of so many Catholic kings and saints, whose name was a glory in itself, and so closely linked to the Catholic glories of the island, was converted, by the education which he had received, into a most cruel oppressor of the Church of his baptism. His expeditions, through the same country which his ancestors had ruled, were characterized by all the barbarities practised at the time by Munro, Coote, and all the parliamentary leaders of the Scotch Puritans, and would have fitted him as a worthy compeer of

Cromwell and Ireton, who were soon to follow. The name of Cashel and its cathedral, where he murdered so many priests, women, and children, around the altar adorned by the great and good Cormac McCullinan, would alone suffice to hand his name down to the execration of posterity.

Ormond and Murrough being the two chiefs of the "peace party," what wonder that the prelates, who had so earnestly labored at the formation of the Kilkenny Confederation, and the Nuncio at their head, refused to have aught to do with projects in which such men were concerned, when it is borne in mind also that several provisions of that "peace treaty" were directly opposed to the oath taken by the Confederates? But, unfortunately, Ormond was a skilful diplomat, had been dispatched by the king, and was supposed to be carrying out the ideas suggested to him by the unhappy monarch. His representations, therefore, could not fail to carry weight, principally with the Anglo-Irish lords of the Pale, many of whom, influenced by his courtly manners and address, declared openly for the proposed peace.

Thus did the peace sow the germs of division and even war among the Irish. The unity among the Catholics, so full of promise, was soon broken up; and those who had met each other in such a brotherly spirit in the day when the native chiefs and Anglo-Irish lords assembled together at Tara, who swore then that the division of centuries should exist no longer, began to look upon each other again as enemies. Without going at length into the vicissitudes of those various contentions, it is enough to say that in the end war broke out between those who had so recently taken the oath of confederation together. Owen Roe O'Neill, the victor of Benburb, and the only man who could direct the Irish armies, was attacked by Preston and other lords of the Pale, and died, as some historians allege, of poison administered to him by one of them.

This was the result of the intrigues of Ormond; nevertheless, Charles continued to place confidence in him, and though he had been twice obliged to resign his lieutenancy, and once to fly the country, the infatuated sovereign sent him back once more.

If was only at the end of the struggle, when the ill-fated king was at length in the hands of his enemies, that Ormond could be brought to consent to conditions acceptable to the national party. But then it was too late; the parliamentary forces had carried every thing before them in England;

England was already republican to the core; and the armies which had been employed against the Cavaliers, once the efforts of the latter had ceased with the death of the king, were at liberty to leave the country, now submissive to parliamentary rule, and cross over to Ireland, with Cromwell at their head, to crush out the nation almost, and concentrate on that fated soil, within the short space of nine months, all the horrors of past centuries.

By the death of Owen Roe O'Neill just at that time, Ireland was left without a leader fit to cope with the great republican general. The country had already been devastated by Coote, Munro, St. Leger, and other Scotch and English Puritans; but the massacres which, until the coming of Cromwell, had been, at least, only local and checked by the troops of Owen Roe, soon extended throughout the island, unarrested by any forces in the field. The Cromwellian soldiers, not content with the character of warriors, came as "avengers of the Lord," to destroy an "idolatrous people."

That their real design was to exterminate the nation, and use the opportunity which then presented itself for that purpose, there can by no doubt. It was only after a fair trial that the project was found to be impossible, and that other expedients were devised. Coote had previously acted with this design in view, as is now an ascertained fact, and had been encouraged in the course he pursued by the Dublin government.[1] The same might be shown of St. Leger, in Munster, toward the beginning of the insurrection. At all events, all doubt in the matter, if any existed, ceased with the landing of Cromwell in 1649, when the real object of the war at once showed itself everywhere.

The result of this man's policy has been painted by Villemain, in his "Histoire de Cromwell," in a sentence: "Ireland became a desert which the few remaining inhabitants described by the mournful saying, 'There was not water enough to drown a man, not wood enough to hang him, not earth enough to bury him.'"

The French writer attributes to the whole island what was said of only a part of it. To this day, the name of Cromwell is justly execrated in Ireland, and "the curse of Cromwell" is one of the bitterest which can be invoked upon a person's head. But, at present, the fidelity of the Irish to the Stuarts

---

[1] See Matthew O'Connor's "Irish Catholics."

concerns us, and a few reflections will put it in a strong but true light before us.

Ever since the restoration of Charles II., many Englishmen have professed great reverence for the memory of the "martyr-king." Even the subsequent Revolution of 1658 left the monument erected to him untouched. Many British families continued steady in their devotion to the Scotch line, and the name of Jacobite was for them a title of honor. Yet what were their sufferings for the cause of the king during his struggle with the Parliament, and after his execution? A few noblemen lost their lives and estates; some went into exile and followed the fortunes of the Pretenders who tried to gain possession of the throne. But the bulk of the nation--England--may be said to have suffered nothing by the great revolution which led to the Commonwealth. On the contrary, it is acknowledged that the administration of Cromwell at least brought peace to the country, and raised the power of Great Britain to a higher eminence in Europe than it had ever known before. As usual, the English made great profession of loyalty, but, as a rule, were particularly careful that no great inconvenience should come to them from it.

Treated with contempt and distrust by Charles and his advisers, so insulted in every thing that was dear to her that it is still a question for historians if, in many instances, the king and the royalists did not betray her, Ireland alone, after having taken her stand for a whole decade of years for God and the king, resolved to face destruction unflinchingly in support of what she imagined to be a noble cause.

After the landing of Cromwell, when to any sensible man there no longer remained hope of serving the cause of the king, when the desire which is natural to every human heart, of saving what can be saved, might, not only without dishonor, but with justice and right, have dictated the necessity of coming to terms with the parliamentarians, and of abandoning a cause which was hopeless, "on the 4th of December, 1649, Eber McMahon, Bishop of Clogher, a mere Irishman by name, by descent, by enthusiastic attachment to his country, exerted his great abilities to rouse his countrymen to a persevering resistance to Cromwell, and to unite all hearts and hands in the support of Ormond's administration. . . . All the bishops concurred in his views, and subscribed a solemn declaration that they would, to the utmost of their power, forward his Majesty's rights, and the good of the nation. . . . Ormond, at last, either sensible that no reliance could be placed on them, or that the treachery of Inchiquin's troops was, at least, on the part of the Irish, a fair ground of distrust and suspicion of the remainder, consented to their removal."-- ("Irish Catholics.")

"At last!" will be the reader's exclamation, while he wonders if another people could be found forbearing enough to wait eight years for the adoption of such a necessary measure.

And the only reward for their fidelity to King Charles I. could under the circumstances be destruction. They waited with resignation for the impending gloom to overshadow them. Terrible moment for a nation, when despair itself fails to nerve it for further resistance and possible success! Such was the position of the Irish at the death of Charles.

Who shall describe that loyalty? After Ormond had met with the defeat he deserved in the field; after the cities had fallen one after another into the hands of the destroyer, who seldom thought himself bound to observe the conditions of surrender; after the chiefs, who might have protracted the struggle, had disappeared either by death or exile, the doom of the nation was sealed; yet it shrank not from the consequences.

The barbarities of Cromwell and his soldiers had depopulated large tracts of territory to such an extent that the troops marching through them were compelled to carry provisions as through a desert. The cattle, the only resource of an agricultural country, had been all consumed in a ten years' war. It was reported that, after every successful engagement, the republican general ordered all the men from the age of sixteen to sixty to be slaughtered without mercy, all the boys from six to sixteen to be deprived of sight, and the women to have a red- hot iron thrust through their breasts. Rumors such as these, exaggerated though they may be, testify at least to the terror which Cromwell inspired. As for the captured cities, there can be no doubt of the wholesale massacres carried out therein by his orders. Of the entire population of Tredagh only thirty persons survived, and they were condemned to the labor of slaves. Hugh Peters, the chaplain of Fairfax, wrote after this barbarous execution: "We are masters of Tredagh; no enemy was spared; I just come from the church where I had gone to thank the Lord."

The same fate awaited Wexford, and, later on, Drogheda. Cromwell, when narrating those bloody massacres, concluded by saying, "People blame me, but it was the will of God."

The Bible, the holy word of God, misread and misunderstood by those fanatics, persuaded them that it would be a crime not to exterminate the Irish, as the Lord punished Saul for having spared Agag and the chief of the Amalekites. Whoever wishes for further details of these sickening atrocities, committed in the name of God, may find them in a multitude of histories of the time, but chiefly in the "Threnodia" of Friar Morrison.

Certain modern Irish historians would seem not to understand the heroism of their own countrymen. "Bitterly," says A. M. O'Sullivan, "did the Irish people pay for their loyalty to an English sovereign. Unhappily for their worldly fortunes, if not for their fame, they were high-spirited and unfearing, where pusillanimity would certainly have been safety, and might have been only prudence."

But the verdict of posterity, always a just one, calls such a high-spirited and unfearing attitude true heroism, and spurns pusillanimity even when it insures safety and may be called prudence, if its result is the surrender of holy faith and Christian truth. Safety and prudence characterized the conduct of the English nation under the iron rule of Cromwell, as under the tyranny of the Tudors. Can the reader of history admire the nation on that account? Who shall affirm that the result of the craven spirit of the English was the prosperity which ensued, and that of Irish heroism destruction and gloom? The history of either nation is far from ended yet; and bold would be the man who dare assert that the prosperity of England is everlasting, and the humiliation of Ireland never to know an end.

However that may be, this at least is undeniable: the opinion current of the Irish character is demonstrated to be altogether an erroneous one by the incontrovertible facts cursorily narrated above. Determination of purpose, adherence to conscience and principle, consistency of conduct, are terms all too weak to convey an idea of the magnanimity displayed by the people, and of their heroic bearing throughout those stirring events.

At last, after a bloody struggle with Cromwell and Ireton, on May 12, 1652, "the Leinster army of the Irish surrendered at Kilkenny on terms which were successively adopted by the other principal bodies of troops, between that time and the September following, when the Ulster forces came to composition." Then began the real woes of Ireland. Never was the ingenuity of man so taxed to destroy a whole nation as in the measures adopted by the Protector for that purpose. It is necessary to present a brief sketch of them, since all that the Irish suffered was designed to punish them for their attachment to their religion, and, be it borne in mind, their devotion to the lawful dynasty of the Stuarts.

First, then, to render easy of execution the stern and cruel resolve of the new government, the defenders of the nation were not only to be disarmed, but put out of the way. Hence Cromwell was gracious enough to consent that they be permitted to leave the country and take service in the armies of the foreign powers then at peace with the Commonwealth. Forty thousand men, officers and soldiers, adopted this desperate resolution.

"Soon agents from the King of Spain, the King of Poland, and the Prince de Conde, were contending for the service of the Irish troops. Don Ricardo White, in May, 1672, shipped seven thousand in batches from Waterford, Kinsale, Galway, Limerick, and Bantry, for the King of Spain. Colonel Christopher Mayo got liberty in September to beat his drums, to raise three thousand more for the same destination. Lord Muskerry took with him five thousand to the King of Poland. In July, 1654, three thousand five hundred went to serve the Prince de Conde. Sir Walter Dungan and others got liberty to beat their drums in different garrisons for various destinations."--(Prendergast.)

To prove that the desperate resolution of leaving their country did not originate with the Irish, notwithstanding what some have written to the contrary, it is enough to remark that their expatriation was made a necessary condition of their surrender by the new government. For instance, Lord Clanrickard, according to Matthew O'Connor, "deserted and surrounded, could obtain no terms for the nation, nor indeed for himself and his troops, except with the sad liberty of transportation to any other country in amity with the Commonwealth."

To prove, if necessary, still further that the expatriation of the Irish troops was part of a scheme already resolved upon, it is enough to remember the indisputable fact that from the surrender at Kilkenny in 1652, until the open announcement in the September of 1653, that the Parliament had assigned Connaught for the dwelling-place of the Irish nation, whither they were to be "transplanted" before the 1st of May, 1654, the various garrisons and small armies which had fought so gallantly for Ireland and the Stuarts were successively urged (and urged by Cromwell meant compelled) to leave the country; and it was only when the last of the Irish regiments had departed that the doom of the nation was boldly and clearly announced.

But these forced exiles were not restricted to the warrior class. "The Lord Protector," says Prendergast, "applied to the Lord Henry Cromwell, then major-general of the forces of Ireland, to engage soldiers . . . . and to secure a thousand young Irish girls to be shipped to Jamaica. Henry Cromwell answered that there would be no difficulty, only that force must be used in taking them; and he suggested the addition of fifteen hundred or two thousand boys of from twelve to fourteen years of age. . . . The numbers finally fixed were one thousand boys and one thousand girls."

The total number of children disposed of in the same way, from 1652 to 1655, has been variously estimated at from twenty thousand to one hundred thousand. The British Government at last was compelled to interfere and put a stop to the infamous traffic, when, the mere Irish proving too scarce, the agents were not sufficiently discriminating in their choice, but shipped off English children also to the Tobacco Islands.

At last the island was left utterly without defenders, and sufficiently depopulated. It is calculated that, when the last great measure was announced and put into execution, only half a million of Irish people remained in the country, the rest of the resident population being composed of the Scotch and English, introduced by James I., and the soldiers and adventurers let in by Cromwell.

The main features of the celebrated "act of settlement" are known to all. It was an act intended to dispose quietly of half a million human beings, destined certainly in the minds of its projectors to disappear in due time, without any great violence-- to die off --and leave the whole island in the possession of the "godly."

Connaught is famed as being the wildest and most barren province of Ireland. At the best, it can support but a scanty population. At this time it had been completely devastated by a ten years' war and by the excesses of the parliamentary forces. This province then was mercifully granted to the unhappy Irish race; it was set apart as a paradise for the wretched remnant to dwell in all Connaught, except a strip four miles wide along the sea, and a like strip along the right bank of the Shannon. This latter judicious provision was undoubtedly intended to prevent them from dwelling by the ocean, whence they might derive subsistence or assis-tance, or means of escape in the event of their ever rising again; and, on the other hand, from crossing the Shannon, on the east side of which their homes might still be seen. This cordon of four miles' width was drawn all around what was the Irish nation, and filled with the fiercest zealots of the "army of the Lord" to keep guard over the devoted victims.

Surely the doom of the race was at last sealed!

But let all justice be done to the Protector. The act was to the effect that, on the first day of May, 1654, all who, throughout the war, had not displayed a constant good affection to the Parliament of England in opposition to Charles I., were to be removed with their families and servants to the wilds of a poor and desolated province, where certain lands were to be given them in return for their own estates. But, who of the Irish could prove that they had displayed a "constant good affection" to the English Parliament during a ten years' war? The act was nothing less than a proscription of the whole nation. The English of the Pale were included among the old natives, and even a few Protestant royalists, who had taken of the cause of the fallen Stuarts. The only exception made was in favor of "husbandmen, ploughmen, laborers, artificers, and others of the inferior sort." The English and Scotch--constituted by this act of settlement lords and masters of the three richest provinces of Ireland--could not condescend to till the soil with their own hands and attend to the mechanical arts required in civil society. Those duties were reserved for the Irish poor. It was hoped that, deprived of their nobility and clergy, they might be turned to any account by their new masters, and either become good Protestants or perish as slaves. Herein mentita est iniquitas sibi.

The heart-rending details of this outrage on humanity may be seen in Mr. Prendergast's "Cromwellian Settlement." There all who read may form some idea of the extent of Ireland's misfortunes.

It is a wonder which cannot fail to strike the reader, how, after so many precautions had been taken, not only against the further increase of the race, but for its speedy demolition, how, reduced to a bare half million, penned off on a barren tract of land, left utterly at the mercy of its persecutors, without priests, without organization of any kind, it not only failed to perish, but, from that time, has gone on, steadily increasing, until to-day it spreads out wide and far, not only on the island of its birth, but on the broad face of two vast continents.

In the space at our disposal, it is impossible to satisfy the curiosity of the reader on this very curious and interesting topic. A few remarks, however, may serve to broadly indicate the chief causes of this astonishing fact, taken apart from the miraculous intervention of God in their favor.

First, then, Connaught became more Irish than ever, and a powerful instrument, later on, to assist in the resurrection of the nation. In fact, as will soon be seen, it preserved life to it. Again, the outcasts, who were allowed to remain in the other three provinces as servants, or slaves, rather, were not found manageable on the score of religion; and, although new acts of Parliament forbade any bishop or priest to remain in the island, many did remain, some of them coming back from the Continent, whither they had been exported, to aid their unfortunate countrymen in this their direst calamity.

As Matthew O'Connor rightly says : "The ardent zeal, the fortitude and calm resignation of the Catholic clergy during this direful persecution, might stand a comparison with the constancy of Christians during the first ages of the Church. In the season of prosperity they may have pushed their pretensions too far"--this is M. O'Connor's private opinion of the Confederation of Kilkenny-- "but, in the hour of trial, they rose superior to human infirmities. . . . Sooner than abandon their flocks altogether, they fled from the communion of men, concealed themselves in woods and caverns, from whence they issued, whenever the pursuit of their enemies abated, to preach to the people, to comfort them in their afflictions, to encourage them in their trials;. . . their haunts were objects of indefatigable search; bloodhounds, the last device of human cruelty, were employed for the purpose, and the same price was set on the head of a priest as on that of a wolf."--(Irish Catholics.)

But, the expectation that the Irish of the lower classes, bereft of their pastors as well as of the guidance of their chieftains, would fall a prey to proselytizing ministers, and lose at once their nationality and their religion, was doomed to meet with disappointment.

Perhaps the cause more effective than all others in preserving the Irish nation from disappearing totally, came from a quarter least expected, or rather the most improbable and wonderful.

No device seemed better calculated to succeed in Protestantizing Ireland than the decree of Parliament which set forth that not only the officers, but even the common soldiers of the parliamentary army should be paid for their services, not in money, but in land; and that the estates of the old owners should be parcelled out and distributed among them in payment, as well as among those who, in England, had furnished funds for the prosecution of the war. Although many soldiers objected to this mode of compensation, some selling for a trifle the land allotted to them and returning to their own country, the great majority was compelled to rest satisfied with the government offer, and so resolved to settle down in Ireland and turn farmers. But a serious difficulty met them: women could not be induced to abandon their own country and go to dwell in the sister isle, while the Irish girls, being all Catholics, a decree of Parliament forbade the soldiers to marry them, unless they first succeeded in converting them to Protestantism. After many vain attempts, doubtless, the Cromwellian soldiers soon found the impossibility of bringing the "refractory" daughters of Erin to their way of thinking, and could find only one mode of bridging over the difficulty--to marry them first, without requiring then to apostatize; and secure their prize after by swearing that their wives were the most excellent of Protestants. Thus while perjury became an every-day occurrence, the victorious army began to be itself vanquished by a powerful enemy which it had scarcely calculated upon, and was utterly unprepared to meet, and finally resting from its labors, enjoyed the sweets of peace and the fat of the land.

But woman, once she feels her power, is exacting, and in course of time the Cromwellian soldiers found that further sacrifices still were required of them, which they had never counted upon. Their wives could, by no persuasion, be induced to speak English, so that, however it might go against the grain, the husbands were compelled to learn Irish and speak it habitually as best they might. Their difficulties began to multiply with their children, when they found them learning Irish in the cradle, irresistible in their Irish wit and humor, and lisping the prayers and reverencing the faith they had learned at their mothers' knees. So that, from that time to this, the posterity of Cromwell's "Ironsides," of such of them at least as remained in Ireland, have been devoted Catholics and ardent Irishmen.

The case was otherwise with the chief officers of the parliamentary army, who had received large estates and could easily obtain wives from England. They remained stanch Protestants, and their children have continued in the religion received with the estates which came to them from this wholesale confiscation. But the bulk of the army, instead of helping to form a Protestant middle class and a Protestant yeomanry, has really helped to perpetuate the sway of the Catholic religion in Ireland, and the feeling of nationality so marked to-day. This very remarkable fact has been well established and very plainly set forth, a few years ago, by eminent English reviewers.

Meanwhile, Ireland was a prey to all the evils which can afflict a nation. Pestilence was added to the ravages of war and the woes of transplantation, and it raged alike among the conquerors and the conquered. Friar Morrisson's "Threnodia" reads to-day like an exaggerated lament, the burden of which was drawn from a vivid imagination. Yet can there be little doubt that it scarcely presented the whole truth; an exact reproduction of all the heart-rending scenes then daily enacted in the unfortunate island would prove a tale as moving as ever harrowed the pitying heart of a reader.

And all this suffering was the direct consequence of two things--the attachment of the Irish to the Catholic religion, and their devotion to the Stuart dynasty. Modern historians, in considering all the circumstances, express themselves unable to understand the constancy of this people's affection for a line of kings from whom they had invariably experienced, not only neglect, but positive opposition, if not treachery. In their opinion, only the strangest obliquity of judgment can explain such infatuation. Some call it stupidity; but the Irish people have never been taxed with that. Even in the humblest ranks of life among them, there exists, not only humor, but a keenness of perception, and at times an extraordinary good sense, which is quick to detect motives, and find out what is uppermost in the minds of others.

There is but one reading of the riddle, consistent with the whole character of the people: they clung to the Stuarts because they were obedient to the precepts and duties of religion, and labored under the belief, however mistaken, that from the Stuarts alone could they hope for any thing like freedom. Their spiritual rulers had insisted on the duty of sustaining at all hazard the legitimate authority of the king, and they were firmly convinced that they could expect from no other a relaxation of the religious penal statutes imposed on them by their enemies. The more frequent grew their disappointments in the measures adopted by the sovereigns on whom they had set their hopes, the more firmly were they convinced that their intentions were good, but rendered futile by the men who surrounded and coerced them.

Religion can alone explain this singular affection of the Irish people for a race which, in reality, has caused the greatest of their misfortunes.

The subsequent events of this strange history are in perfect keeping with those preceding. A few words will suffice to sketch them.

On the death of Oliver Cromwell, his son Richard, being unable and indeed unwilling to remain at the head of the English state, the nation, tired of the iron rule of the Protector, fearful certainly of anarchy, and preferring the conservative measures of monarchy to the ever-changing revolutions of a commonwealth, recalled the son of Charles I. to the throne.

But a kind of bargain had been struck by him with those who disposed of the crown; and he undertook and promised to disturb as little as possible the vested interests created by the revolution, that is to say, he pledged himself to let the settlement of property remain as he found it. In England that promise was productive of little mischief to the nation at large, though fatal to the not very numerous families who had been deprived of their estates by the Parliament. But, in Ireland, it was a very different matter; for there the interests of the whole nation were ousted to make room for these "vested interests" of proprietors of scarcely ten years' standing.

The Irish nobility and gentry, at first unaware of the existence of this bargain, were in joyful expectation that right would at last be done them, as it was for loyalty to the father of the new king that they had been robbed of all their possessions. They were soon undeceived. To their surprise, they learned that the speculators, army-officers, and soldiers already in possession of their estates, were not to be disturbed, short as the possession had been; and that only such lands as were yet unappropriated should be returned to their rightful owners, provided only they were not papists, or could prove that they had been "innocent papists."

The consequences of this bargain are clear. The Irish of the old native race who had been, as now appeared, so foolishly ardent in their loyalty to the throne, were to be abandoned to the fate to which Cromwell had consigned them, and could expect to recover nothing of what they had so nobly lost. So flagrantly unjust was the whole proceeding, that after a time many Englishmen even saw the injustice of the decision, and lifted up their voices in defence of the Irish Catholics who alone could hope for nothing from the restoration of royalty. To put a stop to this, the infamous "Oates" fabrication was brought forward, which destroyed a number of English Catholic families and stifled the voice of humanity in its efforts to befriend the Irish race; and so sudden, universal, and lasting, was the effect of this plot in closing the eyes of all to the claims of the Irish, that when its chief promoter, Shaftesbury, was dragged to the Tower and there imprisoned as a miscreant, and Oates himself suffered a punishment too mild for his villany, nevertheless no one thought of again taking up the cause of the Irish natives.

It is almost impossible in these days to realize what has occupied our attention in this chapter. The unparalleled act of spoliation by which four-fifths of the Irish nation were deprived of their property by Cromwell because of their devotion to Charles I., for the alleged reason that they could not prove a constant good affection for the English regicide Parliament, that spoliation was ratified by the son of Charles within a few years after the rightful owners, who had sacrificed their property for the sake of his father, had been dispossessed, while the parliamentarians, who by force of arms had broken down the power of Charles and enabled the members of the Long Parliament to try their king and bring him to the block, those very soldiers and officers were left in possession of their ill-gotten plunder, at a time when many of the owners were only a few miles away in Connaught, or even inhabiting the out-houses of their own mansions, and tilling the soil as menial servants of Cromwell's troopers.

The case, apparently similar, which occurred in after-years, of the French emigrant nobility, cannot be compared with the result of this strange concession of Charles II. In fact, it may be said that the spoliations of 1792-'93 in France would probably never have taken place but for the successful example held up to the eyes of the legislators of the French Republic by the English Revolution.

As for the share which Charles II. himself bore in the measure, it is best told by the fact that the work of spoliation was carried on so vigorously during the reign of the "merry monarch," that when a few years later William of Orange came to the throne there was no land left for him to dispose of among his followers save the last million of acres. All the rest had been portioned off. Well might Dr. Madden say: "The whole of Ireland has been so thoroughly confiscated that the only exception was that of five or six families of English blood, some of whom had been attainted in the reign of Henry VIII., but recovered flourished ever since. Yet did they not refuse the accessory with the principal. Deluded men they may be called by many; but people cannot ordinarily understand the high motives which move men swayed only by the twofold feeling of religion and nationality.

Nothing in our opinion could better prove that the Irish were really a nation, at the time we speak of, than the remarks just set forth. When all minds are so unanimous, the wills so ready, the arms so strong and well prepared to strike together, it must be admitted that in the whole exists a common feeling, a national will. Self-government may be wanting; it may have been suppressed by sheer force and kept under by the most unfavorable state of affairs, but the nation subsists and cannot fail ultimately to rise.

In those eventful times shone forth too that characteristic which has already been remarked upon of a true conservative spirit and instinctive hatred for every principle which in our days is called radical and revolutionary. Had there existed in the Irish disposition the least inclination toward those social and moral aberrations, productive to-day of so many and such widespread evils, surely the period of the English Revolution was the fitting time to call them forth, and turn them from their steady adherence to right and order into the new channels, toward which nations were being then hurried, and which would really have favored for the time being their own efforts for independence. Then would the Irish have presented to future historians as stirring an episode of excitement and activity as was furnished by the English and Scotch at that time, by the French later on, and which to-day most European nations offer.

The temptation was indeed great. They saw with what success rebellion was rewarded among the English and Scotch. They themselves were sure to be stamped as rebels whichever side they took; and, as was seen, Charles II. allowed his commissioners in his act of settlement so to style them, and punish them for it--for supporting the cause of his father against the Parliament.

Would it not have been better for them to have become once, at least, rebels in true earnest, and reap the same advantage from rebellion which all around them reaped? Yet did they stand proof against the demoralizing doctrines of Scotch Covenanter and English republican. Hume, who was openly adverse to every thing Irish, is compelled to describe this Catholic people as "loyal from principle, attached to regal power from religious education, uniformly opposing popular frenzy, and zealous vindicators of royal prerogatives."

All this was in perfect accord with their traditional spirit and historical recollections. Revolutionary doctrines have always been antagonistic to the Irish mind and heart. This will appear more fully when recent times come under notice, and it may be a surprise to some to find that, with the exception of a few individuals, who in nowise represent the nation, the latest and favorite theories of the world, not only on religion, science, and philosophy, but likewise on government and the social state, have never found open advocates among them. They, so far, constitute the only nation untouched, as yet, by the blight which is passing over and withering the life of modern society. Thus, it may be said that the exiled nobility still rules in Ireland by the recollection of the past, though there can no longer exist a hope of reconstructing an ancient order which has passed away forever. The prerogatives once granted to the aristocratic classes are now disowned and repudiated on all sides; in Ireland they would be submitted to with joy tomorrow, could the actual descendants of the old families only make good their claims. It must not be forgotten that the Irish nobility, as a class, deserved well of their country, sacrificed themselves for it when the time of sacrifice came, and therefore it is fitting that they should live in the memory of the people that sees their traces but finds them not. The dream of finding rulers for the nation from among those who claim to be the descendants of the old chieftains, is a dream and nothing more; but, even still to many Irishmen, it is within the compass of reality, so deeply ingrained is their conservative spirit, and so completely, in this instance, at least, are they free from the influx of modern ideas.

The Stuarts, then, were supported by the Irish, not merely from religious, but also from national motives, inasmuch as that family was descended from the line of Gaelic kings, and, however unworthy they themselves may have been, their rights were upheld and acknowledged against all comers. But, the Stuarts gone, allegiance was flung to the winds.

The success of Cromwell and his republic was the doom of all prospects of the reunion of the two islands; and the subsequent Revolution of 1688, which commenced so soon after the death of the Protector, left the Irish in the state in which the struggles of four hundred years with the Plantagenets and Tudors had placed and left them in relation to their connection with England--a state of antagonism and mutual repulsion, wherein the Irish nation, the victim of might, was slowly educated by misfortune until the time should come for the open acknowledgment of right.

A CENTURY OF GLOOM.--THE PENAL LAWS

WILLIAM III., of Orange, was inclined to observe, in good faith, the articles agreed upon at the surrender of Limerick, namely, to allow the conquered liberty of worship, citizen rights, so much as remained to them of their property, and the means for personal safety recognized before the departure of Sarsfield and his men.

The lords justices even issued a proclamation commanding "all officers and soldiers of the army and militia, and all other persons whatsoever, to forbear to do any wrong or injury, or to use unlawful violence to any of his Majesty's subjects, whether of the British or Irish nation, without distinction, and that all persons taking the oath of allegiance, and behaving themselves according to law, should be deemed subjects under their Majesties' protection, and be equally entitled to the benefit of the law."-- (Harris, "Life of William.")

This first proclamation not having been generally obeyed, another was published denouncing "the utmost vengeance of the law against the offenders;" and the author above quoted adds that "the satisfaction given to the Irish was a source of lasting gratitude to the person and government of William."

It is even asserted that, not only did the new monarch thus ratify the treaty of Limerick, but that "he inserted in the ratification a clause of the last importance to the Irish, which had been omitted in the draught signed by the lords justices and Sarsfield. That clause extended the benefits of the capitulation to "all such as were under the protection of the Irish army in the counties of Limerick, Clare, Kerry, Cork, and Mayo. A great quantity of Catholic property depended on the insertion of this clause in the ratification, and the English Privy Council hesitated whether to take advantage of the omission. The honesty of the king declared it to be a part of the articles."

The final confirmation was issued from Westminster on February 24, 1692, in the name of William and Mary.

But the party which had overcome the honest leanings of James I., if he ever had any, and of his son and grandson, was at this time more powerful than ever, and could not consent to extend the claims of justice and right to the conquered. This party was the Ulster colony, which Cromwell's settlement had spread to the two other provinces of Leinster and Munster, and which was confirmed in its usurpation by the weakness of the second Charles. The motives for the bitter animosity which caused it to set its face against every measure involving the scantiest justice toward its fellow-countrymen may be summed up in two words--greed and fanaticism.

Until the time when the first of the Stuarts ascended the English throne, all the successive spoliations of Ireland, even the last under Elizabeth, at the end of the Geraldine war, were made to the advantage of the English nobility. Even the younger sons of families from Lancashire, Cheshire, and Dorsetshire, who "planted" Munster after the ruin of the Desmonds, had noble blood in their veins, and were consequently subject more or less to the ordinary prejudices of feudal lords. The life of the agriculturist and grazier was too low down in the social scale to catch their supercilious glance. The consequence of which was, that the Catholic tenants of Munster were left undisturbed in their holdings. Instead of the "dues" exacted by their former chieftains, they now paid rent to their new lords.

But the rabble let loose on the island by James I. was afflicted with no such dainty notions as these. To supercilious glances were substituted eyes keen as the Israelites', for the "main chance." The new planters, intent only on profit and gain, thought with the French peasant of an after-date, that, for landed estate to produce its full value, "there is nothing like the eye of a master." The Irish peasant was therefore removed from at least one-half the farms of Ulster, and driven to live as best he might among the Protestant lords of Munster. And in order to have an entirely Protestant "plantation," it became incumbent on the new owners so to frame the legislation as to deprive the Irish Catholics of any possibility of recovering their former possessions. Thus, laws were passed declaring null and void all purchases made by "Irish papists."

Who has not witnessed, at some period in his life, the effect produced on the people in his neighborhood by one avaricious but wealthy man, intent only on increasing his property, and profiting by the slavish labor of the poor under his control? Who has not detested, in his inmost soul, the grinding tyranny of the miser gloating over the hard wealth which he has wrung from the misery and tears of all around him, and who boasts of the cunning shrewdness, the success of which is only too visible in the desolation that encircles him? Imagine such scenes enacted throughout a large territory, beginning with Ulster, spreading thence to Munster and Connaught, and finally through the whole island, and we have an exact picture of the effects of the Protestant "plantation." Each year, almost, of the seventeenth century witnessed fresh swarms of these foreign adventurers settling on the island, interrupted in their operations only by the Confederation of Kilkenny, but multiplying faster and faster after the destruction of that truly national government, until at the time now under our consideration, "Scotch thrift," as it is called, had become the chief virtue of most of the owners of land--Scotch thrift, which is but another name for greed.

It were easy to show, by long details, that this great characteristic of the new "plantation" would suffice to explain that general and terrible pauperism which has since become the striking feature of once-happy Ireland. But only a few words can be allowed.

It is the fanaticism of the new "planters" which will chiefly occupy our attention. These were composed, first, of the Scotch Presbyterians of Knox, whom James I. had dispatched, and afterward of the ranting soldiers and officers of Cromwell's army, more Jew than Christian, since their mouths were ever filled with Bible texts of that particular character wherein the wrath of God is denounced against the impious and cruel tribes of Palestine. It is doubtful whether the ideas of God and man, promulgated and spread among the people by Calvin and Knox, have ever been equalled in evil consequences by the most superstitious beliefs of ancient pagans. Let us look well at those teachings. According to them, God is the author of evil: he issues forth his decrees of election or reprobation, irrespective of merit or demerit; inflicting eternal torments on innumerable souls which never could have been saved, and for whom the Son of God did not die. What any rational being must consider as the most revolting cruelty and injustice, these men called acts of pure justice executed by the hand of God. God saves blindly those whom he saves, and takes them home to his bosom, though reeking with the unrepented and unexpiated crimes of their lives--unexpiable, in fact, on the part of man--merely because they persuade themselves that they are of "the elect."

In that system, man is a mere machine, unendowed with the slightest symptom of free-will, but inflated with the most overbearing pride; deeming all others but those of his sect the necessary objects of the blind wrath of God, cast off and reprobate from all eternity in the designs of Providence; for whom "the elect" can feel no more pity or affection than redeemed men can for the arch-fiend himself, both being alike redeemless and unredeemed.

No system of pretended religion, invented by the perverted mind of man, under the inspiration of the Evil One, could go further in atrocity than this.

Yet such was the pure, undiluted essence of Calvinism in its beginning. In our times its doctrines have been radically modified, as its adherents could not escape the soothing operations of time and calm reason. But, at the period of which we speak, its absurd and revolting tenets were fresh, and taken religiously to the letter.

The new colonists, therefore, believed, and acted on the belief, that all men outside of their own body were the enemies of God and had God for their enemy. What a convenient doctrine for men of an "itching palm!" The papists, in particular, were worse than idolaters, and to "root them out" was only to render a service to God. In the event of this holy desire not being altogether possible of execution, the nearest approach to the goodly work was to strip them of all rights, and render the life of such reprobates more miserable than the death which was to condemn them to the eternal torments planned out for them in the eternal decrees, and so give them a foretaste here of the life destined for them hereafter.

The reader, then, may understand how the Scotch Presbyterians of the time, overflowing as they were with free and republican ideas as far as regarded their own welfare, when it came to a question of extending the same to their Catholic fellow-men, if they would have admitted the term, scouted such a preposterous and ungodly idea. These latter were unworthy the enjoyment of such benefit. And thus the hoot of Protestant ascendancy, "Protestant liberty and right!" came up as war-cries to stifle out all efforts tending to extend even the most ordinary privileges of the liberty which is man's by nature, to any but Protestants of the same class as themselves.

Here a curious reflection, full of meaning, and causing the mind almost to mock at the type of a free constitution, presents itself. The eighteenth century witnessed the development of the British Constitution as now known. It embraced in its bosom all British citizens, raising up the nation to the pinnacle of material prosperity, while at the same time and all through it, whole classes of citizens of the British Empire, both in Great Britain and Ireland, were openly, unblushingly, legally, without a thought of mercy or pity--not to mention such an ugly word as logic--denied the protection of the common charter and the common rights.

Under Cromwell the doctrines of Calvin and Knox did not show themselves quite so obtrusively. The officers and soldiers of his armies, in common with their general, thought the Presbyterian Kirk too aristocratic and unbending. They formed a new sect of Independents, now called Congregationalists. But the chief feature of the new religious system became as productive of evil to Ireland as the stern dogmas of Calvin ever could be. The principle that the Scriptures constituted the only rule of faith was beginning to bear its fruits. It is needless to remark that Holy Scripture, when abandoned to the free interpretation of all, becomes the source of many errors, as it may be the source of many crimes. The historian and novelist even have ere now frequently told us to what purpose the "Word of God" was manipulated by Scottish Covenanter and Cromwellian freebooter.

The Covenanter, or freebooter, saw in the antagonists of his "real rebellion" and opposers of the designs of his dark policy, only the enemies of God and the adversaries of his Providence. He believed himself divinely commissioned to destroy Catholics and butcher innocent women and children, as the armies of Joshua were authorized to fight against Amalek, and possess themselves of a country occupied by a people whose cruel idolatry was ineradicable, and rendered them absolutely irreconcilable. Thus to the stern and odious tenets of Calvinism the new invaders joined the fanaticism of self-deluded Jews, never having received any commission from the God whom they blasphemed, yet bearing themselves with all the solemnity of his instruments.

There is consequently nothing to surprise us in the atrocities committed by the Scotch troops in 1641, when they first invaded the island from the north, as little as there is in the numerous massacres which first attended the march of the troops of Cromwell, Ireton, and other leaders, and which were only discontinued when the voice of Europe rose up in revolt at the recital, and they themselves became thoroughly convinced that the complete destruction of the people was impossible, and the only next best thing to be done was to export as many as could be exported and reduce the rest to slavery.

Thus did the new colony commence its workings, and it is easy to comprehend how such intensely Protestant doctrines, remaining implanted in the breasts of the people who came to make Ireland their home, could not fail to oppose an insurmountable barrier to the fusion of the new and the old inhabitants, and impart a fearful reality to the theory of "Protestant ascendancy" and "Protestant liberty and right"--the liberty and right to oppress those of another creed.

These watchwords form the key to the understanding of all the miseries and woes of Irishmen during the whole of the eighteenth century. We now turn to contemplate the commencement of the workings of this fanatic intolerance which ushered in the century of gloom.

The lords justices had just returned, after concluding the treaty of peace with Sarsfield, when the first mutterings of the thunder were heard that presaged the coming storm. Dr. Dopping, the Protestant Bishop of Meath, while preaching before them on the Sunday following their return to Dublin, reproached them openly in Christ Church for their indulgence to the Irish, and urged that no faith was to be kept with such a cruel and perfidious race. This sort of doctrine has been heard before, and from men of the stamp of Dr. Dopping; it is still heard every day, but it is generally thrown into the teeth of Catholics and saddled on them as their doctrine, however frequently refuted.

The doctor stated broadly that with such people no treaties were binding, and that therefore the articles of Limerick were not to be observed.

William and his Irish government endeavored to check this intemperance; but the feelings of the sectarians were too ardent to be thus easily smothered, and the greater the opposition they encountered, the more they insisted on proclaiming their views, to which naturally they gained many adherents among the colonists of the Protestant plantation.

The Irish Parliament soon assembled in Dublin. The majority, imbued with the gloomy Calvinism of the times, and fearing to face the opposition of the respectable minority of Catholic members, who had come to take their seats, passed an act imposing a new oath, in contradiction to one of the articles of the treaty. That oath included an abjuration of James's right de jure, a renunciation of the spiritual authority of the Pope, and (as though that were not enough to exclude Catholics) a declaration against the doctrine of transubstantiation and other fundamental tenets of their creed. Persons who refused to take this oath were debarred from all offices and emoluments, as well as from both Houses of the Irish Parliament.

The Catholic members were compelled to withdraw at once; and no Catholic ever took part in the legislation of his own country from that day until the Emancipation in 1829.

After this withdrawal, which in the times of the French Convention would have been called an epuration, the Irish Parliament became the bane of the country. In fact, it only represented parliamentary England, and subjected Ireland to every measure required by English ultraists for the attainment of their selfish purposes. Possessed by a gloomy fanaticism, its main object was to root out of the island every vestige that remained of the religion which had once flourished there. All its legislative spirit was concentrated in the two questions: Are the laws already in existence against the further growth of Popery rigidly enforced? and, cannot some new law be introduced to further the same object.?

Many a time were these two questions put in the assembly called the Irish Parliament, until near the end of the eighteenth thunder were heard that presaged the coming storm. Dr. Dopping, the Protestant Bishop of Meath, while preaching before them on the Sunday following their return to Dublin, reproached them openly in Christ Church for their indulgence to the Irish, and urged that no faith was to be kept with such a cruel and perfidious race. This sort of doctrine has been heard before, and from men of the stamp of Dr. Dopping; it is still heard every day, but it is generally thrown into the teeth of Catholics and saddled on them as their doctrine, however frequently refuted.

The doctor stated broadly that with such people no treaties were binding, and that therefore the articles of Limerick were not to be observed.

William and his Irish government endeavored to check this intemperance; but the feelings of the sectarians were too ardent to be thus easily smothered, and the greater the opposition they encountered, the more they insisted on proclaiming their views, to which naturally they gained many adherents among the colonists of the Protestant plantation.

The Irish Parliament soon assembled in Dublin. The majority, imbued with the gloomy Calvinism of the times, and fearing to face the opposition of the respectable minority of Catholic members, who had come to take their seats, passed an act imposing a new oath, in contradiction to one of the articles of the treaty. That oath included an abjuration of James's right de jure, a renunciation of the spiritual authority of the Pope, and (as though that were not enough to exclude Catholics) a declaration against the doctrine of transubstantiation and other fundamental tenets of their creed. Persons who refused to take this oath were debarred from all offices and emoluments, as well as from both Houses of the Irish Parliament.

The Catholic members were compelled to withdraw at once; and no Catholic ever took part in the legislation of his own country from that day until the Emancipation in 1829.

After this withdrawal, which in the times of the French Convention would have been called an epuration, the Irish Parliament became the bane of the country. In fact, it only represented parliamentary England, and subjected Ireland to every measure required by English ultraists for the attainment of their selfish purposes. Possessed by a gloomy fanaticism, its main object was to root out of the island every vestige that remained of the religion which had once flourished there. All its legislative spirit was concentrated in the two questions: Are the laws already in existence against the further growth of Popery rigidly enforced? and, cannot some new law be introduced to further the same object.?

Many a time were these two questions put in the assembly called the Irish Parliament, until near the end of the eighteenth Popery, and, in the next place, it makes evident the necessity there is of cultivating and preserving a good understanding among all Protestants in this kingdom."'

Let the reader bear in mind that language such as this, and its result in the shape of atrocious legislation, continued throughout the whole of the eighteenth century in Ireland, and he will find no difficulty in understanding the meaning of Edmund Burke's words when he said: "The code against the Catholics was a machine of wise and elaborate contrivance; and as well fitted for the oppression, impoverishment, and degradation of a people, and the debasement in them of human nature itself, as ever proceeded from the perverted ingenuity of man." And, elsewhere: "To render men patient under the deprivation of all the rights of human nature, every thing which could give them a knowledge and feeling of those rights was rationally forbidden. To render humanity fit to be insulted, it was fit that it should be degraded."

But it is very pertinent to our purpose to give a sketch of those good laws, as Wharton calls them, before seeing how the Irish preferred to submit to them rather than lose their faith by "conforming." The subject has been already investigated by many writers, and of late far more completely than formerly. But the authors never presented the laws as a whole, contenting themselves, for the most part, by transcribing them in the chronological order in which they were enacted, or, if occasionally they endeavored to combine and thus present a more striking idea of the effect which such laws must have produced on the people, they were never, as far as is known to the writer, reduced to a plan, and consequently fail to bring forth the effect intended to be produced by them.

It is impossible here to give the text of those various laws-- impossible even to give a fairly accurate idea of the whole. They shall be classified, however, to the best of our ability, and as fully as circumstances permit.

Mr. Prendergast seems to consider their ultimate object always to have been the robbing of the Irish of their lands, or securing the plunder if already in possession. That this was one of the great objects always kept in view in their enactment, we do not feel inclined to contest; but that it was their only or even chief cause, we may be allowed to question, with the greatest deference to the opinion of the celebrated author of the often-quoted "Cromwellian Settlement."

We believe those laws to have been produced chiefly by sectarian fanaticism; or, if some of their framers, such as Lord Wharton, possessed no religious feelings of any kind, and could not be called fanatics, their intent was to pander to the real fanaticism of the English people, as it existed at the time, and particularly of the colony planted in Ireland, which hated Popery to the death, and would have given all its possessions and lands for the destruction of the Scarlet Woman.

In order to attain the great result proposed, the aim of the "penal statute" was one in its very complexity. For it had to deal with complex rights, which it took away one after another until the unity of the system was completed by the suppression of them all.

We classify these under the heads of political, civil, and human rights. The result of the whole policy was to degrade the Irish to the level of the wretched helots under Sparta, with this difference: while the slaves of the Lacedaemonians numbered but a few thousands, the Irish were counted by millions.

The system, as a whole, was the work of time, and, under William of Orange--even under Queen Anne--it had not yet attained its maturity, though the principal and the severest measures were carried and put in force from the very beginning. The ingenious little devices regarding short and small leases, the possession of valuable horses, etc., were mere fanciful adjuncts which the witty and inventive legislators of the Hanove-rian dynasty were happy enough to find unrecorded in the statute-books, and which they had the honor of setting there, and thus adding a new piquancy and vigorous flavor to the whole dish.

Toward the middle of the eighteenth century, the system may be said to have reached its perfection. After that time it would, in all likelihood, have been impossible to improve further, and render the yoke of slavery heavier and more galling to the Irish. The beauty and simplicity of the whole consisted in the fact that the great majority of these measures were not decreed in so many positive and express terms against Catholics in the form of open and persecuting statutes. It was merely mentioned in the laws that, to enjoy such and such a particular right, it was necessary that every subject of the crown should take such and such an oath, which no Catholic could take. Thus, the entire Irish population was set between their religion and their rights, and at any moment, by merely taking the oath, they were at liberty to enjoy all the privileges which rendered the colonists living in their midst so happy and contented, and so proud of their "Protestant ascendency."

It was hoped, no doubt, that, if at first and for a certain time, the faith of the Irish would stand proof and prompt them to sacrifice every thing held dear in life, rather than surrender that faith, nevertheless, worn out at length, and disheartened by wretchedness, unable longer to sustain their heavy burden, they would finally succumb, and, by the mere action of such an easy thing as recording an oath in accordance with the law, though against their conscience, become men and citizens. It was what the French Conventionalists of 1793 called "desoler la patience" of their victims.

This unholy hope was disappointed; and, with the exception of a comparatively few weak Christians among their number, the nation stood firm and preferred the "ignominy of the cross of Christ" to the enjoyments of this perishable life.

Their political rights were, as was seen, the first to be taken away. The Parliament of 1691 required of its members the oath referred to, and for the repudiation of which, all the Catholic members were compelled at once to withdraw. But the contrivance of swearing being found such an excellent instrument to use against men possessed of a conscience, the ruling body--now reduced to the former Protestant majority--required that the same oath be taken by all electors, magistrates, and officers of whatever grade, from the highest to the lowest in the land.

The oath itself was an elastic formula, capable of being stretched or contracted, according to circumstances, so that, by the addition of an incidental phrase or two, it might be framed to meet new exigencies, and give expression to the lively imagination of ingenious members of Parliament. It would be curious to collect an account of the variety of shapes it assumed, and to comment on the different occasions which gave rise to these different developments. A long history of persecuting frenzy might thus be condensed into a commentary of a comparatively few pages. Even at the so-called Catholic Emancipation it was not abolished; on the contrary, it was sacredly preserved, and two new formulas drawn up, the one for the Protestant and the other for the Catholic members of the legislature, Lords and Commons, and so it remains, to this day, except that the most offensive clauses of the last century have disappeared.

Imagine, then, the spectacle offered by the island whenever an election for representatives, magistrates, or petty officers, took place; whenever those entitled to select holders of offices which were not subject to election, made known the persons of their choice. This vast array of aristocratic masters was chosen from the ranks of the English colonists, and had for its avowed object to preserve the Protestant ascendency, and consequently grind under the heel of the most abject oppression the whole mass of the population of the island. There was no other meaning in all these political combinations and changes, recurring periodically, and heralded forth by the voice of the press and the thunder of the hustings. Politics in Ireland was nothing else than the expression given to the despotism of an insignificant minority over almost the entire body of the people. For, despite all their repressive measures, the enemies of the Catholic faith could never pretend even to a semblance in point of numbers, much less to a majority, over the children of the creed taught by Patrick. Ireland remained Catholic throughout; and its oppressors could not fail to feel the bitter humiliation of their constant numerical inferiority. Hence the words quoted in the speech of Wharton, the lord-lieutenant.

This has always been the case, in spite of the combination of a multitude of circumstances adverse to the spread of the Catholic population. It may not be amiss to give room for the statistics and remarks of Abbe Perraud on this most interesting subject, contained in his book on "Ireland under British rule."

"In 1672, the total population of Ireland was 1,100,000 (it is to be remembered that this was after the massacres and transportations of Cromwell's period). Of that number

>   800,000 were Catholics.
>   50,000 " Dissenters.
>   150,000 " Church-of-Ireland men.

"In 1727, the Anglican Primate of Ireland, Boulter, Archbishop of Armagh, wrote to his English colleague, the Archbishop of Canterbury, that 'we have, in all probability, in this kingdom, at least five Papists for every Protestant.' Those proportions are confirmed by official statistics under Queen Anne.

"In 1740, according to a kind of official census, confirmed by Wakefield, the number of Protestant heads of families did not exceed 96,067.

"Twenty-six years later, the Dublin House of Lords caused a comparative table of Protestant and Catholic families to be drawn up for each county. The result was the following:

Protestant families . . 130,263
Catholic families   . . 305,680

"In 1834, exact statistical returns being made of the members of each communion, the following was the result: The total population being estimated at 7,943,940, the Church-of-Ireland members amounted only to the number of 852,064. The remaining 7,091,876 were thus divided:

Presbyterians 642,350
Other Dissenters 21,808
Catholics 6,427,718

"The censuses of 1841 and 1851 contained no information upon this important question. Thirty years had therefore elapsed since official figures had given the exact proportions of each Church.

"This silence of the Blue Books had given rise, among the Protestant press of England and Ireland, to the opinion, too hastily adopted on the Continent by publicists of great weight, that emigration and famine had resulted in the equalization of the numbers of Protestants and Catholics in Ireland. The evident conclusion joyfully drawn from this supposed fact by the defenders of the Anglican Church was, that the scandal of a Protestant establishment in the midst and at the expense of a Catholic people was gradually dying away.

"The forlorn hope of the Tory and Orange press went still further. They boldly disputed Ireland's right to the title of Catholic. So, although, ten years and twenty years before, these same journals furiously opposed the admission of religious denominations into the statistics of the census, yet, when the census of 1861 drew near, they quite as loudly demanded its insertion. They made it a matter of challenge to the Catholics.

"The ultramontane journals accepted the challenge. The Catholics unanimously demanded a denominational census. The results were submitted to the representatives of the nation in July, 1861. No shorter, more decisive, or more triumphant answer could have been given to the sarcasms and challenges of the old Protestant party."

We confine ourselves here to the total sums, leaving out minor details:

Catholics 4,490,583
Establishment 687,661
Dissenters 595,577
Jews 322

Thus in this century, as throughout the whole of the century of gloom, the island is truly and really Catholic.

By way of contrast, a few words on the same subject may not be out of place with reference to England. We have already stated, and given some of the reasons for so doing, that, at the death of Elizabeth, England was already Protestant to the core.

In his "Memoirs," vol. ii., Sir John Dalrymple has published a curious official report of the numbers of Catholics in England, in the reign of William of Orange, found after his death in the iron chest of that vigilant monarch. From this authentic document we take the following extract:

Number of Freeholders in England.[1]

	Conformists.	Papists.	Non-Conformists.
Province of Canterbury,	2,123,362	93,151	11,878
Province of York,	353,892	15,525	1,978
Totals	2,477,254	108,676	13,856

It is known also that, under George III., the number of Catholics in the whole of Great Britain did not exceed sixty thousand, so thorough had been the separation of England from the true Church.

To return to the ostracism of a whole nation from its political rights. No individual really belonging to it could take the slightest share in the administration of its affairs. They were all left to the control of aliens,

---

[1] Dr. Madden's "Penal Laws."

whose boast it was that they were English; and whose chief object was to secure English ascendency, and subject every thing Irish to the rule of force.

Yet all this while a new era was dawning on the world; a multitude of voices were proclaiming new social and political doctrines; all were to be free, to possess privileges that might not be intrenched upon--to wit, a voice in the affairs of the nation, trial by their peers, no taxation without due representation, and the like--while a whole nation by the unanimous consent of the loudest of these freedom-mongers was excluded from every benefit of the new ideas, was literally placed in bondage, and left without the possibility of being heard and admitted to the enjoyment of the common rights, because the one voice which would have declared in their favor, which in former times had so often and so loudly spoken, when so to speak was to offend the powers of this world, was deprived of the right of being heard. The doctrine that the Papal supremacy was a usurpation, and the Pope himself an enemy of freedom, was laid down as a cardinal principle. After such public renunciation of former doctrines, all these new and so-called liberal theories were a mere delusion and a snare. There was no possibility of effectually securing freedom, in spite of so much promised to all and granted to some; no possibility of really protecting the rights of all. The public right newly proclaimed ended finally in might. Majorities ruled despotically over the minorities, and, as the despotism of the multitude is ever harsher and more universal than that of any monarch, the reign of cruel injustice was let in upon Ireland. And in her case the injustice was peculiarly aggravated, inasmuch as it was a small alien minority which trampled under foot the rights of a great native majority.

But, although the deprivation of political rights is perhaps more fatal to a nation than that of any other, on account of what follows in its train, particularly in the framing of the laws, nevertheless the deprivation of civil rights is generally more acutely felt, because the grievances resulting from it meet man at every turn, at every moment of his life, in his household and domestic circle. In fact, the penal laws stripped Catholics of every civil right which modern society can conceive, and it was chiefly there that the ingenuity of their oppressors labored during the greater part of a century to make a total wreck of Irish welfare.

Those rights may be classified generally as the right of possessing and holding landed property, the right of earning an honorable living by profession or trade, the right of protection against injustice by equal laws, the right of fair trial before condemnation: such are the chief. It is doubtful if there is any thing of importance left of which a citizen can be deprived, unless indeed he be openly and unjustly deprived of life.

It has been already indicated how the policy of England, with regard to Ireland, from that first invasion, in the time of Henry II., was prompted by the desire of gaining possession of the soil, and how after seven hundred years of struggle it succeeded in attaining its object; so that the whole island had been confiscated, and in some instances two or three times over. The object of the penal laws, therefore, could not be to deprive the Irish of the land which they no longer possessed, but to prevent them acquiring any land in any quantity whatever, and from reentering into possession, by purchase or otherwise, of any portion of their own soil and of the estates which belonged to their ancestors. So harsh and cunning a design, we doubt not, never entered the minds of any former legislators, even in pagan antiquity.

The great stimulus to exertion in civil society consists of the acquisition of property, chiefly of land. In feudal times seignorial estates could be purchased by none but those of noble blood; but with allodial estates it was different all through Europe. Yet just at the time when feudal laws were passing into disuse the Irish were prevented, by carefully-drawn enactments, from purchasing even a rood of their native soil. "The prohibition had been already extended to the whole nation by the Commonwealth government, and when the lands forfeited by the wars of 1690 came to be sold at Chichester House in 1703, the Irish were declared by the English Parliament incapable of purchasing at the auction, or of taking a lease of more than two acres."--(Prendergast.)

The same author adds in a note: "But it was when the estate was made the property of the first Protestant discoverer, that animation was put into this law. Discoverers then became like hounds upon the scent after lands secretly purchased by the Irish. Gentlemen fearing to lose their lands, found it now necessary to conform--namely, to abjure Catholicism. Between 1703 and 1709 there were only thirty-six conformers in Ireland; in the next ten years (after the Discovery Act), the conformists were one hundred and fifty."

But the full object was not only to prevent the Irish from becoming even moderately rich in land; they were to be reduced to actual pauperism. Hence the prohibitory laws did not stop at this first outrage; almost impossible occurrences were supposed and provided for, lest there might be a chance of their realization at some time. It was actually provided that, if the produce of their farms brought a greater profit to the Irish than was expected, notwithstanding all these measures against the possible occurrence of such an evil, the lease was void, and the "discoverer" should receive the amount.

There was no loop-hole by which the people might escape from this degradation. But there was still the chance left of engaging in trade, acquiring personal property by its practice, and becoming the owners of a sum of money in bank, or of a dwelling-house in the city. The English law of succession was understood to be a law for all, and consequently, in some out-of-the-way cases, a stray Irish family might be found in course of time with an elder branch possessed of a fair amount of property, and able to emerge from the dead level of the common misery. Such a possibility could not of course be permitted by the English colonists who ruled the land. So the law of gavelkind, to which the Irish had at one time been so attached, was now to be forced upon them, and upon them alone of all the British subjects. It was decreed that, upon the death of every Irishman, whatever of personal property he left behind him was to be divided equally among all his children, who, being generally numerous, would each receive but a trifle, and so perpetrate the pauperism of the race.

Where the surprise, then, in finding the whole nation reduced since that time to a state of the most abject poverty? It was the will of the rulers that so it should be, and their scheme, guarded and enforced by so many legislative acts, could not fail to succeed in producing the effect intended. Granting even the smallest amount of truth in what is so often flung at the Irish as a reproach--their carelessness and want of foresight--how could it be otherwise, to what cause can such failings, even if they exist, be assigned, save to the utter impossibility of succeeding in any effort which they chose to make?

The true origin of the state in which the Irish at home now appear to the eyes of foreign travellers, is the deliberate intention, sternly acted upon for more than a century, to make the island one vast poorhouse.

The wretched situation in which they have ever since remained, confessed by all to be without parallel on earth, is certainly not to be laid at the door of the present population of England, nor even to the colony still intrenched on Irish soil; but with what right can it be brought forward as a reproach against the Irish themselves, when its real cause is so evident, and when history speaks so plainly on the subject?

All sensible Englishmen of our days will readily acknowledge that, without indulging in mutual recrimination, the duty of all is to repair the injuries of the past, and to do away with the last remnants of its sad consequences. Wounds so deep and many in a nation cannot be healed by half measures; and it is only a thorough change of system, and a complete reversal of legislation, that can leave the English of to-day without reproach.

Pauperism, then, is the necessary misfortune, not the crime of Ireland; we may even go further, and assert that, if millions of Irishmen have lived and died paupers, owing to the barbarous laws enacted for that special purpose, few indeed among them have been reduced even by hard necessity and the extreme of misery to manifest a pauper spirit and a miserly bent.

There is no doubt that the almost invariable result of suffering and want is to create selfishness in the sufferer, and cause him to cling desperately to the little he may possess. Self preservation and self-indulgence, in such a case, form the law of human nature, and no one even expects to find a really poor man generous, when he can scarcely meet his bare necessities and the imperious wants of his family. It is the peculiarity of the Irish to know how to combine generosity with the deprivation almost of the common necessaries of life. When masters of their own soil, a large hospitality and a free-handed "bestowing of gifts"--such, we believe, was the Irish expression--was universal among them; the poorest clansman would have been ashamed not to imitate, in his degree, the liberal spirit of his prince. They often gave all they had, regardless of the future; and, when their chieftains demanded of the clansmen what the Book of Rights imposed upon them, their exclamation was, "Spend me but defend me."

Though the people of Erin have been reduced to the sad necessity of forgetting that old proverb of the nation, the spirit which gave rise to it lives in their hearts and is proved by their deeds. What other nation, even the richest and most prosperous, could have accomplished what the world has seen them bring to-pass during this century? The laws which, so long ago, forbade them to be generous, and prohibited them from providing openly for the worship of their God, for the education of their children, for the help of the sick and needy among them, have at last been made inoperative by their oppressors. But, when they were at length left free to follow the freedom and generosity of their hearts, they found--what? In their once beautiful and Christian country, a universal desolation; the blackened ruins of what had been their abbeys, churches, hospitals, and asylums; the very ground on which they stood stolen away from them, and the Protestant establishment in full enjoyment of the revenues of the Catholics. They found every thing in the same state that they had known for centuries. Nothing was restored to them. They were at liberty to spend what they did not possess, since they were as poor as men could be. Every thing had to be done by them toward the reestablishing of their churches, schools, and various asylums, and they had nothing wherewith to do it.

There is no need of going item by item over what they did. The present prosperous state of the Irish Catholic public institutioris--churches, schools, and all--is owing to their poorly-filled pockets. God alone knows how it all came about. We can only see in them the poor of Christ, rich in all gifts, "even alms-deeds most abundant."

It is only too evident that the degradation which the English wished to fasten upon them forever, could not be accomplished even by the measures best adapted to debase a people. The Celtic nature rose superior to the dark designs of the most ingenious opponents, and continued as ever noble, generous, and openhearted. Nevertheless, the sufferings of the victims were at times unutterable; and one of the inevitable effects of such tyrannical measures soon made itself fearfully active and destructive in the shape of those periodical famines which have ever since devastated the island.

In the days of her own possession, there was never mention of famine there. The whole island teemed with the grain of her fields, consumed by a healthy population, and was alive with vast herds of cattle and flocks of sheep. What were the heca-tombs of ancient Greece compared with the thousands of kine prescribed annually by the Book of Rights? Who ever heard of people perishing of want in the midst of abundance such as this? Even during the fiercest wars, waged by clan against clan, we often see the image of death in many shapes, but never that of a large population reduced to roots and grass for food.

When, later on, the wars of the Reformation transformed Munster into a wilderness, and we read for the first time in Irish history of people actually turning green and blue, according to the color of the unwholesome weeds they were driven to devour in order to support life, at least it was in the wake of a terrible war that famine came. It was reserved for the eighteenth century to disclose to us the woful spectacle of a people perishing of starvation in the midst of the profoundest peace, frequently of the greatest plenty, the food produced in abundance by the labor of the inhabitants being sold and sent off to foreign countries to enrich absentee landlords. Nay, those desolating famines at last grew to be periodical, so that every few years people expected one, and it seemed as though Ireland were too barren to produce the barely sufficient supply of food necessary for her scanty population. The people worked arduously and without intermission; the land was rich, the seasons propitious; yet they almost constantly suffered the pangs of hunger, which spread sometimes to wholesale starvation. This was another result of those laws devised by the English colonists to keep down the native population of the island, and prevent it from becoming troublesome and dangerous. Such was the effect of the humane measures taken to preserve the glory of Protestant ascendency, and secure the rights and liberties of a handful of alien masters.

It is proper to describe some of those awful scourges, which have never ceased since, and at sight of which, in our own days, we have too often sickened. For the Emancipation of 1829 was far from removing all the causes of Irish misery. On the 17th of March, 1727, Boulter, the Protestant Archbishop of Armagh, wrote to the Duke of Newcastle: "Since my arrival in this country, the famine has not ceased among the poor people. The dearness of corn last year was such that thousands of families had to quit their dwellings, to seek means of life elsewhere; many hundred perished."

At the same period Swift wrote: "The families of farmers who pay great rents, live in filth and nastiness, on buttermilk and potatoes."

The following is a short and simple description of the famine of 1741, given by an eye-witness, and copied by Matthew O'Connor from a pamphlet entitled "Groans of Ireland," published in the same year:

"Having been absent from this country some years, on my return to it last summer, I found it the most miserable scene of distress that I ever read of in history. Want and misery on every face, the rich unable to relieve the poor, the roads spread with dead and dying bodies; mankind the color of the docks and nettles which they fed on; two or three, sometimes more, on a car, going to the grave for want of bearers to carry them, and many buried only in the fields and ditches where they perished. The universal scarcity was followed by fluxes and malignant fevers, which swept off multitudes of all sorts, so that whole villages were laid waste. If one for every house in the kingdom died--and that is very probable--the loss must be upward of four hundred thousand souls. If only half, a loss too great for this ill-peopled country to bear, as they are mostly working people. When a stranger travels through this country, and beholds its wide, extended, and fertile plains, its great flocks of sheep and black cattle, and all its natural wealth and conveniences for tillage, manufacture, and trade, he must be astonished that such misery and want should be felt by its inhabitants."

At the time these lines were written, the astonishment was sincere, and the answer to the question "How can this be?" seemed impossible; the phenomenon utterly inexplicable. In our own days, when this same picture of woe has been so often presented in the island, the reasons for it are well known; and what seems inexplicable is that, the cause being so clear, and the remedy so simple, the remedy has not yet been thoroughly applied.

In 1756 and 1757, the same scenes were repeated, with the same frightful results. Charles O'Connor, at that time the champion of his much-abused countrymen, wrote thus, in his letter to Dr. Curry, May 21, 1756:

"Two-thirds of the inhabitants are perishing for want of bread; meal is come to eighteen-pence a stone, and, if the poor had money, it would exceed by--I believe--double that sum. Every place is crowded with beggars, who were all house-keepers a fortnight ago, and this is the condition of a country which boasts of its constitution, its laws, and the wisdom of its legislature."

These words, although sweeping enough, and universally applicable, are far from conveying to our minds, to-day, the real picture of the state of the country. When the writer speaks of "meal," it must be understood to mean rye, oats, and, barley; and even this coarse and heavy food being, as he remarks, inaccessible to the poor, potatoes had become the only bread of the country, and the inhabitants were perishing for the want of it.

For the first time in the history of the two nations, the English Government thought of relieving the distress of the people, and to this purpose applied the magnificent sum of twenty thousand pounds. Such was the generous amount granted by a wealthy and prosperous country to procure food for the inhabitants of an island as large as Ireland is known to be. As to effecting any change in the laws, which were really the cause of this unutterable misery, such an idea never entered into the heads of the legislators. Hence it is not surprising to hear that "the distress in the interior of the country revived the frightful image of the miseries of 1741, nor did the calamity cease, until the equilibrium between the population and the means of subsistence was restored by the accumulated waste of famine and pestilence;" that is to say, until all those had been destroyed whom the laws of the time could, as they had been designed to do, destroy.

These details appear calculated only to shock the feelings of the reader, already sufficiently acquainted with the lot of the Irish cottier and laborer, from the beginning of the last century. Nevertheless, we cannot close this part of our subject without giving publicity to the following description of the mass of the Irish population in 1762, by Matthew O'Connor:

"The popery laws had, in the course of half a century, consummated the ruin of the lower orders. Their habitations, visages, dress, and despondency, exhibited the deep distress of a people ruled with the iron sceptre of conquest. The lot of the negro slave, compared with that of the Irish helot, was happiness itself. Both were subject to the capricious cruelty of mercenary task-masters and unfeeling proprietors; but the negro slave was well-fed, well clothed, and comfortably lodged. The Irish peasant was half starved, half naked, and half housed; the canopy of heaven being often the only roof to the mud-built walls of his cabin. The fewness of negroes gave the West India proprietor an interest in the preservation of his slave; a superabundance of helots superseded all interest in the comfort or preservation of an Irish cottier. The code had eradicated every feeling of humanity, and avarice sought to stifle every sense of justice. That avarice was generated by prodigality, the hereditary vice of the Irish gentry, and manifested itself in exorbitant rack-rents wrung from their tenantry, and in the low wages paid for their labor. Since the days of King

William, the price of the necessaries of life had trebled, and the day's hire--fourpence-- had continued stationary. The oppression of tithes was little inferior to the tyranny of rack-rents; while the great landholder was nearly exempt from this pressure, a tenth of the produce of the cottier's labor was exacted for the purpose of a religious establishment from which he derived no benefit. . . . The peasant had no resource: not trade or manufactures--they were discouraged; not emigration to France--the vigilance of government precluded foreign enlistment; not emigration to America --his poverty precluded the means. Ireland, the land of his birth, became his prison, where he counted the days of his misery in the deepest despondency."

Is it to be wondered at that conspiracies, secret associations, and insurrections, were the result; or should the wonder be that such commotions were less universal and prolonged?

The craving of hunger is perpetual in Ireland. Multitudes of details from a multitude of different and independent sources might be brought forward to show this.

Duvergier de Hauranne, a Frenchman who visited the island in 1826, writes: "Ireland is the land of anomalies; the most deplorable destitution on the richest of soils. . . . Nowhere does man live in such wretchedness. The Irish peasant is born, suffers, and dies--such is life for him."

In 1836, Dr. Doyle, Bishop of Kildare, being asked what was the state of the population, wrote: "What it has always been; people are perishing as usual."

In 1843, Mr. Thackeray, as little a friend to Ireland as he was a foe to his own country, recounting what he saw in his travels, said that, in the south and west of the island, the traveller had before him the spectacle of a people dying of hunger, and that by millions, in the very richest counties.

There is no need of repeating what has been written of the fearful scourge that swept over the country in 1846 and 1847. The details are too harrowing. At last even the London Times had to acknowledge the cause of these calamities: "The ulcer of Ireland drains the resources of the empire. It was to be expected that it should be so. The people of England have most culpably and foolishly connived at a national iniquity. Without going back beyond the Union (in 1800), and only within the last half-century, it has been notorious all that time that Ireland was the victim of an unexampled social crime. The landlords exercise their rights there with a hand of iron, and deny their duty with a brow of brass. Age, infirmity, sickness, every weakness, is there condemned to death. The whole Irish people is debased by the spectacle and contact of beggars and of those who notoriously die of hunger; and England stupidly winked at this tyranny. We begin now to expiate a long curse of neglect. Such is the law of justice. If we are asked why we have to support half the population of Ireland, the answer lies in the question itself; it is that we have deliberately allowed them to be crushed into a nation of beggars!"

The writers of the Times laid the true cause of that appalling misfortune at the door of the landlords. They would not trace back the origin of the evil beyond 1800: they could not or would not appreciate the Christian heroism displayed by the nation while under the infliction of such a fatal scourge. But it must not be forgotten by all admirers of virtue that, in the midst of a distress which baffles description, many of the victims of famine were at the same time martyrs to honesty and faith. "Come here and let us die together," said a wife to her husband, "rather than touch what belongs to another."

The civil right of acquiring land and enjoying its products has so far been the only one considered by us; and the subject has been entered upon at some length, as agriculture has at all times formed the chief occupation of the Irish people. But the penal laws embraced many other objects; and, as their intent was evidently to debase the people and reduce it to a state of actual slavery and want, other civil rights were equally invaded by their tyrannical provisions.

A portion of the population in all countries devotes itself to the intellectual pursuits necessary for the life of every cultivated nation. Whoever chooses must have the right of devoting his life to the professions of medicine and law, of entering the Church or the army, if his tastes run in any one of those directions. Not so in Catholic Ireland. The oath to be taken by every barrister prevented the Catholic Irishman from devoting his powers to such a purpose. There was only one Church for him, and that one proscribed. In the army not only could he not attain to any rank, but he was not allowed to enter it even as a private, the holding of a musket being prohibited to him. So that, through mere fanatical hatred of every thing Catholic, England deprived herself for a whole century of the services of a people, forming to-day more than half of her army and navy, whose efforts have helped to cover her flag with honor, and whose memorable absence from the English ranks at Fontenoy wrung that bitter expression from the heart of George II. when the victorious tide of the English battle was rolled back by the Irish brigade, "Cursed be the laws which deprive me of such subjects!"

These few words are enough to show that the penal laws were in reality a decree of outlawry against the Irish--stamping them, not as true subjects, but as mere slaves and helots, fit only to be hewers of wood and drawers of water at the bidding of their lords and masters.

But there are mere human rights, inalienable in man, and sacred among all nations, which were trampled upon in that desolated land together with all inferior rights. Such are the rights of worshipping God, of properly educating children, of preserving a just subordination in the family and promoting harmony and happiness among its members. These natural rights were more openly and shamelessly violated, if that were possible, than all others; and this in itself would have made the eighteenth century one of gloom and woe for Irishmen.

It was for their religion chiefly that the Irish had undergone all the calamities and scourges which have been described. Had they only, at the very beginning of the Reformation, bowed to the new dogma of the spiritual supremacy of the English kings; had they a little later accepted the Thirty-nine Articles of Queen Elizabeth; had they, at a subsequent epoch, opined in chorus with the Scotch Presbyterians, and given the Bible as their authority for all kinds of absurdities and atrocities, mental and moral; had they, in a word, as they remarked to Sussex, changed their religion four times in twelve years, they would have escaped the wrath of Henry VIII., the crafty and cruel policy of Elizabeth, the shifty expediency of the Stuarts, the barbarity of the Cromwellian era, and finally the ingenious atrocities of the penal laws.

Even if, in the midst of some of the extremities to which they had been reduced, they had at any time resolved to conform and take the oaths prescribed, all their miseries would have been at an end, and their immediate admission to all the rights and privileges of British citizens secured. From time to time, in individual cases, they witnessed the sudden and magical effect produced by conformity on the part of those who gave up resistance altogether, and who, from whatever motive, bowed to the inevitable conditions on which men were admitted to live peaceably on Irish soil, and to the enjoyment of the blessings of this life; such condition being the abjuration of Catholicity. But so few were found to take advantage of this easy chance forever held out to them, that a man might well wonder at their constancy did he not reflect that they set their duty to God above all things. The fact is patent--they had a conscience, and knew what it meant.

Having then surrendered their all for the sake of their religion, the free exercise of that might at least have been left them; and since the choice lay between the two alternatives of enjoying the natural right of worshipping their God or submitting to all the sacrifices previously mentioned (seemingly the meaning of the various oaths prescribed by law), it can only be looked upon as an additional cruelty to violently deprive them of what they chose to preserve at all cost. But the authors of the statutes did not see the matter in this light. They could not lose such an opportunity of inflicting new tortures on their victims; on the contrary, they would have considered all their labor lost had they not endeavored to coerce the very thing least subject to coercion, the religious feeling of the human soul. Accordingly, the resolution was taken to deprive them of every possible facility for the exercise of their religion, that the fire within might give no sign of its warmth.

True, the Irish Catholics were not, as the Christians under the edicts of old Rome, to be summoned before the public courts and there abjure their religion or die. It is strange that the rulers of Ireland stopped short at this; that they invented nothing in their laws at least equivalent, unless the statutes that compelled every person under fine to be present at Protestant worship on Sundays be interpreted to mean, what it very much resembles, an attempt at coercion of the very soul. Still there was no edict openly proscribing the name of Catholic, and punishing its bearer with death.

But the measures adopted and actually enforced were in reality equivalent, and would more effectually than any pagan edict have produced the same result, if the Irish race had shown the least wavering in their traditional steadiness of purpose.

The first of the measures devised for this end would have been completely efficacious with any other people or race. It was a twofold measure: 1. All bishops, priests, and monks, were to depart from the kingdom, liable to capital punishment should they return. 2. All laymen were to be compelled to assist at the Protestant service every Sunday, under penalty of a fine for each offence: the fine mounting with the repetition of the offence, so that, in the end, it would reach an enormous sum. Only let such a policy as this be persevered in for a quarter of a century in any country on earth except Ireland, and, in that country the Catholic religion will cease to exist.

"The Catholic clergy," says Matthew O'Connor--and the reader will remember he was a witness of what he described-- "submitted to their hard destiny with Christian resignation. They repaired to the seaport towns fixed for their embarcation, and took an everlasting farewell of their country and friends, of every thing dear and valuable in this world. Many of them were descending in the vale of years, and must have been anxious to deposit their bones with the ashes of their ancestors; they were now transported to foreign lands, where they would find no fond breast to rely upon, no 'pious tear' to attend their obsequies. Yet their enemies could not deprive them of the consolations of religion: that first-born offspring of Heaven still cheered them in adversity and exile, smoothed the rugged path of death, and closed their last faltering accents with benedictions on their country, and prayers for their persecutors.

"Such as were apprehended after the time limited for deportation, were loaded with irons and imprisoned until transported, to attest, on some foreign shore, the weakness of the government, and the cruelty of their countrymen. Some few, disabled from age and infirmities from emigration, sought shelter in caves, or implored and received the concealment of Protestants, whose humane feelings were superior to their prejudices, and who atoned, in a great degree, by their generous sympathy, for the wanton cruelty of their party.

"The clause inflicting the punishment of death on such as should return from exile was suited only for the sanguinary days of Tiberius or Domitian, and shocked the humanity of an enlightened age. William of Orange, whose necessities compelled him to give his sanction to the clause, would never consent to its execution."

Nevertheless, it was afterward enforced on several occasions, and, during the whole century of penal laws, it not only remained on the statute-book ad terrorem, but whatever clergyman disregarded it could only expect to be treated with its utmost rigor. From Captain South's account, it appears that in 1698 the number of clergy in Ireland consisted of four hundred and ninety-five regulars and eight hundred and ninety-two seculars; and the number of regulars shipped off that year to foreign parts amounted to four hundred and twenty-four--namely, from Dublin, one hundred and fifty-three; from Galway, one hundred and ninety; from Cork, seventy-five; and twenty-six from Waterford.

But such a measure was of too sweeping a character to be carried out to the letter; many of the proscribed priests, seculars for the most part, escaped the pursuit of the government spies, and remained concealed in the country. The bishops had all been obliged to fly; but a few years later, under Anne, several returned, for they knew that, without the exercise of their religious functions, the Catholic religion must have perished; and, in order that they might continue the succession of the priesthood, confirm the children, and encourage the people to stand firm in their faith, they ran the hazard of the gibbet. Of this fact the persecutors soon became aware, and the Commons of Ireland declared openly that "several popish bishops had lately come into the kingdom, and exercised ecclesiastical jurisdiction within the same, and continued the succession of the Romish priesthood by ordaining great numbers of popish clergymen, and that their return was owing to defect in the laws."

To cover this defect, they invented the "registry law." They did not state in express terms their intention of exporting them again, but their object was clearly manifested by the subsequent enactment of 1704. By the registry law "all popish priests then in the kingdom should, at the general quarter sessions in each county, register their places of abode, age, parishes, and time of ordination, the names of the respective bishops who ordained them, and give security for their constant residence in their respective districts, under penalty of imprisonment and transportation, and of being treated as 'high traitors' in case of return."

It is clear that, with the execution of this law, the exertions of the police and of informers would have been superfluous, as the clergy were compelled to act as their own police and inform on themselves. The act, moreover, seems to have been prepared with a view to another bill, which was soon after passed, for total expulsion. It was therefore nothing else than a preliminary measure devised to insure the success of this second act, and prevent the recurrence of the former "defect in the laws."

A new explanatory statute was accordingly drawn up, requiring the clergy to take the oath of abjuration before the 23d of March, 1710, under the penalties of transportation for life, and of high-treason if ever after found in the country. This bill, then, set them the alternative of abandoning either their country or their principles.

At the same time, for the encouragement of informers, the Commons resolved that "the prosecuting and informing against papists was an honorable service." Never before had a like declaration issued from any body in any nation, least of all by legislators, in favor of the confessedly meanest of all occupations; and it is doubtful if the most tyrannical of the Roman Caesars would ever have thought of mentioning the "honorable service" of the delatores whom they employed for the speedy destruction of those whose wealth they coveted. "Genus hominum," says Tacitus, "publico exitio repertum."

While on this subject, it has been remarked that most of the Irish informers amassed wealth by their bills of "discovery," whereas those of the days of Tiberius generally fell victims to their own artifices.

The eagerness for blood-money tracked the clergy to their loneliest retreats, and dragged them thence before persecuting tribunals, by whose sentence they were doomed to perpetual banishment. They must all have finally disappeared from the island, if the people, at last grown indignant at such baseness and cruelty, had not, by the loudness of their execrations, checked the activity of the priest-hunters. Wherever they dared show themselves, they were pelted with stones, and exposed to the summary vengeance of a maddened people.

The detestable "profession" became at last so infamous and unprofitable that foreign Jews were almost the only ones found willing to undertake this "honorable service;" and it is stated in the "Historia Dominicana," that one Garzia, a Portuguese Jew, was the most active of those human blood-hounds, and that, in 1718, he contrived to have seven of the proscribed clergy detected and apprehended.

We cannot speak of the most revolting measure ever intended to be taken against Catholic priests; namely mutilation, so long and with such energy denied by Protestants, who were themselves indignant at the mere mention of it, but now clearly proved by the archives of France, where documents exist showing that the non-enactment of such an infamy was solely due to the severe words of remonstrance sent to England by the Duke of Orleans, regent of France during the minority of Louis XV.

As late as the middle of the century, in 1744, a sudden increase of rigor took place; intentions of conspiracy were ascribed to Catholics as usual, and without any motive whatever, unless it was caused by the sight of some religious houses, which had been quietly and unobtrusively reopened during the few years previous. All at once the government issued a proclamation for "the suppression of monasteries, the apprehension of ecclesiastics, the punishment of magistrates remiss in the execution of the laws, and the encouragement of spies and informers by an increase of reward."

It was a repetition of the old story; a cruel persecution broke out in every part of the island. From the country priests fled to the metropolis, seeking to hide themselves amid the multitude of its citizens. Others fled to mountains and caverns, and the holy sacrifice was again offered up in lone places under the bare heavens, with sentinels to watch for the "prowling of the wolf," and no other outward dignity than that the grandeur of the forest and the rugged mountains gave.

In the cities the Catholics assisted at the celebration of the divine mysteries in stable-yards, garrets, and such obscure places as sheltered them from the pursuit of the magistrates. On one occasion, while the congregation (assembled in an old building) was kneeling to receive the benediction, the floor gave way, and all were buried beneath the ruin; many were killed, the priest among others; some were maimed for life, and remained to the end of their lives monuments of the cruelty of the government. The dead and dying, and the wounded, were carried through the streets on carts; and the sad spectacle at last moved the Protestants themselves to sympathy. The government was compelled to give way, and allow the persecuted Catholics to enjoy without further molestation the private exercise of their religion.

But that this was not a willing concession on the part of the reigning power is manifest enough from the steady, unswerving, contrary policy pursued until that time. It was simply forced to give way to outraged public opinion, then openly opposed throughout Europe to persecution for conscience' sake.

With religion education was also proscribed. Already, under William of Orange, had papist school-masters been forbidden to teach, but the penalty of their disobedience to the law did not go beyond a fine of a few pounds. So that the Irish youth could still, with some precautionary prudence, find teachers of the Greek and Latin languages, of mathematics, history, and geography. In Munster particularly schools and academies of literature flourished; the ardor of the people for the acquirement of knowledge could not be balked by such paltry obstacles as the laws of William III.

But the Irish Parliament under Anne could not rest satisfied with such mild measures. By the "Explanatory Act" of 1710, the school-master in Ireland was subjected to the same punishment as the priest whom he accompanied everywhere. Prison, transportation, death itself, became the reward of teaching. And in proportion as other laws, severer yet, prevented the people from sending their children abroad to be educated, and these laws were renewed occasionally and made more stringent and effective, the result was the total impossibility of Catholic children receiving any education higher than that of the house.

The final result is known to all. The "hedge-school" was established, that being the only way left of imparting elementary knowledge; and it required Irish ingenuity and Irish aptitude for shifts to invent such a system, for system it was, and carry it through for so long a time.

But even the last sanctuary of home was yet to be sacrilegiously invaded; the most sacred of human rights could not be left to the persecuted people, and the strongest bonds of family affection were if possible to be broken asunder. What tyranny had never yet dared attempt in any age or country was to become a law in Ireland; and that holy feeling by which the members of a family are held together, in obedence to one of the most necessary and solemn commandments of God, could not be left undisturbed in the bosom of an Irish child. The father's rule over his children and the honor and love due by the child to its parent, were, in fact, declared by English legislation of no value, and fit subjects for cruel interference, introducing irresistible temptation.

Yes, by the laws enacted in the reign of Anne, the son was to be set against the father, and this for the sake of religion! It was a part of the Irish statutes, and for a long time it took occasional effect, that any son of a Catholic who should turn Protestant at any age, even the tenderest, should alone succeed to the family estate, which from the day of the son's conversion could neither be sold nor charged even with a debt of legacy. From that same day the son was taken from his father's roof and delivered into the custody of some Protestant guardian. No tie, however sacred, no claim, however dear, was respected by those statesmen, who at the very time were the loudest to boast of their love for freedom, while trampling under foot the most indispensable rights of Nature.

The wickedest ingenuity of man could certainly not go beyond this to debase, degrade, and destroy a nation. After unprecedented calamities of former ages, we find millions of men reduced by other men, calling themselves Christians, to a condition of pagan helots, deprived of all rights and treated more barbarously than slaves. And all the while they were allowed, induced, encouraged to put an end to their misery by simply saying one word, taking one oath, "conforming " as the expression had it. Nevertheless they steadily refused to speak that word, to take that oath, to conform; that is to say, to abjure their religion. A few, weak in faith, or carried away by sudden passion, a burst of despair, subscribe to the required oath, assist as demanded at the religious services on Sunday, suddenly rise to distinction, are sure of preserving their wealth, or even enter into sole possession of the family property, to the exclusion of all its other members. But such rare examples, instead of rousing the envy of the rest, excite only their contempt and execration. To them they are henceforth apostates, renegades to their faith, cast out from the bosom of the nation; and their countrymen hug their misery rather than exchange it for honors and wealth purchased by broken honor, lost faith, and cowardly desertion of the cause for which their country was what it was.

While the cowards were so few, and the brave men so many, the latter constituting indeed the whole bulk of the people, they were knit together as a band of brethren, never to be estranged from each other. If any thing is calculated to form a nation, to give it strength, to render it indestructible, imperishable, it is undoubtedly the ordeal through which they passed without shrinking, and out of which they came with one mind, one purpose, animated by one holy feeling, the love of their religion, and the determination to keep it at all hazard.

Yes, at any moment throughout this long century, they might have changed their condition and come out at once to the enjoyment of all the rights dear to men, by what means is best expressed in the few words of Edmund Burke:

"Let three millions of people" (the number of Irishmen at the time he spoke) "but abandon all that they and their ancestors have been taught to believe sacred, and forswear it publicly in terms most degrading, scurrilous, and indecent, for men of integrity and virtue, and abuse the whole of their former lives, and slander the education they have received, and nothing more is required of them. There is no system of folly, or impiety, or blasphemy, or atheism, into which they may not throw themselves, and which they may not profess openly and as a system, consistently with the enjoyment of all the privileges of a free citizen in the happiest constitution in the world."

Thus does the reason of man commend their constancy; but that constancy required something more than human strength. God it was who supported them. He alone could grant power of will strong enough to uphold men plunged for so long a time in such an abyss of wretchedness. To him could they cry out with truth: "It is only owing to Divine mercy that we have not perished;" misericordias Domini, quod non sumus consumpti!

But human reason can better comprehend the effect produced on a vast multitude of people by oppression so unexampled in its severity. An immense development of manhood and self-dependence, an heroic determination to bear every trial for conscience' sake, and a certainty of succeeding, in the long-run, in breaking the heavy chain and casting off the intolerable yoke--such was the effect.

It has been asserted by some authors, who have written on that terrible eighteenth century in Ireland, that the spirit of the people was entirely broken, that there was no energy left among them, and that the imposition of burdens heavier still, were such a thing possible, could scarcely elicit from them even the semblance of remonstrance. It was only natural to think so; but, in our opinion, this is only true of the external despondency under which the people was bowed, but utterly false with respect to a lack of mental energy.

There certainly was no general attempt at insurrection on their part; nor did they take refuge in that last resource of despair-- death after a vain vengeance. If the writers referred to would have preferred this last fatal resource of wounded pride, they are right in their estimate of the Irish; but they forget that the victims were Christians, and could lend no ear to a vengeance which is futile and a despair which is forbidden. There was a better course open before them, and they followed it: to resign themselves to the will of a God they believed in and for whom they suffered, and wait patiently for the day of deliverance. It was sure to come; and if those then living were doomed not to see that happy day, they knew that they would leave it as an inheritance to their children.

Those writers would doubtless have been satisfied of the existence of a will among the people, and their conduct would have met with greater approval, had the attempts of some individuals at private revenge been more general and successful; if the bands of Rapparees, White Boys, and others, had wrought more evil upon their oppressors, although they could not prepare them to renew the struggle on a large scale with better prospect of success.

But this could not be; success could never have been reached by such a road, and it was useless to attempt it. At that time, there existed no possibility of the Irish recovering their rights by force. Meanwhile Providence was not forgetful of those who were fighting the braver moral battle of suffering and endurance for their religion. It was preparing the nation for a future life of great purposes, by purifying it in the crucible of affliction, and preserving the people pure and undebased.

Nowhere has the period of calamity been so protracted and so severe. Ireland stands alone in a history of wretchedness of seven centuries' duration. She stands alone, particularly inasmuch as, with her, the affliction has gone on continually increasing until quite recently, unrefreshed by periods of relief and glimpses of bright hope. The sinking spirits of the people, it is true, have been buoyed up from time to time by sanguine expectations; but only to find their expectations crowned with bitter disappointment and sink deeper again in the sea of their afflictions.

Nevertheless, through all that time the Irish continued morally strong, and ready at the right moment to leap into the stature of giants in strength and resolution. How they did so will be seen, and the simplicity of the explanation will be matter for surprise. But it is fitting first to set in the strongest light the assertion that the Irish were really debased by the calamities of that age, that they possessed no self-dependence at a time when that was the only thing left to them.

This view is thus expressed in Godkin's "History of Ireland:" "Too well did the penal code accomplish its dreadful work of debasement on the intellects, morals, and physical condition of a people sinking in degeneracy from age to age, till all manly spirit, all virtuous sense of personal independence and responsibility was nearly extinct, and the very features-- vacant, timid, cunning, and unreflective--betrayed the crouching slave within."

And the writer, a well-disposed Protestant, did not see how it could well be otherwise, and took it for granted that every one would admit the truth of his assertions without the slightest hesitation.

For he adds, a little farther on: "Having no rights of franchise -no legal protection of life or property--disqualified to handle a gun, even as a common soldier or a game-keeper-- forbidden to acquire the elements of knowledge at home or abroad--forbidden even to render to God what conscience dictated as his due--what could the Irish be but abject serfs? What nature in their circumstances could have been otherwise? Is it not amazing that any social virtue could have survived such an ordeal--that any seeds of good, any roots of national greatness could have outlived such a long tempestuous winter? "

Still Mr. Godkin was mistaken; the Irish had suffered no "debasement of the intellects, of the morals, not even of the physical condition," notwithstanding the plenitude of causes existing to bring such results about.

Their intellect had been kept in ignorance. Unable to procure instruction for their children, except by stealth and in opposition to the laws, few of them could acquire even the first elements of mental culture. But the intellect of a nation is not necessarily debased on that account. As a general rule, it is true that ignorance begets mental darkness and error, and will often debase the mind and sink the intellectual faculties to the lowest human level. But this happens only to people who, having no religious substratum to rest upon, are left at the mercy of error and delusions. One great thought, at least, was ever present to their minds, and that thought was in itself sufficient to preserve their intellect from being degraded; it was this "Man is nobler than the brute and born to a higher destiny." This truth was deeply engraved in their minds; and in defence of it they battled, and fought, and bled, all down the painful course of their history.

Had the intellect of the nation been really debased, would not their religious principles have been the first things to be thrown overboard? Would they not have adopted unhesitatingly all the tenets successively proposed to them by the various "reformers" of England? What is truth, when there is no mind to receive it? It requires a strong mind indeed to say, "I will suffer every thing, death itself, rather thin repudiate what I know comes from God." It is useless to dwell longer on these considerations. The man who sees not in such an heroic determination proof of a strong and noble mind may be possessed of a great, but to common-sense people it will look like a very limited intelligence.

Mr. Godkin cannot have duly weighed his expressions when he spoke of the debasement of morals among the Irish. It is no hyperbole to speak of the nation as a martyr; a martyr in any sense of the word: to the Christian, a Christian martyr. And yet it is by that fact guilty of immorality, or, as he puts it, debased in morals! The point is not worth arguing. But in contrasting the two nations, the nation debased and the nation that wrought its debasement, we are irresistibly reminded of the words used by Our Lord in reference to John the Baptist, then in prison and liable at any moment to be condemned to death: "What went ye out in the desert to see? A man clothed in soft garments? Lo! they that are clothed in soft garments dwell in the houses of kings."

If we would find a people really debased in morals, we must go to those whose material prosperity breeds corruption and gives to all the means of satisfying their evil passions. The orgies of the Babylonians under their last king, of the effeminate Persians later on, of the Roman patricians during the empire, need no more than mention. The cause of the immorality prevailing at these several epochs is well known, and has been told very plainly by conscientious historians, some of them pagans themselves. But, that a people ground down so long under a yoke of iron, gasping for very breath, yet refusing to surrender its belief and the worship of its God as its countless saints worshipped him, to follow the wild vagaries of sectarians and fanatics, should at the same time be accused of corruption and debasement of its morals, is too much for an historian to assert or a reader to believe.

But, beyond all argument, it has been generally conceded, in spite of prejudices, that the Irish, of all peoples, had been preeminently moral and Christian. No one has dared accuse them of open vice, however they may have been accused of folly. Intemperance is the great foible flung at them by many who, careful to conceal their own failings, are ever, ready to "cast the first stone" at them. It would be well for them to ponder over the rebuke of the Saviour to the accusers of the woman taken in adultery; when perhaps they may think twice before repeating the time-worn accusation.

Coming to the "people sinking in degeneracy from age to age;" if by this is meant that, for a whole century, many of them have suffered the direst want and died of hunger, that scanty food has impressed on many the deep traces of physical suffering and bodily exhaustion, no one will dispute the fact, while the blame of it is thrown where it deserves to be thrown. But it will be a source of astonishment to find that, despite of this, the race has not degenerated even physically; that it is still, perhaps, the strongest race in existence, and that no other European, no Englishman or Teuton, can endure the labor of any ordinary Irishman. In the vast territory of the United States, the public works, canals, roads, railways, huge fabrics, immense manufactories, bear witness to the truth of this statement, and the only explanation that can be satisfactorily given for this strange fact is, that their morals are pure and they do not transmit to their children the seeds of many diseases now universal in a universally corrupt society.

There remains the final accusation of the "very features--vacant, timid, cunning, and unreflective--betraying the crouching slave within."

Granting the truth of this--which we by no means do, every school-geography written by whatever hand attesting the contrary to-day--where would have been the wonder that they, subjected so long to an unbending harshness and never-slumbering tyranny, accustomed to those continual "domiciliary visits" so common in Ireland during the whole of last century, dragged so often before the courts of "justice," to be there insulted, falsely accused, harshly tried and convicted without proof--were obliged to be continually on their guard, to observe a deep reserve, the very opposite to the promptings of their genial nature, to return ambiguous answers, full, by the way, of natural wit and marvellous acuteness? It was the only course left them in their forlorn situation. They pitted their native wit against a wonderfully devised legislation, and often came off the victors. Suppose it were true, was it not natural that, under such a system of unrelaxing oppression and hatred toward them, their faces should be "vacant, timid, cunning, and unreflective, betraying the crouching slave within?"

Could they give back a proud answer, when a proud look was an accusation of rebellion? Are prudence, cunning, and just reserve, vacancy and want of reflection? The man who penned those words should remember the choice of alternatives ever present to the mind of an Irishman, however unjustly suspected or accused--the probability of imprisonment or hanging, of being sent to the workhouse or transported to the "American plantations."

The Irishman must have changed very materially and very rapidly since Mr. Godkin wrote. The features he would stamp upon him might be better applied to the Sussex yokel or the English country boor of whatever county. The generality of travellers strangely disagree with Mr. Godkin. They find the Irishman the type of vivacity, good humor, and wit; and they are right. For, under the weight of such a load of misery, under the ban of so terrible a fate, the moral disposition of the Irishman never changed; his manhood remained intact. To-day, the world attests to the same exuber-ance of spirits, the same tenacity of purpose, which were ever his. This indeed is wonderful, that this people should have been thus preserved amid so many causes for change and deterioration. Who shall explain this mystery? What had they, all through that age of woe, to give them strength to support their terrible trials, to preserve to them that tenacity which prevented their breaking down altogether? Something there was indeed not left to them, since it was forbidden under the severest penalties; something, nevertheless, to which they clung, in spite of all prohibitions to the contrary.

It was the Mass-Rock, peculiar to the eighteenth century, now known only by tradition, but at that time common throughout the island. The principal of those holy places became so celebrated at the time that, on every barony map of Ireland, numbers of them are to be found marked under the appropriate title of "Corrigan-Affrion"--the mass-rock.

Whenever, in some lonely spot on the mountain, among the crags at its top, or in some secret recess of an unfrequented glen, was found a ledge of rock which might serve the purpose of an altar, cut out as it were by Nature, immediately the place became known to the surrounding neighborhood, but was kept a profound secret from all enemies and persecutors. There on the morning appointed, often before day, a multitude was to be seen kneeling, and a priest standing under the canopy of heaven, amid the profound silence of the holy mysteries. Though the surface of the whole island was dotted with numerous churches, built in days gone by by Catholics, but now profaned, in ruins, or devoted to the worship of heresy, not one of them was allowed to serve for a place where a fraction even of the bulk of the population might adore their God according to the rites approved of by their conscience. Shut off from these temples so long hallowed by sweet remembrance as the spots once occupied by the saints and consecrated to the true worship of their God, this faithful nation was consecrating the while by its prayers, by its blood, and by its tears, other places which in future times should be remembered as the only spots left to them for more than a century wherein to celebrate the divine rites.

This was the only badge of nationality they had preserved, but it was the most sacred, the surest, and the sweetest. Who shall tell of the many prayers that went up thence from devoted minds and hearts, to be received by angels and carried before the throne of God? Who shall say that those prayers were not hearkened to when to-day we see the posterity of those holy worshippers receiving or on the point of receiving the full measure of their desires?

There, indeed, it was that the nation received its new birth; in sorrow and suffering, as its Saviour was born, but for that very reason sacred in the eyes of God and man. Their enemies had sworn complete separation from them, eternal animosity against them; the new nation accepted the challenge, and that complete separation decreed by their enemies was the real means of their salvation and of making them a People.

As has already been observed, the various attempts to make Protestants of them, attempts sometimes cunning and crafty, at others open and cruel, always persevered in, never lost sight of, began to imbue the people with a new feeling of nationality, never experienced before, and constantly increasing in intensity.

This was witnessed under the Tudors. Their infatuation for the Stuart dynasty served the same end, and it may be said that, from all the evils which that attachment brought upon them, burst forth that great recompense of national sentiment which almost compensated them for the terrible calamities which followed in its train. It was under Charles I. that the Confederation of Kilkenny first gave them a real constitution, better adapted for the nation than the old regime of their Ard-Righs.

But it was chiefly under the English Commonwealth, when they were so mercilessly crushed down by Cromwell and his brutal soldiery, when there seemed no earthly hope left them, that the solid union of the old native with the Anglo-Irish families, which had already been attempted--and almost successfull by the Confederation of Kilkenny yet never consummated was finally brought about once for all; their common misery uniting them in the bonds of brotherly affection, blotting out forever their long-standing divisions and antipathies which had never been quite laid aside.

It was thus that the nation was formed and prepared by martyrdom for the glorious resurrection, the greater future kept in store for it by Providence; the people all the while remaining undebased under their crushing evils.

Lastly, the intensity of the suffering produced by the penal laws, during the eighteenth century, linked the nation in closer bonds of union still, and this time gave them a unanimity which became invincible. Their final motto was then adopted, and will stand forever unchanged. In the clan period it was "Our sept and our chieftain;" under the Tudors, "Our religion and our native lords;" under the Stuarts it suddenly became "God and the King;"--it changed once more, never to change again: it was embraced in one word, the name of Him who had never deserted them, who alone stood firm on their side--"Our God!"

RESURRECTION.-DELUSIVE HOPES

BY delusive hopes are here meant some of the various schemes in which Irishmen have indulged and still indulge with the view of bettering their country. This chapter will aim at showing that, for the resurrection of Ireland, the reconstruction of her past is impossible; parliamentary independence or "home rule," insufficient, physical force and violent revolution, in conjunction with European radicals particularly, is as unholy as it is impracticable.

The resurrection of the Irish nation began with the end of last century. As, to use their own beautiful expression, "'Tis always the darkest the hour before day," so the gloom had never settled down so darkly over the land, when light began to dawn, and the first symptoms of returning life to flicker over the face of the, to all seeming, dead nation. Its coming has been best described in the "History of the Catholic Association" by Wyse. On reading his account, it is impossible not to be struck with the very small share that men have had in this movement; it was purely a natural process directed by a merciful God. As with all natural processes, it began by an almost imperceptible movement among a few disconnected atoms, which, by seeming accident approaching and coming into contact, begin to form groups, which gather other groups toward them in ever-increasing numbers, thus giving shape to an organism which defines itself after a time, to be finally developed into a strong and healthy being. This process differed essentially from those revolutionary uprisings which have since occurred in other nations, to the total change in the constitution and form of the latter, without any corresponding benefit arising from them.

Before entering upon the full investigation of this uprising, it may be well to dispel some false notions too prevalent, even in our days, among men who are animated with the very best intentions, who wish well to the Irish cause, but who seem to fail in grasp in the right idea of the question. Reconstruction, say they, is impossible-at least as far as the past history of the country goes. Where are her leaders, her chieftains, her nobility? Feudalism broke the clans, persecution put an effectual stop to the labors of genealogists and bards. Where, to-day, are the O'Neill, the O'Brien, the

O'Donnell, and the rest? Until new leaders are found, offshoots, if possible, of the old families, more faithful and trustworthy than those who so far have volunteered to guide their countrymen, how is it possible to expect a people such as the Irish have always been, to assume once more a corporate existence, and enjoy a truly national government?

I. That the Irish nobility has disappeared forever may be granted. In giving our reasons for believing in the impossibility of connecting the present with the past through that class, and thus restoring a truly national government, and in strengthening this opinion by what follows, we shall show at the same time that, in that regard, Ireland is on a par with all other nationalities, among whom the aristocratic classes have quite lost the prestige that once belonged to them, and can no longer be said to rule modern nations.

The question of nobility is certainly an important one for the Irish--nay, for all peoples. Up to quite recently, profound thinkers never imagined it possible for a people to enjoy peace and happiness save under the guidance of those then held to be natural guides with aristocratic blood in their veins, who were destined by God himself to rule the masses. We are far from falling in with the fashion, so common nowadays, of deriding those ideas. Men like Joseph de Maistre, who was certainly an upholder of the theory, and who could not suppose a nation to exist without a superior class appointed by Providence to guide those whose blood was less pure, have a right to be listened to with respect, and none of their deliberate opinions should be treated with levity.

And, in truth, no nobility ever existed more worthy of the title, as far as the origin of its power went, than the Irish. Its last days were spent, like those of true heroes, fighting for their country and their God. It is a remarkable fact that they, the truest, were the first of the aristocratic classes to fall. After them, all the aristocracies of Europe, with the exception perhaps of the English, which still exists at least in name, gradually saw their power wrested from them, so that, to-day, it may be said with truth that the "noble" blood has lost its prerogative of rule.

Various are the theories on these superior classes; a few words on some of them may be as appropriate as interesting.

Of all those advanced, Vico's are the least defensible, though they seem to rest on a deep knowledge of antiquity. No Christian can accept his view of a universal savage state of society after the Flood; and his explanation of the origin of aristocratic races, and of the plebeians, their slaves, is purely the work of imagination, however well read in classic lore may have been the author of "Scienza Nuova." To suppose with him that the primeval "nobles" reached the first stage of civilization by inventing language, agriculture, and religion, and by imposing the yoke of servitude on the "brutes" who were not yet possessed of the first characteristics of humanity, is revolting to reason, and contradictory to all sound philosophy and knowledge of history. His aristocracy is a brutal institution which he does well to doom to extinction as soon as the plebs is sufficiently instructed and powerful enough to seize upon the reins of government, before it, in its turn, is brought under by the progressive march of monarchy, with which his system culminates.

The feudal ideas concerning "noble" blood rested on an entirely different basis. The feudal monarch is but the first of the nobles, and the possession of land is the true prerogative and charter of nobility. The inferior classes being excluded from that privilege, are also excluded from all political rights, and are nothing more nor less than the conquered races which were first reduced to slavery. Christianity was the only power which effected a change, and a deep one, in the relations of these two classes to each other; the rigorous application of the system by the Northmen being entirely opposed to the elementary teachings of our holy religion.

From the change thus brought about resulted the Christian idea of aristocratic and monarchical government which had the support of some gifted writers of the last and present centuries. It was in fact a return to the old system realized by Charlemagne in the great empire of which he was the founder--a system whose glorious march was interrupted by the invasion of feudalism in its severest form, which, according to what was before said, came down from Scandinavia in the time of Charlemagne's immediate successors. Under the regime of the noble emperor, the Church, the Aristocracy, and the People, formed three Estates, each with its due share in the government. This mode of administering public affairs became general in Europe, and stood for nearly a thousand years.

But is it the particular form of government necessary for the happiness of a nation, as it was held to be by some powerful minds? If it is, then are we born, indeed, in unhappy times; for the corner-stone of the edifice, the aristocratic idea, has crumbled away, and is apparently gone forever.

Any one, looking at Europe as it stands to-day, must feel constrained to admit that its history for the last hundred years may be summed up in the one phrase: admission of the middle classes of society to the chief seat of government. Russia now makes the solitary exception to this rule; for in England, which seems the most feudal of all nations, the middle classes have attained to a high position, and, through their special representatives, have often taken the chief lead in public affairs, ever since the Revolution of 1688, a lead which is now uncontested. And as individuals of the middle class are often admitted into the ranks of the aristocracy, it would indeed be a hard thing to find purely "noble" blood in the vast majority of aristocratic families now existing in Great Britain.

The history of the gradual decline of what is called the nobility in the various states of Europe would require volumes. In many instances it would certainly be found to have been richly merited, in France particularly, perhaps, where the corruption of that class was one of the chief causes which led to the first French Revolution.

But in Ireland the original idea of nobility was different from that entertained elsewhere; the action of the institution on the people at large was peculiar in its character; and if, in early times, those rude chieftains were often guilty of acts of violence and outrage against religion and morality, they atoned for this by that last long struggle of theirs, so nobly waged in defence of both. But the destruction of the order was final and complete, and seems to have left no hope of resurrection.

In our first chapter, when treating of the clan system, the origin of chieftainship among the Celts was referred back to the family: all the chieftains, or nobles, were each the head of a sept or tribe, which is the nearest approach to a family; all the clansmen were related by blood to the chieftain. The order of nobility among the Celts was therefore natural and not artificial; being neither the result of some conventional under-standing nor of brute force. Nature was with them the parent of nobility and chieftainship; and the ennobling, or raising a person by mere human power to the dignity of noble, was unknown to them: a state of things peculiar to the race.

In Vico's system, aristocracy sprang from physical force or skill; consequently, nobility was founded on no natural right, although the author does his best to prove the contrary, chiefly by ascribing to the aristocratic class the discovery or invention of right (jus) which thus becomes a mere derivative of force.

In feudalism, pure and unmixed, after it had penetrated farther south, under the lead of the Scandinavians, nobility was derived from conquest and armed force. It is true that, by this system, the viking, monarch, or sovereign lord, was the one who distributed the territory, won from conquered nations, among his faithful followers, and thus land and its consequence, nobility, were apparently the award of merit; but the merit in question being equivalent to success in battle, it again resolved itself into armed force. In fact, the power of feudalism proper rested in the army; the chief nobles were duces or combats (dukes or counts), the inferior nobles were equites (knights) and milites (men-at-arms). All power and title began and ended with force of arms, which was the only foundation of right: jus captionis et possessionis--the right of taking and of keeping.

Eventually feudal ideas underwent considerable change among the aristocracy of Christendom, by the gradual spread of Christian manners; and the first establishment of nobility by Charlemagne, which was anterior to pure feudalism, afterward revived, and lasted a thousand years. Then it was conferred by the monarch on merit of any kind, and it was understood that those whom superior authority had raised to the dignity had won their title by their deeds, which were sufficient to prove their noble blood, and that they were empowered to transmit the title to their posterity. The idea was a grand one, and gave proof of its vast political and social usefulness in the immense benefits which it brought upon Europe during so many ages. Unfortunately, the inroad of the Scandinavians, following closely on the death of its great founder, introduced feudalism as better known to us, interfered with the institution which Charlemagne had established in such admirable equipoise, and added to it many barbarous adjuncts, which for a long time entered into the idea of nobility itself. Thus the titles of feudal lords were retained--duce, comites, equites, milites-- with, all the paraphernalia of brute force which the harsh mind of northern despotism had made divine. Thus was the holding of landed property allowed to the nobles alone; the great mass of the population being composed of men--ascripti glebae--who were incapable from their position of rising in the social scale; so that all were duly impressed with the idea that the mass of the people had been conquered and reduced, if not to slavery, to what greatly resembled it--serfdom. From this order of things arose that fruitful source of all modern revolutions, the division of Europe into two great classes antagonistic to each other and separated by an almost impassable gulf--the lords and the "villeins."

To be sure, the supreme lord had the power to raise even a villein to the rank of noble, after he had proved his superior elevation of mind by heroic achievements; but what superhuman exertions did not those achievements call for; what a concourse of fortuitous circumstances rarely occurring, so as to render almost illusory the hope of rising held out by the feudal theory! The Church alone opened her highest grades to all indiscriminately; and, in her, true merit was really an assurance of advance.

Further details are not needed. The difference between the idea of the nobility entertained in Celtic countries, and that held by the rest of Europe, is already in favor of the former.

For this reason the action of the Irish aristocracy on the people at large was happily altogether free from those causes of irritation so common in feudal countries. A close intimacy and personal devotion naturally existed between the chieftain of a clan and his men--an intimacy manifested by the free manners of the humblest among them, and that ease of social intercourse between all classes of people, which was a matter of so much surprise to the Norman barons at their primitive invasion.

At first sight, the Celtic system appears, in one respect at least, inferior to that which prevailed throughout the rest of Europe: the simple clansmen could never indulge in the hope of attaining to the chieftainship, being naturally excluded from that high office. Only the actual members of the chieftain's own family could hope to succeed him after his death, by election, and take the lead of the sept; thus nobility was entirely exclusive, and regulated by the very laws of Nature. The office was really not transferable, and no degree of exertion, of whatever nature, could win it for any person born out of the one family. But the difference was scarcely one in fact; and we know how illusory, often was that ambition which the system of merit inspired in the man born of an inferior class in other races than the Celtic. The broad assertion, that no man could rise from the condition in which he happened to be born, remains true for nearly all cases.

But, on the other hand, there were motives of ambition besides that of becoming chieftain, or entering on the road thereto, by being admitted into the ranks of the nobility, which lay open to the Celt; and if the desire of a mere clansman to become a chieftain lay within the bounds of possibility, the social state of Celtic countries would have been broken up and become intolerable, and society would have been dissolved into its primitive elements. Two considerations of importance:

The whole of Irish history teaches one lesson, or, rather, impresses one fact: that every member of a clan took as much pride in the sept to which he belonged, and labored as zealously for its head, as he could have done had the advantage turned all to himself. The peculiar features engendered by the system were such that each man identified himself with the whole tribe and particularly with its leader; and this is easily understood, as we see the same sort of feeling existing to-day among families. It is in the very essence of natural ties to merge the individual in the community to which he belongs, as in questions which affect the whole family to merge self in the whole, to forget one's own identity, to be ready for any sacrifice, particularly when the sacrifice is called forth in defence of a beloved parent.

To judge by the ancient annals of Ireland which are accessible, this was undoubtedly the sentiment pervading Celtic clans, and it is easy to conceive how, under such conditions, ambitious thoughts of the chieftain-ship or nobility could not well enter there. Moreover, we repeat, had such ambitious thoughts been within the compass of realization, the whole system would have been destroyed.

The greatest source of quarrels, feuds, wars, and general calamities among the Irish people, was the insane aspiration among the inferior members of a chieftain's family after supreme power. The institution of Tanist, or heir-apparent, particularly, which was general for all offices, from the highest to the lowest, was a constant source of trouble and contention to septs which, without it, would have remained united and in harmony. Montalembert has well said that it seems as if an incurable fatality accompanied the Irish everywhere, and condemned nearly all the highest among them to have their blood shed either by others or by their own hand, and that few indeed are those renowned chieftains and kings who died quietly in their beds. Their annals are filled throughout with tales of blood; and, when we know of their strong attachment to religion, of their tenderheartedness for women, children, old and feeble men, it is hard to conceive how they came to shed blood so often, and show themselves proof against the simplest claims of humanity.

But the difficulty is sufficiently explained by their own annals and the state of society under which they lived. The Tanistry was the great source of all those evils. The position of a chieftain was so honorable, so influential, and powerful, that all natural sentiments, even those of family affection, were often extinguished by the insane ambition of attaining to it, in those whom Nature had set on the road toward it.

It looks like a contradiction, yet nothing is so well established as their deep affection for their near relatives and the fury engendered against their nearest of kin when allured by the prospect of the chieftainship. What the case might have been, had all the inferior clansmen been influenced by the same motive, one shudders to think. Happily the possibility of such a position was denied them, and thus were they spared all the crime and horrors which it entailed. Let us now turn to the fall of the Irish nobility, in order to see how that fall was final and decisive, leaving little or no room for the hope of their resurrection.

The great wars of Henry VIII. and Elizabeth upon the island often drove some of the Irish chieftains to quit their country for a time; a thing scarcely ever known before, where the Pale was so contracted and the power of the English kings so limited. But those first voyages of Irish lords to foreign countries had generally no other destination than England itself, whither they sometimes repaired to justify themselves in the presence of the sovereign against the imputations of their enemies, or to pay court to him for the purpose of obtaining some coveted object. Occasionally their children were brought up at the English court, either with the view of instilling Protestantism into their artless minds, or to make them friends of England, so that many of them thus became king's or queen's men. In this manner the Irish nobility first came to look out beyond their own country.

When, as events went on, some great family was crushed or nearly so, as were the Kildares by Henry Tudor and the Geraldines by Elizabeth, the outraged nobility began to think of foreign alliances, and cast their eyes abroad over Spain, Belgium, or France, above all toward Rome, which was the centre of their religion, attachment to which was one of their chief crimes, where the Holy Father was ever ready to encourage and receive them with open arms, Thus history tells us of the narrow escape of young Gerald Desmond.

He was still a child of twelve years, and the sole survivor of the historic house of Kildare, when his life was sought after with an eagerness which resembled that of Herod, but the devotion of his clansmen defeated all attempts at his capture. "Alternately the guest of his aunts, married to the daughter of the chief of Offaly and Donegal, the sympathy everywhere felt for him lead to a confederacy between the northern and southern chieftains, which had long been felt wanting, and never could be accomplished. A loose league was formed, including the O'Neills of both branches, O'Donnell, O'Brien, the Earl of Desmond, and the chiefs of Moylurg and Breffni. The child, object of so much natural and chivalrous affection, was harbored for a time in Munster; then transported, through Connaught, into Donegal; and finally, after four years, in which he engaged more the minds of the statesmen than any other individual under the rank of royalty, he was safely landed in France."-(A. M. O'Sullivan.)

But the intercourse between the Irish nobility and foreign powers was chiefly increased during the reign of Elizabeth, when by the great league of the Desmond Geraldines in the south, which was followed by that of the O'Neills and O'Donnells in the north, they entered into open treaty with the Popes and the Kings of Spain; and, when reverses came, no other resource was left to the outlawed chieftains than flight to the Continent, where they abode till the storm blew over, sometimes for the remainder of their lives.

James Fitzmaurice stayed a long time in Italy, where, on hearing of the imprisonment of his cousins, the Desmonds, he planned the first great league in defence of religion, no longer for the purpose only of righting family wrongs, but of waging a holy war which might draw the cooperation of all the Catholic powers.

These few details are here furnished, because they mark a new starting-point in the history of the race, when the nobility of the land first went abroad to live with a view of finding allies for the Irish cause; while the

Irish at home looked anxiously to their chieftains abroad to return to them with the promised succor.

A few words on the policy exercised toward the Irish nobility by Henry VIII., Elizabeth, and James I., at the beginning of his reign, will give us a sufficiently clear insight into the means adopted for the gradual attack upon them, which resulted first in their partial subjugation, finally in their total destruction. Those monarchs thought that, to reduce Ireland to an English colony, all they had to do was to destroy the chieftains, and the subjugation of the country was complete. They were strengthened in this opinion by the outbreak of Protestantism, which had deprived the lower classes not only of their material comfort and religious consolations, but of all the immunities and liberties which the middle ages had left to them. While the mass of the nation was not only denied all political influence, but even all right to any consideration whatsoever on the part of the state, when the highest nobles were cowering at the feet of royalty, utterly at the mercy of the Tudor despots, how could the plebs of England and Ireland dare show its front even to testify to mere existence?

The English monarchs were aware that the spirit of the Irish nobles was not broken like that of their English vassals; and they resolved on bringing the proud lords of the Pale and the chieftains of the old race to a like submission with their own nobles. But of the common clansmen they made no more account than of the English rabble, and herein lay their great mistake. Subsequent history proved that the national leaders of the Irish race might be utterly annihilated, and yet the Irish question remain as great a difficulty as ever, owing to the stubborn, though sometimes passive resistance of the peasantry. But at that time such a thing was not contemplated.

All the cunning of diplomacy, all the artifice of the law, finally all the material resources of England, were called in, one after the other, or together, to achieve that great object of the policy of the Tudors and of the first Stuart. It is not necessary to go over what every person conversant with the history of the time knows by heart; it is only proper to indicate, as briefly as possible, the gradual results of that crafty and stern policy.

The Geraldine war ended with the total destruction of the Catholic Anglo-Irish nobles of the south, whose place was filled by the younger sons of

Protestant nobles from England. With the Geraldines, or shortly after them, fell the O'Sullivans of Beare, the McGeohegans, the O'Driscolls, and O'Connors of Kerry, whom Spain and Portugal received.

Then the whole efforts of Elizabeth were turned to the destruction of the native chieftains of the north. She failed; and the war resulted in a peace which left their lands and the open practice of their religion to the Ulster chiefs.

But James I., though he seemed willing to abide by the articles of the treaty, was driven by hard pressure to employ deceit, fraud, intimidation, and force, to bring the northern nobility into his power, and "the flight of the earls" was the consequence.

From this date the "Irish exiles" began in good earnest, originally consisting, for the most part, of families belonging to the first blood of the land, with minor chiefs and captains in their retinue. Many letters written at the time, which have been preserved, as well as reports of spies and informers, dispatched to the court of England from Spain, Portugal, Belgium, France, and Italy, give us an insight into the life led by those noblemen in foreign countries. They were sometimes supported by the sovereigns who received them; but at others neglected and reduced to shifts for a living.

The "flight" itself and all its details are given by the Rev. C. P. Meehan. The entire number of souls on board the small vessel which bore them away was, according to Teigue O'Keenan, Ollamh of Maguire, "ninety-nine, having little sea-store, and being otherwise miserably accommodated." This was indeed the first emigration of the Irish nobles and gentry, which was to be followed by many another, to their final extinction.

Sir John Davies took an English view of the subject when he wrote, about that time, to Lord Salisbury: "We are glad to see the day wherein the countenance and majesty of the law and civil government hath banished Tyrone out of Ireland, which the best army in Europe, and the expense of two million pounds sterling, did not bring to pass. And we hope his Majesty's government will work a greater miracle in this kingdom than ever St. Patrick did; for St. Patrick did only banish the poisonous worms, but suffered the men full of poison to inhabit the land still; but his Majesty's blessed genius will banish all those generations of vipers out of it, and make it, ere it be long, a right fortunate island."

Davies's prophecy ought to have been accomplished long ago, for it is long since all the Irish nobility, "those generations of vipers," has been destroyed; yet the poor island is still far from being "right fortunate."

The chief means employed at the time to encompass the destruction of the nobles was the infamous revelations of spies and informers. The existence of these agents has long been known to all; but the extent of their workings was not suspected even until the state papers and the correspondence of political men, and holders of offices at the time, came to be examined by writers desirous of investigating the whole truth.

It was then found that every man in the English Government, beginning from the highest, the king's ministers, through the Lords-Lieutenants and Chief-Justices of Ireland, down to the lowest officials, one and all kept in their pay men of all ranks of life, who, at the bidding of their employers, were ready to circumvent the victims of an odious policy, and under the guise of friendship, interest, common acquaintance, to discover, and even, if needed, to invent facts and circumstances which might be turned against them, or against any other persons obnoxious to England, with the view of destroying them. So that, to England in Europe, and to Elizabeth in England, belongs the dubious honor of having invented that great agent of modern governments--the secret police.

But the operations of those informers were not confined to England and Ireland alone, although those two kingdoms may be said to have literally swarmed with them; all foreign countries were made the scenes of their infamous machinations, wherever in fact the Irish nobles or English Catholics fled for refuge from persecution. At the courts of Spain and Rome they were to be found; in Brussels and Louvain, in Paris and Rheims, as well as in the by-lanes of London and the lowest quarters of Dublin. The ecclesiastical establishments particularly, which were founded by the Irish Catholics for the education of their priesthood, were infested with them: they found means to penetrate into their most secluded recesses, and sometimes the vilest and most shameful hypocrisy was resorted to in order to gain admittance into those holy cloisters devoted to science and virtue.

All the great houses and hotels in foreign countries, where the banished nobility of Ireland passed the tedious hours, months, and years, of their exile, were the places easiest of access to those base tools of the English Government.

On the reports furnished by these men the British policy was based, and the nobility and gentry still left in the island fell into the meshes so cautiously spread around them. How many of their number were cast into the Tower of London or the Castle of Dublin, on the mere word of these pests of society! How many, suddenly warned of the treachery intended, had to fly in haste lest they should fall into the hands of their enemies! We know that the first "flight of the earls" was brought about by such means as these, but our readers would be mistaken in imagining that that was an exceptional case, scarcely ever repeated. It was in reality the ordinary way of getting rid of this hated race of Irishmen.

The great misfortune was that, even among the Irish themselves, nay, among friars and priests belonging to the race, the English Government sometimes, though Heaven be thanked! rarely, found ready tools and most useful informers. Mean and sordid souls are to be found everywhere; our Lord himself was betrayed by an apostle, while giving him the kiss of peace; but among the Irish, people this class was confined to a few needy adventurers, sometimes to men who, from some personal grievance, real or imaginary, were blinded by the spirit of revenge to deliver those whose destruction they thirsted for into the hands of their common enemies, to their own eternal shame and perdition. The common people were too noble-hearted ever to join in such infamy, and to those who would have tempted them with gold to betray the men concealed by them, the response was ever ready: "The King of England is not rich enough to buy me!"

Thus, piecemeal, as it were, during the reign of Elizabeth and James I., and a part, at least, of that of Charles I., numbers of the Irish nobles were imprisoned or slain at home, or compelled to go into exile.

Nor, when James I., going lower in the social scale, began to dispossess the ordinary people, the clansmen, the tenants of Ulster, in order to make room for his Scotch Presbyterians, was, the war on the nobility discontinued on that account. The most prominent and, in its results, universal feature of his reign, was the breaking up of the clans all over the island, whereby he effected a complete change in the social state of the country. But the most efficacious means of bringing that result about was the total destruction of the nobility and gentry. The crafty monarch knew that so long as the Irish could see and converse with their natural chieftains and lords, so long would it be impossible to extinguish or abate, in the slightest degree, the clan-spirit. It was only when the key-stone which held their social edifice together-the head of the sept-had disappeared, that the whole fabric would tumble into ruins.

After a long trial of this policy of treachery and craft, came Cromwell to complete the work with violence and brutal force. There still remained in the island a great number of noble families, and the ollamhs and genealogists kept clear the rolls of the respective pedigrees. There is no doubt, at the time of Cromwell's war of extermination, even when the English Parliament had passed the Act of Settlement, that all the Irish septs still knew where to find their lawful natural chiefs, who, if no longer on the island, were at the head of some regiment in Flanders, France, Austria, or Spain. But, as time went on, the Irish brigades naturally came to identify themselves more and more with the countries into whose service they had passed, and where they had taken up their permanent abode; while in the island itself, force came to degrade what was left of the nobles, and to annihilate forever the national state institutions preserved by the genealogists and bards.

One of the features which most forcibly strikes the reader of the history of those times is, what took place all over the island when the English Parliament issued that celebrated proclamation in which it was declared that "it was not their intention to extirpate this whole nation."-(October 11, 1652.)

By that time the chief officers of Cromwell's army had already taken possession of a great number of the castles and estates of the nobility who had not left the country. The rest had fallen into the hands of the adventurers of 1641, who had advanced money for the purpose of raising a private army to conquer lands for themselves; while the body of Cromwell's troops looked on, awaiting the small pittance of a few hundred acres; which was to be their share of the spoil. Here is the strange and awe-inspiring picture of the conquered island in the seventeenth century:

The nobles, who had survived the fighting and defeat, were allowed to remain a short time until their transportation to Connaught. But, driven away from their mansions, where the new "landlords"-the word then came into use for the first time--occupied what had been their apartments, they had to live in some ruinous out-buildings, and to till with their own hands a few roods of land for the support of their perishing families. A few garans (dray-horses), and a few cows and sheep, were the only aid in labor and production left to them. They were allowed, by sufferance; to raise some small crops of grain and roots, but all their time had to be occupied in purely manual labor.

Such is the image which fixes itself indelibly on the memory of any one who reads attentively the common occurrences of those days. It was a picture presented in every province of the island; in the most distant mountain-fastnesses as well as in the still smiling plains of the lowlands.

The nobles were, as a class, utterly destroyed; few of them fell to the inferior rank of yeomen; while the mass of the people--was at once plunged to the dead level of common peasants and laborers. If some of the former class still retained a few faithful servants, their help was required for the drudgery about the farm or the miserable dwelling. None of them could be spared to keep up "the glory of the house." Would it not have been bitter irony to talk to this remnant of pedigree and their long line of ancestors? And would their enemies, who were now their masters, have countenanced the proscribed offices of files and shanachies, when laws against them specially had been so long enacted if not enforced? Now was the exact time for the rigid execution of those laws so evidently designed for the transformation of the freeborn natives into feudal serfs.

Hence, when the bitter day at last came, which was to deprive them of even the sight of the hereditary territory of the family, which was to transplant them to Connaught-among countrymen, indeed, but none the less strangers to them, whose presence could not fail to be unwelcome, and bring disturbance, confusion, and disorder-how, in such a case, could they hope to retain or revive their prestige as the old lords of the country? It is said that, for this, many of the Munster chieftains preferred to go into exile to Spain, or even to the islands of America, rather than take up their abode in Connaught, where they were sure to find bitter enemies in the old inhabitants of that desolate province.

This state of things knew no change, except with a very few of the Anglo-Irish, when Charles II. came to the throne, after the death of the Protector. He was in truth merely the executor of the great Act of Settlement, and carried into effect what had been enacted by the Parliament which had brought his father to the block, and driven himself into exile.

He only restored their estates to a few families of "innocent papists." Such was the phrase applied to them in derision, doubtless. The generality of the old families continued to sink deeper and deeper in degradation, and the forgetfulness of all they had once been.

It took the greater part of a century, from 1607 to 1689, to effect the almost total disappearance of the Irish nobility. As Colonel Myles Byrne, in his "Irish at Home and Abroad," says: "Few facts in history are more surprising than the rapidity and completeness of the fall of the Irish families stricken down by the penal laws. Reduced to beggary at once, and with habits acquired in affluence, surrounded only by contemporaries similarly crushed, or by the despoilers revelling and rioting in possession of their forfeited lands, friendless and unpitied, regarded as 'suspects' from the reasons for discontent so abundantly furnished them, they seemed struck with stupor, and utterly incapable of any effort to rise out of the abyss into which they had been precipitated. Dispirited, heart-broken, unmanned, they suffered the little personal property left them to melt away; and, on its exhaustion, were compelled to resort to the most humiliating means to prolong existence, and to accept for their helpless offspring the humblest condition which promised them a maintenance. A 'trade' was the general resort sought for the son of the chief of a clan, landholder, or gentleman.

"This gave rise to Swift's observation to Pope: 'If you would seek the gentry of Ireland, you must look for them on the coal-quay or in the liberty.'

"Thus, in my youth, 'the Devoy,' the head of one of the most powerful and distinguished of our septs, was a blacksmith, I have often seen a mechanic, named James Dungan, who was said to be a descendant of James Dungan, Earl of Limerick; and 'the Chevers' (Lord Mount Leinster) was the clerk of Mrs. Byrnes, who carried on the business of a rope-maker.

"Maddened and embittered by humiliation and suffering, renouncing all hope of recovering their stolen lands, those victims of 'bills of discovery,' or of confiscation, burned or destroyed, or threw aside, as worse than useless, the records of their former possessions, the proofs of their former respectability, and seemed, in fact, desirous to efface all evidence of it. I know one case in which the title-deeds of an estate were searched for an important occasion, and in which it appeared that they had been given to tailors to cut into strips or measures for purposes of their trade.

"A claim was set up to a dormant peerage, and a relation of mine having been applied to for information in support of it, he said: 'You are positively in remainder; but you are in the condition of the descendants of many Irish families, whose great difficulty is to prove who was their grandfather.'"

The reader is naturally struck, when the sudden appearance of James II. on the island presents to his eyes another Irish army, and a new Irish nation, fighting again for God and the king, but with few of the old names among those who then appeared on the scene. The leaders throughout the three years' struggle, which decided the ultimate fate of the country, for the most part have names unknown to Ireland, and unassociated with its former history, so completely had the aristocracy of the island perished and disappeared.

It may be well imagined, then, that, after the passage of another century of woe such as was described in the last chapter, it would be impossible to reconstruct the genealogies of the old families who might be entitled to lead the rising generation. Some few names are still advanced as entitled to the hereditary honors of once noble families, and thus we still hear of pretensions to title of "the O'Brien," "the O'Donaghue," and a few others. That such pretensions are acknowledged by the generality of the nation, it would be questionable to assert.

To think, then, of reconstructing the Irish nation out of its former elements, as they once existed, would be an idle dream. Those elements are dissolved and forever destroyed, and all that the nation can do with respect to its past is to preserve in pious remembrance the former race of men who once shed down such a glory over Irish annals. It was a happy and patriotic thought of the antiquarian societies of the island to investigate the old national records; to illustrate, explain, and bring them before the public in a language intelligible to the present generation. It is doubtful if in any other country the aristocracy fell with a heroism and glory so pure and unalloyed. Among all modern nations, as was said previously, the old class of noblemen has either passed out of sight, or is fast disappearing from living history. Ireland, then, does not stand alone in that respect. She was the first to lose her nobility, and she lost it more utterly than any other nation. But in the variety of movements, complications, revolutions, which now go to form the daily current of events in Europe, where do we find the nobles regarded as a power, as an element calculated to restore or even to preserve? The "noblemen" are well enough satisfied nowadays, if they are not persecuted, proscribed, or destroyed; if they are enabled to take their stand amid the crowd of men of inferior rank and share in the affairs of their country; content to see their names once so exclusively glorious, set on a par with those of plebeians, to lead the modernized peoples into the new paths whither they are rapidly drifting. Nay, so low have the mighty fallen, that even dethroned kings and princes sometimes ask to be admitted as simple citizens in the countries which they or their ancestors once ruled.

Here the thought will naturally occur: If the phenomenon is universal with respect to the position allotted now to men of "noble blood"--since it is evident that for those nations which feel no veneration for it a future history is designed, and that future is to be utterly independent of such an idea--then Ireland is no worse off than any other country in that regard, nay, the veneration for noble blood perhaps exists, in its right sense, now in her bosom alone, and, though no longer available for any purpose, is still an element of conservatism worthy of preservation and far from despicable.

Therefore, when we number among false hopes the one entertained by a few Irishmen whose thoughts still cling fondly to the past, and who would fain reconstruct it, it is not with the intention of treating those aspirations slightingly, which we ought to honor and would share, were there only the faintest possibility of calling again to life what we cannot but consider passed away forever.

II. Let us move on to the consideration of our second delusive hope, one of a much deeper import, which to-day of all others occupies public attention--a separate Irish Parliament and home- rule government.

The desire for a separate Irish Parliament is certainly a national aspiration, it may even be called a right; for the people of the island can justly complain of being at the mercy of a rival nation, of which they are supposed to form a part, and are consequently heavily taxed for the support of it without any adequate return. The day may not be far distant when this wish of theirs will have to be complied with, as were so many other rights once as strenuously denied.

Nevertheless it is our opinion, and we say it advisedly, there is no reason for believing that this would prove a universal panacea for Ireland's woes, sure to bring health, happiness, and prosperity to the nation, uniting in itself all blessings, all future success, all germs of greatness; nor is there reason to believe that with it the resurrection of the nation is assured, as without it, it would remain dead.

To speak still more clearly--the representation of a people by its deputies being according to modern ideas an element of free constitution for all nations, and Ireland having for so long a time enjoyed a privilege very similar to it under her own national monarchs, our object cannot be understood to depreciate a political institution which seems to have become a necessity of the times, owing to the eager aspiration of all minds and hearts toward it. But we think it a delusion to imagine that, by its possession, national happiness is necessarily and fully secured.

Whatever may be the general experience of parliamentary rule, its record for Ireland is a sad one. The old Feis of the nation are not here alluded to; they had very little in common with modern Parliaments, being merely assemblies of the chief heads of clans, to which were added in Christian times the prelates of the Church. Neither is the "General Assembly," which was intrusted with legislative and executive powers by the Confederation of Kilkenny, alluded to; this could not be reproduced to-day exactly as it then existed.

The Parliament here meant is such as presents itself at once to the mind of a man of the nineteenth century, with its members of both Houses elected by the people, as in America, or those of the Upper House in the nomination of the crown; its opposing parties often degenerating into mere factions; its views limited to material progress, and its aims and aspirations altogether worldly; deeply imbued with the modern ideas of liberalism, yet knowing very little, if any thing, of true liberty; often following the lead of a few talented members, whose real merits are seldom an index of conscience and sense of right.

Such a liberal institution as this, which, if proposed to-day for Ireland by the English Government, would be hailed with unbounded joy by all ranks of people in that country, would nevertheless be no sure harbinger of happiness to the nation, and, to repeat what was said above, the record of such an institution in Ireland is a sad one.

There is no need of entering upon a history of Irish Parliaments. If an impartial and fair-minded author were to take up such a work, it might serve to open the eyes of many, and show them that it is after all better to rely on Divine Providence than on such an aid to national prosperity.

Dr. Madden, in his "Connection of Ireland with England," conclusively shows that the right of a free and independent Parliament similar to that of England was granted to Ireland by King John at the very beginning of the "Conquest." Such a Parliament was granted to the handful of Anglo-Normans, who were already busy in building their castles for the purpose of reducing the whole mass of the clans to feudal slavery after having deprived them of all their free national assemblies and customs. For nearly four hundred years the Irish Parliaments, when not completely subjected to English control, as they finally were by "Poyning's Act," were mere legislative machines devised for the purpose of subduing, cowing, and finally rooting out every thing Irish in the land. The language of Sir John Davies was very clear on this subject.

This being such a well-known fact to-day, it seems strange that a writer who is so well informed, so acute and discerning, and so thoroughly Catholic, as Dr. Madden undoubtedly is, should attach such great importance to the institution of Parliament as first granted by the English monarchs. They had in their eye only the small English colony settled on the island, with all their feudal customs, and no thought of granting liberty to the mass of the nation. The case of Molyneux, which is so often quoted and praised by Irish writers, should be set aside and forgotten by any man animated by a true love for Irish prosperity. It was merely a revival of the old parties of English by blood and English by birth, without a single thought of the rights of Irishmen. It was a case of siding with one English party against another, both aiming at making Ireland a colony of England, the while the unfortunate country was crushed between them, certain in either case to be the victim. The native race had nothing to say or do in the matter, beyond assisting at the spectacle of their enemies wrangling among themselves.

The same remarks will apply to the pamphlets of Dr. Lucas, which created so much interest at the time, and which Dr. Madden quotes at such length. Lucas, it will be remembered, was a violent anti-Catholic, and consequently anti-Irish partisan.

Yet the Catholic Association made all the use they could of the arguments of Molyneux and Lucas, because these possessed some vestige of the national spirit, inasmuch as they spoke for Ireland, whose very name was hated by the opposite party; and at that time the Association was perfectly right: but matters have altered since then.

It is certainly strange that, when serious attempts were made by Henry VIII. to introduce Protestantism into Ireland, not only were Anglo-Irish Catholics summoned to Parliament, but even native chieftains also, some of whom spoke nothing but Irish, so that their speeches required translating.

But, as was previously shown, this was nothing more nor less than a crafty device to make genuine Irishmen unconsciously confirm, by what was called their vote, former decrees in which the Act of Supremacy had been passed; to make it appear that they had abjured their religion, and were now good Protestants; and, worse still, to set in the statute-book, as acknowledged by all, the law of spiritual supremacy vested in the king, of abjuration of papal authority, of submission to all decrees passed in England with the purpose of effecting an entire change in the religion of the nation.

To such vile uses was the machinery of Parliament reduced. Thenceforth it became an engine for the issuing of decrees of persecution. Catholic members occasionally appeared in it when a lull in the execution of the laws occurred, and they could take their seats without being guilty of apostasy. But, by making close boroughs of his Protestant colonies, James I. secured, once for all, the majority of representatives on the side of the Protestants, and, as a natural consequence, nothing more grinding, sharp, piercing, and strong, could be imagined than this engine of law called the Irish Parliament, as it existed under the Stuarts. "Nothing" would be incorrect: there was something worse; it came in with the Revolution of 1688, and its results have been witnessed in a previous chapter.

Owing to the various oaths imposed upon members in the time of William of Orange, no Catholic could any longer sit in the Irish Parliament without abjuring his faith. And, thence-forth, the state institution sitting in Dublin became more than ever a persecuting and debasing power, intent only on making, altering, improving, and enforcing laws designed for the complete degradation of the people.

There came, however, a period of eighteen years, called "the Rise of the Irish Nation" by Sir Jonah Barrington. It would be a pleasure to set this down as a real exception to the whole previous or later history of Ireland; but such pleasure cannot be indulged in.

At the period referred to France had embraced the cause of the North American colonies of Great Britain, and the English vessels were not the only ones upon the seas. Large French fleets were conveying troops to their new allies, and in 1779 the English Government sent warning to Ireland that American or French privateers were to be expected on the Irish coast, and no troops could be dispatched for the protection of the island. Then arose the great volunteer movement. Every Irishman entitled to bear arms enrolled himself in some regiment raised with the ostensible design of opposing a hostile landing, but really intended by the patriots to force the repeal of Poyning's Act from England, to obtain for the Parliament in Dublin real independence of English dictation.

The result is well known. One hundred thousand Irishmen were soon under arms, who not only took the field as soldiers, and formed themselves into regiments of infantry, troops of horse, and artillery, but, strange to say, as citizens, sent delegates to conventions, and demanded with a loud voice that England should not only grant free trade to the sister isle, but likewise invest the Irish Parliament with independent powers.

This political open-air contest lasted two years, and, on the receipt of the news that the British army had capitulated at Yorktown, and that the American War had come to a successful termination on the side of the colonists, the Ulster volunteers decided to hold a national convention of delegates from every city in the province. On Friday, February 15, 1782, the meeting took place at Dungannon, County Tyrone, and there the delegates swore allegiance to a new and as yet unwritten charter, refusing to acknowledge "the claim of any body of men, other than the King, Lords, and Commons of Ireland, to make laws to bind this kingdom."

The same resolution was adopted in successive meetings of volunteer delegates, municipal corporations, and citizens generally, all over the island.

The English Government could not resist the pressure. After some attempt at temporizing and delaying the concession, on April 15, 1782, by the firmness of Grattan and his supporters in the Dublin House of Commons, the great measure was finally carried unanimously:

"That the kingdom of Ireland is a distinct kingdom, with a Parliament of her own, the sole legislature thereof; that there is no body of men competent to make laws to bind the nation, but the King, Lords, and Commons of Ireland, nor any Parliament which has any authority or power of any sort whatever in this country, save only the Parliament of Ireland; that we humbly conceive that in this right the very essence of our liberty exists, a right which we, on the part of all the people of Ireland, do claim as their birthright, and which we cannot yield but with our lives." The italics are our own.

"The news," says Sir Jonah Barrington, "soon spread through the nation; every city, town, or village, in Ireland blazed with the emblems of exultation, and resounded with the shouts of triumph."

Within a month the whole had been accepted by the new British administration. "The visionary and impracticable idea had become an accomplished fact; the splendid phantom had become a glorious reality; the heptarchy-the old Irish constitution-had not been restored; yet Ireland had won complete legislative independence."

Thus does the kind-hearted author of the "Rise and Fall of the Irish Nation" commemorate the great event. It is a pity that it so soon ended, as it deserved to end, in smoke; for the "unanimous vote" of the Dublin House of Commons was not sincere, but intended to exclude from the benefit of the newly-acquired liberty the great mass of the people; that is, all Catholics, without exception.

Already, during the volunteer excitement, Catholics had looked on at the movement with pleasure and hope that, at least, some relaxation of the barbarous code enacted against them might ensue. Unable to take an active part in the movement, the laws not allowing them to bear arms and enlist, they willingly brought such muskets as they possessed to give to their Protestant neighbors. When the final burst of enthusiasm came at the news that a free and independant Parliament was to meet at Dublin, surely they were justified in expecting that, at last, their natural and civil rights might be restored them in an age so enlightened. They had heard too of the success of the American colonies in winning those rights for all in their happy country, beyond the Atlantic; and we may be sure that not a few of them had heard how, at the conclusion of the War of Indepen-dence, the chief officers of the American army had gone in state with their French allies to the Catholic Church in Philadelphia, there to join in thanksgiving to the Almighty, before a Catholic altar. Moreover, they had Grattan and many of the volunteers on their side.

The all-comprehensive phrase, too, had been inserted in the resolution so unanimously carried, and made law by the British Government: "We humbly conceive that, in this right, the very essence of our liberty consists, a right which we, on the part of all the people of Ireland, do claim as their birthright, and which we cannot yield but with our lives."

Was it possible for the originators and successful promoters of this great change in the government of the nation to interpret such a phrase in a restricted sense? Did not the Irish Catholics, the great bulk of the people, form a part, at least, of "all in Ireland?" One would imagine so: yet what followed soon after showed the preposterousness of such an idea.

The new Parliament met; several measures favorable to the trade and manufactures of the island had been carried; but it was soon found that the electoral law, as it stood, failed to correspond with the altered circumstances of the time. The legislative body was returned by an antiquated electoral system which could not be said to represent the nation. Boroughs and seats were openly and literally owned by particular families or private persons; the voting constituency sometimes not numbering more than a dozen. As a matter of fact, less than one hundred persons owned seats or boroughs capable of constituting a majority in the Commons!

As everywhere else in revolutionary times, the question of parliamentary reform was not debated in the Parliament only; every man in the nation, each in his own sphere, took part in the stormy contest which began to rage all over the island. The volunteers were still in their glory. Flushed with victory, they did not cease from their political agitations. In Septem-ber, 1783, they met once more in convention at Dungannon, the specific object of which, Dr. Madden tells us, was parliamentary reform, and they then determined "to hold another grand national convention of volunteer delegates in Dublin, in the month of November following."

In that extraordinary assembly, the question of the rights of Catholics was naturally brought up, and, to his honor be it said, the Protestant Bishop of Derry proposed to extend the elective franchise to them.

That some fanatics would oppose this motion was only to be expected; and it would have caused no surprise to find the opposition confined to a number of men of inferior station, still deeply imbued with narrow Protestant ideas. But when the leaders of the movement for national independence, Lord Charlemont and Mr. Flood, appeared in the ranks of the determined opponents of the proposition, it was cause for wonder indeed. It was chiefly owing to the exertions and influence of Lord Charlemont that the efforts of the revolution had been finally turned to the side of freedom; while Flood was a greater nationalist than Grattan himself, whose eloquence was so memorable in the last momentous debates of the Irish House of Commons. Flood carried his patriotism so far as to suspect the British Government of not being sincere in its conces-sions, when Grattan thought that "nothing dishonorable and disgraceful ought to be supposed in motives until facts render them suspicious."

Nevertheless, it was Charlemont and Flood who stood firm for the exclusion of Catholics from the franchise demanded for them by a Protestant bishop; and Flood's plan was the one finally adopted.

In order to make a stronger impression on the public mind, a number of delegates, who were also members of Parliament, proceeded, on November 29th, directly from the convention to the House of Commons, some of them dressed in their volunteer uniforms, for the purpose of supporting the plan of Mr. Flood to exclude the Catholics from the franchise.

In the midst of the tumult, the bill of reform failed, seventy-seven voting for, and one hundred and fifty against it. There was therefore no change in the Parliament, and Catholics remained in their old position, in consequence of the blunders of the chiefs of the volunteer movement for independence.

It is true that, at the same time, the whole volunteer movement itself fell to the ground. From that moment it dragged on a doomed life. "One would have thought," says Dr. Madden, "there was national vigor in it for more than an existence of fifteen years, and power to effect more than an ephemeral independence which lasted only eighteen years."

But the Catholics had their eyes opened; they saw that the day of resurrection was not yet come for them. It was not to be brought about by any Irish Parliament. So far, therefore, we were right in stating that the parliamentary record for Ireland is a sad one. It should be said, however, that, from that time, many Protestants, like the Bishop of Derry, Grattan, and others, have always been firm in their demand for freedom to all, and have remained the stanchest supporters of Catholic rights. What we have hitherto called James I's Ulster colony, thus was reduced to the Orange party; and, in that sense, the volunteer movement was a real and permanent benefit to the country. There is no need to mention the names of many distinguished Protestants of our own times, whose whole life has been devoted by act, or speech, or both, to the service of all. All honor to them!

But it is alleged that the Irish Legislature, as framed by the Constitution of 1782, gave to the country an uninterrupted flow of prosperity for eighteen years, and hence the volunteer movement was of great benefit to the race, at least temporarily. We will present the case in the strongest light possible contrary to our own opinion, and for this we can do no better than borrow the arguments of Mr. W.J. O'N. Daunt, in his pamphlet on the "Irish Question" (1869):

"Accustomed as we are," he says, "since the Union-in 1800-to the national distress and chronic disturbance attested by the Devon Commissions, Famine Reports, and other official sources of information, there seems something scarcely credible in the account of Irish pre-Union prosperity-a prosperity which contrasted so strongly with the condition of Ireland under a Parliament which is called 'Imperial,' but which is essentially and overwhelmingly English. But the accounts are given on unimpeachable authority.

"Mr. Jebb, member for Callan in the Irish Parliament, thus speaks of the advance of the country in prosperity, in a pamphlet published in 1798:

"'In the course of fifteen years, our commerce, our agriculture, and our manufactures, have swelled to an amount that the most sanguine friends of Ireland would not have dared to prognosticate.'

"The bankers of Dublin, tolerably competent witnesses, held a meeting on the 18th of December, 1798, at which they resolved, 'that, since the renunciation of Great Britain, in 1782, to legislate for Ireland, the commerce and prosperity of this kingdom have eminently increased.'

"The Dublin Guild of Merchants did the same on the 14th of January, 1797."

But this testimony and that of others whom we could quote was the testimony of men opposed to the "Union." Let us look at a few admissions made by the supporters of that measure:

"First comes its author, Mr. Pitt, who, in his speech in the English House of Commons, January 31, 1799, having alluded to the prosperous condition of Irish commerce in 1785, goes on to say: 'But how stands the case now? The trade is at this time infinitely more advantageous to Ireland.'

"Lord Clare, one of Mr. Pitt's chief instruments in effecting the Union, published, in 1798, a pamphlet containing, as quoted by Grattan, the following account of Irish progress subsequently to 1782: 'There is not a nation on the habitable globe which has advanced in cultivation and commerce, in agriculture and manufactures, with the same rapidity in the same period.'

"Finally, Mr. Secretary Coke, in a Unionist pamphlet, said at that time: 'We have had the experience of these twenty years; for it is universally admitted that no country in the world ever made such rapid advances as Ireland has done in these respects.'"

All this was undoubtedly true; and it is not our intention to admire what was called the Union, nor to advocate it. Those of the various writers cited, who spoke so dogmatically in the above passages, had in their minds only material and external prosperity, and that even of only one class of citizens. Those who wish well to Ireland cannot be satisfied with this.

Not a single name of the favorers or opposers of the Union, here quoted as witnesses, is Celtic. It would be interesting to know what the Celts of the island, that is, the greater part of its inhabitants, thought at the time, not of the Union, but of their own Parliament, and how much of this great material prosperity fell to their portion.

Surely they were all opposed to a Union which for a variety of reasons had grown odious in their sight; but, did they, could they, approve of the acts of their Legislature prior to the Union with England? Were they satisfied with those tokens of prosperity in favor of a class which had systematically oppressed them? Even granting that they were Christian enough not to feel envy at the success of their Protestant fellow- countrymen, did they not, and were they not right to, rue the day which, by an act of that same Legislature, shut them off as a body from all those advantages.

For it must be remembered that it was at the instigation of many of those volunteers who had been so ready to receive the muskets from their Catholic neighbors, for the purpose of striking a blow for liberty, that none of the penal statutes were repealed, and the Irish Catholics continued to groan, at least as far as the law went, under the fearful oppressions of which the last chapter furnished a feeble sketch. Hence, to speak in their presence of their commerce, of their manufactures, of their agriculture, of the increase of their wealth, and so on, was a bitter mockery, which they could not but resent in their inmost soul.

Was the cause of all their miseries removed by such a free and independent Parliament? Where could be the agricultural prosperity of a people which was not entitled, legally, to own an inch of their soil, or lease more than two acres of it? How could they engage in prosperous trade when, at the suit of a "discoverer," they were liable to be compelled to hand over to him the surplus of a paltry income? How could they even contemplate engaging in any manufactures, when the laws reduced them to the frightful state of pauperism which we have shudderingly glanced at? And those laws were preserved, and retained on the statute-book, by the very men who vaunted of the prosperity of Ireland!

It cannot, then, be too strongly reasserted that the social position of Ireland had experienced no change whatever, and that the separation of classes, spoken of with such well-merited rebuke by Edmund Burke, still stood unaltered:

"They divided the nation into two distinct parties, without common interest, sympathy, or connection. One of these bodies was to possess all the franchises, all the property, all the education; the other was to be composed of drawers of water and cutters of turf for them.

Every measure was pleasing and popular just in proportion as it tended to harass and ruin a set of people who were looked upon as enemies to God and man; and, indeed, as a race of bigoted savages, who were a disgrace to human nature itself.

"To render humanity fit to be insulted, it was fit that it should be degraded."

And, even supposing the prosperity of which so much talk was made to have been universal, so that all had a real share in it, how long would it have remained so, if the Irish Parliament had continued to exist, and not become merged in the English, or, as it was termed, Imperial Legislature? How long could the two separated bodies, sitting, the one in Dublin, the other in Westminster, have acted in concert, without breaking out into violent and mutual recrimination, with all its attendant evils?

The difficulty showed itself at the very outset, and when the first question of the relative status of both Legislatures arose.

Mr. Fox, the great Liberal minister of the king, endeavored to solve this difficulty by making a distinction between internal and external legislation: Ireland was never to be interfered with in her Parliament, with respect to her internal questions, while the English legislative body possessed the right to step in in all measures regarding external legislation. This seems very much like what is now proposed by home-rule.

Here is the answer given to this in the tribune of Dublin by Mr. Walsh: 'With respect to the fine-spun distinction of the English minister between the internal and external legislation, it seems to me the most absurd position, and at the same time the most ridiculous one, that possibly could be laid down, when applied to an independent people.

"Ireland is independent, or she is not; if she is independent, no power on earth can make laws to bind her, internally or externally, but the King, Lords, and Commons of Ireland."

Mr. Walsh, a very influential member of the Irish House of Commons, saw, as doubtless did many others, cause of disturbance already for the mutual tranquillity of the two nations. And, indeed, his fears soon showed themselves only too well grounded. Dr. Madden tells the story;

"A month had scarcely elapsed since the opening of the new Irish Parliament in 1782, before Lord Abingdon, in the British House of Peers, moved for leave to bring in a declaratory bill, to reassert the right of England to legislate externally for Ireland, in matters appertaining to the commerce of the latter. A similar motion was made in the British House of Commons by Sir George Young.

"One clause of Lord Abingdon's bill stated that Queen Elizabeth, having formerly forbade the King of France to build more ships than he then had, without her leave first obtained, it is enacted that no kingdoms, as above stated, Ireland as well as others, should presume to build a navy or any ships-of-war, without leave from the Lord High Admiral of England."

It is easy to foresee the pretty quarrel preparing. Once again, then, it may be asserted that the record of Irish Parliaments is a sad one.

But could more have been expected of it? Is the scope of measures, within the capabilities of any legislative assembly of modern times, comprehensive enough to embrace every thing of importance to a Catholic people, such as the Irish nation has ever been?

The general question of parliamentary rule is a very complicated one. The modern Parliament is a very different thing from the old assemblies of the representatives of various orders in any state. With the Church originated those ancient institutions, which in certain parts of Europe partook at once of the twofold nature of councils and political assemblies.

This order has passed away, and no one thinks to-day of reviving those time-honored institutions, however much political writers may be inclined to favor despotism on the one hand, or anarchy on the other. What, then, is the origin of the modern Parliament? It grew into being in England during the seventeenth and eighteenth centuries, emanating as it were, slowly, out of the decomposition of the old Parliaments; the aristocracy, and the Church chiefly, losing more and more the influence once belonging to them, which, in old times, made them paramount in those state deliberations. This is one of the chief features of the newly-modelled British Constitution, which is of very recent growth, and became fixed and settled only after the downfall of the Stuart dynasty, receiving additional modifications in the contest of parties under the Brunswick and Hanover lines of kings.

It is, consequently, an altogether British growth of recent date, particularly well adapted for England, whose prosperity since its establishment has ever been on the increase. But it is very doubtful whether other countries have derived equal benefit from its adoption.

Toward the end of last century, some few Frenchmen of note attempted, with Mounier at their head, to reproduce a feeble copy of it in France. Their failure is too well known to the world: how their English ideas were scouted by the people, while a far more radical revolution swept away every vestige of the old French Constitution, without substituting in its stead any thing save crude and infidel ideas, which resulted in anarchy.

The lamentable failure of the first attempt was no discouragement to other political theorists; and the century has witnessed and still witnesses every day essays at English legislation, as embodied in the constitution of its Parliaments chiefly, all over Europe; and all, as sanguine writers would have us believe, to serve as the stepping-stone for the "Universal Republic," which is to regenerate the world.

The great questions in all those assemblies are of material interests, material prosperity, material projects. Of the moral well-being of the people seldom or never a word is heard; and, whenever a moral question does come up for discussion, the vagueness of the theories advanced and discussed, the indecision of the measures proposed, the want of unity in the views developed, show how unfit are modern legislators for even touching on what concerns the soul of man. The legislators themselves feel that their character is far from being a sacred one, and that the spiritual element is not comprehended in their world. And they are certainly right.

Even the measures of external policy are not universally successful in securing the material well-being of the people. In France, at least, the various legislatures which have succeeded one another have perhaps been productive of as much harm in that regard as the liberty of the press and freedom of public discussion, which have always had and always will have their ardent advocates, and the existence of which is compatible with public order in some countries, but not in others.

The same, with certain reservations, is true of the Spanish-American republics, Brazil, and now of Spain, Italy, and other European nations. The legislative machine which is found to work so well in England, and what were or still are her colonies, seems to get out of order in climates and among nations unaccustomed to it, even as far as material prosperity is concerned.

But it is neither our object to write a history of Parliaments, nor absolutely to condemn those modern institutions by the few words devoted to them. All we wish to insist upon is, that all the evils of nations are not cured by them, and that they should not be taken as in themselves absolutely desirable and all- sufficient.

As to their probable fate in the future, their modern dress is not yet two centuries old, and the seeds of decay already appear in many places. A few questions are sufficient to demonstrate this: Can a Parliament, as understood to-day, last for any length of time and work successfully, when composed for a great part of corrupt legislators who have been returned by corrupt electors? Has not the progress of corruption on both sides, elected and electors, been of late alarmingly on the increase? What space of time is requisite for legislation to come to a stand-still, and prove to modern nations the impossibility of carrying on even material affairs with such corrupt machinery? It requires no great foresight to reply to these questions.

And yet it is on this tottering institution that the Ireland of our days has set her hope. She imagines that, this once gained, prosperity and happiness are insure; that, without it, she cannot but be discontented, as she is and must be if she possesses any feeling. And such is the anomaly of her position that, with this conviction firmly set before us, we believe she is right in demanding home-rule, and that by insisting upon it she will eventually attain it; yet are we convinced that, having obtained it, her evils will not be cured, nor her happiness served. We prize her highly enough to think her worthy of something better, which "something" we are sure God keeps in reserve for her.

Suppose her earnest wish granted, and a home Parliament given her. Suppose even the old question of her relations with the English Legislature determined. A great difficulty has been settled satisfactorily, though it is difficult to see how this may come about. But supposing the questions for her discussion and free-determination being clearly defined, home-rule becomes possible without exciting the opposition of the rival Parliament of Great Britain.

What is likely to be the composition of her state institution? and what the programme of its labors?

In the composition of her two Houses, if she have two, the Catholics will not be excluded as they were in 1782; a great change certainly, and fraught no doubt with great benefit to the country. But will the English element cease to predominate? The native race has been kept so long in a state of bondage that few members of it certainly will take a leading part in the discussions. How many even will be allowed to influence the election of members by their votes or their capacity? Universal suffrage can scarcely be anticipated, perhaps even it would not be desirable. The question is certainly a doubtful one. Of one thing are we certain regarding the composition of an Irish Parliament: it would not really represent the nation.

For the nation is Catholic to the core; the sufferings of more than two centuries have made religion dearer to her than life; all she has been, all she is to-day, may be summed up in one word--Catholic. Nothing has been left her but this proud and noble title, which of all others her enemies would have wrested from her. The nation exists to-day, independently of parliamentary enactments, in spite of the numberless parliamentary decrees of former times; she is living, active, working, and doing wonders, which shall come under notice. See how busy she has been since first allowed to do. Her altars, her religious houses, her asylums, every thing holy that was in ruins--all have been restored.

Not satisfied with working so energetically on her own soil, she has crossed over to England, where the great and unexpected Catholic revival, which has struck such awe and fear into the hearts of sectarians, is in great measure due to her.

Cross the broad Atlantic, and even the vast Southern Ocean, and the contemplation of Irish activity in North America, Australia, and all the English colonies, the intense vitality displayed by this so long down-trodden people is amazing. But all this activity, all this vitality, is employed in establishing on a firm and indestructible basis everywhere the holy Catholic Church.

Looking on all this, say then whether Ireland is truly Catholic, whether the nation is any thing but Catholic.

But can her new Parliament be Catholic?

No! No one imagines such a thing possible; no one thinks, no one dreams of it. It is clear, then, that it cannot represent the nation.

Who will go to compose it? Men who will discard-such is the modern expression-discard their creed, and leave it at the door. Nothing better can be expected. It is true that the bitter feeling engendered for so long a time by religious questions is not likely to show itself again; or though, to speak more correctly, a religious question never was raised in Ireland, the whole people being one on that subject; but it may be hoped that the bitter persecution against every thing Catholic is not likely to recur, whatever may be the composing elements of the new Houses of Parliament.

In the impossibility of even guessing at the probable opinions of the men who are to have the future fate of Ireland in their hands, it may be fairly predicted that, within their legislative halls, religious and consequently moral questions will only be approached in the spirit of liberalism. Probably, the only thing attempted will be the rendering of the people externally happy and prosperous, supposing the majority of the members animated by true patriotic principles; and indeed the aspirations of all who wish well to Ireland are limited to external or material prosperity; and, for our own part, we do not consider this of slight moment. But is this all that the Irish people require?

They have been brought so low in the scale of humanity that every thing has to be accomplished to bring about their resurrection; and the "every thing" is comprised in substituting flesh-meat for potatoes and good warm clothing for rags. Whoever says that the Irish people can be contented with such a restoration as this, knows little of their noble nature, and has never read their heart.

Assuredly, they have a right to those worldly blessings of which they have been so long deprived; and we would not be understood as saying that one of the primary objects of good government is not to confer those material blessings on the people; nay, it is our belief that, when a whole nation has been so long subjected to all the evils which not only render this life miserable, but absolutely intolerable, it is incumbent on those intrusted with the direction of affairs to remedy those evils instantly, and endeavor to make the people forget their misfortunes by, at least, the enjoyments of this life's ordinary comforts. Forgetfulness of the past can be obtained by no other means. And this is a very simple, but, at the same time, very satisfactory answer to the question so often put and so often replied to in such a variety of ways, "Why is Ireland discontented?"

But, while admitting the truth, nay, the necessity of all this, the government of a Catholic people has not fulfilled its whole duty when it has exerted itself to the utmost to procure, and finally succeeded in procuring, the temporal happiness of the nation. In addition to this, it must consult its moral and religious wants, or a great part of its duty remains neglected.

This, indeed, does not nowadays occur to the minds of the majority of men, who have, it would appear, agreed among themselves to consider it an axiom of government that the rulers of a people should have no other object in view than the material comfort and welfare of the masses. They do not reflect that the wants of a nation must be satisfied in their entirety, and that its moral and religious needs are of no less importance, to say the least, than the temporal. This is evident in all those countries where, in imitation of England, or at her instigation, parliamentary governments are now in operation--countries which include not only Europe, without excepting Greece and her chief islands, but Southern Africa at the Cape, America, North and South, Australia, and the, large islands of Jamaica, Tasmania, New Zealand, and several groups of Polynesia, preparing Asia for the boon which, probably, is destined to show itself in Japan first, spreading thence all over the largest continent of the world.

Wherever modern Parliaments flourish, there material interests alone are consulted. This is a new feature of Japhetism; and God alone knows how long nations will be satisfied with such a state of things!

But if non-Catholic nations thus limit their aspirations, there is all the more reason why a Catholic people cannot imitate them in such a course, particularly if that people has for centuries submitted to every evil of this life in order to preserve its religion, showing that, in its eyes, religious blessings rank far above all imaginable material advantages; and we all know such to be the case for Ireland.

But, it may be asked, what are those religious wants which must be satisfied, and how are we to know them? The answer, to a Catholic, is plain, and nothing is easier of recognition. What the spiritual guides of the nation consider of paramount importance and of absolute necessity, is of that character, and the government which neglects to listen to remon-strances coming from such a quarter, shows thereby that it is ignorant of, or slights, its plain duty. Ever since the load of tyranny, which weighed down the Irish people, has been removed, if not entirely, at least suffered a very appreciable reduction, since the rulers of the Church in that unhappy country have been able to lift up their voice, and proclaimed what they considered of supreme importance to those under their charge, is it not a strange truth that their voice has never ceased remonstrating, and that, at this very moment, it is as loud in protestation as ever? When has it been listened to as it should be? Is it likely to meet more regard if Ireland obtains home-rule? It grieves us to say that the only answer which can be given to this last question is still an emphatic "No!"

And for the very simple reason, already given, that Ireland cannot have a truly Catholic Parliament, and that all the great measures which would occupy the attention of the Catholic members, in the event of their meeting at Dublin, would be shemes for the advancement of manufactures, trade, the construction of ships, tenant-right laws, etc.; all very excellent things in their way, and to which Ireland has an undoubted right, which will be strongly contested, and in the struggle for which she may again be worsted; which, even if she obtains, will not enable her to compete with England, and which, after and above all, do not correspond to the heart-beat of the nation--the restoration complete and entire of the Catholic Church all over her broad land.

It may be well to remark that the broad assertion just laid down involves no reprisals against the rights of the minority. That minority, backed by the English Government, has enjoyed nearly three centuries of oppression and tyranny, has taxed human ingenuity to the utmost for the purpose of concocting schemes of destruction against the majority: it has failed. The majority, which at last breathes freely, can well afford not to raise a finger in retaliation, and to leave what is called freedom of conscience to those who so long refused it. The result may be left to the operation of natural laws and the holy workings of Providence. But their religious rights ought, at east, to be secured to them entire; the rights of their Church to be left forever perfectly free and untrammelled.

But, how much has been done against this, even of late? Why has a Protestant university so many privileges, while a similar Catholic institution is refused recognition? To answer what purpose have the Queen's Colleges been established? The Catholic bishops certainly possess rights with regard to the education of their flocks; with what persistence have not those rights been either attacked or circumvented! If the Protestant Establish-ment has been finally abolished, have not its ministers obtained by the very act of abolition concessions which give them still great weight, morally and materially, in the scale opposed to Catholic proselytism, nay, preservation? Is it not a stain even yet, if not in the eye of the law, at least in that of the English colonized in Ireland, to be a "Roman Catholic?" Is "souperism" so completely dead that it never can revive? How many means are still left in the hands of the Protestant minority to vex, annoy, and impoverish the supposed free majority?

Whoever considers the matter seriously cannot but acknowledge that in Ireland there exists still a vast amount of open or silent opposition to the Church of the majority, and a Church which the majority loves with such deep affection that, so long as the least remnant of the old oppression remains, so long must Ireland remain discontented.

And it is more than doubtful whether home-rule would be a sufficient remedy for such a state of things, owing to the fact, already insisted upon, that the new Parliament could not be a Catholic Parliament.

The reader may easily perceive what was meant by saying that the entire restoration of the Catholic Church in the island does not suppose the consequent extirpation of heresy; but it clearly supposes the perfectly free exercise of all her rights by the Church. Nothing short of this can satisfy the Irish people.

III. We pass on to the consideration of a third delusive hope, that of the people regaining all their rights by the overwhelming force of numbers and armed resistance to tyranny-- the advocacy of physical force, as it is called; in other words, the right and necessity of open insurrection, or underhand and secret associations, evidently requiring for success the cooperation of the numerous revolutionary societies of Europe: a criminal delusion, which has brought many evils upon the country, and which is still cherished by too many of her sons. Though we purpose speaking freely on this subject, we hope that our language may be that of moderation and justice.

To a Catholic, who has either witnessed or heard of the frightful evils brought on modern nations by the doctrine of the right of insurrection, of armed force, of open rebellion, against real or fancied wrong, that doctrine cannot but be loathsome and detestable.

True, there is for nations, as for individuals, something resembling the right of self-defence. No Catholic theologian can assert that a people is bound to bow under the yoke of tyranny, when it can shake that tyranny off; and it is this truth which affords a pretext to many advocates of what is called the right of insurrection. Moreover, there is no doubt that, in the case of Ireland particularly, the Irish had for many centuries a legitimate government of their own, and when attacked by foreigners, who landed on their shores under whatever pretext, they had a perfect right, nay, it was the duty of the heads of clans, the provincial kings and princes, to protect the whole nation, and the part of it intrusted to their special care in particular, against open or covert foes. The name of "rebels" was given them by the invaders, with no shadow of possible pretext, and the name was as justly resented as it was unjustly applied.

Under the Stuart dynasty the state of the case is still more clear: for then they were fighting on the side of the English sovereigns to whom they had submitted; and, in waging war against the enemies of their king and country, they were not only enforcing their right, but performing a highly-meritorious and in some cases heroic duty. Yet the name of "rebels" was again applied to them, and its penalty inflicted upon them, as has been seen.

After their complete subjugation, the right of retaliating on their oppressors, even if justifiable in theory, was often illusory and indefensible in fact, because of the impossibility of successful resistance; and the secret associations known under the names of "Tories," "Rapparees," "White Boys," "Ribbonmen," were, with the exception of the first, condemned by the Church.

But in modern times the right of insurrection cannot possibly be defended, if, as can scarcely be avoided, the cause of a Catholic nation is linked with the various revolutionary societies and conspiracies which disgrace modern Europe, endanger society, and have all been condemned by the sovereign Pontiff.

An extensive discussion of both cases--the stubborn resistance made after the fall of the Stuarts, and some of the attempts at independence of later times--would show at once the difference between the two cases, and prevent thinking men from ranking the "Tories" of ancient times with the avowed revolutionists of our days. Mr. Prendergast has given a fair sketch of the former in the second edition of his "Cromwellian Settlement."

The reader who may peruse this very interesting account can notice a remarkable coincidence; one, however, which to our knowledge has not yet been pointed out: the very scenes enacted in Ireland, during the long resistance offered to oppression after the downfall of the Stuart dynasty, were reenacted in France during the Reign of Terror, and for some time after, throughout the districts which had risen in insurrection against the tyranny of the Convention, and both cases were certainly examples of right warring against might.

In fact, to a person acquainted with the history of the violent changes which, during the last century, modern theories, metaphysical systems, and, above all, the working of secret societies, have caused, the reading of the history of England and Ireland, from the Reformation down, offers new sources of interest, by showing how the last frightful convulsion in France was merely a copy of the first in England, at least as far as the means employed in each go, if not in the ultimate object.

In England the revolution was begun by the monarch himself, with a view of rendering his power more absolute and universal by the rejection of the papal supremacy, and, consequently, the destruction of the Catholic Church. In France the revolution was begun by the leaders of the middle classes, who made use of the immense power given them by the secret societies which then flourished, and the influence of an unbridled press, to destroy royalty and aristocracy, that they might themselves obtain the supreme power and rule the country. The object of the two revolutions was therefore widely different; but the means employed in bringing them about, when considered in detail, are found to have been perfectly identical.

In both countries, on the side of the revolutionary party or of the National Assembly, various oaths were imposed and enforced, troops dispatched, battles fought, devastating bands ravaged the country while in a state of insurrection, the same barbarous orders in La Vendee as in Ireland, so that the language even employed in the second case is an exact counterpart of that in the first. There is destruction resolved upon; then the authorities desisting and resolving on a change of policy, though with a rigid continuance of the police measures, including in both cases "domiciliary visits," inquests by commissioners, courts-martial in the first case, revolutionary tribunals in the second--consequent wholesale executions on both sides. There were the decrees of confiscation carried out with the utmost barbarity, resulting in sudden changes of fortune, the class that was aristocratic being often reduced to beggary, while its wealth was enjoyed by the new men of the middle classes. The peasants derive very little benefit from the revolution in France--none whatever, or rather the very reverse of benefit, in Ireland. And, to go into the minutest details, there are the same informers, spies, troops of armed police, or adventurers on the hunt to discover, prosecute, and destroy the last remnants of the insurgents in France as well as in Ireland.

In considering the religious side of the question, the parallel would be found still more striking, as the proscribed ministers of religion were of the same faith in France as in the British Isles, while the means adopted for their destruction were exactly similar.

On the side of the insurgents the same comparison holds good. In both cases there is the first refusal to obey unjust decrees, the same stubborn opposition to more stringent acts of legislature, the emigration of the aristocratic classes, the devotedness of the clergy, with here and there an unfortunate exception, the same mode of concealment resorted to--false doors, traps, secret closets, disguise, etc.; the flying to the country and concealment in woods, caves, hills, or mountains; and, when the burden grows intolerable, and open resistance, even without hope of success, becomes inevitable, there are the same resources, method of organization, attack, call to arms, call to Heaven, the same heroism: yes, and the same approval of religion and admiration of all noble hearts throughout the world.

The only difference consists in the fact that in France the struggle lasted a few years only; in Ireland, centuries. In France the fury of the revolution soon spent itself in horrors; in Ireland the sternness of the persecuting power stood grim and unrelaxing for ages, adding decree to decree, army to army. In France, numerous hunters of priests and of "brigands," as they were called, flourished only for a short decade of years; in Ireland similar hunters of priests and of "Tories" carried on their infamous trade for more than a century.

In the case of the latter country, too, the confiscation was much more thorough and permanent, the emigration complete and final; but, in both cases, the Catholic religion outlived the storm, and lifted up her head more gloriously than ever as soon as its fury had abated.

Finally, to come to the point, which calls now more immediately for attention, if the campaigns of Owen Roe O'Neill, of Brunswick, and Sarsfield, were the models of the great insurrection of La Vendee and Brittany, the bands of "Tories" and "rebels," scattered through Ireland at the time of the Cromwellian settlement, gave an example for the "Chouan" raids which in France followed the blasted hopes of the royalists.

How ought both cases to be considered with reference to the general rules of morality? How were they considered at the time by religious and conscientious men?

There is no doubt that excesses were committed by Tories in Ireland, and Chouans in France, which every Christian must condemn; but there can also be little doubt that such of them as were not deranged by passion, but allowed their inborn religious feelings to speak even in those dreadful times, were restrained, either by their own consciences or by the advice of the men of God whom they consulted, from committing many crimes which would otherwise have resulted from their unfortunate position. All this, however, resolves itself into a consideration of individual cases which cannot here be taken into account.

Our only question is the cause of both Tories and Chouans in the abstract. From the beginning it was clearly a desperate cause, and, admitting that the motive which prompted it was generous, honorable, and praiseworthy, nothing could be expected to ensue from its advocacy but accumulated disaster and greater misfortunes still. Of either case, then, abstractly considered, religion cannot speak with favor.

But, when an impartial and fair-minded man takes into consideration all the circumstances of both cases, particularly of that presented in Ireland, as given by Mr. Prendergast, with all the glaring injustice, atrocious proceedings, and barbarous cruelty of the opposing party taken into account, who will dare say that men, driven to madness by such an accumulation of misery and torture, were really accountable before God for all the consequences resulting from their wretched position?

In the words quoted by the author of the "Cromwellian Settlement:" "Had they not a right to live on their own soil? were they obliged in conscience to go to a foreign country, with the indelible mark left on them by an atrocious and originally illegitimate government?" And, if the simple act of remaining in their country, to which they had undoubtedly a right, forced them to live as outlaws, and adopt a course of predatory warfare, otherwise unjustifiable, but in their circumstances the only one possible for them, to whom could the fault be ascribed? Are they to be judged harshly as criminals and felons, worthy only of the miserable end to which all of them, sooner or later, were doomed? Is all the reproach and abuse to be lavished on them, and not a breath of it to fall on those who made them what they were? Who of us could say whether, if placed in the same position, he would not have considered the life they led, and the inevitable death they faced, as the only path of duty and honor?

We are thoroughly convinced that the first Irish "Tories" deemed it their right to make themselves the avengers of Ireland's wrongs, and consider themselves as true patriots and the heroic defenders of their country, and that many honorable and conscientious men then living agreed with them. And the people, who always sided with and aided them, had after all certainly a right to their opinion as the only true representatives of the country left in those unfortunate times.

Thus far we have considered the right of resistance on the part of the old "Tories;" we now come to what has been called the second case--the right of insurrection advocated by modern revolutionists, chiefly when connected with the unlawful organizations so widely spread to-day. This, indeed, is the great delusive hope of to-day, which must be gone into more thoroughly, in order to show that Ireland, instead of encouraging among her children the slightest attachment to the modern revolutionary spirit, ought to insist on their all, if faithful to the noble principles of their forefathers, opposing it, as indeed the great mass of the nation has opposed it, strenuously, though it has met with the almost constant support of England, who has spread it broadcast to suit her own purposes. Ireland's hope must come from another quarter.

Let us look clearly at the origin and nature of this revolutionary spirit, so different from the lawful right of resistance always advocated by the great Catholic theologians.

The nature of this spirit is to produce violent changes in government and society by violent means; and it originated in first weakening and then destroying the power of the Popes over Christendom. Two words only need be said on both these interesting topics--words which, we hope, may be clear and convincing.

The very word revolutionary indicates violence; and it is so understood by all who use it with a knowledge of its meaning. A revolutionary proceeding in a state, is one which is sanctioned neither by the law nor the constitution, but is rapidly carried on for any purpose whatever. Violence has always been used in the various revolutions of modern times, and, when people talk of a peaceful revolution, it is at once understood that the term is not used in its ordinary significance.

On this point, probably, all are agreed; and, therefore, there is no need of further explanation. On the other hand, many will be inclined to controvert the second proposition; and, therefore, its unquestionable truth must be shown.

That the position held by the Popes at the head of Christendom for many ages was of paramount influence, and that to them, in fact, is due the existence of the state of Europe, known as Christendom, is now admitted almost by all since the investigations of learned and painstaking historians, Protestants as well Catholics, have been given to the world. But had the Popes any particular line of policy, and did they favor one kind of government more than another? This is a very fair question, and well worthy of consideration.

Any kind of government is good only according to the circumstances of the nation subjected to it. What may suit one people would not give happiness to another, and democratic, aristocratic, or monarchical governments, have each their respective uses, so that none of them can be condemned or approved absolutely. No one will ever be able to show that the Roman Pontiffs held any exclusive theory on this subject, and adopted a stern policy from which they did not recede.

But a positive line of policy they did hold to, namely, the insuring the stability of society by securing the stability of governments.

Whoever reads the life of Gregory VII side by side with that of William the Conqueror, is at first astonished to find Hildebrand, who, though not yet Pope, was already powerful in the counsels of the Papacy, favoring the Norman king, although William eventually proved far from grateful. But, when the reader comes to inquire what can have moved the great monk to take up this line of action, he will find that a deep political motive lay at the bottom of it, which throws a flood of light over the policy of the Popes and the history of Europe during the middle ages. He finds Hildebrand persuaded that William of Normandy possessed the true hereditary right to the crown of England, and the policy of the Popes was already in favor of hereditary right in kingdoms, thereby to insure the stability of dynasties, and consequently that of society itself.

Harold, son of Godwin, belonged in no way to the royal race of Anglo-Saxon kings. The Dukes of Normandy had contracted alliances by marriage with the Anglo-Saxon monarchs, and were thought to be more nearly related to Edward the Confessor than Harold, whose only title was derived from his sister.

What had been the state of Europe up to that time? Since the establishment and conversion of the northern races, a constant change of rulers, an ever-recurring moving of territorial limit, and consequently an endless disturbance in all that secures the stability of rights, was common everywhere: in England, under the heptarchy; in France, under the Carlovingians; in the various states of Germany; everywhere, except, perhaps, in a part of Italy, where small republics were springing up from municipal communes, which were better adapted to the wants of the people.

The great evils of those times were owing to these perpetual changes, which all came from the undefined rights of succession to power, as left by Charlemagne; a striking proof that a monarch may be a man of genius, a great and acceptable ruler, and still fail to see the consequences to future times of the legacy he leaves them in the incomplete institutions of his own time. Well has Bossuet said, that "human wisdom is always short of something."

Those rapid, and, to us, wonderful partitions of empires and kingdoms; those loose and ill-defined rules of succession in Germany, France, England, and elsewhere; productive of revolution at the death of every sovereign, and often during every reign, showed the Popes that hereditary rights ought to be clear and fixed, and confined to one person in each nation. From that period, date the long lines of the Capetians in France, the Plantagenets in England; while rights of a similar kind are introduced into Spain and Portugal; likewise into the various states of Northern Germany, or Scandinavia; and Southern Italy, or Norman Sicily--the rest of Italy and Germany are placed on a different footing, the empire and the popedom being both elective.

Such was the grand policy of the Popes inaugurated by Hildebrand, which came out in all its strong features, at the same time, under his powerful influence. Such was the policy which insured the stability of Europe for upward of six hundred years; a set of views to which a word only can be devoted here, but on which volumes would not be thrown away.

In consequence of it, for six hundred years dynasties seldom changed; the territorial limits of each great division of Europe remained, on the whole, settled; and an order of society ensued, of such a nature that any father of a family might rest assured of the state of his children and grandchildren after him.

In this respect, therefore, as in many others, the papacy was the key-stone of Christendom.

But as soon as Protestantism came to contest, not only the temporal, but even the spiritual supremacy of the Popes; when, taking advantage of the trouble of the Church, the so-called Catholic sovereigns, while pretending to render all honor to the spiritual supremacy of the sovereign Pontiffs, refused to acknowledge in them any right of lifting their warning voice, and calling on the powers of the world to obey the great and unchangeable laws of religion and justice, then did the long-established stability of Europe begin to give way, while the whole continent entered upon its long era of revolution, which is still in full way, and, as yet, is far from having produced its last consequences.

England, the most guilty, was the first to feel the effect of the shock. The Tudors flattered themselves that, by throwing aside what they called the yoke of Rome, they had vastly increased their power, and so they did for the moment, while the dynasty that succeeds them sees rebellion triumphant, and the head of a king fall beneath the axe of an executioner.

She is said to have benefited, nevertheless, by her great revolution, and by the subsequent introduction of a new dynasty. She has certainly chanted a loud paean of triumph, and at this moment is still exultant over the effects of her modern policy, from the momentary success of the new ideas she has disseminated through the world, and above all from that immense spread of parliamentary governments which have sprung into existence everywhere under her guidance, and mainly through her agency.

And the cause of her triumph was that, after a few years of commotion, she seemed to have obtained a kind of stability which was a sufficiently good copy of the old order under the Popes, and won for her apparently the gratitude of mankind; but that stability is altogether illogical, and cannot long stand. There is an old, though now trite, saying to the effect that when you "sow the wind you must reap the whirlwind," and no one can fail to see the speedy realization of the truth of this adage on her part. Over the full tide of her prosperity there is a mighty, irresistible, and inevitable storm visibly gathering. At last she has come to nearly the same state of mental anarchy which she has been so powerful to spread in Europe. After reading "Lothair," the work of one of her great statesmen, all intelligent readers must exclaim, "Babylon! how hast thou fallen!" Within a few years, possibly, nothing will remain of her former greatness but a few shreds, and men will witness another of those awful examples of a mighty empire falling in the midst of the highest seeming prosperity.

When a nation has no longer any fixed principle to go by, when the minds of her leaders are at sea on all great religious and moral questions, when the people openly deny the right of the few to rule, when a fabric, raised altogether on aristocracy, finds the substratum giving way, and democratic ideas seated even upon the summit of the edifice, there must be, as is said, "a rattling of old bones," and a shaking of the skeleton of what was a body.

How long, then, will the mock stability established by the deep wisdom of England's renowned statesmen have stood? A century or two of dazzling material prosperity succeeded by long ages of woe, such as the writer of the "Battle of Dorking," with all his imagination, could not find power enough to describe; for no Prussian, or any other foreign army, will bring that catastrophe about, but the breath of popular fury.

But our purpose is not to utter prophecies--rather to rehearse facts already accomplished.

England, then, was the first to feel the shock of the earthquake which was to overthrow the old stability of Europe. It is known how Germany has ever since been a scene of continual wars, dynastic changes, and territorial confusion. What evils have not the wars of the present century brought upon her! Yet, owing to the phlegmatic disposition, one might call it the stolidity of the majority of Germans, the disturbances have been so far external, and the lower masses of society have scarcely been agitated, except by the first rude explosion of Protestantism, and the sudden patriotic enthusiasm of young plebeians, in 1814. But mark the suddenness with which, in 1848, all the thrones of Germany fell at once under the mere breath of what is called "the people!" It is almost a trite thing to say that, where religion no longer exists, there no longer is security or peace.

Impartial travellers, Americans chiefly, have observed of late that, in certain parts of France, there is, in truth, very little religious feeling; while in all Protestant Germany, particularly in that belonging to Prussia, there is none at all. How long, then, is the "new Germanic Empire," so loudly trumpeted at Versailles, and afterward so gloriously celebrated at Berlin, without the intervention of any religion whatever, likely to stand? How long? Can it exist till the end of this century? He would be a bold prophet who could confidently say, "Yes."

As to France, formerly the steadiest of all nations, so deeply attached to her dynasty of eight hundred years, although some of her kings were little worthy true affection; many of whose citizens have been born in houses a thousand years old, from families whose names went back to the darkness of heroic times; which was once so retentive of her old memories, living in her traditions, her former deeds of glory, even in the monuments raised in honor of her kings, her great captains, her illustrious citizens; which was chiefly devoted to her time- honored religion, mindful that she was born on the day of the baptism of Clovis; that she grew up during the Crusades; that a virgin sent by Heaven saved her from the yoke of the stranger; that, on attaining her full maturity, it was religion which chiefly ennobled her; and that her greatest poets, orators, literary men, respected and honored religion as the basis of the state, and, by their immortal masterpieces, threw a halo around Catholicism--France, which still retains in her external appearance something of her old steadiness and immutability, so that to the eye of a stranger, who sees her for the first time, solidity is the word which comes naturally to his mind, as expressive of every thing around him, has only the look of what she was in her days of greatness, and on the surface of the earth there is not to-day a more unsteady, shaky, insecure spot, scarcely worthy of being chosen by a nomad Tartar as a place wherein to pitch his tent for the night, and hurry off at the first appear-ance of the rising sun on the morrow. Can the shifting sands of Libya, the ever-shaking volcanic mountains of equatorial America, the rapidly-forming coral islands of the southern seas, give an idea of that fickleness, constant agitation, and unceasing clamor for change, which have made France a by-word in our days? Who of her children can be sure that the house he is building for himself will ever be the dwelling of his son; that the city he lives in to-day will tomorrow acknowledge him as a member of its community? Who can be certain that the constitution of the whole state may not change in the night, and he wake the next day to find himself an outlaw and a fugitive?

It is a lamentable fact that for the last hundred years a great nation has been reduced to such a state of insecurity, that no one dares to think of the future, though all have repudiated the past, and thus every thing is reduced for them to the present fleeting moment.

And what is likely to be the future destiny of a nation of forty million souls, when their present state is such, and such the uncertainty of their dearest interests? They are unwilling to quit the soil; for they have lost all power of expansion by sending colonies to foreign shores; it is difficult for them to take a real interest in their own soil, for the great moving spring of interest is broken up by the total want of security. May God open their eyes to their former folly; for the folly was all of their own making! They have allowed themselves to be thus thoroughly imbued with this revolutionary spirit--the first revolution they hailed with enthusiasm; when they saw it become stained with frightful horrors, they paused a moment, and were on the point of acknowledging their error; but scribblers and sophists came to show them that it failed in being a glorious and happy one only because it was not complete; another and then another, and another yet, would finish the work and make them a great nation. Thus have they become altogether a revolutionary people; and they must abide by the consequences, unless they come at last to change their mind.

But the worst has not been said. This terrible example, instead of proving a warning to nations, has, on the contrary, drawn nearly all of them into the same boiling vortex. England and France have led the whole European world captive: people ask for a government different to the one they have; revolution is the consequence, and, with the entry of the revolutionary spirit, good-by to all stability and security. Let Italy and Spain bear witness if this is not so.

And the great phenomenon of the age is the collecting of all those revolutionary particles into one compact mass, arranged and preordained by some master-spirits of evil, who would be leaders not of a state or nation only, but of a universal republic embracing first Europe, and then the world. So we hear to-day of the Internationalists receiving in their "congresses" deputies not only from all the great European centres, not only from both ends of America, which is now Europeanized, but from South Africa, from Australia, New Zealand, from countries which a few years back were still in quiet possession of a comparatively few aborigines.

To come back, then, to the point from which we started, it is in this revolutionary spirit, in those conspiracies for revolutions to come, that some Irishmen set their hopes for the regeneration of their country. It would be well to remind them of the sayings of our Lord: "Can men gather grapes from thorns?" "By their fruits ye shall know them."

Let the Irish who are truly devoted to their country reflect well on the kind of men they would have as allies. What has Ireland in common with these men? If they know Ireland at all, they detest her because of her Catholicism; and, if Ireland knows them, she cannot but distrust and abominate them.

It has seemed a decree of kind Providence that all attempts at rebellion on her part undertaken with the hope of such help, have so far not only been miserable failures, but most disgracefully miscarried and been spent in air, leaving only ridicule and contempt for the originators of and partakers in the plots.

If the vast and unholy scheme which is certainly being organized, and which is spreading its fatal branches in all directions, should ever succeed, it could not but result in the most frightful despotism ever contemplated by men. Ireland in such an event would be the infinitesimal part of a chaotic system worthy of Antichrist for head.

But we are confident that such a scheme cannot succeed and come to be realized, unless indeed it enter for a short period into the designs of an avenging God, who has promised not to destroy mankind again by another flood, but assured us by St. Peter that he will purify it by fire.

As a mere design of man, intended for the regeneration of humanity and the new creation of an abnormal order of things, it cannot possibly succeed, because it is opposed to the nature of men, among whom as a whole there can be no perfect unity of external government and internal organization, owing to the infinite variety of which we spoke at the beginning, which is as strong in human beings as elsewhere. No other body than the Catholic Church can hope to adapt itself to all human races, and govern by the same rules all the children of Adam. The decree issued of old from the mouth of God is final, and will last as long as the earth itself. It is contained in Moses' Canticle:

"When the Most High divided the nations, when he separated the sons of Adam, he appointed the bounds of each people, according to the number of the children of Israel," or, as the Hebrew text has it, "He fixed the limits of each people." On this passage Aben Ezra remarks that interpreters understand the text as alluding to the dispersion of nations (Genesis xi.). Those interpreters, were clearly right, although only Jewish rabbies.

When God deprived man of the unity of language, he took away at the same time the possibility of unity of institutions and government; and it will be as hard for men to defeat that design of Providence as for Julian the apostate to rebuild the Temple of Jerusalem, of which our Saviour had declared that there should not remain "a stone upon a stone."

But, though the monstrous scheme cannot ultimately succeed, it can and will produce untold evils to human society. By alluring workmen and other people of the lower class, it draws into the intricate folds of conspiracy, dark projects, and universal disorder, an immense array of human beings, whom the revolutionary spirit had not yet, or at least had scarcely, touched; it undermines and disturbs society in its lowest depths and widest-spread foundations, since the lower class always has been and still is the most numerous, including by far the great majority of men. It consequently renders the stability of order more difficult, if not absolutely impossible; it opens up a new era of revolutions, more disastrous than any yet known; for, as has already been remarked, and it should be well borne in mind, in order that the whole extent of the evil in prospect may be seen, so far, all the agitations in Europe, all the convulsions which have rendered our age so unlike any previous one, and productive of so many calamities, private as well as public, have been almost exclusively confined to the middle classes, and should be considered only as a reaction of the simple bourgeoisie against the aristocratic class. Those agitations and convulsions are only the necessary consequence of the secular opposition, existing from the ninth and tenth centuries and those immediately following, between the strictly feudal nobility, which arrogated to itself all prerogatives and rights, and the more numerous class of burghers, set on the lower step of the social ladder. These latter wanted, not so much to get up to the level of their superiors, as to bring them down to their own, and even precipitate them into the abyss of nothingness below. They have almost succeeded; and the prestige of noble blood has passed away, perhaps forever, in spite of Vico's well-known theory. But the now triumphant burgher in his turn sees the dim mass, lost in the darkness and indistinctness of the lowest pool of humanity, rising up grim and horrible out of the abyss, hungry and fierce and not to be pacified, to threaten the new-modelled aristocracy of money with a worse fate than that it inflicted upon the old nobility.

And, to render the prospect more appalling, the chief means, which so eminently aided the bourgeoisie to take their position, namely, the widespread influence of secret societies, whose workings even lately have astonished the world by the facile and apparently inexplicable revolutions effected in a few days, are now in the full possession of the lower classes, who, no longer rude and unintelligent, but possessed of leaders of experience and knowledge, can also powerfully work those mighty engines of destruction.

In the presence of those past, present, and coming revolutions, the face of heaven entirely clouded, the presence of God absolutely ignored, his rights over mankind denied, the designs of his Providence openly derided, and man, pretending to decide his own destiny by his own unaided efforts, scornfully rejecting any obligation to a superior power, not looking on high for assistance, but taking only for his guide his pretended wisdom, his unbounded pride, and his raging passions; such is now our world.

Is Ireland to launch herself on that surging sea of wild impulse, in whose depths lies destruction and whose waves never kiss a peaceful coast? When she claimed and exercised a policy of her own, she wisely persisted in not mixing herself up with the troubles of Europe, content to enjoy happiness in her own way, on her ocean-bound island, she thanked God that no portion of her little territory touched any part of the Continent of Europe, stretching out vainly toward her shores. So she stood when, under God, she was mistress of her own destiny. If ever she thought of Europe, it was only to send her missionaries to its help, or to receive foreign youth in her large schools which were open to all, where wisdom was imparted without restriction and without price. But to follow the lead of European theorists and vendors of so-called wisdom and science; to originate new schemes of pretended knowledge, or place herself in the wake of bold adventurers on the sea of modern inventions, she was ever steadfast in her refusal.

And now that her autonomy is almost once again within her grasp, now that she can carve out a destiny of her own, would she hand over the guidance of herself to men who know nothing of her, who have only heard of her through the reports of her enemies, and who will scarcely look at her if she is foolish enough to ask to be admitted within their ranks?

Every one who wishes well to Ireland ought to thank God that so far few indeed, if any, of her children have ever joined in the plots and conspiracies of modern times, and that in this last scheme just referred to, not one of them, probably, has fully engaged himself. In the late horrors of the Paris Commune, no Irish name could be shown to have been implicated, and, when the contrary was asserted, a simple denial was sufficient to set the question at rest. Let them so continue to refrain from sullying their national honor by following the lead of men with whom they have nothing in common.

After all, the great thing which the Irish desire is, with the entire possession of their rights, to enjoy that peace and security in their own island, which they relish so keenly when they find it on foreign shores. But no peace or security is possible with the attempt to subvert all human society by wild and impracticable theories, in which human and divine laws are alike set at naught. Further words are unnecessary on this subject, as the simple good sense and deep religious feeling of the Irish will easily preserve them from yielding to such temptation.

Yet, a last consideration seems worthy of note. When, later on, we present our views, and explain by what means we consider that the happiness of the Irish nation may be secured, and its mission fulfilled, a more fitting opportunity will be presented of speaking of the ways by which Providence has already led them through former difficulties, and the consideration of those holy designs and past favors may enable us better to understand what may be hoped and attempted in the future.

Here it is enough to observe that, in whatever progress the Irish have made of late in obtaining a certain amount of their rights, insurrection, revolution, plots, and the working of secret societies condemned by the Church, have absolutely gone for nothing, and the little of it all, in which Irishmen have indulged, really formed one of the main obstacles to the enjoyment of what they had already obtained, and to the securing of a greater amount for the future.

There is no doubt that revolutions abroad and dangers at home have been the greatest inducements to England to relax her grasp and change her tyrannical policy toward Ireland. The success of the revolt of the North American colonies was the main cause of the volunteer movement of 1782, and of the concessions then temporarily granted. The fearful upheaval of revolutionary France, which filled the English heart with a wholesome dread, was also a great means of obtaining for Ireland the concession of being no longer treated as though it were a lair of wild beasts or a nest of outlaws. The act of Catholic Emancipation in 1829 was certainly granted in view of immediate revolutions ready to burst forth, one of which did explode in France in the year following. But, in all those outbursts of popular fury, Ireland never joined; and if she found in them new ground for hope, if she awaited anxiously the anticipated result turning in her favor, she never took any active part whatever in them. She only relied on God, who always knows how to draw good from evil; she, however, profited by them, and saw her shackles fall off of themselves, and herself brought back, step by step, to liberty.

But so soon as any body of Irishmen entered into a scheme of a similar nature, imitating the secret plottings and deeds of European revolutionists, Ireland never gained a single inch of ground, nor reaped the slightest advantage from such attempts. On the contrary, ridicule, contempt, increase of burdens, penalties, and harsh treatment, were the only result which ever came from them, and, worst of all, no one pitied the victims of all those foolish enterprises. There is no need of entering here into details. The first of those attempts failed long ago; the last is still on record, and cannot be yet said to belong to past history.

RESURRECTION.-EMIGRATION

TO the eye of a keen beholder, Ireland to-day presents the appearance of a nation entering upon a new career. She is emerging from a long darkness, and opening again to the free light of heaven. Whoever compares her present position with that she occupied a century ago, cannot fail to be struck with wonder no less at the change in her than at the agencies which brought that change about. And when to this is added the further reflection that she is still young, though sprung from so old-an-origin-young in feeling, in buoyancy, in aspirations, in purity and simplicity-the conclusion forces itself upon the mind that a high destiny is in store for her, and that God proposes a long era of prosperity and active life to an ancient nation which is only now beginning to live.

In such cases, whether it be a people or an individual, which is entering upon its life, crowds of advisers are ever to be found ready to display their wisdom and lay down the plans whose adoption will infallibly bring prosperity and happiness to the individual or people in question.

Ireland, to-day, suffers from no lack of wise counsellors and ardent well-wishers. Unfortunately, their various projects do not always harmonize; indeed, they are sometimes contradictory, and, as their number is by no means small, the only difficulty is where to choose which road the nation should take in order to march in the right direction.

In entering upon this portion of our work, where we have to deal with actual questions of the day, and if not to draw the horoscope of the future, at least to give utterance to our ideas for the promotion of the welfare of the nation, we shall appear to come under the same catalogue of advisers, fully persuaded, with the rest, that our advice is the right, our voice the only one worthy of attention.

Our purpose is far humbler; our reflections take another shape; we merely say

During the last hundred years, Ireland has changed wonderfully for the better; and although the old wounds are not yet quite healed up, though they still smart, though she is still poor and disconsolate, and her trials and afflictions far from being ended; nevertheless, though sorely tried, Providence has been kind to her. Many of her rights have been restored, and she is no longer the slave of hard task-masters. When she now speaks, her voice is no longer met by the gibe and sneer, but with a kind of awe akin to respect, her enemies seeming to feel instinctively that it is the voice of a nation which no longer may be safely despised.

This fact being indisputable, the conviction forces itself upon us that her improved condition is mainly, perhaps solely, due to Providence; and that the career upon which she has entered, and which she is now pursuing with a clear determination of her own, has been marked out, designed, and already partially run, under the guidance of that God for whom alone she has suffered, and who never fails in his own good time to dry up the tears shed for his sake, and crown his martyrs with victory.

Our task is merely to examine the progress made, the manner of its making, the direction toward which it tends, with the aim, if possible, of adding to its speed. We have no new plan to offer, no gratuitous advice to give. The plan is already sketched out--God has sketched it; and our only aim is to see how man may cooperate with designs far higher than any proposed by human wisdom.

The first thing that strikes us, standing on the verge of this new region, opening out dimly but gloriously before our eyes, is one great fact which is plain to all; which is greater than all England's concessions to Ireland, more fruitful of happy consequences, not alone to the latter country itself, but to the world at large; a fact which is the strongest proof of the vitality of the Irish race, which now begins to win for it respect by bringing forth its real strength, a strength to astonish the world; which began feebly when the evils of the country were at their height, but has gone on constantly increasing until it has now grown to extraordinary proportions; and which instead of, as their enemies fondly supposed, wresting Ireland from the Irish, has made their claim to the native soil securer than ever, by spreading strong supporters of their rights through the world. This great fact is emigration.

At this moment, Irishmen are scattered abroad over the earth. In many regions they have numbers, and form compact bodies. Wherever this occurs, they acquire a real power in the land which they have made their new home. That power is certainly intended by Almighty God to be used wisely, prudently, but actively and energetically; not only for the good of those who have been thus transplanted in a new soil, but also for the good of the mother-country which they cannot, if they would, forget. How can they utilize for such a purpose the power so recently acquired, the wealth, the influence, the consideration they enjoy, in their new country? How may such a course benefit the land of their nativity as of their origin? These are important questions; they are not airy theories, but rise up clearly from a standing and stupendous fact. The turning their power of expansion to its right use, the reproduction with Christian aim of that old power of expansion peculiar to the Celtic race three thousand years ago, is what we call the first true issue of the Irish question:- Emigration and its Possible Effects.

In order to judge with proper understanding of the prospective effects of Irish emigration, it is fitting to study the fact in all its bearings; to examine the origin and various phases of the mighty movement, the religious direction it has invariably taken, the immediate good it has produced, and the special consideration of the vast proportions which it has finally assumed. The task may be a long one; but it is certainly important and interesting; and it is only after the details of it have been thoroughly sifted that one may be in a position to judge rightly of the aid it has already furnished, and which it is destine to furnish in a still greater degree, to the uprising of the nation.

The movement originated with the Reformation. It began with the flight of a few of the nobility in the reign of Henry VIII.; their number was increased under Elizabeth, and grew to larger proportions still under James I.; but a far greater number, sufficient to make a very sensible diminution in the population of the country, was doomed to exile by Cromwell and the Long Parliament. It then became a compulsory banishment.

The next following movement on a large scale occurred after the surrender of Kilkenny, when the Irish commanders, Colonel Fitzpatrick, Clanricard, and others, could obtain no better terms than emigration to any foreign country then at peace with England. The Irish troops were eagerly caught up by the various European monarchs, so highly were their services esteemed. The number that thus left their native land, many of them never to return, amounted, according to well-informed writers, to forty thousand men, of noble blood most of them, many of the first nobility of the land, and almost all children of the old race. The details of this first exodus are to be found in the pages of many modern authors, particularly in Mr. Prendergast's "Cromwellian Settlement."

The example thus given was followed on many occasions. The Treaty of Limerick, October 3, 1691, gave the garrison under Saarsfield liberty to join the army of King William or enter the service of France. Mr. A.M. O'Sulli-van has given a spirited sketch of the making of their choice by the heroic garrison as it defiled out of the city:

"On the morning of the 5th of October the Irish regiments were to make their choice between exile for life or service in the armies of their conqueror. At each end of a gently-rising ground beyond the suburbs were planted on one side the royal standard of France, and on the other that of England. It was agreed that the regiments, as they marched out with all the honors of war, drums beating, colors flying, and matches lighted, should, on reaching the spot, wheel to the left or to the right, beneath that flag under which they elected to serve. At the head of the Irish marched the Foot Guards, the finest regiment in the service, fourteen hundred strong. All eyes were fixed on this splendid body of men. On they came, amid breathless silence and acute suspense; for well both the English and Irish generals knew that the choice of the first regiment would powerfully influence all the rest. The Guards marched up to the critical spot, and in a body wheeled to the colors of France, barely seven men turning to the English side! Ginckle, we are told, was greatly agitated as he witnessed the proceeding. The next regiment, however (Lord Iveagh's), marched as unanimously to the Williamite banner, as did also portions of two others. But the bulk of the Irish army defiled under fleur-de-lys of King Louis, only one thousand and forty-six, out of nearly fourteen thousand men, preferring the service of England."

From that time out a large number of the Irish nobility and gentry continued to enlist under French, Spanish, or Austrian colors; and the several Irish brigades became celebrated all over Europe until the end of the eighteenth century. It is said by l'abbe McGeohegan that six hundred thousand Irishmen perished in the armies of France alone. The abbe is generally very accurate, and from his long residence in France had every means at his disposal of arriving at the truth. Some pretend that double the number enlisted in foreign service. There is no doubt that in all a million men left the island to take service under the banners of Catholic sovereigns, and it is needless to dwell on the bravery and devotion of those men whom the persecution of an unwise and cruel Protestant government drove out of Ireland during the eighteenth century-it is needless to dwell upon it, for the record is known to the world.

Without following the fortunes of the Irish brigades, the history of one of which, that in the service of France, has been given us in the very interesting and valuable narrative of John R. O'Callaghan-its various fortunes and final dissolution at the breaking out of the French republic, when the English Government was glad to receive back the scattered remnants of it-the question which bears most on our present subject is: What was the occupation of those Irishmen on the Continent when not actually engaged in war? What service did their voluntary or compulsory exile do their native country? Was that long emigration of a century productive of something out of which Providence may have drawn good?

The first departure of a few under Hugh O'Neill and Hugh O'Donnell had already spread the name of Ireland through Spain, Italy, and Belgium. The reports of the numerous English spies, employed to dog their steps and watch their movements, reports some of which have been finally brought to light, conclusively prove that most of the exiles held honorable positions in Spain and Portugal, at Valladolid and Lisbon, where the O'Sullivans and O'Driscolls lived; at the very court of Spain, or in the Spanish navy, like the Bourkes and the Cavanaghs.

In Flanders, under the Austrian archdukes, were stationed the McShanes, on the Groyne; the Daniells at Antwerp; the posterity of the earls themselves with that of their former retinue. All held rank in the Austrian army, and even in times of peace were occupied in thinking of possible entanglements whereby they might serve their country, while they made the Irish name honored and respected all over that rich land. In Italy, at Naples, Leghorn, Florence, and Rome, in the great centres of the peninsula, the same thing was taking place, and there, at least, the calumnies, everywhere so industriously circulated about Ireland, could not penetrate, or, if they did, only to be received with scorn.

But, when the next emigration, at the end of the Cromwellian and Williamite wars, landed forty thousand soldiers, and twelve thousand more a few years afterward, on the European Continent, these armed men proved to the nations, by their bravery, their deep attachment to their religion, their perfect honor and generosity, that the people from which a persecuting power had driven them forth could not be composed of the outlaws and blood-thirsty cutthroats which the reports of their enemies would make them. How striking and permanent must have been the effect produced on impartial minds by the contrast between the aspect of the reality and the base fabrications of skilfully-scattered rumor!

And be it borne in mind that those men founded families in the countries where they settled; as well as those who continued to flock thither during the whole of the eighteenth century. They carried about with them, in their very persons even, the history of Ireland's wrongs; and the mere sight of them was enough to interest all with whom they came in contact in favor of their country. Hence the esteem and sympathy which Ireland and her people have always met with in France, where the calumnies and ridicule lavished on them could never find an entrance.

It would be a great error to imagine that they were to be found only in the camp or in the garrisons of cities. They made themselves a home in their new country, and their children entered upon all the walks of life opened up to the citizens of the country in which they resided. Thus, at least, the name of Ireland did not die out altogether during that age of gloom, when their native isle was only the prison of the race, where it was chained down in abject misery, out of the sight of the world, the life of it stifled out in the deep dungeon of oblivion.

In all honorable professions they became distinguished-in the Church and in trade, as in the army. Thus, speaking only of France, an Irishman-Edgeworth-was chosen by Louis XVI. to prepare him for death and stand by him during his last ordeal of ignominy; another-Lally Tollendal-would have wrested India from England, if his ardent temperament had not brought him enemies where he ought to have met with friends; another yet-Walsh-during the American War, employed the wealth acquired by trade, in sending cruisers against the English to American waters.

It would take long pages to record what those noble exiles accomplished for the good of their country and religion, quite apart from the heroism they displayed on battle-fields, and their fidelity to principle during times of peace. Their very presence in foreign countries was, perhaps, the best protest against the enslavement of their own. They showed by their bearing that they owed no allegiance to England, and that brute force could never establish right. By identifying themselves with the nations which offered them hospitality and a new right of citizenship, they proved to the world that their native isle could be governed by native citizens. Their honorable conduct and successful activity in every pursuit of life showed that, as they were capable of governing themselves, so likewise could they claim self-government for their country.

The moral condition of France during the eighteenth century, and the depths of corruption into which the higher class sank in so short a time, are known to all. To the honor of the Irish nobility and gentry then in France, not a single Irish name is to be met with in that long list of noble names which have disgraced that page of French history. Not in the luxurious bowers and palaces of Louis XV. were they to be found, but on the battle-fields of Dettingen and Fontenoy. It was a Scotchman- Law-who infected the higher circles of the natives with the rage for speculation, and the folly of gambling in paper. It was an Italian-Cagliostro-who traded on the superstitious credulity of men who had lost their faith. It was an Englishman-Lord Derwentwater-and another Scotchman-Ramsay-who, by the introduction of the first Masonic Lodge into France, opened the floodgates of future revolutions.

Among those of foreign birth, no Irishman was found in France to contribute to the corruption of the nation, and give his aid to set agoing that long era of woe not yet ended.

And needless is it to add that never is one of them mentioned, among those who were so active in propagating that broad infidelity peculiar to that age. If a few of them shared to some extent in the general delusion, and took part with the vast multitude in the insane derision, then so fashionable, of every thing holy, their number was small indeed, and none of them acquired in that peculiar line, the celebrity which crowned so many others. -the Grimms, the Gallianis, and later on the Paines, the Cloots, and other foreigners.

As a body, the Irish remained faithful to the Church of their fathers, honoring her by their conduct, and their respectful demeanor toward holy names and holy things. Eventually they, in common with all Frenchmen, had to share in the misfortunes, brought on by the subversion of all the former guiding principles; but, though sharing in the punishment, they took no part in the great causes which called it down.

These few words will suffice for the emigration of the Irish nobility, and its effects on foreign countries; as well as Ireland itself.

But another class of noblemen had emigrated to the Continent side by side with those of whom we have just spoken; namely, bishops, priests, monks, and learned men. England would not suffer the Catholic clergy in Ireland; she was particularly careful not to allow Irish youth the benefit of any but a Protestant education. Irish clergymen were compelled to fly and open houses of study abroad. Their various colleges in Spain, France, Belgium, and Italy, are well known; they have already been referred to, and it is not necessary to enlarge on the subject. But, though mention has been made of the renown thus acquired by Irishmen then residing on the Continent, it is fitting to speak of them again in their character of emigrants.

They took upon themselves the noble task of making the literature and the history of their nation known to all people; and in so doing they have preserved a rich literature which must otherwise have perished.

What was their situation on the Continent? They had been driven by persecution from their country, sometimes in troops of exiles to be cast on some remote shore; sometimes escaping singly and in disguise, they went out alone to end their lives under a foreign sky. Behind them they left the desolate island; their friends bowed down in misery, their enemies triumphant and in full power. The convents, where they had spent their happiest days, were either demolished or turned to vile uses; their churches desecrated; heresy ruling the land, truth compelled to be silent. All the harrowing details given by the "Prophet of Lamentations" might be applied to their beloved country.

True, they could find peace and rest among those who offered them their hospitality; at least, the worship of God would be free and untrammelled there. But it was not the place of their birth, where they had received their first education; it was not the mission intrusted to them when they consecrated their lives to God. They would bear another language, see around them different manners, begin life anew, perhaps, in their old age.

What a contrast to their former hopes! What a sad ending to the closing days of their life!

Nevertheless, they might be of use to their countrymen. It was not for them now to convert Europe, and preach Christianity to barbarous tribes, as did their ancestors of old. The world which received them was languishing with excess of refined civilization; corruption had entered in, and was fast destroying it; and they could scarcely hope to hold it back from its downward career. But, at least, they might open houses for the reception of the youth of their own country, where they should receive an education according to the teachings of the true Church, which was denied them at home. So they went to Salamanca, to Valladolid, to Paris, Louvain, Douai, Rheims, Rome, wherever there was hope or possibility of directing Irish youth in the ways of true piety and learning.

The labors to which they devoted themselves, though unknown to posterity, were of great utility at the time. They saw the youth they educated grow up under their care; when their studies were concluded, they sent them to labor in the ministry among their countrymen; they heard of them from time to time of their arduous life, the dangers they braved, the many persecutions they underwent, their imprisonment when captured, their conviction, torture often, and death by martyrdom. And thus, through the exertions of those emigrant monks and priests, the true Gospel was preached in Ireland, and the faith of the people kept alive and strong.

A few of them chose another path, and consecrated the remainder of their days to literary labors, which have shed down on their persecuted country a halo of immortal glory.

Some Franciscan friars (two of them the brothers O'Cleary) had already begun this work in the island itself, when driven from their quiet homes to take refuge in the obscure "convents," that is, out-of-the-way farm-houses mentioned before, where they were received and hidden away from the world. The literature of Ireland was fast perishing; the rage of their enemies being as violently directed against their books as against their houses and churches. Precious manuscripts were every day given to the flames and wantonly destroyed, seemingly for the mere pleasure of destruction. A very few years would have sufficed to render the former history of the country a perfect blank. In no spot of the same size on earth had so many interesting books ever been written and treasured up; but before long there would remain no friars on the island to preserve them, no library to contain them, no one to care for them in the least. The brothers O'Cleary saw this with dismay; and they, with two companions, became known as the "Four Masters." They interested in their work the faithful Irish who still retained possession of a farm, or a cabin with a few acres of ground attached; the men, and women even, were to search the country round for every volume concealed or preserved, for every parchment and relic, for vellum manuscripts, even a stray solitary page, did one remain alone. The annals of Ireland were thus saved by the literary patriotism of poor and unknown peasants. All that remains of Irish lore was collected together in the rural convent of the O'Clearys, and an ardent flame was enkindled which lasted the whole of the seventeenth century.

To this initiative must be referred the subsequent labors of Ward, Colgan, Lynch, and others; herculean labors truly, which have enabled antiquarians of our days to resume the thread, so near being snapped, of that long and tangled web of history wherein is woven all that can interest the patriot and the Christian of the island.

Knowing the position in which the writers found themselves, it is astonishing to see what they wrote. It was not a work of fancy to which their pens were devoted: A strong, feeling heart and an active imagination were certainly theirs; but of little service could either prove to them in the ungrateful task of collecting manuscripts, classifying, reading them through, ascertaining their age and authenticity, and finally using them for the purpose of preserving the annals and hagiography of the nation.

The large libraries they found in the various cities which received them could be of little use to them. They had first to collect their own libraries, to summon their authorities from distant lands; many books were to be procured from Ireland itself. With what precautions! It was real, (though lawful) smuggling; for the export of Irish books was not only under tariff, but strictly prohibited; the mere sight of them was more hateful to a British custom-house officer of those days than the sight of a crucifix to a Japanese official of Nagasaki. It would be interesting to know the various stratagems devised to conceal them, tarry them away, and convey them triumphantly to Louvain, Paris, or Rome.

But Ireland was not the only repository of Irish books. Many letters, official documents, copies of old MSS., interesting relics of antiquity, had been gathered ages before and during all the intervening time, in convents, churches, houses of education, on the Continent, along the Rhine chiefly. It is said that even to-day the richest mines of yet unexplored lore of this character are scattered along both sides of the great German river. The frequent movements of various armies, the sieges of cities, the horrors of war which have raged there constantly from the days of Arminius and Varro down, have not destroyed every thing, could not exhaust the rich deposit of Irish manuscripts there concealed. But the labor of striking the mine!-of' opening those musty pages falling to pieces between the fingers and leaving in the hand nothing but illegible fragments of half-blackened parchment; and the further labor of deciphering them, of discovering what they speak about, and if they are likely to prove useful to the purposes.

It is needless to descant on such a theme. It is impossible to give any true idea of the literary labors of those men, without having seen and perused their huge folios, many of which have not yet been published to the world. Poor Colgan could give us little more than his "Trial Thaumaturga and that was only destined to form the portal of the edifice he purposed erecting as a shrine to the memory of the whole host of saints nurtured in the island-the Acta Sanctorum Hiberniae

The grand idea, which first germinated in the minds of those men, expanded afterward in others under circumstances more favorable. Did they not suggest to Bollandus and his fellows the thought whose realization has immortalized them?

In tasks such as these were the Irish emigrant monks of the time employed.

There was yet another class of involuntary Irish exiles those shipped to the "plantations" of America, to the 11 tobacco" and 11 sugar" islands, to Virginia and Jamaica, but principally to the Barbadoes. The origin of this new kind of emigration, already touched upon, is worthy of the times and of the men who called it forth.

After forty thousand soldiers had been allowed, or rather compelled, by Cromwell to enlist in foreign armies, it was found that many had left behind them their wives and children. What was to be done with these "widows" whose husbands and numerous offspring were still living? They could not be sent to Coff as women, with children only, could not be expected to "plant" that desolate province; they could not be expected to "plant" that desolate province; they could not be allowed to remain in their native place, as the decree had gone forth that all the Irish were to "transplant" or be transported: it would have been inconvenient and inexcusable to do what had been so often done in the war-massacre them in cold blood-as the war was over.

To relieve the government of this difficulty, Bristol merchants, and merchants probably from other English cities, trading with the new British colonies of North America, thought it a providential opening for a great profit to accrue to the soils of the benighted Irish women and children, and likely at the same time to add something to their own purses and those of their friends, the West India planters.

It was only under Elizabeth that permanent colonies were sent out from England to the continent and islands of the New World. The Cavaliers of Virginia are as well known in the South as the Puritans of New England in the North. This last colony dated only from the time of the Stuart dynasty. The great question for all those transatlantic establishments was that of labor; but in the South it was more difficult of solution than in the North, where Europeans could work in the fields, a thing scarcely possible in the tropics. The natives as we know, were first employed in the South by the Spaniards, and soon succumbed to the demands of European rapacity.

In the West Indies, natives of two different races existed: the soft and delicate Indian of Hayti and Cuba, and the ferocious Caribs of many other islands. The first race soon disappeared; the other continued refractory, indomitable, choosing to perish rather than labor; and some remnants of it still remain, saved by the Catholic Church. As yet, African negroes had not been conveyed there in sufficient numbers.

A brilliant thought struck the minds, at once pious, active, and business-like, of those above-mentioned Bristol merchants-a thought which was the doom of thousands of Irish women and children.

The names of a few of those Bristol firms deserve to be handed down. Those of Messrs. James Sellick and Leader, Mr. Robert Yeomans, Mr.

Joseph Lawrence, Dudley North, and John Johnson, are furnished by Mr. Prendergast, who tells us that-

"The Commissioners of Ireland under Cromwell gave them orders upon the governors of garrisons to deliver them prisoners of war .... upon masters of work-houses, to hand over to them the destitute under their care, 'who were of an age to labor,' or, if women, those 'who were marriageable, and not past breeding;' and gave directions to all in authority, to seize those who had no visible means of livelihood, and deliver them to these agents of the Bristol merchants; in execution of which latter directions, Ireland must have exhibited scenes in every part like the slave-hunts in Africa."

A contract was signed on September 14, 1653, by the Com missioners of Ireland and Messrs. Sellick and Leader, "to supply them (the merchants) with two hundred and fifty women of the Irish nation, above twelve years and under the age, of forty-five."

The fate reserved for the human cattle, as they must have been looked upon by the godly gentlemen who bartered over them, may be well imagined. It is calculated that, in four years, those English firms of slave-dealers had shipped six thousand and four hundred Irish men and women, boys and maidens, to the British colonies of North America.

The age requisite for the females who were thus shipped off may be noted; the boys and men were not to be under twelve or over fifty. These latter were condemned to the task of tilling the soil in a climate where the negro only can work and live. As all the cost to their masters was summed up in the expense of transportation, they were not induced to spare them, even by the consideration of the high price which, it is said, caused the modern slave-owners of America to treat their slaves with what might be called a commercial humanity. It is easy to imagine, then, the life led by so many young men forced to work in the open fields, under a tropical sun. How long that life lasted, we do not know; as their masters, on whom they entirely depended, were interested in keeping the knowledge of their fate a secret. It is well understood that, when the unfortunate victims, had once left the Irish harbor from which they set sail, no one ever heard of them again; and, if the parents still lived in the old country, they were left to their conjectures as to the probable situation of their children in the new.

Sir William Petty says that "of boys and girls alone"-exclusive, consequently, of men and women-" six thousand were thus transplanted; but the total number of Irish sent to perish in the tobacco-islands, as they were called, was estimated in some Irish accounts at one hundred thousand."

The "Irish accounts" may have been exaggerated, but the English atoned for this by certainly falling below the mark, as is clear from the fact that, according to them, the Commissioners of Ireland required the "supply" for New England alone to come from "the country within twenty miles of Cork, Youghall, Kinsale, Waterford, and Wexford;" that "the hunt lasted four years," and was carried on with such ardor by the agents of many English firms that those men-catchers employed persons "to delude poor people by false pretenses into by-places, and thence they forced them on board their ships; that for money sake they were found to have enticed and forced women from their husbands, and children from their parents, who maintained them at school; and they had not only dealt so with the Irish, but also with the English." For this reason, the order was revoked, and the "hunt" forbidden.

When agents were reduced to such straits after the government had used force, as Henry Cromwell acknowledged, the large extent of country mentioned above must have been well scoured and depopulated; and certainly a far greater number of victims must have been secured by all those means combined than is given in the English accounts. We believe the Irish.

One other source of supply deserves mention. Not only women and children, but priests also, were hunted down and shipped off to the same American plantations; so that persons of every class which is held sacred in the eyes of God and man for its character and helplessness, were compelled to emigrate, or rather to undergo the worst possible fate that the imagination of man can conceive.

In 1656 a general battue for priests took place all over Ireland. The prisons seem to have been filled to overflowing. "On the 3d of May, the governors of the respective precincts were ordered to send them with sufficient guards, from garrison to garrison, to Carrickfergus, to be there put on board of such ships as should sail with the first opportunity to the Barbadoes. One may imagine the sufferings of this toilsome journey by the petition of one of them. Paul Cashin, an aged priest, apprehended at

Maryborough, and sent to Philipstown, on the way to Carrickfergus, there fell desperately sick; and, being also extremely aged, was in danger of perishing in restraint from want of friends and means of relief. On the 27th of August, the commissioners having ascertained the truth of his petition, they ordered him sixpence a day during his sickness, and (in answer, probably, to this poor prisoner's prayer to be saved from transplantation) their order directed that the sixpence should be continued to him in his travel thence (after his recovery) to Carrickfergus, in order to his transplantation to the Barbadoes."-- (Cromwellian Settlement.)

In that burning island of the West Indies, deprived of all means, not only of exercising their ministry among others, but even of practising their religion themselves, of fulfilling their holy obligation of prayer and sacrifice, these victims of such an atrocious persecution were employed as laborers in the fields: their transplantation had cost money, and the money had to be repaid a hundred-fold by the sweat of their brow.

Ship-loads of them had been discharged on the inhospitable shore of that island; each with a high calling which he could no longer carry out; each, therefore, tortured in his soul, with all the sweet or bitter memories of his past life crowding on his mind, and the dreary prospect spreading before him, to the end of his life, of no change from his rude and slavish occupation under the burning sun, hearing no voice but that of the harsh taskmaster; his eyes saddened and his heart sickened by the open and daily spectacle of immorality and woe, with no ending but the grave.

It seems, however, that these holy men found some means of fulfilling their sacred duty as God's ministers, for the inhuman traffic in such slaves as these to the Barbadoes lasted but one year. In 1657 it was decreed that this island should no longer be their place of transportation, but, instead, the desolate isles of Arran, opposite the entrance to the bay of Galway, and the isle of Innisboffin, off the coast of Connemara. Mr. Prendergast thinks that this change of policy in their regard may have been caused by the price of their transportation, which probably mounted to a high aggregate sum. But he must be mistaken. They certainly cost no more than women and children, and their labor in the West Indies surely covered this expense. The reason for the change is more plainly visible in the nature of the site substituted for the Barbadoes as their place of exile. The "holy isles" of Arran and the isle of Innisboffin were then, as now, bare of every thing--almost of inhabitants. The priests could be there kept as in a prison, and, though they might be of no profit to their masters, they could not hear a voice or see a face other than those of their fellow-captives. In the West India islands there existed an already thick population, and the very women and children who had been transported thither before them would be consoled by their ministry, though practised by stealth, and streng-thened in their faith, which might thus have not only been kept alive among them, but spread over the whole country.

Who can say if the faith, preserved among the many Irish living in the island until quite recently, was not owing to their exhortations?

"The first Irish people who found permanent homes in America," says Thomas D'Arcy McGee, "were certain Catholic patriots banished by Oliver Cromwell to Barbadoes. . . . In this island, as in the neighboring Montserrat, the Celtic language was certainly spoken in the last century,[1] and perhaps it is partly attributable to this early Irish colonization, that Barbadoes became 'one of the most populous islands in the world.' At the end of the seventeenth century, it was reported to contain twenty thousand inhabitants."

Although Barbadoes is the chief island concerned in the present considerations, nevertheless nearly all the British colonies then existing in America, received their share of this emigration. Several ship-loads of the exiles were certainly sent to New England, at the very time that New-Englanders were earnestly invited by the British Government to "come and plant Ireland;" Virginia, too, paid probably with tobacco for the young men and maidens sent there as slaves. The "Thurloe State Papers" disclose the fact that one thousand boys and one thousand girls, taken in Ireland by force, were dispatched to Jamaica, lately added to the empire of England by Admiral Penn, father of the celebrated Quaker founder of Pennsylvania.

Thus, then, began the first extensive emigration of the Irish to various parts of British America--a movement quite compulsory, which in our days

---

[1] The Celtic language-- that sure sign of Catholicity--was not only spoken there last century, but is still to-day. The writer himself heard last year (1871), from two young American seamen, who had just returned from a voyage to this island, that the negro porters and white longshoremen who load and unload the ships in the harbor, know scarcely any other language than the Irish, so that often the crews of English vessels can only communicate with them by signs.

has become voluntary, and is productive of the wonders soon to claim our attention.

The involuntary emigration of soldiers and clergymen to the Continent of Europe during the seventeenth and eighteenth centuries, was, as has been seen, the cause of great advantages to Ireland, and became, in the designs of a merciful Providence, a powerful means of drawing good from evil. At first sight, it seems impossible to discover a similar advantage in this other most involuntary emigration to the plantations of America.

A pagan has declared that "there is no spectacle more grateful to the eyes of God than a just man struggling with adversity;" and where, except in the first ages of Christianity, could more innocent victims, and a more cruel persecution, be witnessed?

After the horrors of a civil war, horrors unparalleled perhaps in the annals of modern nations, the children and young people of both sexes are hunted down over an area of several Irish counties, dragged in crowds to the seaports, and there jammed in the holds of small, uncomfortable, slow-going vessels. What those children must have been may be easily imagined from the specimens of the race before us to-day. We do not speak of their beauty and comeliness of form, on which a Greek writer of the age of Pericles might have dilated, and found a subject worthy of his pen; we speak of their moral beauty, their simplicity, purity, love of home, attachment to their family, and God, even in their tenderest age. We meet them scattered over the broad surface of this country--boys and girls of the same race, coming from the same counties, chiefly from sweet Wexford, the beautiful, calm, pious south of Ireland. Who but a monster could think of harming those pure and affectionate creatures, so modest, simple, and ready to trust and confide in every one they meet? And what could be said of those maidens, now so well known in this New World, of whom to speak is to praise, whom to see is to admire? Such were the victims selected by the Bristol firms, by "Lord" Henry Cromwell, Governor-General of Ireland, or by Lord Thurloe, secretary and mouth-piece of the "Protector." They were to be violently torn from their parents and friends, from every one they knew and loved, to be condemned, after surviving the horrible ocean-passage of those days, the boys to work on sugar and tobacco plantations, the girls to lead a life of shame in the harems of Jamaica planters!

Such of them as were sent North, were to be distributed among the "saints" of New England, to be esteemed by the said "saints" as "idolaters," "vipers," "young reprobates," just objects of "the wrath of God;" or, if appearing to fall in with their new and hard task-masters, to be greeted with words of dubious praise as "brands snatched from the burning," "vessels of reprobation," destined, perhaps, by a due imitation of the "saints," to become some day "vessels of election," in the mean time to be unmercifully scourged by both master and mistress with the "besom of righteousness" probably, at the slightest fault or mistake.

Such was the sorrowful prospect held out to them; there was no possibility of escape, no hope of going back to the only country they loved. In the South they soon, very soon, sank into an obscure grave. In the North a prolonged life was only a prolongation of torment. For, who among them could ever think of becoming a "convert?" They had been taken from their island-home when over twelve years of age; they had already received from their mothers and hunted priests a religious education, which happily could never be effaced; they were to bury in their hearts all their lives long the conviction of their holy faith, supported by the only hope they now had, the hope of heaven.

Could the eyes of God, looking down over the earth, and marking in all places with deep pity his erring children, find souls more worthy of his vast paternal love? Can we imagine that the ears of Heaven were deaf to their prayers poured out unceasingly all those long days and nights of trials and of tears? Can we read in the designs of Providence the blessed decrees which such scenes called forth? Blind that we are, unable often to judge rightly of our own thoughts, often an enigma to ourselves, how shall we dare to judge of what is so far above us? No Christian at least can pretend that all those miseries, accumulated on the heads of so many innocent victims, had no other object than to make them suffer. Ireland will yet profit by all the merits, unknown and untold, gained by so many thousand human hearts and souls and bodies given over to misfortunes which baffle expression.

And as yet we have said nothing of those cargos of priests shipped from Carrickfergus to Barbadoes, and afterward to Arran and Innisboffin. Deprived of all means of making their new country in America a witness of Catholic prayer and worship--not one of them probably being able to offer the holy sacrifice even for a single day, nor administer any sacrament unless perhaps that of penance-by stealth; not one dared open his mouth and preach the truth publicly to all. What could they do? They offered the sacrifice of themselves; the very sight of them possessed almost the virtue of a sacrament, and their lives preached a sermon more eloquent than any of those which entrance the vastest audience of a solemn cathedral.

No! the first emigration of 'the Irish to America was not unfruitful in its results. And were we to attribute the great progress made by Catholicity on the American Continent in the present age to the merits of those numerous victims of persecution, who could prove us to be in error, and say that between the sufferings of innocence in the seventeenth and the glorious success of their countrymen in the nineteenth century there is no connection? The old phrase of Tertullian, "Sanguis martyrum, semen Christianorum," has been proved true too often in the annals of the Catholic Church to be falsified in this one instance; yet, if what our days witness be not the result of former sufferings and sacrifices, those trials were barren, and are consequently inexplicable. Every cause must have its effect; and it is a truth which no Christian can hesitate to admit, that the most efficacious source of blessings is the tear of the innocent, the anguish of the pure of heart, the humble prayer of the persecuted servant of God.

When we come to speak of the emigration of the race to the American Continent, which is now in progress, the stupendous facts which will make our narrative and excite our admiration must be regarded and accounted for from a religious and Catholic stand point, and we shall then be able to refer to this first and apparently barren emigration. Many losses, spiritual as well as temporal, may stagger the unreflecting, particularly when the whole designs of Providence are as yet scarcely in their inceptive stage; but the more they are developed before our eyes, the more the truth is made clear; every difficulty vanishes; and the soul of the beholder exclaims "Yes, God is truly wise and merciful!"

But it is time at last to enter on the consideration of what we esteem the first great issue involved in the resurrection of Ireland, namely, all the probable consequences of the present emigration, which is the true point we are aiming at, as our purpose is to show the benefit that Ireland has already derived, and is sure to derive later on, from that incessant flow of the great human wave starting from her shore to oversweep vast continents and islands of the sea. What aid will it afford to her own resurrection at home, in order to render that complete and lasting? This may be said to have been our main object in writing these pages; for, although it may be impressive enough for those who regard the subject attentively, and although it will certainly be a source of wonder to those who come after us, nevertheless it fails to strike as it ought the great mass of beholders.

Often in the history of nations, while the mightiest revolutions are in progress, they are scarcely perceptible to the actors in them; all their circumstances, their most active and effective operations, being like the silent workings of Nature, scarcely sensible to those around, until the end comes and the great result is achieved; then history records the event as one fraught with the greatest blessings, or misfortunes, to mankind. So will it be, we have no doubt, with that strange concatenation of small domestic facts which now form the universal phenomenon of all English-speaking countries: the spread of the Irish everywhere.

What were its beginnings? Nothing at all. What good effects followed it? None perceptible for a long time. These two reflections claim our attention first, for we must study the phenomenon, in all its circumstances and bearings.

This new emigration we call voluntary, to distinguish it from the first, which was forced upon large portions of the Irish race. But, in reality, the Irish undertook it at the beginning with reluctance; the intolerable state of existence which they were compelled to undergo in their own land acting upon them with a kind of moral compulsion amounting to an almost irresistible force. For it was either the famine or persecution of the century preceding which first drove them to emigrate.

Necessity of expansion is a great characteristic of their race, an instinctive impulse which three thousand years ago carried a part of it into the heart of Asia. But this particular branch had been rooted to the soil for so many centuries, by the stern necessity of repelling a series of successive invasions, that this great characteristic appeared for a long time to be totally extinct in it. They seemed neither to know nor care any more for foreign countries; and no race in Europe, from the ninth to the eighteenth century, showed itself so completely wedded to the soil, and incapable of the thought of spreading abroad.

At last they began to move. And what was the first origin of the new movement? No one can say precisely. Only, in various accounts of occurrences taking place in the island during the last century, we occasionally meet with such entries as the following by Matthew O'Connor, in his "Irish Catholics:"

"The summer of 1728 was fatal. The heart of the politician was steeled against the miseries of the Catholics; their number excited his jealousy. Their decrease by the silent waste of famine must have been a source of secret joy; but the Protestant interest was declining in a proportionate degree by the ravages of starvation. . .

"Thousands of Protestants took shipping in Belfast for the West Indies. . . . The policy that would starve the Catholics at home would not deny them the privilege of flight."

This is the first mention of emigration, on any extensive scale, which we could find in the records of last century; and, at the time when the Protestant Irish went to America, where they doubtless met with congenial minds in the Puritans of New England, the Catholics still turned, as before, to Spain and France.

But a new entry in 1762 unfolds a new aspect. This time Catholics alone are spoken of: "No resource remained to the peasantry but emigration. The few who had means sought an asylum in the American plantations; such as remained were allowed generally an acre of ground for the support of their families, and commonage for a cow, but at rents the most exorbitant."

This is the first instance we meet with of Irish Catholics emigrating to America, at least in comparatively large bodies. They were no doubt encouraged to take this step by the accounts which reached them of the success of the Ulster Protestants who had gone before, and whose posterity is now to be found in the South chiefly, as low down as Carolina and Georgia.

But the relative prospects of the Protestants and Catholic were at that time far from being equally good. The first, driven from home by famine, found a land of plenty awaiting them, a genial climate, perfect toleration of their religious tenets everywhere, and in some districts they gained real political influence. They were received with open arms by the colonists, who were unable to occupy the land alone, and ready to welcome new fellow- citizens, who would aid them in their contests with the Indians, and add materially to their prosperity and resources. All persons and all things then smiled on the new-comer, and within a very short time he found himself possessed of more than he had ever expected. Thus others were induced to follow from the north of Ireland, and famine was no longer the only motive power which impelled them to leave their native land. Mr. Bancroft tells us they were called Scotch-Irish.

On the other hand, the Irish Catholics found a fertile soil and an inviting climate; Nature welcomed them, but man recoiled, inflamed by a bitter hostility against their faith and their very name. This feeling of opposition, on both accounts, was already fast wearing away in Europe; but the "liberality" springing up in the Old World, owing to a variety of circumstances, had not yet penetrated into the British colonies of North America. They were still, in this respect, in the state in which the Revolution of 1688 had left them: Catholicity was proscribed everywhere, and the penal laws of the Old World were attempted to be enforced in the New, as far as the different state of the country would permit. A few details, taken mainly from Mr. Bancroft's history, will give us a tolerably exact idea of the situation in which the newly-arrived Irish Catholic found himself in that future land of liberty.

The consequences of the downfall of James II. were soon fully accepted by the British colonies, throughout which changes of greater or less degree took place in the laws, not only without any great opposition, but in the main with the full applause of all parties. The Stuart dynasty was thrown over more easily in America than it had been in the British Isles.

It is universally admitted that one of the greatest consequences of that downfall was the renewed persecution of Catholics in England and Ireland. In the words of Mr. Bancroft:

"The Revolution of 1688, narrow in its principles, imperfect in its details, frightfully intolerant toward Catholics, forms an era in the liberty of England and of mankind."

465

It will be no surprise, then, on coming to review the various colonies, to find the oppression of the Catholic Church common to all without one exception.

Beginning with the South, we find the new governor of South Carolina, Archdale, a Quaker, and, on that account, personally well disposed toward all, desirous of showing that a Quaker could respect the faith of a "Papist," commencing his administration by sending back to the Spanish Governor of Florida four Indian converts of the Spanish priests, who were exposed as slaves for sale in Carolina. He likewise enfranchised the Huguenots of South Carolina, who, up to this time, had been kept under by the High Church oligarchy. Yet, when he came to urge the adoption of liberal measures toward all in the state, the colonial Legislature consented to confer liberty of conscience on all Christians, with the exception of "Papists."

In North Carolina, the Church of England was actually made the state Church, in 1704, and the Legislature enacted that "no one who would not take the oath prescribed by law should hold a place of trust in the colony."

Of Virginia, Spotswood, the governor, could write to England, in 1711: "This government is in perfect peace and tranquillity, under a due obedience to royal authority, and a gentlemanly conformity to the Church of England."

Of Maryland, Mr. Bancroft writes that the English Revolution was a Protestant revolution.

"A convention of the associates 'for the defence of the Protestant religion' assumed the government, and, in an address to King William, denounced the influence of the Jesuits, the prevalence of popish idolatry, the connivance by the previous government at murders of Protestants, and the danger from plots with the French and Indians."

Hence, a little farther on, we read: "The Roman Catholics alone were left without an ally, exposed to English bigotry and colonial injustice. They alone were disfranchised on the soil which, long before Locke pleaded for toleration, or Penn for religious freedom, they had chosen, not as their own asylum only, but, with Catholic liberality, as the asylum of every persecuted sect. In the land which Catholics had opened for Protestants, the Catholic inhabitant was the sole victim to Anglican intolerance. Mass might not be said publicly. No Catholic priest or bishop might utter his faith in a voice of persuasion. No Catholic might teach the young. If the wayward child of a Papist would but become an apostate, the law wrested for him from his parents a share of their property. The disfranchisement of the proprietary related to his creed, not to his family. Such were the methods adopted 'to prevent the growth of Popery.'"

Mr. Bancroft adds with much truth and force: "Who shall say that the faith of the cultivated individual is firmer than the faith of the common people? Who shall say that the many are fickle, that the chief is firm? To recover the inheritance of authority, Benedict, the son of the proprietary, renounced the Catholic Church for that of England; the persecution never crushed the faith of the humble colonists."

Pennsylvania appears to form an exception to that universal animosity against Catholics. It is said that, owing to William Penn, "religious liberty was established, and every public employment was open to every man professing faith in Jesus Christ. . . . In Pennsylvania human rights were respected: the fundamental law of William Penn, even his detractors concede, was in harmony with universal reason, and true to the ancient and just liberties of the people."

Such may have been the written law--the theory; but the law as executed--the fact--was far from realizing those fine promises. As late as the end of the Revolutionary War, the Catholics of Philadelphia were compelled to hide away their worship in a small chapel, surrounded by buildings whose only access was a dark and winding alley still in existence a few years back.

It is known, moreover, that Penn himself, in 1708, forbade mass to be celebrated in the colony. According to T. D. McGee, Governor Gordon, in 1734, prohibited the erection of a Catholic church in Walnut Street; and, in 1736, a private house having been purchased at the corner of Second and Chestnut streets for the same object, it was again prohibited.

New Jersey showed her liberality in the form sacred to all the other colonies: "Liberty of conscience was granted to all but papists."

There was as yet no homogeneity in New York, the Dutch still preserving great power, and, consequently, "the idea of toleration was still imperfect in New Netherlands; equality among religious sects was unknown." If this was the case with several Protestant organizations, what must it have been with the Catholics? It is well known that no one dared openly avow his faith in the true Church, and that John Ury was hanged in 1741 for being a priest, though whether he was a priest or not is still a question.

Rhode Island had proclaimed in the beginning "entire freedom of mind;" but, after the Revolution of 1688, the colony "interpolated into the statute-book the exclusion of papists from the established equality."

The spirit of Connecticut is well expressed in the words of the address sent by the colony to King William of Orange, on his accession: "Great was the day when the Lord who sitteth upon the floods did divide his and your adversaries like the waters of Jordan, and did begin to magnify you like Joshua, by the deliverance of the English dominions from popery and slavery." We wonder how the taciturn Hollander received this effusion of Connecticut? There is nothing more to add on the situation of the Catholics in the land of the "blue laws."

In Massachusetts it will be no surprise to hear that "every form of Christianity, except the Roman Catholic, was enfranchised."

This short sketch is eloquent enough with reference to the position in which the poor Irish immigrant found himself on landing on the shores of the New World. His faith he found proscribed as severely almost as in his own country. He was compelled to conceal it; and, even had he been free to make open profession of it, he could find no minister of his creed tolerated anywhere. The country was a perfect blank as far as the ceremonies of his religion went. In his native land he knew where to find a priest; he was advised of the day and of the precise place where he might assist at the sacred mysteries of his religion; and, were it in the cave or on the mountain-top, in the bog or the morass, he knew that there he could adore and receive his God as truly and as worthily as in the magnificent domes looking proudly to heaven under Catholic skies. But in British North America, except in a few counties of Maryland, where the true faith had once been openly planted and taken root, where some clergymen of his own creed were even still to be found, though forced to conceal, or at least not expose themselves too freely, he knew that elsewhere it was useless for him to inquire, not only for a sacred edifice where he might go to thank his God on landing, but even to look for a priest should he find himself at the point of death.

At the present day it is almost impossible to give any details and move the reader by a picture of the complete spiritual destitution of the Irish immigrant in his new home. Here and there, however, we meet, in reading, facts apparently insignificant in themselves, which at first sight seem to have no connection whatever with the subject on hand, yet which, with the aid of reflection, throw quite a flood of light on it, as convincing as it is unexpected. Take, for instance, the following:

"In the last year of the administration of Andros in Massachusetts," says Mr. Bancroft, "the daughter of John Goodwin, a child of thirteen years, charged a laundress with having stolen linen from the family. Glover, the mother of the laundress, a friendless immigrant, almost ignorant of English, like a true woman, with a mother's heart, rebuked the false accusation. Immediately, the girl, to secure revenge, became bewitched. The infection spread. Three others of the family, the youngest a boy of less than five years old, soon succeeded in equally arresting public attention. . . . Cotton Mather went to pray by the side of one of them, and, lo! the child lost her hearing till prayer was over. What was to be done? The four ministers of Boston and the one of Charlestown assembled in Goodwin's house, and spent a whole day of fasting in prayer. In consequence, the youngest child, the little one of five years old, was 'delivered.' But if the ministers could thus by prayer 'deliver' a possessed child, there must have been a witch. The honor of the ministers required a prosecution of the affair; and the magistrates, William Stoughton being one, with a 'vigor' which the united ministers commended as 'just,' made 'a discovery of the wicked instrument of the devil.' The culprit was evidently a wild Irishwo-man, of a strange tongue. Goodwin, who made the complaint, 'had no proof that could have done her any hurt;' but the 'scandalous old hag,' whom some thought 'crazed in her intellectuals,' was bewildered, and made strange answers, which were taken as confessions, sometimes, in excitement, using her native dialect. . . . It was plain the prisoner was a Roman Catholic; she had never learned the Lord's Prayer in English; she could repeat the Pater Noster fluently enough, but not quite correctly; so, the ministers and Goodwin's family had the satisfaction of getting her condemned as a witch and executed."

The position of this poor woman, who had never openly declared herself a Catholic, but which fact the people were led to infer from various circumstances, expresses the condition of all Irish immigrants at the time. A further fact recorded by the same historian shows what the feeling toward Catholics was at the time in Massachusetts:

"The girl, who knew herself to be a deceiver, had no remorse, and to the ministers it never occurred that vanity and love of power had blinded their judgment."

The reason was plain: Glover was a Catholic. How could the girl be expected to feel remorse for having brought about her death? How could the ministers feel the least concern because their "vanity and love of power" had effected the hanging of such a creature?--"a vessel of wrath," in any case; a "predestined reprobate," beyond doubt, whose ignominious death on earth and eternal punishment afterward were "a true source of joy in heaven and an increase of glory for the infinite justice of God," if there was any truth in Calvinism.

Another fact, as suggestive as the above, is found in McGee's "Irish Settlers in America:" "The first Catholic church that we find in Pennsylvania, after Penn's suppression of them in 1708, was connected with the house of a Miss Elizabeth McGauley, an Irish lady, who, with several of her tenantry, settled on land on the road leading from Nicetown to Frankfort. Near the site of this ancient sanctuary stood a tomb, inscribed, 'John Michael Brown, ob. 15th December, A. D. 1750. R. I. P.' He had been a priest residing there incognito."

Miss E. McGauley was not poor, like Glover. On coming to America with some of her tenantry, she secured herself beforehand against the difficulty of practising her religion; and, knowing well that no priest was to be found in the country, she brought one with her. All the remainder of his life did this minister of God reside in her house incognito, keeping the ministry intrusted to him for the service of all a profound secret. He never attempted, probably, to enlighten his prejudiced and ignorant neighbors; the knowledge of his character and the benefits arising from his presence were confined to the lady of the house and her faithful tenantry. Even after his death the secret was still kept, and only the cabalistic characters "R. I. P." remain to tell an intelligent reader that he was neither Quaker nor Protestant; and, probably, tradition alone, preserved doubtless in the neighborhood, could assure us that he was a priest.

How many Catholics scattered over the broad colony of Pennsylvania, immigrants like Miss McGauley, but unlike her in their poverty, and therefore unable to hire a clergyman, never knew that they might unburden their consciences and enjoy the consolations of their religion, by travelling a hundred miles or so to the house "on the road leading from Nicetown to Frankfort?" How many lived and died within a short distance, and never knocked at the door, owing to their ignorance of the class of inmates? Thus, although there were some ministers of God in the country, their number was so small, and they were so far distant from each other, that their labors were utterly unavailing for the great body of the Catholic immigrants, who would have rejoiced to throw themselves at their feet, and ease their hearts and purify their souls by confession.

Some Irishmen, it is true, had emigrated before such concealment was requisite, in Maryland at least, where an asylum for all had been opened by Lord Baltimore, a Catholic. Thus, the Carrolls had settled in Prince George County. They were at liberty to make open use of the services of the English fathers of the Society of Jesus, who for a long time officiated undisguisedly among their English Catholic flocks; but, as was seen, after the Revolution of 1688, Catholics were disfranchised in Maryland even, their religious rites proscribed, and penalties enacted against the open profession of their worship.

Thus, concealment became a necessity, there also; the policy of keeping the existence of clergymen and the celebration of the holy mysteries secret had to be adopted there as in other colonies. The Carroll family, like Miss Elizabeth McGauley, gave refuge in their house to a minister of their own religion, and it was in such a chapel-house that John Carroll was born, on the 8th of January, 1735--the first Bishop and Archbishop of Baltimore.

It is therefore no matter for wonder that the number of children of the Church in North America did not increase in proportion to the number of Catholic immigrants; on the contrary, the posterity of the majority of those who chose the British colonies, for their home was lost to her. The immigrants themselves, we are confident, never lost their faith. Although living for years without any exterior help, without receiving a word of instruction or advice, without the celebration of any religious rite whatever, or the reception of any sacrament, yet, faith was too deeply rooted in their minds and hearts to be ever eradicated, or shaken even.

But, though they themselves clung fast to their faith in the midst of so many adverse circumstances, what of their children?

There is no doubt that many of them did, individually, every thing possible to transmit that faith to their children; but all they could do was to speak privately, to warn then against dangers, and set up before them the example of a blameless life. Not only was there no priest to initiate them into the mysteries, granted by Christ to the redeemed soul; there was not even a Catholic school-master to instruct them. Even the "hedge-school" could not be set on foot. Books were unknown; Catholic literature, in the modern sense, had not yet been born; there was no vestige of such a thing beyond, perhaps, an occasional old, worn, and torn, yet dearly-prized and carefully-concealed prayer-book, dating from the happy days of the Confederation of Kilkenny.

There is no reason, then, for surprise in the fact that, although the families of those first Irish settlers were numerous and scattered over all the district which afterward became the Middle and Southern States, only a faint tradition remained among many of them that they really belonged to the old Church and "ought to be Catholics." How often was this the case thirty years ago, particularly in the South!

It would not be right to conclude that all this was a pure and unmitigated loss to the Church of Christ. Later on, we shall have to speak of more numerous and serious losses: but a few words on this first one may not be thrown away.

As in the material world an infinite number of germs are lost, and quantities of seeds, wafted on the breeze from giant trees and humble plants, fall and perish on a barren rock, in the eddies of a swift-running brook, or, oftener still, on the hard and unkind soil on which they have happened to alight; so that, out of a thousand germs, a few only find every thing congenial to their growth, and attain to the full size allotted them by Nature--nevertheless, despite this loss, the species is not only preserved, but so multiplied as to produce on the beholder, in after-time, the impression that, not only no loss has been sustained, but that much has been gained. So is it with the Catholic Church in general, and in particular with the momentous events now being considered.

The cultivated field of the "father of the family" was about to be extended over a new and vast area. A whole continent was to be "fenced around," and "olive-trees," and "fig-trees," and all plants useful and ornamental, were destined to flourish in that vast garden to the end of time. The great and eternal Father was, by his providence, directing the mighty operation from above, and marking the various points of the compass to which the floating germs were to be wafted. He knew that he was planting a new garden for his Son, who would, as usual, be the first husbandman, and employ many workmen to help him.

How could it be expected that all would be gain without loss, when the harvest-time had not yet arrived, and the "enemy" was busy sowing "tares" in all directions? Was not the work human as well as divine? and, as human, did not the work partake of the imperfection of human things?

The continent had evidently been predestined to form one of the strongest branches of the great Catholic tree. Discovered before the modern heresies of Protestantism had shown themselves, it was to bring into the fold of Christ new nations, when some old ones were to be cut off and wither away. This has long ago been pointed out; but another mighty design of Providence there was which only now begins to show itself.

Columbus was in search of Asia and the holy sepulchre when he stumbled on the New World. Nor was the idea of his great mind altogether a delusion. The new continent was in future ages to be used as the highway from Europe to the Orient; China, Japan, India, vast regions filled with innumerable multitudes of human beings, had, so far, scarcely been touched, could scarcely be touched, by Catholicism coming from Europe. In fact it was too far away, and the means of intercommunication were too inadequate. The holy Catholic Church increases as "things which grow;" a few husbandmen--missionaries--are required to set the first seedlings and plants in the soil, to water them, watch over them, and see that they thrive and flourish; the rest of the process is a matter of seeds wafted by the wind, falling and taking root in a fertile soil, which has been already prepared for their reception. If there were no other means of propagation than the toil and sweat of the husbandman, how long would it take to cover the whole earth with vegetation? The first propagation of Christianity was done in this way; hence it took more than ten centuries to Christianize Europe. In the fifth century, Rome was still thoroughly pagan. Were the vast regions of that dim, far-away East to undergo a similar slow and painful process, necessitating an immense amount of labor, centuries and centuries in duration? God hastened the process by adding to it the wafting of seeds, and America was to be the vast nursery from which those seeds were to come. It was from that long and alternately widening and narrowing belt of land, running down the sea from north to south, that the Japhetic race was to invade the "tents of Sem."

Thus was the dream of Columbus to be realized. Asia would be reached by Europe, of which America would form a part. The east of Asia would become contiguous to a real European population, large masses of which would easily come in contact with the Mongolian and Malay races of their immediate neighborhood, steam and modern improvements in travel reducing the intervening distance to a matter of a few days. Thus the Japhetic movement could be carried out on a large scale, and European civilization come to supersede the obsolete manners of those old and effete races of Eastern Asia. The unity of mankind would be vindicated against its blasphemers; and, to crown the whole, Christianity would find its way back to the cradle of man, then, to its own birthplace, Calvary and the sepulchre of Christ. Thus would the conjectural vision of the great Genoese become only an explanation of the old prophecy of the second father of mankind.[1]

Thus would the Church at last become rigorously Catholic, and not as some theologians imagined, in their desire to make actual, incomplete facts coincide with a far wider theory, only Catholic by approximation.

If it were allowed us to read the designs of Providence reverently, we might say, without presumption, that it seems such is to be future history, although simple conjecture may produce too strong an impression on our minds. But, at the period of which we speak, shortly after the middle of the last century, any one who would have spoken thus would have been justly deemed a visionary. The south of America, though possessed of the true religion, seemed inert; the North was already showing signs of an intense future activity, but all opposed to the truth. God was about to

---

[1] The reader will understand that all this is merely "a view, " and not given as a pure interpretation of Scripture or past history.

change those appearances, and, by infusing the Irish element into the North, produce, in a comparatively short space of time, the wonderful phenomenon which we witness.

Yet, so short-sighted are we, that some are almost staggered in their faith, because the children of the earliest Irish emigrants to this country, were apparently lost to the Church.

Nevertheless, several circumstances might be brought forward to show that a real gain accrued to the Church from these lost children of the first Irish settlers. How many prejudices, so deeply rooted in the country as to seem ineradicable, owe their destruction to them! How many harsh and uncharitable feelings against Catholics were smoothed away or softened down by their instrumentality!

Those men who, in after-life, remembered that they "ought to be Catholics," were not ready to accept, on the word of a "minister," all the absurd calumnies spread against the Church throughout those vast regions. They had heard, by a kind of tradition, kept alive in their families, of what their ancestors had formerly suffered, and they at least were not inclined to join in the universal denunciation of a creed which they were conscious "ought to be" their own.

Who shall say whether it is not the old Catholic blood, running in the veins of these children of Irish Catholic parents, which has been mainly instrumental in creating that spirit of true liberality which inspires the honorable conduct of the majority of the American people, and in which the Church has at all times found her safety?

It is certain that there is a vast difference between that American spirit and the atmosphere of distrust pervading other countries, and that the rapid spread of the Church throughout the broad regions of the Union has been singularly favored by the soft breeze of a liberal and kindly feeling so common to those even who are not born within the fold. And that the children of Irish parents, themselves lost to the Church, have exercised great influence from the start, in that regard, cannot, we think, be denied.

But, perhaps, too much space has been devoted to that first emigration from Ireland; it is time to come to a more recent period of which there are more certain and positive accounts.

There is no need to speak of the happy change effected in the position of the Catholic Church in America by the Revolution; Washington, in his reply to the address of the Catholics of the country, has given expression to the feelings of the nation in terms so well known that they require no comment.

From that date commences the real history of the Catholic Church in North America, outside of the provinces originally settled by the French and Spaniards. The influx of Irish immigrants now attracts our chief attention.

From the year 1800, when the "Union" was effected between England and Ireland, the number of immigrants increased suddenly and rapidly, and the situation of the new-comers on their arrival was very different from that of their predecessors. They found liberty not only proclaimed, but established; few churches indeed, but, such as there were, known and open, and a bishop and clergymen already practising their ministry.

Before entering upon the extent, nature, and effects of this second Irish immigration--which may be studied from documents existing--it will be well to say a few words on the elements which constituted the Catholic body when first organized. We are concerned, it is true, with the new element introduced by the great movement of which we begin to speak; but we are far from undervaluing other sources of life, which not only affected the Church at its birth in the United States, but have continued to act upon her ever since with more or less of energy. The reader should not imagine that, by not speaking of them, we are unjust or blind to their efficiency; they simply lie without the scope of our plan.

In the North the French, and in the South the Spanish missionaries, had imparted to Catholicity a vitality which could not be extinguished; but its operations were almost entirely confined to limits outside those which circumscribe the field of our investigations. The French element, however, grew into prominence even at the outset within those limits, either through the acquisition of Louisiana, or in consequence of the French immigration during the terrible revolution of last century. It is only necessary to open the pages of Mr. R. H. Clarke's recently-published "Lives of the American Bishops," to be struck with the importance of that element. It may be said that, for the first twenty-five years of the republic, French prelates and clergymen, together with several American Marylanders, were intrusted with the care of the infant Church. Ireland seems to have had scarcely any office to fulfil in that great work, save through the humble exertions of a few devoted but almost unknown missionaries; so that, when bishops of Irish birth were first chosen, they were either taken from Ireland itself, as was Dr. England, Bishop Kelly, of Richmond, or Conwell, of Philadelphia, or from the monasteries of Rome, as were Bishops Connolly and Concanen, of New York. Bishop Egan, of Philadelphia, can scarcely be called an exception, as he had only spent a very few years in this country when he was elevated to the episcopal dignity. The German element showed itself only in Pennsylvania.

It was under circumstances such as these that that stream of desolate people began to flow, spreading gradually through immense regions, and bringing with it only its unconquerable faith.

From the "mustard-seed" a noble tree was to spring up; but as yet it was only a weak sapling. In 1785, Bishop Carroll made an estimate of the Catholic population of the States: "In Maryland, seventeen thousand; in Pennsylvania, over seven thousand; and, as far as information could be obtained, in other States, about fifteen hundred." New York City could not yet boast of a hundred Catholics.

Like all things durable and mighty, the first swelling of that great wave was slow and silent, and scarcely perceptible, until little by little the ripple spread over the vast ocean.

The first apparent causes have been well expressed by T. D. McGee, in his "Irish Settlers:" "The breaking out of the French War in 1793, and the degrading legislative Union of 1800, had deprived many of bread, and all of liberty at home, and made the mechanical as well as the agricultural class embark to cross the Atlantic.

"Hitherto the Irish had colonized, sowed and reaped, fought, spoken, and legislated in the New World, if not always in proportion to their numbers, yet always to the measure of their educational resources. Now they are about to plant a new emblem--the Cross--and a new institution--the Church--throughout the American Continent. For, the faith of their fathers they did not leave behind them; nay, rather, wheresoever six Irish roof-trees rise, there you will find the cross of Christ reared over all, and Celtic piety and Celtic enthusiasm, all sighs and tears, kneeling before it."

Let us look at a few particular signs of the coming of this great wave in its first scarcely perceptible movement.

"John Timon was born at Conewago, Pennsylvania, February 12, 1797, and baptized on the 17th of the same month; his parents, James Timon and Margaret Leddy, had quite recently arrived in this country from Ireland, and were from Belturbet, County Cavan. A family of ten children, of whom John was the second son, blessed the Catholic household of these pious parents."--(Lives of American Bishops.)

"Francis Xavier Gartland was born in Dublin, Ireland, in 1805; he came to America, while yet a child, and made his studies at Mount St. Mary's, Emmettsburg."--(Ibid.)

"John B. Fitzpatrick was born in Boston, November 1, 1812. His parents emigrated from Ireland, and settled in Boston in 1805."-- (Ibid.)

What did the parents of the future bishop find on their arrival at Boston? In the year previous, the first Catholic congregation was assembled in that city by the Abbe La Poitre, a French navy-chaplain, who had remained in America after the departure of the French fleet, which rendered such powerful assistance in the struggle for American independence. In 1808, four years before the birth of him who was destined to wear the mitre, the Catholics had obtained the old "French Church" in School Street, which was probably a Calvinist meeting house.

Another wavelet of a precious kind was the following: "Bishop Lanigan was meditating" (in Ireland) "the establishment of a religious community in the city of Kilkenny, and designed Miss Alice Lalor for one of its future members. But, in 1797, her parents emigrated from Ireland and settled in America, and she felt it to be her duty . . . . to accompany them. But she promised the bishop to return in two years. On arriving at Philadelphia, she became acquainted with the Reverend Leonard Neale. . . . Feeling convinced that it was not the design of Providence that she should abandon America for Ireland, Father Neale released her from her promise to return to Kilkenny, in order that she might become his cooperator in the foundation of a religious order in the United States (the Visitation Nuns)."-- (Ibid.)

Already was the young church robbing the old of some of its best members, who were to give some weight to the Irish element in this country.

"George A. Carrell was born at Philadelphia. . . . He was the seventh child of his Irish parents, and the house they occupied, and in which he was born, was the old mansion of William Penn, at the corner of Market Street and Letitia Court."-- (Ibid.)

Two short observations naturally present themselves here. Philadelphia is the city oftenest mentioned whenever foreigners are spoken of as landing in North America at that time. It was then the great harbor of the country, New York not having attained the preeminence she now enjoys. Hence, the Church counted seven thousand children in Pennsylvania; but very few north of that city. Thither came the German Catholics, also, in great numbers to spread themselves chiefly West and South. Such was the direction then taken by the Catholic wave.

Our second remark only concerns the house in which he who became Bishop Carrell was born. It seemed only fitting that an Irish Catholic family should thus early take possession of the very dwelling-place of the founder of the colony, as the Catholic Church was destined, through the Irish element chiefly, to supplant and outlive the little church of the "Friends."

All the facts, however, just quoted are exceptional, and regard only the select few. What became of the mass, meanwhile? As usual, history for the most part is silent with regard to it. A very few words constitute the only record which can afford us a glimpse of the real situation of the vast majority of those poor, friendless, obscure immigrants, on whom, nevertheless, the great hopes of the future were built.

We have, happily, some means left us of forming an opinion; and it will be seen that their situation was much the same as that of their earlier compatriots. For instance, in the "Lives of American Bishops" we read the following startling story:

"The Abbe Cheverus very frequently made long journeys to convey the consolations of religion or perform acts of charity. About this time (1803) he received a letter from two young Irish Catholics confined in Northampton prison, who had been condemned to death without just cause, as was almost universally believed, imploring him to come to them and prepare them for their sad and cruel fate. He hastened to their spiritual relief, and inspired them with the most heroic sentiments and dispositions, which they persevered in to the last fatal moment of their execution. According to custom, the prisoners were carried to the nearest church, to hear a sermon preached immediately before their execution; several Protestant ministers presented themselves to preach the sermon; but the Abbe Cheverus claimed the right to perform that duty, as the choice of the prisoners themselves, and, after much difficulty, he was allowed to ascend the pulpit. His sermon struck all present with astonishment, awe, and admiration."

Here, in 1803, we have almost a repetition of the death of the poor woman Glover; and, had it not been for the high character of the admirable man who hastened to their assistance, those two young Irish Catholics would have had for their only religious preparation before death a sermon from one or more Protestant ministers; and, as the great and good Cheverus could not be everywhere in New England, there is little doubt but that such was the fate of more than one of the newly-arrived immigrants.

In 1800 and the following years a comparatively large number of Irishmen landed at New York, and the future terrible scourge of their race, ship-fever, soon broke out among them. Dr. Bailey, the father of Mrs.Seton, was Health Physician to the port of New York at the time, and he allowed his daughter to visit and do good among them. She was deeply impressed by the religious demeanor of the Irish just landed. The Rev. Dr. White relates in her "Life:" "'The first thing,' she said, 'the poor people did when they got their tents was to assemble on the grass, and all, kneeling, adore our Master for his mercy; and every morning sun finds them repeating their praises.' In a letter to her sister-in-law she describes their sufferings under the 'plague' in the following golden words:

"'Rebecca, I cannot sleep; the dying and the dead possess my mind--babies expiring at the empty breast of their mother. And this is not fancy, but the scene that surrounds me. Father says that such was never known before; that there are actually twelve children that must die from mere want of sustenance, unable to take more than the breast, and from the wretchedness of their parents deprived of it, as they have laid ill for many days in the ship, without food, air, or changing. Merciful Father! Oh, how readily would I give them each a turn of my child's treasure, if in my choice! But, Rebecca, they have a provider in heaven, who will soothe the pangs of the suffering innocent.'"

When she wrote the above, Mrs. Seton was not yet professedly a Catholic; but how truly animated with the spirit of the Church of Christ! Happy would the poor immigrants have been had they only met with Protestants of her stamp on landing, and of her father's, who, although he prevented her becoming foster-mother to those poor children, as her first duty regarded her own child, died himself, a victim to his charity toward their parents, contracting, in the fulfilment of his office, the fever they had brought with them, which he was striving to allay!

The following fact, which will conclude this portion of our inquiry, happened a little later, but, on that very account, will serve as a connecting link with the considerations which are to follow, and will open our eyes to the real position of that already swelling mass of immigrants.

"During the year 1823, Bishop Connolly (of New York) made the visitation of his entire diocese. . . . He extended his journey along the route of the Erie Canal, which was commenced in 1819, where large numbers of Irish laborers had been attracted, and among whom the bishop labored with indefatigable zeal." At that time the clergy of the whole diocese consisted of eight priests with their bishop.

At last we find the "Irish people" at work. The spectacle is full of sadness; and the only emotion which can fill the heart is one of deep pity. In that vast wilderness of the West, for such it then was, along public works extending hundreds of miles, large gangs of men--such is the expression we are compelled to use--are hard at work along that dreary Mohawk River; blasting rocks, digging in the hard clay, uprooting trees, clearing the ground of briars, tangled bushes, and the vast quantity of debris of animal and vegetable matter accumulated during centuries. This was the work which "attracted" large numbers of Irish laborers. They had left their country, crossed the ocean under circumstances that should come under our notice, and landed on these (at that time) inhospitable shores, to find work; and they found the occupation just mentioned. We can picture the "shanties" in which they lived, the harpies who thrived on them, the innumerable extortions to which they were subjected. Bearing in mind that, in the immense State of New York and in one-half of New Jersey, there were just eight priests with their bishop, we may form some idea of the way in which they lived and died.

How they must have blessed this bishop, who had left Rome, his second country, and the noble associations which surrounded him in the Eternal City, to come to the succor of his unfortunate countrymen scattered away in a New World! And well did he deserve that blessing!

But his passage along the Erie Canal could be nothing more than a veritable passage--a transient sojourn of a few days or weeks at most. What became of those gangs of men after, what had happened to them before, no one has said, no one has told us, no one now can ascertain; we are only left to conjecture, and the spectacle, as we said, is too sad to dwell upon.

But, hidden within this melancholy view, lies a great and glorious fact. It was the beginning of an "apostolic mission" on the part of a whole people, a mission which will form one of the most moving and significant pages of the ecclesiastical history of the nineteenth century. Every Christian knows that apostolic work is rough work; the brunt of the battle must be borne by the earliest in the field, that it may be said of their successors in the words of the Gospel: "Vos in labores eorum introistis."

Such being the hard lot of the immigrants in the interior of the country, was that of those who remained in the cities much more enviable? On this point we are enabled to judge, at least as regards New York. In a letter written by Bishop Dubois, and published in vol. viii. of the "Annals of the Propagation of the Faith," we meet with the following exhaustive description:

"At the beginning of this century, the newly-arrived immigrants were employed as day-laborers, servants, journeymen, clerks, and shopmen. Now, the condition of this class here is precisely the same as its condition in England; it is entirely dependent upon the will of the trader: not because by law are they forced thereto, but because the rich alone, being able to advance the capital necessary for factories, steam-engines, and workshops, the poor are obliged to work for them upon the masters' own conditions. These conditions, in the case of servants especially, sometimes degenerate into tyranny; they are frequently forced to work on Sundays, permission to hear even a low mass being refused them; they are obliged betimes to assist at the prayers of the sect to which their masters belong, and they have no other alternative than either to do violence to their conscience, or lose their place at the risk of not finding another. Add to this the insults, the calumnies against Catholics, which they are daily forced to hear--a kind of persecution at the hands of their masters, who do every thing to turn them away from their religion; consider the dangers to which are exposed numbers of orphans who lose their fathers almost immediately upon landing; add to this the want of spiritual succor, a necessary consequence of the scarcity of missionaries; and you will have a feeble idea of the obstacles of every kind which we have to surmount. . . . Supposing an immigrant, the father of a family, to die, the widow and orphans have no other resources but public charity; and if a home is found for the children, it is nearly always among Protestants, who do every thing in their power to undermine their faith."

This picture of immigrant-life in New York was certainly repeated through all the other large cities. Under such a combination of adverse circumstances it is most probable that men and women of any other nation would have entirely lost their faith. Such, then, was the dreary prospect for the new-comers. Who at that time would have dared hope to witness the consoling spectacle which followed soon after? To begin with the dawn of that bright day, we must pass on to a new period of immigration, commencing in 1815 or shortly after, and continuing down to the "exodus" of 1846.

It may be well, before entering upon it, to look at the causes which drove so many to leave the shores of Ireland. From the year 1815 the number of immigrants increased considerably and kept on a steady increase until it swelled to the startling proportions of 1850 and the following years.

It is easy to demonstrate that the causes were twofold: 1. The wretched state of the vast majority of the Irish at the best of times. 2. The periodical famines which have regularly visited the island since the beginning of last century. At any time it was in the power of the English to remedy both causes by effecting certain changes in the existing laws. The first of these is evidently the necessary result of the penal laws which had converted the Irish, designedly and with the wilful intent of the legislators, into a nation of paupers. The second can only be the result of the laws affecting the tenure of land and the trade and manufactures of the country.

To attribute the pauperism which now seems a part and parcel of the Irish nation while in their own country to the indolence and want of foresight on the part of the natives themselves, as it is a fashion with English writers to do, is wilfully to close the eyes to two very important things: their past history in their own land, and their present history outside of it.

As to their past history in their own land, it is an established fact that pauperism was unknown in the island, until Protestant legislators introduced it by their confiscations and laws with the manifest intent of destroying, rooting out, or driving away the race. What has been previously stated on this point cannot be gainsaid; and it suffices for the vindication of a falsely-accused people. There might be some hope for a speedier and happier solution of the vexed "Irish difficulty" did the grandsons of those who wrought the evil only honestly acknowledge the faults of their ancestors--the least that might be expected of them; and it would not be too much to imagine them honest enough to repair those faults in these days of severe reckoning and self-scrutiny.

As to the present history of the race outside their own land, now that it has been scattered, by these grievous calamities, all over the world, whatever characteristics its children may present, indolence and want of foresight can scarcely be numbered among them, in view of the success which attends their march everywhere. And if these qualities would seem to be rooted in the native soil, they are only "importations" like the men who fastened them there, and due only to the cramped position in which their legislators so carefully confined them. Where should there be energy, when every motive that could urge it has been taken away? How is it possible to improve their condition, when every improvement only imposes an additional burden upon them in the shape of rack-rent or eviction?

In his work on "The Social Condition of the People," Mr. Kay quotes from the Edinburgh Review of January, 1850, the evidence on this point given by English, German, and Polish witnesses before the Committee of Emigration, and the proofs gathered from every source as to the rapid improvement of the Irish emigrant, wherever he goes, are certainly convincing.

As for the foolish (for it is nothing else, unless it be wicked) assertion that those frightful famines referred to are to be attributed to the sufferers themselves, it is only necessary to say in refutation that in the very years when thousands were being swept away daily by their ravages in Ireland--1846 and 1847--the harbors of the island were filled with English vessels, loaded with cargoes of provisions of every kind to be transported to England in order to pay the rents due to absentee landlords: and all these provisions were the product of the famine-stricken land, won by the toil of the famine-stricken nation. This has invariably been the case when famine has swept over the island: the island's riches were in her harbors, stored in the holds of foreign vessels, to be carried away and converted into money that these noble Anglo-Irish landlords might be enabled to "sustain" life

Others have ascribed these periodical visitations to a surplus population; but, without entering into a discussion on the subject, Sir Robert Kane, in his "Industrial Resources of Ireland," shows that, taking the island in her present state and under the existing system of cultivation, she could support with ease eighteen million inhabitants; that, if the best methods of farming were generally adopted, the soil, by double and even triple crops, could feed without difficulty, not only twenty-five million, the figure stated by Mr. Gustave de Beaumont, a French publicist of eminence, but as many as from thirty to thirty-five million inhabitants.

But, as the same judicious writer observes, "the enormous quantity of cattle annually shipped off from Ireland to England would, in that case, be consumed in the country which produces it."

It is clear, therefore, that the pretended surplus population of Ireland is, as Sir Robert Kane says, a piece of pure imagination, perfectly ideal, and that it is its unequal and not its aggregate amount which is to be deplored.

But no one has presented the question more clearly and solved it more precisely than Mr. Gustave de Beaumont in his admirable work on Ireland, from which we note one or two telling passages, as given in Father Perraud's "Ireland under English Rule."

"The celebrated French publicist, who was the first to present to us (in France) a complete picture of the condition of Ireland, examining in 1829 how emigration might or might not do away with all the misery he had witnessed, proposed to himself the following questions:

"I. To what extent ought emigration to be carried, in order to bring about a material change in the general state of Ireland? namely, by taking away the pretended surplus population.

"II. Would it be possible to carry it out to the proposed extent?

"III. Supposing it practicable, would it be a radical and final solution of existing difficulties?

"The advocates of emigration replied to the first question by estimating at a minimum of two million the number of individuals who would have to leave Ireland, at one time, in order to produce there that kind of vacuum which would improve the conditions of labor and the existence of the rest of the agricultural population.

"Upon these data the solution of the second question was easy. It was by no means difficult to prove that the system was impracticable on so large a scale; impracticable on account of the insufficiency of the means of transport at disposal; impracticable on account of the enormous sums required to carry it out.

"In fact, supposing an emigrant-ship to carry a thousand passengers--a very high figure--two thousand vessels would be required to attain the end in view, namely, the sudden and universal emigration of the whole so-called surplus population. That is to say, the whole merchant navy of Great Britain would have to be drawn off from the commerce of the world, and chartered for the execution of this very chimerical plan. Where was the sum required for the most necessary expenses and urgent wants of two million passengers to be got? And what country in the world would have submitted to a monster invasion like those of barbarous times? Unless, indeed, these two million individuals were beforehand coldly devoted to death by hunger, was there a single country in which it could be hoped they would immediately find work or the means of subsistence?"

All those impossibilities, genuine indeed and at the time, 1829, of unforeseen solution, became, under Providence, possible by extending the period of transportation from one year to twenty; so that, instead of two, in reality three million and a half were thus transported.

But, where M. de Beaumont displayed all his talent for appreciation and keen reasoning was, when he came to consider the third and most embarrassing question of all. Was it certain that, the system of renting and cultivating land always remaining the same, emigration would suffice to heal those inveterate sores, and effect, in conformity with the wishes of its partisans, a social transformation?

On this point, he showed, in a manner admitting of no reply, that the emigration of a third or even of half the population would not radically put an end to the misery of the country. The difficulty with Ireland does not consist in being unable to produce wherewith to feed her population; it lies in the manner in which landed property is managed, a system which no amount of emigration can possibly modify; for, "if one of the first principles of the landlord be that the farmer should gain by tilling no more than is strictly necessary to support him--if, in addition, this principle is, as a general rule, rigidly followed out, and all economical means of living resorted to by the farmer necessarily induce a rise in the rent--what, upon this supposition (of the sad reality of which every one knowing Ireland is perfectly conscious), can be the consequence of a decrease of population?"

Always obliged to live as sparingly as possible, in order to escape a rise in the rent, and forced to undergo daily privations in order to meet his engagements, how is the Irish farmer to gain by the departure of his neighbor? "Thus, after millions of Irishmen have disappeared, the fate of the population which remains is in no wise changed; it will forever be equally wretched."

Then, glancing at the past, making a sad enumeration of Ireland's losses during the last three centuries, and evoking from these too eloquent figures the accents of a touching eloquence, the writer asks himself how far so much bloodshed, such armies of individuals, stricken down by death, or hurried out of the country by transportation--so many families extinct, and the like--had contributed to restore and save Ireland?

"Open the annals of Ireland, and see the small amount of influence which all those violent enterprises and all those extraordinary accidental causes of depopulation have had upon the social state of the country. Calculate the number of souls that perished during the religious wars; count the thousands of Irishmen that perished under the sword of Cromwell; to all that the victor massacred add the myriads that he transported; think of the hundreds of thousands who sank under famine, the number of whom exceeded in one year, 1741, forty thousand; do not overlook the formerly considerable number who yearly died by the hand of the executioner; in fine, to this add the twenty-five or thirty thousand individuals who emigrate from the country every year" (this was written before 1830); "and, having laid down these facts, you look for the consequences: when, in the midst of these different crises, you see Ireland always the same, always equally wretched, always crammed with paupers, always bearing about with her the same hideous and deep wounds, you will then recognize that the miseries of Ireland do not arise from the number of her inhabitants; you will conclude that it is the nature of her social condition to generate unmitigated indigence and infinite distress; that, supposing millions of poor swept out of her by a stroke of magic, others would be seen rising up in abundance out of a well-spring of misery, which in Ireland never dries up; and that the fault does not lie in the number of her population, but in the institutions in force in the country."

The celebrated French writer had certainly pointed out what were the real causes of the distress in Ireland. He had shown how false were the pretended causes then assigned for it by Englishmen; he touched the key-note--the land tenure; and, as a well-wisher to Ireland, deprecating any new calamities, he was firmly opposed to those various fancy projects of emigration en masse, suggested by numerous British writers, many of whom, such as the editors of the London Times, were induced to promulgate them by their deep hatred for the old race, which led them to represent under a modern garb the old Norman and Puritan philanthropic desires of rooting out and sweeping off the Irish from the land.

The projects of emigration, therefore, were most eagerly advanced by the enemies of the Irish, their real friends being, on the whole, opposed to the movement at the time. But, the true causes of Irish misery being either unseen or unappreciated, or, if known, studiously fostered, with a view of bringing about the one aim which ran all through the English policy, of emptying the island and destroying the race, eventually it did actually become a dire necessity for the people to fly; and therefore, from 1815 to 1845, the wave of emigration began to rise fast, and go on swelling in volume and widening in extent from year to year. Midway between the two extreme points, about 1830, it amounted to between twenty-five and thirty thousand. M. de Beaumont could not see how two millions could be transported at once. Nor were they. But he did not foresee that in the twenty years succeeding that in which he wrote more than three millions and a half would actually be shipped from the island; and all the difficulties that he anticipated--the number of ships requisite, the immense amount of money needed, the countries where such numbers might be received--were furnished by Providence for the spread of the Irish in many lands. But these considerations can only be briefly touched upon here; they will form the interesting subject of the next chapter. What we have now to consider is the commencement of the great exodus, confined so far to Canada and the United States, but already working wonders over the vast stretch of country which spreads away between the St. Lawrence and the Gulf of Mexico.

According to the official records of emigration from the "United Kingdom," from 1815 to 1860 inclusive, we find that, in general, the greater number emigrated to Canada up to 1839; from that epoch, but chiefly after 1845, the greater number went directly to the United States. Let us first look for a reason for this change of destination, and afterward for its result.

Homer, wiser than many modern philosophers, tells us that "there are beings which have a certain name among men and another quite different among the gods." What is true of names, is true likewise of what they represent, motives and things in general. Men often assign to actions motives far different from those known to God; and, in like manner, the motives of men, visibly impelled by the Spirit of God, are often far beyond the comprehension of "philosophers." We are far from presuming to dive into the divine thoughts with the certainty of bringing to the surface what lies hidden in their mysterious depths; but every Christian should endeavor humbly to penetrate them, and modestly set forth what he gathers from them.

What object can be assigned for the Irish emigrating in such large numbers to Canada for a quarter of a century, from 1815 to 1840? It cannot be because Canada is, as it then was, a British colony: the English Emigration Commissioners had the honesty to confess, later on, that the rush to the United States was in consequence of their desire to avoid dwelling under the English flag. It was not because, in Canada, a greater facility opened up for obtaining good land; for, in Lower Canada, where they tarried for a long time, the land was already occupied by French-Canadians, and, in that severe climate, the soil is not over-productive. It cannot have been the facility for transportation--during about six months of every year, the mouth of the St. Lawrence is closed to ships, and travel through a frozen land is not the most desirable thing, particularly to homeless and moneyless immigrants. Last of all, it was not the similarity of climate and language with those of their own island. What, then, can it have been?

In our own opinion, the human motive of the Irish can have been no other than a religious one; in the Divine mind, the motive was of a still higher and more merciful character. The Irish had heard, from the few of their countrymen who had already emigrated to the United States, of the great difficulty they experienced in practising their religion. On the other hand, they knew that, throughout Lower Canada, there was not a village without its Catholic church and priest, and that Quebec and Montreal were important and entirely Catholic cities. This great fact blinded them to the many disadvantages they would have to undergo in emigrating to such a country; or, rather, they saw the disadvantages, but the thought that their religion and that of their children would be safe in Canada was enough for them. It is the same people ever, in the nineteenth century as in those which preceded it, and all noble minds must respect them for thus first looking to the supernatural.

But, had the Almighty a design in directing them to the north of the continent, and establishing so great a number of them permanently in that country? We are fully persuaded that the Irish race is now, and ever has been, predestined to fulfill a high mission on this earth. What is now transpiring under our eyes is too clear to be denied by any Christian; and admitting the general fact that the race must be an instrument in the hands of God to spread his Church throughout, in English-speaking countries particularly, to correct, by their presence and influence in every quarter of the globe, the evil effects of the spread of what we call Japhetism among Oriental races--let us endeavor to see how their coming to settle in Canada served for that great end.

The Gospel of our Lord was first preached in those dreary regions by religious of the Gallic race. The labors of Catholic missionaries in Canada, of the members of the Society of Jesus particularly, are now well known and appreciated. The French colony in Canada was from the first a Catholic colony: It was not a conquest; it was not a commercial enterprise; it was not a transatlantic garden for luxurious Frenchmen: it was what Mr. Bancroft has well called it, "a mission." The desire of winning souls to

Christ had begun the work, had run all through it almost to the end. The blood of martyrs had consecrated it; that of Rasles, shed by heretics; of Lallemant, Brebeuf, and Jogues, by pagans. But, after the surrender of the colony to England, although the terms of the cession were as favorable to religion as could be desired, and the British power could not introduce there any of the penal laws still pressing so hard on English and Irish Catholics, nevertheless, a great danger arose in consequence, which is particularly visible now after more than a century has passed away. Though Catholicity could not be persecuted, and, for once, England faithfully observed the terms of a capitulation which involved a religious side, as little could heresy be excluded or denied some of the privileges which it enjoys in the mother country. The government was to be administered mostly by Protestant officials; the new-comers from England would be composed, for the greater part, of Protestant merchants and artisans. The Anglican Church would soon gain the prestige of wealth and influence. The country in the east, it is true, thickly settled by Catholic farmers, would long remain Catholic; but in the large towns, Quebec and Montreal chiefly, an influx of Protestants of every sect was to be expected; while in the west, where the French had scarcely occupied the country, the numerical majority would soon lean to the side of the new arrivals from England and Scotland. The English tongue would gradually supersede the French, and it might have been foreseen from the beginning that, within a given time, notwithstanding the rapid increase of French-Canadians by birth, Catholicity would lose first its preeminence, and, perhaps, after a while, occupy a very inferior rank.

The religion professed by the many millions connected with the centre of unity has never shrunk from an equal contest, and is sure of victory when left free and untrammelled; but in Canada it should be observed that, had it not been for the coming of the Irish, the whole of the Catholic population would have spoken French, being surrounded and absorbed almost by sectarians of every hue, all speaking English. The strange spectacle would there have shown itself--a spectacle, perhaps, never witnessed hitherto--of a Catholic and Protestant language. The separation of the two camps would have rested chiefly upon this peculiar basis; and there can be no doubt that, with the vigorous youth of the United States, developing so rapidly in the South, and destined to carry with it the English tongue over all the Northern continent, together with the spread of the English and Scotch North and West, the French language was destined to become circumscribed within narrower and narrower limits, and its final disappearance in America would be probably only a work of time.

If it is permitted us to study, love, and admire the designs of Providence among men, who shall say that it is presumption to assert that God's was the hand which directed the Irish exiles and set them in their place, in order to prevent the sad spectacle of a land settled by holy people, belonging almost exclusively to God and to Christ, endeared to the true Church by so many labors endured for the spread of truth, and memorable by so many heroic virtues practised in those frozen wilds and dreary forests, from falling sooner or later into the hands of the most unrelenting enemies of the papacy?

It cannot be presumptuous to attribute it to the designs of Providence, as otherwise it is impossible to discover any reason whatever which might influence the Irish in selecting that desolate spot for their place of exile. They came, therefore, in great numbers, to set themselves under the spiritual control of priests unable to understand either their native language or the borrowed English they brought with them; they came, confident that all the Catholic churches built prior to their coming would be open to them, and that the pastors of those French congregations would receive them, not as strangers, but as long-lost children, at last let loose from a land of bondage, come to share the freedom secured by the settlers.

The statistics of immigration having been accurately kept since 1815, it is easy to ascertain the number of Irish people who landed in Canada during the precise period under investigation. And, although a certain number, which increased with the years, did not remain in the country where they first landed, but pushed on immediately, or shortly after, south to the United States, still, a large proportion settled permanently in the country.

Half a million English-speaking persons arrived in Canada between the years 1815 and 1839. At that time there was no distinction made between the three different classes coming respectively from England, Scotland, and Ireland; but, when this classification afterward came to be made, the Irish formed a steady three-fourths of the whole. Applying this proportion to the time under consideration, we have the large amount of three hundred and seventy-five thousand. The number was afterward considerably increased, although a greater number still went directly to the United

States; so that it is ascertained that within ten years, from 1839 to 1849, four hundred and twenty-eight thousand Irish people arrived in Canada; that is to say, at a rate of fifty thousand a year.

The country in which they settled was certainly large, as it comprised not only Canada proper, but also the British provinces of New Brunswick, Nova Scotia, and the large islands in the vicinity. But, as the Irish, contrary to their former custom, now prefer to dwell in large towns and assemble together rather than find themselves, as it were, lost in a sparsely-peopled district, the population of important cities, such as Quebec and Montreal, and of the growing western towns of Toronto, Kingston, and others, was very sensibly affected by their arrival. The English was no longer to be an exclusively Protestant tongue; and, as the more rapid increase of the Irish by birth would soon equalize numbers, and give them eventually the preponderance, it was clear that the country would ultimately remain Catholic, even supposing that the French tongue should be finally forgotten.

The first extensive emigration to the large cities of Canada was also owing to the fact that, the eastern provinces not having come under the stipulation of the capitulation treaty, the penal laws were still unrepealed in that district. Toward the beginning of this century we find Father Burke, wishing to open a school for Catholic children at Halifax, Nova Scotia, threatened with the enforcement of the law by the then governor of the province, if he persevered in his attempt, a threat which was only prevented from being carried into execution by the liberal spirit of the Protestant inhabitants. The flow of emigration to the colonies south and east of the St. Lawrence was, consequently, of a much later, in fact, for the most part, of quite recent date.

In Newfoundland the case was still worse. That region had been ceded to Great Britain by France, in 1713, at the Treaty of Utrecht; and, although that treaty stipulated that freedom of worship should be guaranteed, nevertheless, the country remained closed to Catholic clergymen, the stipulation being nullified by the treacherous clause "as far as the laws of England permitted. "Hence, the French Catholics with their clergy were soon obliged to leave the colony, and as late as 1765, according to Mr. Maguire ("Irish in America"), the governor of the island was issuing orders worthy of the reign of Queen Anne. In the words of Dr. Murdock, Bishop of St. John's, Newfoundland, "the Irish had not the liberty of the birds of the air to build or repair their nests; they had behind them the forest or the rocky soil, which they were not allowed, without license difficultly obtained, to reclaim and till. Their only resource was the stormy ocean, and they saw the wealth they won from the deep spent in other lands, leaving them only a scanty subsistence."

The Irish had therefore to fall back on the cities of Lower Canada, where, moreover, they found numerous churches and priests. Hence, Quebec was their first place of refuge, and they soon formed a large percentage of the population. Montreal was their choice from the first, where they arrived in crowds, attracted by the intense pleasure they felt at the happy chance of living and dying in a really Catholic city, where, turn in what direction they would, their eyes were gladdened by the sight of magnificent churches, colleges, convents, hospitals, with the cross, the symbol of their faith, surmounting nearly all the public edifices of the city.

Western Canada was as yet an uninviting field for the Irish. A large number of Scotchmen and "Orangemen" had already settled there, when the British Government, having adopted the scheme of emigration for Ireland, offered them favorable conditions for transport and settlement. It was on the west chiefly that an invasion of English Protestantism threatened, and the Catholics of Ireland were, in the dispensation of Providence, to meet that danger. It is no surprise, then, to find the English Government itself made subservient to designs very different from its own, offering in 1825 to bear the whole expense of establishing large bodes of Irishmen on these wilds-- wilds then, but full of promise for the future. Among other colonies transported bodily, Mr. Maguire tells of four hundred and fifteen families, comprising two thousand individuals, all from the south of Ireland, genuine "Irish in birth and blood," transported from Cork harbor to Western Canada, on board British ships, under the auspices of the government. Their story will well repay the reading, and above all their remonstrance to the governor of the province, after they had surmounted the first difficulties of their new position: "We labor under a heavy grievance, which, we confidently hope, your Excellency will redress, and then we will be completely happy, viz., the want of clergymen to administer to us the comforts of our holy religion, and good schoolmasters to instruct our children."

In spite, however, of the efforts made by British statesmen to direct the flow of Irish emigration to the northern part of the American Continent, the number of those who voluntarily crossed the Atlantic to settle directly in the United States was steadily increasing. Not only did they find there perfect freedom of religion, but the absence of clergymen was being gradually less felt, and each new bishopric created became a centre of religious life and vigor.

Moreover, the new republic had turned out to be the most energetic and enterprising nation which the world had yet seen. A whole continent lay before it to subdue, and at once the young giant prepared to grapple with the truly gigantic difficulty. With the arrival of every "packet-boat," Europe was astonished to hear of the amazing vitality displayed by a nation of yesterday, composed of a few millions of individuals, who had already spread their frontiers as far north as the whole line of the great lakes, as far west as the Pacific coast, and southward to the Gulf of Mexico. Louisiana fell in, and, from a state of torpidity in which it had slumbered, the vast territory which then went by that name waked suddenly into a prodigiously active life. At the very beginning of the century, the Missouri had been navigated to its source, and Lewis and Clarke, crossing the high ridge of the Rocky Mountains, had descended the Columbia to its mouth, and settled the boundary of the United States along the far-spreading Pacific. The mighty Mississippi, in the midst of that splendid domain, belonged from source to mouth to the republic, and, with its tributaries, was already alive with numerous steamboats, passing up and down, bearing their life and all its belongings with them, and the (at that time more numerous still) flatboats, carried down the stream, to reach, in due time, New Orleans.

There was small thought of hindering "foreigners" from coming to take a share in the giant enterprise. All the inhabitants were in fact foreigners to the soil; and the new-comers, no matter from what country they came, had just as good a right to sit at the common board as the first-landed. It was felt and wisely acknowledged to be the real interest of the young nation to welcome as great a number as Europe could send.

Thus have we already seen large numbers of Irishmen laboring along the Erie Canal. There was not a public work undertaken at the time in which they did not bear a welcome hand. And what race of men could be found better fitted for such work? It would indeed be interesting to show from good statistical tables what share Irishmen have really had in building up the prosperity of the Union by their labor, skilled and unskilled.

At the period we have now come to, they were already crowding in at the harbors of the Atlantic, so astonishing to the newly- arrived European by the extraordinary activity which characterizes them; they were numerous in the factories just starting into life, from the desire of not depending on England for all manufactured goods; they were multiplying in large hotels, in private families, in the fields outside the large cities. Above all, the buildings erected at the time, in such great numbers, employed many of them as mechanics and laborers; and whenever some grand undertaking, which looked to the future welfare of the country, demanded a large draft of men, there were they to be seen as they had never been seen before, even in their own country, where all labor was reduced to the individual efforts of each, just sufficient to eke out a miserable life.

At this time, about 1820, the Irish immigrants settled, for the most part, on the Atlantic seaboard; few had yet crossed even the ridge of the Alleghanies. In the Eastern States they found occupation enough, and the steady growth of the country required their willing aid. From that time the North formed their chief point of attraction, and the States of Pennsylvania, New Jersey, and New York, were their great resorts. Even New England was no longer forbidden ground to them, and they began to spread themselves over its rocky and unpromising surface, to effect there a greater moral change than probably anywhere else in the country. In 1827, during the first pastoral visitation of Bishop Fenwick, when he erected, on the spot made memorable by the apostolic labors of Father Rasles, a monument to the memory of that saintly man, we read that "he then went in search of some Irish Catholics living at Belfast, Maine, whom he found suffering both for the necessaries of life and for the sustenance of the soul. He relieved both their temporal and spiritual wants, and imparted them his blessing, and some wholesome advice."

He was enabled to do more for them in the following year at Charlestown, Massachusetts. On the 15th of October, 1828, according to the Boston Gazette, "he laid the corner-stone of a Catholic church near Craigie's Point, designed to accommodate the Catholics of that place and of Charlestown, who were said to be already numerous." There is no doubt that the several churches built about that time in Maine, New Hampshire, Massachusetts, Connecticut, and Rhode Island, were filled rather by Irish immigrants than by American converts, although not a few consoling examples of this latter method of the Church's increase took place about this period.

But New York was taking the lead as the landing of predilection for the desolate children of Ireland. Thus, at the installation of Bishop Dubois, in St. Patrick's Cathedral, November 9, 1826, he addressed himself particularly to the Irish portion of his congregation, observing that "he entertained for them the liveliest feelings of affection. He reminded them of the persecutions they had undergone in defence of their religion, of the sacrifices many of them had made on leaving their native country, and conjured them always to manifest that attachment to the religion of their forefathers which had hitherto so prominently distinguished them among their brother Catholics."

The whole State was beginning to swarm with new arrivals from the Green Isle. This detachment, however, only formed the scarcely perceptible head of the great army which was to follow. We shall soon return to see its masses steadily treading their way on toward the West, and never halting till they reached the Pacific coast; we will see for what purpose.

Meanwhile, it is fitting to look at another wing of this army taking its position directly south of Asia, the great continent which holds the first dwelling of man on earth, and toward which all the tendencies of modern civilization seem to turn.

An immense island, to which geographers have now given the name of the fifth continent, from the dawn of creation lay sleeping between the seas known as the Indian and Pacific Oceans. A few thousand savages, said to be the lowest type of the human family, roamed aimlessly over its extensive wilds. Out of the ordinary route of circumnavigating explorers, few European ships had reached its coast, when the Dutch attempted to form establishments on its southern and western sides, giving it the name of New Holland. At the end of last century the English Captain Cook formed the first successful European settlement--Botany Bay--in what he called New South Wales, at the south-eastern extremity of the island. The French surveyed a considerable portion of the western coast at the beginning of this century. But finally, as has so far generally been the case with other colonies, the English remained in possession of the whole, and, though their first thought was to use it merely as a penal settlement, they soon saw the importance of removing their convicts to Van Diemen's Island, and now no less than four or five distinct British colonies embrace the entire coast-line of the continent, the interior still remaining an unknown desert.

Immigration, other than the transport of criminals, began only in 1825; and the white population of New South Wales, which in 1810 was only eight thousand three hundred, in 1821 only thirty thousand, increased rapidly after the discovery of the gold-fields in 1851, so that in 1861 more than seven hundred thousand free colonists had been landed from British ships on the continent and large islands of Van Diemen and New Zealand, notwithstanding their enormous distance from Great Britain.

The importance of this vast colony, or, rather, of this agglomeration of colonies, should not be estimated from their extent and productions alone, but chiefly from their proximity to Asia toward the north, and to America toward the east. Already lines of steamers connect the new continent with China on the one side and San Francisco on the other; and when we reflect that the English tongue is the only one spoken through-out that vast territory; that English political institutions, with all their attendant machinery of parliaments, elections, municipal governments, and liberties, toleration, a free press and free discussion, are day by day becoming more deeply rooted in the habits of the people, it is easy to perceive how soon the peculiarities of Japhetism, starting from that centre, will invade the whole line of Southern and Eastern Asia and the countless island-groups of Polynesia. The Catholic reader will at once perceive how the true religion must have been left to struggle, hopelessly almost, in its mission of enlightenment and mercy, surrounded as it was by so many adverse circumstances, had not the Irish element been at hand to fall back on.

Our information on this important branch of the subject is unfortunately not extensive; nor is this to be wondered at, since it is only from 1851 that Irish immigration really began to show itself in Australia, and take an active part in the European rush toward that quarter of the world, or, rather, to use the phrase of Holy Writ, "to dwell in the tents of Sem."

When Great Britain sent out her first cargoes of convicts to Australia, it never entered into the ideas of that enlightened power that such an attendant as a minister of religion might be wanted, and, as Mr. Marshall says in his book on "Christian Missions:" "The first ship which bore away its freight of despair, of bruised hearts, and woful memories, and fearful expectations, would have left the shores of England without even a solitary minister of religion, but for the timely remonstrance of a private individual. The civil authorities had deemed their work complete, when they had given the signal to raise the anchor and unloose the sails; the rest was no concern of theirs. "He adds something more extraordinary and more to our purpose still:

"Among the emigrants to the new continent, soon some of those children of Ireland, whom Providence seems to have dispersed through all the homes of the Saxon race, that they might one day rekindle among them the light of faith, which their own long misfortunes have never been able to quench, were carried as the first fruitful seeds of the ever-blooming tree of the Church."

To these exiles it was necessary to convey the succors of religion. The first Catholic priest who arrived in Australia on his mission of charity, and whom the policy of self-interest, at least, might have prompted the authorities to greet with eager welcome, was treated with derision, and "was directed," as one of his most energetic successors relates, "to produce his permission," or "hold himself in readiness for departure by the next ship." He was alone, and consequently a safe victim; and though, as the latest historian of the colony observes, "his ministrations would have been not less valuable in a social than in a religious point of view," he was seized, put in prison, and finally sent back to England, because his presence was irksome to men who seem to have felt instinctively that his proffered ministry was the keenest rebuke to their own cruelty and profaneness.

This first Catholic priest was the Rev. Mr. Flynn, on whom the Holy See had conferred the title of archpriest, with power to administer confirmation. Arrived at Sydney in 1818, he did much good there in a short time. Mr. Marshall has told us how the colonial authorities treated him.

But a circumstance, not mentioned in this clever author's work on "Missions," shows who and what were those Irish exiles whom the priest had come to serve and direct in his spiritual capacity. When suddenly carried off to prison, he left the Blessed Sacrament in their little church at Sydney. There the faithful frequently assembled during the two years which followed his departure, as large a number as could muster, to offer up their prayers to God, and look for consolation in their affliction. The visible priest had been violently snatched away from them; the Archpriest of souls, Christ, remained.

The Rev. W. Ullathorne, now Bishop of Birmingham, England, was afterward made Vicar-General Apostolic of that desolate mission by the Holy See. He informs us, in a letter published among the "Annals of the Propagation of the Faith," how these poor Irish people were treated by their "masters" in Australia.

"It was forbidden them to speak Irish, under pain of fifty strokes of the whip; and the magistrates, who for the most part belonged to the 'Protestant clergy,' sentenced also to the whip and to close confinement those who refused to go hear their sermons, and to assist at a service which their consciences disavowed."

In 1820 two fresh missionaries replaced Mr. Flynn. They found the little church where their predecessor had left our Lord two years before still in the same state; and soon the insignificant flock, which ever multiplies under persecution, began to increase wonderfully, so that twelve years later, out of the whole population of the colony--one hundred thousand-- there were from twenty to thirty thousand Catholics.

Meanwhile, their emancipation in England had secured their rights in the British colonies. There was no longer the threat of the whip hanging over those who refused to hear Protestant sermons; there was no longer fear of their missionary being sent back by the first ship to England. Hence the Holy See immediately established the hierarchy of the Church, on a regular and permanent basis, there, Dr. Polding being the first bishop.

This may be called an era in the history of the Catholic Church. A hierarchy, independent of the state in heretic and even infidel countries, is a modern thought inspired by the Holy Spirit to the rulers of the flock of Christ to meet modern requirements. By this new system the long list of so-called Protestant countries was at once swept away. For no country can be called Protestant which has its regularly-established bishops of Holy Church, with their authority permanently secured. Their dioceses cover the land, and the land consequently belongs to the Church, however great may be the number of heretics or infidels, and however powerful the organizations antagonistic to Catholicity. The "people of God" is there, to multiply with the years, and finally absorb all heterogeneous bodies. The Church, as we saw, is a growth; other bodies are crystallized and do not grow; more, they become materially and necessarily disintegrated by the action of time and the friction of surrounding bodies, of spreading roots and living organisms.

This plain, unmistakable, eventual truth was the real cause which brought about the violent explosion of fear and hatred following directly the reestablishing of the Catholic hierarchy in England. The opposing forces felt that their hour was come, and they could not but shiver at their approaching annihilation, small as was the body of the English Catholics at the time. But it is not for us to enter here on these considerations, which would call for long developments, and which belong more fittingly to the general history of the Church than to Irish emigration to Australia.

The few facts glanced at above afford ample grounds for picturing the state of the first Irish exiles who set foot on that broad island of the Antipodes. It was only a repetition of the scenes witnessed at the same time wherever the Irish strove to propagate the true faith. Later on it will be our pleasure to come back to this field and wonder at the growth of a blooming garden which has replaced the old sterility.

Of the other British colonies wherein a certain number of Irishmen began to settle at the time of the present investigation, no details can yet be furnished. It is easy to suppose, however, without fear of mistake, that the spiritual destitution and state of more or less open persecution which we have found existing in America and Australia, prevailed also at the Cape Colony, at Natal, in Guiana, Labuan, Ceylon, etc. A very different spectacle is about to be unfolded before our eyes, and we hasten on to behold its wondrous development and splendor--a splendor, however, ushered in by scenes of extreme woe.

THE "EXODUS" AND ITS EFFECTS

THE stream of Irish emigrants, starting from the one source, separated now and continued flowing to the four quarters of the globe, and, at length, its influence was beginning to be felt in England itself, the last of the lands whither the Irish exiles could think of turning. The poorest, unable to pay their passage-money to North America, began to show themselves among the thick populations of the great manufacturing centres of Great Britain. More than fifty thousand departed annually to settle in other climes and plant Catholicity in regions that, from a religious point of view, were wildernesses.

In 1846 came an awful calamity, to impart to the movement an impetus of which no one could have dreamed, and which went very far to realize what M. de Beaumont had a few years before declared to be an impossibility-- the almost sudden transportation of millions of starving Irish. This was the great famine, still so fresh in memory, and now appearing to those who witnessed its effects like that terrible passage of the destroying angel in the night.

There is no better mode of accounting for this visitation than that given by T. D. McGee, in his "Irish Settlers in America:"

"The famine (of 1846) is to be thus accounted for: The act of Union in 1800 deprived Ireland of a native legislature. Her aristocracy emigrated to London. Her tariff expired in 1826, and, of course, was not renewed. Her merchants and manufacturers withdrew their capital from trade and invested it in land. The land! the land! was the object of universal, unlimitable competition. In the first twenty years of the century, the farmers, if rack-rented, had still the war prices. After the peace, they had the monopoly of the English provision and produce markets. But in 1846 Sir Robert Peel successfully struck at the old laws imposing duties on foreign corn, and let in Baltic wheat and American provisions of every kind, to compete with and undersell the Irish rack-rented farmers.

"High rents had produced hardness of heart in the 'middleman,' extravagance in the land-owner, and extreme poverty in the peasant. The poor-law commission of 1839 reported that two million three hundred thousand of the agricultural laborers of Ireland were 'paupers;' that those immediately above the lowest rank were ' the worst-clad, worst-fed, and worst-lodged ' peasantry in Europe. True indeed! They were lodged in styes, clothed in rags, and fed on the poorest quality of potato.

"Partial failures of this crop had taken place for a succession of seasons. So regularly did those failures occur, that William Cobbett and other skilful agriculturists had foretold their final destruction years before. Still, the crops of the summer of 1846 looked fair and sound to the eye. The darkgreen, crispy leaves, and yellow-and-purple blossoms of the potato-fields, were a cheerful feature in every landscape. By July, however, the terrible fact became but too certain. From every town-land within the four seas tidings came to the capital that the people's food was blasted--utterly, hopelessly blasted. Incredulity gave way to panic, panic to demands on the Imperial Government to stop the export of grain, to establish public granaries, and to give the peasantry such productive employment as would enable them to purchase food enough to keep soul and body together. By a report of the ordnance-captain, Larcom, it appeared there were grain-crops more than sufficient to support the whole population--a cereal harvest estimated at four hundred millions of dollars, as prices were. But to all remonstrances, petitions, and proposals, the imperial economists had but one answer: 'They could not interfere with the ordinary currents of trade.' O'Connell's proposal, Lord Georga Bentinck's, O'Brien's, the proposals of the society called 'The Irish Council,' all received the same answer. Fortunes were made and lost in gambling over this sudden trade in human subsistence, and ships laden to the gunwales sailed out of Irish ports, while the charities of the world were coming in.

"In August, authentic cases of death by famine, with the verdict, 'starvation,' were reported. The first authentic case thrilled the country, like an ill wind. From twos and threes they rose to tens, and, in September, such inquests were held, and the same sad verdict repeated, twenty times in a day. Then Ireland, the hospitable among the nations, smitten with famine, deserted by her imperial masters, lifted up her voice, and uttered that cry of awful anguish which shook the ends of the earth.

"The Czar, the Sultan, and the Pope, sent their rubles and their pauls. The Pacha of Egypt, the Shah of Persia, the Emperor of China, the Rajahs of India, conspired to do for Ireland what her so-styled rulers refused to do--to keep her young and old people living in the land. America did more in this work of mercy than all the rest of the world."

The sudden effect of this fearful trial was to increase the total emigration from the British Isles from ninety-three thousand in 1845 to one hundred and thirty thousand in 1846; to three hundred thousand in 1849; to nearly four hundred thousand in 1852. In ten years from 1846, two million eight hundred thousand had fled in horror from the country once so dear to them. From May, 1847, to the close of 1866, the number of passengers discharged at New York alone amounted to three million six hundred and fifty-nine thousand!

Those immense fleets of transports, which M. de Beaumont thought necessary, but not to be found, were found. On such a sudden emergency, every kind of tub afloat was thought suitable for the purpose; and, all being sailing-vessels, the voyage was proportionately long, the provision made for such numbers insufficient, and the emigrants, already weakened by privations, were fit subjects for the plague which, under the form of ship-fever, rapidly spread among those receptacles of human misery, so that, when the great caravan arrived in the St. Lawrence, whither that first year all seemed to tend, the following was the picture presented:

"On the 8th of May, 1847, the Urania, from Cork, with several hundred immigrants on board, a large proportion of them sick and dying of the ship-fever, was put into quarantine at Grosse Isle, thirty miles below Quebec. This was the first of the plague-smitten ships of Ireland which that year sailed up the St. Lawrence. But, before the first week of June, as many as eighty- four ships, of various tonnage, were driven in by an easterly wind; and of that enormous number of vessels there was not one free from the taint of malignant typhus, the offspring of famine and of the foul ship-hold."

The effects of that awful misfortune may be found vividly described in Mr. Maguire's book, from which the above extract is taken, on the long line of march of that desolate army of immigrants, leaving its thousands of victims at Grosse Isle, near Quebec, at Pointe St. Charles, a suburb of

Montreal, in Kingston, in Toronto, Upper Canada, and, finally, at Partridge Island, opposite St. John's, New Brunswick.

America was thus destined to witness some of those scenes so often enacted on the soil of Ireland, to compassionate the people of the holy isle, to open her friendly bosom for the reception of the unfortunate beings, who in return gave her all they possessed--their faith.

But what M. de Beaumont so emphatically insisted upon, although at first seemingly contradicted by the event, was nevertheless true. England, the mighty mistress of the seas, did not possess ships enough for the purpose of transportation; and her entire navy added to all her merchant-vessels would scarcely have sufficed. Ships had to be built, steamers chiefly, in order to effect the transportation speedily, and diminish the dangers of the passage.

Then Providence worked upon the ingenuity of worldly-wise men, and set them planning and studying the question in all its bearings, to devise new schemes of transportation on a scale not dreamed of hitherto. Watt, the Stephensons, Brunel, A. Maury, and others, rose up to perfect the various steam-machines already known and in use; to investigate the currents of the ocean, the different qualities of its waters, its depth and soundings, in order to make the paths of the deep easier and surer to navigators. The ingenuity of ship-builders effected a revolution in naval architecture, and rendered possible the construction of vessels of from ten thousand to twenty-five thousand tons burden. Merchant companies and capitalists arose to embrace the whole world in their mighty speculations, studying the capabilities of all countries for trade, the most desolate as well as the most inviting, the meanest as keenly as the mightiest, linking the whole world in one vast commercial circle, that the European race might be borne on to the mercantile conquest of the universe; and all this came about, doubtless, to effect its deeper and more permanent moral conquest by the despised, doom-trodden, starving, dying Irishman, who laid claim to one arm, one possession only--his faith and the blessing of the Church.

Was not the Irish exodus intimately connected with all those events? Was it not one of the mightiest causes of all those gigantic enterprises?

But where were the funds to be found for such immense undertakings? The treasury of nations is continually drained of vast sums at home, and dare not draw away a part of its metallic basis sufficient for such a purpose. Moreover, it is limited, and needs the precious metals as a solid foundation whereon to rest, or the fabric built upon it will be the fabric of a dream, as was that of Law in France at the beginning of the eighteenth century. The gold and silver mines of Mexico and Peru seem exhausted; the new ones of the Ural Mountains in Northern Asia, of the Atlantic coast of North America, were not adequate to meet the demands of such mighty operations.

Suddenly, in the year 1846, a Swiss captain, transformed into a California settler, while endeavoring to turn a water-fall in his new home to some account, discovers gold-dust in the sand. As if by magic, the coast of California, hitherto neglected, difficult of access at the time, and consequently ignored by mankind, notwithstanding its wealth in mineral and vegetable productions, becomes at once the cynosure of all eyes, the hope of all hearts, the most renowned of all countries. Thither they flock in crowds prom all parts of Europe and America, and a steady flow of seventy million dollars annually is secured as a basis for the new designs of capitalists and merchants.

Other gold-fields are soon discovered all along the American coast, on the Pacific, from Lower California to Alaska, inviting men to go thither and settle, just opposite to the Asiatic Continent, separated from it only by the broad but easily- navigated Pacific Ocean.

Soon also, far away south in the antipodes, opposite to another portion of Asia, rich gold-fields are opened up in the newly- discovered Continent of Australia, attracting immigration toward another spot, whence the Asiatic nations may also be reached with greater facility and dispatch.

Whoever believes that Providence has something to do with the affairs of men; whoever is wise enough to see that this universe is not the result of chance, and that its destinies are ruled by a superior power, must admit that when events as unexpected as they are unprepared by man come to pass--events which are so connected together as to reveal the workings of a single mind and a great object at once, foreshadowed if not positively foretold, God is the designer, and a stronger hand is at work than the combined power of men and devils could successfully oppose. This is a truth which was not unknown to Homer, centuries ago, when he described Jove holding our globe suspended in space at the end of a chain, and defying all the inferior gods to move the world in a direction contrary to that given by his mighty arm.

The image, striking and poetical as it is, for a Christian is too material. We speak more correctly when we say that Mind -- the Divine Mind--is the great invincible and invisible Force of which all material forces are but the created agents, and by which all inferior minds must stand or fall, conquer or fail. A man must be blind with that incurable blindness--of will--who cannot see it acting in and on the universe, and even controlling the lower designs of puny intellects. The reverent eye which sees the vastness of the plan, the multitude of its agents, aiding and seconding it consciously and unconsciously, recognizes it, and the supreme object of its workings, Love, infinite Love.

And we distinguish with grateful surprise all those circumstances visibly appearing in the great fact which has just been so imperfectly sketched, and which will come home to us still more forcibly when the workings of its lesser details come to be examined. Here, for instance, at the moment of writing these lines (March, 1872) we learn from the morning newspapers of the recent arrival of the Japanese embassy at San Francisco; that its members had been dispatched to this country to study European, or, as we call them, Japhetic institutions, for the purpose of copying and adapting them to their own wants. The embassy, detained at Salt Lake City by the snow-blockade on the Pacific Railroad, refused to go back, temporarily, to California, and made up their mind to wait in Utah, until it is possible for them to proceed.

Pacific Railroad, Salt Lake City, San Francisco, Japanese embassy, adoption of European manners by the Mikado and daimios--who can fail to gather from these words and details the conception of means to an end, and that end the one we now begin to study?

The first circumstance coming under our review and indicative of a loving design on the part of Providence, a circumstance not marked sufficiently at the time, is the preservation by the English themselves of the poor remnants of the Irish race, which the first working of the plan had so frightfully decimated and left in danger of being utterly wiped out. Had they disappeared, would Japhetism have become a blessing to the Asiatic nations? The Catholic, looking abroad and casting his mind's eye over the vast European field, to all seeming so rich in every production, yet in reality so sterile morally, peering with awe and horror into the Japhetic caldron--for such it is--seething and bubbling to the brim, full of the most deadly poisons and noxious substances, ready at any moment to overflow in infected waves and sweep over the unfortunate countries which look to it so anxiously for blessings, a torrent of black destruction, spreading around naught but desolation and barrenness--the Catholic eye, seeing all this, can find but one answer to our query. The Asiatic races cannot hope to be benefited by the introduction of European manners among them, unless the same great movement carries in its train the holy Catholic Church: and as that introduction must be brought about by English-speaking leaders, the only English-speaking Catholics of numerical significance must be the instruments of the adorable designs of Providence.

That this assertion may not appear too sweeping, it is only enough to instance the example of India, which England has held long enough to convert, at least in part, had she so desired and been moved by the Spirit of God, yet to-day India stands in a worse relation toward Protestantism than when Protestantism in the name of Christianity, but in the person of a British trader, settled down in its midst. What good has Hindostan derived?

But, at this very moment, the whole Irish race is at the mercy of the English Government and people. Only let the same kind of vessels continue to be dispatched filled with Irish emigrants, and the whole race must disappear within a short period, or become so reduced in numbers that its operations as a race, on a large scale, will be unproductive of sufficient results.

And it is well to mark that at the time of this outpouring of the race, as long before, and almost constantly since, there were Englishmen rejoicing at the glorious result which death by plague and famine was about to produce. It were easy to quote many a barbarous passage from the London Times, expressive of the most satanic joy, not only at the departure of the Irish from the "United Kingdom," but at the prospect of their ultimate, or rather proximate disappearance out of the world altogether.

Yet it was the same English Government and people which, feeling, let us hope, some compassion at the sight of this new woe of the "Niobe of nations," determined to try and save her children, as, if they must cast them out, at least it should he alive and full of health on a foreign shore.

Laws, therefore, were passed, regulating the quantity and quality of provisions, particularly of drinkable water, the number of the crew and working-men, the ventilation of the vessel, the number of passengers to be received, etc.

Still, these first attempts at humanity seem to have been rather faint-hearted, as the following passage from Mr. Maguire's "Irish in America," showing how they were carried out, and how inadequate was the remedy applied in 1848, will explain:

"The ships, of which such glowing accounts were read on Sunday by the Irish peasant near the chapel-gate, were but too often old and unseaworthy, insufficient in accommodation, not having even an adequate supply of water for a long voyage, and, to render matters worse, they, as a rule, were shamefully underhanded. True, the provisions and the crew must have passed muster in Liverpool; . . . but there were tenders and lighters to follow the vessel out to sea; and over the sides of that vessel several of the mustered men would pass, and casks, and boxes, and sacks would be expeditiously hoisted, to the amazement of the simple people who looked on at the strange and unaccountable operation. And, thus, the great ship, with its living freight, would turn her prow toward the West, depending on her male passengers, as on so many impressed seamen, to handle her ropes or to work her pumps in case of accident. What with bad or scanty provisions, scarcity of water, severe hardship, and long confinement in a foul den, ship-fever reaped yet a glorious harvest between-decks, as frequent splashes of shot-weighted corpses into the deep but too terribly testified. Whatever the cause, the deaths on board the British ships enormously exceeded the mortality on the ships of any other country. According to the records of the Commissioners of Emigration for the State of New York, the quota of sick per thousand stood thus in 1848 British vessels, 30; American, 9 3/5; German, 8 3/5. It was yet no unusual occurrence for the survivor of a family of ten or twelve to land alone, bewildered and broken-hearted, on the wharf at New York; the rest, the family, parents, and children, had been swallowed in the sea, their bodies marking the course of the ship to the New World."

It would seem, then, that those first English regulations, by which British ships were to pass muster at Liverpool before sailing, were not very efficient; the figures of mortality quoted by Mr. Maguire are too eloquent; and it would be a pleasure to us to be able to say with certainty that the more stringent and better executed laws afterward enforced did not proceed from the Commission of Emigration, which originated in New York with some generous-hearted Irish-Americans.

Our readers will have noticed that, even in 1848, with all the apparent desire on the part of England to save the remnants of the Irish nation, the mortality on board British ships was more than three times that on board American vessels, and nearly four times greater than that on board German ships. Why this difference? And why should it be so enormous?

It is possible that to the Legislature of New York State chiefly, and soon after to the Congress of the United States at Washington, which enacted stringent laws for the protection of immigrants at sea, belong the chief honor of saving hundreds of thousands of Irish lives, and that England, whether urged by the effects of good example, or for very shame, soon followed in their wake.

But, whatever the cause may have been, it is a heart-felt pleasure to record the fact that from 1849, when an act of Parliament, entitled the "Passengers Act," imposed on ship-owners and captains of vessels strict conditions for the welfare of emigrants, government control on this subject became every year more immediate and severe.

Not only were the vessels, provisions, water, medicine chests, etc., more carefully examined, but the passengers themselves were compelled to undergo a careful inspection as to their health and wardrobe.

And, a thing which had never been done before, the space allotted to each emigrant on deck and between-decks was determined and subjected to serious control, so that no overcrowding of passengers should take place. The penalties, also, on delinquents became even severe; heavy fines were imposed, and in some cases transportation to a penal settlement was decreed against the more offensive outrages on humanity.

If all abuses failed to be corrected by such laws, it is because the most stringent enactments can, to a greater or less extent, always be evaded by those desirous of evading them; but there is every reason to believe that the legislators were honest in their intent of remedying the glaring evils which previously obtained, and, to a great extent, their efforts met with success, as is evidenced by the fact that the mortality on board of British vessels has shown yearly a remarkable diminution since that time. According to the "Twenty-fourth General Report," the mortality was: In 1854, 0.74 per cent., already a very remarkable diminution on previous averages; in 1860, it was reduced to 0.15 per cent. This was the percentage for vessels going to North America only.

The first operation of the missionary people was to plant the living tree of Catholicism in the United States, and so powerfully forward its growth, that other spiritual plants of a noxious kind, and weeds that go by the name of creeds, should gradually be choked up; finally, let us hope, to disappear. While speaking on this subject, and laying before the reader the necessary details, we desire not to be held forgetful of the efforts made in a like direction by Catholic immigrants of other nationalities. A word has already been said of the early influence of the French in the North and of the Spaniards in the South, in establishing the Church in North America. The German children of the true Church, though at first not so conspicuous, have for a long time taken, and are now particularly taking, an active part in the dissemination of the faith, and there can be no doubt that, with the daily increase of German immigration, their large numbers must in course of time make a lasting impression on the territory where they settle. But the French, the Spaniards, and the Germans, must forget their language before they become widely useful in the great work before them; and thus the Irish form the only English-speaking people on whom the brunt of the battle must fall. Moreover, we treat only of the Irish race.

The wonderful history of the spread of Catholicity in North America by the Irish, in the northern part of the United States particularly, would call for an array of details which it would be impossible to furnish here in extenso. An imperfect sketch must suffice.

First comes the consideration that, when the wave of immigration touched the continent, it might have been feared that, by its absorption into a dry and parched soil, the aggregate loss would have reduced to a mere nothing the ultimate gain. There were no churches for the new worshippers, no priests to administer to them the sacraments of Christ, no Catholic school-teachers to train their children. That is to say, these means of preservation and of propagation were so few and so far between, that many of the newly-arrived immigrants were forced to establish themselves in places where they could find none of those, to them, priceless advantages.

The spiritual dearth was not indeed so great as that previously described. The zeal of bishops and priests, and teachers from regular orders, had been so active in its labors, that, aided by the liberty which the institutions of the country afforded, results, astonishing indeed, had already rewarded their efforts. But, after all, what were these compared with the demands so suddenly laid upon them by such a rapid increase of numbers? It might be said with truth of multitudes of immigrants, that the position in which they then found themselves was very little different from that of their predecessors at the beginning of the century.

As late as 1834, Archbishop Purcell, of Cincinnati, wrote: "There are places in which there are Catholics of twenty years of age, who have not yet had an opportunity of performing one single public act of their religion. How many fall sick and die without the sacraments! How many children are brought up in ignorance and vice! How many persons marry out of the Church, and thus weaken the bonds that held them to it!"-- (Annals of the Propagation of Faith, Vol. viii.)

To the same annals, three years later, Dr. England, of Charleston, sent the long letter in which he detailed the innumerable losses sustained by the Church in America in consequence of the want of spiritual assistance. The letter was, in fact, a cry of anguish wrung from him by the sight he witnessed.

Such was the universal feeling among those who could rightly appreciate the fatal consequences of the rush of Catholics to the New World without any provision prepared for their reception. And yet all these laments and apprehensions preceded the vast inpouring of immigrants subsequent to the year 1846. What must have been the consequent losses then? Yet, looking now, in 1872, at the present state of the Church in the Union, who can say that this inpouring and rush, unprepared as the country was for its reception, was not one of the greatest means devised by Providence, not only for establishing the Catholic Church in this country for all time, but likewise as a preparation for further developments, not only on this continent, but on the part of many a nation now sitting in "the shadow of death!" Deplorable, indeed, were the losses, but permanent and wonderful the gain.

The first effect of the great calamity which occurred along the St. Lawrence and its tributaries, in 1847, was to reduce the immigration to Canada to insignificant numbers, and, proportionately increase that to the United States in a quadruple ratio. Massachusetts and Connecticut, in New England, and the great States of New York and Pennsylvania, were now the chief places of resort for the new-comers; and from New York, principally, they began to pour, in a long, steady stream, away by the Erie Canal, westward to the great lakes.

All along these lines, congregations were, providentially, already formed; and, in the passage of the stream, they were immediately, as by magic, increased in some instances, to a tenfold proportion. The labors of the clergy were correspondingly multiplied, and efforts were immediately made to obtain new recruits for its ranks. Then appeared a very strange fact, which, at the time, was remarked upon by everybody, but has never been satisfactorily explained. Wherever the number of worshippers in a church induced the chief pastors to have another constructed in the neighborhood, upon the completion of the new edifice, the old one seemed to suffer no diminution in attendance, and the congregation attending the new one gave no evidence of having hitherto been uncared for. This very remarkable fact was of such frequent occurrence that it could not be a delusion, or an exceptional case having its origin in some extraordinary cause; it was evidently a providential dispensation, akin, in a spiritual sense, to the miraculous multiplication of loaves, twice mentioned in the Gospel.

There have certainly been numerous examples of this, in the city of New York particularly, for more than twenty years; and probably the same thing is occurring at the time of the present writing.

Then, another fact occurred, deplored by many, chiefly by Mr. Maguire, in the interesting work already quoted from, yet, evidently of a providential character also, and consequently eminently fruitful, and, it may be said, adorable in its depth. The Catholic immigrants, although in their own country agriculturists for the most part, forgot the tilling of the soil as soon as they reached their new home, and settled down in great numbers in all the large cities, on the line they pursued toward the West. Many special evils resulted from this, detailed at length by those whose wonder it excited, and who strove, for excellent motives, to thwart this providential movement. But the immense good which immediately followed from it, and which, within a short time, was to be greatly increased, was never mentioned in reply to the reasons advanced by these well-meaning complainants. The first result of it was the sudden and necessary creation of many new episcopal sees in all large cities, where churches were being rapidly built, or had already been erected in astonishing numbers.

Suppose the Catholics had, following the old bent, turned themselves chiefly to the tillage of the soil, and buried themselves away in scattered country villages and farms, how long would the creation of those new sees have been delayed? Who is ignorant of the effect of a new see on the propagation of Catholicity? Cities which otherwise would have numbered among their population only a few hundred Catholics, scarcely sufficient for the filling of one small edifice, saw at once one-third, one-half, or even the larger portion of their population clamoring for a Catholic bishop, and all the institutions a bishopric brings in its train. It is unnecessary to furnish examples of this; they are around us.

Yet one difficulty seems to cast some doubt on this view of the subject, and strengthen the opposition of those who ardently advocated the country as the true home for Irish Catholics; and, as the point involves a universal interest, it is better to discuss it at once in its chief bearings.

At the time when those wonderful events were being enacted, any one opening a copy of those general State Directories, with which New England is particularly blessed, wherein not only the great commercial and industrial enterprises of each State are enrolled, but also correct lists of the educational establishments and various churches of all cities, towns, and villages, are given--a cursory glance, even, would show him the striking fact that, as far as the great centres of population were concerned, Catholic churches, educational establishments, and primary schools were found in respectable numbers; but many a page had to be turned when the reader came to places of lesser importance, to rural populations chiefly, before he met with any indication of the Catholic Church entering yet upon that large country domain. This experience was encountered by the writer at the time, and caused him a moment of doubt.

But beyond the reflection that, in matters of this kind (of the propagation of a doctrine or a creed), the first thing to be looked to is the centre, and that this, once mastered, will in course of time draw under its influence the outer circles; that all things cannot be effected at once, and the best thing to be done is to begin with the most important; that, moreover, those statistics are often incorrect with respect to Catholic matters, whether from malicious design, or inadvertence, or want of knowledge, on subjects to which the compilers attached very little importance, so that, if their statements be compared with Catholic official intelligence with regard to the same places, it will be found that many towns and villages which, according to the State Directories would seem to have been altogether forgotten by the Church, were actually in her possession, at least by periodical or occasional visits; apart from all these considerations, there is one more important remark to be made, which includes in its bearing not only the present point of consideration, but, it may be said, the whole life of the Church from the beginning; so that it is really a law of her birth, existence, and propagation.

To illustrate our meaning, let us see how the Christian religion first forced its way in heathen lands, throughout the whole Roman Empire, whether in its Oriental division where Greek was spoken, or among its Western, Latin-speaking populations.

All the apostles fixed their sees in the largest or most important cities of the ancient world; St. Peter, under the special guidance of God, taking possession of the capital and mistress of the whole. All the bishops ordained by the first apostles did the same by their direction; and it is needless to add that the like law has been followed down to our own times whenever the Church has had to spread herself in a new country.

In accordance with this plan, the cities of the Roman world were the first to be evangelized, and their populations were converted with greater or less difficulty, according to the dispositions of the inhabitants, before almost an effort had been made for the conversion of the rural populations, except as they happened to come in the way of the "laborers in the vineyard." Hence the result, so well known: heathenism remained rooted in the country for a much longer time than in the cities, so that the heathen were generally called pagans--pagani--as if it were enough, when desiring to convey the intimation that a man was a worshipper of idols, to designate him as a dweller in the country.[1] And if the word "pagans" became synonymous with heathens in all European countries, it is a proof that the fact underlying the name was universal wherever Christianity spread. It is known, moreover, that the dissemination of the Gospel in those rural districts was a work of centuries, and that, for nearly a thousand years after Christ, pagans were to be found in villages of countries already Christian.

The fundamental reason which governs and regulates these strange facts is that already given, namely, that Christianity-- that is, Catholicity--is a growth, and follows the laws of every thing that grows. True, its first increase is from without, by the conversion of infidels or erring men; but even in that first stage of its existence, its growth is the faster where the numbers are greater; hence its establishment invariably in large cities. But when it has passed beyond this first stage, it increases from within, like all growths, and the work is accomplished by the increase of families agglomerated in the same large towns.

How true is it that the Church, once firmly planted in the midst of one of those agglomerations of men called cities, is sure in the end to invade the whole as "the yeast that leavens the whole! "How easy is it to see that in the course of time those cities of the Union, among which a large proportion of Catholics is found, will belong almost exclusively to the true Church, if for no other reason by the births in families, even supposing that the flow of immigration should finally cease! If any one entertains some doubt on this point, he has only to consult the records containing the number of children baptized in her bosom, and compare it with the corresponding number in families still outside her.

Hence the really astonishing fact, whose truth is recognized to-day in all the Northern States along the Atlantic coast, that suddenly almost in the cities of New England, for instance, where the number of Catholics was simply insignificant, they took an apparently unaccountable prominence, and in the course of a few years, increasing steadily by birth as well as by immigration, the fact became the most curious though evident of the times, completely changing the moral and social aspect of the country, and foretelling still greater changes to come. For, in the face of this wonderful

---

[1] Another meaning is given to the word paganus by some writers; but the old and common interpretation is the surest, and is confirmed by the best authorities.

increase to the ranks of Catholicity, appears another significant fact, but very different as to direction and energy--the gradual disappearance of names once prominent in those parts, and the daily narrowing area of Protestantism in the numerous sects of which it is composed.

At the same time a great danger was averted (or at least wonderfully lessened and modified), from the whole country, by the settlement of those immigrants in the large centres of population. The manufacturing enterprises, which at that time assumed such vast developments in North America, received among their workers, men and women, a large proportion of Catholics, and the fear of future political and social peril to the peace and security of society at large could never, on this continent, reach the extreme point witnessed in Europe to-day. The great danger of the European future nestles principally in those vast hives of industry with which that continent abounds. Our eyes have witnessed, our ears have been affrighted at those stupendous plans and projects in which, not only the great questions of capital and labor are involved, but the whole fabric of society is threatened with downfall. Religion, government, property, the family, the state--all those great principles and facts on which the security of mankind depends, enter now into the programme of artisans and laborers enlisted in gigantic and many-ramified secret societies, while the whole world trembles at the awful aspect of this unwelcome phantom, that no government, however powerful, can lay.

Suppose that on this continent the numerous bands of workingmen, so actively engaged everywhere in developing the resources of the country, should aim at extending their solicitude beyond their immediate and material welfare to the reformation and reorganization of mankind on a new basis; and suppose that, with this aim in view, they should combine with those of Europe, and enter into an unholy compact with them, what hope or refuge would remain in the whole world for harmony, peace, justice, and happiness? And when the great upheaval, so generally expected in Europe, and which sooner or later must take place, shall come to pass, where could those men fly, who cannot but look upon those satanic schemes with horror? Where on this earth would be found a spot consecrated to the acknowledgment of the only social principles which can secure the real good of mankind, by rendering safe the stability of society?

It is our firm belief that the vast number of true children of the Church, occupied honestly and actively in the many factories of the North, will, when the contest commences, even before it commences, when the question of connecting the "unions" of this country in a band of brotherhood with those of Europe shall be gravely mooted, make their voices loudly and unmistakably heard on the right side.

Enough has now been said on the locality chosen by preference as the dwelling- place of the Irish immigrants at the period under consideration. Let us now see those armies of new-comers at work. They have been called a missionary people; let us see how they understand their "mission."

In this new country every thing had to be done for the establishment of religion, education, help for the poor, the aged, the infirm, on a lasting and sufficiently broad basis. And, strange to remark, it was found that the previous persecutions they had undergone fitted them admirably for their work, not only by giving them a strong faith, the true foundation of Christian energy, but in a manner more curious, if not more effective. It fitted them to give money freely and abundantly, poor as they were! One may smile incredulously at the conceit; but it has become a most powerful and incontestable fact.

Suppose the Irish never to have been persecuted in their own country: suppose that they had found there a benevolent government to supply them with churches, schools, hospitals--homes for the poor--every thing that they, as Catholics, could desire. Suppose them to have been in a similar position with the Frenchmen, Spaniards, and Italians, of those days, how bitterly would they have felt the inconvenience of building all these things up for themselves in their new homes with the labor of their own hands, by their own individual efforts, unaided by the government! Their ardor would have been damped, their energy cramped, their inclination to give would have fallen far below the necessities of the time: for money was sorely needed--no niggard offerings, but immense sums.

But happily--happily in the result, not in the fact--not only had the British Government never done any thing of the kind for them in their old home; not only, on the contrary, had it been particularly careful to rob them of all the buildings and estates left by their ancestors for those great objects; but, until very recently, the passing of the Emancipation Act of 1829, it had studiously and most persistently hindered them from doing voluntarily for themselves what it refused to do for them. There were numerous penal statutes enacted, in the course of two centuries, to prevent them from building churches, opening schools, erecting asylums and hospitals of their own, nay, from possessing consecrated graveyards for their dead. Thus did fanatic hatred pursue them even to the grave, and, as far as it could, beyond the gates of death. Every one had to surrender the mortal remains of his relatives to the Protestant minister for burial; as though what the government called its religion would snatch from them whatever it could lay hands on--the body at least since the soul had escaped and passed beyond its reach.

But in their new country they found every thing altered. Not only was prohibition of this kind utterly unknown, but there existed there the greatest amount of liberty ever enjoyed by man for acting in concert with a religious, educational, or charitable object in view. No law devised by the old Greek republics, by the Roman fisc, by modern European intermeddling was ever attempted in the country which with justice boasted of being the "asylum of the oppressed." Thus as the liberty so long denied to the Irish was at last opened up, as no barrier existed to cramp and confine the natural generosity of their hearts, no sooner did they find that they might contribute as they chose to those great and holy objects, than they rushed at the chances offered them with what looked like recklessness.

We hope that the reader may understand, from this, our meaning in saying that persecution had admirably fitted them for the mighty work that lay before them. It was the first time for centuries that they were allowed to give for such sacred purposes.

Another thing which disposed than toward it was, the lingering fondness for the old customs of clanship, still harbored in their inmost soul, never entirely dead and ready to revive whenever an opportunity presented itself. There can be no doubt of this; the great adjuration of the clansman to his chieftain--"Spend me, but defend me"--tended wonderfully to consecrate in their eyes the act of giving and giving constantly, as though their purse could never be exhausted. The chieftain has been replaced by the bishop, the priest, the educator; the nobility has gone, but these have come; and unconsciously perhaps, but none the less really, does this feeling lie at the bottom of their hearts, which are ever ready to burst out with the old expression, though in other form: "Spend me, eat me out, but help my soul, and save my children."

This feeling has always run in the blood of the race. St. Paul long ago detected it in the Galatians, a branch of the Celtic tribes, when he wrote to them: "You received me as an angel of God, even as Christ Jesus. . . . I bear you witness that, if it could be done, you would have plucked out your own eyes, and given them to me."--Epistle to the Galatians, iv. 15.

Few, perhaps, have reflected seriously on the large sums required for the establishment of the Catholic Church in so vast a country, with all her adjunct institutions; therefore the stupendous result has scarcely struck those who have witnessed and lived in the midst of it. The same is the case, though on a much smaller scale, with respect to the money sent back to Ireland by newly-arrived immigrants. People were aware that the Irish, women as well as men, were in the habit of forwarding drafts of one, two, or three pounds to their relatives and friends, but in such small amounts that the whole could not reach a very high figure. But when it came to be discovered that many banking associations were drawing large dividends from the operation, that new banks were continually being opened which looked to the profit to be derived from such transmission as their chief means of support, some curious people set to work collecting information on the subject and instituting inquiries, when it was found that the aggregate sum amounted to millions, and would have become a serious item in the specie exports of the country, if what was transmitted did not in the main come back with those to whom it had been forwarded.

So was it, but in much larger proportions with respect to the amounts annually spent in the purchase of real estate, the building of churches, schools, asylums, hospitals, for the support of clergymen, school-teachers, clerks, officials, servants, which were called for all at once, over the surface of an extensive territory, for the service of hundreds of thousands of Catholics arriving yearly with the intention of settling permanently in the country. Could the full statistics be furnished, they would excite the surprise of all; the few details which we would be enabled to gather from directories, newspapers, the reports of witnesses, and other sources, could give but a faint idea of the whole, and are consequently better omitted.

One single observation will produce a more lasting impression on the reader's mind than long statistics, and the enumeration of buildings and other undertakings. It is a fact, without the least tinge of exaggeration, that in the States of Pennsylvania, New Jersey, New York, Connecticut, Massachusetts, Ohio, Indiana, Illinois, Iowa, Missouri, Wisconsin, and several other Western States, nearly every clergyman, who had the care of a single parish before 1840, if alive to-day, could show in his former district from ten to twenty parishes, each with its own pastor and church, now flourishing, and attached to each a much larger number of useful educational and charitable establishments than he could have boasted of in his original charge. Let one reflect on this, and then imagine to himself the sums requisite to purchase such an amount of real estate, for the erection of so many edifices, and for placing on an efficient footing so many different establishments.

It is true that, to-day, a number of these institutions are still in debt; but, if the list of what is actually paid for be made out, and separated from what still remains indebted, the result would stand as a most wonderful fact.

The question will naturally present itself, "How was it possible for newly-arrived immigrants, who often landed without a penny in their pockets, to become all at once so easy in their circumstances as to be enabled to contribute, so generously and enormously, to so gigantic an enterprise?" The details in reply to this might be given very simply and satisfactorily; but, as it is a real work of God, who always acts simply and satisfactorily, though in a manner worthy of the deepest attention and gratitude, it is proper to examine the question in all its bearings, and then even those who have seen, and can account for it very easily, will wonder, admire, and thank, the infinite Providence of God.

First, it is certain that nowhere else in this world could it have been accomplished at all; and nowhere else in this world has any thing like it been accomplished in a like manner. This may appear strange, but it is so; let us see.

All know how, in infidel countries, every thing necessary for the material help of Catholic missions must be supplied by the missionaries themselves; that, in fact, they have not only their own support to consider, but, often also, the feeding, clothing, and education of the natives at their own expense. It is thus in all the barbarous countries of Asia, Africa, and the new continent and islands in the South Sea. It is thus in the old, effete, but once civilized countries of Asia, such as Syria, Hindostan, China, and others. In all those countries, money must come from without, not only to begin, but to continue, the work of evangelization, even when it has been going on for centuries. Details on this subject are unnecessary, the truth of what has just been said is so well known.

In Christian countries, as in Europe, the various governments have so far contributed to the aid of the mission of Christianity, or have been gracious enough to allow such of the wealthy classes as were willing to take this task off their shoulders and set it up on their own, the lower classes being scarcely able to help toward it. What the case will be when the halcyon days come of the separation of Church and state, and the latter succeeds in the object at which it seems so earnestly striving now, of making the people godless like itself, when the rich will no longer be willing to undertake this work, God only knows. But in those countries, as is well known, the government, formerly, and latterly up to quite recent times, or rich families by large contributions laid down at once, have built churches, founded universities, colleges, and schools, erected hospitals and asylums; founded--such was the expression--all the religious, charitable, or literary institutions in existence. The "people" have scarcely effected any thing in this direction, for the very good reason that they were unable to do so.

In the United States alone, and among Catholics alone, it is "the people," the poor, who have taken and been able to take this matter into their own hands.

That they--the Irish particularly--have done this, redounds to their honor, and it will receive its reward from God; nay, has already in a great measure received it, by filling the land with the temples of their faith, with schools where their children are still taught to believe in God and grow up a moral race, and with the various Catholic asylums and institutions established for the glory of religion, or the comfort of those who are comfortless. That they have been able to do this is owing to the unique, exceptional, marvellous prosperity of the country which offered them an asylum. And let us add with reverence that the country owes this singular prosperity, which has been the source of so many blessings, to the designs of a loving Providence, who looks to the welfare of the whole of mankind, and has therefore endowed this young and gigantic nation with the necessary qualities of energy, activity, "go-aheaditiveness," as it is called, added to the fixed principle that every individual throughout these vast domains shall enjoy liberty, facility of acquiring a competency, and the right to make what use of it he pleases, as well as generosity enough to applaud the one who devotes his surplus earnings to useful public undertakings.

In no other country of the world has this been the case, and in no other country is it the case at the present moment. And, as the fact is mighty in its results, unprepared by man, unlooked for a hundred years ago, requiring for its fulfilment a thousand agencies far beyond the control of any man or inferior mind, following the line of reasoning previously indicated, we ascribe, are constrained to ascribe, it all to the great infinite Mind, to God himself, and to him alone!

And now we turn to the workings of the Irish, and to a consideration of a few of the details. The first crying need was churches and orphan asylums: churches for the all-important worship of God; orphan asylums to receive the numbers of children left homeless by the death of immigrants soon after their arrival, and who were immediately snatched up by the proselytizing sects.

The style of architecture displayed in those first temples of the great God was homely indeed and humble. Nevertheless, it might favorably compare with similar buildings erected by wealthy Protestant congregations. This fact alone is sufficient to convict Protestantism of want of faith, namely, that its adherents have never been struck by the thought that the majesty of God, if really felt, calls for a profusion of gifts on the part of those who have superabundant means. Not that man can by his feeble exertions in that regard give adequate honor to the divine Omnipotence, but that love and gratitude are naturally profuse in their demonstrations, and whoever loves ardently is ever ready to give all he has for the object of his love, even to the sacrifice of himself. The reflection that God is too great, and that it is useless, even presumptuous, to offer to him what must seem so infinitely mean in the light of his greatness, is but the flimsy pretext of an avaricious soul, and can be nothing but a lie, even in the eyes of those who utter it. From the beginning all truly religious nations have endeavored to make their external worship correspond with their internal feeling, and give expression, as far as man can do, to their idea of the worth and majesty of God; and that thought is a true measure of a religion; for, when the external is but a cold and sordid worship, we may be sure that the internal corresponds; and, when little or nothing is done in that way, it is clear that the heart feels not, and the mind is empty of true convictions and of faith.

And what has been the invariable conduct of Protestant nations in this regard? They became possessed of splendid churches built by their

Catholic ancestors, and, after stripping them of all their beauty, they retained them as "preaching-halls" or "meeting-houses." The number of those who remained attached to a frigid and unattractive service gradually diminished; the edifices were found to be too large, and in many instances what had been the sanctuary, where art had exhausted itself in embellishment, partitioned off from the rest of the church, was kept for their dwindling congregations, while the vast aisles and roomy naves went slowly to ruin, or became deserted solitudes. As for the idea of building new religious edifices, the old ones were already too numerous for them, or if, as was not unfrequent, a new sect started into spasmodic life, and its votaries found it necessary to open a new "place of worship," the temple they erected to God generally took the form of a hired hall. Let the floor be carpeted and the benches covered with soft, slumber-inviting cushions, the room wear a general air and aspect of comfort, the "acoustics" duly considered, so that the voice of the preacher might reach to the door and half- way to the galleries, and nothing more was required. The man who asked for something more solemn, and answering better to the cravings of a religious heart, would be laughed at as a visionary, if his person did not distil, to the keen-scented organs of these religious folk, a strong flavor of "popery " and of "the man of sin."

So that in the United States at the time spoken of, although the number of churches was extraordinary, because of the number of sects, they were mere shells of buildings, capable of accommodating from three to eight hundred people (very few of the latter capacity); and, although many of the members of the congregations who built them were rich men, adding to their wealth daily, one seldom encountered any of the structures, then common, showing much more than four walls, enclosing four lines of clumsy pews.

Consequently, the Catholic Church had no reason to blush by comparison at the poverty of her children; nay, the extreme simplicity of the edifices raised by them was in keeping with every thing around, and what they did in the hurry of the moment, with the scanty means at their disposal, at least might vie with what wealthy Protestants had done deliberately with all the leisure and wealth at their command.

Already, even at that epoch, in the centre of Catholicity in this country, the love of the true worshipper of God began to display something of that feeling which is naturally alive in the heart of the sincerely religious man;

and the Cathedral of Baltimore, long since left so far behind by other monuments of true devotion, created throughout the country a genuine excitement and admiration, when its doors were first opened for the worship of God. It was clear, from the universal acclaim of the people, non-Catholics included, that at least one class of men in the country had a true idea of what was worthy of God in his worship, and what was worthy of themselves in their worship of him.

But, though, with some rare exceptions, the architecture displayed in those edifices constructed by the children of the true Church was poor indeed, the number of those which were commenced and so speedily completed and devoted to their holy use was so extraordinary, that it is doubtful if the annals of Catholicity have ever recorded the same thing occurring on the same scale, in the same extent of country. If the ecclesiastical history of the United States ever comes to be written, it is to be hoped that, in the archives of the various episcopal sees, authentic documents have been preserved, which may furnish future writers with comprehensive statistics on the subject, that the posterity of the noble-hearted men and women who undertook and carried out, with such a wonderful success, so arduous a task, may be stimulated to religious exertion of the same kind by the memory of what their forefathers have accomplished. The reflection already suggested by another idea may serve here likewise, and be usefully repeated. If, in the course of twenty-five years, over the surface of at least ten of the largest Northern States, every clergyman who, at the beginning of that period, officiated in a very small church, is, to-day, supposing him living, gladdened by the sight of ten to twenty collaborators, with a corresponding number of newly-built churches, it is easy to judge of the vastness of the effort made by the greatness of the undertaking and the unexampled success with which God has been pleased to crown it. The other States of the Union are omitted here, not because the Catholics residing in them were then idle, but because, their growth being less remarkable, the external result could not be so striking. Nevertheless, the actual increase among them would compare favorably with that of other growing Catholic countries.

Could details, at this present time, only be gathered from all the States, in the area referred to, the vast diffusion of Catholicity by the influence of immigration would come home to us with far greater force, as would the conception of the corresponding work demanded of the immigrants for the creation of all the objects of worship, charity, and education. Let the reader look to what is related in the "Life of Bishop Loras," who was at that time charged with the founding of religion in Iowa and Minnesota. It will at the same time bring under our notice the march of the Irish toward the West, after having seen them solidly established in the Atlantic States.

"He was consecrated at Mobile by Bishop Portier, assisted by Bishop Blanc, of New Orleans, on December 10, 1837. His diocese was a vast region unknown to him. The unfinished Church of St. Raphael, at Dubuque, was the only Catholic church in the Territory, and the Rev. Sam. Mazzuchelli, its pastor, was the only Catholic priest. The Catholic population of Dubuque was about three hundred. . . . But there must be, thought the new bishop, some members of the flock in distant, isolated, and unfrequented localities, who were in danger of wandering from the faith; besides, the future waves of population would certainly set in toward this fine expanse of meadow, prairie, and forest. . . . With prudent foresight he purchased land . . . . three acres at Dubuque; later, St. Joseph's Prairie, one mile square, near the same city. . . . A valuable property was acquired in Davenport, on the Mississippi, with the view of applying the revenue from it to the support of the missions.

"To his regret he saw large numbers of the European immigrants tarrying in the Atlantic cities, where want, sickness, and crime, beset their path, and he became deeply interested in giving to this worth population the more healthful and vigorous direction of the West. . . . Articles were prepared and published, setting forth the attractions of the country. . . . An immense correspondence, with persons in this country and in Europe, resulted from the well-known interest Bishop Loras took in these subjects. . . . He undertook the settlement of colonies. . . . Germans in New Vienna, in 1846 . . . Irish on the Big-Maquokety. . . . He organized them in congregations and commenced in person the work of building for them churches. . . . establishing schools and academies, laboring for the temporal and eternal welfare of the people."

Thus did the tide of Catholic population begin to flow into Iowa and Minnesota, to be brought under the influence of the Church as soon as it arrived.

Meanwhile associations were being formed in the East, in New York chiefly, for the purpose of inducing Irishmen to go west as far as Illinois, and the Territories west of the Mississippi. Several zealous clergymen placed themselves at the head of the movement. Their main object was to rescue the Catholic immigrants from the dangers surrounding them in large cities, and to make farmers of them. We have seen why these plans, though prompted by the best intentions, failed to succeed; their immediate effect was to give a fresh impetus to the great movement westward, and, by relieving the Atlantic coast of a sudden excess of population, to extend the Church along the line marked out by Providence toward the coast of the Pacific.

At the same time, on the very shores of that vast ocean, California was receiving directly from Europe large detachments of the voluntary exiles who were then leaving Ireland in a compact body in the full tide of the "Exodus." The Catholic Church was thus early taking up a commanding position at the extreme point whither the main "army" was tending, and soon to arrive with the completion of the great Pacific Railroad.

The following extract, taken from the "Life of Bishop Loras," will be sufficient to give an idea of the rapid increase of the Catholic population in the West, in consequence of the workings of so many agencies employed by God's providence for his own holy ends:

"In 1855, the Catholic population of Iowa increased one hundred and fifty per centum in a single year. It seems almost incredible to relate, that the churches and stations, provided for their accommodation, increased in the same time nearly one hundred per centum. The Catholic population reported in 1855 was twenty thousand, and the churches and stations fifty-two; the Catholic population in 1856 was rated at forty-nine thousand, and the churches and stations at ninety-seven.

"Bishop Loras commenced his episcopate (in 1837) with one church, one priest, and the only Catholic population reported, that of Dubuque, was three hundred. In 1851, Minnesota was taken from his diocese, yet in 1858, the year of his death, the diocese of Dubuque alone possessed one hundred and seven priests, one hundred and two churches and stations, and a Catholic population of fifty-five thousand."

There can be little doubt that, if similar statistics were drawn up for all the Western States of the Union during a corresponding period, they would give very similar results; and it is only by reflecting and pondering over such astonishing facts as these, that the mind can come to grasp the idea of the magnitude of the work assigned by Providence to the Irish race. This, we have no hesitation in saying, will form one of the most remarkable features of the future ecclesiastical history of the age, and will appear the more clearly when all the consequences of this stupendous movement shall stand out fully developed, so as to strike the eyes of all.

It may be well to reflect a moment upon the activity displayed by that zealous hive of busy immigrants, who, soon after landing, when the thoughts of other men would have been exclusively and, as men would think, naturally, occupied by the thousand necessities arising from a new establishment on a foreign soil-- while not neglecting those necessities-- found time to enter heart and soul into projects set on foot everywhere for buying up landed property, making contracts with builders, supervising the work already going on, attending above all to the collection of money, forming lists of subscribers to that end, visiting round about for the same purpose, and attending to the fulfilment of promises sometimes made too hastily, or with too sanguine an expectation of being able to accomplish what in the future was never realized to the extent expected.

But, much sooner than might have been hoped, the desire, so congenial to the Catholic heart, of beholding more suitable dwellings erected to the honor of God and to the reception of his Divine presence, was fulfilled, or aroused, rather, in a quarter least expected, and consequently more in accordance with the (to man) mysterious ways of Providence. The sudden increase of the Church in England, in consequence of remarkable conversions and principally of the little-remarked flow of emigrants thither from the sister isle, induced some pious and wealthy English Catholics, now that they found themselves free to follow their inclinations unmolested, to devote their means to the construction of churches worthy of the name. The splendid structures, now the lifeless monuments of the old faith, which their fathers had raised, rested in the hands of the spoiler, and they could not worship, save privately and inwardly, at the shrine of Thomas of Canterbury, or before the tomb of Edward the Confessor. Yet were their eyes ever afflicted with the presence of those noble edifices, that resembled the solemn tombs of a buried faith, yet still cast their lofty spires heavenward, while the structure beneath them covered acres of ground with the most profuse and elaborate architecture. They looked around them for a builder, who might raise them such again. But there was none to be found capable of conceiving, much less building such vast fabrics as the old churches, which owed their existence not to the ingenuity of a designer, but to the inspired enthusiasm of a living faith. Nevertheless, a man, full of energy and reverence and love for the beauty of the house of God, came forward at the very moment he was wanted. Welby Pugin soon became known to the world, and was still in the full vigor of his enterprising life, when all over the American Continent the immigrants were engaged in satisfying the first cravings of their hearts, and covering the country with unpretending edifices crowned, at least, by the symbol of salvation. Among them arrived pupils of Pugin, who speedily found Irish hearts to respond to theirs, and Irish purses ready to carry their designs into execution.

There is no need of going into details. Puritan New England even has seen its chief cities one by one adorned with true temples of God, and its small towns embellished by stone edifices devoted to Catholic worship, their form pleasing to the eye, and their interior spacious enough, at least temporarily, for the constantly-increasing congregations. But perhaps the most remarkable result of all has been the sudden zeal which sprang up among the sectarians themselves, who had hitherto expressed such contempt for any thing of the kind, of outstripping the Catholics in Christian architecture. They have even gone so far as to discover that the cross, the emblem of man's salvation, is not such a very inappropriate ornament, after all, to the summit of a Christian temple, and that the statues of angels and of saints are possessed of a certain beauty. So that what in their eyes hitherto had borne the semblance of idolatry--such, according to themselves, was their way of looking at it--suddenly became an aesthetic feeling, if not an act of true devotion.

And, singularly enough, it was just at the time when the erection of so many episcopal sees necessitated the building of cathedrals, that the thought, natural to the Catholic heart, of making the house of God a place of beauty and magnificence, could begin to be realized by the arrival of true artists and the increasing wealth of the Catholic body.

It is in the true Church only that the meaning of a cathedral can be fully grasped. Those sects which acknowledge no bishops and deride the title certainly can form no conception of it, and even those who imagine that they have a bishop at their head, have so little idea of what are true episcopal functions, of the greatness of the position which a see occupies, of the importance of the place where it is established, that in their eyes the pretended dignitary can scarcely rank much higher, either in position or degree, than a wealthy parish minister, and the church wherein "his lordship" officiates is very much the same as an ordinary parish church. If in England a show of dignitaries is attached to each of those establishments, it is merely a form well calculated to impress the solemn Anglo-Saxon character; but even that very form would scarcely have existed were it not one of those few semblances of the Catholic reality which the wily founders of the Protestant religion found it convenient to retain for the purpose hinted at. The Catholic Church alone can understand what a cathedral ought to be.

This is not the occasion to enter upon an explanation of all the meanings and uses of a cathedral, least of all to penetrate the sublime mystical significance embodied in its conception. Here it is enough to insist upon the least important, yet most sensible and more easily-recognized object of the building, which is, not simply the seat of honor of the first pastor of the diocese, who is a successor of the apostles, but likewise the place of adoration and sacrifice common to all the faithful of the diocese. Strictly speaking, no special congregation is attached to it; but it is the spiritual home of all the faithful; its doors are open to all the congregations of that part. There the common father resides and officiates; there his voice is generally to be heard; there he is to be found surrounded by all those whose duty it is to assist him in his sublime functions. When he appears in any parish church, the clergy of that special temple are his only attendants, unless others flock thither to do him honor. But the cathedral is his fixed seat and permanent abode; there the appointed dignitaries of the diocese find their allotted places, and there alone are his officers permanently attached to him by their functions.

Hence it is the cardinal church upon which the whole spiritual edifice called the diocese is hinged. Therefore is it the natural resort of the whole flock, as well as of the pastor himself. This will explain the vastness of those edifices which strike us with wonder in old established Catholic countries. In accordance with their primitive intention and purpose, there should be in them standing and kneeling room for all who have a right to enter there; and it is purely on account of the impossibility of exactly fulfilling this intent that the edifice is allowed to be built smaller. We are thus enabled to understand why the great temple which is the centre-spot of Catholic worship can contain only fifty thousand worshippers at a time, and why many other sacred edifices consecrated to episcopal functions can find room for no more than twenty or thirty thousand.

But even those structures, which strike with wonder the puny minds of this "advanced" age, have consumed centuries in their construction, and the number and the faith of those who raised them were, we may say, exceptional in the life of the Church. There were no dissenters in those days; and, as all were possessed of a firm faith, all labored with a common will and contributed with a common pleasure to their construction.

Times having changed for the worse, the same ardor and generosity could not be looked for; but something at least was required which should give some idea of the old, splendor and vastness. So, throughout all the new dioceses projects were set on foot for raising real cathedrals, which should quite overshadow the buildings hitherto known by that name.

Thus, a cathedral was promised to New York City, three hundred and thirty feet in length, and one hundred and seventy-two in breadth across the transept; while that of Philadelphia was soon completed, and all might gaze on the massive and majestic edifice, by the side of which every other public building in a city containing eight hundred thousand souls appeared dwarfish and unsubstantial. Boston was soon to behold within its walls a Catholic cathedral, three hundred and sixty-four feet long, and one hundred and forty broad in the transept, though the same diocese was already filled with large stone churches, built solely by the resources of the immigrants.

The Archbishop of New York, when preaching the sermon at the laying of the foundation-stone of this edifice in 1867, was able to say in the presence of many who might have borne personal testimony to the truth of his words: "There are those most probably within the sound of my voice who can remember when there was but one Catholic church in Boston, and when that sufficed, or had to suffice, not alone for this city, but for all New England; and how is it now? Churches and institutions multiplied, and daily continuing to multiply on every side, in this city, throughout this State, in all or nearly all the cities and States of New England; so that at this day no portion of our country is enriched with them in greater proportionate number, none where they have grown up to a more flourishing condition, none where finished with more artistic skill, or presenting monuments of more architectural taste and beauty."

Had any one predicted this to the good and gifted Bishop Cheverus, when leaving America for France, he might perhaps have not refused altogether to believe or hope for it, but he would certainly have pronounced it a real and undoubted miracle of God, to happen within a century.

But the Archbishop of New York, in that same sermon, pointed out the true cause, when he attributed it to "God's blessing," and to "the never-ceasing tide of immigration that has been and still continues to be setting toward the American shores."

The history of the Church certainly contains many a page where the traces of the finger of God are clearly marked; nay, we may say that such traces are apparent throughout, as we know that God alone could have originated, spread out, supported, multiplied, and perpetuated the Church through all the centuries of her existence; but it is doubtful if in all her annals a single page shows where the action of Providence is more clearly visible, as it was least expected, than in the few facts just cursorily and briefly enumerated.

Yet have we mentioned only a part of the work to which the poor immigrants were called to contribute immediately after their arrival, and at the vastness of which they never murmured nor lost heart, as though a greater burden had been laid upon them than human shoulders could endure.

The worship of God and the care of souls were the first things to be attended to, and, with these, other necessary objects were not to be neglected. There was the care of the poor, whom the Church of Christ was the first public body to think of relieving; the tending of the sick in hospitals, where their own clergy might not only have access, but where it should be made sure that the management be one of true Christian charity and tenderness; the orphan children, always so numerous under circumstances like those of the present, were to be saved from falling into the hands of sectarians, and being educated by them, as were formerly the Catholic wards, in hatred of their own faith, and of the customs, habits, and modes of thought of their ancestors. This last great and incalculable source of loss to the Church was to be put a stop to at once, if not completely--for that was then impossible--at least as perfectly as zeal, generosity, and true love of souls, could effect. All these works required money, an incalculable amount; as it was not in a single city, not in a small particular State, but throughout the whole Union, through as many cities as it contains, that the undertaking was to be straightway set on foot and simultaneously acted upon.

Nor was the question one of the erection of buildings merely, but also of the support of an immense number of inmates, and of their constant support without a single day's intermission. Who can calculate the sums required for such immediate and most pressing needs?

In a nation where Christianity has been long established, taxes imposed upon all for the constructing, repairing, maintaining, and carrying on so many and such large establishments are easily collected. For all are bound by law to contribute to such purposes, and the question generally reduces itself merely to a continuance of the support of institutions long standing, and which can be no longer in need of the large disbursements necessary at the first period of their existence. But here it was a question of providing, without any other law than that of love, without the help of any other tax-gatherer than the voluntary collector, for all those necessities at once, including the vast outlays requisite for the first establishment of those institutions, and imposing, by that very act, the necessity and duty of supporting forever all the inmates gathered together at the cost of so much care and expense, within those walls consecrated to religion and charity. The government had no share whatever in it; too happy were they at the government interposing no obstacle to its carrying out! That was all they asked for on its part--non-interference.

On this subject, Mr. Maguire remarks justly, without, however, bringing the matter of expenditure into sufficient prominence:

"For the glorious Church of America many nations have done their part. The sacred seed first planted by the hand of the chivalrous Spaniard has been watered by the blood of the generous Gaul; to the infant mission the Englishman brought his steadfastness and resolution, the Scotchman, in the northeast, his quiet firmness, . . . the Irishman his faith, the ardor of his faith. And, as time rolled on, and wave after wave of immigration brought with it more and more of the precious life-blood of Europe, from no country was there a richer contribution of piety and zeal, of devotion and self-sacrifice, than from that advanced outpost of the Old World, whose western shores first break the fury of the Atlantic; to whose people Providence appears to have assigned a destiny grand and heroic--of carrying the civilization of the Cross to remote lands and distant nations.

What Ireland has done for the American Church, every bishop, every priest, can tell. Throughout the vast extent of the Union there is scarcely a church, an academy, a hospital, or a refuge, in which the piety, the learning, the zeal, the self- sacrifice, of the Irish--of the priest or the professor, of the Sisters of every order or denomination--are not to be traced; there is scarcely an ecclesiastical seminary for English- speaking students in which the great majority of those now preparing for the service of the sanctuary do not belong, if not by birth, at least by blood, to that historic land to which the grateful Church of past ages accorded the proud title, Insula Sanctorum."

To this may be added the remark that it is still further beyond doubt that all the establishments mentioned, almost without one exception, owe their existence, at least partially, and very often entirely, to the generous and never-failing contributions of the Irish.

The Rev. C. G. White, in his "Sketch of the Origin and Progress of the Catholic Church in the United States of America," which is appended to the translation of Darras's "History of the Catholic Church," says still more positively:

"In recording this consoling advancement of Catholicity throughout the United States, especially in the North and West, justice requires us to state that it is owing in a great measure to the faith, zeal, and generosity of the Irish people who have immigrated to these shores, and their descendants. We are far from wishing to detract from the merit of other nationalities; but the vast influence which the Irish population has exerted in extending the domain of the Church is well deserving of notice, because it conveys a very instructive lesson. The wonderful history of the Irish nation has always forced upon us the conviction that, like the chosen generation of Abraham (previous to their rejection of the Messiah, of course), they were destined, in the designs of Providence, to a special mission for the preservation and propagation of the true faith. This faith, so pure, so lovely, so generous, displays itself in every region of the globe. To its vitality and energy must we attribute, to a very great extent, the rapid increase in the number of churches and other institutions which have sprung up and are still springing up in the United States, and to the same source are the clergy mainly indebted for their support in the exercise of their pastoral ministry. It cannot be denied, and we bear a cheerful testimony to the fact, that hundreds of clergymen, who are laboring for the salvation of souls, would starve, and their efforts for the cause of religion would be in vain, but for the generous aid they receive from the children of Erin, who know, for the most part, how to appreciate the benefits of religion, and who therefore joyfully contribute of their worldly means to purchase the spiritual blessings which the Church dispenses."

To this we may add that what Mr. White so expressly states of the generous support given by the Irish people to the clergy is equally true when extended to the thousand inmates of orphan asylums, reformatories, schools, convents, and of all the charitable institutions generally which are specially fostered by the Church for the common good of humanity. To quote only one fact recorded in a note to Mr. Maguire's book, a Sister of Mercy tells us what the Irish working-class has done for the order in Cincinnati: "The convent, schools, and House of Mercy, in which the good works of our Institute are progressing, were purchased in 1861 at a considerable outlay. This, together with the repairs, alterations, furnishing, etc., was defrayed by the working-class of Irish people, who have been and are to us most devoted, and by their generosity have enabled us up to the present time to carry out successfully our works of mercy and charity."

It may be stated, without fear of contradiction, that the same thing might be asserted by the superior of almost every Catholic establishment in the country, were an opportunity afforded them of coming forward in like manner.

All this is well known to those who are in the least acquainted with the history and workings of those institutions; but very little noise is made about it, according to the rule of the Gospel which recommends us to do good in such a manner that "the left hand may not know what the right hand doeth." Nothing is more Christian than such silent approval, and the eternal reward, which must follow, is so overwhelmingly great that the applause of the world may well be disregarded. But as constant good offices are apt to beget indifference in those who benefit most by them, there are not wanting some good people who seem to labor under the impression that really the Irish deserve scarcely any thanks; that every thing which they do comes so naturally from them, it is only what one could expect as a matter of course, and that, it being nothing more, after all, than their simple duty, it becomes a very ordinary thing.

It may be superfluous to say that if all this was expected from them, and if it be, as it really is, after all only a very ordinary thing on their part, this fact is precisely what makes them a most extraordinary people, as expectations of this nature which may be most natural are of that peculiar kind of "great expectations" magnificent in prospect, but very delusive in fact; and certainly they would not be looked for as a matter of course in any other nation. Let any one reflect on the few details here furnished, let him add others from his own information, and the whole thing will appear, as it truly is, most wonderful, and only to be explained by the great and merciful designs of God, as Dr. White has just indicated-- designs intrusted on this occasion to faithful servants whose generous hearts and pure souls opened up to the mission intrusted to them, to its glorious fulfilment so far, and to a greater unfolding still in time to come.

In order to understand, as ought to be understood, more fully the weight of the burden they so cheerfully undertook to bear, a few reflections on the subject of religious and charitable institutions will not be considered out of place.

The Romans--those master-organizers, who reduced to a perfect system every branch of government, legislation, war, and religion--never abandoned, never intrusted to the initiative of the people, the care of providing the means for any thing which the state ought to supply. The public religious establishments were all endowed, the colleges of the priests enjoyed large revenues, and the expenses of worship were supplied from the same source. To the fisc in general belonged the duty of supporting the armories, the courts of law, and the large establishments provided for the comfort and instruction of the people, the baths, libraries, and regular amusements. The private munificence of emperors, great patricians, and conquerors, undertook to supply occasional shows of an extraordinary character in the theatres, amphitheatre, and the circus.

There was no room left for charity in the whole plan. Indeed, the meaning of that word was unknown to them; for it cannot be properly applied to the regular distribution of money or cereals to the plebs; as this was one of those generosities which are necessary, and was only practised in order to keep the lower orders of citizens in idle content and out of mischief, as you would a wild animal which you dare not chain: you must feed him. The really poor, the saves, the maimed, the helpless, were left to their hard fate, they being apparently unworthy of pity because they excited no fear.

Yet the system was fruitful in its results. As soon as Christianity was seated on the throne, nothing was easier than to transfer the immense sums contributed by regular funds, or which were the product of taxes, from one object to another; and thus the Christian clergy and churches were supported as had been the colleges and temples of the pagan priests, by the revenues derived from large estates attached to the various corporations. Thus did Constantine and his successors become the munificent benefactors of the Church in Rome and through-out the whole empire.

Meanwhile, the 11 collections of money" among the faithful, which were first organized, as we read in the epistles of the apostles, and afterward systematized still better in Rome under the first popes, soon grew into disuse, at least to the extent to which they once prevailed; the new charitable institutions, such as the care of the poor, of widows and orphans, being under- taken by the Church at large, while the expenses of the whole were defrayed by the revenues accruing from the donations of princes, or the bequests of wealthy Christians.

The consequence was that, throughout the whole Christian world, all religious, literary, and charitable institutions enjoyed large revenues, and there was no need of applying to the generosity of the common people for contributions.

After the successful invasion of the barbarians, the same system held good; and history records how richly endowed were the churches built, the monasteries founded, the universities and colleges opened, by the once ferocious Franks, Germans, or Northmen even, tamed and subdued by the precepts and practices of Christianity.

We know how the immense wealth, which had been devoted to such holy purposes by the wise generosity of rulers or rich nobles, became in course of time an eyesore and object of envy to the worldly, and that the chief incentive to the `~ Reformers" for doing their work of 11 reformation" thoroughly was the prospect of the golden harvest to be reaped by the destruction of the Catholic Church.

But the very large amounts required to satisfy the aspirations introduced into the heart of humanity, by the religion of Christ, may give us an adequate idea of what Christian civilization really costs. It is foolish to imagine a sane man really believing that those generous founders of pious institutions, who devote by gift or bequest, such large estates and revenues to the various

****
This E-text is missing paper pages 457-472.
****

We cannot afford to transfer any more of his experiences among the Irish. From all his accounts, they are the same in London as everywhere else, most firmly attached to Catholicity, and, as a general rule, most exemplary in the performance of their religious obligations.

It is fitting, however, to give the conclusion of a long description of what he saw among them while visiting them in the company of a clergyman: "The religious fervor of the people whom I saw was intense. At one house that I entered, the woman set me marvelling at the strength of her zeal, by showing me how she continued to have in her sitting-room a sanctuary to pray every night and morning, and even during the day when she felt weary and lonesome."

II. Passing from religion to morality, let us look at this writer again: "Only one-tenth, at the outside, of the couples living together and carrying on the costermongering trade (among the English) are married. . . . Of the rights of legitimate or illegitimate children, the English costermongers understand nothing, and account it a mere waste of money to go through the ceremony of wedlock, when a pair can live together, and be quite as well regarded by their fellows without it. The married women associate with the unmarried mothers of families without scruple. There is no honor attached to the married state and no shame to concubinage.

"As regards the fidelity of these women, I was assured that in any thing like good times they were rigidly faithful to their paramours; but that, in the worst pinch of poverty, a departure from this fidelity--if it provided a few meals or a fire--was not considered at all heinous."

Further details may be read in the book quoted from, which would scarcely come well in these pages, though quite appropriate to the most interesting work in which they appear. From the whole, it is only too clear that the class of people referred to is profoundly immoral and corrupt, their very poverty only hindering them from indulging in an excess of libertinism.

On the other hand, when Mr. Mayhew speaks of the street Irish in London, he is most emphatic in his praise of the purity of the women in particular, and the care of the parents in general to preserve the virtue of their daughters, in the midst of the frightful corruption ever under their eyes. The only remark he passes of a disparaging character is the following:

"I may here observe"--referring to the statement that Irish parents will not expose their daughters to the risk of what they consider corrupt influences --"that, when a young Irish woman does break through the pale of chastity, she often becomes, as I was assured, one of the most violent and depraved of, perhaps, the most depraved class."

It is evident, from the mere form in which this phrase is put, that such a thing is of very rare occurrence, and that the violence and depravity spoken of offer all the stronger contrast to the general purity of the whole class, and are merely the result of the open and unreserved character of the race.

But the whole world knows that chastity is the rule, and perhaps the most special virtue of the Irish, a fact which their worst enemies have been compelled to confess. In this same work of Mr. Mayhew's a still more surprising fact than the last--for that is acknowledged by all--is brought into astonishing prominence; a fact opposed to the general opinion of their friends even, and yet supported by incontrovertible evidence. It relates to another contrast between the English and Irish costermongers on the score of temperance.

III. The result arrived at by his inquiries among liquor-dealers in that part of London inhabited by about equal numbers of both nationalities, Mr. Mayhew gives us as twenty to one in favor of the Irish with respect to the consumption of liquor. In most "independent," that is to say, "not impoverished" Irish families, water is the only beverage at dinner, with punch afterward; and estimating the number of teetotallers, among the English at three hundred, there are six hundred among the Irish, who constitute, it may be remembered, only one-third of the whole costermonger class, and those Irish teetotallers, having taken the pledge under the sanction of their priests, look upon it as a religious observance and keep it rigidly. The number of Irish teetotallers has been considerably increased since Mr. Mayhew made his returns, in consequence of the energetic crusade entered upon against drink by the zealous London clergy, under the powerful lead of Archbishop Manning.

It is true that an innkeeper told Mr. Mayhew that "he would rather have twenty poor Englishmen drunk in his tap-room than a couple of poor Irishmen, who will quarrel with anybody, and sometimes clear the room." But this remark, if it shows any thing, shows only how and why the Irish have obtained that reputation of being a nation of drunkards, which is slanderous and false.

IV. Yet another, and perhaps as surprising a result as any, is the contrast between both classes of people with respect to economy and foresight: The English street-sellers are found everywhere spending all their income in the satisfaction often of brutish appetites; the Irish, on the contrary, save their money, either for the purpose of transmitting it to their poor relatives in Ireland, or bringing up their children properly, or--if they are young--to provide for their marriage-expenses and home. Such cares as these never seem to afflict the English costermonger. So strongly did Mr. Mayhew find these characteristics marked among the Irish, that he is at times inclined to accuse them of carrying them too far, even to the display of a sordid and parsimonious spirit. According to him, they apply to the various "unions," or to the parish, even when they have money, or sometimes go with wretched food, dwelling, or clothing, in order to have a small fund laid by, in case of any emergency arising.

But the general result of his observations is clear: that the Irish are most provident and far-seeing; a surprising statement, doubtless, to the generality of Mr. Mayhew's readers, but one which, after all, only accords with the testimony of many unexceptionable witnesses of their life in other countries. And, if in England, in London especially, they at times appear sordid in their economy, is not this the very natural result of the misery they had previously endured in their own impoverished land, and therefore a proof that, at least, they have profited by the terrible ordeals through which they were compelled to pass?

We have spoken only of the Irish in London; the same facts are most probably true of them in all the large cities of Great Britain. Unfortunately, Mr. Mayhew's most interesting work has found no imitators in other parts of the kingdom. F. Perraud's remarks, however, in his "Ireland under English Rule," extend almost over the whole country.

After giving his own experience, and that of many others whom he had consulted, or whose works he had read; after having set forth the dangers which beset the Irish in that (to them) "most foreign country"--England-- and also the success which had attended the labors of many proselytizing agents among them, and even in some cases the progress of immorality in their midst resulting from the innumerable seductions to which they were exposed, a success and a progress which Mr. Mayhew's personal observation would lead us to think the good father has exaggerated, he concludes as follows:

"We must not overlook the fact that the Irish emigration to England and Scotland produces in many individual cases results which cannot be too deeply deplored.

"But there, also, as well as in America and Australia, through the economy of an admirable providence, God makes use of those Irish immigrants for the propagation and extension of the Catholic faith in the midst of English and Scotch Protestantism. What progress has not the Catholic religion made within the last thirty years in England? And might not the Catholics say to their separated brethren what Tertullian said to the Caesars of the third century: 'Our religion is but of yesterday; and behold, we fill your towns, your councils, your camps, your tribes, your decuriae, the palace, the senate, the forum . . . . You have persecuted us during centuries, and behold, we spring up afresh from the blood of martyrs!'

"At the beginning of the reign of George III., England and Scotland scarcely contained sixty thousand Catholics who had remained true to the faith of their fathers. Their number in 1821 was, according to the official census, five hundred thousand. In 1842, they were estimated at from two million to two million five hundred thousand. At present (1864) they number nearly four million, and of this total amount the single city of London figures for more than two hundred and fifty thousand."

In a note he adds the following figures, furnished him by Dr. Grant, the late Bishop of Southwark:

Total No. of Catholics.	No. of Irish.

Manchester	80,000	60,000
Liverpool	130,000	85,000
Birmingham	30,000	20,000
Preston	24,000	4,300
Wigan	18,000	6,000
Bolton	12,000	4,000
St. Helen's (Lancashire)	10,000	6,000
Edinburgh	50,000	35,000
Glasgow	127,000	90,000

"Finally, we must not forget that about one-half the army and navy is composed of Irish Catholics.

"In 1792 England and Wales counted no more than thirty-five chapels; in 1840 the number amounted to five hundred, among which were vast and splendid churches, such as St. George's, Southwark, and the Birmingham Cathedral. At present (1864) the number is nearly one thousand.

"In connection with the movement of individual conversions, which yearly brings within our ranks from those of Protestantism the most upright, the sincerest, the best-disposed souls, the Irish immigration in England is then destined to play an important part in the so desirable return of that great island to the faith which she received in the sixth century from St. Gregory the Great and St. Austin of Canterbury," and, let us add, from Aidan and his Irish monks of Lindisfarne and Iona, as Montalembert has shown.

If we examine closely the figures just furnished by F. Perraud, and consider that the number of Catholics in Great Britain was only five hundred thousand in 1821, which, following his calculation, mounted to four million in 1864, if we look closely into the gradations of the increase marked in the various censuses taken between those dates, we shall find that the Irish immigration has indeed played a most important part in the return of England toward Catholicity. We are surprised to find that he seems to estimate the number of Irish in England at only one million; there can be no doubt that they and their offspring compose the majority of Catholics there, and that many of the Englishmen who come back to the true faith are induced by their example and influence, particularly among the lower orders, and that the real work of the conversion of the English nation rests in the hands of the Irish immigrants. Mr. Mayhew has informed us of the disposition of the English costermongers on religious matters.

We have now examined the three great waves which bore the Irish to foreign countries; the lesser streamlets, which wandered away into other English colonies, may be dismissed, as to trace and follow up their course would involve more time and trouble than they really call for. We now see the Irish race disseminated in large groups over many and vast territories; and, although the home population has been considerably diminished by that great exodus, and is now reduced to about five millions, nevertheless, to count them as they are dispersed throughout the world, their number is far higher than it has ever been before; and we now proceed to offer some considerations tending to show the effects of that vast emigration on the resurrection of the race, and on the future progress of the country from which the race comes.

First, then, emigration has given Ireland and Irishmen an importance in the eyes of the world which they and it would never have acquired unless that emigration had taken place; so that England, on whom in a great measure their future fate depends, is now compelled to respect and render them justice; and justice is all that is wanting to bring about their complete resurrection.

In order to form a true idea on this point, it is necessary to consider them in their twofold aspect, as emigrants to the United States, residing under and citizens of a government distinct from that of England; and, secondly, in countries which are under the control of Great Britain, one of these being England itself.

In the Union they become for the greater part citizens of the country which they have made their home, and the first condition necessary for the obtaining of this right of citizenship is the renunciation of all allegiance to their former English rulers. The readiness and joy even with which they perform this task need no mention. But, as Christians, the new obligations under which they bind themselves involve something more than the mere oath of allegiance; the spirit no less than the letter of the oath prescribes that they acknowledge no other country as theirs than that which offered them a refuge, and consequently, by the very fact of becoming American citizens, they cease to be Irishmen.

But their oath does not bind them to forget their former country, as little as it forbids them to benefit it as far as lawfully lies in their power. Far otherwise. Their new allegiance would indeed be a poor thing if, in its very conception, it could only bind hearts so cold as to renounce at once all affection for the land of their birth, and banish in a day memories that the day before were sacred. This is not required of them; and, were it, they could never so understand their allegiance. They remain, and justly, firmly attached to Ireland, and look anxiously for any lawful occasion on which they may manifest their affection by their acts.

Meanwhile, in their new country, position, influence, wealth, consideration, often fall to their lot; their numbers swell, and they become an important factor in the republic. Something of the power wielded by the great nation of which they are now citizens attaches to them, and shows them to the astonished gaze of England under a totally new and unexpected aspect. In war, the effect is most telling, and, even so far back as 1812, the part played by "saucy Jack" Barry, for instance, already gave rise to very grave considerations and forebodings on the part of British statesmen. But, even in time of peace, the high position held by many Irishmen in the United States, and the aggregate voice of a powerful party, where every tongue has a vote, cannot fail to tell advantageously on questions referring to their former country.

Can it be imagined that this exercises no influence on the treatment of Ireland by the ruling power? To afford a true conception of the alteration brought about by Irish emigration, suppose for an instant the ruling power using again its old recklessness in abusing Ireland--not that we imagine the English statesmen of to-day capable of such a thing and anxious to restore what, happily, has passed away forever--but merely to show the utter impossibility of such a contingency again arising, suppose one of the old penal laws to be again enacted and sanctioned by a British sovereign, what would the effect be on the multitude of Irishmen now living in America? What, independently of the Irish, would be the effect on all the organs, worthy of the name, of public opinion in America? How would the great majority of the members, not of Congress only, but of the Legislature of each State, speak? Public opanion is now the ruler of the world, and when public opinion declares against a flagrant and crying injustice, its voice must be heard, its mandate obeyed, and lawlessness cease. This extreme and, as we believe, impossible example, is merely adduced as a proof of the advantage which Ireland has reaped from the dispersion of her scattered children--an advantage falling back on her own head, in return, perhaps, for the mission they are working.

But, over and above the supposition of such an extreme case, there is surely a silent power in the mere standing of millions of free men who would resent, as done to themselves, a recurrence of an attack on their old country. And there are, beyond question, three millions of former Irishmen, citizens to-day of the United States, on whom the glance of many an English statesman, with any just pretension to the name, must fall. Therefore do we say that now England must respect Ireland.

That respect is daily heightened by the greater comfort and easier circumstances, though still far too wretched on the whole, of the Irish at home, which have been mainly brought about by the help received from their exiled countrymen. As was seen, the old policy of their oppressors had for chief object the pauperization of the country, and, as was also seen, that policy was eminently successful. We know how deeply the effects of that former policy are still felt, and how far from completion still is justice in that regard; how they still complain, and with only too much reason, of many laws which are as so many gyves still binding them down in their old degradation; but, of this, the following chapter will speak.

Yet, it is undeniable that their situation is considerably improved, and that the excessive sufferings which formerly seemed their privilege, are scarcely possible in our days. This change in their circumstances for the better may be ascribed to a variety of causes, one of which, we acknowledge, has been the repairing of many previous injustices. But we must acknowledge also that the main lever in a nation's resurrection, once the ground is cleared round about--her treasury--has, as far as Ireland is concerned, been chiefly replenished from abroad. Absentee landlords still drain the country; but the money which has gone into it has been certainly owing greatly to the immense sums transmitted yearly from America by the exiles, all of which has certainly not returned to the place from which it went out. It is impossible to estimate the amount which was kept in Ireland and that which floated back, but the balance must be considerably on the side of what remained, as the distress at home was so great, and in millions of instances immediate relief came from the distant friends who had acquired a competency in their new country, and, knowing the dire distress of their relatives at home, sent generally what they could spare, by the speediest means at their command.

There is no doubt that thousands of families have thus been benefited by that first sad emigration of their friends, and that the visible improvement in the condition of the Irish at home is in a great measure due to it. We hear, moreover, that the working of the new "Encumbered Estates Court " has already placed in the hands of native Irishmen many parcels of the lands of their fathers, and probably many of the ample estates belonging to what was the Irish Church Establishment, which are to be sold, will find their way back in the same manner.

The Irish are thus being slowly reinstated in possession of their own soil, and, that once accomplished, the respect of England is secured-- respectability in England being in its essence equivalent to real estate.

Thus is the uprising of the nation being gradually, silently, but surely brought about by the emigration to the United States; and this effect is considerably heightened when the emigration to countries under English control is taken into consideration--Canada, Australia, England itself.

In those places the same results followed which we have just witnessed in the United States, but another and far greater result remains for them. Not only did they slowly aid in awakening the respect for their countrymen at home in the English breast by their own rising importance and improved condition, but in Canada and Australia they possess a privilege which, in the British Isles, is theirs only in theory, but abroad becomes a very powerful fact.

Ever since the Union of 1800, the Irish are supposed to form a part and parcel of the empire at home, and to have fair representation of their native country in the members they return to the Imperial Parliament. But it is well known that the Irish influence in that Parliament is almost null, and that their presence there frequently is productive of no other result than to countenance laws injurious to their own country. Does, can Ireland hope to derive any political or social benefit from her representatives in London beyond whatever may accrue to her from their vain remonstrances and ineffective speeches? But in the colonial Parliaments the case is very different.

It is not our desire to be understood as saying that Irishmen, by meddling with politics, can effect a certain improvement in their condition and that of their country, beyond giving tokens of the life which is in them. We believe, on the contrary, that too great an eagerness in such pursuits has injured them on many occasions; and they ought to beware of flattering themselves that they are rising because their votes are clamored for, and they themselves exhorted to enter into the contest as fierce partisans. This, too often, leads them into making themselves the mere tools of shrewd men.

But, in the colonies, they muster in considerable force, and, with prudence and sagacity, may have their desires and measures fairly considered and conceded; for, unfortunately, the style of measures fair and favorable to them as Irishmen and Catholics, is completely at variance with that of those opposed to them, whom, go where they will, they encounter, and always in the same form. In Ireland, they are at liberty, apparently, to do the same by reason of their superiority in point of numbers; the result of the late Galway elections proves what a farce is this show of liberty, and even the members whom they would and do sometimes elect possess a very feeble influence, or none, in what is called the Imperial Parliament. But, in the colonies, if they, as electors, outnumber their political opponents, they can and must return the majority to the House of Representatives and of officers to the various departments of the colonial administration. Such is the law of election in really representative governments which are truly free; the majority of electors returns the majority to the government; and rightly so. Of course, there is room here, particularly where the majority happens to be Irish, for a vast quantity of frothy bluster about drilled and intimidated voters, and all that sort of thing. With that we have no concern at present, and merely remark en passant that it is a pity a little more of it was not wasted on the recent Galway elections, already alluded to, on both sides; and for the rest, that the world has not yet been apprised of Irish majorities in the Australian Parliament abusing their power by either accidental or systematic misrule; and it may, therefore, be safely conceded that, on the whole, the government has rested in safe hands. However, what concerns us at present is the state of Canada and Australia, where, among the highest public dignitaries, are found men who are Irish, not simply by birth, but in feeling and in truth. And the conclusion which we wish to draw from that fact is, that Ireland is greatly benefited by the high positions which her sons assume in those distant colonies; and probably no one will be rash enough to deny or controvert in any way this point.

The truth is, that by emigration Ireland has suddenly expanded into vast regions formerly ignorant of her name; regions which swell the power and wealth of England, and which are destined to play a very important part in her future history. In these districts Irishmen have found a new country;

something of the ubiquity of the English belongs to them, and the influence, power, and weight, thus thrown into their hands, need no further comment. To show this in extenso would be only to travel over ground already trodden in previous pages, enumerating the various countries they have touched upon in their Exodus. Thus have our seemingly long digressions had a very direct object in view, and served powerfully to solve our original question. We may now see that the resurrection of Ireland was intimately involved in the emigration of her children; that much of what has already taken place to aid in that resurrection may be ascribed to this emigration, and that much brighter days are yet in store for the nation, resulting mainly from this constant and powerful cause. Let no one, then, lament the perseverance of those hardy wanderers who, though their country has already been depleted by millions, still leave her to the figure of seventy thousand annually. It seems that in Ireland much surprise is expressed at the movement never ceasing. Providence will end it in its own good time; if God still allows it, it is surely for the accomplishment of his own mighty and benevolent designs.

To conclude, then, this long chapter, there is only one question to be put, which demands a few words, but words, in our opinion at least, of vast importance, and which we would give all that is ours to give, to see promptly and energetically attended to: Has Ireland profited by this so-often mentioned emigration to the extent she should have profited? And what ought Irishmen to do in order to increase the advantages derived from it?

We must confess that, up to the present, the benefit is far from what it ought to have been, and the cause of this lies in want of organization and association. They have seemed to let God work for them without any cooperation on their part; for God's, as we saw, was the plan, and he forced them, as it were, to carry out his design. They went at the work blindly, merely following the impulse of circumstances, with no preparatory organization, and less still of association. And even now, when they are spread out over such vast territories in such mighty multitudes, as yet they have given no sign of the least desire of attempting even something like a combined effort to accelerate the work of Providence. The only signs of life so far given have been violent and spasmodic, directly opposed to the genius of the race, which, as we have endeavored to prove, has nothing revolutionary in its character, and is not given to dark plots and godless conspiracies.

Unfortunately, also, they do not seem naturally adapted to a spirit of steady and long-continued or systematic association. In this, chiefly, does their race differ from the Scandinavian stock, which is grafted on system, combination, and steadiness, in pursuit of the object in hand.

But why not begin, at least, to make an effort in that direction? The Latin races, in which runs so much Celtic blood, are powerful to organize, as the Romans of old, and the French and Spaniards of to-day, have so often proved. The Irish have been infused with plenty of foreign blood, after their many national catastrophes, although we believe that their primitive characteristics have always overcome all foreign elements introduced among them; and, what the race could scarcely attempt ages ado, is possible now. Moreover, there is nothing in the leanings of race which may not be overcome, and sure without any radical change a nation can adapt itself to the necessities of the time, and to altered circumstances. Let the Irish see what they might effect toward the resurrection of their native country, if they only seriously began at last to organize and associate for that purpose. They would thus turn the immense forces of their nation, now scattered over the world, to the real advantage of their birthplace. In union is strength; but union can only be promoted by association, particularly when the elements to be united are so far apart.

For such an object do we believe that God gave man in these late days the destroyers of space--the steam-engine and the electric telegraph. Those powerful agents of unification were unknown to mankind until God decreed that his children dispersed through the earth should be more compactly united. To the Catholic they were given, in the first place, to serve God's first purpose by making the Church firmer in her unity and more effective in the propagation of truth; but, after all, the mission of the Irish to-day is only a branch of the mission of the Church, and, if only on that account, are the missionaries deserving of all honor and respect.

If in the designs of Providence the time has at last arrived for the dwelling of the children of Japhet in the tents of Sem, and for putting an end to the terrible evils dating from the dispersion at Babel and the confusion of tongues, the object of these great scientific discoveries is still more apparent. At all events, organization and association are clearly needed for the resurrection of Ireland, and the sooner a step is taken in that direction the better.

But, what association would we propose? What should be its immediate and most practicable objects? These questions we do not feel competent to answer. Let Irishmen be once convinced that organization is the great lever to work for the raising up of their down-trodden nation, and they will know best how to use this powerful instrument. The leaders of the nation in that holy enterprise should, in our own opinion, be its spiritual leaders. They know their country, and they love it; they undoubtedly possess the confidence of their countrymen: they, then, should be the natural originators of those great schemes. And what other leaders does Ireland possess, what body like them, acceptable to the nation, and neither to be bought by money nor office?

This first remark naturally presupposes another: that the object of those associations, being approved of by the religious guides of the people, cannot be other than holy, and consequently require no secrecy of any kind. They must be patent to the world, as not being antagonistic to any established law or authority. Every man desirous of becoming a member of the association should know beforehand what is proposed to be done, and how far his consent is to be given.

One other important point strikes us: the centre of organization should be in Ireland. Ireland is to be benefited by it, and there the effort should naturally begin, where its results will fall. As for the particular direction which those efforts should take, the detail of the whole enterprise, the plan of the campaign--all this lies beyond us, and a sketch of it would most probably be a mere chimera.

One concluding word may be said, however, on a subject which has often been present to the writer's mind: The fearful oppression of the nation began by robbing the people of their lands and making them paupers: one of the first aims of association, then, should evidently be the raising of the people up by the restoration, in great part at least, of the soil to the native race.

It is not our purpose to propose a new confiscation now, by way of remedying the old ones; but England has allowed them to buy back the land of their fathers in the "Encumbered Estates Courts," and by the law recently passed which disestablished the Irish Protestant Church? Is there no room for a plan whereby Irishmen, who have grown rich in foreign countries, may become purchasers of the land thus offered for sale? And, in reply to the natural and powerful objection to such a plan on the score of distance from their native land, and the natural repugnance to return and live there, and break up new ties, which are now old, and have made them what they are, could not the fathers spare one son at least, whom they might devote to the noble purpose of becoming Irish again, and settling on an Irish estate, and marrying there? This would seem an easy and simple manner of recreating a Catholic gentry in the island.

This is merely a hint thrown out to exemplify what we mean by associations for the purpose of raising Ireland up again; the many possible objects of national organization will occur to any mind giving a moment's reflection to it. This subject will occupy our attention at greater length in the next chapter.

MORAL FORCE ALL-SUFFICIENT FOR THE RESURRECTION OF IRELAND

THIS chapter will be devoted to the island itself. For many centuries it was happy in its seclusion and separation from the rest of Europe: in these days it necessarily forms a part of the whole mass of Japhetic races; its isolation is no longer possible; and, in the opinion of many, it is destined once again to become a spot illustrious and happy. The consideration of how that lustre and happiness are to come upon it is the only task still left us.

Whoever takes into consideration the advantages it already enjoys, and compares its present situation with that of a hundred years back, cannot fail to be struck with the remarkable change for the better which has taken place between the two periods. Ireland still suffers, and suffers sorely, and the world still speaks with justice of her wrongs; but, in whatever light they may appear to those who love their country, no one can pretend that it still groans under the weight of tyranny which has formed the burden of her history. And, while acknowledging this beneficial change in her condition, they must wonder at the same time how small was the share which the natives themselves had in bringing it about, although their activity never relaxed, and they had great and good men working for their cause. What, in truth, did it?

The first point which claims our attention is how effectually the moral force of what is called liberal thought dealt a death-blow to the penal laws half a century before any of them were erased from the statute book.

Liberal thought may be said to have originated in England, whence it passed over to France, to be disseminated and take root throughout Europe by means of the mighty influence then exercised by the great nation. The chief object which animated the minds of those who first labored for its admission into modern European principles is not for us to consider here. There is no doubt that this chief object was of a loosening and deleterious nature: namely, to ruin Christian faith, to change all the old social and political axioms held by Christendom, and to create a new society imbued with what now goes by the name of modern ideas. It is not necessary to point out the frightful imprudence as well as criminality of many of those who were the pioneers of the movement. We must only take the new principles as a great fact, destined yet to effect a radical change in the ideas of men of all races, a change already begun in Europe.

Liberal thought, we say, originated in England; and it would be easy to show that there it was the result partly of Protestantism, partly of indifferentism, the ultimate consequence of the great principle of private judgment.

This became manifest in Great Britain, from the beginning of the eighteenth century, and, as was previously shown, what is called the British Constitution was the result and outgrowth of deep political thought matured in minds indifferent to religion, of men who were as little Protestants as any thing else. But they were deeply possessed by a sense of conservatism and moderation in the application of the most radical principles, which later on the fiery Gallic mind carried to their final and most disastrous consequences.

But, in whatever garb it may have appeared, liberalism was clearly the essence of the British Constitution, as established after all the civil and dynastic wars of the sixteenth and seventeenth centuries. The leaders of the English nation happened at the time to be fully wedded to aristocratic ideas, and accordingly they refused to recognize all the consequences of their principles, and to see them carried out to the full.

It was admitted that the king reigned, but did not govern; that the nation governed by its representatives; that those representatives were created by election; that a nation could not be taxed without its free consent; that thought, religious thought chiefly, was free; that toleration, therefore, could admit of no exception in point of religious doctrine; and all the other modern principles which have at length been admitted, though not always observed, as governmental axioms by all European nations.

As long as those axioms were in the close keeping of English patricians, some of their consequences were far from being fully evolved; but certain Frenchmen, Voltaire among others, happening to cross the Straits of Dover, returned with them, and, the wretched government of Louis XV being not only too weak to withstand, but even conniving at, the boldness of the new philosophers, the French language, which was then spoken all over Europe, carried with it from mouth to mouth the new and fascinating doctrine of the emancipation of thought.

None of those writers, indeed, undertook to plead the cause of unfortunate Ireland. Voltaire threw the whole of France into agitation, nay, all Europe, to the wilds of Russia, by taking up the case of the Protestant Calas, who was condemned to death and executed unjustly, as it seems, for the supposed murder of a son who was inclined to embrace Catholicity; but never a word did he speak of the suffering which at that time had settled down over the whole Irish nation solely for the crime of its religious convictions.

Nevertheless, toleration became the catchword with all. It rang out loudly from a thousand French pamphlets and ponderous tomes; it was caught up and echoed back from England; it penetrated the unkindly atmosphere of Russia even, and was silently pondered over under the rule of an unbelieving despot.

It was impossible for Ireland not to derive some benefit from all this. It took a long time, indeed, for emancipation of thought to cross that narrow channel which divided the "sister" islands; for, at the precise period when the doctrine was loudest in France, the most atrocious penal laws were being executed in Ireland, and there seemed no hope for the suffering nation.

But, toward the end of that eventful eighteenth century, the breath of that magic word, toleration, at last was felt on the shores of Erin. When it was in the mouths of all Europe, when English clergymen had thoroughly imbibed the new doctrine, when even Scotch ministers began to thaw under its genial influence, and become "liberal theologians," how could an Irish magistrate think of hanging a friar, or transporting a priest, or imposing a heavy fine on a Catholic who committed the heinous offence of hearing mass, or absenting himself from the services of the Established Church? At last, the "Mass-rock" was no longer the only spot whereon the divine victim of expiation could be offered up; and it soon came to be known that, to by-lanes and obscure houses in the cities numbers of persons flocked on Sundays, presided over by their own Sogarth Aroon. On one occasion, already noticed, the floor of a rickety house, where they were worshipping, gave way, to the killing and maiming of many; thenceforth, Catholics were allowed to assemble in public to the knowledge of all, and, though "discoverers" were still legally entitled to denounce and prosecute them, there was small chance of a verdict against them.

Thus was it owing to a great moral force--whether good or bad is not the question now--that the penal laws first became obsolete; and Irishmen had absolutely nothing whatever to do in the matter. Not a single pamphlet, demanding toleration, and proclaiming the rights of religious freedom, ever, to our knowledge, issued from the Irish press at the time. No book, written by an Irish author, advocating the same, was ever printed clandestinely, as were so many French books, at first appearing in Holland, or covertly in France, with a false title-page.

When the Volunteer movement took place, toleration was in full sway in Ireland. As was seen, the question debated in the Dungannon Convention referred solely to the extension of the elective franchise to Catholics; and, though this was unjustly denied them by the majority of the Volunteers, under the guidance of the leaders of the movement, there was no question of any longer refusing to the native Irish Catholics the right of practising their religion freely. This the moral sense of the century had secured to them.

The attainment of the political franchise was also the result of purely moral force, though it required a much longer time in its acquisition, as it was a question, not merely of a right individual in its nature, as all natural religious rights are, but one affecting external society, and productive of material results of great import.

In this the Irish were not merely passive; they launched themselves heart and soul on the sea of political agitation. From 1810 to 1829, the Catholic Association, which embraced men of all classes of society, was incessant in its clamor for emancipation. The chief object of this association being the political franchise, it was felt by all that, sooner or later, that privilege must be granted. Meanwhile, the secular enemies of Ireland were not idle. Emancipation--that is the political franchise--they called a "Utopian dream," which they asserted England could not grant. Was it not directly opposed to the coronation-oath, nay, to the English Constitution? The king himself was, and publicly declared himself to be, of this opinion. According to your thorough-bred Englishman, the state would rather spend its last shilling, and sacrifice its last man, than suffer it. How many spoke thus, even up to the very day on which Wellington, changing his mind perforce, at last proposed the measure!

All this opposition was perhaps only to be expected; but the strange thing was that many excellent patriotic Irishmen, Catholics, laymen as well as clerics and prelates, were opposed to the agitation set on foot by O'Connell and his friends; they also thought it a "Utopian dream," likely only to bring new calamities upon their country. They seemed not to see that the refusal of emancipation meant in fact the continuance of the small Protestant minority as the ruling power--the state--in Ireland, which, owing to moral force, was no longer so, save in theory. In fact, already the majority, that is, almost the whole of Ireland, was an immense power. Its members were at liberty to combine openly, to show themselves, to speak, to write, to agitate; they were, in a word, a people, and the Protestant minority no longer really constituted the state.

It is true that the majority of Irishmen had for centuries continued to act unanimously in their resistance to oppression; as was seen, they had been a people from the moment that the English kings and Parliaments strove to coerce their religious faith, and more particularly from the destruction of clanship. They were truly a nation, though without a government of their own, and for the greater part of the time bending under the most intolerable tyranny. Religion had given them one thought and one heart. And now that, owing to the mighty, the irresistible moral force of liberalism, they could no longer be openly persecuted for wishing to remain Catholics, the question arose: Were they still to be absolutely nothing in the state? This was the real demand of the Catholic Association, and every one ought to have seen its importance and the certainty of success.

Nevertheless, a great number of sincere Irishmen did not see the question in this light, and were covertly or openly opposed to the agitation. Ireland appeared to be divided just at a momentous crisis.

The leaders of the association were not themselves altogether agreed as to the best mode of putting their question. Some were for armed opposition, thinking they could beat England in the open field. But the great originator and leader of the movement sternly opposed so mad a proposition. He was for moral force, seeing how clearly and irresistibly, even if unwittingly, it was working for their cause. In spite of all adverse circumstances, although the English party and the English nation stood up en masse against him, although many Irishmen refused to join in the agitation, while some of his best friends wished to risk all in a desperate venture, he stood calm, firm, and so confident of success, that he caused himself to be returned as member for the County Clare to the English Parliament, before even emancipation had given him the right of candidature. It was immediately after this "unconstitutional" election that the boon of emancipation was suddenly granted, contrary to all expectation and probability, and O'Connell proudly took his seat among the repre-sentatives of Ireland in the Imperial Parliament.

If this measure was not carried by a purely moral force, it is hard to see how that phrase can be applied to any thing in this world. This is not the place to write a history of that memorable struggle. It is still fresh in the memory of many living men. We merely draw a conclusion from what has happened in our own time, and one which may be said to be a clear inference from the circumstances of the case, and to which no one can offer any serious objection. This conclusion is, the omnipotence of moral force in gaining for Ireland so much of liberty, of political, and social privileges, as was finally granted her.

This victory won for the Irish Catholics the acknowledgment on the part of England that they were a factor in the state. The next question which naturally presented itself was, "What was to be their exact position in the state?"

There are many answers to this, even in modern ideas. In purely democratic countries suffrage is universal, all have a political vote, and the majority is supposed to rule. In countries where the government is oligarchical or aristocratic, rank, wealth, and position, are "privileged;" the great mass is deprived of a vote. Yet, even in those countries, in accordance with the modern idea, blood is not every thing; a certain number of plebeians are admitted to a share in public affairs, and their number is greater or smaller as the struggle, which is always going on between the few and the many, wavers to this side or to that. Thus, in the English Parliament there is often an "electoral" or "reform" question discussed and agitated. But the leaders of the Catholic Association boldly advocated a question prior to those-- what at the time was called the repeal of the Union, and is now known as "home-rule."

Must Ireland continue to be governed by laws enacted in England? The number of her special representatives is comparatively so small, her Catholic aspirations meet with such deaf ears in the majority of the members, that, as long as Ireland is without her own Parliament, she cannot be called a free country.

Moreover, according to modern ideas, self-government seems to be admitted as an axiom; all countries have a right to it, under the limitation of constitutional enactments, either in "confederacies" or in "imperial states." Why should Ireland alone be deprived of such a boon?

It is known how O'Connell suddenly grasped the question and mastered it. His first repeal association was suppressed on the instant by a proclamation of the Irish Secretary. O'Connell bowed to the proclamation, and for the first organization substituted another called "the Irish Volunteers for the Repeal of the Union." This met with the same fate as the first. The great agitator then took refuge in "repeal breakfasts," and declared his intention, if the government "thought fit to proclaim down breakfasts, to resort to a political lunch, and, if political luncheon be equally dangerous to the peace of the viceroy, he would have political dinners; if the dinners be proclaimed, we must, said he, like certain sanctified dames, resort to tea and tracts."

The "breakfasts" were suppressed, and O'Connell was arrested. The prosecution, however, was soon abandoned, and for the moment, despairing of success in advocating repeal, he came down to the "Reform party," from which he obtained at first some great advantages for Ireland-- the administration of Lord Mulgrave, the best the island had known for centuries, and the appointment of many Catholics to high offices in the state.

It is not necessary to relate the circumstances which finally drove O'Connell back upon his original plan, and the formation, in April, 1840, of the "Loyal National Repeal Association."

Within a short time three million associates were contributing annually to the national fund, and a scene was witnessed which the most devoted lover of Erin could never have anticipated. It would be useless to search the annals of mankind for a more startling exhibition of purely moral force.

The causes of its failure will appear causes altogether of a temporary and unexpected character, when we come to examine them.

But the stupendous spectacle itself was enough to impress the beholder with the irresistible effect which it could not fail to produce. A whole nation obedient to the voice of one man! --and that a man who had never been invested with a state dignity, proud only of having once represented a poor Irish county in the English Parliament; who was eminently a man of the people, identified in every way with the people, speaking a language they could all understand, speaking to hundreds of thousands who had come at his call to listen to him: at one time nearly a million of them surrounded him on the hill of Tara.

Had a demagogue stood in his place, how could he have resisted the temptation of using such power to effect a thorough revolution? O'Connell had only to utter the word, and those immense masses of men would have swept the whole island as with a besom of destruction. The impetuosity of the Irish character when placed in such circumstances is well known, and O'Connell knew it better than any man living at the time. He showed himself truly heroic in the constant moderation of his words, even in scenes the most exciting, when a look from him might have lashed the nation into madness.

To bring out more clearly the stamp and greatness of the man, compare his conduct with that of the leaders in the great French Revolution of 1793. Not one of them ever possessed a tithe, not merely of the great Irishman's honesty of purpose, but even of his real authority over the people; yet, what frightful convulsions did they not bring upon the state in the days of their brief popularity? Throughout the whole repeal movement, when millions of people obeyed implicitly one leader, ready to do his will at any moment, there was never a single breach of the peace, never an attempt at outrage, never a threat of retaliation.

The only difficulty is where to bestow the greater admiration, on O'Connell or the people; for, if O'Connell towered almost above humanity in his never-varying moderation, with such a powerful engine in his hands, the people offered a spectacle which would be looked for in vain elsewhere in the history of man, that of a whole nation swayed by the most excited feelings, one in thought, in aims, in the bitter memory of the past, conscious of their irresistible power in the present, yet never yielding to passion, but dispersing quietly after listening to the impassioned harangues of their leader, to return to their homes and resume their ordinary occupations. Any impartial man, who has read history at all, must acknowledge that this spectacle is unexampled, and in itself vindicates the Irish character from the foolish aspersions so lavishly cast upon it, and so thoughtlessly repeated still.

One great fact was brought out by those demonstrations which afterward appeared so barren of result, namely, the existence of a nation full of life and energy, of a surprising vigor, and at the same time governed by stern principles as well as swayed by emotion. It would be idle to pretend that they were a non-entity, save as forming a part of the British Empire, existing on sufferance as it were, merely to add to the greatness and the glory of the English nation. They possessed a life of their own. That life had, as was seen, been instilled into them by their religious convictions alone; it had lain dormant for more than a century; and now it burst forth in the view of the world, to proclaim that the Irish nation still existed. And this wonderful resurrection was due to moral force alone.

Though the Irish people then appeared so different from that humbled, crushed mass of oppressed beings, who, a hundred years before, lay so completely at the mercy of their masters, it was, nevertheless, the same people, and the difference was purely one of circumstances. Had they been allowed in the previous century to manifest their feelings, as a happy change in the state of affairs now permitted them, they would assuredly have acted in exactly the same manner. And this reflection tends to confirm the opinion, several times here expressed, that the Irish people existed all along, and that the most adverse circumstances had never succeeded in destroying it.

Meanwhile, O'Connell was the sovereign of that nation, and one whose power over his subjects was greater than that of any of the kings or emperors who occupied the various thrones of Europe at the time. Later events proved how precarious was the authority of all those who appeared to hold the fate of millions in their hands; the authority of O'Connell alone was deeply rooted in the heart of his nation. From the humble position of a Kerry lawyer, he had gradually risen to the proud preeminence which he occupied in the eyes of Europe, and he owed it solely to that moral force of which he was so sincere an advocate, and which he knew so well how to wield.

But how came all the high hopes then so ardently entertained by the friends of Ireland to be so suddenly dashed to the ground, and O'Connell to die of a broken heart?

It seems, indeed, to be the opinion of Irishmen even, that O'Connell's theory was faulty; that moral force alone could not restore Ireland to her lawful position among nations; that, in fact, he failed by his very moderation, and that the bitterness which clouded his last days was the natural consequence of his false and delusive expectations. Such seems now to be the almost universal opinion.

Yet, in all his wonderful career, only one fault can be brought against him. Yielding, on one occasion, in 1843, to the exuberance of his feelings, "he committed himself to a specific promise that within six months repeal would be an accomplished fact."

This promise, rashly given, and showing no result, is said to have cooled down the enthusiasm of the people, who, from that time, lost confidence in their leader; and to this alone is the utter failure of the great agitation ascribed.

But there is so little of real truth in this assertion that, when, on his well-known imprisonment, after the law lords, in the British House of Peers, declared that the conviction of O'Connell and his colleagues was wrong, he was restored to liberty, the writer just quoted confesses that "overwhelming demonstrations of unchanged affection and personal attachment poured in upon him from his countrymen. Their faith in his devotion to Ireland was increased a hundred-fold."

It is true that the same writer, Mr. A.M. O'Sullivan, adds that "their faith in the efficiency of his policy, or the surety of his promise, was gone;" but to reconcile this phrase with what precedes it, it must not be taken absolutely. The want of faith here spoken of was restricted to the members of a new party, which had been organized chiefly during the imprisonment of the great leader, the "Young Ireland party," the new advocates of physical force against England, composed of the ardent and, most surely, well-intentioned young men, who failed so egregiously a few years later.

This party was the chief cause of O'Connell's failure, coupled with the awful famine which followed soon after, and left the Irish small desire for political agitation with grim Death staring them in the face, and the main question before them one of avoiding starvation and utter ruin.

Both causes, however, were purely of a temporary nature, and the efficacy of moral force remained strong as ever, and, in fact, the only thing possible.

The Young Ireland party could not exist long, as its avowed policy was so rash, so ill-founded, and poorly carried out, that the mere breath of British power was enough to dissipate it hopelessly in a moment. Moreover, it placed itself in open antagonism to the mass of the Catholic clergy, and appeared to have so ill studied the history of the country that its members did not know the real power which religion exercised over their countrymen. They could not but fail, and their futile attempt only served to render worse the condition of the country they were ready to die for.

It would be enough to add here, of other subsequent attempts of the same nature, that no real hope for the complete resurrection of Ireland could be looked to from such abortive and stillborn conspiracies; especially when the alliance entered into by some of them with the revolutionary party of European socialists and atheists is taken into account, men from whom nothing but disorder, anarchy, and crime, can be expected. Thus, those who wish well to the Irish cause have only moral force to fall back upon.

It is needless to do more than mention the passing nature of the frightful calamity of famine and consequent expatriation, which have been sufficiently dwelt upon. The Irish race has passed through ordeals more trying than either of these; it has survived them, and increased in numbers after all previous calamities, as it doubtless will after this last, when God thinks proper to abate in the people the eagerness they still feel for leaving their native country.

All the progress made by Ireland, so far, is due, therefore, solely to the kind action of Divine Providence, which is generally called the "logic of events," aided by men endowed with prudence and energy. It would be superfluous for our purpose to detail at length several other progressive steps made subsequently, which the mad attempt of the party of physical force would have effectually prevented if open tyranny were as easy a thing in these days as it once was. The establishment of the "Encumbered Estates Courts," and the disestablishment of the Irish Protestant Church, are the chief measures alluded to: the first so fruitful of good to Ireland since its adoption, and the second destined to be no less so. It is useless to remark that physical force had nothing to do with their introduction, and that the British statesmen who advocated and carried them through were swayed only by that unseen power which is said by Holy Scripture to "hold the heart of kings in its hands." Let the Irish do their part, and Heaven will continue to smile on them.

Since it is to this unseen power that all the improvement now visible in the condition of the Irish nation is due, it is only natural to expect from it every thing that is still wanting. For we are far from thinking that nothing more is to be done, and that all to be desired has been obtained. That the nation is still dissatisfied, is plain enough; and it must be right in not feeling contented with the various measures for its improvement tendered it so far. The voice of its natural leaders--of the prelates and clergy-proclaims that there are many things to change, and many new measures to be introduced.

The first and foremost of these is a thorough remedy for the disgraceful state of pauperism to which the great majority of the Irish nation is yet reduced. That pauperism was wilfully established, and this national crime of England stands unatoned for still. It would be unjust to say that the policy which produced it is pursued to-day by the English Government; we sincerely believe, on the contrary, that the state of things which has existed for the last two centuries is seriously deplored by many of those who, under God, hold in their keeping the destiny of millions of men. But it is surprising that so many projects, so many attempts at legislation, the writing of so many wise books, discussions so many and so exhaustive of the evil, should all result in leaving the evil almost as it stood.

If we listen to those who know Ireland perfectly, who have either spent their lives in the country, or traversed its surface leisurely and intelligently, it would seem as though the old descriptions of her in the time of her greatest misfortunes would still be appropriate and true.

"No devastated province of the Roman Empire," said Father Lavelle, but yesterday, in his "Irish Landlord," "ever presented half the wretchedness of Ireland. At this day, the mutilated Fellah of Egypt, the savage Hottentot and New-Hollander, the live chattel of Cuba, enjoy a paradise in comparison with the Irish peasant, that is to say, with the bulk of the Irish nation."

But, as this short passage deals only in generalities, and as there may be some suspicion of the warm nature of the writer having given a higher color to his words than was warranted by the facts, let us listen to the less impassioned utterances of travellers who have recently visited the island: let us see the Irish at home in their towns and in the country.

I. In towns and cities: The most Rev. Archbishop of Dublin, writing in 1857 to Lord St. Leonards, on the state of his flock in Dublin, says: "Were your lordship to visit some of the ruined lanes and streets of Dublin, your heart would thrill with horror at the picture of human woe which would present itself."

And in a pastoral letter, November 27,1861, he spoke of "tens of thousands of human beings, destitute of all the comforts of life, who are to be met with at every step in all great towns and cities. If you enter the wretched abodes where they live, you will find that they have no fuel, that they are unprovided with beds and other furniture, and that generally they have not a single blanket to protect them from the cold."

Abbe Perraud, after a thorough examination of the subject, wrote, in 1864, in "Ireland under English Rule:"

"The poor quarters of Cork, Limerick, and Drogheda, present the same spectacle as Dublin, and justify the sad proverbial celebrity of `Irish rags.' Dirt, negligence, and want of care, doubtless, go a long way in giving to destitution in Ireland its repulsive and hideous form; but who is unaware that continued and hopeless destitution engenders, as of necessity, listlessness and carelessness, and that, to enter into a struggle with poverty, there must be at least some chance of carrying off the victory?"

A German Protestant, Dr. Julius Rodenberg, writing in 1861, expressed his astonishment at the sight of Ireland's poverty, as he saw it in the streets of Dublin, although he had doubtless read a great deal about it previously. "You are in a country," he says, "whence people emigrate by thousands, while fields, of such an extent and power of production as would support them all, lie fallow."

And with respect to the progress already made, M. de Beaumont had remarked many years before that in Ireland a certain relative progress was quite compatible with the continued existence of pauperism among the lower classes. "One single cause," he remarks, "suffices to explain why the agricultural population becomes poorer, while the prosperity of the rich is on the increase: it is that all improvement in the land is profitable solely to the proprietor, who exacts more rent from the farmer in proportion as he works the land into a better state."

Since M. de Beaumont wrote, the pauperism in the cities has assumed a more wretched and repulsive form, in consequence of the crowding there of poor peasants who had been evicted from their small farms and fled to the nearest city or town with the hope of finding there at least charity.

"For the last ten years," wrote Abbe Perraud, in 1864, "there has been taking place in the large cities an accumulation of poor as fatal to their health as to their morality. They are mostly country people whom eviction has driven from the country, who have been unable to emigrate, and who were unwilling to shut themselves up immediately in the workhouses. The resources they procure for themselves, by doing odd work, are so completely insufficient, that it is impossible to be surprised at their destitution."

Dr. Rodenberg, describing the state of the poor country people crowded in the "Liberties of Dublin," says of the rooms in which they live: "In those holes the most wretched and pitiable laborers imaginable live; they often lie by hundreds together on the bare ground."

Such citations might be sadly multiplied, but those given are sufficient as descriptive of the state of the poor Irish in the cities. Let us now see how the peasants live in the country in many parts of Ireland:

II. "The destitution of the agricultural classes," writes Abbe Perraud, from personal observation, "in order to be rightly appreciated, must be seen in the boggy and mountainous regions of Munster, of Connaught, and of the western portion of Ulster.

"The ordinary dwelling of the small tenant, of the day-laborer, in that part of Ireland, answers with the utmost precision the description of it twenty years ago given by M. de Beaumont: 'Let the reader picture to himself four walls of dried mud, which the rain easily reduces to its primitive condition; a little thatch or a few cuts of turf form the roof; a rude hole in the roof forms the chimney, and more frequently there is no other issue for the smoke than the door of the dwelling itself. One solitary room holds father, mother, grandfather, and children. No furniture is to be seen; a single litter, usually composed of grass or straw, serves for the whole family. Five or six half-naked children may be seen crouching over a poor fire. In the midst of them lies a filthy pig, the only inhabitant at its ease, because its element is filth itself.'

"Into how many dwellings of this kind have we not ourselves penetrated--especially in the counties of Kerry, Mayo, and Donegal--more than once obliged to stoop down to the ground, in order to penetrate into these cabins, the entrance to which is so low that they look more like the burrows of beasts than dwellings made for man!

"Upon the road from Kilkenny to Grenaugh, in the vicinity of those beautiful lakes, at the entrance of those parks, to which, for extent and richness, neither England nor Scotland can probably offer any thing equal, we have seen other dwellings. A few branches of trees, interlaced and leaning upon the slope in the road, a few cuts of turf, and a few stones picked up in the fields, compose these wretched huts--less spacious, and perhaps less substantial, than that of the American savage."

At the time of Abbe Perraud's visit, a correspondent of the Dublin Saunders News-Letters, who was commissioned to inquire into the condition of the peasants, gave the following reply, which, as the abbe justly remarks, is but the faithful echo of all the descriptions made within the last half-century:

"The inhabitants of Erris appear to be the most wretched of all human beings. Their cabins, their patched and tattered clothes, their broken-down gait--every thing bears witness to their poverty. Their beds consist of a few bits of wood crossed one upon the other, supported by two heaps of stones, and covered with straw; their whole bedclothes a miserable, worn-out quilt, without any blankets . . . . But there is nothing in Ireland like the habitations which the people of the village of Fallmore have made for themselves, who have been evicted by Mr. Palmer. They are composed of masses of granite, picked up on the shore, and roughly laid one by the other. These cabins are so low that a man cannot stand upright in them; so narrow that they can hardly hold three or four persons."

After all, F. Lavelle was guilty of no exaggeration in stating that the hut of the Hottentot was better than that of the Irish peasant. But, in the district of Gweedore, northeast of County Donegal, the state of the peasantry is more deplorably wretched still than in any other part of Ireland. At the time of a celebrated parliamentary inquiry in to the matter in 1858, a Londonderry newspaper stated that "there are in Donegal about four thousand adults, of both sexes, who are obliged to go barefoot during the winter, in the ice and snow--pregnant women and aged people in habitual danger of death from the cold . . . . It is rare to find a man with a calico shirt; but the distress of the women is still greater, if that be possible. There are many hundreds of families in which five or six grown-up women have among them no more than a single dress to go out in . . . . There are about five hundred families who have but one bed each-- in which father, mother, and children, without distinction of age or sex, are crowded pell-mell together."

If from the dwellings and clothing of the peasantry we pass to their food, there is no need of adding any thing to what was said on this point when describing the periodical famines. One detail, however, not yet mentioned, deserves to be recorded:

"In the district of Gweedore," says Abbe Perraud, "our eyes were destined to witness the use of sea-weed. Stepping once into a cabin, in which there was no one but a little girl charged with the care of minding her younger brothers, and getting ready the evening meal, we found upon the fire a pot full of doulamaun ready cooked; we asked to taste it, and some was handed to us on a little platter.

"This weed, when well dressed, produces a kind of viscous juice; it has a brackish taste, and savors strongly of salt water. We were told in the country that the only use of it is to increase, when mixed with potatoes, the mass of aliment given to the stomach. The longer and more difficult the work of the stomach, the less frequent are its calls. It is a kind of compromise with hunger; the people are able neither to suppress it nor to satisfy it; they endeavor to cheat it. We have also been assured that this weed cannot be eaten alone; it must be mixed with vegetables, since of itself it has no nutritive properties whatever."

How long is such a state of things likely to continue? It has already existed long enough to be a disgrace to the much-vaunted benevolence of the nineteenth century. A sure and radical remedy must be found for it; and, as it has been already so long delayed, it should be found the more promptly.

It seems that the tenure of land lies at the bottom of the question, and that respect for what are called "established rights" offers the main difficulty. Those rights, indeed, were founded on the cruellest wrong and the most flagrant injustice; but as possession is "nine points of the English law," and so long a time has passed since the land changed hands, prescription must be admitted and let them be called rights; nor can any man in his senses ask for a violent subversion of society for the sake of righting an old wrong.

But it has ever been a maxim of jurisprudence that summum jus, summa injuria; and this axiom finds its full explanation in the present case, when it is considered that the jus is on the side of a comparatively small number of men, for the most part absentee landlords, while the injuria leans to the great mass of the primitive owners of the soil. The time-honored policy of the English Government, that all the open abuses of landlordism should be watched over and protected with the most jealous care, while, on the other hand, the wretched farmer and cottier is supposed to have no rights to defend and guard, should be abandoned at once and forever, with a firmness that can leave no room for doubt or equivocation, if the restoration of confidence on the part of the Irish is esteemed any thing worth.

But, if for no other motive, at least for the sake of securing peace and order in Ireland, a remedy must be found. There is no reason why the Irish should longer remain a nation of paupers; and, although some may still pretend that the fault and its remedy lie with themselves, unprejudiced men will readily acknowledge that the fault lay first, at least, at England's door--a fact which the London Times has conceded often and proclaimed loudly enough.

Let British statesmen, then, devise proper means for such an end without social commotion, with as little disturbance of private rights as possible; for the object is an imperious necessity. It seems that the latest law enacted with this view is not the measure that was required; is totally inadequate in its provisions, scope, and extent. In such a case it is always open to legislators to introduce a new and more satisfactory measure; and moral force will surely bring this about, provided it is true to itself. We confess to having no scheme of our own to set forth; but Irishmen are free, nay entitled, to speak, to write on, and discuss the subject; and a serious, steady, but lawful agitation of the question will surely find its true and final solution. The last Galway election, notwithstanding the temporary triumph of Judge Keogh, was a beginning in the right direction.

There is no need here of revolution, of what the French call une jaquerie, of arming the populace for the purpose of violently ejecting the great landowners. No Irishman has ever stood for so calamitous a remedy. The aid of the Internationalists will certainly never be called in by the true children of Erin for any purpose whatever. It seems that the great and holy Pontiff, Pius IX., made this remark to the Prince of Wales, at their last interview at the Vatican, and, according to the report, the prince fully admitted its truth as far, at least, as he, by any outward sign, could show.

The question is one of pure justice, to be settled within the limits of order and law; and surely, when all admit that the evil is so crying, that a remedy must be found, one will be found, which, while it does no real injury to any person, will bring comfort and relief to the most deserving and suffering race of men--the Irish peasantry. We will soon see how.

But the Irishman is not only physically destitute; he is also destitute mentally; and, if the first case calls for a prompt remedy, the second is no less urgent. Pauperism and ignorance were the two terrible engines so long worked by England for the degradation and final destruction of the Irish race. Our readers have seen how persistently was education, of any kind, refused to the natives. The Universities of Dublin and Drogheda in the fourteenth century, the cathedral schools, founded by the Anglo-Normans, in the same age, carefully excluded the Irish from their benefits. And, when the Reformation set in, with its long series of oppressions, no Catholic could share in the new foundations of the Tudors and the Stuarts without first abjuring his religion. Penal statute after penal statute made of all the shifts, to which the Irish were driven in order to educate their children, so many crimes, punishable by death or transportation. That, under such a state of things, they could remain Catholics without becoming idiots is one of the most remarkable instances on record of buoyancy of spirit and soundness of mind on the part of a whole nation.

From the end of the last century the policy of England changed completely in appearance. The foundation and endowment by the state of the great college of Maynooth, destined for the education of the Irish clergy, in 1795, was certainly a step on the right road, and if only primary schools for the people had, at the same time, been spread all over the island on the same principle of true liberality, the old injustice on the matter of education would have been atoned for and remedied, to a great extent.

But the Kildare Peace Society and the Church Education Society, founded in 1839, showed that the antagonism to the Catholic Church in Ireland was far from being dead; nay, was as rife as ever.

Lord Stanley's National Education System, in 1831, at first seemed of a character altogether above Protestant or infidel proselytism. But, the composition of the various boards under that system, and some of the measures adopted, gave evidence clearly and soon enough that the education proposed for the Irish was not in accordance with the true spirit of the nation, so eminently Catholic and religious as it is. Hence, the total failure--for such it is now admitted by all to have been--of that system ought to have opened the eyes of all impartial Englishmen to the necessity of starting from the principle that Ireland is Catholic, and that the Irish are true children of the Catholic Church. But this fact seems not yet recognized or acknowledged by those who rule the nation, since, at this very moment, a bill lies before Parliament against which all the bishops of Ireland have united in raising their voice. The queen's colleges all confess to be a wretched failure.

The injustice of centuries, then, is not, even in these free days, when there is such a talk about educating the masses, repaired by the English Government; and this sad fact seems to militate against the power of moral force. However, it is but right to remember that only those establishments are here spoken of which are supported by state aid, and that complete freedom of education, independent of such assistance, does actually exist in Ireland. Have not the bishops all necessary power to open schools of their own? Have they not even founded a university? Does the state dare to interfere in whatever educational establishments they think proper to set on foot? They are now, in that regard, as free as the Catholic bishops in the United States; and if the degrees granted by the faculties under their control have no value in the eyes of the state, they can easily dispense with a concurrence, which is certainly unjustly denied, but which, even if granted, would not, in the eyes of the Church, increase in the slightest the real value of the diplomas they themselves approve. They can afford to wait for the time when complete justice will be done; meanwhile they are freer than Catholic bishops at this moment are in all Catholic countries of Europe; and the freedom they enjoy is entirely owing to that moral force which, we allege, is sufficient to insure, sooner or later, all the advantages that can be desired. When the present situation of the native Irish, from an educational point of view, is compared with the oppression under which they lay a hundred years ago, one cannot but wonder how so much has been obtained, and the hope, that every thing still wanting is sure to come by the agency of the force that has already won so much, cannot be deemed vain and illusory.

Let not, however, what is here said be construed as advising Ireland to stand still while schemes of education, evidently godless, are concocted, matured, and passed into laws for their special benefit. On the contrary, they must not only continue but increase their efforts to cry them down, till they compel a blind and deaf government to open its eyes and ears to a national want and a national voice. This is what is meant by the use of moral force.

But, can the complete remedy for pauperism and the solid establishment and endowment of truly Catholic schools be expected to come from any hands but those of an Irish Legislature? Can they be hoped for as long as the destiny of Ireland rests in the hands of an Imperial Parliament whose great majority can have no real sympathy with the long-oppressed race? In a word, is home-rule necessary to bring about those two great measures, which seem absolutely indispensable for the complete resurrection of the nation?

Our readers already know that, in our opinion, an Irish Parliament would not be a sure panacea for the evils of the country, particularly those of pauperism and ignorance, even though that Parliament sat in Dublin, and was composed of Irishmen bred and born. The evils would not be struck out promptly and utterly, although many great improvements would immediately follow.

Some of our reasons for being chary of confidence in the success of home-rule have been already given. But we have also insisted on the necessity of leaving the question open, and admitted that Irishmen have a right to discuss it, and take whatever side they may think proper, provided always they stand, as they are standing, within the limits of law and order.

Surely, the Irish have a right to be fairly represented; modern doctrines, as far as they can go, consecrate that right; and, if fair representation is an impossibility in the present state of affairs in Ireland, that state should be so altered as that the Irish nation might obtain all the advantages which a truly representative government bestows.

It is clear that the difficulty consists in the paramount importance of the union--of the empire; and this is not the place to discuss so large a question. It may be said, however, that the union of the British Empire does not and cannot consist in the absorption into one whole of the three integral parts which compose it. England, Scotland, and Ireland, are still three distinct national entities, each inhabited by a peculiar race, and each race cannot, in such a political organization, be in justice ignored, for a mere abstraction called the state.

Certainly the question is a very complicated one; and to offer a dogmatic solution of it would be pretentious. It is better to leave it to a future which is not far distant. What may be insisted on is, that moral force is strong enough to bring about a satisfactory decision, and that to resort to revolution for such a purpose would be as fatal as it is criminal.

A right discussion of the question must make clear the fact that Ireland is entitled to fair dealing as a component part of the empire. Many other political organizations embraced within the vast limits of the British power are allowed to discuss and decide on questions peculiar to themselves, and which they are at full liberty to pronounce upon for themselves by a wise adjustment and concession on the part of the mother-country as necessary to their well-being. Canada is almost entirely independent; the Australian colonies have all their own legislatures; it is the same more or less with all the distant dependencies of England, yet there have been no complaints heard so far of these late concessions threatening the union of the Empire.

But the objection is urged: "If such a concession be made to Ireland, where can you stop? The Scotch may ask the same, and the Welsh; one has as much right to home-rule as the other; where can you draw the line?"

An easy answer to this is, that the Scotch have never asked for home-rule, for the very good reason that they never had to complain of unfair treatment at the hands of the English Government; their special wants and desires having been always duly considered from the moment of their union with England. But the union of Ireland with England is not yet a century old, was brought about perforce, and by chicanery and fraud, and from the moment of its enactment to the present has been loudly protested against by the Irish nation--the nation, that is, which we have followed all through, joined in this instance by numbers of their Protestant fellow-countrymen. A long list of pamphlets and books might be drawn up, as showing the fact that multitudes of Irish writers, not of a revolutionary but of a truly conservative character, who cannot be accused of disloyalty to England, have deplored, protested against, and clamored for the repeal of, the Union of 1800.

Such is not the case with Scotland. But suppose it were, and proofs furnished showing that Scotland is not fairly represented in a Parliament which meets at Westminster, then that country would have just as much right to see itself fairly represented, its special wants satisfied and met, as all the other branches of the great British organization.

Certain it is that the empire cannot be sound when an important, a vital part of its political frame is incurably sore. Let that sore be healed by justice, large, generous, and complete; let Ireland be truly and really represented, in whatever manner her representation may be carried out, and the sudden rise of the little western isle in wealth, contentment, true prosperity, and happiness, will redound to the general good of the whole. As it now stands, its still miserable condition is as great and constant a danger to Great Britain as it is a reproach and a shame upon the maternal government which suffers the child, for whose session it would stake its all, to continue in a state of almost hopeless poverty, materially and intellectually, and to struggle unaided in its efforts to rise.

If home-rule be the measure which is to heal Ireland's wounds, it must be granted, and the voice of reason and right must rise above the stupid clamor which says that it cannot, must not, shall not be granted! Such expressions were common in inflammatory pamphlets which flooded the country on the eve of Catholic Emancipation, in 1829; and possibly many were issued even after the granting of this (from a certain English point of view) suicidal act of justice to Catholics.

But whatever may be the ultimate issue of the home-rule movement, the question of education, which is so closely allied to, as to seem dependent on it, is of such importance that it brooks no delay. Ireland is, as it may be hoped it will ever continue, a truly Catholic nation, and for such education must be special, and cannot be left to the direction of a non-Catholic state, not to use a worse expression. The result of the so-called national system, as exhibited by the Queen's Colleges and the rest, ought to be enough to open the eyes of real statesmen. But non- Catholic legislators need a sense which they do not possess, to appreciate the blunders they must fall into when proposing to touch such delicate interests as spiritual things. Thirty years ago, when those Queen's Colleges and schools were established in Ireland, the Catholic hierarchy raised up their voice to warn the British Government against so rash an attempt; for the very few who appeared willing to give the system a trial had their own doubts and forebodings. The warning, as usual, was not heeded, and the consequence is, that the partisans of the system now confess that their darling scheme has turned out a complete failure. Yet, strange to say, they do not in the least seem to have changed their ideas on the subject. On the contrary, they wish to secularize education more completely than ever, and to extend their project to the whole British Empire; though at this moment the warning comes to them also from the Presbyterians of Scotland, who refuse to submit to the scheme, universal in its scope, of educating the young according to state notions and worldly ideas.

In this the British Government only follows the lead of all European cabinets and legislatures; for this great iniquity is not confined to the British Isles, but is attempted everywhere, with the evident design of taking the government of souls out of the hands to which Jesus Christ confided it--the Church. The Sovereign Pontiff was compelled to protest, and, as is the custom in these days, his protest fell unheeded. It remains to be seen whether men, who call themselves Christians, will consent to see their children educated by secular bodies, which are not only void of all authority over the souls of men, but imbued, as all know, with doctrines the most pernicious and disorganizing. The just complaint made by the Irish hierarchy is unfortunately not restricted to their own body; their complaint is one with that of all the rulers of the Church throughout the world. It seems to us that there is greater hope of establishing a thorough Christian system of education in Ireland than in any other country, because the Irish nation will always take a more determined attitude, and gather in a more compact and united body around her natural leaders, the bishops and priests of God, than any other modern Catholic nation; and, in this age, where there are unanimity and a fixed purpose among any body of men, they cannot fail to result in a victory over all obstacles and opponents.

Of one thing England may be sure, that the Irish bishops would never submit to the project now on foot in England, as to do so would be to fail in their most sacred duty; and the mass of the Irish people is at their back. The Catholic hierarchy is always ready to support the secular power so long as that power remains within its province and does not step out of it to encroach on their unquestionable domain; but, when duty calls on them to resist, the experience of centuries is before the world, in Ireland at least, to show how far they can carry their resistance. In this they will stand united as one man, and it is vain for the English Government to flatter itself that it will find tools among them, should it foist on them the Birmingham scheme.

But a more threatening fact still is the compact union of all Irishmen in support of their bishops, against schemes which have already excited such bitter opposition on their part, and on which they have already pronounced and given their solemn verdict in unmistakable tones. If in our days Irishmen have been so eager to uphold many projects of a doubtful character, because those projects were opposed to England; if they have shown in the most emphatic manner that the memory of the past is still fresh, and that they are not yet prepared to accept the British Government as a friend; if they have seized every occasion, the most trifling as well as the most important, to show that the union with England was distasteful to them--what will be their attitude when the question admits of no doubt, and can give rise to no apprehension in a Christian conscience; when, indeed, they know that they stand where their duty to God bids them, urged at the same time by their natural feelings of opposition to a power which they detest and to which they are irreconcilable? We do not say that we altogether approve of their dogged opposition to England; it is only alluded to as a fact which it would be folly, in treating of questions between England and Ireland, to shut one's eyes to or doubt.

When such is the state of feeling, how can a scheme of godless education hope to succeed, which, after all, requires the consent of fathers and mothers of families? It is only natural to suppose that the English Government, in the event of its success, is scarcely prepared to employ such a numerous, watchful, and determined police as shall march the children off to school every lay by force--to schools which to them would be prisons, presided over by jailers in the shape of instructors. Nevertheless, the scheme now agitated by British statesmen must culminate in some such measure, if they would have their schools attended; and the inference is natural that education viewed from such a stand-point becomes a design criminal and oppressive in its nature, as well as a sheer impossibility in its carrying out. Once again the whole British power would launch itself in vain against the unyielding rock of as stubborn a will as ever animated human beings, as durable and unshrinking almost as the inner rock upon which it is built--Catholic faith.

Much space has already been devoted to the consideration of what are here considered as the two great measures necessary and sufficient for the complete resurrection of the Irish race--the lifting of the load of pauperism under which they have so long labored, and the establishment among them of a sound and thorough Christian education; and that those measures will undoubtedly be carried without any attempt at social convulsions, without any violation of law and order. But, as, unfortunately, many side-issues have been raised in Ireland of very inferior importance, but of a nature almost exclusively to engage the attention of Irishmen, to the great detriment of real progress, it may be well to dwell a little longer on the consequences which must infallibly follow from a higher state of physical comfort and mental culture among them:

I. A higher state of physical comfort will naturally produce a stronger attachment to their native soil and a corresponding reluctance to leave it, as they now do by wholesale emigration. The thought has been dwelt upon that emigration was a design of Divine Providence, and even the first step in the resurrection of the nation and in the establishment of its power within as well as without. That the object of emigration is not yet fully attained may be inferred from the fact that it still continues on so large a scale; that it must ultimately dwindle to much smaller proportions, if not cease utterly, is pretty certain. This is our wish and hope: for the home population of the island must be large enough to invest it with deserved importance in the eyes of foreigners. Our title-page sets forth the words of Dr. Newman, expressive of the firm belief that the time will come when the Catholic population of Erin will be as thick and prosperous as that of Belgium? Why should it not be so? Pauperism alone prevents it. Let their existence be one of comfort--mere comfort, not luxury--and there is no limit to the increase of their numbers. In such an event Protestantism would contract into such narrow limits that in Ireland it would become a thing unknown; the few sectarians still abiding there would themselves share in the general prosperity, and would possibly of their own accord return to the bosom of the common mother of Christians.

The question, then, of increase of physical comfort for Irishmen is one of the utmost importance, and, as the tenure of land is so closely connected with it, not to this question is the term side-issue applied. The land-question should be thoroughly exhausted until the true solution, the real measure, which has not yet appeared, may be brought to the surface and carried out to the full. The land-question in all its bearings lies beyond our competence; not so, certain reasons for believing that the possession of land is necessary for the complete restoration of the nation. Manufactures and commercial pursuits are of secondary importance in a country like Ireland, which is eminently agricultural. This should not be taken to mean that such matters are to be neglected, and the Irish to be discouraged in engaging in them, particularly in their home manufactures; nor in calling for better laws to help them, at least for fair dealing as far as legislation goes. But supposing them completely independent and masters of themselves; supposing not only the repeal of the Union, but even the separation from the British organization effected, how could they hope to compete in manufacturing skill, and science, with the inventive genius of the American, the systematic comprehensiveness of the Englishman, or the artistic taste of the French? Goods are manufactured for the markets of the world, and the Irish are not yet prepared for such extensive enterprises; and, taking the characteristics of the race into consideration, it is doubtful whether they will ever be successful in such ventures.

The same may be said of commerce. When are they likely to have a navy of their own? They are still Celts, and would it be well for them to cease to be Celts? The oceans of the globe are covered with ships bearing the flags of many nations. Suppose them to unfurl a national flag to the breeze, which is saluted, wherever met, by the crafts of other civilized nations, when would it become perceptible among the crowded fleets which already hold possession of the seas? The broad thoroughfares of the ocean know two or three national colors; all the others are so seldom seen, that their presence or absence is alike unnoticed by the world at large. Among these would the Irish be numbered, if they engaged in commerce on their own account, and sailed no longer under British colors.

It is for them, then, to turn their attention to the land, which is their chief source of wealth. Let them buy it up, or gain it by long leases, inch by inch and acre by acre, until not only the bleak bogs and wild mountains of Connaught are again their own, but the rich meadow-lands and smiling wheat-fields of Munster and Leinster. Let their brethren in America and Australia associate with them in this, and thus will they build up again a true Irish yeomanry and nobility--for nobility has a new meaning to-day-- more glorious, perhaps, than the old one. Poverty and rags will give place to prosperity and comfort, even in the lowliest cottages, and mirth and glee will be heard again in the country from which they have so long been banished.

Is such a picture a dream, and its realization an impossibility? It is our belief that, to make it a reality, only requires steadiness of purpose, perseverance, energy, and association. Fifty years ago it would certainly have seemed a dream; but matters have advanced within the last half-century, and every thing is now prepared for such a hoped-for consummation.

II. Together with physical comfort, the culture produced by a sound and thorough education is the second thing absolutely necessary for the resurrection of the nation. Education has, at all times, been of the utmost importance; in our age it is more so than ever. It may be said that, in the opinion of mankind, it tends more and more to replace blood. The privileges that once belonged to rank and birth are now everywhere freely accorded to a truly-educated man. And here, wealth, which is almost worshipped by many, cannot altogether take the place of education. Consequently, a great effort should be made in Ireland to raise the standard of the intellectual scale of society. Owing to former tyranny and oppression, the rising must begin at the lowest grade. But the first impulse has already been given by the Church of God, and that impulse must continue and increase with a constantly-accelerated force.

Unfortunately, a false direction has been given it by the state. The means which will surely defeat this action of the state have been seen. Nevertheless, it works mischievously for the general result; and the money paid by the nation has been and still is squandered for a most unholy purpose, when, if properly applied, it would be so fruitful of good.

Should the government persevere in its project, one course only lies open before all true Irishmen; and that is, to ignore the action of the government, and follow a plan of their own. They have only to do what the Catholics in France would most willingly do if the state allowed them; what Catholics in the United States have been doing for some time, and will have to do for some time longer--not murmur too loudly at the taxes paid by them for educational purposes and used so lavishly by the state without any profit to them; but with steady purpose raise funds which the state cannot touch, devoted to an object with which the state cannot interfere, namely, the solid Christian education of their children under the eyes and chief control of the Church, with competent and truly religious masters.

Let them reflect that until recently education in Christian countries was always imparted by the Church of Christ, and that its secularization is but a work of yesterday; that the effect of that secularization is manifest enough in the mental anarchy which grows more prevalent in Europe every day; that the nation which comes back to the old system, and places again the care of youth in the hands of religious teachers, is sure to obtain a far sounder and more effective education than those who take for teachers of their children men void of faith and remarkable only for a false and superficial polish, which sooner or later will be reckoned by all at its true value, and meet only with well-merited neglect and contempt.

No one will deny that moral training, the first and most important part of education, is far surer and safer in the care of religious teachers than in that of mere laymen, whose morality is often doubtful, and whose reputation is not of the best. With regard to scientific teaching, the mind of the religious is not, to say the least, lowered by the holy obligations which he has contracted: and it is an awkward fact for those who in a breath uphold secular education and abuse the religious, that in former ages the men who excelled in arts and sciences, the geniuses whose works will live as long as the earth, were either themselves monks or the pupils of monks. A list of them would fill many pages, and their names are not unknown to the world.

For the mass of the people, the common level of primary education with which so many are now satisfied may at least be as satisfactory in its results when imparted by religious, male and female, as when under the direction of young men and women who have received every possible diploma which is at the disposal of school commissioners or boards of gentlemen invested with an office, worthy of the gravest attention, but to which they can devote but very little time.

But the subject may be said to have passed beyond discussion. The true and authorized leaders of the Irish in such matters, the Catholic bishops, have already taken the matter into their own hands; and in a very short time have covered the island with their schools, with every prospect of a university. It rests with the government to give or refuse its aid in imparting a true national education to a nation which is Catholic; but, with or without this aid, the Irish will have the means of educating their children rightly; and the culture they receive will favorably compare with that imparted by rival establishments fostered by the state, whose pupils will not know a word even of their own national history, since, in the authorized books, Ireland has no existence other than that of an unworthy subject of the great British Empire.

It was necessary to give prominence to what is here considered as the most effective means of bringing about the great result which engages our attention in this chapter. There are secondary objects which might be treated, but which, in the final working of the divine will, may be insignificant. For, to repeat what has been said before, the restoration of the nation which is now progressing so steadily almost unaided by any action of man, however much he may indulge in agitation, is the work of God, and before long will so manifest itself to all. Meanwhile it is enough to assert in general terms that Ireland is entitled to all those things which render a people happy and contented. That wished-for state is not far off; let them continue to be active in its pursuit. A previous chapter has already touched upon the great means to be employed in bringing this about: association, whose centre should be Ireland, and whose branches should spread wherever Irishmen have established themselves; whose guides should be the clergy, but its chief workers, intelligent and energetic laymen. On this point it is desirable particularly to be rightly understood; it is not our purpose to say that in such a work laymen ought not to cooperate, or even to lead; with the memory of O'Connell before us, such a thing would be impossible; on the contrary, the external working of the whole scheme should be placed in the hands of good, active, and intelligent laymen. They are the proper instruments for carrying on such a work actively and efficaciously; they form, at least numerically, the principal part of the moral power of the nation, and that power should be developed on a larger scale than it has ever yet been. But the first impulse should be given by the moral leaders, rulers of the Church. Let the nation work under the guidance, the leadership of the men who alone stood by them when all else had been lost, who, in fact, by preserving their religion, preserved to them their nationality; let them work under their eyes and with their sanction, and assuredly their labor will not be labor in vain.

What will the final result be of such a cooperation of workers? The formation or rather consolidation of a truly Christian and Catholic people; a most remarkable phenomenon in this wonderful nineteenth century! It would seem that they have thus far been deprived of a government of their own only to win a government at last which shall be, what is so sadly wanted in these days, Christian and Catholic. Modern governments have broken loose from Christianity; they have declared themselves independent of all moral restraint; they have pronounced themselves supreme, each in its own way; and, to be consistent, they have become godless. Donoso Cortes has shown this admirably in his work on "Catholicism, Liberalism, and Socialism." The sad spectacle which in our age meets the eye of the Christian, is universal; there is no longer a Catholic nation; Christendom has ceased to exist. This is held by the statesmen of to-day to be a vast improvement on the old social system. Medieval barbarism, as they term it, has, according to them, met with just condemnation; and to return to it now, would be to drag an advanced age centuries backward, a horror which no sane man could contemplate.

Undoubtedly there were many abuses under the old regime, which the most sincere Christian regrets, and could not wish to see restored, or again attempted. But, its great feature, the inner link which bound the system together, its unity under the guidance of the universal Church, was the only safeguard for the general happiness of mankind. This admirable unity has been broken into fragments; each part does for itself, and thus the world lies at the mercy of Might, and each nation goes about like "a strong man armed, keeping his house."

Even Heeren, a writer who is strongly Protestant and liberal, is driven to confess in his "History of the Political System of Europe," that the reign of Frederick the Great, in Prussia, was "immediately followed by those great convulsions in states, which gave the ensuing period a character so different from the former. The contemporary world, which lived in it, calls it the revolutionary; but it is yet too early to decide by what name it will be denoted by posterity, after the lapse of a century."

After a brief review of the various states as they existed toward the middle of the last century, he adds: "The efforts of the rulers to obtain unlimited power had overthrown the old national freedom in all the states of the Continent; the assemblies of the states had disappeared, or were reduced to mere forms; nowhere had they been modelled into a true national representation."

He does not see that, in order to obtain that "unlimited power," the rulers had thrown off the yoke of Church authority everywhere, and that Christendom disappeared with the "old national freedom" as soon as the key-stone of the edifice, the papacy, was ejected from its place.

Nevertheless, he was keen enough to perceive it necessary to call in armed force to uphold that usurped power of rulers:

"For the strength of the states no other criterion was known than standing armies. And, in reality, there was scarcely any other. By the perfection which they had attained, and which kept pace almost with the growing power of the princes, the line of partition was gradually drawn between them and the nations; they only were armed; the nations were defenceless."

This great German historian carries his views further still, and confesses that, "if the political supports were in a tottering condition, the moral were no less shattered. The corner-stone of every political system, the sanctity of legitimate possession, without which there would be only one war of all against all, was gone; politicians had already thrown off the mask in Poland; the lust of aggrandizement had prevailed . . . . The indissoluble bond connecting morals and politics being broken, the result was to make egotism the prevailing principle of public as well as private life."

Admirable reflections, doubtless, but incomplete; the Protestantism of the writer not allowing him to perceive that, the only sure defender of morality having been discarded, egotism could not but prevail. Therefore does he complain, being blind to the true cause of the disorder, that "democratic ideas, transported from America to Europe, were spread and cherished in the midst of the monarchical system--ready materials for a conflagration far more formidable than their authors had anticipated, should a burning spark unhappily light upon them. Others had already taken care to profane the religion of the people; and what remains sacred to the people when religion and constitution are profaned?"

This last observation, thrown in at the end of some very sound considerations, would have made them far more striking, had it appeared at their head as the great source of all the catastrophes which ensued. But it requires a Catholic eye to take in the whole truth, and a Catholic tongue to give the right explanation of history, as of all things else.

Many reflections similar to those above quoted have been made by non-Catholic writers, and the defenders of the Church have spoken with clearness and energy throughout. Nevertheless, the evil has continued to grow more universal and more alarming, until, to-day, no principle on which the social fabric can securely stand is acknowledged by those who rule the exterior world. And of what Heeren calls the violation of "the sanctity of legitimate possession," let Poland and many other states speak, nay, those of the Father of the faithful himself, to whose warning voice rulers have now so long persistently turned a deaf ear. Where are now even the fragments of that "corner-stone" of the old "political system?"

Such is the state of affairs, not only in Europe, but generally throughout the world, so that the Catholic Church has at length entered fully upon that stage of her existence when she possesses individual subjects full of tender affection and devotedness, whose number, thank God! increases every day, but not a single State which acknowledges her as its director and teacher.

Ireland may be destined to become the first one which shall acknowledge her, and set an example to the rest. If ever she enjoys self-government, she will surely do so, for Catholic she is to the core, and Catholic she cannot but remain.

When it was said that home-rule would not serve as a sure panacea for all her evils, it will be understood as applying to the actual moment and nothing else. That it would not be a good thing for her ever to enjoy real self-government was never in our mind. Moral force is bringing this nearer to her; and step by step she is learning how to walk without support.

Already, she possesses something of political franchise, and enjoys municipal government more truly than Frenchmen do after all their social convulsions.

There are men, Irishmen even, who pretend that she would subside into anarchy if her destiny were confided to her own care. They point to the constant wranglings which have been her bane for centuries, and the "prophet" who wrote the "Battle of Dorking" represents her, as soon as the humiliation of England left her free, struggling painfully in the throes of anarchy. That this general opinion of men with regard to Ireland is but too true, was conceded in another place, yet only so far as concerned interests which were trifling, or, at best, of no high character; that when the object at stake is one of great importance, there was more steadiness, unanimity, energy, and true heroism in the Irish people, than in any other known to history in modern times. And this reflection is certainly borne out by the issues of all the secular struggles of the Irish with Scandinavianism, feudalism, and Protestantism.

Surely is there in them the right material for a nation; and, when the day comes for the country to take in hand, under Providence, her own destiny and work it out, the "prophet" will find himself sadly mistaken when, freed forever from the degradation of pauperism, she is at liberty to raise her thoughts above food and raiment; when her children, lifted by a solid Christian education to the high level of intellectual foresight, shall be able to discuss the great objects of their national interests, with no question of clan and clan; then wrangling will cease, as far as public questions are concerned, and be merely left to matters of minor importance, or private affairs, as with all other nations. But that concentrated energy which has marked the race throughout that long fight of centuries against such overwhelming odds, will still continue as their distinguishing characteristic, but turned now to the question of their own national welfare, and no longer to the aversion of doom.

Then will Europe see what a truly Christian people is, for then there will be no other left; and the superiority of principles, of strength of mind, energy of character, naturally fostered by deep religious convictions, will afford another proof of Montesquieu's reflection, that "the Christian faith, which seems to have for its object only the future life, is likewise the best calculated to make people happy and prosperous during this."

If ever men are brought to acknowledge the fatal error they made in rejecting the sacred safeguard which Christ left them in his Church, it will be by looking on the example of a nation actually existing, governed by the great principles which alone can insure the happiness of the individual and the prosperity of the whole people.

In all the foregoing considerations Ireland has been looked upon as a nation full of vigor and energy; but, as this vital point is denied by some, who bear the reputation of thoughtful writers, it is well to establish it clearly before our minds.

Is Ireland a nation? Some say, No; others, among them Mr. Froude, say she is divided into two nations.

The first of these assertions, that she is not a nation, is in appearance so self-evident and true that it seems folly to deny it. She has no government of her own; her destinies seem to be altogether in the hands of a hostile race, which rules her by a Parliament, where her voice is scarcely heard. She has no army nor navy, no commerce, no treasury, not the lowest prerogative of sovereignty. There is a green flag still somewhere with a harp on it and a crown above the harp, reserved for state occasions, and unfurled now and again, when a show of loyalty and a little enthusiasm is called for; but that flag never waves the Irish to battle, not even when fighting for England. There is no Irish standard-bearer for it, as there was under the Tudors, when the flag of Ulster was seen amid the armies of Elizabeth. The name of Ireland is never mentioned in any treaty with foreign powers; and, when the sovereign of England, Scotland, and Ireland, signs a treaty, a convention, nay, a poor protocol, with any foreign state, the name of Ireland is not to be seen on the parchment, save at its head, among the titles of the monarch. There is no Irish seal even to affix to the document: the country is a national non-entity.

But other men, and wise men too, discover a strange anomaly in this curious country. They hold that it is composed of two distinct nations, and furnish excellent reasons in support of their theory.

They talk in this fashion: "Look at the people; travel the country north and south, and converse with them as you go. What do you find? Unity of feeling, aims, agreement of opinion on all possible subjects? Just the opposite! You find Jacob and Esau on every side struggling in the womb of their mother. The quarrel between Sassenach and Gael still goes on. What two figures can be found more antagonistic than the Orangeman of Ulster and the Milesian of Connaught? Yet they are both children of the same country."

And so deep-grained is the difference between them that, although they have lived side by side for centuries, they are still as hostile to each other as when they first met in battle array. The Danes, after a struggle of a little more than two centuries, gave up the contest and became Celts. Strongbow's Normans soon adopted the manners of the old inhabitants, intermarried with them, and, after a lapse of four centuries, though quarrels often broke out between the one and the other, they were to all intents and purposes Celts, the old race, as it were, absorbing the Norman blood, and always showing itself in the children.

But, when will the children of James's Scotchmen or Cromwell's Covenanters coalesce with the descendants of the Milesians? The longer they dwell together, the farther they seem apart, the more they seem to hate each other; and every 12th of July, 5th of November, 17th of March, or even 15th of August, brings danger of bloodshed and strife to every city, hamlet, and town. Surely, this fact speaks of two nations in the country.

The question here presented is indeed a complicated one, requiring solid distinctions in order to elucidate it; and, strange to say, this last difficulty of the presence of two nations in Ireland offers greater obstacles to the firm establishment of our opinion than the first assertion, so clear and undeniable in appearance, that there is no Irish nation!

If true nationality existed only in the externals of government, in an army, navy, commerce, a public seal and flag, and recognition by foreign powers, further discussion would clearly be useless, and the subject might as well at once be dropped.

But the true idea of a nation embraces much more than this; there is such a thing as a national soul, and all the array of accidents alluded to above constitute only the body, or, more truly, the surroundings. As a writer in the North American Review (vol. cxv., p. 379) has well expressed it, a nation is "a race of men, small or great, whom community of traditions and feeling binds together into a firm, indestructible unity, and whose love of the same past directs their hopes and fears to the same future."

In this sense nationality assuredly belongs to Ireland. More, perhaps, than among any other people on earth, is there for the great bulk of them "community of traditions and feeling," binding them together into "a firm and indestructible unity;" and who shall say that they feel no love for their past, because that past has been clouded with sorrow? Nay, this fact makes the past dearer, and tends all the more to direct their hopes and fears to the same future; a future, indeed, still dim and uncertain, and not to be named with perfect certainty, but wrapped in mists like the morning; yet the faint flush of the dawn is already there that shall pale and die away when the full orb of the sun appears.

The reader may remember what was said of the unanimity so striking in all Irishmen, wherever they may be found; that, though private disputes may be taken up among them with such ardor that their quarrels have become proverbial, when the question refers to their country or their God, in a moment they are united, suddenly transformed into steady friends, ready to shed their blood side by side for the great objects which entirely absorb their natures.

This feeling it is which forms the soul of a nation. Wherever this is to be found, there is an indestructible nationality; wherever it is absent, there is only a dead body, however strong may seem its government, however vast its armies, however high its so-called culture and refinement.

These reflections being kept in view, judicious men will agree that, among Europeans at least, there is scarcely any other nationality so strong and vigorous as the Irish. Their traditional feeling keeps their past ever present to their eyes; their ardent nature hopes ever against hope; misfortunes which would utterly break down and dishearten any other people, leave them still full of bright anticipations, and, as they seem to weep over the cold body of a dear mother--Erin, their country--they think only of her resurrection.

But are there not two nations among them--two nations radically opposed to each other and incapable of coalescing? Supposing a resurrection of the people, which of the two is to prevail--the numerical majority, or the so far influential minority? In either event, it is fair to suppose a new state of helotism for the one party or the other. Is this the spectacle which the regenerated nation is likely to present?

In speaking of the resurrection of Ireland, the old, massive, compact body of the people, the venerable race, Celtic in its aspirations and tendencies, if not altogether in its origin, has always been kept in view; and that anomalous, foreign excrescence which has so steadily refused to assimilate with the mass, and has until our days remained "encamped" in Ireland, as the Turks are justly said to have remained "encamped" in Europe, has never entered into our reckoning.

The true Irishman has ever been catholic--the word is used in its grammatical and not in its religious sense--in fellowship. The race, as now constituted, is assuredly of mixed origin, and large drafts of foreign population have been added from time to time to the primitive stock, which has always been kind to admit, absorb, and make them finally Celtic. Strong-bow's Normans were not the last who submitted to that process; as was seen, many Cromwellians became the fathers, or grandfathers at least, of as sturdy an Irish branch as ever flourished in the strong air of the country.

But a comparatively small body of men has doggedly refused to submit to this process, and continued to this day an English or Lowland Scotch colony on the Irish soil. The future of Ireland does not take them in, for the very simple reason that they are not of her, they do not belong to her, they are as much foreigners to-day as they ever were. Therefore do we admit the existence of two nations, if people are pleased to call them so, in Ireland, but of one nation only have we written. The only question in regard to this second "nation" is: What will become of them in the future? Are they, in their turn, to become helots, after having vainly striven so long to make helots of the others? God forbid! No true Irishman nourishes in his soul such feelings of retaliation or revenge.

Assuredly, they will be prevented from disturbing any longer the public order, and forced at length to respect the majority, or rather, the mass of their countrymen. No one can object to having such a necessary measure imposed upon them. In the many civil discords which, for more than a century and a half, have disgraced the north of Ireland, they have almost invariably been the aggressors. The government openly taking their part for a long time, they had the whole field to themselves, and what use they made of their privilege, and how they improved their opportunity, is known to all. When, at last, the public authorities could no longer pretend to ignore their hateful spirit, and began to show some signs of protecting the hitherto much-abused majority, by forbidding those odious processions to which the others always attached such importance, they gave themselves the airs of a persecuted body of men, and pretended that henceforth their lives, and those of their wives and children, were no longer safe.

The province of Ulster being closed to them as a field of operations, they transferred to Upper Canada the exhibition of their blood-thirsty hatred, and on several occasions the Catholic population of the country had to protect their churches, musket in hand. Even in the United States they have rendered themselves odious to the people by foisting their spirit of strife on a land where they cannot but be strangers, and by staining some of the streets of New York with blood, in order to gratify their senseless animosity.

It is surely time that an end be put to such absurd and dangerous antics, not abroad only, but at home. In the new order of things now dawning upon Ireland, there can no longer be room for them; and the very name of Orangeman must disappear forever from the vocabulary of the new nation, to the joy of all peaceful and law-abiding citizens.

That is all the persecution they need expect. Not only will there be room for them still in the country of their birth, but of course they will have their due share in all the privileges of citizenship. Political distinctions between themselves and the old race will be unknown; social distinctions will be a question for themselves to settle. Should they show the slightest desire of combining with the majority of their countrymen, these latter will be generous enough to forget the past, and perhaps the others may imitate their predecessors, the Danes, the Normans, and even some of their Cromwellian kin, and become, at last, Hibernis hiberniores.

What is said of political and social distinctions will hold good also for religious tenets. Let them, if they choose, continue to stand by their Presbyterian dogmas, provided they do not quarrel with the majority for professing what they love to believe; but that belief must come to an external and public profession. They will often hear the bells of Catholic churches; as they pass outside, if they do not enter, the strains of the glorious music and noble anthems, resounding within, will fall on their ears; they will see the statue of the Blessed Virgin borne through the streets on the 15th of August, amid showers of snowy blossoms, falling from the innocent hands of children; all this they must endure, if it be so hard to endure it; but this is not persecution. Even to their eyes, if their heart be not frozen by a cold belief, the sight will bear some attractions. And if they come to think, that what is oldest in Christianity is the best, and that, after all, Catholicity has something in it which makes life sweet and pleasant, it can scarcely be held a crime in the universal Church to open her arms and receive back to her bosom those wandering and so long obstinate children.

When will all this come to pass? Who can tell? But stranger things than these have already taken place in Ireland, and we are confident that future historians of the race will have to record greater wonders still, and facts more stubborn and difficult of explanation.

At all events, should the inflexible Puritanism of the Scotch colony stand proof against the allurements of a motherly and tender-hearted Church, they must at least become subject to the iron laws of population and absorption. When the public statutes are no longer drawn up for their special benefit, when no new swarms of brethren come to swell their ranks, when they are abandoned to the merciless laws of loss and gain in numbers, then will people soon see on which side is true morality, and by which the ordinances of God are really respected; then will many vapid accusations against the holy Catholic Church of themselves disappear, and the eyes of men will open to the great fact that Ireland must be and remain one in race, feeling, and, above all, in religion. The foreign element will have dwindled to insignificance, if it shall not have utterly disappeared. Indeed, it may be safely predicted that the day will arrive when the announcement of the natural demise of the last Puritan in Ireland will appear in the daily newspapers as a curious piece of intelligence, not devoid of a certain interest.

Though moral force, as the agent of the regeneration of Ireland, has been our theme all through, we would not have our readers infer that Irishmen should adopt the do-nothing policy, and leave to God alone the work of raising them up. The moral force spoken of is that of human beings endowed with activity and determination; steady and persevering in the pursuit of well-organized plans of their own conception.

Let Irishmen lift up their eyes and behold what they might do, did they only appreciate their strength and husband it. Dire calamities, which God designed from the first to convert into blessings, have scattered them over the world, and brought out that power of expansion which was always in their nature, but lay dormant and cramped under the pressure of terrible circumstances. They again show themselves as that old race which three thousand years ago spread itself all over Europe and Asia. They now bear in their hands an emblem which they had not then--the cross of Christ! And the cross is the sign of universality in time and space. To that sign, since the triumph of the Saviour on the day of his resurrection, is given the rule of the world till the end of time. Now that our globe is known at last, the cross must be planted all over its surface, and in this great work the Irish race is clearly destined to bear a conspicuous part.

In the fulfilment of that divine vocation they are dispersed, and whatever is dispersed is deprived of a great part of its strength. How can the disjecta membra, scattered far and wide by Typhon, become again Osiris? Under the guidance of God, by that great instrument of modern times, the power of association and organization, aided by a steady, energetic will.

Ezekiel has admirably described the process in his thirty-seventh chapter. The Lord must first speak: "Ye dry bones, hear the word of the Lord. . . . Behold, I will send spirit into you, and ye shall live; and I will lay sinews on you, and will cause flesh to grow over you, and will cover you with skin; and I will give you spirit, and ye shall live."

All this seems to be the work of God alone, yet, in the very words of the prophet, the dry bones have their part to perform:

"As I prophesied, there was a noise, a commotion, and the bones came together, each one to his joint."

There is the whole process; it supposes a noise, a commotion, a rising, an assembling together, and a fitting each one into his own joint. They possess an activity of their own, which they must use. And the phenome-non is to take place in the midst of "a vast plain"--two great continents--over the surface of which the "bones" are found on every side, appearing "exceeding dry."

With what a power will that army be invested when it rises up and stands upon its feet! We may form some faint idea of it, when in our large cities any thing occurs to excite the interest and warm up the feeling of that apparently inert Celtic mass. The largest halls constructed cannot contain the multitudes who have only read the announcement of a meeting, a lecture, or a charitable undertaking. Such scenes are witnessed every day along the banks of the St. Lawrence, the Hudson, and the Delaware Rivers; by the shores of Chesapeake Bay; in all the great centres of population dotting the Atlantic coast; in the heart of the continent along the winding course of the Mississippi and Missouri; and already, even in the far West, on the spreading shores of the Pacific Ocean. The same is occurring all over the inhabited portion of Australia and the adjacent islands. What power, then, would be theirs did those "bones" know how to come together each in his own joint!

How is it that we hear of no concerted action among them for their country's sake? Is each man so busy, and lost in his own little sphere of interest and speculation, that he cannot spare a moment's thought for the claims of his native country? Who can say this? Moreover, the best means of promoting their own private interests would be to raise before the eyes of all the status of the country with which they are naturally identified. The truth is, each one waits for another to set the example, the mass being ever ready to follow a lead and show its good-will. Association is needed.

When they turn their eyes to the incessant struggle going on in the mother-country, when they read in their own newspapers the discussions of the Irish press, of the questions debated on the soil most dear to them, and the agitation of the momentous interests pending and awaiting a final decision among their former countrymen, no doubt their feelings are strongly moved; the hopes and fears of their youth, before they left their native shores, are revived with renewed force, and their love for their green island is as ardent as ever.

But is this all? Is it enough that the heart of each one is stirred within him? Is it not for them to see that the influence of their new name, new position, and bettered circumstances, be brought to bear, however far away they may be, upon the great home questions of land-tenure, education, the elective franchise, a native Parliament, commerce, manufactures, and all matters touching on the general welfare of Ireland? If, having become adopted citizens of a new country, they can no longer act as citizens of Erin, they may and ought at least to interest themselves in these matters as far as true loyalty to their adopted country may allow them; and this they can best do by association.

The bonds of a wise organization would give firmness and compactness to the whole moral force of the dispersed nationality. By association, the scattered "dry bones" would be speedily changed into a solid array of living warriors standing upon their feet, and the startling spectacle would astonish the whole world, and win for the race the involuntary respect of all who should witness or hear of it. Nothing would be easier than to set such a thing on foot, for, although so far apart in appearance, the majority of Irish families, from the very fact of emigration, have half of their members at home and half abroad, joined together by an active correspondence and a constant transmission of funds. The managers of the movement would only have to organize for a general object, what already is organized in fact, and direct to the common good what is now done privately.

A word has already been said on the possible management of such an organization: that the movement should begin at home, in the island; that its supervision should be left to the true leaders of the nation; and that all the workings, details, and executive part, may be safely intrusted to the active members of the association.

The class here designated as leaders of the nation is already known to the reader. The old nobility having been destroyed, there is no other body which truly represent the Irish people to-day save the clergy. This is, no doubt, a misfortune, but none the less a fact. It offers the anomaly of clergymen meddling to a certain extent in politics; but, in Ireland, this is unavoidable.

How does the whole body of the European Catholic clergy understand its position in all those Catholic congresses and unions, which are now, thank God! starting up in all Christian countries? How do the laymen, on their side, appreciate the share they have to take in those various movements? How do they act under the lead of their spiritual advisers? Are any odious distinctions ever known in those associations? Can any misunderstanding arise among men animated with a true love for religion? And why should not the same be true of Ireland, among a people so full of love for country? This is what is meant when the terms leaders and followers, clergy and laity, are here used.

Another consideration will show still more forcibly the importance of the great measure here proposed. One circumstance must have struck those who read the detailed reports of the Catholic congresses mentioned above--the sudden appearance of a large array of laymen, illustrious by their birth, wealth, political power, or literary attainments; but, for the most part, not so well known for their deep attachment to the cause of the Church. A new channel of activity was suddenly opened up to them; they threw themselves into it, and became the bold champions of a cause to which, undoubtedly, they had been individually attached, but of which they now became the public men. And there is little doubt that many young men, lukewarm before, and perhaps with nothing more than the remembrance of the Christian education they had once received, suddenly revived in spirit and made a solemn profession of a cause which, perhaps, they would not have had the courage openly to advocate, did not the number and names of the first originators of the movement encourage them to join in it heart and soul.

Now, it is said, perhaps too truly, that the warm religious feeling which has been all along claimed as the most striking characteristic of the Irish race, is no longer shared alike by all classes of Irish Catholics; that, too often, when individuals among them rise in the social scale, and reach a step in the social ladder from which they imagine that they can look down upon the despised mass below, they no longer feel that deep reverence for their religion which had characterized their youth, and, after all, are not very different from the mass of non-Catholics among whom they prefer to move. This class of men has been well described by Moore in his own person, in various passages of his "Irish Gentleman in search of a Religion."

The fact is, indeed, too true; but what is the chief cause of it? One of the most active means of bringing about such a result we take to be the complete isolation in which young men of the class referred to find themselves in their own sphere of life. There is, in fact, no motive for displaying their attachment to their religion, and no respectable means of doing so. They do not feel their souls moved by sufficient proselytic ardor to induce them, of their own accord, to originate any thing of that kind, and the generality of them have, probably, not received from Nature the talents requisite to make them leaders in any cause whatever. No one around them moves in that direction; hence their apathy and consequent lukewarmness in the practice and outward profession of their faith.

But change all the surroundings; present them an influential body to which it is an honor to belong--a body marching openly under the banner of the true Church of Christ and of their country, bound together as of old--and then will it be seen whether or not they indeed are the degenerate sons of martyred ancestors they now appear to be.

It is indeed very remarkable that, of all countries, Ireland seems to make the least show in those Catholic unions and congresses now so widely spread throughout Europe. The reason for this, perhaps, is, that there seemed less cause for their existence in Ireland than elsewhere. But, as, in Ireland, their object would not only embrace the interests of religion, but likewise those of the country itself, it seems natural to think that there they are particularly wanted.

Let the leaders of the nation, then, bestir themselves. Long ages of oppression unfortunately have rendered them somewhat timid and seemingly afraid of jeopardizing the important interests confided to their care. Let them lift up their eyes and see that the time for timidity has passed away: the enemy is reckless and open in his attacks; their resistance must be equally undisguised and fearless. The people themselves understand this and occasionally display a boldness which shows that the old heroism still lives in them; but they want leaders, and, if the right ones are not fast to take hold of them, they may fall into the hands of wrong-headed guides. Let the true guides look out and see how broad are the lines which divide the good from the evil, and that victory is sure to the stout of heart, when backed by the serried masses of a united people.

The principle of association and the machinery of organization must be applied to all subjects connected with the resurrection of the country. What has been done so effectually for the cause of temperance must be done likewise for education, for the purchase or tenure of land, for the development of agriculture, manufactures, and commerce, for the true representation of the nation, for free municipal government, for the securing of a truly Irish yeomanry and gentry, for a thousand objects on which the future welfare of the nation depends. All classes of society, persons of every age and of either sex, yes, women and children, ought to be induced to take an interest in what concerns all alike. Every possible occasion should be taken advantage of to insure the attainment of the ultimate object. When such a work is really entered upon in earnest, the results will be astonishing.

This is the complete development of moral force, and, until all these means have had fair trial, no one can say that moral force has been fully tried and has failed.

Such a system would, we firmly believe, result in the ultimate restoration of Ireland's rights and would surely culminate in her final resurrection at no distant date. That the Irish would enter with spirit into those various associations has been sufficiently demonstrated by previous examples, particularly under O'Connell; and it is impossible to see how surer, greater, and speedier results could be obtained by any amount of physical force of which Ireland is capable. What array of physical force can the Irish muster to compete at all with their powerful rivals, situated as they are with the chains of centuries still binding them down, for, though the shackles may be actually removed, their effect is still there. The very statement of the terms, Ireland versus England, is enough to show the hopelessness of such a combat. It is a very easy thing to magnify the old heroism of the Irish, and cast opprobrium on the present bearers of the name, as did several newspaper writers recently, for not displaying the "pluck" of their ancestors who fought against Elizabeth, Cromwell, and William of Orange. It is forgotten that circumstances have altered considerably since those days when the Irish possessed a regular army led by experienced generals: restore those circumstances, and the Irish of to-day might outdo their ancestors; at all events, there is no reason for supposing that they would be inferior. However, there is such a thing as impossibility, and any attempt of such a nature, with such surroundings, must be deemed by all sensible men not merely rashness, but folly.

In concluding these pages, the author begs to be allowed a word as to their general character, in reply to a dogmatic and comprehensive criticism which it is easy to foresee will be passed on them. It will undoubtedly be asserted that an undue prominence has been given to the religious side of the Irish question, while its many political aspects have been left in the background. This charge will be laid at the door of the clerical and religious character of the writer, and may give rise to the notion that the view here taken of the subject is not the right one, but a radical failure.

The answer to this objection is, in brief, that no one can treat seriously and properly of the Irish race without taking a religious view of it. Whoever adopts a different method of treating the matter would, in our opinion, go completely astray; would take in only a few side-views; would, in fact, pretend to have made a serious study of it, which he offered to the public as such, while ignoring the chief and almost only feature.

The Irish is a religious race, and nothing else. It seems that such was its character thousands of years ago, even when pagan. At the time when Hanno was sent by the Carthaginian senate beyond the Pillars of Hercules to explore the western coast of Africa, toward the south--of which voyage the short narrative is still left us--Himilco, brother to Hanno, was similarly commissioned to form settlements on the European coast, toward the north. The account of this latter expedition, which was extant in the time of Pliny the Elder, is unfortunately lost; but, in the poem of R. Festus Avienus, entitled "Ora Maritima," there are copious extracts from it, in which, at least, the sense of the original is preserved. Avienus, after speaking of the "Insulae OEstrimnides," which Heeren thinks must be the Scilly Islands, goes on to say:

> "Ast hinc duobus in Sacram (sic insulam
> Dixere prisci) solibus cursus rati est.
> Haec inter undas multam caespitem jacet,
> Eamque late gens Hibernorum colit."

The passage runs almost into literal English as follows:

> "Thence in two days, a good ship in sailing
> Reaches the Holy Isle[1]--so was she called of old--
> That in the sea nestles, whose turf exuberant
> The race of Hibernians tills."

---

[1] Dr. Lingard, evidently perplexed by this expression, asks himself, "What might its origin have been?" and suggests that the name of Ierne--the same as Erin--having been given to Ireland by the ancients, and the Greek iepa--holy-- bearing a great resemblance to it, Avienus might have thus fallen into a very natural mistake of confounding the one with the other. But, in the first place, Himilco's report was certainly not written in Greek, but in Phoenician, and Avienus seems merely to have translated that report. Moreover, the word iepa begins with a very strong aspirate, equivalent to a consonant, while there are few vowels softer in any language than the first in Erin or Ierne. Heeren does not attempt such an explanation, but concedes that the Carthaginians, as well as the Phoenicians before them, called Ireland the Holy Isle.

In the time of Himilco, therefore, five hundred years before Christ, Ireland was called the Holy Isle, a title she had received long before: Sic insulam discere prisci. In what that holiness may have consisted precisely, it is impossible now to say; all we know is, that foreign navigators, who were acquainted with the world as far as it was then known, whose ships had visited the harbors of all nations, could find no more apt expression to describe the island than to say that, morally, it was "a holy spot," and physically "a fair green meadow," or, as her children to this day call her, "the green gem of the sea."

But we have better means of judging in what the holiness of the people consisted after the establishment of Christianity in their midst; and the description of it given in the fourth chapter of this book, taken from the most trustworthy documents, shows how well deserved was the title the island bore.

From that day forth the religious type was clearly impressed on the nation, and has ever remained deeply engraven in its character. The race was never distinguished for its fondness for trade, for its manufactures, for depth of policy, for worldly enlightenment; its annals speak of no lust of conquest among its people; the brilliant achievements of foreign invasion, the high political and social aspirations which generally give lustre to the national life of many a people, belong not to them. But religious feeling, firm adherence to faith, invincible attachment to the form of Christianity they had received from St. Patrick, formed at all times their striking characteristics.

From the day when their faith was first attacked by the Tudors did it chiefly blaze forth into a special splendor, which these pages have striven faintly to represent. Before taking up the pen to write, after the serious study of documents, only one great feature struck us--that of a deep religious conviction; and, after having seen what some writers have had to say recently, the same feature strikes us still. We will not deny that this fact moved us to write, and the task was the more grateful, probably, because of our own personal religious character; but we are confident that any layman, whatever might be his talent and disposition for describing worldly scenes, who took up Irish history, could find nothing else in it of real importance to render the annals of the race attractive to the common run of readers.

And is not religion more capable of giving a people true greatness and real heroism than any worldly excellence? Men of sound judgment will always find at least as much interest attached to the history of the first Maccabees as to that of Epaminondas; and the self-sacrifice of the Vendean Cathelineau, with his "beads" and his "sacred heart," will always appear to an impartial judge of human character more truly admirable than that of any general or marshal of the first Napoleon. Religious heroism, having for object something far above even the purest patriotic fervor, can inspire deeds more truly worthy of human admiration than this, the highest natural feeling of the human heart; and, for a Christian, the most inspiring pages of history are those which tell of the superhuman exertions of devoted knights to wrest the sepulchre of our Lord from the polluted hands of the Moslem.

But religion did not confine her influence over Irishmen to the bravery which she breathed into them on the battle-field. Religion truly constituted their inner life in all the vicissitudes of their national existence; it was the only support left them in the darkest period of their annals, during the whole of the last century; and, when the dawn came at last with the flush of hope, religion was the only halo which surrounded them. Their emigration even, their exodus chiefly, was in fact the sublime outpouring of a crucified nation, carrying the cross as their last religious emblem, and planting it in the wilds of far-distant continents as their only escutcheon, and the sure sign which should apprise travellers of the existence of Irishmen in the deserts of North America and Australia.

Truly, those men are very ignorant of the Irish character who would abstract the religious feature from it, and paint the nation as they would any other European people, whose great aim in these modern days seems to be to forget the first fervor of their Christian origin. With the Irish this cannot be. The vivid warmth of their cradle has not yet cooled down; and, if it would be indeed ridiculous to represent the English of the nineteenth century as the pious subjects of Alfred or Edward, it would be equally foolish to depict the Irish of to-day as the worldlings and godless of France, Italy, or Spain. The Irish patriot could not be like them, without deserting his standard and the colors for which his race has fought. The nation to which he has the honor of belonging is still Christian to the core; and, if some few have really repudiated the love of the religion they took in at their mother's knee, the only means left them of remaining Irishmen, at least in appearance, is not to parade their total lack of this, the chief characteristic of their race.

www.ingramcontent.com/pod-product-compliance
Lightning Source LLC
Chambersburg PA
CBHW051541010526
44118CB00022B/2540